"At last! A systematic entryway into covenant theology. I have been waiting for a book like this one, a book that does not merely regurgitate the storyline of Scripture but summons systematic theology to make covenantal connections across the canon. To our detriment, the covenant of redemption, the covenant of works, and the covenant of grace have been sidelined today in the name of being 'biblical.' But without these covenants we strip Scripture and its good news of its Trinitarian author, confuse and conflate law and gospel, and stumble over the sacramental tapestry of typology that culminates with Christ. But Harrison Perkins has accomplished more still—like Reformed theologians of old he reads the Bible with the church catholic (universal). Few theologians are so capable of bringing the Reformed tradition into conversation with the history of biblical interpretation. Whether you agree or disagree with Perkins, this book is an achievement."

MATTHEW BARRETT, Midwestern Baptist Theological Seminary, Kansas City, MO

"This book is at once a thorough historical and biblical discussion of covenant theology with all its nooks and crannies, and one that is easy to understand. Perkins demonstrates the internal consistency of covenant theology, along with its practical implications. If you've ever wondered what covenant theology teaches or whether its teaching is arbitrary, here is a positive presentation that shows its internal coherence and also addresses common misunderstandings. Perkins writes with a deep familiarity with what he discusses, enabling him both to explain difficult concepts for modern readers and to highlight areas of disagreement even among the Reformed. A model of pastoral scholarship written in service to the church."

BRANDON D. CROWE, Westminster Theological Seminary, Glenside, PA

"In this volume, Harrison Perkins presents the Bible's teaching on covenant theology with the precision of a systematician, the knowledge of an historian, and the warmth of a pastor. The result is not only impressive but immensely helpful. Ministers in particular will benefit from this exhaustive aid as they teach the riches of covenant theology to God's people."

JONATHAN LANDRY CRUSE, Community Presbyterian Church, Kalamazoo, MI

"There are any number of books on covenant theology currently available. Many address specific dogmatic, historical, exegetical, or pastoral concerns. Harrison Perkins has given us a definitive volume which addresses all of these, yet which is highly accessible, engaging, and drawn from the wealth of Christian reflection across time on this important topic."

KIM RIDDLEBARGER, Christ Reformed Church, Anaheim, CA

"We're witnessing a renaissance of covenant theology, which is to say, classic Reformed theology. Taking into account key debates, Perkins weaves biblical, historical, and systematic theology into a rich tapestry. And, as a pastor, he displays its relevance for our lives. With this book we have the best contemporary account of the Bible's own unifying structure."

MICHAEL HORTON, Westminster Seminary California, Escondido, CA

"Readers expecting just another book on covenant theology may be surprised as they read this work, but they will not be disappointed. Harrison Perkins has approached the topic of covenant theology in a unique way here and provided a theological feast in the process. One does not have to agree with all of his conclusions to recognize what a gift this book is to the church."

KEITH A. MATHISON, Reformation Bible College, Stanford, FL

"No less clear than it is comprehensive, Harrison Perkins's *Reformed Covenant Theology* surveys covenant theology in a way that will benefit student and scholar alike. Warmly recommended."

GUY PRENTISS WATERS, Reformed Theological Seminary, Jackson, MS

"Thinking through how the covenants work in Scripture is no small thing. It takes us to the heart of who our glorious Triune God is, why and how our Lord Jesus Christ is central to all of Scripture, and what the gospel is. … In *Reformed Covenant Theology*, Harrison Perkins masterfully helps us understand God's covenants and redemptive plan by expounding and applying the venerable tradition of Reformed, classic covenant theology. This is simply the best current introduction of this view. It faithfully and carefully explains what covenant theology is and also shows its practical relevance for our lives. Although those from other theological traditions, specifically covenantal Baptists like myself, will not agree with some of its biblical and theological formulations and conclusions, this book will allow for continuing conversations on these significant issues that still divide us. After all, we agree more than we disagree on main gospel truths including the centrality of Christ to the covenants. This is why after reading this book you will not only know Scripture better, but also you will be led to know, worship, and love our covenant-making and keeping God more. I highly recommend this work."

STEPHEN J. WELLUM, The Southern Baptist Theological Seminary, Louisville, KY

Reformed Covenant Theology

Reformed Covenant Theology

A SYSTEMATIC INTRODUCTION

Harrison Perkins

LEXHAM ACADEMIC

Reformed Covenant Theology: A Systematic Introduction

Lexham Academic, an imprint of Lexham Press
1313 Commercial St., Bellingham, WA 98225
LexhamPress.com

Print ISBN 9781683597339
Digital ISBN 9781683597346
Library of Congress Control Number 2023940134

Lexham Editorial: Todd Hains, Brittany McComb, Kaeli Joyce
Cover Design: Jim LePage
Typesetting: Mandi Newell

24 25 26 27 28 29 30 / IN / 12 11 10 9 8 7 6 5 4 3 2

For John V. Fesko
Superlative scholar, matchless mentor, wonderful friend
Scruffy looking aside, he's no nerf herder

Contents

PART FOUR:
THE ADMINISTRATION OF THE COVENANT OF GRACE

PART FIVE:
LIVING IN GOD'S COVENANT OF GRACE

Foreword

We are enjoying a happy explosion of both academic and popular books on covenant theology in our time. I became interested in the history of covenant theology over forty years ago when as a university history major I encountered "the Perry Miller thesis" (that the Puritans were the inventors of federal theology) in a US history course. I instinctively knew that something was wrong with the way Miller was approaching and framing the subject, but I didn't know enough then to quite put my finger on it. I have been studying covenant theology and its historical development ever since. But back then (early 1980s), before the work of Richard Muller, there was not a lot being written on classic Reformed covenant theology. Little did I know that all of that was about to change.

In those days and in my theological neck of the woods, the names Murray, Kline, and Robertson dominated the discussions of covenant theology. Professor John Murray of Westminster Seminary (Philadelphia) wrote articles on various aspects of covenant theology and published an influential booklet, *The Covenant of Grace* (1954), in which he took issue with some aspects of traditional Reformed covenant theology (including rejecting the terminology of covenant of works, while retaining much of the idea under the name "Adamic administration"). Murray also emphasized the unilateral or monergistic aspect of divine covenants in ways that are dependent on Geerhardus Vos and which are somewhat typical for twentieth-century Reformed theology. Alongside Murray was a younger contemporary, an Old Testament scholar (and expert in Assyriology and Egyptology), Meredith Kline (who taught at Gordon-Conwell, and the two Westminsters). Kline's books, *Treaty of the Great King* (1963) and *By Oath Consigned* (1968), as well as numerous articles and a sustained teaching and research focus on covenant theology, made him a fountainhead of the renewed interest in covenant theology in the last quarter of the twentieth century. Both Kline and Murray had more than quibbles with the Westminster Confession's formulation of covenant theology (Kline famously scrupled God's "voluntary condescension" in WCF 7.1 in relation to the covenant of works), but on the whole, they and those who followed them had fairly high views of our confessional inheritance of covenant theology.

Enter Palmer Robertson (who taught at Reformed, Westminster, and Covenant seminaries), whose book *The Christ of the Covenants* (1980) incorporated insights from both Murray and Kline and popularized covenant theology again not only in the Presbyterian and Reformed community, but the wider Reformed and evangelical world. Robertson's treatment of covenant theology followed a mostly biblical theological outline of the subject and sparked forty years of writing and teaching on the topic in Reformed circles. Robertson adopted Kline's terminology for the covenants of works and grace (creation and redemption), but held to the majority Reformed view on the status of the Mosaic covenant (while omitting from his exposition the idea of a pretemporal *pactum salutis*, covenant of salvation). Robertson's work (which he has continued adding to in a series that will eventually cover the entire canon) anticipated and contributed to four plus decades of research and writing on the history of covenant theology and expositions of the biblical covenants.

So today we enjoy a surfeit of riches when it comes to covenant theology. Some notable highlights of what has been published in the last four decades include the following. Andrew Woolsey wrote *Unity and Continuity in Covenantal Thought: A Study in the Reformed Tradition to the Westminster Assembly* as a thesis at the University of Glasgow in 1988, which was subsequently published in 2012 with a foreword by none other than Richard Muller—who has been just as responsible as Kline and Robertson for the explosion of interest in the history of covenant theology especially because of his overall research project on the relation between sixteenth- and seventeenth-century Reformed theology, his critique of the "Calvin vs. the Calvinist" historiography, and specifically his works *Christ and the Decree* (1986), *Post-Reformation Reformed Dogmatics* (1987–2003), and *The Unaccommodated Calvin* (2001). I met Andrew Woolsey while I was doing my PhD at the University of Edinburgh, looking at some of the patristic sources to which the sixteenth-century Reformers appealed for their exposition of the biblical covenants. While in Edinburgh, I sat at the feet of Donald Macleod who had spent years studying historic Scottish covenant theology, interacting with its Barthian critics (especially the Torrances), and advocating for classic confessional covenant theology. Macleod wrote numerous articles on the topic, including his entry on "covenant theology" in the *Dictionary of Scottish Church History and Theology* (1993). In the mid-1990s Francis Turretin's *Institutes of Elenctic Theology* was published in an updated English translation (1992–1997). They contain Turretin's robust and influential formulation of covenant theology that informed, for instance, nineteenth-century confessional American Presbyterian theology. Their republication helped fuel the increasing interest in historic covenant theology going on in our time.

J. I. Packer wrote an introduction to covenant theology (1990), which has since been published separately, that prefaced a reprinting of Herman Witsius's *The Economy of the Covenants between God and Man* (1693). Packer also wrote an entry on "Covenant" in his *Concise Theology* (1993). Packer's influence in commending covenant theology should not be overlooked. Rowland Ward produced a history of the formulation and development of the doctrine of the covenant of works in *God and Adam: Reformed Theology and the Creation Covenant* (2003). Peter Golding wrote a popular exposition called *Covenant Theology: The Key of Theology in Reformed Thought and Tradition* (2004). Michael Horton provided his own Kline-influenced overview of the subject in *Introducing Covenant Theology* (2006). Jonty Rhodes composed another short, popular treatment, *Covenants Made Simple: Understanding God's Unfolding Promises to His People* (2014). The faculty of Reformed Theological Seminary coauthored a massive and extensive treatment of the subject in *Covenant Theology: Biblical, Theological, and Historical Perspectives* (2020). Dick Belcher of RTS Charlotte expounds the Westminster Confession's version of covenant theology in *The Fulfillment of the Promises of God: An Explanation of Covenant Theology* (2020), and then critically interacts with a number of significant scholars of the covenants: Robertson, Murray, Dumbrell, Williamson, Kline and others. John Fesko, who taught at RTS Atlanta, then Westminster California, and now is my (prolific!) colleague at Reformed Theological Seminary in Jackson, has made a number of major contributions to the subject: *The Trinity and the Covenant of Redemption* (2016), *The Covenant of Works: The Origins, Development, and Reception of the Doctrine* (2020), and *Adam and the Covenant of Works* (2021). John's discussions and taxonomy of views of the relation of the covenant of works to Sinai in the Reformed tradition are helpful and clarifying. Stephen Myers, an RTS graduate who now teaches at Puritan Reformed Theological Seminary, recently wrote *God to Us: Covenant Theology in Scripture* (2021), which contains maybe the best short historiographical survey of covenant theology that I have read.

Which brings me to Harrison Perkins. I have been following Dr. Perkins's academic work with appreciation for some time and greatly enjoyed reading the publication of his thesis in the book *Catholicity and the Covenant of Works: James Ussher and the Reformed Tradition* (2020). In this book, *Reformed Covenant Theology: A Systematic Introduction* (2024), Dr. Perkins aims to explore and recover aspects of traditional Reformed covenant theology that have been underdiscussed by scholars and books that have taken a more biblical-theological approach. Perkins deliberately emphasizes covenant theology's categories rather than its narrative. He explores and outlines his subject intentionally from the standpoint of systematic rather than biblical theology (without in any way disagreeing with, downplaying, or denigrating the latter). He is especially concerned to show that the major premises of Reformed covenant theology develop out of the catholic tradition, and particularly, the ancient church. He makes the case that covenant theology codifies how the church has always read the Bible.

Perkins understands covenant theology as about how God himself has provided a way for our communion with God. He acknowledges the covenant of works and covenant of grace, as well as the pretemporal intra-Trinitarian covenant of redemption. He argues that the categories of the covenant of works and grace explain why grace and works cannot be mixed as the basis for our relationship with God, and he connects this law-gospel distinction to Paul's contrast of the Mosaic and Abrahamic covenants in Galatians 3–4 (more on this later).

He makes a case for the traditional Reformed view of the covenant of works, replete with citations from Reformed confessions, major theologians, and church fathers. In the standard Reformed manner he links the content of the law given to Adam with the Ten Commandments, and shows how the covenant of works requires perfect and personal obedience to it, but also how it demonstrates God's love by his promise of reward for that obedience. Devoting an entire chapter to the application of the doctrine (which also further extends his apologetic for it), Perkins shows why the covenant of works is indispensable to Reformed covenant theology.

Perkins defends and advances the traditional Reformed view of the covenant of redemption, fully aware of how recent Trinitarian discussion comes to bear on that doctrine, and affirming the doctrines of divine simplicity, the unity of the divine will, and inseparable operations. He also helpfully assembles the testimony to the covenant of redemption found in the Reformed confessions (which is admittedly less explicit than their witness to the covenants of works and grace), concluding with a discussion of three ways the covenant of redemption helps us read our Bibles better.

He maintains and demonstrates the unity of the covenant of grace, in Old Testament and New, with Christ as its substance in each, and faith as the sole condition or alone instrument (WCF 11.2), thereby highlighting why the Reformed are enabled and concerned to preach Christ from all the Scriptures. He highlights a classic Reformed presentation of union with Christ that affirms the *ordo salutis,* including justification, adoption, sanctification, and glorification, and explains why it matters. Addressing the vexed question of the relation of the Mosaic covenant to the covenant of works, Perkins acknowledges that the Mosaic covenant is an administration of the one covenant of grace, and he acknowledges its salvific continuity with the Abrahamic covenant, but also asserts that it resembles or has points of similarity with the covenant of works especially at the national level for Israel. My own view on this matter is different. I follow Anthony Burgess, an influential member of the Westminster Assembly, who emphasizes the Mosaic covenant as a covenant of grace, and that the giving of the law at Sinai was as a rule of life (the so-called third use of the law), not a covenant of works. But Perkins argues his view as carefully here as I've seen it done, and all Reformed theologians will appreciate his irenicism and judiciousness on the matter. I tell my students that relating the Mosaic covenant to the new is one of the most difficult and demanding theological tasks in biblical interpretation. It is no wonder that Burgess can remark on the confusion and perplexity on the issue even among sound and learned men.

Perkins concludes the book with edifying pastoral deployments of the doctrine of the covenant of grace, and his "Six Theses about Reformed Covenant Theology" (and his exposition of them) are worth the price of the book. This volume and its approach provide a welcome entry in the growing body of literature analyzing and expounding historic Reformed covenant theology. Perkins is an expert in his field and very much a pastor, and both show in the product. You will not be disappointed that you have taken the time to carefully and prayerfully walk through the outline, arguments, and applications of this book.

Ligon Duncan

Jackson, MS, 2023

Preface

This book aims to recover aspects of covenant theology that the resurging interest in biblical covenants has underdiscussed. Recent research focuses on how covenants develop Scripture's historical narrative, an indispensable investigation nonetheless gridlocking discussion on Reformed and Baptist disagreement about new covenant membership. Traditional Reformed covenant theology addresses far more than simply baptism, focusing on Christ, salvation's nature, the law-gospel distinction, and the distribution of God's promises. This book emphasizes these issues, omitting a climactic joust over infant baptism, hoping that various Protestant traditions can appreciate anew some fundamental aspects of covenant theology and deploy them well within distinct confessional traditions as we focus on communion with God, Christ, salvation, assurance, and the church's necessary role in the Christian life.

This work's approach is distinct by emphasizing covenant theology's *categories* rather than the covenants' narrative. The shape of each argument starts with statements from Reformed confessions as accepted expressions of covenantal doctrine, exegetically defends those statements, and then draws confirmation from the Christian tradition. The historical arguments prioritize Reformed confessions then the ancient church, seeking to demonstrate that the major premises of Reformed covenant theology did not originate in the Reformation but developed out of the catholic tradition. This preference for patristic writers marks how the Reformed are hard to persuade to abandon our methods of covenant theology *because* we believe that the church has read Scripture essentially this way since Christ's ascension.

We have a Great Tradition of interpreting Scripture and should delight to remain part of the conversation between Scripture and our confession of its meaning. This book's approach integrates confessional statements and exegetical discussions to demonstrate the mutually informing relationship between understanding Scripture and confessing its meaning. The goal is a resource well organized for quick reference, rooted in Reformed confessions, and thorough in explanation of biblical texts. Because pastors should teach this material to their congregations, I regularly abandon the academic tone to illustrate, apply, and address the heart. The historical quotes from the ancient and Reformed tradition put rich and trusted phrasing directly at hand for pastors lacking time to dig through everything cited in the footnotes.[1] In this respect, the abbreviations are truly crucial for following the citations in the footnotes, as they compress even the most important sources into streamlined references. Nonetheless, I hope that this book provides all the explanation, exegesis, historical formulations, illustrations, and applications that pastors need to teach their churches about covenant theology.

This book's notable accent is on the covenants from the perspective of systematic theology. I believe that, although biblical theology makes invaluable contributions to our understanding of Scripture concerning various author's distinct emphases and the progress of revelation, a rut has formed regarding studies of the covenants. The biblical theological outline of investigating each covenant (usually focusing nearly exclusively on the covenant's initiation passage) for only its redemptive-historical contribution has become overly rehearsed and has begun to exclude clear and precise *doctrinal* conclusions concerning our major systematic topics. This book, although drawing thoroughly upon biblical theology and in no way aiming to displace it, emphatically stresses the covenants' value for systematic theology, hoping to overturn that rut and set new directions in future discussions.

My favorite thing about this book is its thorough connection to my life as a pastor, as every section grew directly out of churchly endeavors.

---

1. I have modernized the language in almost every quote, including confessions, and freshly translated most ancient church citations since the nineteenth-century translations often read poorly and use unfamiliar terms.

I am immensely privileged to pastor Oakland Hills Community Church (OPC) and profusely blessed to be part of this wonderful body of believers, who are hungry for God's word and very gracious in granting me time to write. Every chapter gathers exegetical work primarily from preparation to preach for Sunday worship, Bible studies, or lectures for Edinburgh Theological Seminary, aimed at training pastors. As a pastor, the chapters on the administration of the covenant of grace were the most enriching to write. Contemplating how God uses the ordinary means of grace as his very instruments for us to commune with him and to receive his promises inflamed my heart with new joy to be a pastor who, although a *very* mere clay pot, has been entrusted to distribute these magnificent treasures of the gospel to God's people each week. This book has an academic flavor but was born out of churchly labors.

This book is dedicated to John V. Fesko as a small token of my great appreciation for his scholarship and friendship. He has made significant contributions to the study of covenant theology, often writing the books that I wished I had. The church is better because he got to the task first. Readers will see his fingerprints all over this book, and I don't hide that I follow him on a great many points. I am thankful for his support over the years and hope this book blesses him with at least a laugh that someone else tried hard to say things as well as he does.

There are many who read at least sections of this book and offered helpful feedback: Dave VanDrunen (whose much-appreciated feedback prompted a genuine overhaul of the first draft), John Fesko, Scott Clark, Ryan McGraw, Matthew Barrett, Adonis Vidu, Ryan Hurd, Keith Mathison, Bryan Estelle, Jonathan Cruse, Chad Vegas, Kim Riddlebarger, Bob Akroyd, Matt Bingham, Richard Barcellos, Mary Reid, and Alastair Herd. Special thanks to Stephen Wellum, Richard Lucas, and Sam Renihan for their extensive interactions and feedback, which has delighted me in building friendship with them.

Some miscellaneous but well-deserved gratitude: Deep thanks to Todd Hains and the Lexham team for taking on this project, particularly the reviewer for his very encouraging feedback about this book's pastoral worth and obvious love for Jesus. Thanks to the *Evangelical Presbyterian Magazine* and *Modern Reformation* for permission to reuse material. Thanks must go to Bob Ackroyd for letting me lecture on covenant theology for his systematic theology courses at Edinburgh Seminary and especially for being a good friend. Thanks also to Philip Stewart, Andy Longwe, and Andrew Mullan, friends who continually encourage me and whose support is an incredible help.

A great many thanks to Faith Crawford for producing the indices!

A very special thanks to Ligon Duncan for so graciously (and quickly) writing a very kind foreword for this book. I remember hearing Dr. Duncan preach in Birmingham early in my days of learning Reformed theology, and having appreciated his ministry ever since, I am deeply honored by his endorsement of this work.

I must thank my precious family: my son, Scott, who brings much joy to me as I live in God's promise to be God to me and my children after me, and my wife, Sarah, who has endless patience as I invest myself for too long in writing. She is the greatest earthly gift I have, and it is no small thing to be in covenant with her. I am ever grateful to belong to her with an oath.

Harrison Perkins
Detroit, MI, 2023

Abbreviations

ACW	J. V. Fesko, *Adam and the Covenant of Works* (Fearn, UK: Mentor, 2021)
ANF	Alexander Roberts and James Donaldson (eds.), *Ante-Nicene Fathers*, 10 vol. (Buffalo: The Christian Literature Publishing Co., 1885)
AP	Michael W. Holmes (ed.), *The Apostolic Fathers: Greek Texts and English Translations*, 3rd ed. (Grand Rapids: Baker Academic, 2007)
BC	Belgic Confession
BOC	Meredith G. Kline, *By Oath Consigned: A Reinterpretation of the Covenant Signs of Circumcision and Baptism* (Grand Rapids: Eerdmans, 1968)
BRD	Herman Bavinck, *Reformed Dogmatics*, ed. John Bolt, trans. John Vriend, 4 vol. (Grand Rapids: Baker Academic, 2003–2008)
BTA	Chris Bruno, Jared Compton, and Kevin McFadden, *Biblical Theology According to the Apostles: How the Earliest Christians Told the Story of the Old Testament* (Downers Grove, IL: IVP Academic, 2020)
CC	John Calvin, *Calvin's Commentaries*, 22 vol. (Grand Rapids: Baker, 2009)
CD	Michael Allen and Scott R. Swain (eds.), *Christian Dogmatics: Reformed Theology for the Church Catholic* (Grand Rapids: Baker Academic, 2016)

CDT	Brent E. Parker and Richard J. Lucas (eds.), *Covenantal and Dispensational Theologies: Four Views on the Continuity of Scripture* (Downers Grove, IL: IVP Academic, 2022)
CF	Michael Horton, *The Christian Faith: A Systematic Theology for Pilgrims on the Way* (Grand Rapids: Zondervan, 2011)
CG	John Colquhoun, *A Treatise on the Covenant of Grace* (Edinburgh, 1818)
CMT	Johann Heinrich Heidegger, *The Concise Marrow of Theology*, trans. Casey Carmichael (Grand Rapids: Reformation Heritage Books, 2019)
CO	John Calvin, *Opera quae superunt omnia*, ed. Edouard Cunitz, Johann-Wilhem Baum, and Eduard Wilhem Eugen Reuss, 58 vol. (Corpus Reformatorum; Brunsigae: C. A. Schwetschke, 1863)
COC	Philip Schaff (ed.), *The Creeds of Christendom*, 3 vol. (New York: Harper and Brothers, 1877)
CRS	Wilhelmus à Brakel, *The Christian's Reasonable Service*, trans. Bartel Elshout, ed. Joel R. Beeke, 4 vol. (Grand Rapids: Reformation Heritage Books, 1992)
CT	Guy Prentiss Waters, J. Nicholas Reid, and John R. Muether (eds.), *Covenant Theology: Biblical, Theological, and Historical Perspectives* (Wheaton, IL: Crossway, 2020)
CTJ	*Calvin Theological Journal*
CUL	Cambridge University Library
CW	John Colquhoun, *A Treatise on the Covenant of Works* (Edinburgh: Thomsons Brothers, 1821)
DIALIC	J. V. Fesko, *Death in Adam, Life in Christ: The Doctrine of Imputation* (Fearn, UK: Mentor, 2016)
DLGTT	Richard A. Muller, *Dictionary of Latin and Greek Theological Terms Drawn Principally from Protestant Scholastic Theology*, 2nd ed. (Grand Rapids: Baker Academic, 2017)

EC	Herman Witsius, *The Economy of the Covenants between God and Man*, trans. William Crookshank, 2 vol. (Edinburgh: Thomas Turnbull, 1803)
GWM1	John Webster, *God without Measure: Working Papers in Christian Theology Volume I: God and the Works of God* (London: T&T Clark, 2016)
GWM2	John Webster, *God without Measure: Working Papers in Christian Theology Volume II: Virtue and Intellect* (London: T&T Clark, 2016)
HC	Heidelberg Catechism
IJST	*International Journal of Systematic Theology*
JETS	*Journal of the Evangelical Theological Society*
JRT	*Journal of Reformed Theology*
KP	Meredith G. Kline, *Kingdom Prologue: Genesis Foundations for a Covenantal Worldview* (Overland Park, KS: Two Age Press, 2000)
KTC	Peter J. Gentry and Stephen J. Wellum, *Kingdom through Covenant: A Biblical-Theological Understanding of the Covenants*, 2nd ed. (Wheaton, IL: Crossway, 2018)
LC	John R. Bower, *The Larger Catechism: A Critical Text and Introduction* (Principal Documents of the Westminster Assembly; Grand Rapids: Reformation Heritage Books, 2010)
LG	John Colquhoun, *A Treatise on the Law and the Gospel* (Edinburgh: J. Ogle, 1816)
LNF	Bryan D. Estelle, J. V. Fesko, and David VanDrunen (eds.), *The Law Is Not of Faith: Essays on Works and Grace in the Mosaic Covenant* (Phillipsburg, NJ: P&R, 2012)
MAJT	*Mid-America Journal of Theology*
MMB	Francis Roberts, *Mysterium & Medulla Bibliorum* (London: George Calvert, 1657)
MS	Manuscript
MT	William Ames, *The Marrow of Theology*, trans. John Dykstra Eusden (Grand Rapids: Baker, 1968)

NPNF1	Philip Schaff (ed.), *Nicene and Post-Nicene Fathers, Series 1*, 14 vol. (New York: Christian Literature Company, 1887)
NPNF2	Henry Wace and Philip Schaff (eds.), *Nicene and Post-Nicene Fathers, Series 2*, 14 vol. (New York: Christian Literature Company, 1895)
OHRT	Michael Allen and Scott R. Swain (eds.), *The Oxford Handbook of Reformed Theology* (Oxford: Oxford University Press, 2020)
PG	Jacques Paul Migne (ed.), *Patrologia Cursus Completus: Series Graeca*, 161 vol. (Paris: Amboise, 1857–66)
PL	Jacques Paul Migne (ed.), *Patrologia Cursus Completus: Series Latina*, 221 vol. (Paris: Amboise, 1844–64)
RHBI	Geerhardus Vos, *Redemptive History and Biblical Interpretation: The Shorter Writings of Geerhardus Vos*, ed. Richard B. Gaffin Jr. (Phillipsburg, NJ: P&R, 1980)
RST	Joel R. Beeke and Paul M. Smalley, *Reformed Systematic Theology*, 4 vol. (Wheaton, IL: Crossway, 2019–)
SBJT	*The Southern Baptist Journal of Theology*
TI	Francis Turretin, *Institutes of Elenctic Theology*, trans. George Musgrave Giger, ed. James T. Dennison Jr., 3 vol. (Phillipsburg, NJ: P&R, 1992–97)
TCR	J. V. Fesko, *The Trinity and the Covenant of Redemption* (Fearn, UK: Mentor, 2016)
VBT	Geerhardus Vos, *Biblical Theology: Old and New Testaments* (Grand Rapids: Eerdmans, 1988)
VRD	Geerhardus Vos, *Reformed Dogmatics*, 5 vol. (Bellingham, WA: Lexham Press, 2012–14)
WCF	Westminster Confession of Faith
WLC	Westminster Larger Catechism
WSC	Westminster Shorter Catechism
WTJ	*Westminster Theological Journal*
WWG	Herman Bavinck, *The Wonderful Works of God: Instruction in the Christian Religion according to the Reformed Confession*, trans. Henry Zylstra (Glenside, PA: Westminster Seminary Press, 2019)

WWP	William Perkins, *The Works of William Perkins*, 10 vol. (Grand Rapids: Reformation Heritage Books, 2014–20)
WWS	J. V. Fesko, *Word, Water, and Spirit: A Reformed Perspective on Baptism* (Grand Rapids: Reformation Heritage Books, 2010)

Prayer to Our God Who Covenants with Us

In the name of the Father and of the Son and of the Holy Spirit. Amen.

> The friendship of the Lord is for those who fear him,
> and he makes known to them his covenant. *Psalm 25:14*

Our Triune God, who is the ancient of days overseeing every age of your world, make us delight in how everything written in the Law, the Prophets, the Psalms, and our new covenant Scripture was all written about and gives Christ.

Cause us to love how even from creation, you made Adam as our representative to give us a type of the one to come, namely, Christ, seeing that all things were created through and for him in whom all things hold together.

Prompt joy in our hearts at knowing that the eternal covenant, founded upon satisfaction of our mediator Jesus Christ, was established in your own triune counsel before the world's foundations.

Move us to rejoice at how the promises, types, and ordinances of your old economy applied Christ to your people.

Make your manifold wisdom be further displayed in the church, so that glory goes to Christ in the church throughout all generations.

We are glad to belong to you, our covenant Lord, who is Father, Son, and Spirit working all things for our good and your glory and from whom all blessings flow. We pray you hear us because of Christ. Amen.

1

Meeting God in the Covenants

The friendship of the Lord is for those who fear him,
and he makes known to them his covenant.
—*Psalm 25:14*

Covenant theology, quite simply, concerns our relationship with God, making it about our understanding of ultimate matters. Among the creatures who inhabit the physical realm, we humans alone have walked with the Lord, had opportunity to pray to him, and enjoy his intimate fellowship, prompting us to marvel with David, as he wrote in Psalm 8:3–4, "What is man that you are mindful of him, and the son of man that you care for him?" All the more, Psalm 25:14 teaches us how those who fear the Lord and have his friendship know what it means to be *in covenant* with him. We are the creatures made for communion with God, and covenants are the way that God facilitates that communion with us.

God is then the foremost end of all our hopes and needs. For this reason, theology's supreme investigation is the doctrine of God's triune life, in some ways taking preeminence even over the doctrine of salvation.[1] Although this book is not about theology proper, it fits within the scope of theology's

1. John Webster, "*Rector et Iudex Super Genera Doctrinarum?* The Place of the Doctrine of Justification" in *GWM1*, 159–61; John Webster, "'It Was the Will of the Lord to Bruise Him': Soteriology and the Doctrine of God," in *GWM1*, 143–57.

highest endeavor—contemplation of God—by explaining God's works that provide the place where we encounter him in his love: the covenant. As John Webster (1955–2016) highlighted, "The gospel, that is, concerns the history of fellowship—covenant—between God and creatures."[2] This book, therefore, focuses on covenant theology through the lens of communion with God.

Reformed theologians have long understood how covenant theology is the best way to discuss our communion with God. Francis Roberts (1609–1675) highlights, "The Lord God brings man into communion with himself, by that sweet familiar way of covenant, in all ages, from the foundation to the consummation of the world."[3] Likewise, Francis Turretin (1623–1687) writes, "As God wished in every age to have a church in which he might dwell and which might cherish communion with him for the fruition of happiness, so it pleased him to institute that communion in no other way than that of a covenant."[4] So, as the Reformed have grasped, to understand covenant theology is simply to explore the depths of our relational communion with God.[5]

Knowing *that* covenant characterizes our relationship with God is one thing, but knowing *how* covenant theology shapes, defines, and informs our life as we traverse this pilgrim land on the short side of glory is another matter. This book unpacks what it means to live in covenant with God by exploring the major biblical themes connected to covenant as they have been articulated in traditional Reformed theology. The most important emphasis is that the covenant delivers Christ to his people, so that sinners encounter God in grace only through the Lord Jesus in all times and places. Even in eternity's depths, God established the covenant as the place where we would meet Jesus Christ, forging even his covenant with Adam before the fall in such a way as to provide "a type of the one to come," namely, Christ himself (Rom 5:14). As John Owen (1616–1683) writes, God delivers all his promises to us through the one covenant of

2. Webster, "Will of the Lord to Bruise Him," 143; also D. Glenn Butner Jr., *Trinitarian Dogmatics: Exploring the Grammar of the Christian Doctrine of God* (Grand Rapids: Baker Academic, 2022), 1–10.

3. *MMB*, sig. A3v–A4r.

4. *TI*, 12.2.1.

5. Geerhardus Vos, *The Teaching of the Epistle to the Hebrews* (Grand Rapids: Eerdmans, 1956), 41–45.

grace: "But whereas all the promises belong unto the same covenant, with all the grace contained in them and exhibited by them, whoever is interested by faith in that covenant is so in all the promises of God that belong thereunto, and hath an equal right unto them with those unto whom they were first given."[6] To say that we have communion with God by covenant, therefore, is simply to affirm that sinners have fellowship with the Lord because of Christ. So, this book explains how the whole Bible is about God's one, unified, unfolding plan of salvation through the work of our Savior Jesus Christ, expressed through covenant.

Covenant theology should then delight God's people's hearts, even seeing how Scripture often describes our life in covenant with God in moving language. For example, Psalm 105:8–11 uses the theme of covenant to remind God's people of how faithful our Lord is to us.

> He remembers his covenant forever,
>   the word that he commanded, for a thousand generations,
> the covenant that he made with Abraham,
>   his sworn promise to Isaac,
> which he confirmed to Jacob as a statute,
>   to Israel as an everlasting covenant,
> saying, "To you I will give the land of Canaan
>   as your portion for an inheritance."

God remembers his covenant, not as if he forgot and now recalls it, since God is all-knowing and unchanging, but in the sense that his previous promises prompted him to act for his people. God's acts of remembering his covenants signify his commitment to enact his covenant promises.[7] God's covenants are then a moving source of hope that he will faithfully do what he has promised for his people.

Believers should find immense comfort in knowing that God does not determine his faithfulness to us by how he might feel at any given moment but has made infallible promises to people of ages past and has kept those

---

6. John Owen, "Work of the Holy Spirit in Prayer," in *The Works of John Owen*, ed. William H. Goold, 16 vol. (Edinburgh: T&T Clark, 1862), 4:261.

7. Bruce K. Waltke with Cathi J. Fredericks, *Genesis: A Commentary* (Grand Rapids: Zondervan, 2001), 141.

promises even to believers today.[8] Covenant theology then reminds us that our God is unchanging in who he is and in his faithfulness to us.[9] When our unchanging God makes a promise—Psalm 105 reminds us how he did so for Abraham, Isaac, and Jacob—then God's promise is also unchanging.

The Bible itself highlights the comfort we should find in God by emphasizing his covenant with us. Every Christian knows something about feeling overwhelmed, crushed, and distressed. The psalmist reminds us in Psalm 106:44–45 that when God's people are in distress, God's covenant is an unshakeable foundation that prompts God into action on our behalf:

> Nevertheless, he looked upon their distress,
> when he heard their cry.
> For their sake he remembered his covenant,
> and relented according to the abundance of his steadfast love.

In the context of Psalm 106:40–43, God's people had been remarkably unfaithful, bringing God's discipline upon their rebellion. Despite their self-inflicted distress, God was good to them, freeing them from it because they were his people with whom he had covenanted.

The importance and helpfulness of exploring covenant theology should then be clear. Covenant theology's doctrines concern what it means to live before God and in fellowship with him. Covenant theology is about knowing how we relate to our Maker and Redeemer and especially how we, as sinners, might know that we are accepted in his sight and have the guarantee of his eternal love. We have communion with God by covenant. Covenant then helps us see the full scope of God's one plan to create a treasured people for himself, and about how, as Paul said in 2 Corinthians 1:20, all of God's promises find their yes and amen in our Lord and Savior, Jesus Christ.

---

8. Michael S. Horton, "Covenant," in *OHRT*, 435–36.
9. WCF 2.1 makes this point by stating that God is without passions; *COC*, 3:606.

WHAT IS COVENANT THEOLOGY?

A covenant is most simply a formal relationship.[10] Although they might sound exotic, covenants daily surround us. Covenants have analogies to the agreements we sign to buy a home, lease a car, or accept a new job. We certainly make a covenant by committing ourselves in love to a spouse when we are married. Covenants are not exactly contracts, since commercial exchanges may not do full justice to the relational aspect of covenants, but these examples still embody relationships where people become *bound* to one another in some fixed way.[11]

Covenants entail agreements, but many are made between parties, one of whom may be superior in authority.[12] Covenants are then flexible, diverse in kind, capable of relational dynamics, but also fundamentally legal and binding.[13] They include some sort of obligatory terms, making them committed arrangements, even when those committed terms are to love one another unconditionally, as in marriage. Most importantly, though, they are a biblical way of describing relationships, since God made covenants across the Scripture with his people as individuals or as a collective body, with varying types of functions and foundations.

Covenants further inform every relationship that God has with us. In other words, human beings cannot have a relationship with God that is not covenantal.[14] Although Reformed theologians disagree about whether God created Adam in covenant (as suggested here) or added the covenant relationship to Adam's created state, the issue is ultimately beside the present point that God has used covenants to define his relationship with us in every state of our existence.[15] Covenant has always been that aspect of our relationship with God that lets us know where we stand

---

10. *TI*, 8.3.1, 3; *EC*, 1.1.9; *MT*, 1.10.9–11; *CMT*, 62; *CW*, 1–4; *KP*, 1–6; *BOC*, 16; *KTC*, 164–66, 172–73; O. Palmer Robertson, *The Christ of the Covenants* (Phillipsburg, NJ: P&R, 1981), 4–7; Richard C. Barcellos, *The Covenant of Works: Its Confessional and Scriptural Basis* (Palmdale, CA: RBAP, 2016), 64–67; Thomas R. Schreiner, *Covenant and God's Purpose for the World* (Wheaton, IL: Crossway, 2017), 13–14; Daniel I. Block, *Covenant: The Framework of God's Grand Plan of Redemption* (Grand Rapids: Baker Academic, 2021), 1–2.

11. *ACW*, 55–76.

12. *MMB*, 14–15.

13. *MMB*, 16–17.

14. Walter Eichrodt, *Theology of the Old Testament*, trans. J. A. Baker, 2 vol. (Philadelphia: The Westminster Press, 1961), 1:36–45.

15. *ACW*, 385–88.

with him. Robert Rollock (1555–1599) argued that "all the Word of God appertains to some covenant, for God speaks nothing to man without the covenant."[16] If, therefore, God had not made a covenant with us, then we would have been left without a way to know what to expect from him. Certainly, creatures never have the right to demand something from God, as Luke 17:10 says, "So you also, when you have done all that you were commanded, say, 'We are unworthy servants; we have only done what was our duty.' " But because God is good, kind, and loving, he made a covenant even with Adam in the garden of Eden, so that we might always know exactly how we relate to him and so that there is a foundation to our relationship with him.

The Westminster Confession of Faith describes the general premise of God's covenanting with humanity: "The distance between God and the creature is so great that although reasonable creatures do owe obedience unto him as their Creator, yet they could never have any fruition of him as their blessedness and reward but by some voluntary condescension on God's part, which he has been pleased to express by way of covenant" (WCF 7.1).[17] As creatures, we inescapably owe allegiance and obedience to God, but we could never expect anything in return just because we did what we were supposed to do. God, who is kind and loving, made a covenant, attaching a promise to reward our obedience with further blessing, namely, everlasting life in the new creation—a point explored throughout part 1. For now, we see that God uses covenants to facilitate our communion with him. He forges communion with us by covenant, also using covenants to offer us even greater blessings in communion with him.

This covenantal principle is like when a mother tells her son to clean his room but promises to take him for ice cream if he cleans it well. The mother owns the home where her son lives and has authority to impose obedience without the reward of ice cream. In kindness, however, this mother condescends to offer that reward to her son upon fulfillment of the agreement. God too condescended to offer reward to humankind, doing so by means of covenants.

---

16. Robert Rollock, *A Treatise of God's Effectual Calling*, trans. Henry Holland (London: Felix Kyngston, 1603), 6.

17. *COC*, 3:616.

Reformed theology has long emphasized how the biblical theme of covenant importantly informs the scriptural storyline's full breadth, having fulfillment in Jesus Christ. Scripture describes how God made many covenants with individuals, such as Noah (Gen 6:18; 9:1–17), Abraham (Gen 12:1–3; 15; 17:1–14), and David (2 Sam 7:1–17), and with his corporate people, such as the Sinai covenant (Exod 19–24) and the new covenant (Jer 31:31–34). Each historical covenant plays a special role in advancing God's one story of salvation, which he authors for his own glory and for our benefit.[18] Alongside recognizing the important role that each covenant plays in the unfolding but unified drama of redemption, Reformed theology has also summarized the main points of this drama and the main aspects of theology under the heading of three doctrinal covenants. Two of these covenants occur in history involving God and humanity, and one is eternal involving the Triune God alone.

First, *the covenant of works* was a covenant that God made with Adam, offering reward based on Adam's perfect obedience. In this covenant, God appointed Adam as the representative of all humanity, meaning that Adam's success or failure determined whether all humanity would receive reward or condemnation. Christians know that Adam failed, fell into sin, and so plunged the rest of us into sin with him.[19]

Second, *the covenant of redemption* is a pact among the Father, Son, and Holy Spirit in which each person participates in executing the plan of salvation, their personal properties clearly shining forth as the Triune God works salvation for his people. The Father arranges salvation by electing some from the mass of fallen humanity and giving them to the Son to redeem. The Son accomplishes salvation by completing his mission to fulfill all the requirements of salvation on our behalf and so procure everlasting life for us. Finally, the Spirit applies salvation by joining us to Christ by faith.[20] This covenant was made among the Trinity in eternity, so in that regard it precedes the covenant of works. Still, this covenant addressed the need created by Adam's breach of the covenant of works. In this respect, the covenant of redemption was a covenant of works for

18. *KTC*, 34–37 *mutatis mutandis*.

19. WSC 16; *COC*, 3:679.

20. WSC 30; *COC*, 3:682.

the Son but is a covenant of grace for us. Although other outlines could be used effectively, this book explains the covenant of redemption after the covenant of works to highlight how it expounds God's plan of rescuing us from the situation created by Adam's fall.

Third, *the covenant of grace* is God's one way of saving his people from their sin by Christ's work, which is applied to believers in history through each biblical covenant, which unifies the Triune God's saving work from Genesis 3 to Revelation 22. God has always saved his people by administering the same promise of grace through various historical covenants, but the underlying premise of the entire covenant of grace is that God has been our God because of Christ's work. James Ussher (1581–1656) explained: "What then is the sum of the covenant of grace? That God will be our God and give us Life everlasting in Christ, if we receive him, being freely by his Father offered unto us."[21] This book focuses on unpacking these three doctrinal covenants from the texts of Scripture.

Before progressing, we should note two reasons why covenant theology should be helpful for Christ's disciples, drawing from Exodus 2:23–25: "During those many days the king of Egypt died, and the people of Israel groaned because of their slavery and cried out for help. Their cry for rescue from slavery came up to God. And God heard their groaning, *and God remembered his covenant with Abraham, with Isaac, and with Jacob*. God saw the people of Israel—and God knew." First, covenants clarify our relationship with God, providing confidence that he will act for us. Abraham's descendants were in distress, but God would act to rescue them. They were unlikely the only people struggling in the world at that time as, undoubtedly, other peoples even felt the Egyptian empire's weight. Nonetheless, God acted particularly to free Abraham's descendants from their plight, precisely because he had covenanted with Abraham. God's covenant, therefore, establishes a special promissory bond with his people, which even the passing centuries cannot break. God's promise is unchangeable because he makes his promises within covenants that obligate him—of course by his own choice—to be faithful to those promises. "God saw the people of Israel—and God knew" precisely in the sense that he knew them as the people who were special to

21. James Ussher, *A Body of Divinitie* (London: Thomas Downes and George Badger, 1645), 159.

him as his own treasured possession *because* he had covenanted with their forefather Abraham. God's promise to Abraham still applies to his people today, as the apostle Paul clearly explained in Galatians 3–4, entailing that Christians can be equally as sure that God will act on our behalf and has done so in Christ. So, covenants are a source of clarity and assurance about how you relate to God.

Second, covenants unite the biblical storyline. As we will see particularly regarding the covenant of grace, covenant theology at least in part concerns Scripture's narrative about the drama of redemption. That concern helps us understand that God has been writing one unified story of salvation from Genesis 3 to the actual events described in Revelation 22. The principles of covenant theology unify the Bible's story about God redeeming a people for himself. Even though we have to read our Bibles well to discern the doctrines of covenant theology, in return covenant theology helps us to read our Bibles more deeply.

Covenant theology makes us more aware of how the God who is sovereign has been directing history, certainly toward his people's redemption, but particularly toward their redemption in Christ. Christ is the scope of all Scripture in that all Scripture points to him who achieved the forgiveness of our sins and grants us access to God's throne of grace. Christ was not God's backup plan but first plan of salvation at every point of the biblical narrative. So, covenants also help us read our Bible with depth and clarity.

TWO COVENANTAL PRINCIPLES

This chapter's remainder explains one of Reformed covenant theology's fundamental principles, namely, that our relationship with God must be *founded* on only one of two distinct premises: law or gospel. The point is not to oversimplify each historical covenant as each neatly belonging to one category but that two thoroughly distinct covenantal principles—namely, works and grace—undergird the two mutually exclusive ways of relating to God.[22] Although the biblical covenants' features vary their emphases concerning obligation and promise, the principle basis by which we relate to God, personal obedience or God's grace, cannot be mixed. To be clear, these principles of works and grace are opposed,

22. Horton, "Covenant," 436–41.

not in themselves or in God, but regarding us as sinners.[23] The following discussion does not, then, erase the complexities concerning the historical features of the biblical covenants nor believers' experience within them. Rather, it highlights that however these complexities may be present in a covenant's *administration*, contributing in various ways to the developing biblical narrative, ultimately, a person's relationship with God necessarily rests *in principle* upon the *basis* of either law or gospel—specifically, concerning how to be right with him and obtain his blessings.

Reformed theology has historically emphasized that our categories of the covenants of works and grace explain why grace and works cannot be mixed concerning the basis for our relationship with God, undergirding the law-gospel distinction.[24] Even at the confessional level, the Second Helvetic Confession 13.1 states, "The gospel is certainly opposed to the law. For the law works wrath and announces the curse, but the gospel proclaims grace and blessing."[25] The law-gospel distinction is then a confessional issue rather than a matter of private opinion.

Interestingly, the Reformed commentary tradition prominently features this law-gospel distinction, showing its nature as a biblical deduction more than simply a doctrinal construct. John Calvin (1509–1564), commenting on Galatians, said the principles of law and grace are a "contradiction of the premises," since "the law binds every human under the curse" making it "vain to strive for blessing by it."[26] In other words, "salvation by the law and by the promise are contrary," so that "establishing one destroys the other certainly because the promise has respect to faith, but the law to works."[27] William Perkins (1558–1602), arguing that this law-gospel distinction is an essential part of what Jude 1:3 calls the faith once for all delivered to the saints, wrote, "The law and gospel are two parts of the Word of God and are divers kinds of doctrine. By the law, I understand that part of God's Word which promises life to the obeyer. By the gospel, that part which promises it to the believer."[28] Perkins saw

23. *ACW*, 199.

24. Michael S. Horton, "Covenant Theology," in *CDT*, 36–41.

25. *COC*, 3:260.

26. *CO*, 50:208; *CC*, 21:1.88–89.

27. *CO*, 50: 214; *CC*, 21:1.98.

28. *WWP*, 4:53 (commentary on Jude 3).

the same teaching in Paul's letter to the Galatians as well, writing: "Let us again mark here the difference between the law and the gospel. The law promises life, but to the worker for his works, or upon condition of obedience. The gospel called by Paul "the promise" offers and gives life freely without the condition of any work and requires nothing but the receiving of that which is offered."[29] Likewise reflecting on Galatians 3:12, Rollock explained the significance of "the law is not of faith" by arguing "these two—law and faith—thus far fight, so that if a person would be righteous by faith, now he would not be so by the law ... certainly, when someone seeks for the meritorious cause of justification and its principal effect, surely then, at this point, these two are reciprocally split apart from each other, so that if you set up one, it is necessary that you refuse the other."[30] The Reformed exegetical tradition, then, saw the principles of law and gospel as a thoroughly biblical doctrine.

The law-gospel distinction was also part of the Reformed dogmatic heritage. Herman Witsius (1636–1708) explained:

> The Apostle teaches us this distinction (Rom. 3:27) where he mentions the law of works, and the law of faith; by the law of works, understanding that doctrine which points out the way in which, by means of works, salvation is obtained; and by the law of faith, that doctrine which directs by faith to obtain salvation. The form of the covenant of works is, "the man, which doth those things shall live by them," (Rom. 10:5). That of the covenant of grace is, "whosoever believeth in him, shall not be ashamed," (Rom. 10:11).[31]

Connecting his point to that Reformed exegetical tradition, Witsius commented on Galatians 3:11–12, "For, in vain would any seek for eternal life by the law, if never promised in it. But the Apostle places the whole difference, not in the thing promised, but in the condition of obtaining the promise."[32] Herman Bavinck (1854–1921) put it similarly, "Grace and works stand at opposite poles from each other and are mutually exclusive."[33]

---

29. *WWP*, 2:193 (commentary on Galatians 3:18).

30. Robert Rollock, *Analysis Logica in Epistolam Pauli Apostoli ad Galatas* (London: Felix Kyngston, 1602), 54.

31. *EC*, 1.1.15.

32. *EC*, 1.4.7.

33. *WWG*, 254; *BRD*, 4:453.

Geerhardus Vos (1862–1949) then overtly connected these distinct principles to Reformed covenant theology: "In Scripture, then, the antithesis between law and gospel is meant such that the law as the condition of the covenant of works and the gospel exclude each other."[34] The Reformed consensus then is that the principles of works and grace contrast in regard to our right standing with God.[35]

Exegetical considerations demonstrate why the Reformed so readily appropriated this distinction as a fundamental part of our doctrinal system. Paul crisply summarized how grace and works cannot both ground our relationship with God in Romans 11:6: "But if it is by grace, it is no longer on the basis of works; otherwise grace would no longer be grace." Paul contrasted works and obedience on the one hand with grace and gift on the other, showing why the distinction between the covenant of works and covenant of grace is useful and *biblical*.[36] Romans 5:15–19 highlights this contrast:

> But the *free gift* is not like the trespass. For if many died through one man's trespass, much more have the grace of God and the *free gift* by the *grace* of that one man Jesus Christ abounded for many. And the *free gift* is not like the result of that one man's sin. For the judgment following one trespass brought condemnation, but the *free gift* following many trespasses brought justification. For if, *because of* one man's *trespass*, death reigned through that one man, much more will those who receive *the abundance of grace and the free gift* of righteousness reign in life through the one man Jesus Christ. Therefore, as one trespass led to condemnation for all men, so one act of righteousness leads to justification and life for all men. For as by the *one man's disobedience* the many were made sinners, so by the *one man's obedience* the many will be made righteous.

Paul emphasized the *free gift* and how this free gift, which comes entirely through grace, results in justification, so it is *not like* the original trespass that Adam committed by breaking God's law. Adam's relationship with

---

34. *VRD*, 5:86.

35. *TI*, 8.3.4; *CW*, 12–13, 63.

36. Belcher, *Fulfillment*, 33–35; Horton, *Covenant Theology*, 35–50; Barcellos, *Covenant of Works*, 88–89.

God was tied to his obedience, contrasting his failure by disobeying with Christ's victory by obeying. Believers receive grace and life, not because we obey, but because someone else obeyed for us.[37]

The biblical narrative shows how these principles apply in the history of God's people, tying this law-gospel distinction to the covenants. Genesis records the story of Abraham, a supremely important figure in the history of God's covenants. God promised to make Abraham the father of countless descendants, even as many as the stars of heaven or sands on the shore (Gen 22:17). Abraham and his wife, Sarah, were elderly though and struggled to believe God's promise, so they acted to bring God's promises about by their own works. Abraham had a son with one of Sarah's handmaids, Hagar, and this son's name was Ishmael. Despite Abraham's lack of faith and his sinful efforts to claim God's promise by his own works, God still blessed Abraham with a son through Sarah, whom they named Isaac. In Galatians 4:24–26, Paul, interpreting the difference between the two mothers of Abraham's children, connected the issues of promise and works to the covenants: "Now this may be interpreted allegorically: *these women are two covenants*. One is from Mount Sinai, bearing children *for slavery*; she is Hagar. Now Hagar is Mount Sinai in Arabia; she corresponds to the present Jerusalem, for she is in slavery with her children. *But the Jerusalem above is free*, and she is our mother." Paul's point was that although we can relate to God only by covenant, there are two kinds of covenants, one placing sinners in slavery and one making us free.[38]

Redemptive history unfolded so that these two covenants, one with Abraham and one with Israel at Mount Sinai, would teach about the two covenantal principles that are opposed concerning the foundation of our relationship with God. Even in Galatians, Paul addressed errors about justification because the Galatians had bought the lie that sinners could and must do some act of obedience in order to be right with God, namely, in their case, circumcision.[39] In Galatians 3:9–19, as he explained God's

---

37. Michael Horton, *Justification*, 2 vol. (Grand Rapids: Zondervan, 2018), 2:57–60.

38. Herman Ridderbos, *The Epistle of Paul to the Churches of Galatia* (Grand Rapids: Eerdmans, 1953), 172–76; Richard N. Longenecker, *Galatians* (Grand Rapids: Zondervan, 1990), 210–11; *BTA*, 105–11; Rollock, *Treatise*, 6–7; *CW*, 5–6.

39. F. F. Bruce, *The Epistle to the Galatians* (Grand Rapids: Eerdmans, 1982), 19–32; David A. deSilva, *The Letter to the Galatians* (Grand Rapids: Eerdmans, 2018), 7–26; Thomas R. Schreiner, *Galatians* (Grand Rapids: Zondervan, 2010), 390–92.

redemptive-historical purposes for the Abrahamic and Mosaic covenants, Paul defended why we cannot combine the mutually exclusive principles of works and faith regarding the basis on which we relate to God.

This redemptive-historical point highlights how the lived experience of God's people often includes the temptation to categorize wrongly our endeavors to obey God as the need to keep his law to maintain our right standing with him. Those who lived under the Mosaic covenant—and especially those who tried to keep living under it after Christ came—experienced the continual threat of God's curse lingering over them as a warning against any breach against the law.[40] Although individually saved by grace alone, Israel's national experience under the law pointed to the theological reality that everyone who trusts in their works is condemned and cursed by the law (Gal 3:10; Rom 2:17).[41]

Christians often believe that God's law and our obedience to it serves no purpose unless we keep it to gain something from God. Some Galatians had come to think that the Mosaic law's purpose was to add the condition of obedience to faith for obtaining God's blessings. They were greatly confused about why Christians seek to obey God's law, a problem remaining today. As Calvin explained, "Where we hear that the law has no influence for conveying justification, various thoughts immediately creep up, either it is therefore useless, or it is opposed to God's covenant, or something of that sort."[42] In truth, the Mosaic covenant served at least in part to "make transgressions known, and in this way [to] compel people to admit their guilt."[43] So, the law shows us how we need the promise because sinners cannot obtain God's blessings but by grace.

The principles of works and grace are then entirely opposed concerning the foundation of our relationship with God. We cannot look to our obedience as a reason for God to accept us because we need to relate to him by the kind of covenant founded on grace, which then cannot be

---

40. T. David Gordon, *Promise, Law, Faith: Covenant-Historical Reasoning in Galatians* (Peabody, MA: Hendrickson Academic, 2019), 7–25, 39–41; J. V. Fesko, *Galatians* (Grand Rapids: Reformation Heritage Books, 2012), 63–66; Gordon, *Promise*, 114–118.

41. *WWP*, 2:169 (commentary on Galatians 3:10); *LG*, 19, 25, 41, 64–65, 139–40; Longenecker, *Galatians*, 115–16, 128–30; Ridderbos, *Galatians*, 136–37; Brian S. Rosner, *Paul and the Law: Keeping the Commandments of God* (Downers Grove, IL: IVP Academic, 2013), 89.

42. *CO*, 50:214; *CC*, 21:1.99.

43. *CO*, 50:215; *CC*, 21:1.100.

established by works. We still strive to keep God's law as an expression of our new life and gratitude for redemption. Indeed, Christians who believe that salvation is by grace alone should long most deeply to improve in holiness. All the same, we remember that this growth in godliness is not the principle of our relationship with God, since we must know him by the covenant of grace, not the covenant of works.

CONCLUSION

Covenant theology is about our communion with God, importantly drawing our attention to the way that we live life before him, since he uses covenants to facilitate our relational communion with him. Covenant is then the context in which we find ourselves bound to our Maker, and as Christians the context in which we find ourselves bound to our Maker who is also our Redeemer and our Savior, Jesus Christ. An exploration of the biblical doctrines of the covenant, therefore, enriches and deepens our understanding of our relationship with our Triune God. Just as a child needs to understand her relationship with her parent to fathom love, discipline, and guidance, we must understand the structure of our relationship with our God in order to appreciate the deepest and most joyful relationship for which we were created. In other words, the Christian life circles around our awareness that we belong to God in Christ.

These two covenant principles show how God is supremely committed to giving his blessings to his people. Although sinners cannot obtain God's favor by our works, God has offered his gifts to us on the basis of his free grace. This distinction between two covenantal principles undergirds the difference between what the Reformed tradition has termed the covenant of works and the covenant of grace. Before the fall, God made a law covenant with Adam that established the patterns, structures, types, and a foundation for the tensions that would occur in redemptive history, all anticipating Christ and concerning what he would achieve for his people and distribute to us on the principle of grace alone.[44]

44. Stephen J. Wellum, "Progressive Covenantalism," in *CDT*, 90; Stephen J. Wellum, "A Progressive Covenantalism Response," in *CDT*, 205–7; cf. *KTC*, 675.

Part One

THE COVENANT OF WORKS

11

The Covenant with Adam and Its Law

The law of his God is in his heart; his steps do not slip.
—*Psalm 37:31*

When God created humanity, he formed Adam fit for communion with his Maker, suiting us for relationship with him. God shaped his relationship with Adam by a covenant, making Adam's rich and blessed communion covenantal. *Love* was at this covenant's heart.

The covenant of works, based on that *covenantal principle* of law and works rather than grace and promise, concerns God making a covenant with Adam regarding his everlasting destiny. The Westminster Confession outlines the basic premises of this covenant: "The first covenant made with man was a covenant of works, wherein life was promised to Adam, and in him to his posterity, upon condition of perfect and personal obedience" (WCF 7.2).[1] From this description, this chapter unpacks how Scripture teaches of God's covenant with Adam, its offered reward of life and its legal conditions. Centrally, the covenant of works is the context for God and Adam to demonstrate love for one another. God created Adam to be his friend

1. *COC*, 3:616–17.

in communion and, although not obligated to do so, offered everlasting rewards if Adam would reciprocate the love that he had already received by keeping God's law.

ADAM'S ORIGINAL RIGHTEOUSNESS

Before examining specific aspects of the covenant of works, understanding Adam's created condition informs its important contours. Some readers might find it odd that Adam in the covenant of works might have received reward from God by his works, since Reformed theology clearly excludes salvation by works. On the one hand, truly, *salvation* is God's gracious rescue of sinners who are fallen, condemned, and in rebellion against God. On the other hand, the covenant of works is about God's relationship with humanity *before the fall,* preceding our need of salvation from sin's consequences and corruption. Critically, before the fall, God made human nature upright and very good. In contrast to fallen sinners, Adam's upright condition allowed him to give pure expression to his love for God through good works.

In that created state, Adam had the ability to keep and to fulfill God's law.[2] In Genesis 1:31, when God completed creation by making humankind in his image, he assessed his whole work and affirmed that creation was "very good," excluding sinful rebellion since God cannot affirm sinful things as good and certainly not as very good.[3]

The Reformed confessions reflect upon creation's goodness, providing insight that brings together creation's original goodness and the image of God. The Heidelberg Catechism explains the difference between our condition before and after the fall:

> 6. *Did God create man thus wicked and perverse?*
>
> No; but God created man good, and after His own image—that is, in righteousness and true holiness; that he might rightly know God his Creator, heartily love him, and live with him in eternal blessedness, to glorify and praise him.[4]

2. *CW*, 3, 29–31, 41–43.

3. Cf. John H. Walton, *The Lost World of Adam and Eve: Genesis 2–3 and the Human Origins Debate* (Downers Grove, IL: IVP Academic, 2015), 128–39.

4. *COC*, 3:309.

The Canons of Dort give a fuller description to this pre- and post-fall contrast:

> Man was originally formed after the image of God. His understanding was adorned with a true and saving knowledge of his Creator, and of spiritual things; his heart and will were upright, all his affections pure; and the whole Man was holy; but revolting from God by the instigation of the devil, and abusing the freedom of his own will, he forfeited these excellent gifts, and on the contrary entailed on himself blindness of mind, horrible darkness, vanity, and perverseness of judgement; became wicked, rebellious, and obdurate in heart and will, and impure in [all] his affections.[5]

The Westminster Confession 4.2 says,

> After God had made all other creatures, he created man, male and female, with reasonable and immortal souls, endued with knowledge, righteousness, and true holiness, after his own image, having the law of God written in their hearts, and power to fulfill it; and yet under a possibility of transgressing, being left to the liberty of their own will, which was subject unto change. Beside this law written in their hearts, they received a command not to eat of the tree of the knowledge of good and evil; which while they kept were happy in their communion with God, and had dominion over the creatures.[6]

Our tradition has united opinion about humanity's original goodness.[7]

That God made humanity with the law written on our hearts "and the power to fulfill it" is significant. God's image entails original righteousness and holiness, along with an original knowledge of God's law and ability to keep it by our natural strength.[8] As early as the fifth century, Augustine (354–430) wrote, "Nature was made intact, only afterward

5. Canons of Dort 3/4.1; *COC*, 3:587–88.

6. *COC*, 3:611–12.

7. See also BC articles 14–15; *COC*, 3:398–401.

8. Concerning the importance of Adam's *natural* strength, see Harrison Perkins, *Righteous by Design: Covenantal Merit and Adam's Original Integrity* (Fearn, UK: Mentor, forthcoming).

being corrupted by sin."[9] John Colquhoun describes how God entered the covenant with Adam who was "without standing in need, for that purpose, of any further supplies of habitual grace."[10] James Ussher also argues that Adam's obedience "should be natural according to that strength God put into him at the beginning."[11] So too, William Perkins explains, "When God first gave the law, He also gave power to fulfill the law. If the law be impossible, it is not God's fault, but man's, who by his own fault has lost this power of keeping the law."[12] In other words, grace is opposed to sin rather than human nature.[13]

A web of biblical statements undergirds the Reformed confession about human nature's original integrity. In Ephesians 4:24, Paul exhorts believers "to put on the new self, created after the likeness of God in true righteousness and holiness," clearly linking our renewal *in the likeness of God* to righteousness and holiness. In Colossians 3:10, he grounds his instruction that Christians ought not to lie to one another in how we "have put on the new man, which is being renewed *in knowledge* after the image of its creator." Bearing God's image entails a certain knowledge, righteousness, and holiness.[14]

Emphatically, this description of bearing God's image pertains to our life *before the fall*. After the fall, sin tarnishes God's image in us and damages our ability to keep God's law. Ecclesiastes 7:29 reflects upon the quest to find wisdom among the human race: "See, this alone I found, that God made man upright, but they have sought out many schemes." God's creation of an originally good, upright, and righteous humanity shines in shocking contrast to our quest after wickedness. The contrast is shocking because, as the Westminster Confession 4.2 notes, God made Adam in his image with the natural ability to keep the law.[15]

Notably, Adam's creation in God's image entailed knowledge of the law. God's law describes not a list of rules invented without reason, but his

9. Augustine, *Concerning Nature and Grace*, §3, in *PL*, 44:249; *NPNF1*, 5:122.

10. *CW*, 29–30.

11. CUL MS Mm. 6.55, fol. 228v (sermon on Galatians 3:12 dated June 29, 1651).

12. *WWP*, 2:173–74 (commentary on Galatians 3:10).

13. *BRD*, 3:516–17, 573–79.

14. *BRD*, 2:557–59.

15. See also *TI*, 8.3.5, 11, 14; 8.6.10.

own righteous character.[16] The Westminster Larger Catechism 95 reads, "The Moral Law is of use to all men, to inform them *of the holy nature and will of God*."[17] Herman Bavinck explained, "The law, after all, is an expression of God's being."[18] Even as God summarized the moral law in the Ten Commandments at Mount Sinai, he prefaced them by announcing his own name: "I am the Lord your God, who brought you out of the land of Egypt, out of the house of slavery" (Exod 20:2). This announcement links the following commandments to God's identity as descriptions of his divine character.[19] God is faithful, so we should not commit adultery. God is generous, so we should not covet. God is life, so we should not murder. Since the moral law describes God's character and since we are made in God's image to reflect his goodness into the world, we inescapably have knowledge of what the law requires.[20] God's law is inherently connected to God's character, so too God's image stamped into human nature also conveys awareness of God's character.[21]

Since Adam was stamped as God's image and had inescapable knowledge of God's character, he also had natural knowledge of God's law. Romans 1:18–23 explains that, even though sin tarnishes God's image, we still retain knowledge of that law through God's natural revelation.[22] After all, "what can be known about God is plain to them, because God has shown it to them"—specifically by making us in his image (Rom 1:19). Further, God's "invisible attributes, namely, his eternal power and divine nature, have been clearly perceived, ever since the creation of the world, in the things that have been made," particularly in our own nature constituted in God's image (Rom 1:20). Paul concludes that our sin means we "are without excuse" because God has revealed his law's requirements

16. *CMT*, 62; *CRS*, 1:17, 356–58; *EC*, 1.3.8–19; *TI*, 3.18.1–12; 11.1.4, 9; 11.2.4–7.

17. *LC*, 84 (emphasis added).

18. *BRD*, 4:455.

19. *KTC*, 379–80.

20. *CF*, 387–406; *KTC*, 225–32, 551; Schreiner, *Covenant*, 23–25.

21. Webster, "*Rector et Iudex*," 171–72; Andrew Davison, *Participation in God: A Study in Christian Doctrine and Metaphysics* (Cambridge: Cambridge University Press, 2019), 106–8; Richard C. Barcellos, *Getting the Garden Right: Adam's Work and God's Rest in Light of Christ* (Cape Coral, FL: Founders Press, 2017), 123–33, 137–44.

22. Jonathan Burnside, *God, Justice, and Society: Aspects of Law and Legality in the Bible* (New York: Oxford University Press, 2011), 81–84.

by making us in his image. God's covenant with Adam, requiring perfect works, was premised on Adam's good and upright created state. God is a loving God, generous and kind in how he made Adam, fashioning human nature with the capacity to understand righteousness and so to know how to return God's love.

THE COVENANT WITH ADAM

Since God made Adam with original righteousness so that humans would have the capacity to have a loving relationship with God, the covenant of works was the first context for us to express that love for God. We first need to establish that the Bible attests to a covenant between God and Adam as the first premise directly about the covenant of works. Admittedly, Genesis does not say, "and then God made a covenant with Adam," so a case must be made that this covenant was present.[23] Still, if you walk into a venue where the audience is focused on a band playing on stage, you know that this is a concert even without a marquee saying so. The same is true of a covenant in Genesis 1–3.

Hosea 6:7 is one text traditionally understood to teach a covenant with Adam: "But *like Adam* they transgressed the covenant; there they dealt faithlessly with me." In addressing Israel's sin, Hosea indicates that their manner of covenant violations was "like Adam." Many Reformed theologians have seen this verse as a reference to a covenant involving the first man.[24]

---

23. Charles Hodge, *Systematic Theology*, 3 vol. (New York: Scribner, Armstrong, and Co., 1877), 2:117–18; *MMB*, 20; J. V. Fesko, *Last Things First: Unlocking Genesis 1–3 with the Christ of Eschatology* (Fearn, UK: Mentor, 2007), 82–95; *BOC*, 26–29; John Bolt, "Why the Covenant of Works Is a Necessary Doctrine: Revisiting Objections to a Venerable Reformed Doctrine," in *By Faith Alone: Answering the Challenges to the Doctrine of Justification*, eds. Gary L. Johnson and Guy P. Waters (Wheaton, IL: Crossway, 2006), 171–89; *KTC*, 211–15; Barcellos, *Covenant of Works*, 7–28, 57–68; Schreiner, *Covenant*, 19–23; Pieter de Vries, "Can the Relationship between God and Man/Creation Before the Fall Be Characterized as a Covenant?" *MAJT* 30 (2019): 73–83.

24. Westminster Assembly, *Annotations upon all the Books of the Old and New Testament* (London, 1645), *ad loc.*; B. B. Warfield, *Selected Shorter Writings of Benjamin B. Warfield*, ed. John E. Meeter, 2 vol. (Phillipsburg, NJ: P&R, 1970), 1:116–29; C. F. Keil, *The Twelve Minor Prophets*, trans. James Martin, 2 vol. (Edinburgh: T&T Clark, 1878), 99–100; Thomas Edward McComiskey, "Hosea," in *The Minor Prophets: An Exegetical and Expository Commentary*, ed. Thomas Edward McComiskey (Grand Rapids: Baker Academic, 1998), 95; Richard P. Belcher Jr., "The Covenant of Works in the Old Testament," in *CT*, 66–67; Jeremiah Burroughs, *An Exposition with Practical Observations continued upon the Fourth, Fifth, Sixth, and Seventh Chapters of the Prophesy of Hosea* (London, 1649), 621–26; Brian C. Habig, "Hosea 6:7 Revisited," *Presbyterion* 42/1–2 (Fall 2016): 13–20; *TI*, 8.3.8; *CW*, 6–7;

Not all have accepted this meaning of Hosea 6:7, suggesting alternative translations. An older view suggests that Israel broke the covenant "like men," pointing to humanity's general rebellious inclination.[25] Although linguistically possible, this translation does not dodge the issue that the only covenant involving *every* member of humanity was made with our first father Adam.[26] More recently, scholars have preferred translating this phrase as "at Adam," suggesting there was some well-known violation of the Mosaic covenant in a city called Adam.[27] Problematically, this translation involves changing the preposition in the Hebrew text from "like" to "at," which the manuscript tradition does not support.[28] Further, this change presumes widespread knowledge of an event not recorded in Old Testament or extrabiblical literature.[29] Even concerning the history of interpretation, this understanding was only recently proposed. It first arose in higher-critical circles, having significance because many higher-critical exegetes assume that the prophetic books were written prior to the Pentateuch, entailing that the prophet Hosea could not have referred to the man Adam from Genesis.[30] In their view, Genesis had not been written for Hosea to cite.[31]

Despite these alternatives, good reason remains to understand Hosea 6:7 as referring to the Adam of Genesis. First, some of the earliest Christian interpreters see the man Adam as Hosea's referent. Jerome (d. 420) renders the phrase, "but they like Adam have transgressed the covenant" (*ipsi autem sicut Adam transgressi sunt pactum*). Jerome argues

---

Fesko, *Last Things First*, 88–91; *KTC*, 254–57; Wellum, "Progressive Covenantalism," 89; Schreiner, *Covenant*, 20–21; Barcellos, *Covenant of Works*, 77–88.

25. William Rainey Harper, *A Critical and Exegetical Commentary on Amos and Hosea* (Edinburgh: T&T Clark, 1905), 288; John Murray, *Collected Writings*, 2:47–59; *CC*, 13:2.233–35.

26. Habig, "Hosea 6:7 Revisted," 11–13.

27. E.g. Francis I. Andersen and David Noel Freedman, *Hosea* (New York: Doubleday, 1980), 435–39; A. A. Macintosh, *Hosea: A Critical and Exegetical Commentary* (Edinburgh: T&T Clark, 1997), 236–39.

28. The conjectural emendation is from כ to ב. Admittedly, the two letters look very similar, and it is not impossible that scribes may have confused the two. Still, any emendation lacking manuscript support is speculative, this one resting on erroneous assumptions about the Old Testament canon's development; Byron G. Curtis, "Hosea 6:7 and Covenant-Breaking like/at Adam," in *LNF*, 176–88.

29. Curtis, "Hosea 6:7," 195–97.

30. Julius Wellhausen, *Prolegomena to the History of Ancient Israel* (New York: Meridian, 1957), 1–13, 295–308.

31. Habig, "Hosea 6:7 Revisited," 7–11.

that Hosea meant "they were imitators of Adam, just as the one who acted in paradise by transgressing my covenant and law, so they acted in the land."[32] Likewise, Cyril of Alexandria (376–444) argues against the generic reference to humanity in favor of the proper name Adam: "The Hebrew edition, rather than 'like *man*,' has 'like *Adam* transgressing the covenant,' so that the Israelites' transgression is understood to be of the same quality as Adam's."[33] Even very early Christian exegetes argue for the reference to Adam.

Second, contextual features support a reference to Adam. In contrast to higher-critical studies, more recent scholarship has recognized that the prophetic literature, including Hosea, makes sense only within the context of the earlier books of Moses.[34] In addition to this recent insight about the prophetic books generally, Hosea regularly alludes to Genesis, making a reference to Adam more probable.[35]

Third, the other occurrence of the Hebrew phrase "like Adam" also mostly likely refers to the first man. Job 31:33 says: "If I have covered my transgressions *like Adam* by hiding my iniquity in my heart …"[36] If one rejects the higher-critical assumption that Genesis was written later in Israel's history, no reason stands to doubt that Job would have known Adam's story. In that case, the obvious allusion in the phrase "like Adam" is when Adam tried to cover his sin by sewing leaves together to hide his nakedness (Gen 3:7). Given that Job's allusion in the phrase "like Adam" is to the first man, Hosea also very likely uses the same phrase to refer to the man Adam.[37]

Hosea 6:7 does not prove the entire doctrine of the covenant of works, nor does the argument that God was in covenant with Adam rest entirely on this verse. Still, Hosea's reference to Adam offers plausible reason that he was in covenant with God, which further biblical evidence confirms.

---

32. Eusebius Hieronymus, *Commentaria in Osee*, §2.6, in *PL*, 25:869–70.

33. Cyril of Alexandria, *Commentarius in Oseam Prophetam*, §66, in *PG*, 71:169–70.

34. Curtis, "Hosea 6:7," 171–75.

35. Duane Garrett, *Hosea, Joel* (Nashville: B&H, 1997), 162–63; Curtis, "Hosea 6:7," 188–93; Harper, *Amos and Hosea*, 288.

36. My translation. The occurrence of the same lexeme כְּאָדָם in Job 31:33 and Hosea 6:7 provides some evidence against the conjectural emendation of כ to ב.

37. For a more extensive defense of Hosea 6:7 along the same lines, *ACW*, 239–62.

Two more considerations suggest a covenantal relationship between God and Adam. First, although Genesis 1–3 does not explicitly refer to a covenant between them, other instances occur where Scripture, referring to a past event, states that a covenant was made, even though the original narrative does not. A prominent example relates to God's promises to David concerning David's kingly dynasty, recorded in 2 Samuel 7:8–16:

> Now, therefore, thus you shall say to my servant David, "Thus says the Lord of hosts, I took you from the pasture, from following the sheep, that you should be prince over my people Israel. And I have been with you wherever you went and have cut off all your enemies from before you. And I will make for you a great name, like the name of the great ones of the earth. And I will appoint a place for my people Israel and will plant them, so that they may dwell in their own place and be disturbed no more. And violent men shall afflict them no more, as formerly, from the time that I appointed judges over my people Israel. And I will give you rest from all your enemies. Moreover, the Lord declares to you that the Lord will make you a house. When your days are fulfilled and you lie down with your fathers, I will raise up your offspring after you, who shall come from your body, and I will establish his kingdom. He shall build a house for my name, and I will establish the throne of his kingdom forever. I will be to him a father, and he shall be to me a son. When he commits iniquity, I will discipline him with the rod of men, with the stripes of the sons of men, but my steadfast love will not depart from him, as I took it from Saul, whom I put away from before you. And your house and your kingdom shall be made sure forever before me. Your throne shall be established forever."

This passage about how God will establish David's heir with an eternal throne over God's people does not designate these promises a covenant. Psalm 89:3–4, however, says, "You have said, 'I have made a covenant with my chosen one; I have sworn to David my servant: "I will establish your offspring forever, and build your throne for all generations." ' " This Psalm cites from 2 Samuel 7, clarifying after the fact that God's promise to David was a covenant, which confirms that Scripture need not mention that a covenant was made in its first narrative for a covenant to be present.

Further, other passages name the creation events covenants, although they are not called such in the early Genesis account. For example, Jeremiah 33:20-21: "Thus says the LORD: If you can break my covenant with the day and my covenant with the night, so that day and night will not come at their appointed time, then also my covenant with David my servant may be broken, so that he shall not have a son to reign on his throne, and my covenant with the Levitical priests my ministers." The early Genesis narratives do not say that God covenanted with the sun, moon, day, or night, but Jeremiah does. This passage also reconfirms that God's promises to David were covenantal. In addition to this evidence from Jeremiah, Malachi 2:14 gives us information about marriage that God did not initially reveal in Genesis 1–3: "But you say, 'Why does he not?' Because the LORD was witness between you and the wife of your youth, to whom you have been faithless, though she is your companion and your wife by covenant." Genesis itself does not describe Adam and Eve's relationship as a covenant, but they were married, and Scripture says marriage is a covenant.

Second, Moses depicts the garden of Eden as the first temple.[38] Most pointedly, Genesis 2:15 says that God put Adam in the garden "to work it and to keep it." The Hebrew words behind these terms are used together elsewhere to mark the priestly task to serve and to guard the temple (e.g., Num 3:6–8; Num 18:5–6; Ezek 44:14), marking Adam's role as a priest in the garden.[39] Further, the gold and onyx found near Eden (Gen 2:10–14) were used in the priestly garb (Exod 39:8–14), which forges a link

---

38. Fesko, *Last Things First*, 56–75; Benjamin L. Gladd, *From Adam and Israel to the Church: A Biblical Theology of the People of God* (Downers Grove, IL: IVP Academic, 2019), 6–12; Waltke with Fredericks, *Genesis*, 81; G. K. Beale, *A New Testament Biblical Theology: The Unfolding of the Old Testament in the New* (Grand Rapids: Baker Academic, 2011), 614–648; G. K. Beale, *The Temple and the Church's Mission: A Biblical Theology of the Dwelling Place of God* (Downers Grove, IL: IVP Academic, 2004), 32–33, 66–67; G. K. Beale, "Adam as the First Priest in Eden as the Garden Temple," *SBJT* 22.2 (2018): 9–24; John H. Walton, *Ancient Near Eastern Thought and the Old Testament: Introducing the Conceptual World of the Hebrew Bible* (Grand Rapids: Baker Academic, 2006), 123–27; John H. Walton, *The Lost World of Genesis One: Ancient Cosmology and the Origins Debate* (Downers Grove, IL: IVP Academic, 2009), 71–91, 101–6; Walton, *Lost World of Adam and Eve*, 46–52; *KTC*, 245–53.

39. G. K. Beale, *The Book of Revelation* (Grand Rapids: Eerdmans, 1999), 1110–11; Gordon J. Wenham, *Genesis 1–15* (Grand Rapids: Zondervan, 1987), 67; Fesko, *Last Things First*, 71–73; Gladd, *From Adam and Israel to the Church*, 15–18; Walton, *Lost World of Adam and Eve*, 104–15.

between Adam's surroundings and the priestly role.[40] That God appointed specifically cherubim to guard the garden of Eden after Adam's fall also indicates Adam's priestly role by marking the garden as a temple sanctuary (Gen 3:24), since cherubim guard God's presence in the tabernacle (Exod 26:1; 36:35), in the Solomonic temple (1 Kings 6:22–24), and even atop the ark of the covenant itself (Exod 25:17–22; 36:8; 37:7–9). The priesthood and the temple are always tied to a covenant.[41] If Adam was a priest in a temple, then he was the priest of a covenant.[42] Most decisively, Jesus is the high priest of the new covenant (Heb 9:15), with a direct parallel between his representative role and Adam's (Rom 5:12–21).[43]

The biblical evidence, then, indicates a covenantal relationship between God and Adam. Although that does not yet reveal anything about what that covenant was like, this covenant was the first context of loving communion between God and Adam.[44]

ADAM HAD THE LAW

Since the Reformed confessions teach that God made a covenant with Adam, requiring perfect obedience, the natural question is, "Obedience to what?" So, this section contends that God gave the moral law to Adam in paradise.

The law functioned not as some cold and removed list of rules, but as a guide for Adam in how to express his love for God well. God hardwired the law into Adam's nature, not only as an expression of his own divine character in his image bearer, but also as faithful direction for how Adam could demonstrate his love-fueled gratitude to his Maker. Too often we think of the law as hard legislation, handed down as a demanding task master. Certainly, sinners who want to try to earn God's favor by their works should think of the law precisely in this way.

---

40. Meredith G. Kline, *God, Heaven, and Har Magedon: A Covenantal Tale of Cosmos and Telos* (Eugene, OR: Wipf & Stock, 2006), 45–46, 65–66. Thanks to my friend Tim Graham for his feedback and helpful insight on this point and the following point about cherubim.

41. Geerhardus Vos, "The Priesthood of Christ in the Epistle to the Hebrews," in *RHBI*, 126–60.

42. Horton, *Justification*, 2:68–69; Barcellos, *Getting the Garden Right*, 125–33; Schreiner, *Covenant*, 25–26.

43. Schreiner, *Covenant*, 22.

44. *VRD*, 2:93.

On the other hand, another sense applies to those who belong to God in love, as with Adam in the covenant of works—namely, that God has kindly made known his law so that we are not left without direction in how best to express our love for him. So, God said in Deuteronomy 6:5–6: "You shall love the LORD your God with all your heart and with all your soul and with all your might. And these words that I command you today shall be on your heart." God reminded his people to *love* him fully, then pointed them to his revealed law as the means by which they might know how to show their love. Likewise, in John 14:15, Christ taught, "If you love me, you will keep my commandments." Of course, we must take account of how sinners are never fully able to perform the duties of the law.[45] Still, Christ clearly meant that our obedience to the law manifests our love for him. The same was true even in the Garden as the law directed Adam in how to show his love for his covenant God.[46]

As an illustration, every year near my wedding anniversary, I always hope to get a list of things that my wife might want as a present. In this case, I want to express my love for her by giving her something. I hope to have a list of what she wants because that would help me express my love for her. I want her to have what is truly pleasing to her because I love her, and the best way for me to know what pleases her is if she tells me. The same applies in Adam's (and our) relationship with God. We know best how to show our love for him if he tells us what pleases him. So, he revealed his law even in our nature to guide our expression of love.[47]

The connection of a covenant between God and Adam to Adam's reception of the law is an ancient idea. Even before the New Testament period, Jewish writers linked the creation story to both covenant and law. Although not inspired Scripture, Ben Sirach exemplifies how God's people interpreted Scripture during the intertestamental period, beginning: "The LORD created human beings from the earth, and makes them return to earth again" (Sir 17:1). Then, he connected Adam and Eve's first state to covenant and law:

45. WSC 82; *COC*, 3:694.

46. *CMT*, 63; *CRS*, 1:359.

47. WSC 39–40; *COC*, 3:684.

> He set before them knowledge,
> and allotted to them the law of life.
> An everlasting covenant he made with them,
> and his commandments he revealed to them.
> (Sir 17:11–12; NAB)

Ben Sirach understood that Adam's upright state included knowledge of the law, linked to the law of life and the commandments.[48] So, God's people have long seen the connection among Adam, covenant, and the law.

Romans 1:19–21 and 32 highlight Adam's possession of the law by addressing some important principles about our natural accountability before God.

> For what can be known about God is plain to them, because God has shown it to them. For his invisible attributes, namely, his eternal power and divine nature, have been clearly perceived, ever since the creation of the world, in the things that have been made. So they are without excuse. For although they knew God, they did not honor him as God or give thanks to him, but they became futile in their thinking, and their foolish hearts were darkened. … Though they know God's righteous decree that those who practice such things deserve to die, they not only do them but give approval to those who practice them.

All people are under condemnation because they are without excuse before God, meaning that all people *know* that all sins deserve death, since God revealed himself, his own character, and his righteous decrees about what is right and wrong to humanity by making it known to us "in the things that have been made." God's creation testifies to our liability to God's standard of righteousness.[49]

The aspect of the covenant of works in focus is, then, as described in the Westminster Confession 7.2, the "condition of perfect and personal obedience."[50] The argument is that God gave to Adam the law, which was

48. Thanks to John Fesko for alerting me to this passage.

49. Guy Prentiss Waters, *For the Mouth of the Lord Has Spoken: The Doctrine of Scripture* (Fearn, UK: Mentor, 2020), 22–26, 30–31.

50. *COC*, 3:617.

the standard of his obedience. The Reformed tradition has long taught this point: "God gave to Adam a law, as a covenant of works, by which He bound him and all his posterity to personal, entire, exact, and perpetual obedience; promised life upon the fulfilling, and threatened death upon the breach of it; and endued him with power and ability to keep it."[51] Some already noted important points are present: Adam's need for obedience, the promise of life, and Adam's natural ability to keep the law. Additionally, we also see the present point that God gave the law to Adam, giving it to him as the covenant of works.[52] These confessional observations establish this doctrine's historically Reformed pedigree, prompting consideration of the more important scriptural teaching.

The consideration of Romans 1:18–21 and 32 already indicated that God made the world in such a way that we know him and his righteous decrees through the creation itself—through what we call natural or general revelation—leaving sinners without excuse before God as our judge.[53] Paul reconfirms that point in Romans 2, where he attempts to convict the Jewish people that their possession of God's *written oracles* did not automatically secure their justification—their right standing before God.[54] Their possession of the written law rendered them without excuse since it is not the hearers but "the doers of the law who will be justified" (Rom 2:13).[55] Remembering the difference between God's law as it was built into creation, as described in Romans 1, and the written law given to Israel, then Romans 2:14 makes clear sense: "For when Gentiles, who do not have the [written] law, *by nature do what the [natural] law requires*, they are a law to themselves, even though they do not have the [written] law." The bracketed words clarify Paul's different ways of referring to the law regarding what every person knows by nature and what some know more

---

51. WCF 19.1; *COC*, 3:640.

52. *CW*, 46–47.

53. Guy Prentiss Waters, "Romans," in *A Biblical-Theological Introduction to the New Testament: The Gospel Realized*, ed. Michael J. Kruger (Wheaton, IL: Crossway, 2016), 182–83; J. V. Fesko, *Reforming Apologetics: Retrieving the Classic Reformed Approach to Defending the Faith* (Grand Rapids: Baker Academic, 2019), 11–48.

54. Waters, "Romans," 183–84.

55. Waters, "Romans," 183n64.

clearly through biblical revelation.[56] John Calvin comments, "It is as if Paul had said that knowledge of the written law is not necessary for the just condemnation of a sinner."[57] So, there is a natural law that explains why all human beings are without excuse and know that those who break God's law are owed the death penalty.[58]

The way we live in our societies illustrates this distinction between knowing the law by nature and having the written law. Most households do not own a personal copy of their town's legal codes. Still, everyone who lives in that town has a general, almost innate, sense of what behavior accords to their community's legal standards. Certainly, law enforcement assumes that every citizen knows the law well enough so that there is accountability to that law even when families do not own a written copy. On the other hand, those families who do own a copy of the town's legal codes are beyond excuse in reference to knowing the law. A town lawyer, for example, cannot plead ignorance about what he or she should have done.

The point is that knowledge of the law is similar in our relationship with God. Human beings have a fundamental understanding of what God's law requires simply because we are God's image and have been especially marked in his likeness.[59] In addition to that natural awareness of God's requirements, God also wrote down his moral law and gave it to Israel at Mount Sinai. Israel had natural *and* written knowledge of God's law, rendering them all the more accountable, but every person has that natural knowledge.

In Romans 5:12–14, Adam's role as a covenant head more directly confirms this notion of the law given to humanity by nature.

---

56. Richard Muller explained the Reformed Orthodox view of the moral law as that "which is primarily intended to be the rule of morals." So, "the *lex moralis* is identical with the *lex naturalis* (q.v.), but unlike the natural law, it is given by revelation in a form that is clearer and fuller than what is otherwise known to the reason." So too, the Reformed consensus was that the natural law "rests on the righteous and utterly holy divine nature—and is good because God is good, in contrast to the positive law (*lex positiva*, q.v.) of God, which is good because God commanded it." These principles are commonly known by rational creatures, so that the natural law was known even by those who did not receive the revelation of the Mosaic law; *DLGTT*, 196–98; *TI*, 9.9.17; 10.4.28.

57. *CO*, 49:36; *CC*, 19:2.95.

58. Burnside, *God, Justice, and Society*, 76–81; *ACW*, 161–81; *CRS*, 1:358, 360; *LG*, 7–14.

59. Barcellos, *Getting the Garden Right*, 137–44.

> Therefore, just as sin came into the world through one man, and death through sin, and so death spread to all men because all sinned—for sin indeed was in the world before the [written] law was given, but sin is not counted where there is no law. Yet death reigned from Adam to Moses, even over those whose sinning was not like the transgression of Adam, who was a type of the one who was to come.

Death is the consequence of sin, which was in the world before God gave the *written* law at Sinai, yet sin is counted only where a law is present. Clearly, Paul again had in mind that distinction between the law as known by nature and the law as written at Sinai because of the time frame "from Adam to Moses."[60] Sin, which results in death, is the lack of conformity to or the breaking of God's law.[61] Adam, then, had a law because Paul said death results from sin, Adam certainly sinned and died, and yet sin requires a law.[62] Paul had said as much in Romans 4:15: "Where there is no law there is no transgression." So, Adam clearly possessed a law, which we will see is a crucial feature of the covenant of works.

THE CONTENT OF ADAM'S LAW

What did that creation law command? This section argues that the law that God gave to Adam, of which even other nations besides Israel maintained some possession, was essentially summarized in the Ten Commandments.[63] These commandments *summarize* the law that God built into us by nature, explaining one reason why they remain important to God's people in all ages: they are hardwired into us as creatures made

60. *TI*, 5.9.17.

61. WSC 14; *COC*, 3:678.

62. Richard N. Longenecker, *Paul, Apostle of Liberty*, 2nd ed. (Grand Rapids: Eerdmans, 2015), 86–87; David VanDrunen, "Israel's Recapitulation of Adam's Probation under the Law of Moses," *WTJ* 73 no 2 (Fall 2011): 306–10; Meredith G. Kline, "Gospel until the Law: Rom 5:13–14 and the Old Covenant," *JETS* 34 no 4 (Dec 1991): 433–46; Horton, *Justification*, 2:63–65; *CW*, 10–12.

63. *MT*, 1.10.5–7, 16, 26–29; *EC*, 1.3.7; *CRS*, 1:356–60; *CW*, 45–46; Horton, *Justification*, 2:75. For discussion of lists of ancient Near Eastern law as summarizing a wider network of covenantal expectation, see Walton and Walton, *Lost World of the Torah*, 25–53. I would emphasize that the point about the Ten Commandments as a summary of the natural law should highlight that the natural law is not less than its summary, making plenty of room for applications of the Ten Commandments like those found in HC 94–113, WLC 103–148, and WSC 45–81.

in God's image.[64] Again, this notion is not new in the Reformed tradition, as the Westminster Confession 19.2 shows: "This law [that God had given to Adam as a covenant of works], after his [Adam's] fall, continued to be a perfect rule of righteousness; and, as such, was delivered by God upon mount Sinai in ten commandments, and written in two tables; the first four commandments containing our duty towards God, and the other six our duty to man."[65] The confession summarizes how God did not invent new rules at Mount Sinai but simply wrote down the same law principles that he had always made known to humankind, especially as we were created in his image.

The church, then, unsurprisingly values the Ten Commandments as a guide to living the Christian life. The idea that God revealed these laws before he wrote them on stone tablets at Mount Sinai might be new to some, but the idea is actually ancient. Even prior to Christ's coming, intertestamental Jewish writers taught that the Torah had an eternal basis and was known before its revelation at Sinai.[66] After the apostolic period, Irenaeus of Lyons (c. 130–c. 202) argued, "For from the beginning, God certainly was admonishing them *through the natural precepts which he had built into humanity from the start*, that is *through the Decalogue*."[67] Irenaeus understood that God wrote the law into humanity by creation and gave this natural law again in the Ten Commandments.[68] In this respect, Irenaeus, although not connecting it directly to a works principle, believed that God made a covenant with Adam.[69] Chapter 7, however, discusses how Irenaeus's arguments have remarkable similarity to how the Reformed understand the covenant of works. Regardless, the point that these laws reliably summarize in writing what people as made in God's image know by nature provides tremendous help in understanding why the biblical authors hold everyone from any nation and people

64. *CMT*, 62–63; *MMB*, 20–21; Brandon D. Crowe, *The Path of Faith: A Biblical Theology of Covenant and Law* (Downers Grove, IL: IVP Academic, 2021), 46–50.

65. *COC*, 3:640.

66. DeSilva, *Galatians*, 311.

67. Irenaeus, *Against Heresies*, 4.15.1 in *PG*, 7.1:1012; *ANF*, 1:479 (emphasis added).

68. Irenaeus, *Against Heresies*, 4.16.3 in *PG*, 7.1:1017; *ANF*, 1:481.

69. Irenaeus, *Against Heresies*, 3.11.8 in *PG*, 7.1:389; *ANF*, 1:429.

group accountable to the standards of God's moral law, even if they have not read the Bible.

This point prompts a reconsideration of biblical passages that otherwise may seem obscure or imprecise. For example, Amos 1:1–2:5 contains a lengthy chain of indictments against various nations for their transgressions.[70] Amos 1:3 opens the first formal accusation by saying, "Thus says the LORD: 'For three transgressions of Damascus, and for four, I will not revoke the punishment, because they have threshed Gilead with threshing sledges of iron." Throughout Amos 1, the prophet rebukes the nations that surrounded Israel for their transgressions.[71] Poignantly, after the long series of rebukes against those surrounding nations, in Amos 2:4 the prophet says, "Thus says the LORD: 'For three transgressions of Judah, and for four, I will not revoke the punishment, because they have rejected the law of the LORD, and have not kept his statutes, but their lies have led them astray, those after which their fathers walked.' " As another example, the prophet Isaiah likewise announces that the whole world's inhabitants have ruined the world by transgressing God's law and breaking his everlasting covenant: "The earth lies defiled under its inhabitants; for they have transgressed the laws, violated the statutes, broken the everlasting covenant" (Isa 24:5).[72] God's rebuke against his own people *and foreign nations* for their sin will not surprise most Christians but still raises the question how he could hold those other nations accountable for their sin when he had not revealed the written law to them as he had to Israel.[73]

The answer is that God gave a law to Adam and hardwired that law into us as those made in his image. That explains *how* everyone is without excuse before God, but not *what law* held everyone accountable. Petrus van Mastricht (1630–1706) explained that "all the Decalogue's obligations are demanded from man by the covenant of nature" because they are the law "naturally, then divinely, then humanly so far as man bears God's

---

70. For detailed exegesis for this understanding of Amos 1:1–2:5, see David VanDrunen, *Divine Covenants and Moral Order: A Biblical Theology of Natural Law* (Grand Rapids: Eerdmans, 2014), 167–78.

71. Interestingly, "transgressions" is a technical term that denotes sins that are violations of a covenant; *ACW*, 233–36, 282–91, 299.

72. *ACW*, 217–37.

73. VanDrunen, *Divine Covenants*, 178–90.

image."[74] Amos could then legitimately pronounce God's rebuke against the surrounding nations because they were accountable to the same basic law as Israel, since all people everywhere, made in God's image, have an in-built knowledge of God's *moral* law. This point comes to new clarity when we consider Paul's words in Romans 10:5: "For Moses writes about the righteousness that is based on the law, that the person who does the commandments shall live by them." The righteousness that Moses described, which Romans 10 makes clear no sinner can achieve, is about doing the commandments. God did not invent these commandments at Sinai, but wrote them in our hearts at creation, and *then* wrote them on stone tablets at Sinai.

Paul's explanation of the law, again in Romans 5:12–14, further clarifies the relationship of the natural and Mosaic law. Here, Adam and Moses are the two figures structuring this consideration of the law. Death as the consequence for transgressing *the law* equally afflicted those who lived "from Adam to Moses." Significantly then, the law which was given to Adam had some connection to the law which Moses had, at least in that the same penalty for violating the moral law as revealed at Sinai applied to everyone since Adam's first sin. In other words, the Ten Commandments were linked both to Adam and to Moses.

The fourth commandment, which concerns remembering the Sabbath as a day of restful communion in worship with our God, may provide a helpful example to corroborate the point that the Ten Commandments belong to humanity by nature. Arguably the fourth commandment—possibly along with the second, prohibiting images of the Godhead—is the most contested among contemporary evangelicals.[75] Some theologians argue that the fourth commandment does not bind the weekly practice of new covenant believers because, in their view, it is strictly associated

74. Petrus van Mastricht, *Theoretica-Practica Theologia* (1699), 3.12.28.

75. For defense of the Reformed understanding of the second commandment, see David VanDrunen, "Iconoclasm, Incarnation and Eschatology: Toward a Catholic Understanding of the Reformed Doctrine of the 'Second' Commandment," *IJST* 6 no 2 (April 2004): 130–47; David VanDrunen, "Pictures of Jesus and the Sovereignty of Divine Revelation: Recent Literature and a Defense of the Confessional Reformed View," *Confessional Presbyterian* 5 (2009): 214–27; Harrison Perkins, "Images of Christ and the Vitals of the Reformed System," *Confessional Presbyterian* 14 (2018): 201–15, 272–74.

with the Mosaic covenant and not creational.[76] The purpose of using this debated command as an example is that if there is a reasonable argument that one of the debated commands was built into nature and abides into the new covenant, it is then all the more justified to see the less debated commands in the same manner.[77]

The Scripture paints a holistic picture of the Sabbath as a principle that belongs to nature.[78] After all, the creation week itself culminates with God consecrating the seventh day as a holy day of rest (Gen 2:1–3).[79] Indeed, the Bible describes the creation week as it does so that God's image bearers would understand that we are supposed to imitate God in the pattern of work and rest.[80] Far from being a ceremonial burden, this point shows us that God ordered humanity *by nature* toward everlasting communion with him in restful worship.[81] In addition to the creation narrative, other passages confirm that the Sabbath is more than a disposable aspect of the Mosaic covenant.[82] In Exodus 20:11, God grounds the Sabbath command

---

76. E.g. D. A. Carson (ed.), *From Sabbath to Lord's Day: A Biblical, Historical, and Theological Investigation* (Eugene, OR: Wipf & Stock, 1999); Thomas R. Schreiner, "Good-bye and Hello: The Sabbath Command for New Covenant Believers," in *Progressive Covenantalism: Charting a Course between Dispensational and Covenantal Theologies*, eds. Stephen J. Wellum and Brent E. Parker (Nashville: B&H, 2016), 159–88; Thomas R. Schreiner, *40 Questions about Christians and Biblical Law* (Grand Rapids: Kregel, 2010), 209–18; Andrew David Naselli, "What Is a Biblical Theology of the Sabbath?" in Jason S. DeRouchie, Oren Martin, and Andrew David Naselli, *40 Questions about Biblical Theology* (Grand Rapids: Kregel Academic, 2020), 257–66; Craig Blomberg, "The Sabbath as Fulfilled in Christ," in *Perspectives on the Sabbath*, ed. Christopher John Donato (Nashville: B&H Academic, 2011), 305–58; D. A. Carson, "The Tripartite Division of the Law: A Review of Philip Ross, *The Finger of God*," in *From Creation to New Creation: Biblical Theology and Exegesis: Essays in Honor of G. K. Beale*, eds. Daniel M. Gurtner and Benjamin L. Gladd (Peabody, MA: Hendrickson, 2013), 223–36. Thanks to my friend Richard J. Lucas for his help in clarifying this point and for pointing me to some of the sources cited here.

77. R. Scott Clark, *Recovering the Reformed Confession: Our Theology, Piety, and Practice* (Phillipsburg, NJ: P&R, 2008), 295–305.

78. Barcellos, *Getting the Garden Right*, 110–269.

79. Burnside, *God, Justice, and Society*, 69–73. *KTC*, 382–83 dismissively rejects the connection between the Sabbath and the creation covenant but does not exegetically reckon with Genesis 2:1–3, presuming that the Sabbath is merely Mosaic rather than *also* creational.

80. *VBT*, 139–143; Barcellos, *Getting the Garden Right*, 156–80.

81. C. John Collins, *Genesis 1–4: A Linguistic, Literary, and Theological Commentary* (Phillipsburg, NJ: P&R, 2006), 88–94; *KP*, 33–40; Waltke with Fredericks, *Genesis*, 71–73; *VRD*, 1:176; *TI*, 11.13.6–44.

82. On the ceremonial dimensions of the Mosaic Sabbath, Colossians 2:16–17 concerning abrogated features of the Mosaic covenant refers to plural "Sabbaths" (σαββάτων). This grammatical observation is important because the singular reference to the Sabbath marks the statute of the moral law, but the plural indicates the wider ceremonial system of festivals. So, Exodus 20:8 commands remembering the singular Sabbath day (יוֹם הַשַּׁבָּת). Even in the Septuagint, the Sabbath command's

upon its standing as a creation ordinance. Just like marriage belongs to the creation order, so does the fourth commandment. The argument that because Deuteronomy 5:15 grounds the fourth commandment's Sabbath principle in redemption, the Decalogue applies to those whom God has saved fails to reckon with the wider creational considerations. Rather, God has ordered humanity toward the Sabbath principle of communion with him in restful worship by *both* creation and redemption.[83]

Further, God expected Israel already to know and keep even this commandment before he gave them the written law. Exodus 16:22–30 shows that God's people were responsible to honor the Sabbath well before God delivered that command atop Mount Sinai.[84] God's people, who would leave Egypt, were not yet responsible to observe *Mosaic* ceremony but were responsible to keep God's commands that obliged them by creation.[85] Hebrews 3:7–4:13 confirms that the promise of everlasting Sabbath rest *still* awaits God's people. Hebrews 4:3–7 explicitly appeals to the creation principle to undergird the prospect of Sabbath rest but later also commends us not to forsake assembling together (Heb 10:25). In other words, certainly Christians have our everlasting rest in Christ and presently

head noun is singular (*τὴν ἡμέραν τῶν σαββάτων*). In contrast, references to the Sabbath in the plural are tied into the wider festival observance, as in 1 Chronicles 23:29–31 (וְלַמֹּעֲדִים לַשַּׁבָּתוֹת לֶחֳדָשִׁים; *ἐν τοῖς σαββάτοις καὶ ἐν ταῖς νεομηνίαις καὶ ἐν ταῖς ἑορταῖς*). In this instance, the plural Sabbaths are linked to the new moons and festivals that are tied to Levitical sacrifices. Again, in Ezekiel 45:17, the same pattern appears of "feasts, the new moons, and the Sabbaths" (בַּחַגִּים וּבֶחֳדָשִׁים וּבַשַּׁבָּתוֹת; *ἐν ταῖς ἑορταῖς καὶ ἐν ταῖς νουμηνίας καὶ ἐν τοῖς σαββάτοις*), but this time joined to "the burnt offerings, grain offerings, and drink offerings." These repeated combinations indicate that the plural references to the Sabbath are bound into the whole Mosaic ceremonial system; see Guy Prentiss Waters, "Covenant in Paul" in *CT*, 235–36. The exegetical background for *this* use of the plural distinguishes it from the uses of *σάββασιν* that have singular meaning; William L. Lane, *The Gospel of Mark* (Grand Rapids: Eerdmans, 1974), 71n109. Accordingly, the ceremonial aspect of yearly Sabbaths tied to other festivals and the sacrificial system is certainly abrogated, since the substance to which those types pointed is Christ (Col 2:16–17). On the other hand, the singular Sabbath day of the moral law remains an abiding creation ordinance. Schreiner, without exegetical argument, conflates the Mosaic sign of the explicitly *plural* Sabbaths system—which was the sign of the Mosaic covenant—with the Sabbath principle as such; "Good-bye and Hello," 164, 179–80.

83. Collins, *Genesis 1–4*, 89–90; Clark, *Recovering the Reformed Confession*, 300–304; cf. Schreiner, "Good-bye and Hello," 164–65.

84. WCF 19.2; *COC*, 3:640. Schreiner misses that Israel's Sabbath keeping in Exodus 16 was decisively prior to the cutting of the Mosaic covenant, so not part of its structures at that point. The argument that the patriarchs would have been required to keep the Sabbath if it were a creation ordinance misses that obligations may be in force, even when people do not keep them; "Good-bye and Hello," 161–66, 168–69.

85. Barcellos, *Getting the Garden Right*, 181–87.

experience some of that rest, but, since the full enjoyment of that rest awaits Christ's future return, we should still abide by the Sabbath principle because that creation ordinance always pointed forward to another rest that we receive in everlasting life. We mark and take part in that future rest by presently observing the Sabbath law of nature.[86] The creation ordinance of the Sabbath principle as it is repeated in an appeal to nature (Exod 20:11) is one example of how the *whole* moral law was given to humanity since the beginning of the world.[87] As chapter 4 argues, the rest given in the Sabbath even from creation held forth the promise of everlasting rest in the new creation, conditioned upon Adam's fulfillment of the covenant of works.

This link between Adam and Moses, namely, in how both possessed the Ten Commandments, clarifies why prophets like Amos could rebuke the nations for breaking God's law, despite not having it written. Amos did not rebuke Damascus, Gaza, Tyre, Edom, Ammon, or Moab for breaking Israel's ceremonial or civil laws—for example, the prohibition against eating fish that do not have fins or scales (Lev 11:9–12) or the civil penalty of death for manslaughter and the provision of a city of refuge to avoid that death (Exod 21:12–14). Those ceremonial and civil laws were specific to Israel. On the other hand, God's moral law, which "is summarily comprehended in the ten Commandments," regulates our relationship first to God and then to fellow people and is universal for those made in God's image.[88] That is why Amos could fire God's judgment for breaking the moral law equally at Judah, Israel, and the surrounding nations. God wrote the natural law on Adam's heart.[89]

---

86. Barcellos, *Getting the Garden Right*, 231–59.

87. Barcellos, *Getting the Garden Right*, 187–89.

88. WLC 98; *LC*, 85; Walton and Walton, *Lost World of the Torah*, 25–45.

89. Progressive covenantalism dismisses the distinction of moral, civil, and ceremonial law apparently because they presume that the moral law is inherently Mosaic and they have not reckoned with Reformed arguments about natural law; Jason C. Meyer, "The Mosaic Law, Theological Systems, and the Glory of Christ," in *Progressive Covenantalism*, 69–99; *KTC*, 393–95. Even still, they come close to suggesting the abiding moral value of the Decalogue by arguing that we should understand these commandments "not merely as fundamental requirements determining divine-human and human-human relationships as moral principles but as the foundation of true social justice and the basis of what it means to be a son or daughter of God, an Adamic figure—that is, truly and genuinely human." *KTC*, 395. Had they grappled with the Reformed understanding of the natural law's covenantal dimension, they might have recognized the connection between their own claims, the creation covenant, and the moral law. The Reformed need not refute all their exegetical points to

THE LAW ABOUT THE TREE OF THE KNOWLEDGE OF GOOD AND EVIL

In addition to the moral law that God wrote into Adam's nature, summarized in the Ten Commandments, God gave Adam the specific command about the tree of knowledge of good and evil. The Westminster Confession 4.2 explains: "Beside this law written in their hearts, they received a command not to eat of the tree of the knowledge of good and evil; which while they kept they were happy in their communion with God, and had dominion over the creatures."[90] Scripture records God's announcement of this prohibition in Genesis 2:15–17:

> The LORD God took the man and put him in the garden of Eden to work it and keep it. And the LORD God commanded the man, saying, "You may surely eat of every tree of the garden, but of the tree of the knowledge of good and evil you shall not eat, for in the day that you eat of it you shall surely die."

God clearly commanded Adam not to eat a specific fruit in the Garden of Eden—that from the tree of the knowledge of good and evil. Having already considered how Adam knew God's moral law, now we examine the function of God's specific prohibition against eating from the tree of knowledge of good and evil in connection to the covenant of works.[91] Even before the specific tree prohibition, God had already commissioned Adam to be his righteous servant. Scripture recounts this broader task that God gave to Adam in Genesis 1:26–28:

> Then God said, "Let us make man in our image, after our likeness. And let them have dominion over the fish of the sea and over the birds of the heavens and over the livestock and over all the earth and over every creeping thing that creeps on the earth." So God created man in his own image, in the image of God he created

---

prove the moral, civil, and ceremonial distinction, since we have established the additional exegetical connection between the moral law and the natural law; cf. *KTC*, 785–88. Indeed, natural law rather than the "tripartite distinction" as such is truly the principle on which covenant theology grounds the moral law's abiding role; cf. Stephen J. Wellum, "Progressive Covenantalism and the Doing of Ethics," in *Progressive Covenantalism*, 215–16, 218–21; Meyer, "Mosaic Law," 87.

90. *COC*, 3:612.

91. *ACW*, 183–98.

> him; male and female he created them. And God blessed them. And God said to them, "Be fruitful and multiply and fill the earth and subdue it, and have dominion over the fish of the sea and over the birds of the heavens and over every living thing that moves on the earth."

Again, the Ten Commandments describe God's character.[92] God is truth, so the ninth written commandment forbids lying. God is life, so the sixth written commandment prohibits murder. Since the Ten Commandments describe God's character, which cannot be otherwise, we who are made in God's image are stamped by our very nature with an understanding of those laws. Adam, then, is commissioned to be fruitful, multiply, and fill the earth with replications of God's image so that God's righteousness and holiness would cover the globe.

After God created and initially commissioned Adam in his image, he placed him in the garden and issued the command about the tree. This command was, then, additional to the natural law and tied to a specific purpose in Eden. Notably, whereas the Ten Commandments express God's immutable character, this command is not grounded in God's nature but was simply from God's will, making it a "symbolic law."[93] This added command, or positive law, was linked to God's covenant with Adam because the covenant of works required Adam to fulfill the law, as the Westminster Confession 19.1 says, by rendering "perfect, personal, and *perpetual* obedience."[94] God added this tree command in order to create a moment of testing, so that Adam's period of perpetual probation would have a decisive ending.[95]

In contrast to the natural law embedded in human nature, the command attached to the tree was not inherently linked to God's image.[96] The tree-law's moral principle was obedience to God, but no power or reason for the command resided in the tree itself, making God's authority the driving factor in this positive law. God appointed this tree as a

---

92. *EC*, 1.3.8–19.

93. *MMB*, 32–33.

94. *LC*, 70.

95. Hodge, *Systematic Theology*, 2:119–20; *KTC*, 667n29, 676.

96. *EC*, 1.2.7.

way for Adam to prove his obedience if he passed the serpent's test.[97] So, Athanasius (d. 373) argues that, "having brought them into his paradise, God gave the law," which would result in "the promise of immortality in heaven and life empty of grief, pain, and anxiety in paradise" if they kept it.[98] Likewise, Augustine argues, "For the first covenant, which was made with the first man, is just this: 'In the day ye eat thereof, ye shall surely die.' " He concluded that it was by Adam's sin that "God's first covenant was broken," and the human race was plunged into the state of death.[99] Thomas Aquinas (1225–1274) interprets Genesis 2:17 in this way: "And God did not thus forbid eating of the latter tree because the eating as such was evil, but so that human beings, at least in this slight matter, observed something for the sole reason that God commanded it. And so eating from the aforementioned tree became evil because it was prohibited."[100] Similarly, Calvin comments on Genesis 2:16 that God "assigned to him as a sign of his subjection" so that "the prohibition of the one tree was an examination of obedience."[101] Roberts explains the point of the tree of knowledge of good and evil in a very similar way as a "positive law" or "symbolical precept" since it was the "outward Testimony of his Obedience and service to God."[102] So, God added the law concerning the tree as a symbolic test of Adam's obedience.

This symbolic law was nonetheless not entirely disconnected from the moral law. Tertullian (c. 155–c. 240) helpfully explains how this probationary command summarily represents the moral law, writing: "Every command that later came forth when given through Moses was contained in this law given to Adam" such that "the primordial law was given to Adam and Eve in paradise, just as the mother of all of God's commands." He connected this command to the moral law by analogies to the Ten Commandments. For example, "If they had loved the Lord their God,

97. *EC*, 1.3.20–22.

98. Athanasius, *Oratio de Incarnatione Verbi Dei*, §3, in *PG*, 25b:102.

99. Augustine, *The City of God*, 16.27 in *The Works of Aurelius Augustine*, trans. Marcus Dods, 15 vol. (Edinburgh: T&T Clark, 1913), 2:142.

100. Thomas Aquinas, *Compendium of Theology*, trans. Richard J. Regan (New York: Oxford University Press, 2009), §188.

101. *CO*, 23:44; *CC*, 1:1.125–26; Schreiner, *Covenant*, 26–28.

102. *MMB*, 31; Ussher, *Body*, 124.

then they would not have gone against his command." So too, they did not love their neighbors and even murdered them by committing sin and plunging us all into death. Tertullian similarly connects this law about the tree to each precept of the Ten Commandments. His point was that the whole law was at stake in symbolic law about the tree.[103] The symbolic law symbolized specifically the whole moral law by encapsulating the rule of love. If Adam had passed the test concerning the tree, which came to a head in the serpent's temptation, then he would have fulfilled the covenant of works and earned its reward for himself and his posterity.[104] So then, this probationary law also directed Adam about how best to show his love for others. The tree ultimately represented all the natural law's obligations by encapsulating the moral law in this symbolic command, explaining why some Reformed theologians have thought that the natural law is the covenant of works while also reckoning with the place of this tree in that covenant.

The command about the tree heightened the crisis moment of pass or fail. God issued this command to limit Adam's probation in the covenant of works, to a set period of time with a clear end point.[105] In other words, God in his kindness added this tree test to shorten Adam's probationary period.[106] As Francis Turretin puts it, "God gave this precept to man for his trial."[107] Johann Heidegger (1633–1698) explains: "The prohibition was positive and fit for testing because God wished to test man through [it] and explore his obedience."[108] God's prohibition concerning the tree of knowledge had a specific testing function as part of the covenant of works.[109]

In light of Adam's relationship of blessed communion with God from the beginning, the claim that Adam was in a probation period under the law in Eden may sound harsh if we associate probation with needing to prove our innocence when someone assumes that we are guilty. Adam's

103. Tertullian, *Adversus Judeos*, §2 in *PL*, 2:599; *ANF*, 3:152.

104. *EC*, 1.6.26–24.

105. *WWG*, 199–201.

106. Waltke with Fredericks, *Genesis*, 87–88; Wenham, *Genesis 1–15*, 67, 87.

107. *TI*, 8.4.7.

108. *CMT*, 63. I omitted the Greek word for "testing" from this quote simply to keep the text non-technical.

109. *TI*, 5.9.17, 8.4.3–7; *BRD*, 2:500, 566, 571–72, especially 574; *CW*, 47–53, 115–17; *KP*, 103–7.

probation was not like that though.[110] Good teachers do not make their students take exams on the assumption that students are stupid and that the test will make them intelligent. Rather, good teachers test students on the assumption that students are capable people and should have the opportunity to demonstrate their intelligence. Adam's probation worked in this manner as an opportunity to demonstrate how God had created him "very good" with full ability to fulfill every responsibility that God gave him.

As Olympians compete because they are already the most able, longing to demonstrate their ability publicly with the prospect of earning golden reward, so too Adam's probation was the opportunity to showcase how God had created him with the inherent ability to show perfect love in perfect law keeping with the prospect of spiritual reward. As Turretin writes, Adam "willingly sinned and freely and of his own accord without any compulsion or external force transgressed the command of God, though he was furnished with such strength and helps that he might easily have avoided sin, if he had wished."[111] Adam's test with the serpent ought to have resembled an Olympic runner racing a turtle, but Adam squandered the opportunity. God gave Adam, his beloved son (Luke 3:38), the opportunity to showcase his ability for his Father.

In sum, the natural law as summarized in the Ten Commandments was Adam's fundamental law in the covenant of works to guide his commission to be fruitful, multiply, and fill the earth, but God added the command about the tree of knowledge of good and evil to shorten and intensify Adam's probation and bring about the outcome of the covenant of works.

CONCLUSION

This chapter introduces the covenant of works in which God had a rich and blessed relationship with Adam, one of communion by covenant. So, the covenant of works was a relationship fundamentally characterized by love between God and Adam.[112] The covenant contained that law which described the way that Adam should have expressed his committed love

---

110. Cf. Henri Blocher, *In the Beginning: The Opening Chapters of Genesis* (Downers Grove, IL: InterVarsity Press, 1987), 133–34.

111. *TI*, 9.7.8.

112. *ACW*, 391–96.

for God.[113] After all, the summary of the law is to *love* God with all of our heart, soul, mind, and strength and to *love* our neighbor as ourself (Matt 22:37–40). God's prohibition in the covenant of works against eating from the tree of knowledge of good and evil was added to Adam's responsibilities to God's moral law in order to create a specific end point to Adam's probation in the covenant of works. The next chapter furthers these ideas by explaining the legal nature of the covenant of works and the reward that God offered to Adam in it.

The pastoral use of the material in this chapter is that it shows two things about our relationship with God, which ought to benefit God's people. First, God is not a whimsical lover. He has always related to us by covenant, by a fixed bond. So, God is trustworthy, even when we are not. His love is settled and committed, rather than fleeting or even subject to change. He is the God "with whom there is no variation or shadow due to change" (Jas 1:17). Second, this material also shows how God created us for a certain model of holiness. Certainly, we will never be perfect in this life and we should not feel as though our holiness earns God's favor. The point, however, is that Christian moral standards are not arbitrary. Pastors especially, but Christians generally, should not invent standards of righteousness based on the culture or human preference. Rather, God built us for specific ways of holiness, so we should attend to God's Word to understand what the moral law is that he hardwired into us as his image bearers.

113. *EC*, 1.4.18; Horton, *Justification*, 2:61–62.

III

The Covenant's Legal Character and Reward

He will render to each one according to his works:
to those who by patience in well-doing seek for glory and honor
and immortality, he will give eternal life.
—*Romans 2:6–7*

God's first relationship to humanity was a covenant in his loving communion with Adam. William Strong (d. 1654) describes the covenant of works in this way: "To give our first Parents a being, and so glorious a Covenant, and all the Creatures for their use, to have dominion over them all, *was great love from God*."[1] In this covenantal communion, Adam had the law plaited into his constitution as the divine image bearer, serving as his trusted guide for expressing his love for God. God fit us for communion with him, and that first communion was guided by his law's standards.

This chapter shows how the covenant of works' legal aspect offered the prospect of even deeper communion with God than we had by nature. The covenant of works fully displayed God's kindness and rich generosity, as

1. William Strong, *A Discourse of the Two Covenants: Wherein the Nature, Differences, and Effects of the Covenant of Works and of Grace Are Distinctly, Rationally, Spiritually and Practically Discussed* (London, 1678), 32 (emphasis added).

he created Adam with righteousness and holiness to have a relationship with his Maker but also offered the possibility of even deeper communion to Adam if he fulfilled the covenant's terms. The Belgic Confession teaches that "God created man ... after his own image and likeness, good, righteous, and holy, capable in all things to will agreeably to the will of God" with "*the commandment of life*" that was the condition for everlasting, incorruptible life with "God, who was his true life" (BC 14).[2] This chapter argues that the condition in the covenant of works was perfect obedience to the law and the reward was heavenly life in communion with God.

In the covenant of works, as the Westminster Confession describes, "life was promised to Adam, and in him to his posterity, upon condition of perfect and personal obedience" (WCF 7.2).[3] God created Adam to have communion with him but, further, offered greater communion in an even more blessed new creation, if Adam kept the law. Geerhardus Vos explains that for man to bear God's image "means above all that he is disposed for communion with God, that all the capacities of the soul can act in a way that corresponds to their destiny only if they rest in God."[4] Humanity's existence as God's image entails a fitting fellowship with God—apart from sin. Vos also says, "According to the deeper Protestant conception, the image does not exist only in correspondence with God but in being disposed toward God."[5] God created humanity naturally fit for supernatural communion with him in the new creation. Even though Adam had wonderful communion with God by creation, God is so rich in his generosity and goodness that he offered to Adam even deeper communion with him upon his fulfillment of the covenant of works.[6] The covenant of works is,

2. *COC*, 3:398 (emphasis added).

3. *COC*, 3:616–17. Concerning the covenant of works' implicit presence in the Three Forms of Unity, see J. Mark Beach, "Some Observations about the *Three Forms of Unity* and the Doctrine of the Covenant of Works," *MAJT* 21 (2010): 103–19; also Michael G. Brown, "The Covenantal Foundation of the Heidelberg Catechism," *Puritan Reformed Journal* 7 no. 1 (2015): 88–102. For the same concerning the Second London Baptist Confession, see Barcellos, *Getting the Garden Right*, 38–52; also Barcellos, *Covenant of Works*, 29–56; and Pascal Denault, "By Farther Steps: A Seventeenth-Century Particular Baptist Covenant Theology," in Richard C. Barcellos (ed.), *Recovering a Covenantal Heritage: Essays in Baptist Covenant Theology* (Palmdale, CA: RBAP, 2014), 71–75.

4. *VRD*, 2:13. Thanks to Tony Faggiano from the New Geneva Podcast for alerting me to this quote.

5. *VRD*, 2:13–14; *BRD*, 2:539–53, 571–72. On this point, see the considerations about natural and supernatural ends in Perkins, *Righteous by Design*.

6. *TI*, 8.3.2; 8.6.10; *EC*, 1.4.13–17.

then, not a cold, merely contractual relationship but a means to facilitate the deepest love between God and his creatures. The legal conditions for reward demonstrate God's rich goodness in offering Adam even more blessings for the obedience that Adam was required to render anyway. This chapter looks precisely at this issue, that the condition for Adam to fulfill the covenant was perfect obedience and that his reward would have been incorruptible life.

THE LEGAL COVENANT

God's law requires perfect obedience, which was Adam's condition to obtain reward in the covenant of works. The Westminster Confession clarifies the covenant of works' legal character by stating, "God gave to Adam a law, *as a covenant of works*" (WCF 19.1).[7] Since God's character is unchanging and the law expresses God's character, the same moral law always remains binding upon God's image bearers, grounding why the Westminster Confession affirms that after the fall the same law "continued to be a perfect rule of righteousness" (WCF 19.2).[8] The law always functions as a guide to express our love for God but operates *as a covenant* or *as a rule* when given, marking a crucial distinction.[9] In creation, God gave his law to Adam as a covenant in which the law "bound him and all his posterity to personal, entire, exact, and perpetual obedience."[10] The law itself requires perfect obedience but as a covenant "promised life upon the fulfilling, and threatened death upon the breach of it."[11] Vos explains that the law "can also indicate a specific obligation, determined by a pact, to which certain consequences are linked if it is kept or transgressed."[12] So, the law as a covenant requires perfect obedience but, additionally, offers a reward.[13]

This distinction between the law as a covenant and as a rule could be illustrated by giving a ring as a gift to my wife. If I purchase a gold band

---

7. *COC*, 3:640.
8. *COC*, 3:640.
9. Michael Horton, *Introducing Covenant Theology* (Grand Rapids: Baker Academic, 2006), 174–77.
10. *COC*, 3:640.
11. *COC*, 3:640.
12. *VRD*, 5:86.
13. Hodge, *Systematic Theology*, 2:119–20; *BOC*, 29–35.

to give to her, that very ring could have different kinds of significance depending on the occasion on and purpose for which I gave it to her. If I give her a golden band on Valentine's Day, it might simply show my affection, serving as reminder of my love. On the other hand, I did give her a gold band on our wedding day, saying, "With this ring I thee wed," using it to initiate our new relationship, giving it to signify the covenant of marriage. In both situations, I could have used the same exact golden band—although not after I used it once! In one instance, it carried all the privileges and obligations of our marriage covenant.

The law itself was the covenant of works for Adam but remains the rule to direct us in godliness even after Adam broke that covenant. Petrus van Mastricht affirms that "the Decalogue has the substance of the covenant of works so that it speaks a renewal of the covenant of works that came down upon Sinai."[14] For Mastricht, the moral law as revealed through Moses contained the premises of the covenant of works, not meaning that the people of Israel were required to earn their salvation but that God had given this exact law *as the covenant of works* to Adam at creation. Mastricht continues, writing, "This inscription on the heart according to the law has maintained the exact knowledge of moral obedience."[15] The law containing the covenant of works still describes the universal requirements of our obedience to God. In other words, God gave the law as the covenant of works, but the moral law remains the rule or guide for the godly life.

The difference between law and grace as opposing covenantal principles grounds this distinction between the law as a covenant and as a rule. Zacharius Ursinus (1534–1583) drew on this distinction in his larger catechism, writing that the divine law teaches "the kind of covenant that God entered with man in creation." Still, the law also teaches "what God requires of him after beginning the new covenant of grace with him."[16] The law defined the covenant of works but remains our rule of godliness in the covenant of grace. Ursinus further clarifies the distinction between the law and the gospel in that "the law contains the natural covenant, which God began with men in creation, that is, it is known by men by nature and

14. Mastricht, *Theoretica-Practica Theologia*, 3.12.28.

15. Mastricht, *Theoretica-Practica Theologia*, 3.12.28.

16. Zacharius Ursinus, *Catechesis, Summa Theologiae*, in *Opera Theologica*, 3 vol. (Heidelberg: Johannes Lancellot, 1612), 1:10.

requires from us perfect obedience toward God, and promises everlasting life to those who keep it but threatens everlasting death to those who do not keep it."[17] So, Ursinus argues that the law itself contains the covenant of works. As God gave it to humanity in creation, the law demands perfect obedience, but in that situation, before the fall, it offered Adam the potential to earn the reward of everlasting life. By contrast, "the gospel contains the covenant of grace" which "displays Christ's fulfillment of that righteousness which the law requires from us." So, the law is a distinct type of covenant from the gospel, having a different covenantal principle for inheriting reward. The covenant of works had a legal character insomuch as, even though Christians are still bound to keep the moral law today, the law offered Adam the potential to earn rewards.

In that respect, the distinction between the two different covenantal principles—works and grace—is pivotal. We who trust in Jesus obey the law, not as an attempt to earn rewards from God, but "to show ourselves thankful to God for his blessing" and as "fruits and evidences" of having received God's favor by faith.[18] Adam's situation was very different in that, even though he certainly did have God's favor and blessing, he was required to render perfect obedience to earn further rewards from God.[19]

Paul's interpretation of the Mosaic law in Romans 10:5 displays the law's demand for perfect obedience: "For Moses writes about the righteousness that is based on the law, that the person who does the commandments shall live by them." The law as such offers life only to those who do—fulfill, complete, and perform—the whole law.[20] Herman Bavinck writes, "If there had not been sin, therefore, it [the law] would also have been able to grant life through works (Rom 10:5; Gal 3:12)."[21] Although sinners cannot earn life by the law, Adam as the upright man in the covenant of works could have obtained the law's reward of everlasting life.[22]

17. Ursinus, *Catechesis*, 1:14.

18. *COC*, 3:338, 633. See also HC 86 and WCF 16.2.

19. *CW*, 28, 54–65; *TI*, 8.3.5, 8.6.12–13.

20. *VRD*, 4:153; *CRS*, 1:475; Guy Waters, "Romans 10:5 and the Covenant of Works" in *LNF*, 210–239; *ACW*, 212–15.

21. *BRD*, 4:184.

22. Brian S. Rosner, *Paul and the Law*, 59–73.

Adam, then, had a positive job to fulfill the law. In Genesis 1:28 God said to man, "Be fruitful and multiply and fill the earth and subdue it, and have dominion over the fish of the sea and over the birds of the heavens and over every living thing that moves on the earth." God tasked Adam to conquer the earth as his representative king.[23] This was to be the clearest expression of the image-bearing constitution with which God created Adam. God made Adam in his image with knowledge, righteousness, and holiness (Col 3:10; Eph 4:24), and that meant that Adam should fulfill the law, not just avoid sinning.[24]

Further passages confirm that the condition for Adam to earn his reward was perfect obedience. Paul's point in Romans 10:5 becomes clearer by considering his Old Testament citation, Leviticus 18:5: "You shall therefore keep my statutes and my rules; if a person does them, he shall live by them: I am the LORD." Although surrounded by ceremonial laws, Leviticus 18:5 explains why many Jewish people failed to attain salvation. They failed because they pursued justification—their righteousness before God—by the law.[25] Interestingly, Paul said that Moses wrote about *works* righteousness, which required perfect obedience if the one who relies on the law would obtain life by it.[26]

The apostle was not the first person to understand the "do this and live" principle in this way, as many Old Testament writers interpreted it to refer to an offer of everlasting life, resulting from obedience.[27] Paul

---

23. Fesko, *Last Things First*, 95–102. Christ consummates this need for kingship built into God's covenantal structure for creation, but that theme is addressed more fully in chapters 8 and 14.

24. *CMT*, 63.

25. Rosner, *Paul and the Law*, 71–72.

26. Francis Watson, *Paul and the Hermeneutics of Faith*, 2nd ed. (London: Bloomsbury T&T Clark, 2016), 303–14; Bryan D. Estelle, "Leviticus 18:5 and Deuteronomy 30:1–14 in Biblical Theological Development: Entitlement to Heaven Foreclosed and Proffered," in *LNF*, 109–146; Waters, "Romans 10:5 and the Covenant of Works," 210–239.

27. Simon Gathercole, "Torah, Life, and Salvation: Leviticus 18:5 in Early Judaism and the New Testament," in *From Prophecy to Testament: The Function of the Old Testament in the New*, ed. C. A. Evans (Peabody, MA: Hendrickson, 2004), 126–45; Joel Willitts, "Context Matters: Paul's Use of Leviticus 18:5 in Galatians 3:12," *Tyndale Bulletin* 54.2 (2003): 115–17; Watson, *Hermeneutics of Faith*, 289–303, 314–24; Rosner, *Paul and the Law*, 59–64; *ACW*, 199–216; for less-than-exegetical assertions, cf. Bradley G. Green, *Covenant and Commandment: Works, Obedience and Faithfulness in the Christian Life* (Downers Grove, IL: IVP Academic, 2014), 68–72.

did not dispute that principle but only that sinners can fulfill the terms.[28] Righteousness that is based on the law requires a person to fulfill the law. Augustine argues,

> Faith in Christ is not necessary for salvation if a person without it is able to live righteously. On account of this, the nature of the human race, being born from the flesh of the one transgressor, if he were able in himself to make complete satisfaction in fulfilling the law and to execute righteousness perfectly, then he must be secure concerning the reward, that is concerning everlasting life, even if in any nation or any previous time faith in Christ's blood was unknown to him. For, certainly, God is not unjust as if he would cheat a righteous person out of the wage for righteousness, if the mystery of Christ's divinity and humanity, that he has been manifested in the flesh, has not been announced to him.[29]

Someone's best efforts at keeping the law are insufficient to achieve righteousness by the law.[30] For works righteousness, the law must be done, completed.

Paul's use of Leviticus 18:5 clarifies one of the covenant of works' crucial principles. Reformed theologians have understood that Leviticus 18:5 teaches the principle of "do this and live," entailing that the law offered everlasting life to the one who perfectly kept the law.[31] John Calvin comments on Romans 10:5 that Leviticus 18:5 "promises everlasting life to those who keep his law," summarizing, "Since no one can obtain the righteousness that is commanded by the law unless they exactly fulfill its every demand, but every person is invariably so incredibly far away from that

---

28. *WWP*, 2:173–74 (commentary on Galatians 3:10); Schreiner, *Galatians*, 203–14; Rosner, *Paul and the Law*, 66–71.

29. Augustine, *Nature and Grace*, §2, in *PL*, 44:248–49; *NPNF1*, 5:122.

30. *CW*, 28.

31. *WWP*, 1:244 (commentary on Matthew 5:17); John Owen, *An Exposition of the Epistle to the Hebrews*, 4 vol. (London: : Thomas Tegg, 1839), 3:715–16; *MT*, 1.10.32; Robert Rollock, *Some Questions and Answers about God's Covenants and the Sacrament That Is a Seal of God's Covenant: with Related Texts*, trans. Aaron Clay Denlinger (Eugene, OR: Pickwick, 2016), 21-22; Mastricht, *Theoretica-Practica Theologia*, 3.12.28; *TI*, 5.12.4, 8.3.7, 8.5.4, 11.3.4; *EC*, 1.2.1; *CRS*, 1:360; *BRD*, 2:565; 3:174, 182–85, 224–28; 4:601–2; *VRD*, 2:41, 94, 130; Richard A. Muller, "'Either Expressly Set Down…or by Good and Necessary Consequence,'" in *Scripture and Worship: Biblical Interpretation and the Directory for Worship* ed. Richard A. Muller and Rowland S. Ward (Phillipsburg, NJ: P&R, 2007), 69–81; *ACW*, 13–42.

perfection, anyone strives vainly for salvation by this method."[32] Calvin's commentary exemplifies how many Reformed thinkers understand that the web of biblical evidence linked to Leviticus 18:5 teaches that the law requires perfect righteousness to earn everlasting life.

James Ussher also draws heavily upon Leviticus 18:5 as he discusses the premise of the covenant of works, arguing that the law requires "all such duties as were required of Adam in his innocence (Lev. 18:5) and all such as are required since by reason of his fall (Deut. 27:26) binding us to eternal death for our least defect therein." So, the covenant of works "is a conditional Covenant between God and man, whereby on the one side God commands the perfection of godliness and righteousness, and promises that he will be our God if we keep all his Commandments; and on the other side man binds himself to perform entire and perfect obedience to God's Law, by that strength wherewith God hath endued him by the nature of his first creation." The sum of this law was, "Do this, and thou shalt live, if thou does it not, thou shalt die the death."[33] Even though sinners cannot meet the standard of "do this and live," Adam in his original, upright state could fulfill the law.

This principle that the law requires complete and perfect obedience appears more explicitly in Galatians 5:3–4: "I testify again to every man who accepts circumcision that he is obligated *to keep* the whole law. You are severed from Christ, you who would be justified by the law; you have fallen away from grace." If we rely on any one point of the law to be justified, then we are obligated to complete the law in every point.[34] Witsius comments on Galatians 5:3 that, "even by the promulgation of the new gospel covenant, the breakers of the covenant who are without Christ, are not set free from that obligation of the law, which demands perfect obedience, but continue [to be] debtors to do the whole law."[35] The phrase

---

32. *CO*, 49:198; *CC*, 19:2.387.

33. Ussher, *Body*, 124–25. It is confusing that Letham would refer to Ussher, citing the very pages quoted here, as one who "did not mention the pre-fall covenant"; Robert Letham, *Systematic Theology* (Wheaton, IL: Crossway, 2019), 457; cf. Perkins, *Catholicity and the Covenant of Works*, which is a monograph-length analysis of Ussher's view of the pre-fall covenant of works.

34. *LG*, 18–19, 24, 41.

35. *EC*, 1.9.6.

"to keep" or "to obey" in many English versions indicates the requirement to complete the law, to fulfill its every principle.[36]

So then, the law given to Adam as the covenant of works requires perfect obedience to earn blessings by it. God did not inherently owe Adam further blessings for his obedience (Luke 17:10) but, because of his rich and abundant love for Adam, promised to reward Adam if he perfectly fulfilled the terms of the covenant. Many Reformed theologians have called Adam's ability to earn a blessing from God by his works "covenantal merit."[37] This category emphasizes that Adam could merit his reward only because God in his goodness had voluntarily promised to grant a reward according to the terms of the covenant.[38] Once God appointed the conditions and the reward that would follow the conditions, the covenant established the terms of justice, so enabling Adam to merit, at least in a sense, his reward.[39]

Romans 2:12–15 clearly teaches that the law as the covenant of works requires perfect obedience.

> For all who have sinned without the law will also perish without the law, and all who have sinned under the law will be judged by the law. For it is not the hearers of the law who are righteous before God, but the doers of the law who will be justified. For when Gentiles, who do not have the law, by nature do what the law requires, they are a law to themselves, even though they do not have the law. They show that the work of the law is written on their hearts, while their conscience also bears witness, and their conflicting thoughts accuse or even excuse them.

---

36. S. M. Baugh, "Galatians 5:1–6 and Personal Obligation: Reflections on Paul and the Law," in *LNF*, 259–80.

37. Harrison Perkins, "*Meritum ex Pacto* in the Reformed Tradition: Covenantal Merit in Theological Polemics," *MAJT* 31 (2020): 57–87.

38. *LG*, 21–23; *BRD*, 2:544; Cornelis P. Venema, *Christ and Covenant Theology: Essays on Election, Republication, and the Covenants* (Phillipsburg, NJ: P&R, 2017), 32–35; Carl R. Trueman, *Grace Alone: Salvation as a Gift of God* (Grand Rapids: Zondervan, 2017), 98–102; *EC*, 1.4.13–17, 20–22; John Halsey Wood Jr., "Merit in the Midst of Grace: The Covenant with Adam Reconsidered in View of the Two Powers of God," *IJST* 10 no. 2 (April 2008): 133–48.

39. For further defense of Adam's covenantal merit, see Perkins, *Righteous by Design*.

The law was built into creation as the standard of righteousness before God.[40] God is the judge, and the ones who would be righteous before him—justified—must do the law. One sin breaks the law and brings condemnation. Justification, therefore, requires fulfilling—keeping, completing, doing—the law. As Calvin comments, "Thus, so far this present passage's effect is: If righteousness is sought by the law, then the law must be completely fulfilled, because the righteousness of the law is located in the perfection of works."[41] Adam was created with the ability to achieve that perfection. The Westminster Assembly, in their biblical annotations, comment that glory "follows good works: which he lays not out before us as though there were any that could attain salvation by his own strength; but by laying this condition of salvation, which no man can perform; to bring men to Christ, who alone justifies believers."[42] The covenant of works' legal character meant Adam needed to render perfect righteousness to fulfill the covenant of works. But what would Adam's reward have been had he succeeded in that task?

THE REWARD OFFERED TO ADAM

God's immense love for Adam was fully displayed in his offer to reward Adam's obedience with even higher blessings than he gave in creation. Truly, as God's handiworks, "reasonable creatures do owe obedience unto him as their Creator." Still, God voluntarily condescended by a covenant to accept humanity's obedience as the means to obtain "the fruition of him as their blessedness and reward."[43] God was abundant in his kindness to appoint that naturally owed obedience as the condition of a covenant offering rich and everlasting communion with him in heavenly life. This section then explores the Westminster Confession's claim that "life was promised to Adam" in the covenant of works.[44]

The covenant of works demands perfect obedience but also offers the prospect of plentiful communion with God as our blessedness. The first

40. *CRS*, 1:360.

41. *CO*, 49:37; *CC*, 19:2.95.

42. Westminster Assembly, *Annotations upon all the Books of the Old and New Testament* (London, 1645), *ad loc.*

43. WCF 7.1; *COC*, 3:616.

44. *COC*, 3:617; Hodge, *Systematic Theology*, 2:118–19.

premise concerning this reward is that personal righteousness according to the law results in justification. Paul writes in Romans 2:13, "For it is not the hearers of the law who are righteous before God, but the doers of the law who will be justified." If someone perfectly fulfills the law by performing all its conditions, then God would justify them—declare them fully righteous—on the basis of their works. As Calvin comments, "Indeed, the apostle urges upon the Jews only the judgment of the law, which he had mentioned, because they were not able to be justified *by the law* unless they fulfill it. ... Since it is only those who fulfill the law who are justified by the law."[45] Adam would have been justified if he had fulfilled the law, meaning he could have obtained the right to everlasting, incorruptible life.[46]

The biblical tapestry firmly links doing the law and justification, even for Adam. "Justification" means the declaration that we are completely righteous in God's sight—"righteous before God" (Rom 2:13). It is God's verdict that we have kept and fulfilled all righteousness. Robert Rollock highlights how justification was structured even into the covenant of works:

> There is a twofold righteousness to be considered in the covenant of works. The first is original righteousness, which is nothing other than that holiness and condition of nature. It is beyond controversy that this righteousness is not promised in the covenant of works because it had indeed been the foundation of the covenant. The second righteousness is that which follows the good works of the [original] holy and just nature, and so can be called the righteousness of works. Because after the man had already performed well and justly according to his just and good nature, then it was just

45. *CO*, 49:37; *CC*, 19:2.95–96.

46. *TI*, 1.4.15–16; 8.6.4–5; 12.7.32; 16.2.2; *ACW*, 357–76; *CW*, 184–90; John Calvin, *Institutes of the Christian Religion*, trans. Ford Lewis Battles, ed. John T. McNeill, 2 vol. (Louisville: Westminster John Knox, 1960), 3.17.12; Geerhardus Vos, "The Alleged Legalism in Paul's Doctrine of Justification," in *RHBI*, 393–98; David Dickson, *An Exposition of All St. Paul's epistles* (London, 1659), 5; Thomas Cartwright, *A Confutation Of The Rhemists Translation, Glosses And Annotations On The New Testament* (Leiden: W. Brewster, 1618), 331–34; *CRS*, 1:7–8, 128, 326, 411, 417, 577; James Buchanan, *The Doctrine of Justification* (London: The Banner of Truth Trust, 2016), 249–70; Charles Hodge, *Romans* (London: The Banner of Truth Trust, 1972), 53–57; Douglas J. Moo, *The Epistle to the Romans*, 1st ed. (Grand Rapids: Eerdmans, 1996), 125–57; Waters, "Romans," 183n64; Leon Morris, *The Epistle to the Romans* (Grand Rapids: Eerdmans,1988), 123–24; VanDrunen, *Divine Covenants*, 233–51; Horton, *Justification*, 1:275–76; 2:126–33, 378–94.

> as if he might become righteous a second time, and God would declare him righteous by good works and the things that he had done, being pleasing and acceptable to his God, and in this way at that point God would grant everlasting life by justification.[47]

Since God made Adam upright, just, and perfect (Rollock's first way that Adam was righteous) he could live in such a way as to obtain an even higher righteousness (Rollock's second way of being righteous) resulting in his justification and the further consequent reward of everlasting life.

In this respect, Romans 2:13 pinpoints the connection between performing righteousness and justification: "For it is not the hearers of the law *who are righteous before God*, but the *doers of the law who will be justified*." As Calvin indicts sinners, "When Paul says, that *the doers of the law are justified*, (Rom. 2:13) he excludes all from *the righteousness of the law*."[48] Likewise, Rollock comments, "The discussion is certainly about men outside Christ seeking justification in themselves, that is, the justification by works."[49] The issue is righteousness before God, which results in justification, but that can happen only if we meet the condition for that kind of justification by doing—fulfilling, completing, performing—the law.[50]

Two passages in the Gospels underscore this connection between fulfilling the law and justification. First, Matthew 19:16–19 narrates a man wanting Jesus to tell him what good deed would earn everlasting life.

> And behold, a man came up to him [Jesus], saying, "Teacher, what good deed must I *do to have eternal life*?" And he said to him, "Why do you ask me about what is good? There is only one who is good. If you would enter life, *keep the commandments*." He said to him, "Which ones?" And Jesus said, "You shall not murder, You shall not commit adultery, You shall not steal, You shall not bear false witness, Honor your father and mother, and, You shall love your neighbor as yourself."

---

47. Robert Rollock, *Tractatus de Vocatione Efficaci* (Edinburgh: Robert Waldgrave, 1597), 10–11; Rollock, *Treatise*, 8.

48. CC, 16:2.395 (italics original).

49. Robert Rollock, *Analysis Dialectica … in Pauli Apostoli Epistolam ad Romanos* (Edinburgh: Robert Waldgrave, 1594), 27.

50. For further defense for this interpretation of Romans 2:13, see the appendix.

Note that the man's question to Christ was about obtaining everlasting life.[51]

Further, this man wanted to know what "good deed" he had to do to obtain everlasting life. Jesus did not deny the absolute possibility that one could obtain everlasting life by good deeds but simply said that if this man wanted to obtain life by his good deeds, then he must keep the commandments.[52] As Calvin comments, "Any man who kept the law perfectly—if there were such a man—would obtain life for himself." The problem is that "we are *all destitute of the glory of God,* (Rom. 3:23)" so "nothing but cursing will be found in the law." There is then "a twofold righteousness, *the righteousness of the law,* (Rom. 10:5), and the righteousness of faith (Rom. 10:6)."[53] Calvin recognizes that perfect performance of the law would warrant the reward of everlasting life, and this works principle of inheritance sharply contrasts with the principle of righteousness by faith.

Those two principles, after all, belong to two different types of covenants. Rollock comments that in Matthew 19:17, "the Lord put forward the formulation of the covenant of works." Thus, "the pact of legal works and the standard of legal works is put upon everyone who is outside Christ and is seeking righteousness by the law and by works of the law" so that "a person is prepared by the awareness of his sin and misery so that he would grasp the covenant of grace in Christ."[54] The law, according to Rollock and Calvin, genuinely offers the reward of life but only on exacting conditions.

Regarding the law's content, Christ even specified that the commandments he meant were the Decalogue, confirming that Adam needed to keep those same commandments to obtain life.[55] Now, the man who approached Jesus mistakenly assumed that he, a sinner, had kept and could keep the commandments well enough to earn everlasting life. Still,

51. Horton, *Justification*, 2:183–84.

52. Donald A. Hagner, *Matthew 14–28* (Dallas, TX: Word Books, 1995), 557; *CRS*, 1:362; *CW*, 67–68, 74–76; *LG*, 67–68, 164.

53. *CC*, 16:2.394 (italics original).

54. Rollock, *Tractatus*, 13; Rollock, *Treatise*, 9–10.

55. David L. Turner, *Matthew* (Grand Rapids: Baker Academic, 2008), 469; Hagner, *Matthew 14–28*, 557.

Christ pointed to the "do this and live" principle of the covenant of works as the condition for earning everlasting life.[56]

The other particularly pertinent passage from the Gospels, Luke 10:25–29, concerns a lawyer trying to test Christ about the legal requirements to obtain everlasting life:

> And behold, a lawyer stood up to put him [Jesus] to the test, saying, "Teacher, *what shall I do to inherit eternal life*?" He said to him, "What is written in *the Law*? How do you read it?" And he answered, "You shall love the Lord your God with all your heart and with all your soul and with all your strength and with all your mind, and your neighbor as yourself." And he said to him, "You have answered correctly; *do this, and you will live*." But he, desiring to justify himself, said to Jesus, "And who is my neighbor?"

Just like the question posed to Jesus in Matthew 19:16–19, the lawyer again queried about obtaining everlasting life by doing something.[57]

As before, Jesus pointed to the law.[58] This time he summarized the moral law with, not the Decalogue, but a further abridgement combining Deuteronomy 6:5—"You shall *love the Lord your God* with all your heart and with all your soul and with all your might"—and Leviticus 19:18—"You shall not take vengeance or bear a grudge against the sons of your own people, but you shall *love your neighbor as yourself*." Still, the requirement to obtain life is keeping the law, since Jesus quoted Leviticus 18:5, "You shall therefore keep my statutes and my rules; if a person does them, he shall live by them: I am the Lord."[59] So, Jesus precisely encapsulated that principle that the Reformed tradition has recognized as a summary of the covenant of works: "You have answered correctly; *do this, and you will live*."[60] The lawyer, Calvin notes, asked not for the best way to enter ever-

---

56. Mastricht, *Theoretica-Practica Theologia*, 3.12.28; *TI*, 8.3.7, 8.6.4, 12.3.8, 15.15.6; *BRD*, 3:174, 226; *CW*, 185; Horton, *Justification*, 1:278–79; Hagner, *Matthew 14–28*, 558; Belcher, "Covenant of Works in the Old Testament," 70.

57. *ACW*, 208–12; Morris, *Romans*, 282.

58. *BRD*, 3:174, 226; *CW*, 74, 196; *LG*, 20–21, 273.

59. Charles Hodge, *1 & 2 Corinthians* (London: The Banner of Truth Trust, 1974), 433; J. V. Fesko, "The Republication of the Covenant of Works," *Confessional Presbyterian* 8 (2012): 208.

60. Brandon D. Crowe, *The Last Adam: A Theology of the Obedient Life of Jesus in the Gospels* (Grand Rapids: Baker Academic, 2017), 179–82.

lasting life but what work he must do to obtain it.[61] Christ accommodated the question as the lawyer asked it and indicated that the requirement was to fulfill the principle of the covenant of works.[62] It is impossible for sinners who live after the fall to achieve this righteousness, but Adam in his integrity could have.[63]

In considering the Westminster Confession's claim that "life was promised to Adam" in the covenant of works, so far, Romans 2:13, Matthew 19:16–19, and Luke 10:25–29 establish the connections between perfect fulfillment of the law, justification, and obtaining everlasting life. The next premise establishes that these connections inform the character of the inheritance of everlasting life. Adam could have earned justification by perfectly fulfilling the law, but his further consequent reward of justification would have been everlasting, incorruptible life. Although the Westminster Standards do not specify that the life offered to Adam in the covenant of works was spiritual or heavenly, canon IX of the Helvetic Consensus Formula codified this specification at the confessional level:

> Wherefore we can not agree with the opinion of those who deny that a reward of heavenly bliss was offered to Adam on condition of obedience to God. We also do not admit that the promise of the Covenant of Works was any thing more than a promise of perpetual life abounding in every kind of good that can be suited to the body and soul of man in a state of perfect nature, and the enjoyment thereof in an earthly Paradise. For this also is contrary to the sound sense of the Divine Word, and weakens the power of the law considered in itself.[64]

As Reformed theologians continued to reflect on the covenant of works, they affirmed that the life offered to Adam was specifically spiritual life,

61. *CC*, 17:3.56–57.

62. R. Scott Clark, "Do This and Live: Christ's Active Obedience as the Ground of Justification," in R. Scott Clark (ed.), *Covenant, Justification, and Pastoral Ministry* (Phillipsburg, NJ: P&R, 2007), 245.

63. *EC*, 1.4.5–13.

64. Martin I. Klauber, "The Helvetic Consensus Formula (1675): An Introduction and Translation," *Trinity Journal* 11 (1990): 117.

better elevated eschatological life.[65] What Scripture confirms this confessional idea?

God created humanity for this eschatological life. Hebrews 2:5–10 describes how God made humanity even since creation for the world to come. Hebrews' preceding point was an exhortation to pay close attention to the message of Christ's preeminence because it is the message of great salvation (Heb 2:1–4). The author then defends this exhortation on the grounds that "it was not to angels that God subjected the world to come, of which we are speaking" (Heb 2:5).[66] Clearly, the discussion is about *the world to come*—the new creation.[67] In verses 6–8, he then quotes Psalm 8:4–6 as evidence:

> "What is man, that you are mindful of him,
>   or the son of man, that you care for him?
> You made him for a little while lower than the angels;
>   you have crowned him with glory and honor,
>   putting everything in subjection under his feet."

The author saw how David's words address the world to come. Man was made just slightly lower than the angels by creation, but only for a little while, since he was destined for glory with everything in subjection to him. Hebrews then notes that Psalm 8 testifies that man was meant to attain more glory than he possessed at creation.[68]

More pointedly, the problem in Hebrews is that man has not attained this glory, which is why we must pay close attention to Christ.[69] The world to come is not for the angels but for man, as the reflections in Psalm 8 about creation show: man is to be crowned with glory with the world

---

65. For the background for this confession, and even this particular canon of the Formula, as a refutation of growing Arminian and Socinian problems in the Reformed churches, see Fesko, *Covenant of Works*, 119–22, 126–30; also Klauber, "Helvetic Consensus Formula," 103–14.

66. Luke Timothy Johnson, *Hebrews* (Louisville: Westminster John Knox, 2012), 89; cf. Paul Ellingworth, *The Epistle to the Hebrews* (Grand Rapids: Eerdmans, 1993), 145.

67. *BTA*, 173–74; Peter T. O'Brien, *The Letter to the Hebrews* (Grand Rapids: Eerdmans, 2010), 93–94; Johnson, *Hebrews*, 89–90.

68. Johnson, *Hebrews*, 90; cf. Ellingworth, *Hebrews*, 150–52.

69. Ellingworth, *Hebrews*, 146–47; O'Brien, *Hebrews*, 97.

to come in subjection to him.[70] Since the Son came in human nature, so becoming temporarily lower than the angels, Christ has thereby been "crowned with glory and honor because of the suffering of death, so that by the grace of God he might taste death for everyone" (Heb 2:9).[71] Christ's death brought his exaltation after he endured sin's penalty for his people.[72] His exaltation, however, was not exclusively for himself because "it was fitting that he, for whom and by whom all things exist, in bringing many sons to glory, should make the founder of their salvation perfect through suffering" (Heb 2:10). So, Christ's suffering and exaltation both aimed to bring his people with him into glory.

Strikingly, the author of Hebrews proves our future glory in the world to come from a Psalm about humanity's creation. Christ is the man who brings humanity, more specifically believers, to our destiny in the world to come, which God intended for us in creation. God created us to be oriented by nature toward our supernatural end in the world to come. Had Adam completed his task in the covenant of works, he would have victoriously entered the new creation. Since Adam failed, Christ brings his people into that eschatological communion.[73] If God created humanity for glorious communion with him in the world to come, how then do we link that destiny to Adam and the covenant of works?

God created humanity for eschatological communion with him in glory, but that incorruptible life is the consequent reward of justification, as in Romans 3:21–24: "Now though, the righteousness of God has been shown apart from the law—even though the law and the prophets still bear witness to it—namely, the righteousness of God that comes through faith in Jesus Christ to everyone who believes. For there is no distinction because all have sinned and *failed to obtain the glory of God*, so are justified freely in his grace through the redemption that is in Christ Jesus" (my translation). Sinners' need for justification clearly has a legal context,

70. O'Brien, *Hebrews*, 94–96; cf. John Goldingay, *Psalms*, 3 vol. (Grand Rapids: Baker Academic, 2006–8), 1:160–61.

71. Ellingworth, *Hebrews*, 153–55; Johnson, *Hebrews*, 90–91.

72. Johnson, *Hebrews*, 91–92.

73. David VanDrunen, *Living in God's Two Kingdoms: A Biblical Vision for Christianity and Culture* (Wheaton, IL: Crossway, 2010), 40–43, 54–56, 59–60, 100; Stephen J. Wellum, *The Person of Christ: An Introduction* (Wheaton, IL: Crossway, 2021), 81–82; *KTC*, 669, 672, 729, 734–35, 779–80; Block, *Covenant*, 422–23.

since we need to obtain righteousness but also need a method to do so apart from the law. Sin means that we have "failed to obtain the glory of God." Paul's point in this passage is not that we have tarnished God's image by sinning, but that we never obtained the glory that God offered to us in the covenant of works as a reward for our obedience.[74] There was a higher "glory and honor and immortality" that Adam could have sought and obtained "according to his works" (Rom 2:6–7), but sin short-circuits our ability to pursue these rewards by the covenant of works.[75] Thankfully, God grants it to us by faith. This assertion of justification by faith is then in stark contrast to the method of justification by doing the law that Paul outlines in Romans 2:6–16.[76]

The connection between justification and incorruptible life is clear when Paul writes that "all have sinned and failed to obtain the glory of God." If a runner falls short of the finish line, it does not mean that he reached the finish line and then left it. Rather, he never got there at all. So, too, Adam fell short of glory by never obtaining it.[77] The life that results from justification is the glorious life that we have "in the presence of God," the incorruptible, new creation life.[78] As Vos explains, "If Adam had remained unfallen and kept the probation command, then God would have justified him—that is, God would have taken into account Adam's holy and steadfast condition and would have had a state of immutable righteousness follow."[79] The link between glory and justification is clear in that, despite of how we fall short and do not obtain glory by our sin, we are nevertheless freely justified because of God's grace. What Adam failed to achieve by his works, God freely grants to believers by his grace.[80]

The connection between justification and the glorious life is further highlighted in Romans 5:12–21, contrasting the poor results that afflict humanity because of Adam's failed work with the amazing results that

74. Barcellos, *Getting the Garden Right*, 70–77; Barcellos, *Covenant of Works*, 95–111; *TI*, 17.1.11.

75. CC, 19:2.89–90; Hodge, *Romans*, 49–51; Moo, *Romans*, 142; Frank Thielman, *Romans* (Grand Rapids: Zondervan, 2018), 129–33; and Richard N. Longenecker, *The Epistle to the Romans* (Grand Rapids: Eerdmans, 2016), 254–57.

76. Thielman, *Romans*, 197–98, 202.

77. Morris, *Romans*, 176–77; Hodge, *Romans*, 90.

78. CC, 19:2.141.

79. *VRD*, 4:138.

80. CC, 19:2.139–41.

bless believers because of Christ's successful work. Especially in Romans 5:18, the ultimate contrast is between the work of those two covenant representatives: "Therefore, just as one trespass led to condemnation for all men, in the same way one act of righteousness leads to the justification that results in life for all men" (my translation). Adam's sin that resulted in condemnation, which entails death, contrasts with Christ's righteousness that brings about justification. Notably, justification results in life (Rom 5:9–10).[81]

The crucial phrase is "the justification *that results in life*," highlighting how life comes as the consequent reward of justification.[82] Justification guarantees that this eschatological life comes to us. Newer English versions often read "justification *and life*," seemingly separating justification and life as two disconnected benefits of Christ's work, but older translations better express the link. The Geneva Bible (1599) reads "unto justification of life" and the King James Version says "to the justification of life." Both translations better convey the Greek than "justification and life." The form of the Greek word that the Geneva Bible and KJV translate "of life," at its most basic root, indicates that there is a relationship between "life" and the word that proceeds it, which happens to be "justification." The translation "the justification related to life" is true, yet unspecific, but at least it indicates some sort of connection between justification and life. The rendering "justification and life" in newer translations severs that relationship, even though the literal rendering "justification of life" in older versions is not very specific about the meaning.

To clarify then, "justification of life" indicates the results of justification. As Bavinck specifies: "the act of justification that carries life with it (Rom. 5:18)."[83] To illustrate, if I had a bowl of ice cream, I could point to it and say that it is the ice cream "of my delight." If asked what "of my delight" means, I would explain that this ice cream brings about my delight or causes my delight. My delight results from this ice cream. In a similar fashion, we should understand Romans 5:18 to teach that justification

81. Longenecker, *Romans*, 596–97; *CW*, 72–73.

82. The genitive relationship that I am trying to express is probably closest to Wallace's genitive of product; Daniel B. Wallace, *Greek Grammar Beyond the Basics: An Exegetical Syntax of the New Testament* (Grand Rapids: Zondervan, 1997), 106.

83. *BRD*, 4:211.

brings about everlasting life. Everlasting life results from justification.[84] So, Paul summarizes grace's reign as "righteousness leading to eternal life through Jesus Christ our Lord" (Rom 5:21).[85]

Reformed theologians have regularly understood this to be Paul's point. Calvin comments, "The justification of life is understood as absolution, which restores life to us, as though he had said life-giving. … Life, therefore, results from justification."[86] So, too, William Perkins explains, "For righteousness is the foundation of life eternal. And therefore it is called 'justification of life' (Rom. 5:17)."[87] Elsewhere, Perkins argues concerning justification that "after that God has absolved a sinner and reputed him as just, there must follow this acceptation to life, which is therefore called 'justification of life' [Rom. 5:18]," since "as Adam's sin is imputed unto all, by which death entered, so Christ's obedience imputed to believers brings life and justification."[88] So, too, Rollock affirms, "God would grant everlasting life by justification."[89] In Bavinck's words, "Justification brings life in its train (5:18)."[90] Just like eating this ice cream has the effect of giving me delight, justification has the effect of granting everlasting life.

This connection explains why Paul can write in various places about the law in association both with righteousness and with life.[91] Righteousness, or justification, is a result of keeping the law connected to life. Fulfilling the law results in the status of righteousness, further resulting in the possession of life. Everlasting spiritual life is justification's consequent reward. Paul can say that keeping the law leads to righteousness or to life because both are true according to the terms of the covenant of works, but the status of righteousness is the first result, having life as its further reward.

---

84. *VRD*, 4:154; *CMT*, 64–65.

85. *BOC*, 31.

86. *CO*, 49:101; *CC*, 19:2.212.

87. *WWP*, 2:175 (commentary on Galatians 3:11).

88. *WWP*, 4:62 (commentary on Jude 3).

89. Rollock, *Tractatus*, 11; Rollock, *Treatise*, 8.

90. *BRD*, 4:249.

91. Watson, *Hermeneutics of Faith*, 146; Rosner, *Paul and the Law*, 71–72.

The contrasting results of Adam's work and Christ's links this life of Romans 5:18 more thoroughly to the covenant of works.[92] In this respect, Christ is "the last Adam" (1 Cor 15:45), demonstrating that the Adamic commission informs the biblical depiction of our two leading covenant representatives.[93] The parallel between Adam and Christ in Romans 5:18 highlights how righteousness, if and when attained, results in justification that further results in life. The link between the law—the covenant of works—and this reward of life is explicit in Romans 7:10: "The very commandment *that promised life* proved to be death to me."[94] Calvin argues, "The commandment demonstrates the way unto life in the righteousness of God, and for that reason was given so that we might obtain everlasting life by keeping the Lord's law, if our every depravity would not prevent it."[95] Although our sin warrants death by the law, Christ, the last Adam, was able to and did earn justification for us, implying that the first Adam as our original covenant representative also had the potential before his fall to earn justification by his obedience, even though he failed.

With the link between perfect righteousness, justification, and everlasting life established, what would that everlasting life have looked like had Adam earned it? The "do this and live" principle from Leviticus 18:5, which is the premise of the covenant of works, indicates that if someone fulfills God's commandments, he or she would obtain everlasting life by

92. *CRS*, 1:361–62.

93. Block, *Covenant*, 419–22.

94. Morris, *Romans*, 282; Hodge, *Romans*, 225; *TI*, 8.6.4. Substantial arguments posit that Romans 7:7–12 concerns Adam. More specifically, the whole human race would not have known what sin is had God not revealed his law. God's commandment to Adam promised life but resulted in his death. In Romans 7:13–25, Paul then shifts from Adam's perspective to his own, explaining his struggle to keep the law even as a Christian precisely because Adam had sold humanity into sin and death rather than obtaining life. Although this interpretation has some validity, it is far from the settled consensus, and so appears in the notes, while the main text emphasizes clearer passages. Regardless of one's conclusion about this passage's Adamic perspective, the argued premise—specifically that the law promised life to the one who keeps it—is clear. If that promise ties directly to an Adamic setting, then it further confirms the covenant of works' premises. For the exegetical case, see Watson, *Hermeneutics of Faith*, 325–30; Francis Watson, *Paul, Judaism and the Gentiles: A Sociological Approach* (Cambridge: Cambridge University Press, 1986), 152; VanDrunen, "Israel's Recapitulation," 310–12; Dennis E. Johnson, "The Function of Romans 7:13–25 in Paul's Argument for the Law's Impotence and the Spirit's Power, and Its Bearing on the Identity of the Schizophrenic 'I,' " in *Resurrection and Eschatology*, 31–36; and Herman Ridderbos, *Paul: An Outline of His Theology*, trans. John Richard de Witt (Grand Rapids: Eerdmans, 1975), 143–44.

95. *CO*, 49:126; *CC*, 19:2.256.

their works.[96] The present argument is that if Adam had fulfilled the covenant of works, rather than remaining in the condition wherein he was created, he would have obtained a better, heightened existence in even richer communion with God than he previously enjoyed.[97] If he had been justified and received everlasting life, then Adam would have received an incorruptible body.[98] Adam's fulfillment of the covenant of works would mean confirmation in everlasting righteousness, total inability ever to sin, and the glorified existence that believers now anticipate receiving at Christ's return.[99] His communion with God would have been exponentially deepened had he fulfilled the covenant.

The common assumption is that Adam and Eve had absolutely perfect life in paradise. Certainly, nothing was defective or deficient about them or their condition. They were truly sinless. They had a life of unbroken fellowship with God, everything that they could want to satisfy them, and no burden or toil in their work. Still, although their life was not defective, it was in a sense incomplete. It lacked perfection specifically in the sense of not yet being fully what it could be. The creation world was not the world to come. In the covenant of works, God offered to make it perfect in that sense if Adam completed his task.

This offer of even deeper communion with God in everlasting, incorruptible life marks God's inexhaustible goodness and immense love for Adam.[100] God was by no means stingy in showering Adam with good gifts by creation. Still, no matter how good his gifts have been, God is continually able to outgive himself.[101] The covenant of works' legal nature does not reduce God's relationship with Adam to a cold, merely contractual arrangement, since it was a "covenant of friendship."[102] Since the law describes God's character, Adam as God's image needed to keep the law anyway, but God was richly kind to offer higher blessings to Adam by

96. *CO*, 49:198; *CC*, 19:2.387; Rosner, *Paul and the Law*, 59–72.

97. *BRD*, 2:563–88; *CF*, 381–87.

98. Beale, *New Testament Biblical Theology*, 29–45.

99. *TI*, 5.10.14; Schreiner, *Covenant*, 27.

100. Davison, *Participation in God*, 113–31.

101. *EC*, 1.4.8–11, 20–22; *CW*, 26–27.

102. *CW*, 4.

the covenant.[103] Law and love are, then, fully compatible, complementary companions. Even with its legal character, the covenant of works did not burden Adam in his natural strength because God meant it "for promoting his manifested glory *in the happiness of mankind*," showing its fundamental relational and loving character.[104]

What does God's offer to make Adam's life completely perfect mean? Adam was good and upright by creation but capable of sinning, as is clear from the fact that he did sin. Sin's effects include bodily death, meaning, at least, that Adam's body could become corruptible. The offer to live forever entailed that God would make Adam and his posterity incorruptible. We all would have become incapable of sinning. We all would have received glorified bodies incapable of injury or decay. Linking this idea to Christ's work, Thomas Aquinas argues, "And the incapacity to suffer and die that the first man had differs in this respect from the incapacity to suffer and die that the saints will have after the resurrection. The saints, with their will altogether confirmed in God ... will never be capable of suffering or dying."[105] Just as Jesus Christ, the last Adam, will bring the new creation at his return and grant new creation bodies to his people, so too the first Adam could have obtained the new creation and our new creation bodies.

The idea that Adam could have attained a better, heightened kind of existence, even beyond what he experienced in paradise, has firm biblical support in the premises of Paul's argument for the resurrection of our bodies at Christ's return. Adam's potential to gain a better, incorruptible existence seems clear in 1 Corinthians 15:42–46:

> So is it with the resurrection of the dead. What is sown is perishable; what is raised is imperishable. It is sown in dishonor; it is raised in glory. It is sown in weakness; it is raised in power. It is sown a natural body; it is raised a spiritual body. *If there is a natural body, there is also a spiritual body.* Thus it is written, "The first man Adam became a living being"; the last Adam became a life-giving spirit. But it is not the spiritual that is first but the natural, and then the spiritual.

103. *TI*, 8.3.16–17.

104. *CW*, 2, 53–54; *TI*, 8.3.2, 5.

105. Thomas, *Compendium*, §186.

Among these principles for the resurrection, it is essential that, "If there is a natural body, there is also a spiritual body." God created the natural body but made it capable of becoming spiritual. Adam then had capacity for everlasting life and supernatural communion with God built into his nature.[106]

The logical progression is that if one thing is true, then the other must also be true. If God made the natural body, which obviously he did, then there is a spiritual body to obtain. Certainly, our bodies do not become nonphysical—i.e., ghosts or disembodied spirits—since the argument proves the necessity of *bodily* resurrection. Rather, Adam even in his original condition had potential to obtain a better body, a higher existence.[107]

A butterfly's life cycle provides an apt illustration. Some butterflies rank among nature's most beautiful creatures, sporting bright and pleasing colored wings while bobbing delicately through the air. Every butterfly, however, begins life as a caterpillar. God designed the same creature to have two modes of existence, two different types of bodies for two stages of its life. A caterpillar has nothing wrong with it as it stands, although it clearly has a lower form in its slimy or hairy worm-like state than after it turns into a butterfly. Still, while keeping its same brain and other internal organs, the same creature drastically changes from its lower form to its better body. God designed it for this beautiful progression, as he did with seeds that grow into flowers (1 Cor 15:35–41). This illustration of God-designed life cycles for one creature to change from a lower body into a greater body also applies to how God made humanity to be able to exist first in our natural body and then obtain our higher spiritual body.

We need not speculate about what this spiritual body is like because Paul describes it as imperishable and characterized by glory. In other words, human nature will be unable to decay or ever fall into unrighteousness. This spiritual body, which the first man Adam could have obtained, is glorified for unending, heightened, and consummate fellowship with

106. Geerhardus Vos, "The Eschatological Aspect of the Pauline Conception of the Spirit," in *RHBI*, 105–7; *ACW*, 325–26; Gladd, *Adam and Israel to the Church*, 110–14.

107. Roy E. Ciampa and Brian S. Rosner, "1 Corinthians," in *Commentary on the New Testament Use of the Old Testament*, ed. G. K. Beale and D. A. Carson (Grand Rapids: Baker Academic, 2007), 747.

God.[108] The reception of this sort of spiritual existence, as it is inherently linked to the Holy Spirit as "the Spirit of life" (Rom 8:2), is usually called glorification.

This description of the body that Christ will grant at the resurrection closely links the natural body's potential for spiritual existence to the first Adam. Paul's reference to Adam's creation through his quotation of Genesis 2:7 proves that he was reflecting upon Adam's existence before sin.[109] Just as in Romans 5, also about the inheritance of everlasting life, Paul here links our future destinies to the contrast between the two Adams.[110] The first Adam received the natural body and was capable of advancing it to incorruptible life, even though he failed to do so.[111]

In the second century, Irenaeus argued that God's goodness shines in offering to Adam the opportunity to grow above his created condition as God's image into the more perfect image bearer.[112] He notes that in "his great kindness," God "made men like himself in their own power." Further, from the outset "what is mortal must be excelled to and absorbed by immortality, what is corruptible by incorruptibility."[113] God made humanity so that our nature could be advanced to immortality, but Adam's sin threw us into the clutches of the knowledge of good and evil. Irenaeus even tied the test for receiving this immortality to the law about the tree of knowledge of good and evil.[114]

In this respect, the last Adam, God the Son, assumed a natural body but succeeded in advancing it to incorruptible life, which is clear in his

---

108. Beale, *New Testament Biblical Theology*, 29–45; Guy Prentiss Waters, "1–2 Corinthians," in *Biblical-Theological Introduction to the New Testament*, 212–14; Hodge, *Corinthians*, 347–48; Gordon D. Fee, *The First Epistle to the Corinthians*, rev. ed. (Grand Rapids: Eerdmans, 2014), 869–70; and Anthony C. Thiselton, *The First Epistle to the Corinthians* (Grand Rapids: Eerdmans, 2000), 1276–81.

109. Richard B. Gaffin Jr., *Resurrection and Redemption: A Study on Paul's Soteriology* (Phillipsburg, NJ: P&R, 1987), 80–91; Guy Prentiss Waters, "The Covenant of Works in the New Testament," in *CT*, 85.

110. Thiselton, *Corinthians*, 1281–83.

111. James McKeown, *Genesis* (Grand Rapids: Eerdmans, 2008), 33; Wenham, *Genesis 1–15*, 60–61.

112. Irenaeus, *Against Heresies*, 4.38.1–4, in *PG*, 7.1:1105–9; *ANF*, 1:521–22.

113. Irenaeus, *Against Heresies*, 4.38.4. in *PG*, 7.1:1109; *ANF*, 1:522; and Denis Minns, *Irenaeus: An Introduction* (London: T&T Clark, 2010), 72–76.

114. Irenaeus, *The Demonstration of the Apostolic Preaching*, trans. J. Armitage Robinson (London and New York: Aeterna Press, 2015), §15.

glorious resurrection.[115] Irenaeus again helpfully ties our sinful estate to Adam's disobedience but our rescue to the last Adam's obedience.

> And because in the original formation of Adam all of us were tied and bound up with death through his disobedience, it was right that through the obedience of Him who was made man for us we should be released from death. … And therefore our Lord took that same original formation as (His) entry into flesh, so that He might draw near and contend on behalf of the fathers, and conquer by Adam that which by Adam had stricken us down.[116]

The connection between Adam's possibility of and Christ's victory in obtaining the spiritual body clarifies how Christ is not confused or identified *directly* with the Holy Spirit by becoming a "life-giving spirit." Rather, Christ is the man who obtained that spiritual—glorified and incorruptible—body and has earned the position to distribute that indestructible life to all those whom he represents, which of course is a condition rewarded by the Holy Spirit.[117] Calvin comments on Genesis 2:7 that Moses describes

---

115. *VRD*, 2:18–20; 3:223, 225–28.

116. Irenaeus, *Demonstration*, §31.

117. In the phrase "life-giving spirit," Paul draws upon his word contrast of *natural* and *spiritual* from within the context of 1 Corinthians 15:35–58. Verses 44–45 could be translated to stress the linguistic parallels in the Greek, so to alleviate the confusion in what seems like odd terminology:

> It is sown a *natural* (ψυχικόν) body, it is raised a *spiritual* (πνευματικόν) body. If there is a *natural* (ψυχικόν) body, then there is also a *spiritual* (πνευματικόν) body. Thus, it is written: "The first Adam became a living *natural man* (ψυχήν)"; the last Adam became the life-giving *spiritual man* (πνεῦμα).

The use of "spirit" (πνεῦμα) in verse 45 should be understood in light of how Paul uses the concept of "spiritual" within his surrounding discussion. Adam was created in a *natural* (ψυχικόν) condition and exemplified that state. On the other hand, Christ exemplifies the spiritual (πνευματικόν) condition. Each represents a different mode of human existence: protological or eschatological. The Holy Spirit is tied to that eschatological life as the source of glorification or imperishable existence and thereby characterizes the age to come. In verse 45, Paul then refers indirectly to the Spirit by noting that Adam potentially could obtain, and Christ truly has obtained, that spiritual condition. The point then is not to divorce "the life-giving Spirit" from the Holy Spirit, since the Spirit is fully tied to this identity, but to show how Christ obtained the spiritual condition, still linked to the Spirit's work, that was always the reward of the covenant of works. The first Adam was alive, but was in that initial, unglorified, *natural* (ψυχικόν) state, but the last Adam obtained the *spiritual* (πνευματικόν) state of not merely being alive, but of being that glorified man who could even give incorruptible life to others. In that respect, the contrast is not merely between natural and spiritual but also between the one who just lived and the one who gives life. For further argument and more technical detail for this exegesis, see Peter Jones, "Paul Confronts Paganism in the Church. A Case Study of First Corinthians 15:45," *JETS* 49.4 (December 2006): 713–27; Collins, *Genesis 1–4*, 146–47; Gordon D. Fee, *Pauline Christology: An Exegetical-Theological Study* (Grand Rapids: Baker Academic, 2007),

how God gave life to humanity, and that Paul's interpretation then "stated an antithesis between this living creature and the life-giving spirit which Christ confers upon believers" to show "that the human condition was not completed in the person of Adam; but it is a singular benefit from Christ that we may be renewed unto heavenly life."[118] The first Adam *could have* won incorruptible life for all humanity, but the last Adam *has* and grants incorruptible life to his people. So, Christ became the life-giving spirit.

Adam's sin resulted in our natural bodies becoming perishable, but God built human nature with the potential to become a spiritual body.[119] Christ will resurrect his people into this condition, having earned it for us as the second Adam. Christ's designation as the second Adam implies that the first Adam could also have obtained that spiritual body for us.[120] If Adam had fulfilled the covenant of works, he would have been justified and thereby glorified. To tie together 1 Corinthians 15 and Romans 5—the two most explicit passages about the first and last Adam—the "justification that results in life" (Rom 5:18) shows how life is justification's consequent, but this life received as justification's consequent is incorruptible life, or, in other words, glorification.[121]

Adam's justification and glorification would have been tied together as one event, as was certainly the case for Christ when he was both justified and glorified in his resurrection (Rom 4:25; 1 Tim 3:16). Still, Romans 5:18–21 grounds the justification that results in life in Christ's obedience, so that the status of righteousness leads to that glorified life.

> Therefore, as one trespass led to condemnation for all men, so one act of righteousness leads to *justification unto life* for all men. For as by the one man's disobedience the many were made sinners, so

116–19; Gaffin, *Resurrection and Redemption*, 80, 85–89, 108–12; Fee, *Corinthians*, 872–75; Thiselton, *Corinthians*, 1281–85; *VRD*, 225–28; *BRD*, 2:564; *TI*, 5.8.3–4; Waters, "Covenant of Works in the New Testament," 83; and Waters, "1–2 Corinthians," 212–13; cf. Hendrikus Berkhof, *The Doctrine of the Holy Spirit* (Richmond, VA: John Knox, 1964), 25–28.

118. *CO*, 23:36; *CC*, 1:1.112–13.

119. *CW*, 73.

120. N. Gray Sutanto, "Consummation Anyway: A Reformed Proposal," *Journal of Analytic Philosophy* 9 (Summer 2021): 223–37.

121. Richard B. Gaffin Jr., "The Work of Christ Applied," in *CD*, 275; Brandon Crowe, "The Passive and Active Obedience of Christ: Retrieving a Biblical Distinction," in *The Doctrine on Which the Church Stands or Falls: Justification in Biblical, Theological, Historical, and Pastoral Perspective*, ed. Matthew Barrett (Wheaton, IL: Crossway, 2019), 448–52.

> *by the one man's obedience the many will be made righteous.* Now the law came in to increase the trespass, but where sin increased, grace abounded all the more, so that, as sin reigned in death, grace also might reign through *righteousness leading to eternal life* through Jesus Christ our Lord.

The connection between obedience and justification has already been argued, but this passage further states that the justification unto life is grounded in *Christ's obedience* that makes us righteous in God's sight. This status of righteousness—justification—leads to or has the consequent reward of everlasting life, namely, glorification.

Although justification and glorification would have been bound together for Adam and were for Christ, the conceptual distinction between them remains in that justification is the prerequisite for glorification. One results in the other, at least logically speaking, even though Christ experienced them as one event. We can illustrate the point in two ways.

In terms of the relationship of prerequisite to consequent, if a runner comes first place in a race, he receives a gold medal for his victory. When he finishes first, his status as victor guarantees his reward, even though he does not receive it at the moment he crosses the finish line. Still, the gold medal is inherently linked to his victorious status since it announces and even confirms that status in public fashion. So, too, justification is the prerequisite victorious status—"winning" at fulfilling the law—that guarantees the consequent reward of glorification that follows upon that status but announces and confirms that status publicly. This illustration shows how a status and its inherent reward are bound together even if not conferred simultaneously.

On the other hand, a graduation ceremony illustrates how a status and its reward remain conceptually distinct even if they are conferred in the same act. A student must satisfy all the school's requirements to graduate, meaning conditions or terms must be fulfilled. Once she has fulfilled those terms, she will be rewarded with the status of graduate and the token of a diploma. Theoretically, the status of graduate can be granted to her separately from receiving her diploma. After all, she could graduate *in absentia*, not attending the ceremony. Still, she would be declared a graduate at the ceremony and her diploma would then be mailed to her later. In practice, as she attends her graduation ceremony, she is declared a graduate in the same act of receiving her diploma. The status is distinct from the reward in that she had fulfilled the terms, the school had acknowledged that completion, and she would need to be a graduate legitimately to receive a diploma. Still, in practice, the event of handing the reward of the diploma is the act of declaring her a graduate.

If Adam had fulfilled the covenant of works, then he would seemingly have been justified and glorified in the same act, even if the status and consequent token of his reward are distinct. Certainly, Christ's resurrection was both his justification and glorification bound into one act.[122] There is, then, an inherent link between justification and glorification, between righteousness and incorruptible life. Since justification and glorification are both benefits that believers receive from Christ, their relationship remains as two aspects of our salvation in union with Christ. The discussion in chapters 9 and 10 about the benefits of Christ in the covenant of grace further explains how believers receive these two related aspects of salvation.

It should not be odd to think that God would give Adam good blessings by creation and offer him even greater blessings of communion with God for his obedience. Truly, God is that generous and good. Think of an instance of parents reminding their son that tonight is family movie night together. In addition to that fellowship, if the son cleans his room before the movie, he will also get ice cream. The communion as a family is already in place, but the parents have offered to sweeten that communion if the condition of obedience is fulfilled. Adam was in communion with God but God offered to make that communion even sweeter if Adam fulfilled the terms of the covenant of works.

CONCLUSION

The legal character of the covenant of works again reminds us of God's immense love and kindness for Adam and the whole human race. God not only gave Adam the gift of existing in the divine image but also offered him the potential to intensify the communion that he had with God by

---

122. Gaffin, "Work of Christ Applied," 275–76; Gaffin, *Resurrection and Redemption*, 119–24, 126–27.

covenant. Adam was to demonstrate his love for God by perfectly obeying the law, but God showed the inexhaustible riches of his kindness by offering to reward Adam with incorruptible life in the new creation. Despite how Adam had to obey the law simply because he is God's creature, God put his love for Adam on full display by offering to reward Adam for his obedience.

The pastoral use of the doctrines in this chapter relates to God's attributes. God's people need to know that God is perfectly righteous, which is why he cannot accept anything other than perfect obedience as the standard for earning rewards from him. Although that is bad news for every sinner who tries to earn God's favor by being good enough, it is wonderful news for sinners who would depend upon God's promises. Because God is righteous, he must honor his promises to receive those who come to him in Christ. That is why John writes, "If we confess our sins, he is *faithful and just* to forgive us our sins and to cleanse us from all unrighteousness" (1 John 1:9). God's justice would be compromised if he broke any of his promises.

Further, the doctrines in this chapter also remind God's people of his goodness. In the modern era, many people often take God's love for granted. The rise of mysticism, wherein someone claims to be "spiritual but not religious," has embedded the assumption in the modern West that God almost *had* to have a relationship with us, most probably because we are so lovable. The covenant of works reminds us of God's goodness, first, in that God did not even need to create us but was so rich and overflowing in his goodness and love that he *wanted* creatures on whom to shower his love. It reminds us of God's goodness, second, in that God is not a distant God or an impersonal force but is the God who bound himself to his people in covenant, so by a *personal* bond of communion. It reminds us of God's goodness, third, in that God is inexhaustible in his goodness to his people. He created Adam and gave paradise to him as a home, so seemingly a perfect life. God was still able to offer even higher blessings to him of supernatural, eschatological communion in the new creation. Our God can always outgive himself, no matter how rich his blessings have already been.

IV

Applying the Covenant of Works

The fruit of the righteous is a tree of life,
and whoever captures souls is wise.
—*Proverbs 11:30*

When you order at the counter in a fast-food restaurant, one question that you must answer is, "For here or to go?" indicating a difference in how you will receive your food. If you opt for "for here," then your food will come on a tray. On the other hand, if you opt for "to go," then your food will come in a bag. In this case, the same food—the same substance—is given in two different methods. The same benefits can be presented—administered—through multiple means.

We have seen the type of communion that Adam had with God in the covenant of works, and how God offered him even greater communion for fulfilling the terms of the covenant. Nevertheless, our covenant relationship with God is not an abstract notion but a lived experience. Believers today should remember that the covenant is still where we find ourselves before God, walking with him in Christ's grace. In the covenant of works, Adam had a genuine historical and lived experience as he began his time on earth.

This chapter looks at two aspects of how the covenant of works intersects with lived experience. First, it addresses how God applied the covenant to Adam. We have seen *that* God offered incorruptible life as the covenant reward but must see *how* he presented this offer. The Reformed tradition has often differentiated between a covenant's substance and administration. In our fast-food illustration, the ordered food is the substance, given to you in some container, and the tray or the bag is the administration, meaning the method of delivering the substance. In the covenant of works, the substance was the offered reward of incorruptible life in communion with God, but, as we will see, God used two features of Adam's life in the garden as its administration, the ways in which God presented that offer to Adam. This substance-administration distinction is important as we think about Adam's lived experience in the covenant of works but will become even more important when considering the covenant of grace.

After ordering at that fast-food restaurant, we know that, whether receiving our food via tray or bag, we still need to apply that food to ourselves by eating it. So, this chapter also addresses some ways that the covenant of works addresses our lived experience in the Christian life. The covenant of works may be a precisely formulated doctrine, but it still has value for our walk with the Lord to help us understand our lived experience in covenant with God.

HOW GOD OFFERED INCORRUPTIBLE LIFE TO ADAM

Genesis 1–3 records Adam's lived experience in the covenant of works, detailing several interesting features of how God offered to Adam the reward of deeper communion. In particular, God proffered Adam the reward of everlasting life through features of ordinary life, in the consecration of the seventh day for Sabbath rest and in the tree of life. This section outlines the significance of these two features of Adam's life in the garden for how they indicate the methods by which God offered potential reward to Adam.

Amidst various modern debates about the creation week, the seventh day has perhaps received the least reflection. This neglect unfortunately underplays the seventh day's profound importance for the narrative's theological point, for God's relationship with Adam, and for the culmination of Scripture's storyline. Genesis 1 records how creation's first six days contain God's work activities, each day being clearly marked with beginning and end. Then, regarding the seventh day, Genesis 2:1–3 says, "Thus the heavens and the earth were finished, and all the host of them. And on the seventh day God finished his work that he had done, and he rested on the seventh day from all his work that he had done. So God blessed the seventh day and made it holy, because on it God rested from all his work that he had done in creation." Differing from the first six, the seventh day lacks a marked ending. The first six days contain "morning" and "evening," but this seventh day has no such noted end.[1] Some theologians suggest that the seventh day's lack of ending relates to how God consecrated it as the end of his work and the beginning of his rest.[2] The creation Sabbath's unending nature, in lacking an evening to transition it into another day, indicates that God himself entered an unending rest. Accordingly, God's consecration of the Sabbath as the one holy day for his people also marks how an everlasting rest waits for those who complete their assigned work.[3] God completed the pattern of his work and so rests forever, establishing by example the principle that Adam too would enter everlasting rest if he completed his work.[4] Although Adam failed, to get slightly ahead of ourselves, Christ would fulfill this Sabbath principle and earn everlasting rest for his people.

God's institution of the Sabbath day shows that he made the world in such a way that he built directly into the creation an offer for those made in his image to join him in unending rest.[5] Herman Witsius explains that God and man both resting on the seventh day marks that "the rest of the glory of God is then to be expected," but also "that man is not to enter into rest, till he has finished his course of probation, and God upon strictly examining it by the rule of his law, finds it complete and in every

---

1. Waltke with Fredericks, *Genesis*, 68.

2. *WWG*, 198–99; *VBT*, 139–143; *KP*, 33–41.

3. Fesko, *Last Things First*, 183–203; Wenham, *Genesis 1–15*, 40; Waltke with Fredericks, *Genesis*, 71–73; McKeown, *Genesis*, 28; Derek Kidner, *Genesis* (Downers Grove, IL: IVP Academic, 1967), 60.

4. Fesko, *Last Things First*, 102–3, 168–75; Barcellos, *Getting the Garden Right*, 110–55; *EC*, 1.7.8.

5. Beale, *New Testament Biblical Theology*, 775–802.

respect perfect."[6] This understanding of the creation Sabbath, however, is not limited to inferences drawn from the lack of morning and evening in Genesis 2:1–3.

Hebrews 3:7–4:14 interprets the creation week's Sabbath principle from new covenant perspective, explaining how the prospect of permanent Sabbath rest remains before us. As Hebrews elaborates, disobedience disqualifies sinners from entering that everlasting rest by their own works, meaning that only believers in Christ will join God in that unending rest.[7]

> For we who have believed enter that rest, as he has said, "As I swore in my wrath, 'They shall not enter my rest,' " although his works were finished from the foundation of the world. For he has somewhere spoken of the seventh day in this way: "And God rested on the seventh day from all his works." And again in this passage he said, "They shall not enter my rest." Since therefore it remains for some to enter it, and those who formerly received the good news failed to enter because of disobedience. (Heb 4:3–6)

Although raising many rich and interesting threads, the clear but pertinent point for the creation Sabbath and reward is God's resting from his works "from the foundation of the world"—the creation week—was an offer for God's people to join him in that unending rest.[8] Disobedience prevents one from joining God in that rest, which is exactly how the covenant of works ended. Adam and his posterity can no longer join God in his rest by works, but we can by faith in the second Adam who has earned everlasting Sabbath rest for us. Although in Christ we are presently able to rest from our works as a condition for inheriting everlasting rest, our full possession of that rest awaits when we enter the new creation.[9] This understanding of the Sabbath as indicating an eschatological reward in Hebrews 3:7–4:16 follows clearly from (and is further supported by) the

6. *EC*, 1.7.16.

7. Johnson, *Hebrews*, 126; Ellingworth, *Hebrews*, 246, 255.

8. O'Brien, *Hebrews*, 162–73; Johnson, *Hebrews*, 124–30; Ellingworth, *Hebrews*, 247, 249–51; Michaels, "Hebrews," 17:359–61; *EC*, 1.7.17.

9. Thanks to my friend, Steve Wellum, for highlighting the need to indicate here that Christ has presently provided rest to believers.

recognition that Hebrews 2:5–10, as the previous chapter argues, indicates an eschatological reward for humanity tied to creation.

This understanding of the Sabbath as connected to the covenant of works highlights the creation week's theological significance in indicating the link between the works principle and its reward. Reformed theologians have frequently implemented this very traditional interpretation, but even Augustine drew the same connection while preaching on John 5:19.[10] He explains that Scripture refers to God's seventh-day rest "to admonish us that we should only rest after good works," so that the narrative enjoins that we, "on observing that God rested after having done good works, should only hope for rest after performing good works."[11] Augustine may not have held the exact doctrine of the covenant of works—although he did believe in a covenant between God and Adam as well as Adam's headship and probation—but he clearly shared the view that the Sabbath presented the offered reward of everlasting life.[12] He emphasized that this reward was offered upon the completion of a works requirement, which is the covenant of works' fundamental premise. In this respect, the Heidelberg Catechism notes how the Sabbath command's requirement to rest every day from evil works is to "begin in this life the everlasting Sabbath" (HC 103).[13] The covenant of works, channeled through the Sabbath command, established our principal hope for the new creation as rest in blessed communion with God.

In addition to how the creation's Sabbath principle, which offered everlasting rest to Adam upon the completion of his works, the tree of life, featuring specially in the garden narrative, also offered the reward to Adam. The way that the tree of life offered the covenantal reward to Adam comes into clearer perspective if we survey each point of the story involving that tree. This aspect about the tree of life fittingly refocuses our discussion of the covenant of works on the events as they unfolded. The story's first point concerning the tree of life occurs in Genesis 2:8–9: "And the Lord God planted a garden in Eden, in the east, and there he put the

---

10. *WWG*, 198–99; *VBT*, 139–143; *KP*, 33–41.

11. Saint Augustine, *Homilies on the Gospel of John 1–40*, trans. Edmund Hill, ed. Allan D. Fitzgerald (Hyde Park, NY: New City Press, 2009), 358.

12. Augustine, *City of God*, 16.27 in *NPNF1*, 2:749.

13. *COC*, 3:345.

man whom he had formed. And out of the ground the Lord God made to spring up every tree that is pleasant to the sight and good for food. The tree of life was in the midst of the garden, and the tree of the knowledge of good and evil." The garden narrative about Adam's covenant revolves around the two trees. God made Adam, then planted a garden in Eden, then put Adam in that garden to be confronted with the choice between two trees. These trees highlight the tension of Adam's probation in the covenant of works. As Peter Lombard (1096–1160) writes, "To preserve what he had given and for the deserving of what he had promised, God added the command of obedience to the natural reason that had been placed in the soul of man at creation, by which he was able to discern between good and evil. By observing this command, man would not lose what he had been given and would obtain what had been promised, so that he might come to his reward through merit."[14] Adam was permitted to eat of all the trees in the garden but forbidden to eat from the tree of knowledge of good and evil, giving him opportunity to prove his obedience (Gen 2:16–17).

Although permitted to eat from all the other trees, Adam first had to earn the right to eat from the tree of life, encapsulating the second way that God offered the reward of incorruptible life in the covenant of works.[15] Adam's perfect obedience would have secured the right to eat from the tree of life, which would mean that he had been justified in God's sight, and he would enter confirmed incorruptible life as he joined God in consecrated and everlasting Sabbath rest.

The second point of the story about Adam's relationship to the tree of life describes the results of the covenant of works. Just after Adam's fall, in reaction to Adam's sin, God responds in Genesis 3:22–23: "'Behold, the man has become like one of us in knowing good and evil. Now, lest he reach out his hand and take also of the tree of life and eat, and live forever—' therefore the Lord God sent him out from the garden of Eden to work the ground from which he was taken." God wanted to prevent sinful Adam from eating of the tree of life since then he would live forever,

---

14. Peter Lombard, *The Sentences Book 2: On Creation*, trans. Giulio Silano (Ontario: Pontifical Institute of Medieval Studies, 2008), 20.6.2.

15. *CW*, 75, 111–15.

showing that this tree itself was an offer of living forever if Adam partook of it. Taco Hajo van den Honert (1666–1740), who happened to have the best name in Reformed theology, clarifies how the tree of life was aptly named because it sealed how Adam could merit life according to the terms of the covenant of works. He explains that it was named the tree of life "because, provided that Adam fulfilled obedience in the manner according to perseverance in good works, God was obliged by the covenant to keep the promise that he would have confirmed to him his spiritual life through eating of this tree (or orchard), he would have confirmed to him his bodily life, and he would have granted safety from all condemnation and death (Gen. 3:22, 24)."[16] That connection between the tree and living forever clarifies that God used the tree of life as a way to administer the offered reward to Adam in the covenant.[17]

Both that Adam had to earn the right to eat from that tree and that the tree of life symbolized that heightened everlasting life are indicated in Genesis 3:22: "Now, lest he reach out his hand and take also of the tree of life and eat, and live forever." First, the word "lest" demonstrates that Adam had to earn the right to eat from this tree. The Hebrew word most often means preventing something from happening that had not previously occurred. For example, Judges 18:25: "And the people of Dan said to him, 'Do not let your voice be heard among us, *lest* angry fellows fall upon you, and you lose your life with the lives of your household.' " The angry fellows had not yet attacked Micah, since then the warning would be nonsense. So, "lest" indicates precisely that this event had not yet occurred. Isaiah 36:18 is another example: "Beware *lest* Hezekiah mislead you by saying, 'The LORD will deliver us.' " This warning would also be nonsense if the deception had already occurred, again showing that "lest" is normally about preventing something that had not already occurred.[18]

Furthermore, God did not want Adam to take *also* from the tree of life, highlighting how Adam had to choose which fruit from the two special

16. Taco Hajo van den Honert, *Dissertationes Historicae 1. de Creatione Mundi 2. de Situ Edenis et Horti* ... (Leiden: Apud A. Kallewier, 1738), 138.

17. *MMB*, 21–22; *KP*, 93–96.

18. For other instances of פֶּן, see Genesis 19:19; 26:7, 9; Exodus 13:17; 34:12, 15; Numbers 16:34; Judges 7:2; 1 Samuel 13:19; 27:11; and Job 32:13.

trees in the Garden he would eat and could not rightfully eat from both.[19] Since he chose to eat the probationary fruit from the tree of knowledge of good and evil, he could not also eat the reward fruit from the tree of life. Again, the tension within the garden narrative and Adam's probation within the covenant of works centered on his decision between these two trees.

At the end of *Indiana Jones and the Last Crusade*, the villain drinks from a golden cup that he thinks is the holy grail. That cup turns out not to be the grail, and his wrong choice results in his body disintegrating. The elderly knight in the room—in one of cinema's bigger understatements, as the villain's skin and body melts—simply says: "He chose poorly." His words could equally apply with amplified understatement to Adam's choice. Adam had not yet eaten of the tree of life, so had not been confirmed in his ability to live forever, but God had offered to Adam the potential for better, glorified, everlasting life, if he passed the covenant of works.

Second, God said in Genesis 3:22 that the consequence of eating from the tree of life would be living forever, showing how the right to eat from the tree of life signified the reward of everlasting life. Certainly, the tree did not have magic powers to make Adam live forever if he ate its fruit. Rather, this tree was the sacrament of the covenant of works, meaning that it was the tangible marker setting forth in a physical way God's promised reward if Adam met the conditions.[20] So, Bavinck concludes, "Thus sometimes, in the covenant of works before the fall (when there really were no means of *grace*), they [the Reformed] listed the Sabbath and paradise, the tree of knowledge and the tree of life, as sacraments."[21] At least the Sabbath and the tree of life were means by which God offered a reward to Adam.

The book of Revelation confirms the tree of life's sacramental role. That the tree of life features in Scripture's opening narratives and returns in its account of history's end is significant. Revelation 21 describes the arrival of the New Jerusalem when Christ returns, and Revelation 22 expands upon what that new creation looks like. "Then the angel showed me the river of the water of life, bright as crystal, flowing from the throne of God

---

19. Wenham, *Genesis 1–15*, 85.

20. Kidner, *Genesis*, 67; McKeown, *Genesis*, 33; Walton, *Lost World of Adam and Eve*, 120–25; *TI*, 8.5.1–5; *CRS*, 1:379–80.

21. *BRD*, 4:490.

and of the Lamb through the middle of the street of the city; also, on either side of the river, the tree of life with its twelve kinds of fruit, yielding its fruit each month. The leaves of the tree were for the healing of the nations" (Rev 22:1–2). Some features of this account of the tree of life indicate its role in offering the reward to Adam in the covenant of works.[22] In Genesis, the tree was in the midst of the garden but, in Revelation, has grown to span the river. Whereas Adam was supposed to fill the earth with the new creation kingdom as part of his task, but left the garden as a small patch of paradise blocked to his posterity by angels, Christ installs the global new creation kingdom that Adam was supposed to achieve, signified in the expanded tree of life.[23] John symbolically describes this global blessing, which Christ will grant, by referring to the tree of life's return: "The leaves of the tree were for the healing of the nations." At history's end, the blessing of everlasting rest, which the tree of life signifies, will extend to people of every tribe, tongue, and nation because of Jesus Christ's work as Savior.[24]

Revelation also crystalizes that requirement to earn the right to eat of the tree of life: "Blessed are those who wash their robes, so that they may have *the right to the tree of life* and that they may enter the city by the gates" (Rev 22:14). In our present circumstances as sinners this side of Adam's fall, we need justification that includes the forgiveness of sins, which Jesus grants to us. In this respect, the washed robes indicate this aspect of our salvation by implementing the Old Testament's metaphor wherein the cleansing of polluted garments represents the forgiveness of sins (Isa 1:18; 64:6; Zech 3:3–5).[25] In our justification, Christ gives us the clean robe of his righteousness, thereby bestowing the right to eat from the tree of life, which then includes the right to enter God's everlasting kingdom. Just as Isaiah 62:10–12 depicts the Savior going "through the gates" so that God's people may enter into the city of their salvation, so too, in Revelation, obtaining the right to eat from the tree of life because of Christ's work for us allows us to "enter the city by the gates."[26] This understanding of the tree of life ties into why Paul would write in Philippians

22. *TI*, 8.5.6–7.

23. Beale, *Revelation*, 1103.

24. Beale, *Revelation*, 1106–11.

25. Beale, *Revelation*, 436; cf. 1139.

26. Beale, *Revelation*, 1139–40.

3:20–21: "But our citizenship is in heaven, and from it we await a Savior, the Lord Jesus Christ, who will transform our lowly body to be like his glorious body, by the power that enables him even to subject all things to himself." Being a citizen is a legal right, which we are given because Jesus Christ justifies us. We may enter the gates of the New Jerusalem at Christ's return because he has made us clean, given us clean robes, and granted us the status of heavenly citizen as he makes us righteous before God's throne. That citizenship, our justification and guaranteed entry, also ensures that we will receive a transformed, glorified body. So, this citizenship means that we are allowed to enter God's everlasting kingdom in incorruptible bodies.

Paul's picture of justification as citizenship and entry into the kingdom clearly parallels John's image of those who are clean before God (justified) receiving the right to eat from the tree of life—which in Eden signified the right to live forever—and enter the New Jerusalem. In Revelation 22:19, having a share in the tree of life symbolizes participation in everlasting life in the New Jerusalem. Although John warns that those who falsely profess faith and participate in the church community in name only will not finally eat the tree of life's fruit, that warning still holds out the wonderful prospect to true believers that we wait for a glorious feeding from that tree as we enter the holy city.[27] The immensely rich theology within the intersections of these texts about salvation, citizenship/entering the gates, and glorified bodies/eating from the tree of life underscores how the tree of life signified the reward offered to Adam in the covenant of works.

These means by which God offered the reward to Adam in the covenant of works demonstrate that God and his promises are not disconnected from his people's daily lives. God makes his goodness known to us in the everyday things he gives us to point us to the blessing of living in communion with him. God reminded Adam that he walked with him and had wonderful blessings in store for him through a special day of the week and a tree in the garden where he lived. These ordinary things sealed God's amazing promises to Adam.

God has not changed and still puts everyday things in his people's lives to remind us of the communion that we have with him in the covenant of

27. Beale, *Revelation*, 1153.

grace. We too have a day of the week on which we gather as the church to hear of God's goodness and rest from our worldly engagements. On that day, we are reminded of the blessings that come to us in Christ, of which that day of rest is only a small foretaste. Those blessings continue to roll out to us throughout the rest of the week, because we know that whatever our work is, we do it in gratitude to serve our family, friends, and neighbors, rather than to obtain our everlasting reward.

THE COVENANT BROKEN

Before considering how the covenant of works is a helpful doctrine in our Christian life, we should examine the actual outcome of this covenant. The preceding outlines of the covenant of works, its terms, its potential reward, and its administration, have delved deeply into the scriptural principles about the law, righteousness, the new creation, and the tree of life. Still, Adam did not obtain that possible outcome. As most readers will already know, Adam committed the first sinful act by eating from the tree of knowledge of good and evil. Adam's sin brought the covenant of works to its end point, in that Adam forfeited by his disobedience any right that he might have obtained to eat of the tree of life and enter the new creation.

Since Adam was made good and upright and had the full and natural ability to fulfill the law and earn his covenantal reward, the question remains why we are in such a sinful condition and struggle to achieve even a meager appearance of personal holiness. The Heidelberg Catechism 7 says that "this depraved nature of man" comes "from the fall and disobedience of our first parents, Adam and Eve, in Paradise, whereby our nature became so corrupt that we are all conceived and born in sin."[28] We have already outlined Adam's probationary situation and his choice between the two trees, but the encounter with the serpent makes clear which tree Adam chose and the consequences for his disobedience.

Genesis 3 records how the serpent approached Eve and prompted her to eat the forbidden fruit. Although Eve was the first to eat, several factors put the ultimate blame for this defeat squarely upon Adam. First and practically, Adam was responsible for the failure. In the wake of the serpent tempting Eve, "she took of its fruit and ate, and she also gave some to her

28. *COC*, 3:310–11.

husband *who was with her,* and he ate" (Gen 3:6). Adam, even though Eve engaged the serpent and ate first, was present the whole time. He, as the covenant head, should have gotten involved, killed the serpent, cast out his body, and chosen the life-giving fruit.[29] After all, God had given the probationary command to Adam before he created Eve (Gen 2:15–17), making him responsible to pass on God's law to his wife. Adam was to blame both because he was negligent in upholding the law and because he participated in the sin. Second, Adam was ultimately to blame for the defeat in the covenant of works because he—no one else—was the covenantal representative for all humanity. Paul clearly states in Romans 5:12 that "sin came into the world through one man," baldly blaming Adam, as the first covenantal head, for all that is wrong in the world.

Although God offered the world, the new creation, and incorruptible life in fullest communion with himself in the covenant of works, Adam rejected those rewards in favor of the serpent's temptation. Rather than submitting to what God instructed him to do, Adam pretended to have the right to determine what is good and what is evil.[30] The accurate meaning of the test concerning the tree of knowledge of good and evil requires a consideration of the tree's name, the serpent's test in Genesis 3:4–5, and God's verdict: "Behold, the man has become like one of us in knowing good and evil" (Gen 3:22). God's verdict entails that the tree's test could not have been about man becoming a mix of good and evil, since that mixture is opposite of being like God. The tree was also not a test of *simply* whether Adam could properly discern good and evil—although that was certainly a factor, since he did not properly discern what was good, in which respect also he was not like God. In the end, Adam tried to usurp the authority to determine what is truly good and evil, but God alone has that right. Instead of a global paradise and indestructible life with God, Adam chose the illusion of false authority.

Adam's sin, as a transgression of God's law, was fundamentally breaking the covenant. Since the covenant of works was God's means of facilitating communion with Adam and his posterity, sin is inherently relational. Sin is a lack of conformity to or a transgression of God's law, but breaking *God's*

29. *KP*, 121, 128.

30. Blocher, *In the Beginning*, 126–33.

law is legal *and relational* rebellion against God.[31] Sin, therefore, makes us guilty before God but also alienates us from God, fracturing our communion with God in every sense.[32]

Pivotally, Adam acted not only on his own behalf, but as the representative of all humanity.[33] Just as Adam would have earned the rewards for us all if he had fulfilled the terms of the covenant of works, so he likewise warranted the condemnation and punishment that accompanied his defeat. Reformed theology has said that Adam's sin was *imputed* to us. "Imputation" simply means that Adam's sin was legally credited to each of us as our sin.[34] By way of illustration, if we cosign on a loan but the primary signer defaults on his or her debt, then that debt becomes ours and we must pay everything accrued by the person who took out the loan. Their debt and also their penalties are credited to us as the one legally joined to them by the covenant of the loan contract. It is imputed to us. So too, as those joined to Adam in the covenant of works, his debt, guilt, and penalties were all credited or imputed to us upon his breach of the terms that God set for him.[35] The fall was not just Adam's bad choice but the end of innocence for all humanity, since Adam's sin was imputed to us.[36]

Because Adam broke the covenant of works and we all became sinners because of his sin (Rom 5:12–21), the offer of the covenant of works no longer stands as a viable option for any who are fallen in Adam.[37] The law still demands perfect fulfillment, promising the reward of the first covenant to the person who succeeds (Rom 2:6–16). The problem is that sin prevents us from being able to fulfill the law (Gal 3:10–11). Even if we were somehow to perform all the law's obligations, we still must bear the punishment for sin. No one who is already a sinner can attain perfect righteousness and bear the law's curse in such a way to obtain the

31. WSC 14; *COC*, 3:678.

32. WSC 19; *COC*, 3:679–80; Richard B. Gaffin Jr., *By Faith, Not by Sight: Paul and the Order of Salvation*, 2nd ed. (Phillipsburg, NJ: P&R, 2013), 34–40.

33. WSC 16; *COC*, 3:679.

34. *MT*, 1.17.3; *VRD*, 2:64–69; *TI*, 9.9.1–45; *CW*, 159–82.

35. Letham, *Systematic Theology*, 374–96. Although Letham's discussion is helpful overall, primary source evidence shows that he at least overstated his criticisms of Charles Hodge; see *TI*, 9.9.9–21; and *CW*, 159–82.

36. *DIALIC*; John Murray, *Imputation of Adam's Sin* (Phillipsburg, NJ: P&R, 2012).

37. Hodge, *Systematic Theology*, 2:122.

covenant of works' reward by their own deeds. Adam's first sin means that no one can fulfill the covenant of works or perform perfect, personal, and perpetual obedience to the law.[38] The consequence of sin is everlasting death rather than everlasting life.[39] Because of our status as sinners, we are cursed and owed a penalty of enduring God's wrath.[40] We, therefore, must look for a way to obtain everlasting life other than through the covenant of works.

APPLICATIONS FOR CONTEMPORARY RELEVANCE

The covenant of works is a helpful doctrine in the Christian life in several ways. First and most generally, it provides a principle to explain the difference between the two covenantal principles: works and grace, law and gospel. The covenant of works, especially its legal character, demonstrates one side of that distinction, namely, the law requires perfect obedience to obtain a reward *by works*. That means that a law covenant contrasts in principle with grace. In Herman Bavinck's words, "Grace and works stand at opposite poles from each other and are mutually exclusive."[41] Or as Robert Rollock puts it, "For these two—law and faith—thus far fight, so that if a person would be righteous by faith, now he would not be by the law. And from the contrary, if by the law, now it is not by faith. Just as the Apostle discussed in Romans 11:6 regarding grace and works."[42] The covenant of works, then, fundamentally establishes the principles by which we try to relate to God.

In light of the Reformed exegesis of Galatians 3 and the subsequent elaboration of the covenant of works, the suggestion that the law *simply* regulates life under grace is gravely mistaken.[43] On the contrary, although law and grace are not *absolutely* opposed in that a person now under the promise of grace must endeavor after new obedience, they are opposed as *principles* by which we related to God. As the covenant of works stipulates,

38. *EC*, 1.9.19–23.

39. *MMB*, 53–58.

40. *EC*, 1.5.1–42.

41. *BRD*, 254.

42. Rollock, *Galatas*, 54.

43. Letham, *Systematic Theology*, 359–65.

the law played a fundamental part in how God intended us to relate with him—in Bavinck's words, "without the assistance of supernatural grace."[44] The case is not, therefore, that in every instance God made a grace covenant with us to which he added the law. As Paul explains in Galatians 3:15, a covenant means that "no one annuls it *or adds to it* once it has been ratified." Throughout Galatians 3:15–4:31, Paul's point is that the two covenants under discussion were explicitly *different* (3:12; 4:24), not that the law supplemented grace by adding Moses to Abraham.[45] As chapter 13 argues, that interpretation potentially supports *both* antinomianism and legalism.

That God intended us to relate to him by the law reminds us of the distinction between the law as a covenant and as a rule. In this respect, the contrast between law and grace does not undermine the law's importance. On the contrary, since the law describes God's character and since we are made in God's image, the law has stratospheric importance. As a covenant, the law must be perfectly fulfilled, which was possible only for Adam before his fall into sin while he was still upright in nature, having the strength to perform the law's requirements. As Witsius argues, "Eternal life, promised by the covenant, can be obtained upon no other condition, than that of perfect, and in every respect complete obedience."[46] In order to uphold the law's importance, we do not need to restructure the Reformed view to integrate grace and law together. Rather, we need to recognize that the gospel makes sense only in light of the law that sinners have broken.[47]

So, the law does not supplement grace. Instead, as Paul explains in Romans 3:31, faith establishes the law.[48] Witsius, unpacking this verse, explains that the covenant of grace is "the confirmation of the covenant of works, in so far as the mediator has fulfilled all the conditions of that covenant, so that all believers may be justified and saved, according to the covenant of works, to which satisfaction was made by the mediator."

44. *BRD*, 2:567.

45. *LG*, 66–70; *CW*, 5–6; cf. Letham, *Systematic Theology*, 361–62.

46. *EC*, 1.9.2.

47. *BOC*, 26–38.

48. *CW*, 186–87; Buchanan, *Justification*, 265; Hodge, *Romans*, 101–3; Horton, *Justification*, 2:242; Michael Allen, *Sanctification* (Grand Rapids: Zondervan, 2017), 277–78.

When Romans 8:4 says "that the righteousness of the law might be fulfilled in us," Witsius also took this to mean "that what the law accounts for righteousness is fully bestowed on us; and consequently, that what merits the reward of the law, becomes perfectly ours."[49] So, someone must fulfill the law for us if we are to obtain everlasting reward.

The law does not add to grace, but the gospel upholds the law, and does so in the sense that Christ has fulfilled the law's requirements on our behalf so that we can be reconciled to God.[50] The law was the first means by which God related to us, so the law must be upheld and established. As William Perkins explains in explicit reference to the distinction between the law and the gospel,

> First, the law is natural, and was in man's nature before the fall, but the gospel is spiritual, revealed after the fall, in the covenant of grace.... Thirdly, the law requires a perfect righteousness within us, but the gospel reveals our acceptance with God, by imputed righteousness.... Lastly, the law promises life to the worker and doer of it: "Do this, and thou shalt live" [Rom. 10:5; Lev. 18:5]. But the gospel offers salvation to him that "worketh not, but believeth in him that justifieth the ungodly" [Rom. 4:5], not considering faith, as a work, but as an instrument apprehending Christ, by whom we are made righteous.[51]

Perkins clearly saw the law as preceding grace in humanity's original relationship with God, and that Christ *by grace* fulfilled the law for us, since the law was the first principle by which we were made to reach everlasting life in the new creation.

The covenant of works is, then, not some disposable doctrine but has paramount importance. John Colquhoun argues that it is "a fundamental doctrine of Divine revelation" for understanding our relationship with God and "without admitting the reality of such a covenant, we cannot

49. *EC*, 1.9.23. Although not naming him in the text, Witsius was interacting with Johannes Cocceius's view about the abrogation of the covenant of works; see Willem J. van Asselt, "The Doctrine of the Abrogations in the Federal Theology of Johannes Cocceius (1603–1669)," *CTJ* 29 no. 1 (1994): 101–16.

50. *LG*, 191–213; *CC*, 19:2.151–52; *BOC*, 30–31.

51. *WWP*, 1:244 (commentary on Matthew 5:17).

consistently with our doing so, believe any article of that glorious gospel, which is an exhibition of the covenant of grace, to sinners of mankind."[52] Wilhelmus à Brakel (1635–1711) contends that,

> Acquaintance with this covenant is of the greatest importance, for whoever errs here or denies the existence of the covenant of works will not understand the covenant of grace, and will readily err concerning the mediatorship of the Lord Jesus. Such a person will very readily deny that Christ by His active obedience has merited a right to eternal life for the elect. This is to be observed with several parties who, because they err concerning the covenant of grace, also deny the covenant of works. Conversely, whoever denies the covenant of works, must rightly be suspected to be in error concerning the covenant of grace as well.[53]

As Brakel clearly understood, the covenant of works' critical role in Reformed theology underscores the distinction between the law and the gospel and forms the basis for how we understand not only our works but also, more importantly, Christ's work in saving us. The law *as a covenant*, namely, the covenant of works, clarifies the principles by which we have a relationship with God and explains Christ's saving work for us.

On the other side of that covenant-rule distinction, the covenant of works also helps us understand why Christians still love the Decalogue, even though those commands were first written during Moses's time.[54] The law that was given to humanity by nature as a covenant remains a rule to guide the Christian life. The moral law summarizes God's will for humanity since creation.[55] God's moral law is not an arbitrary list of rules but a summary reflection of God's own character. We, as God's image, necessarily have this summary reflection hardwired into our human existence, perhaps most commonly known as our conscience. The covenant of works reminds us that God did not invent the Ten Commandments at Mount Sinai but embedded those commands, which describe his own

52. *CW*, iii–v, 23.

53. *CRS*, 1:355; cf. Letham, *Systematic Theology*, 353–54.

54. *EC*, 1.9.23; 2.5.6, 13.

55. Walton and Walton, *Lost World of the Torah*, 25–53.

character that we are meant to reflect as those made in his image, into our very nature. The Decalogue is part of the fabric of creation, showing what it means to live out our identity as God's image. The Ten Commandments are, then, not archaic legislation but a fundamental description of what it means to be human. The covenant of works provides strident explanatory power to the law's abiding role as a rule for directing the godly life. The law has always been our guide to how best to express our love for God.

In addition to that general framework, the covenant of works also has more specific relevance for the Christian life. First, the covenant of works explains why we deal with sin. The whole world is filled with sinners, and no one is exempt. This reality relates to the outcome of the covenant of works, in that Adam failed the covenant of works by eating from the forbidden tree and sinning against God. Adam's failure, however, was not relevant simply for himself, but actually plunged the whole world into its present fallen condition. As Paul writes in Romans 5:12, "Therefore, just as sin came into the world through one man, and death through sin, and so death spread to all men because all sinned." The covenant of works reminds us that Adam was not a figure out there on his own but that he was all humanity's covenantal representative. Sin entered the world through him, not simply as he sinned first and then became a bad example that everyone followed, but death spread to all men in his first sin because all men were counted as sinners in Adam's action.

The Olympics illustrate this point. I am an American, so I want the American Olympians to win gold medals. In something like the one-hundred-meter dash, one person represents every American on that track. Although one man runs that race, what will *I* say if *he* wins a gold medal? *We* won! I include myself in his victory because he represents me in that task. On the other hand, if he trips, falls, and finishes dead last, then his loss, too, includes me and I am credited with his defeat. That I enjoy loss much less than victory does not change the representative principle. In reality, that same principle holds true for Olympians who ran the one-hundred-meter dash even long before I was born. Their victory or loss is still credited to me even though I did not yet exist because they represented the group of people to which I belong. That was like Adam's role. He was meant to be our champion who would win on behalf of everyone but failed, and his one violation of the law, his first sin, was credited to everyone he represented—namely, everyone. That is what Paul meant that death came to us all when sin entered through Adam "because all sinned."[56] Adam's sin made us all sinners because he was our representative.

Second, the covenant of works shows how God always accomplishes his purposes for his people. The reward in the covenant of works was life in the new creation, and now believers anticipate receiving that same life at Christ's return. As Witsius puts it, "To Adam, in the covenant of works, was promised the *same eternal life*, to be obtained by the righteousness which is of the law, of which believers are made partakers through Christ."[57] He argues the same point elsewhere, indicating how the same reward was offered on two different covenantal principles: "Here we are to observe a remarkable difference between the promises of the covenant of works, and those of the covenant of grace. The same eternal life is promised in both, which can be but one, consisting in the communion and enjoyment of God; but it is promised in a manner quite different in the one, from what is in the other."[58] Bavinck likewise explains that "because Adam's destiny lay in eternal blessedness, Christ could acquire it for us in his place." Still, "grace does not give us any more than what, if Adam had not fallen, would have been acquired by him in the way of obedience." Marking again the two principles of relating to God, he notes, "The covenant of grace differs from the covenant of works in method, not in its ultimate goal. It is the same treasure that was promised in the covenant of works and is granted in the covenant of grace."[59] God offered Adam incorruptible life, namely, the glorified bodies that believers receive at the resurrection, and Adam could have covered the entire world in complete paradise, which Christ will do at his return, as seen in how the tree of life returns and expands so that its leaves are healing all the nations. The covenant of works provides context to understand how the new creation is not God's plan B, dreamed up after the fall, but was always his purpose for us.[60]

56. *ACW*, 281–300; *CW*, 8–12; Letham, *Systematic Theology*, 387–96; Murray, *Imputation of Adam's Sin*.

57. *EC*, 1.4.7.

58. *EC*, 3.1.7.

59. *BRD*, 3:577.

60. Belcher, *Fulfillment*, 41; *KP*, 145–48; *CW*, 75–76.

Third, the covenant of works helps us understand why legalism (the notion that we can earn God's favor by keeping the law) and antinomianism (the notion that Christians have no responsibility to keep the moral law since we are under grace) are both deeply rooted but problematic temptations. Legalism is a default to our natural programming. The covenant of works explains why we are hardwired to assume that our works should earn God's reward: because that was how God dealt with us in our original state.[61] The problem is that sinners are no longer good or upright. Legalism is a failure to remember that the option to earn God's blessing by our obedience is no longer open to those who have broken the law at all. Legalists remember that the law was first given to us as a covenant but forget how that covenant was broken.

On the other hand, antinomianism is full rebellion against our natural programming, the belief that even Christians have no reason to obey God's moral law since we cannot earn reward by our works. Antinomianism disregards that those made in God's image should still strive to be like the God whom they image even if we cannot earn reward by that obedience. For those who are justified, the law from the covenant of works is no longer the condition for their relationship with God but is the guide to living for God, which is necessary fruit in the Christian life as a consequence of our salvation. Antinomians remember that the covenant of works was broken but forget that the same law remains as a rule for our lives.

The difference between legalism and antinomianism can be hard to split because of these issues tied to the covenant of works. Rollock helpfully navigates the subject, arguing that "good works be required of them which be in Christ, and justified by him, but such works belong to grace and regeneration," meaning that for believers "the covenant of works to them is abolished, and none effect so far forth as by it justification and salvation is obtained." Still, "the law abides which is the rule of those works, which properly and specially did first appertain to the covenant of works" since "it serves for our direction in the works of grace and sanctification."[62] Legalists ignore how sin has too severely damaged our abilities to keep

61. *CW*, 25.

62. Rollock, *Treatise*, 10.

the law as a covenant of works, but antinomians neglect the important point that our role as God's image bearers permanently ties us to the law as a rule for living in godliness. In both respects, the covenant of works clarifies the underlying problems with legalism and antinomianism and gives us some reasons why we must quickly and firmly reject both errors.

Finally, despite the terrible outcome of Adam's work as our representative, the covenant of works is actually very good news because it establishes the principle that God deals with his people through a representative. The comfort of Christ as our representative before God, since he was our victorious champion, is far more encouraging than humanity's universal condemnation before God because of Adam's transgression. Christ's representation seems like obviously great news to people who understand the gospel, but Adam's representation can seem unfair. Despite how Adam failed, however, his representative role was a good thing because it established the principle that God deals with us through a representative. We can have a champion who runs in our place because the covenant of works set the representative principle in place for God's relationship with humanity. Christians can legitimately have Christ as our representative before God now without bringing God's justice or fairness into question precisely because God has always dealt with humanity through a representative. In this way, the covenant of works helps us understand Christ's work on our behalf, which will be the topic addressed throughout part two.

CONCLUSION

In John 14:15, Jesus says, "If you love me, you will keep my commandments." Despite the modern distaste for legality, structure, and rules, law and love are unbreakably linked. Far from being antithetical, the law describes the purest expressions of love. So Francis Roberts writes, "The covenant of works is deservedly styled *foedus amicitiae*, a covenant of amity or friendship, because God and man, at the making thereof were upon terms of perfect friendship, with each other."[63] The covenant of works as the legal arrangement between God and Adam that required perfect obedience was, therefore, the original opportunity for Adam to express his fullest love for God when he was fully able to do so according

63. *MMB*, 70.

to the strength that God had given to him by nature. Without sin's hindrance, Adam had complete capability to love God to the fullest by abiding by the standards that, as God's image bearer, he knew simply reflected God's character back to his Maker. If imitation is flattery's sincerest form, Adam's fulfillment of the law of the covenant of works would have been a sincere means of loving his God by honoring him as the God worth reflecting into the world.[64] In this way, the covenant of works was a deeply meaningful relationship, built on communion between God and Adam, and offering even greater communion with God by covenant.

This chapter already tries to name several pastoral uses and implications for the doctrine of the covenant of works. So, here we might just remind ourselves of the pastoral implications of the creation Sabbath and the tree of life. In the covenant of works, God made his blessings known to Adam through features of his everyday life. God still acts this way today. He reminds us of his blessings through a book, through baptismal water, through bread and wine. He reminds us of his blessings through the fellowship we have with fellow church members as we bear one another's burdens in the Christian life. We need not seek some abstract, other-worldly encounter with God to have true spirituality. God meets us in the everyday affairs of our lives and walks with us in communion as his creatures made for a relationship with him.

64. *KP*, 62–66.

Part Two

THE COVENANT OF REDEMPTION

V

The Trinity and Their Covenant

I am the LORD; I have called you in righteousness;
I will take you by the hand and keep you; I will give you as a covenant
for the people, a light for the nations, to open the eyes that are blind,
to bring out the prisoners from the dungeon, from the prison
those who sit in darkness.
—Isaiah 42:6–7

God made us for an endless loving relationship with him, but Adam's violation of the covenant of works shattered our original communion with him and sent the entire race into exile away from his presence. So, the Westminster Standards explain that the fall resulted in "the loss of Communion with God, his displeasure and curse" (WLC 27).[1] Since perfect obedience was the premise of that first covenant with God, our sin making us now unable to fulfill those terms, we are alienated from God in condemnation. Our sinful inability further prevents us from ever restoring or fulfilling that initial communion by covenant. Since sinners cannot earn back God's favor, we need a new champion, a better Adam, going before us to recover and renew our covenantal relationship with God, so that we might obtain that everlasting communion with God in supernatural life. We

1. *LC*, 71.

need a way to relate to God by a grace covenant rather than a law covenant. The covenant of redemption is the foundation for that way.

The covenant of redemption is the Triune God's plan to restore his people's communion with him, the Father, Son, and Spirit each contributing their own distinct mission. More specifically, in the Triune God's decreed plan for salvation, the relations among the Father arranging salvation, the Son accomplishing salvation, and the Spirit applying salvation are covenantal. As God predestined his people's salvation before the world's foundations (Eph 1:3–5), he decreed the covenant of redemption before Adam existed in the covenant of works. Despite that priority, the covenant of redemption addresses our need as sinners requiring rescue under the broken covenant of works' curse.[2] The covenant of redemption is the "other side of the doctrine of the covenant of works," explaining Christ's work as our mediator saving us from Adam's wreckage.[3] Geerhardus Vos argues, "In back of the covenant of grace lies the covenant of works, which may not just be pushed aside but must be removed judicially—that is, the debt incurred through the breaking of the covenant of works must be discharged. At the same time, however, this covenant of works, which was violated by Adam, must be carried out. The benefits of the covenant of works must be obtained."[4]

The covenant of redemption, being a covenant of works for Christ but a covenant of grace for us, explains how Christ fulfilled the covenant of works for believers rescued in the covenant of grace.[5] Even though God decreed the covenant of redemption before history began and before Adam fell, one sensible approach is to explain it after explaining the covenant of works.[6]

The covenant of redemption broaches the depth of Trinitarian theology, displaying the riches of love that the Father, Son, and Spirit have for each other and for us. Because this doctrine concerns the Trinity, the

---

2. Patrick Gillespie, *The Ark of the Covenant Opened: or A Treatise on the Covenant of Redemption* (London: Thomas Parkhurst, 1677), 33–35.

3. Geerhardus Vos, "The Doctrine of the Covenant in Reformed Theology," in *RHBI*, 245.

4. *VRD*, 3:2.

5. Clark, "Do This and Live," 243–44.

6. Not all Reformed writers follow this approach, and no criticism is meant by taking another order. There is wisdom in various pedagogical outlines.

Trinity must set bounds for formulating the covenant of redemption. This chapter, therefore, first discusses Trinitarian premises that must frame the plan of salvation, then argues biblically for a covenantal relation among Father, Son, and Spirit for that plan.

THE TRIUNE GOD, THE INCARNATE CHRIST, AND THE PLAN OF SALVATION

The one God exists as Father, Son, and Holy Spirit sharing one divine essence, unified in having every attribute that God necessarily possesses.[7] Each person is equally all-powerful, all-knowing, all-glorious, and present everywhere—to name just a few things God is, the point being that each person is equally God.[8]

The Westminster Larger Catechism explains who God is. Concerning the one God's attributes, he "is a Spirit" having infinite "being, glory, blessedness, and perfection," being "allsufficient, eternal, unchangeable, incomprehensible, every where present, almighty, knowing all things, most wise, most holy, most just, most merciful and gracious, long-suffering, and abundant in goodness and truth." Further, the true God is triune so that Father, Son, and Spirit are "the same in substance, equal in power and glory; although distinguished by their Personal Properties." These personal properties are the distinct characteristics for each divine person since they are otherwise equal and the same by essence. So, "It is proper to the Father to beget the Son, and to the Son to be begotten of the Father, and to the Holy Ghost to proceed from the Father and the Son from all eternity." Scripture teaches that the Son and Spirit are equal with the Father by ascribing "unto them such Names, attributes, works, and worship, as are proper to God only" (WLC 7–11).[9] The three persons' shared unity is one of "substance" and equality of attributes like power and glory, but each person has something special about them—namely,

---

7. Speaking of God as "possessing attributes" does not intend to deny the doctrine of divine simplicity, which teaches that God is not composed of parts. God's attributes are not individual "things" that taken together make up God. The point is merely to affirm that everything that must be said of God as God must be said of each of the persons of the Trinity; James E. Dolezal, *All That Is in God: Evangelical Theology and the Challenge of Classical Christian Theism* (Grand Rapids: Reformation Heritage Books, 2017), 37–58, 105–34; Butner, *Trinitarian Dogmatics*, 75–99.

8. Butner, *Trinitarian Dogmatics*, 15–44.

9. *LC*, 67–68.

their personal procession or relation of origin, distinguishing Father as Father, Son as Son, and Spirit as Spirit.[10]

Two particular aspects of this Trinitarian theology must shape a precise formulation of the covenant of redemption. The first Trinitarian premise is that the Triune God has one will common to the three persons.[11] Every *human* person has the individual capability to want things—to will—independently. If our will is understood as the center of our desires, then every human person has a separate "wanter." We may agree with one another about what is right or about what we want, but each still has our own "wanter," our own faculty of willing. The common will among Father, Son, and Spirit is not merely limited to agreeing with one another. Rather, the three divine persons all have the exact same "wanter," the exact same will.[12]

Christians have emphasized this point since the ancient period. Justin Martyr (AD 100–165) wrote concerning instances when the Son appeared on earth prior to his incarnation that he "is called God by the Scripture, being distinct from the one who created all things, namely I mean distinct by number *not by will*."[13] Tertullian explains God's unity by arguing that God's "monarchy means nothing other than the singular and unified authority." The divine monarchy is not divided when the Son—and Sprit—share it with the Father because it "is that which is commonly possessed by two who are all the same of one substance."[14] John of Damascus (c. 675–749) connected the singular divine will to the one divine nature: "since there is but one divine nature, there is, likewise, only one natural will. Moreover, since, again, the Persons are not at variance, there is one

10. St. Thomas Aquinas, *Summa Theologica*, trans. Fathers of the English Dominican Province, 5 vol. (1948; repr. Notre Dame: Christian Classics, 1981), 1.27.1–5, 1.28.1–4, 1.29.1–4; Thomas, *Compendium*, §37–67; Butner, *Trinitarian Dogmatics*, 47–72, 101–28.

11. J. N. D. Kelly, *Early Christian Doctrines*, 4th ed. (London: Adam and Charles Black, 1968), 272–74; Matthew Barrett, *Simply Trinity: The Unmanipulated Father, Son, and Spirit* (Grand Rapids: Baker, 2021), 54–57; *TI*, 3.22.3; 4.1.7.

12. Stephen J. Wellum, *God the Son Incarnate: The Doctrine of Christ* (Wheaton, IL: Crossway, 2016), 395–419; Wellum, *Person of Christ*, 127–44; Matthew Barrett, *None Greater: The Undomesticated Attributes of God* (Grand Rapids: Baker, 2019), 86–87; Barrett, *Simply Trinity*, 227–30, 291–93.

13. Justin Martyr, *Dialogue with Trypho*, §56, in *PG*, 6:599; *ANF*, 1:223 (emphasis added).

14. Tertullian, *Adversus Praxeam*, §3 in *PL*, 2:158; *ANF*, 3:599; also Butner, *Trinitarian Dogmatics*, 83, 177–83.

thing willed and one movement of the three Persons."[15] In the medieval period, Richard of St. Victor (d. 1173) writes that if the Trinity shares one true and most intimate love, "how much more *the sameness of will* in them must belong to the persons with whom it is the same being who wills and who accordingly acts, just as one being, therefore also *one will*? Thus, in the whole Trinity, there is *one single will*, one single love, one single and undifferentiated goodness."[16] Likewise, John Owen affirms that the "Father, Son, and Spirit have not distinct wills" since they "are one God, and God's will is one, as being an essential property of his nature."[17] The divine persons are not three separate centers of consciousness with ability to want, desire, and will independently from one another.[18] Rather, they all share the same, singular, unified divine will so God's will "is single and totally one in him."[19] Even the Second Council of Constantinople (553) requires that Christians believe that "the Father and the Son and the Holy Spirit are one nature or essence, one power or authority."[20] Even in its mystery, Christians necessarily confess this truth.[21]

---

15. John of Damascus, *The Orthodox Faith*, 2.22, in *The Fathers of the Church: Saint John of Damascus: Writings*, trans. Frederic H. Chase Jr. (Washington DC: The Catholic University of America Press, 1958), 251.

16. Richard of St. Victor, *De Trinitate*, 5.23, in *PL*, 196:965 (emphasis added).

17. John Owen, "Exercitation XXVIII," in *Hebrews*, 1:468.

18. Letham, *Systematic Theology*, 97–147; *CF*, 296–306; Stephen R. Holmes, "Three Versus One? Some Problems of Social Trinitarianism," *JRT* 3 (2009): 77–89; Kevin Giles, *The Eternal Generation of the Son: Maintaining Orthodoxy in Trinitarian Theology* (Downers Grove, IL: IVP Academic, 2012), 91–204; Fred Sanders, "The Trinity," in *The Oxford Handbook of Systematic Theology*, eds. John Webster, Kathryn Tanner, and Iain Torrance (New York: Oxford University Press, 2007), 37–48; Karen Kilby, "Perichoresis and Projection: Problems with Social Doctrines of the Trinity," *New Blackfriars* 81 no 956 (Oct 2000): 432–45. This classical position runs contrary to, e.g., J. Scott Horrell, "The Eternal Son of God in the Social Trinity," in *Jesus in Trinitarian Perspective: An Introductory Christology*, eds. Fred Sanders and Klaus Issler (Nashville: B&H, 2007), 44–79; Gijsbert van den Brink, "Social Trinitarianism: A Discussion of Some Recent Theological Criticisms," *IJST* 16 no 3 (July 2014): 331–50; Jürgen Moltmann, *The Trinity and the Kingdom: The Doctrine of God*, trans. Margaret Kohl (Minneapolis: Fortress Press, 1981), 47; Jürgen Moltmann, "The 'Crucified God:' A Trinitarian Theology of the Cross," trans. Keith R. Crim, *Interpretation* 26 no 3 (1972): 280–86; Jürgen Moltmann, *The Crucified God: The Cross of Christ as the Foundation and Criticism of Christian Theology* (New York: Harper & Row Publishers, 1974), 222–28; and Bruce A. Ware, "Alleging Heresy Where There Is None," in *Journal for Biblical Manhood and Womanhood* 16 no. 2 (Fall 2011): 42–46.

19. *MT*, 1.4.58; also *VRD*, 1:21.

20. "Anathema I" in *Creeds of the Churches: A Reader in Christian Doctrine from the Bible to the Present*, ed. John H. Leith (Garden City, NY: Anchor Books, 1963), 46; also Wellum, *Person of Christ*, 56–57. 148–49; again, contra Bruce A. Ware, *Father, Son, and Holy Spirit: Relationships, Roles, and Relevance* (Wheaton, IL: Crossway, 2005), 46–51.

21. Thomas, *Summa Theologica*, 1.32.1.

The second Trinitarian premise necessary to formulate the covenant of redemption precisely is the doctrine of *inseparable operations*. God as Father, Son, and Spirit act together in every work outside themselves, since, as Gregory of Nyssa (c. 335–c. 395) argues, "any difference of operation, so that the Father worked in one way but the Son in another," would entail also that "diverse effects were produced by more than one being."[22] This doctrine rests upon the distinction between God's internal (*ad intra*) and external (*ad extra*) works. As seen in the Wesminster Larger Confession, God in his essence is three persons. The persons are relations within the Godhead, distinct in their mode of subsistence according to certain personal properties, which are the eternal *processions* occurring within the divine essence. God's internal (*ad intra*) operations, also called "immanent activities," are these processions.[23] More specifically, the Father eternally generates the Son (active generation), the Son is eternally begotten from the Father (passive generation), the Father and Son both eternally spirate the Spirit (active spiration), and the Spirit eternally proceeds from the Father and Son (passive spiration).[24] These relations, which are the personal properties of each person in the Godhead, are God's *ad intra* operations.[25]

Whereas God's *ad intra* operations concern the eternal relations within the divine essence that distinguish each person, God's external (*ad extra*) operations concern God's works that terminate outside the divine essence, namely, those works toward creation or his "transitive activities."[26] As an example, again, eternal generation is an *ad intra* operation that occurs within (hence internal) the Godhead, but providence is an *ad extra* work directed from God toward (hence external) creatures. The only *ad intra* works are those processions of relation among the persons. On the other

---

22. Gregory of Nyssa, *Against Eunomius*, 1[.27], in *PG*, 45:373–74; *NPNF2*, 5:72.

23. Andreas J. Beck, "God, Creation, and Providence in Post-Reformation Reformed Theology," in *The Oxford Handbook of Early Modern Theology, 1600–1800*, eds. Ulrich L. Lehner, Richard A. Muller, and A. G. Roeber (New York: Oxford University Press, 2016), 196–97, 202–4, 207–8; Willem J. van Asselt, "Christ, Predestination, and Covenant in Post-Reformation Reformed Theology," in *Oxford Handbook of Early Modern Theology*, 218–19.

24. Barrett, *Simply Trinity*, 155–211, 261–85.

25. Technically speaking, the Father's personal property is unbegottenness, meaning that he has no eternal relation *of origin*. Thanks to my friend Steve Wellum for his advice, clarifying the language in this paragraph and to Matthew Barrett for his, in regard to this point about the Father.

26. Barrett, *Simply Trinity*, 175–76.

hand, all God's works toward creation are *ad extra*. So then, we have the distinction of God's *ad intra* (internal/essential) and *ad extra* (external/economic) operations.[27]

To illustrate: Our bodies contain our organs, necessarily functioning to keep us alive. My heartbeat is an internal operation performed involuntarily, which is necessary for my existence. On the other hand, I also perform works toward other people, such as hugging my wife. Those external operations are not necessary to my being as they happen outside me, are directed elsewhere. Although every illustration has qualified application to God, the point simply clarifies the difference between God's operations *ad intra,* which are necessary to who he is, and *ad extra,* which are directed toward creatures. God by nature, involuntarily, must be Father, Son, and Spirit, each procession operating essentially *ad intra* but also performing voluntary operations toward creation *ad extra.*

With the *ad intra* and *ad extra* distinction established, the doctrine of inseparable operations affirms that the Triune God together executes all *ad extra* works. This affirmation relates to how there is only one will common among the Father, Son, and Spirit. Those *ad intra* works are not voluntary works, but essential works, meaning that God is necessarily triune and so the processions of Father, Son, and Spirit must occur within the divine essence. In contrast, all God's *ad extra* works are voluntary. God did not have to create, nor act in any certain way toward creation. The Father, Son, and Spirit have *one* will in common, so decree and, identically by essence, execute all God's *ad extra* works.[28]

To specify inseparable operations further, the point is that no one divine person can act without the others. The Father cannot perform any *ad extra* work without the Son and Spirit coworking in that operation.[29] So, even as the Apostles' Creed credits the Father as the "Maker of heaven and earth," we also confess with Colossians 1:16 that Christ is the divine Son by whom "all things were created, in heaven and on earth, visible

---

27. Fred Sanders, *The Triune God* (Grand Rapids: Zondervan, 2016), 130–33; Butner, *Trinitarian Dogmatics*, 183–89.

28. Adonis Vidu, *The Same God Who Works All Things: Inseparable Operations in Trinitarian Theology* (Grand Rapids: Eerdmans, 2021), 91–125; Barrett, *Simply Trinity*, 290–93. Thanks to Ryan Hurd for his help in clarifying my expressions about inseparable operations.

29. Cornelis van der Kooi, "Creation and Providence," in *OHRT*, 421–22.

and invisible," so that "all things were created through him and for him."[30] So, the Son—and the Spirit too (Gen 1:1–2; Ps 104:30; Job 26:13)—acted jointly with the Father in the work of creation because all of God's *ad extra* works must execute according to the one divine will.[31] God's works, such as creation or grace, as Athanasius explains, are not "given differently and separately by each Person ... but all are from the one God."[32] Basil the Great (330–379) elaborates that God's unity of action—in his argument pertaining to the Son—is "because if the Word possesses essence identically [to the Father], then he also possesses power identically. Again, since being equal in power, they are also equal in all way in operation."[33] Accounting for how Scripture (and the later creeds) appropriates the work of creation to the Father, Irenaeus illustrates that the Father created by his "two hands," namely, the Son and Spirit.[34] So, the Westminster Confession affirms, "It pleased God the Father, Son, and Holy Ghost ... to create or make of nothing the world, and all things therein" (WCF 4.1).[35] Thus, because God is one in essence, having one knowledge and one will among the persons, one divine person *cannot* will or perform one work external to the divine essence while one or both of the other persons performs a different work.[36]

These two Trinitarian premises require our formulation of the covenant of redemption to explain carefully how the three persons can *covenant* together as they share one will, and how each person can perform distinct missions in the plan of salvation if the three persons cannot work independently of one another. The covenant of redemption cannot suggest

---

30. *COC*, 2:45.

31. John Webster, "Trinity and Creation," in *GWM1*, 83–98; Vidu, *Same God*, 23–31, 126–57; Barrett, *Simply Trinity*, 300–304.

32. Athanasius, "A Letter of Athanasius to Bishop Serapion concerning the Holy Spirit," in *The Letters of Saint Athanasius Concerning the Holy Spirit*, ed. C. R. B. Shapland (London: The Epworth Press, 1951), 142.

33. Basil the Great, *Book on the Holy Spirit*, 8.19 in *PG*, 32:103–4; *NPNF2*, 8:13–14.

34. Irenaeus, *Against Heresies*, 5.6.1, in *PG*, 7.2:1136–38; *ANF*, 1:531–32.

35. *COC*, 3:611.

36. *TI*, 3.23.5, 3.27.3; *DLGTT*, 245–46; Tyler R. Wittman, "On the Unity of the Trinity's External Works: Archaeology and Grammar," *IJST* 20 no. 3 (2018): 359–80; Vidu, *Same God*, 52–90; Barrett, *Simply Trinity*, 218–20; cf. Emil Brunner, *Dogmatics Volume 1: The Christian Doctrine of God*, trans. Olive Wyon (London: Lutterworth, 1949), 234; Ware, *Father, Son, and Holy Spirit*, 55–59.

more than one will in the Godhead nor violate the doctrine of inseparable operations.[37]

Regarding God's singular will, if a covenant usually involves some sort of agreement, how can persons who do not have separate minds or wills make an agreement?[38] Some Reformed theologians have tried to get around this problem by appealing to the distinct "manner of working" within the one divine will that accords with the Father, Son, and Spirit's interpersonal relations.[39] Owen expresses the principle that "where there is but one nature there is but one will: but in respect of their distinct personal actings, this will is appropriated to them respectively, so that the will of the Father and the will of the Son may be considered [distinctly] in this business." He affirms that the divine will is "essentially one and the same" but "the work distinctly carried on by them" accords to their distinct personalities.[40]

Some theologians apply this nuance on how each person relates to the one divine will to the covenant of redemption. Wilhelmus à Brakel affirms that "the Father and the Son are one in essence and thus have one will and one objective" but "the one divine will can be viewed from a twofold perspective." More specifically, "It is the Father's will to redeem by the agency of the second Person as Surety, and it is the will of the Son to redeem by His own agency as Surety."[41] The principle of distinct inflections on the divine will according to each person's personal properties, although having useful applications, does not fully solve our problem.[42]

37. Richard A. Muller, "The Spirit and the Covenant: John Gill's Critique of the *Pactum Salutis*," *Foundations* 24 no. 1 (1981), 4–14.

38. The Reformed have long known that this is an issue to explain; Owen, "Exercitation XXVIII," 1:460–76; *VRD*, 3:84. Letham claims that the covenant of redemption violates the principle of inseparable operations; *Systematic Theology*, 432–39.

39. *DLGTT*, 245; Owen, "Exercitation XXVIII," 1:468–69; Wittman, "Unity of the Trinity's External Works," 372–79.

40. John Owen, *Vindiciae Evangelicae*, in *Works*, 12:497; also *WWP*, 2:197 (commentary on Galatians 3:19); Scott R. Swain, "Covenant of Redemption," in *CD*, 121–22; Keith E. Johnson, *Rethinking the Trinity and Religious Pluralism: An Augustinian Assessment* (Downers Grove: InterVarsity Press, 2011), 101–19; and Barrett, *Simply Trinity*, 304–10. Owen's point can be pressed too far to suggest that although the persons act together in an act, it is not one inseparable act executed by the singular divine will; see Vidu, *Same God*, xiii–xix, 106–16.

41. *CRS*, 1:252.

42. Vidu, *Same God*, 62–63, 101–6, 146–57. Brakel's explanation is likely what Vidu termed a "soft" version of inseparable operations, whereas Vidu correctly argues that the "hard" version is the

Our formulation of the covenant of redemption cannot suggest that the Father, Son, and Spirit could contract together in the divine nature (*ad intra*) as separately willing agents in the way that humans do. If our application of the personal properties to the one divine will even hints that each person could will independently and compact as individuals, then the covenant of redemption is not well expressed.

This problem becomes more focused regarding the Son's obedience during his incarnation. Since obedience is at least in some way a submission of one person's will to another, we affirm that God's Son, as the divine Son, necessarily cannot obey God.[43] Herman Witsius highlights this exact point when explaining the covenant between the Father and Son: "The Son, as precisely God, neither was, nor could be subject to any law, to any superior; that being contrary to the nature of the Godhead, which we now suppose the Son to have in common with the Father."[44] God does not obey but is to be obeyed. So, the Reformed affirm in the Second Helvetic Confession:

> We likewise condemn all heresies and heretics teaching that the Son and the Holy Spirit are God in name only, and likewise that one is created *and serving* or *subordinate to another in the Trinity*, and even *that there is inequality in it, a greater or a lesser*, a body or something bodily portrayed, *a difference in character or will*, something out of order or separate, as if the Son and Holy Spirit are the affections and properties of the one God the Father like the Monarchians, Novatians, Praxeas, Patripassians, Sabellius, Paul of Samosata, Aetius, Macedonians, Anthropomorphites, Arius, and those like them have thought. (3.5)[45]

The Son as the Son does not have ability to submit to the Father in the divine essence, since Father, Son, and Spirit will everything together using the same will.

---

biblical and traditional formulation.

43. *WWP*, 2:114–15 (commentary on Galatians 2:15–16); D. Glenn Butner Jr., "Eternal Functional Subordination and the Problem of the Divine Will," *JETS* 58 no. 1 (2015): 131–49; Barrett, *Simply Trinity*, 213–59; cf. Ware, *Father, Son, and Holy Spirit*, 76–83.

44. *EC*, 2.3.6.

45. *COC*, 3:241 (emphasis added).

The resolutions to the problems about the Father, Son, and Spirit covenanting and about the Son's obedience are both grounded in God's decree concerning salvation for his elect. A proper application of the decree to the covenant of redemption not only preserves the divine will's unity but also harmonizes our formulation with the doctrine of inseparable operations. The Triune God decrees the plan of salvation and how that plan will be brought about in a thoroughly Trinitarian way.[46]

The one Triune God commonly decrees the plan of salvation that then includes differing contributions from the Father, Son, and Spirit in that plan—in that *economy* of redemption. God's decree is an essential work willed by the entire Trinity, being necessarily a Trinitarian decree precisely because the Godhead has only one will.[47] Francis Turretin writes, "As this work [the decree] is eternal, it is common and undivided to the whole Trinity with this distinction, however—that each person has his own proper and peculiar mode of operation here, agreeable to this saving economy (1 Pet. 1:2)."[48] The Father, Son, and Spirit together will and decree in unity that, in redemption's outworking, the Son acts as the one mediator between God and man (1 Tim 2:5–6), the Father gives the elect to the Son as the mediator (John 10:29), the Son procures salvation for the elect (John 17:4), and the Spirit ensures that the elect come to partake of that salvation by faith (Eph 1:13).[49] As Owen explains, God's will concerning each person and his specific role in the plan of salvation belongs to the Father, Son, or Spirit specifically "though not exclusively," since they share that will "by reason of their mutual inbeing." Each person decrees the plan of salvation but not independently of the others.[50] The Triune God, as such, decrees by a single will how each person of the Godhead

---

46. On this doctrine of *opera interna ad extra* in connection to the covenant of redemption, see Katherine Sonderegger, "The Doctrine of God," in *OHRT*, 396–402.

47. *DLGTT*, 245; Wittman, "Unity of the Trinity's External Works," 362–79; Guy M. Richard, "The Covenant of Redemption," in *CT*, 60–61.

48. *TI*, 12.2.7.

49. *DLGTT*, 246.

50. Owen, "Exercitation XXVIII," 1:468; Tyler R. Wittman, "The End of the Incarnation: John Owen, Trinitarian Agency and Christology," *IJST* 15 no. 3 (July 2013): 284–300; T. Robert Baylor, "'He Humbled Himself': Trinity, Covenant and the Gracious Condescension of the Son in John Owen," in *Trinity without Hierarchy: Reclaiming Nicene Orthodoxy in Evangelical Theology*, eds. Michael F. Bird and Scott Harrower (Grand Rapids: Kregel Academic, 2019), 165–93; Beck, "God, Creation, and Providence," 205.

has a mission that distinctly contributes to salvation within the plan of redemption.[51]

The covenant of redemption exists within and explains the relations that each Trinitarian person has to one another, *not within the divine essence*, but within that decreed plan. More precisely, the covenant of redemption concerns not the Trinity's *processions*, but *missions*.[52] The category of divine *missions* further clarifies how God still works truly triunely in the world, so that a particular aspect of God's work of salvation in history focuses upon one person without disrupting inseparable operations.[53]

In contrast to a divine person's procession, which eternally subsists in God's essence, his *mission* extends his procession to an effect in creation.[54] For example, the Son has the procession of eternal generation but has the temporal mission of coming in the incarnation. In respect to the mission, the Son is properly the subject of the incarnation, as *his* procession extends into creation via that work, since neither Father nor Spirit assumed a human nature. At the same time, the incarnation as a work of God must be a work of the entire Godhead.[55] In this regard, although the whole Godhead works in the incarnation, it *terminates* upon the person of the Son, and other works *terminate* upon Father or Spirit.[56] God's external works are then inseparable even when *appropriated* to a specific person in his mission.[57]

The procession-mission distinction protects God's immutability and inseparable operations while explaining how God truly works in history. The Son did not come into existence at his incarnation nor change as a divine person by assuming a new relation to creation. As Aquinas explains, a "mission is a temporal procession," suggesting that the sent

---

51. Petrus van Mastricht, *Theoretical-Practical Theology Volume 2: Faith in the Triune God*, trans. Todd M. Rester, ed. Joel R. Beeke (Grand Rapids: Reformation Heritage Books, 2019), 1.2.15.10; *TI*, 3.22.2–3, 6, 11; 4.1.7, 17; 4.2.6; Swain, "Covenant of Redemption," 107–8, 111; *RST*, 1:897.

52. Barrett, *Simply Trinity*, 344–46n92.

53. Thanks to my friend Adonis Vidu for his help clarifying this discussion of the divine missions.

54. Butner, *Trinitarian Dogmatics*, 153–72.

55. *TI*, 13.4.1–11; *VRD*, 3:188; Wellum, *Person of Christ*, 140–41.

56. Vidu, *Same God*, 158–216; Wellum, *Person of Christ*, 153–58.

57. Butner, *Trinitarian Dogmatics*, 189–97; Geerhardus Vos, "Doctrine of the Covenant," 246; *BRD*, 3:214–16; *TI*, 3.27.20, 13.4.2; *VRD*, 2:87; *WWG*, 251–52; *TCR*, 174–81; Laurence R. O'Donnell III, "Not Subtle Enough: An Assessment of Modern Scholarship on Herman Bavinck's Reformulation of the *Pactum Salutis* contra 'Scholastic Subtlety,' " *MAJT* 22 (2011): 89–106.

person "begins to exist where he was before, but in a new way, in which sense mission is ascribed to the divine persons."[58] Divine persons appear in history through their missions while remaining unchanged by it.

The relations in the covenant of redemption, then, concern not the processions belonging properly to God's being (since they do not explain how the persons relate *as the divine essence*), but God's missions, explaining how God acts in creation for salvation. Although the covenant of redemption regards relations among the persons, *these* relations are not properly about how they relate as God but how they work together in creation for the plan of salvation.[59] The covenant of redemption is, then, not part of God's *ad intra* works, which are only the eternal relational operations in the Godhead that distinguish each person's personal properties and in no way even involve God's creatures.[60] Rather, the covenant of redemption belongs to God's *ad extra* works, which are his acts directed to the creation, namely, in the decree.[61]

The covenant of redemption does not divide the Trinity because God works inseparably in establishing—decreeing in the one divine will—that plan of salvation. Bavinck explains specifically in reference to the Son: "Together with the Father He designates Himself as the Mediator of redemption and as the Head of His church."[62] Even though each person has a distinct mission in completing the plan of salvation, each person of the Triune God, commonly, hence equally, decreed by their singular

58. Aquinas, *Summa Theologica*, 1.43.3, 6.

59. Vos, "Doctrine of the Covenant," 245–46.

60. Barret, *Simply Trinity*, 343–46n92; Wellum, *Person of Christ*, 150–53.

61. Sanders, *Triune God*, 121–53. Alternatively stated, the covenant of redemption belongs to the economic rather than the immanent Trinity. That said, Sanders convincingly argues that the processions-missions distinction is clearer terminology than economic and immanent Trinity because it avoids suggesting that God's eternal relations do not to some degree shape the Trinitarian character of God's works in history; see also Barrett, *Simply Trinity*, 116–19; and Butner, *Trinitarian Dogmatics*, 164–68. Essential processions have created effects that explain how each person can contribute their own role in the covenant of redemption while still working together inseparably; see Vidu, *Same God*, 92–106. Each person's mission, as a created effect of his procession, is bound together with the other persons' missions to accomplish the singular divine will by the covenant of redemption. So, the covenant of redemption helps solidify the doctrine of inseparable operations in tandem with the doctrine of appropriations wherein each mission has a terminus in one person; see Barrett, *Simply Trinity*, 297–300; and Barrett, *None Greater*, 84–88.

62. *WWG*, 250; also *WWP*, 2:197–98 (commentary on Galatians 3:19); and Letham, *Systematic Theology*, 417–20.

will what those distinct missions would be.[63] So Bavinck further argues, "In the decrees, also in those of predestination, the one will of God occupied the foreground, and their Trinitarian character was still blurred. But here, in the pact of salvation, the work of redemption stands out in its full divine splendor. It is *the* divine work par excellence."[64] The covenant among Father, Son, and Spirit is, therefore, not so much properly within God's being as it is within God's plan for how the Triune God orchestrates our redemption.

How did the incarnate Son render obedience if he shares one will with Father and Spirit, working inseparably with them, so cannot rightly be said to be obedient as the Son of God?[65] God—whether Father, Son, or Spirit—does not obey but is to be obeyed, since God is one in essence, glory, majesty, power, and *rule*.[66] As the Athanasian Creed says, "The divinity of the Father, and of the Son, and of the Spirit is *one*, equal glory, coeternal majesty. ... And in this Trinity, none is before or after, *none greater or lesser*."[67] Or in Witsius's words, "The Son, as precisely God, neither was, nor could be subject to any law, to any superior; that being contrary to the nature of the God-head, which we now suppose the Son to have in common with the Father."[68] Within the covenant of redemption, however, the Son acts, not as the Son properly, according to his procession, but according to his mission as the mediator between God and the elect.[69]

The Reformed tradition and its antecedents clearly affirm this point. Owen argues concerning how Christ said the Father was greater than him, this subordination was only "in respect of that work of mediation which he had undertaken" since "the inequality in office does not destroy the

63. CG, 13–19.

64. *BRD*, 3:215 (italics original).

65. Tyler R. Wittman, "*Dominium naturale et oeconomicum*: Authority and the Trinity," in *Trinity without Hierarchy* (Grand Rapids: Kregel, 2019), 151–58.

66. Lewis Ayres, *Nicaea and Its Legacy: An Approach to Fourth-Century Trinitarian Theology* (Oxford: Oxford University Press, 2004), 279.

67. *COC*, 2:66, 68 (emphasis added). Thanks to Matthew Barrett for suggesting this reference.

68. *EC*, 2.3.6.

69. Fred Sanders, *Fountain of Salvation: Trinity and Soteriology* (Grand Rapids: Eerdmans, 2021), 18–27, 32–53; Adonis Vidu, *The Divine Missions: An Introduction* (Eugene, OR: Cascade Books, 2021), 15–21; *CF*, 398; *WWG*, 249.

equality in nature."[70] Turretin likewise explains how, just because Christ as our priest and intercessor is a servant, "it does not follow that the divine nature in Christ is inferior to the Father." Rather, "Christ was made less than the Father not in nature, but in economy."[71] For this reason, the Athanasian Creed confesses that Christ is "equal to the Father according to his divinity, lesser than the Father according to his humanity."[72] Anselm of Canterbury (c. 1033–1109) rightly asserts, "That particular man, Christ, owed this obedience to God his Father, and his humanity owed it to his divinity, and the Father was demanding this from him."[73] Thomas Aquinas argues that, in contrast to the Son's eternal procession, "*mission* implies inferiority in the one sent," showing that Christ's subjection to the Father accorded to his humanity rather his deity.[74] In this respect, Witsius also argues that Christ's mission to save the elect by his obedience "was nothing but the most glorious act of the divine will of the Son," but still "it implies therefore no manner of subjection."[75] Witsius continues, "And by undertaking to perform this obedience, in the human nature, in its proper times, the Son, *as God*, did no more subject himself to the Father, than the Father with respect to the Son, to the owing that reward of debt, which he promised him a right to claim."[76] In this respect, John Colquhoun explains about the Son's obedience, "While he still continues, and must forever continue, in his state of *Divine equality* with the Father, he willingly agreed to enter upon a state of *mediatorial inferiority* to him."[77] The Triune God appointed the Son to become the new representative of those whom the Father gave to him in the covenant of redemption. Still, the Son *as God* did not owe obedience to anyone, but the Son *in his saving office as our*

70. Owen, *Vindiciae Evangelicae*, in *Works*, 12:202. Owen cites a Latin maxim, which I have translated above: "inaequalitas officii non tollit aequalitatem naturae." Cf. Saint Augustine, *The Trinity: De Trinitate*, trans. Edmund Hill, 2nd ed. (Hyde Park, NY: New City Press, 2015), 1.6.

71. *TI*, 14.2.17.

72. *COC*, 2:69.

73. Anselm of Canterbury, *Why God Became Man*, in *The Major Works*, ed. Brian Davies and G. R. Evans (Oxford: Oxford University Press, 1998), 1.9.

74. Aquinas, *Summa Theologica*, 1.43.1; also *Summa Theologica* 3.20.1, 3.26.2.

75. *EC*, 2.3.7.

76. *EC*, 2.3.7 (emphasis added).

77. *CG*, 25 (italics original).

mediator undertook the obligation to fulfill the law on our behalf by virtue of the covenant of redemption.[78]

The book of Hebrews contains profound reflections along these lines. Hebrews 5:8 says, "*Despite* being the Son, he [Jesus] *learned obedience* through the things that he suffered."[79] The author was very clear that Jesus's obedience during his humiliation on earth was despite the fact that he is God's Son (Phil 2:5–8). Charles Hodge (1797–1878) summarizes, "Notwithstanding his being a son he still learned obedience by what he suffered. ... Christ cannot be said to learn what he already knew."[80] In other words, the Son first experienced obedience when he became incarnate, and thereby also had a human will with which he could obey and submit to God.[81] The Son's mediatorial obedience for us according to his mission cannot be read back into his procession because that conflation neglects the *ad intra-ad extra* distinction and how both Hebrews 5:8 and Philippians 2:5–8 insist that his obedience was learned *through his suffering*, which is not proper to the divine essence.[82] His obedience was then *for us* rather than tied to his divine Sonship per se.[83]

The tradition also has categories to explain how Old Testament passages can depict this covenant relation as a present reality before the Son came in human nature. The problem needing resolution here is twofold: (1) We need a cogent explanation for how Christ's work applies to Old Testament believers before his incarnation to support the covenant of grace's unity. (2) The category of missions, whereby the Father can address the Son for his obedience from the presumed premise of Christ's human

---

78. Richard A. Muller, *Post-Reformation Reformed Dogmatics: The Rise and Development of Reformed Orthodoxy, Ca. 1520 to Ca. 1725*, 2nd ed., 4 vol. (Grand Rapids: Baker Academic, 2003), 4:278–81; Baylor, "He Humbled Himself," 165–92.

79. My translation. The opening conjunction makes the participial phrase explicitly concessive in force: καίπερ ὢν υἱός. I have taken υἱος as referring to the definite identity of Christ as *the Son* rather than generically referring to "a son." Regardless, the contrast between Christ's sonly existence and his obedience is built into the grammar; see Ellingworth, *Hebrews*, 292–93; and Amy Peeler, "What Does 'Father' Mean? Trinity without Tiers in the Epistle to the Hebrews," in *Trinity without Hierarchy*, 77.

80. Charles Hodge, *Exegetical Lectures and Sermons on Hebrews*, ed. William VanDoodewaard (London: The Banner of Truth Trust, 2019), 40.

81. Barrett, *Simply Trinity*, 213–60; Vidu, *Same God*, 74–82.

82. Barrett, *Simply Trinity*, 344–46n92. Thanks to Matthew Barrett for his helpful comments on this point.

83. Clark, "Do This and Live," 261.

nature, particularly his human will, coheres with classical Trinitarianism. The resolution to both is that while the Son's mission (and the Spirit's) is temporal, his appointment as mediator for all the elect is eternal, belonging to God's eternal decree.[84] In the mystery that is God's being, his decree's eternality makes room for categories that allow the effects of the persons' temporal missions to transcend the bounds of their appearance in history.

The classic distinction between the Son *incarnandus* (who would become incarnate) and *incarnatus* (who has become incarnate) provides eternal and temporal perspectives on the Son's economic office as mediator in God's plan of salvation.[85] God's eternal decree for the covenant of redemption includes Christ's *sponsorship*, or his appointment as the elect's mediator so that he bears the penalty of their sin and procures righteousness for them.[86] In this respect, Peter Martyr Vermigli (1499–1562) argues, since the Son serves as mediator for all the elect according to both his divine and human nature, that "before the incarnation, moreover, God's same Son illumined men, taught them, and dwelled together with them but nevertheless at the proper time was going to suffer and be crucified. As long as the saints, the believing fathers, trusted in that sacrifice, they were granted the right to the saving benefits."[87] More recently, Vos explains, the Son, "although having not yet assumed human nature," was still "the same person who later became flesh, suffered, and died" so that he had the office of mediator in eternity.[88] More specifically, "the Son of God assumed His suretyship not as the *Logos* in the abstract, but as the *Logos* who would become flesh in time. He did this as *Logos incarnandus* [to be incarnate], and His human nature was thereby taken into account as if

84. Gillespie, *Ark of the Covenant*, 176–79.

85. Owen, "Exercitation XXVIII," 1:467–68, 472; *EC*, 2.2.8, 2.3.2–4; *TI*, 12.9.5–20; *CRS*, 1:252; *BRD*, 3:214; *DLGTT*, 169; Jeff Fisher, "Protestant Scholastics on Trinity and Persons," in *Trinity without Hierarchy*, 205–10; cf. Letham, *Systematic Theology*, 433, 436–37.

86. Van Asselt, "Christ, Predestination, and Covenant," 216–17, 224–25.

87. Peter Martyr Vermigli, Heinrich Bullinger, et al., *Epistolae Duae, Ad Ecclesias Polonicas* (Zurich, 1561), 5. For Vermigli as the named author and for his wider argument that Christ is the mediator according to both natures, see K. J. Drake, *The Flesh of the Word: The* extra Calvinisticum *from Zwingli to Early Orthodoxy* (New York: Oxford University Press, 2021), 155–64.

88. *VRD*, 3:41, 49.

it were really present."[89] The Son's office as mediator assigned in eternity, therefore, always has his human nature in view even before he assumed it.[90]

The *incarnandus-incarnatus* distinction then protects two doctrinal fronts. Concerning salvation, this *incarnandus* category will be crucial throughout part three about the covenant of grace's substance because the Son's appointment as mediator *in eternity* explains how he acts as Savior of all God's people before and after he came in his incarnation. Concerning theology proper, it guards divine immutability. When the Son comes in his incarnate mission, his new assumed relation to creation is not a true change in God because it has an eternal background. His office as mediator appears in history as *history* changes but has eternally been the office appointed for the Son to play in redemption.

More specifically, in his office as mediator, Christ was the sponsor for the elect as *expromissor* rather than *fideiussor*. For Christ to be the elect's *expromissor* means that he fully assumed their covenantal debts, so becoming the party now truly responsible to pay them. By contrast, *fideiussor* would imply that Old Testament believers remained personally liable for their sin until Christ paid for them on the cross. Because the Son was appointed as mediator for all the elect in the covenant of redemption, with his work's merit resting upon the eternal decree, the virtue and efficacy of his satisfaction could be distributed even before he accomplished it in history. So, Aquinas writes, since the Son's "invisible mission was directed to the Old Testament Fathers," then "the Fathers of old were justified by faith in Christ's passion, just as we are. … The Fathers of old had faith in the future passion of Christ, which, inasmuch as it was apprehended by the mind, was able to justify them. But we have faith in the past passion

89. *VRD*, 3:84.

90. This point clarifies how we can affirm that the Spirit performed his mission to apply the effects of the Son's mission even prior to his incarnation. Vidu argues that the Son and Spirit's missions must follow sequentially upon one another; see Vidu, *Divine Missions*, 27–48. Although, truly, the Spirit's mission is dependent upon the Son's, the Triune God's eternal decree concerning the missions and the application of the virtue of the Son's mission prior to his incarnation—a point chapter 8 explores—enable us to argue that the Spirit's mission is logically contingent upon the Son's but the benefits of both missions were distributed to believers historically before those missions were accomplished; see Harrison Perkins, "Reconciling the Divine Processions-Missions Relationship with Confessional Reformed Theology: An Engagement with Adonis Vidu's *The Divine Missions: An Introduction*: Part 2—The Covenant of Grace," at *The Heidelblog*, June 30, 2022, https://heidelblog.net/2022/06/reconciling-the-divine-processions-missions-relationship-with-confessional-reformed-theology-an-engagement-with-adonis-vidus-the-divine-missions-an-introduction-part-2/.

of Christ, which is able to justify."[91] Believers who trusted in Christ *incarnandus* received the full remission of sin in their time, just as we who trust in Christ *incarnatus* do today.[92]

To illustrate the *expromissor-fideiussor* distinction, imagine that you took out a loan but could not pay it. Your brother then promises that he will pay it for you. Now, one repayment method would be that the loan remains in your name, but he submits the payments. In this situation, you remain liable for the debt until it is paid, but someone else is paying it. In this approach, your brother is the *fideiussor*. On the other hand, you could go into the bank and legally transfer the loan into his name, so that the debt truly became his to pay, leaving you no longer liable at all. Even if he does not immediately pay off the debt, you are forgiven of it because he has taken full legal responsibility for it. This transfer makes him the *expromissor*, the true guarantor now responsible for your debt.

God's decree of the covenant of redemption appointed Christ as *expromissor* for the elect in all ages, so that they would be fully justified and forgiven of their covenantal debts at the moment they trust in Christ, regardless of whether he had yet paid those debts in history. Christ's office as *expromissor* is precisely why the Westminster Confession states, "Although the work of redemption was not actually wrought by Christ till after his incarnation, yet the virtue, efficacy, and benefits thereof were communicated unto the elect, in all ages successively from the beginning of the world" (WCF 8.6).[93] The efficacy of Christ's work could be credited to every believer even before he paid off their covenantal debt in history because their covenantal debts had been imputed to him in the covenant of redemption, so that his covenantal merits—regardless of whether the believer lived before or after the incarnation—are imputed to us by faith.

---

91. Aquinas, *Summa Theologica*, 1.43.6; 3.62.6.

92. The issue concerns whether Old Testament saints received the full remission of sin (ἄφεσις) or, as Johannes Cocceius argued, merely had their sins passed over until Christ paid for them during his incarnate mission (πάρεσις). Christ's *expromissio* sponsorship means they had the full remission of sins (ἄφεσις) in their own time. The notion of eternal justification does not legitimately follow from this view, since justification occurs in time by faith; see *DLGTT*, 33–34, 116, 120, 254, 342; Willem J. van Asselt, "Expromissio or Fideiussio?: A Seventeenth-Century Theological Debate between Voetians and Cocceians about the Nature of Christ's Suretyship in Salvation History," *MAJT* 14 (2003): 37–57; *VRD*, 4:144–50, 160–66; *TI*, 16.9.2–6, 8; and *EC*, 4.12.27–43; 4.13.2–4.

93. *COC*, 3:621–22.

The Triune God's singularly-willed appointment of the Son as mediator for the elect forges his mission as their representative.[94] According to God's *ad extra* decree, this mission extends from or follows the Son's *ad intra* procession but cannot be collapsed into or conflated with it.[95] With this mission decreed, even before the Son historically executed it, the Scripture glimpses the Father addressing the Son *in his mission* prior to the incarnation. These "conversations" specifically concern the Father's interaction with the Son concerning his mediation, so pertaining to the Son *in his mission* as *incarnandus*.[96]

Hebrews' wider discussion about Christ's priesthood importantly situates the point concerning the nature of his Sonship. Priests represented the people in God's presence, offering sacrifices and interceding on their behalf. In the covenant of redemption, as the Westminster Confession says, the Father called Christ to be the mediator of the covenant of grace, which office includes the three duties to act as the consummate prophet, priest, and king (WCF 8.3).[97] Concerning his duty as high priest, the Westminster Shorter Catechism explains, "Christ executes the office of a Priest, in his once offering up of himself a sacrifice to satisfy divine justice, and reconcile us to God, and in making continual intercession for us" (WSC 25).[98]

Hebrews frames Christ's priesthood both within our general need as sinners for an effectual high priest and within the context the Old Testament's description of God's appointment of the Son as high priest from eternity. Hebrews 5:1–10 reads,

> For every high priest chosen from among men is appointed to act on behalf of men in relation to God, to offer gifts and sacrifices for sins. He can deal gently with the ignorant and wayward, since he himself is beset with weakness. Because of this he is obligated to offer sacrifice for his own sins just as he does for those of the people. And no one takes this honor for himself, but only when called by God, just as Aaron was.

---

94. *TI*, 14.2.10–15.
95. Webster, "Will of the Lord to Bruise Him," 152–57; Wellum, *Person of Christ*, 153–54.
96. *VRD*, 3:90; Butner, *Trinitarian Dogmatics*, 115–18.
97. *COC*, 3:620; Gillespie, *Ark of the Covenant*, 202–20.
98. *COC*, 3:681.

> So also Christ did not exalt himself to be made a high priest, but was appointed by him who said to him,
>
> "You are my Son, today I have begotten you";
> as he says also in another place,
> "You are a priest forever, after the order of Melchizedek."
>
> In the days of his flesh, Jesus offered up prayers and supplications, with loud cries and tears, to him who was able to save him from death, and he was heard because of his reverence. Although he was a son, he learned obedience through what he suffered. And being made perfect, he became the source of eternal salvation to all who obey him, being designated by God a high priest after the order of Melchizedek.

Our sin makes us need a priest to act on our behalf before God, but the old covenant priests were ineffectual because of their own sin. Just as God had appointed the old covenant priests to their office, so God appointed Christ as the final and effectual high priest.

Hebrews' use of Psalm 2:7 contextualizes Christ's priesthood within his Sonship. Although Hebrews 1:5 already applies Psalm 2:7 to Christ's divine Sonship as preeminent even over the angels, this royal Psalm also displays the king's coronation, or God's begetting him into his royal position. In Hebrews 5, the royal Son—the Son fulfilling God's covenantal promises to David about an everlasting heir—is begotten into his covenantal office as head of God's people.[99] As mediator, Christ's kingly duty then also connects to his priestly work.

Hebrews further connects Christ's installation as the covenantal royal Son to his appointment as the high priest by quoting Psalm 110:4. God appoints the eternal priest who will forever intercede for his people, which Hebrews applies to the Son's commission as the mediator of the new covenant. Melchizedek was the priest-king whom Abraham encountered in Genesis 14, so Christ's appointment according to the order of Melchizedek links his priesthood to the Abrahamic covenant's foundational promises, rather than the Mosaic covenant's later temporary priesthood.[100] In regard

99. *TCR*, 79–94; Barrett, *Simply Trinity*, 194–98.

100. *TCR*, 95–106.

to the covenant of redemption, Hebrews states that these Old Testament passages record God's appointment of Christ as the mediator and priest, although written long before Christ was born. These passages speak from the eternal perspective about Christ *incarnandus*. The Son, although he had not yet come in the incarnation, was already appointed the covenant mediator, priest, and king.

This context for Christ's priesthood again highlights Christ's obedience precisely as obedience as the mediator for God's people. The Son as God cannot obey but as our mediator "learned obedience through what he suffered." His suffering, although culminating in the cross, was not limited to it (Phil 2:8).[101] Christ's obedience ties to his office as the covenant mediator representing us.

A covenant—an agreement—among the persons of the Godhead or one person's obedience to another *seems* nonsensical because of the Triune God's common will. As argued, however, the mutuality of the covenant of redemption should not be mapped into the singular divine will itself but kept within God's economic activity. Within the triunely decreed plan of salvation, the persons have a covenantal arrangement whereby the Father appointed Christ as mediator from eternity, the Son assumes a human nature in history so rendering perfect obedience, and the Spirit rests upon Christ to anoint him as the Messiah and applies his messianic work to the elect.[102] The Canons of Dort summarize:

> Indeed God the Father's *sovereign counsel*, and most gracious *will and purpose* was, that the quickening and saving efficacy of the most precious death of his Son should extend to all the elect for bestowing upon them alone the gift of justifying faith, thereby to bring them infallibly to salvation: that is, it was God's will, that Christ by the blood of the cross, *whereby he confirmed the new covenant*, should effectually redeem out of every people, tribe, nations, and language, all those, and those only, who were *from eternity chosen unto salvation and given to him by the Father; that he should confer upon them faith, which together with all the other saving gifts of the Holy Spirit*, he purchased for them by his death; should purge them

101. WSC 27; *COC*, 3:681.

102. WCF 8.3; *COC*, 3:620.

> from all sin, both original and actual, whether committed before or after believing; and having faithfully preserved them even to the end, should at last bring them free from every spot and blemish to the enjoyment of glory in his own presence forever. (Canons of Dort 2.8)[103]

With careful thought, the covenant of redemption coheres well with Trinitarian orthodoxy.

THE COVENANT AMONG FATHER, SON, AND SPIRIT

Why such effort to retain the doctrine of the covenant of redemption in light of the preceding complexities in traditional Trinitarianism? Simply, scriptural evidence pressures us to see such an eternal intra-Trinitarian pact to make proper sense particularly of prophetic texts and intra-canonical exegesis. The biblical testimony indicating the specific relation among Father, Son, and Spirit in the plan of salvation is rightly called a covenant.

In Isaiah 49:8–9, God promised that the coming Savior would be a covenant to his people as the one who would obtain a dwelling place for his people and free them from bondage. "Thus says the LORD: 'In a time of favor I have answered you; in a day of salvation I have helped you; I will keep you and *give you as a covenant* to the people, to establish the land, to apportion the desolate heritages, saying to the prisoners, "Come out," to those who are in darkness, "Appear." ' " Christ's work as the Messiah is, therefore, firmly related to the notion of covenant. Covenant theology is simply about our relationship with God, since God makes covenants with his people to bind us to himself in formal and official ways. After Adam broke the covenant of works and plunged us all into sin, our relationship with God must be founded on something entirely other than our own personal obedience. So, God has given Christ as a covenant for his people.[104]

In one sense, Scripture explicitly identifies God's covenant with Christ. In Galatians 3:15–20, Paul frames the history of redemption with the illustration of an irrevocable promise *covenant*. Pointedly, this promise

103. *COC*, 3:562 (emphasis added).

104. Hodge, *Systematic Theology*, 2:359–61.

covenant was made to Abraham and his singular offspring, "who is Christ" (Gal. 3:16). So, Christ overtly received this covenant. Moreover, Paul appealed to God's unity to show how this promise covenant with Christ had priority over the Mosaic law. Referring to Moses's role of mediating the law from God through angels to Israel, Paul writes: "Now an intermediary implies more than one, but God is one" (Gal 3:20). Since God made this promise covenant with Abraham and his singular descendant Christ, and since Christ is God subsisting in the one divine essence according to his deity, this covenant needed no mediator. The covenant was between God and Christ.[105]

Other passages confirm this covenantal arrangement among the Trinity. Zechariah 6:13 is a classic prooftext in the Reformed tradition for the covenant of redemption, and good reasons still exist to support recognizing an agreement between the Father and Son in this passage.[106] "It is he who shall build the temple of the LORD and shall bear royal honor, and shall sit and rule on his throne. And there shall be a priest on his throne, and *the counsel of peace* shall be between them both." Witsius comments: "There is a remarkable prophecy concerning the Messiah, whose person, offices, and glory, the Prophet truly describes in a short but lively manner, subjoining at last the cause of all these; namely, why the Messiah appeared as such a person, executed offices, and obtained such a glory; namely, because of that counsel which was between him and the Father, the fruit of which with respect to us, is *peace*."[107] Reformed interpreters have understood Zechariah's "counsel of peace" to be about the covenant between Father and Son in the plan of salvation.[108]

On its surface, this reading might seem like special pleading of specific phrasing, but the context of Zechariah 6:9–14 substantiates the point. This passage addressed exiles in Babylon about their future restoration, including some surprising features. These surprising features reside in the relations between God, the royal figure, and the priest. God told Zechariah to "make a crown, and set it on the head of Joshua, the son of

---

105. S. M. Baugh, "Galatians 3:20 and the Covenant of Redemption," *WTJ* 66 (2004): 49–70.

106. David VanDrunen and R. Scott Clark, "The Covenant Before the Covenants," in *Covenant, Justification, and Pastoral Ministry*, 187–89, 192–93.

107. *EC*, 2.2.7 (italics original); cf. *VRD*, 2:84.

108. *TCR*, 53–77.

Jehozadak, the high priest." The high priest's reception of the sign of royalty already signals something unusual. Since kings were from the tribe of Judah, and priests were from the tribe of Levi, this kind of overlap in roles was not supposed to occur. This action performed toward Joshua is prophetic of "the man whose name is the Branch," reminding us of Isaiah 11 about the root from the stump of Jesse, and this stump is the Branch who has God's Spirit upon him and is the great messianic figure. So, in Zechariah this combined royal and priestly figure is God's Messiah who will build the Lord's temple.

As should already be clear, some tension is building in this prophecy that needs resolution. So, Zechariah writes, "It is he [the Messiah] who shall build the temple of the Lord and shall bear royal honor, and shall sit and rule on his throne." The Messiah builds the Lord's temple and bears royal honor, and "shall sit and rule on his throne." The context is the Lord's temple, and Zechariah continues: "And there shall be a priest on his throne, and the counsel of peace shall be between them both." This priest will be on *his* throne, but the question is *whose* throne? Since the context is the Lord's temple, this throne is the Lord's, and the messianic priest is upon it. Now, a counsel of peace is between the Lord and the messianic priest-king.[109] Clearly, the counsel of peace cannot be between a king and a priest because Zechariah's king and priest are the same person. So, the counsel is between God and the Messiah, which exactly suggests a covenant between Christ and the Lord.[110]

Luke 22:29 confirms this interpretation of Zechariah 6:13, posing a covenantal relation between the Father and Christ in his royal and priestly offices. Jesus says to the disciples, "And I assign to you, as my Father assigned to me, a kingdom." Interestingly, the word translated here as "assign" is the Greek verb *diatithemi*, which appears throughout the Greek translation of the Old Testament and in the New Testament with the meaning that God made a covenant.[111] In fact, this word *diatithemi* is

109. *TI*, 14.6.7; M. G. Kline, *Glory in Our Midst: A Biblical-Theological Reading of Zechariah's Night Visions* (Overland Park, KS: Two Age Press, 2001), 219–240.

110. *VRD*, 3:8; Richard, "The Covenant of Redemption," 51–53.

111. *KP*, 139–40; Samuel Renihan, *The Mystery of Christ: His Covenant and His Kingdom* (Cape Coral, FL: Founders Press, 2020), 175–76.

simply the verb form related to the Greek noun for covenant, *diatheke*.[112] It might be helpful to illustrate how related verbs and nouns might work together with a more relatable English example. So, I might say, "I am running a run," or, "I am living my life." Both sentences use a verb (running, living) and noun (run, life) version of the same root word. The Greek Old Testament uses this verb *diatithemi* for "covenanting" with the noun *diatheke* for a "covenant" in this way.[113]

Specific Old Testament passages establish this verb's important relationship to covenant. This verb and noun combination appears, for example, in the Greek translation of Jeremiah 31:31–33. As translated from the Hebrew, it reads:

> Behold, the days are coming, declares the LORD, when I will make a new covenant with the house of Israel and the house of Judah, not like the covenant that I made with their fathers on the day when I took them by the hand to bring them out of the land of Egypt, my covenant that they broke, though I was their husband, declares the LORD. For this is the covenant that I will make with the house of Israel after those days, declares the LORD: I will put my law within them, and I will write it on their hearts. And I will be their God, and they shall be my people.

The relevant repeated phrase concerns God making the covenant, wherein the verb "make" is actually *diatithemi* and the noun "covenant" is *diatheke*. There are a few examples from this passage: "when I will make [*diatithemi*] a new covenant [*diatheke*] with the house of Israel and the house of Judah"; "not like the covenant [*diatheke*] that I made [*diatithemi*] with their fathers"; "this is the covenant [*diatheke*] that I will make [*diatithemi*] with the house of Israel."[114] The same word pattern appears when the book of Hebrews cites this passage concerning its fulfillment in Christ (Heb 8:10; 10:16).[115]

---

112. More technically, the verb διατίθημι and its cognate noun διαθήκη appear throughout the Greek Old Testament and the New Testament in polyptoton figures of speech.

113. Block, *Covenant*, 395–96, 428; *VRD*, 2:85.

114. In the actual Greek version of the Greek translation of the Old Testament, the Septuagint, this passage is numbered Jeremiah 38:31–33.

115. Other passages that confirm the same relationship of *diatithemi* and *diatheke* are Exodus 24:8, Deuteronomy 4:23, Joshua 9:15, and Acts 3:25.

The word *diatithemi*, therefore, fully links to God's actions of forming a covenant with his people. We might easily translate phrases from Jeremiah 31 as "God covenanted a covenant."

So, when Jesus says in Luke 22:29 that the Father had "assigned" to him a kingdom, he used a Greek word thoroughly linked to God's actions of covenant making. In other words, Christ used this covenantal verb to say that the Father had covenanted a kingdom to him, which was exactly the point in Zechariah 6:13. In Zechariah, God made a counsel of peace—an arranged relationship or simply a covenant—with the priestly Messiah as the king on the throne, and we know that Christ is the one who fulfills that office of the priestly and royal Messiah. As many Reformed writers recognize, Christ confirmed in Luke 22:29 that the Father had made that relation with him to bestow the kingdom upon him as the priestly and royal Messiah by means of a covenant.[116]

This point about the covenant among the persons of the Godhead in the plan of salvation is not limited to the intersection of Zechariah 6:13 and Luke 22:29, being threaded into other passages that speak about the Son's appointment as the effectual mediator of salvation. In a very pointed way, Psalm 110 confirms the intersection between the royal and priestly offices in the Messiah and that God appointed this historical Messiah in eternity.[117] In Matthew 22:41–46, Christ himself explained that Psalm 110:1—"The LORD says to my Lord: 'Sit at my right hand, until I make your enemies your footstool' "—was about him as the Messiah who is also the divine Lord himself. In this case, the Father spoke to the Son. Calvin writes that Psalm 110 "sets forth the perpetuity of Christ's reign, and the eternity of his priesthood," specifically in that "God conferred upon Christ supreme dominion" and installed him "into the priestly office with all the solemnity of an oath," with the result that "this shall be a new priesthood, whose introduction shall put an end to the Levitical priesthood, which was temporary, and that it shall be everlasting."[118] Calvin rightly summarizes Christ's own point from Matthew 22 about how Psalm 110's opening verse is about the eternal Son's saving kingship, but other portions of Scripture

116. Richard A. Muller, "Toward the *Pactum Salutis*: Locating the Origins of a Concept," *MAJT* 18 (2007): 11–65; *TI*, 12.2.14; *EC*, 2.2.3; *CRS*, 1:255.

117. *TCR*, 95–106.

118. *CC*, 6:1.295.

indicate just as much that Psalm 110 tells us about God's eternal appointment of the Son as priest. The distinction concerning the Son *incarnandus* and *incarnatus* helpfully explains these Old Testament passages that speak so directly about the Son's mission.

Like Matthew's Gospel, Hebrews 7:15–22 also provides inspired interpretation of Psalm 110 as about Christ. This passage in Hebrews concerns Christ's work as the guarantor of the new covenant but raises some profound points about *when* Christ was appointed as the guarantor. Remembering that Psalm 110 began by describing a conversation between two persons whom David could call "Lord," which indicates that both are divine, God's address to David's Lord now outlines his priestly office:

> The LORD has sworn
> and will not change his mind,
> "You are a priest forever
> after the order of Melchizedek." (Ps 110:4)

Hebrews 7:20 points out that God's address to the Messiah in Psalm 110:4 was an oath—a binding covenantal declaration—meaning that it cannot be broken or overturned.[119] It may not be immediately obvious, but Scripture depicts the act of swearing an oath as bound with the making of a covenant.[120] In other words, when someone takes an oath, they have also made a covenant. In 2 Kings 11:4–8, Jehoiada the priest bound the guards by covenant to the king's son, but his actions in ratifying that covenant show the link between making a covenant and taking an oath: "And he made a covenant with them and put them under oath in the house of the LORD" (11:4). Even within Hebrews, the author describes the Abrahamic covenant in terms of God's act of swearing an oath, which inherently binds one of the paradigmatic covenants to the notion of oath (Heb 6:13–18). Oaths and covenants are inseparably linked, but the author of Hebrews says God made an oath concerning his appointment of the Son as the everlasting high priest.

Regarding the use of Psalm 110:4 in Hebrews 7, God will not change his mind because he made an oath, which is a covenantal act that is part

119. *TCR*, 99–101.

120. Williamson, *Sealed*, 39–43; *BOC*, 16–21.

of what makes the Messiah's priesthood so much better than that of the old covenant.[121] This priesthood will be effective forever. The point that needs to be noted is that the inspired narratives about Jesus's life never record God stating this oath to Christ during his earthly ministry. The New Testament often refers to Psalm 110, but never in such a way that indicates the Father said these words to the Son during his time on earth. Psalm 110, therefore, is not simply prophetic about Christ's ministry but also records God's eternal counsel whereby the Father appointed the Son as the everlasting priest to save his people. In Psalm 110 the Father speaks to Christ *incarnandus* about his incarnate mission. Hebrews 7:22 says, "This," which refers to God's statement in Psalm 110:4, "makes Jesus the guarantor of a better covenant." God from eternity appointed Christ as the effectual covenant mediator. Psalm 110 provides another instance of how the New Testament sheds light on how passages in the Old Testament actually describe a covenantal relation among the persons of the Godhead within the plan of salvation.[122]

Although some aspects of Reformed covenant theology are not explicitly stated in one given passage, comparing several texts of Scripture often demonstrates how the Bible presents a unified portrait of God's plan of salvation in covenantal hues.[123] Far from being foreign to biblical interpretation, the task of theology demands that we reflect upon Scripture in light of other parts of Scripture in order to digest more useful categories for explaining the Bible's whole message. In reference to the covenant of redemption, we now see how the New Testament interpretation of Old Testament themes and texts suggests that there was a covenant involved between God the Father and Christ the mediator.

CONCLUSION

The Triune God dwells in eternal communion as Father, Son, and Spirit. Whereas Adam broke the covenant of works and shattered humanity's original communion with God, the persons of the Trinity decreed a

121. Hodge, *Hebrews*, 65–66.

122. Richard, "Covenant of Redemption," 53–54.

123. *KTC*, 77–79; Wellum, "Progressive Covenantalism Response," 202; Wellum, *Person of Christ*, 39; Peter J. Gentry and Stephen J. Wellum, *Kingdom through Covenant: A Biblical-Theological Understanding of the Covenants*, 1st ed. (Wheaton, IL: Crossway, 2012), 59–60, 654–56.

covenantal plan to bring God's people back into communion with them. That plan is structured as the covenant of redemption.

The covenant of redemption forces us to contemplate the endless majesty of God's being. There are complexities to formulating the covenant of redemption precisely regarding particular aspects of Trinitarian theology. We should not shy away from those complexities, however, but run full speed into the reflection upon the glory of our God who is Father, Son, and Spirit. Sometimes this work is difficult but it should lead us to fuller and deeper love of who our God is. The Triune God is beyond our full comprehension. Relationships, however, are about knowing one another increasingly well as the love between parties grows. It is, therefore, highly fitting that the covenant of redemption—as one part of the explanation of our covenant relationship with God—would push us to think deeply about God himself so that we might know him better and love him more richly.

The pastoral application of this chapter's material is, as we do theology as pilgrims traversing this age, we marvel at the inexhaustible and incomprehensible majesty of our God. Moreover, we marvel at how the Triune God as such has so deeply loved us. God's single decree, commonly willed by Father, Son, and Spirit, shows us the depth, riches, and magnitude of God's love for his people. Too often, we might mistakenly think that Christ's cross means that the Son won over the angry Father to love believers. In truth, Father, Son, and Spirit together so loved the elect that by their common will, they appointed the Son as our mediator, the Father then giving us to our Savior to redeem the divinely-beloved. Just as the covenant of works underlined God's love for Adam and Adam's opportunity to return God's love, so the covenant of redemption highlights God's infinite inner triune love—as this plan of redemption shows Father, Son, and Spirit working in love for one another to display their triune glory—and immense love for his people, since God is his decree and has decreed his love for us in Christ.

VI

The Father, Son, and Spirit in the Fulfillment of Salvation

In him we have redemption through his blood, the forgiveness of our trespasses, according to the riches of his grace, which he lavished upon us, in all wisdom and insight making known to us the mystery of his will, according to his purpose, which he set forth in Christ as a plan for the fullness of time, to unite all things in him, things in heaven and things on earth.

—Ephesians 1:7–10

Christian faith thrives on contemplating the immeasurable riches received by faith from Christ. In our daily life, we likely think most about our experience and assurance of those blessings. The preaching we hear in corporate worship should weekly point to Christ's work as our Savior during his earthly ministry and, now, his intercession in heaven. Probably, we less often focus on the eternal foundations explaining why Christ is our salvation's surety and why that foundation so richly assures us as we walk before God. Our salvation's eternal foundation is the covenant of redemption.

Building on the previous chapter's introduction of the procession-mission distinction, this chapter considers each divine person's *mission* in effecting our salvation. Without overturning the unity of God's singly willing but triune decree about salvation's plan, Scripture reveals its outworking in history with several *appropriations* to specific persons and as their missions. In Irenaeus's words, we are brought to God again "by the Father well knowing and ordering, and the Son executing and forming, and the Spirit nourishing and advancing" us to God's planned end of restoration in his image.[1] More specifically, three triads of A's structure the particular functions that the Father, Son, and Spirit fulfill to bring about the elect's redemption: (1) the Father *arranges* redemption by *appointing* the Son as mediator and *assigning* the elect to him; (2) the Son *accomplishes* redemption by *accepting* his Father's will and *attaining* righteousness for the elect; and (3) the Spirit *applies* redemption by *accompanying* the Son in his earthly mission and *administering* Christ's benefits to the elect.

THE FATHER ARRANGES REDEMPTION

Scripture clearly teaches that Christ, in his mediatorial office rather than as God per se, did the Father's will, entailing that the Father's mission was *arranging* what the Son would *accomplish* during his incarnation, which the Spirit would then *apply*. Strictly speaking, since a divine mission is the effect of a procession in creation, the Father's part in this redemptive plan is not properly a mission. The Father's personal relation is unbegotten, meaning he does not proceed like the Son proceeds from him and the Spirit proceeds from Father and Son. Processionally and missionally, the Father is properly only sender. Further, the Father's part is not properly a mission because his person does not manifest in creation like the Son and Spirit do for their missions. Given that the Triune God together decreed the covenant of redemption, clearly the Father's whole arranging role in appointing the Son as mediator and assigning the elect to him is an example of *appropriation* of operation rather than a proper mission. Nonetheless, his person has relation to the Son and Spirit's missions as the one sending them economically, making his role a necessary part of a complete portrait of the *pactum salutis*. With this caveat in place, the discussion still, albeit improperly, applies "mission" to the Father's relation to the Son and Spirit's missions, mainly over lack of another suitable

1. Irenaeus, *Against Heresies*, 4.38.3 in *PG*, 7.1:1108; *ANF*, 1:521–22.

term. This section focuses on the Father's arranging role in the covenant of redemption.

The first aspect of the Father's mission in arranging redemption is *appointing* the Son as mediator. In some ways, the previous chapter broaches this point by looking at how Hebrews 7 cited Psalm 110 as the Father's words to the Son in eternity, although the argument can be further supplemented.[2] In his office of mediator, Christ is high priest of the better covenant, as Hebrews repeatedly affirms.[3] That Christ is the final high priest simply means that he is the one who can enter God's direct presence, bringing a sacrifice that effectively forgives our sin before God.[4] As Hebrews 9:11–14 explains, Christ's sacrifice is truly effective unto forgiveness because he offered not the blood of mere animals, but *his own* blood, indeed God's own blood (Acts 20:28). Although Christ also executes the offices of prophet and king, because of his priestly office Hebrews 9:15 says, "Therefore he is the mediator of a new covenant, so that those who are called may receive the promised eternal inheritance, since a death has occurred that redeems them from the transgressions committed under the first covenant." As mediator, Christ stands between two parties, God and humanity, for the sake of reconciliation (1 Tim 2:5–6).

Scripture, moreover, clearly indicates that the Father appointed the Son to this office as mediating high priest.[5] Hebrews 5:4 states, "And no one takes this honor for himself, but only when called by God, just as Aaron was." Men cannot select themselves for the role of high priest. As children may whine to be first in line, but, ultimately, the teacher appoints the leader, so we lack the authority to nominate ourselves as the mediator between God and humanity (Heb 5:1–4). God must appoint that person, so the Father addressed the Son, appointing him as high priest and final, consummate mediator (Ps 110:4; Heb 5:5–6; Heb 7:15–22).[6]

The Father arranges redemption by appointing the Son as the mediator but also by *assigning* the elect to him.[7] Jesus describes part of his mission

---

2. *CRS*, 1:255–56.
3. *MT*, 1.19.18–19.
4. *CF*, 492–520.
5. Owen, "Exercitation XXVII," in *Hebrews*, 1:455–60.
6. *CG*, 65–67; *MT*, 1.19.3–6.
7. *CRS*, 1:252–53.

for salvation by explaining the certainty of everlasting resurrection life for the elect. In John 6:38–40, he teaches, "For I have come down from heaven, not to do my own will but the will of him who sent me. And this is the will of him who sent me, that I should lose nothing of all that he has given me, but raise it up on the last day. For this is the will of my Father, that everyone who looks on the Son and believes in him should have eternal life, and I will raise him up on the last day." A primary point of Christ's mission in the covenant of redemption was to do his Father's will. Clearly, this obedience specifically concerns the plan of salvation because he had to come from heaven to earth in order to perform it.[8] The Father's will that Christ accomplished was that he lose nothing that the Father had given him but raise it on the last day. Although that language *might* seem impersonal, and therefore vague, Jesus clarified that he was speaking of the elect because he meant "everyone who looks on the Son and believes in him." The Father's will that the Son came to accomplish was that all of those whom the Father gave to him—the elect—would believe in the Son, would never be lost, and would certainly have everlasting life when they are resurrected at Christ's return.[9] In his role, the Father had given these elect to the Son.

Other Scripture confirms the Father's role in assigning the elect to the Son. In John 10:25–30, Jesus rehearses his teaching about how he will ensure that those whom the Father had given to him will certainly receive everlasting life.

> Jesus answered them, "I told you, and you do not believe. The works that I do in my Father's name bear witness about me, but you do not believe because you are not among my sheep. My sheep hear my voice, and I know them, and they follow me. I give them eternal life, and they will never perish, and no one will snatch them out of my hand. My Father, who has given them to me, is greater than all, and no one is able to snatch them out of the Father's hand. I and the Father are one."

8. Butner, "Eternal Functional Subordination," 143–46; CG, 63–65.

9. Herman Ridderbos, *The Gospel according to John: A Theological Commentary*, trans. John Vriend (Grand Rapids: Eerdmans, 1997), 231.

That Jesus knows these sheep who follow him confirms that they are believers. Still, his people *are* his sheep and *therefore* come to faith, rather than first coming to faith and then becoming Christ's sheep. Election clearly features in Christ's relationship to his sheep, especially as he asserts that he *will* give his sheep everlasting life so they cannot be lost. He cannot lose these sheep because the Father has given them to him and the Father is greater than anything that might try to snatch them away.[10] In respect only to the Son's incarnate ministry, the Father is greater than he, ensuring their jointly decreed plan of salvation.[11]

Throughout Christ's "high priestly prayer" in John 17, Jesus repeats the same emphasis on his work on behalf of those whom the Father had given to him. Jesus is the one who has the authority to give everlasting life to all those given to him (John 17:2), which is that work which the Father assigned him to do (John 17:4). Most clearly for the covenant of redemption: "I have manifested your name to the people whom you gave me out of the world. Yours they were, and you gave them to me, and they have kept your word. Now they know that everything that you have given me is from you" (John 17:6–7). In eternity via the covenant of redemption, the Father gave the elect to the Son so that he might reveal salvation to them and that they might be adopted into God's family through the Son (Eph 1:5). So, the Westminster Shorter Catechism says that, as mediator, "Christ executes the office of a Prophet, in revealing to us by his Word and Spirit, the will of God for our salvation" (WSC 24).[12] In more particular regard to the covenant of redemption as indicating that the Father *arranged* and the Son *accomplished* the specifics of the plan of salvation, Jesus performed his earthly mission and now prays only for those whom the Father gave to him (John 17:9). The Father assigned the elect to the Son as those specific people whom Christ would certainly save, and the Son faithfully executed that assignment so that he is able to pray not for the whole world, but for the elect alone.

The passages examined about the Father's part in *arranging* salvation reveal an emphasis upon how the Father's commissioning of the Son as

---

10. Ridderbos, *John*, 369.

11. Ridderbos, *John*, 370–71; Wittman, "*Dominium naturale*," 151–58; Adesola Akala, "Sonship, Sending, and Subordination in the Gospel of John," in *Trinity without Hierarchy*, 25–26.

12. *COC*, 3:681.

mediator relates to the Son's incarnate mission to save the elect. Just as God commissioned Adam in the covenant of works as the first representative of humanity to fulfill the law and earn everlasting new creation life on behalf of himself and his posterity, so the Father commissioned the Son in the covenant of redemption, as the final representative of the redeemed humanity, to fulfill the requirements of the first covenant on behalf of the elect given to him.[13]

THE SON ACCOMPLISHES REDEMPTION

This section argues that the Son's mission in the covenant of redemption was to *accomplish* redemption through his incarnate work. Through his perfect obedience as our mediator, Christ merited everlasting life for those whom the Father gave to him in their eternal covenant. In terms of our three triads of A's, the Son *accomplishes* redemption by *accepting* the will of his Father and *attaining* righteousness for the elect.

First, Christ accomplishes salvation by accepting his mission from the Father to come and secure salvation for the elect whom the Father gave to him.[14] This acceptance clearly presumes the Son's mission in his incarnation because it requires his human will as distinct from the Triune God's common will. Some passages explored in the previous section also inform the Son's acceptance of his mission. Throughout John's Gospel, Christ repeatedly affirms that he came to do his Father's will.

In John 4:1–30, Jesus converses with the woman at the well, revealing and proving to her that he is the Christ, so the woman went to go tell the other townspeople that she had encountered the Messiah. As the disciples returned to where Jesus was, they were more concerned about eating than about how this woman had understood the gospel. This context situates Jesus's comments in John 4:31–38 about his devotion to his Father's will.

> Meanwhile the disciples were urging him, saying, "Rabbi, eat." But he said to them, "I have food to eat that you do not know about." So the disciples said to one another, "Has anyone brought him something to eat?" Jesus said to them, "My food is to do the will of him who sent me and to accomplish his work. Do you not say,

13. CG, 69–71.

14. Hodge, *Systematic Theology*, 2:361–62; Owen, "Exercitation XXVIII," 1:467–68; *CRS*, 1:256–67.

> 'There are yet four months, then comes the harvest'? Look, I tell you, lift up your eyes, and see that the fields are white for harvest. Already the one who reaps is receiving wages and gathering fruit for eternal life, so that sower and reaper may rejoice together. For here the saying holds true, 'One sows and another reaps.' I sent you to reap that for which you did not labor. Others have labored, and you have entered into their labor."

Although the disciples prompted him to worry about lunch, Christ said that his sustenance is to do his Father's will and to accomplish his Father's work. Strikingly, this clarification about accomplishing the Father's work is sandwiched between the event of bringing the woman at the well to understand the gospel and the statement that informed the disciples of the need for workers for the harvest. In other words, Christ's sustenance in doing and accomplishing his Father's will inherently relates to the gospel.[15]

Jesus's discussion in John 5:19–47 about his authority and the witness about him develops this theme of Christ doing the Father's will. As he began this discourse, Christ's opening remarks show his fundamental unity with the Father in the plan of salvation. He affirms that "the Son can do nothing of his own accord, but only what he sees the Father doing. For whatever the Father does, that the Son does likewise" (5:19). Christ as God is not less than the Father but is the Father's Son, so works in conjunction with the Father.[16] This idea becomes clearly linked with Christ's mission to do the Father's will: "I can do nothing on my own. As I hear, I judge, and my judgment is just, because I seek not my own will but the will of him who sent me" (5:30). Now the Son's unity with the Father shows itself in his coming into the world to accomplish the divine mission by accepting the Father's will. Christ then furthered the importance of his mission and how that mission shows his identity: "For the works that the Father has given me to accomplish, the very works that I am doing, bear witness about me that the Father has sent me" (5:36).[17] Although Christ

15. Ridderbos, *John*, 166–69.

16. Augustine, *John 1–40*, 359–65, 372–77; Ridderbos, *John*, 192–93.

17. Ridderbos, *John*, 203. Christ confirmed this interpretation of his words in John 5 in what he said about his authority and the Father's commandment in John 12:44–49.

may not have added much new to this theme yet, its importance for understanding Christ's incarnate work should be clear.

Jesus's bread of life discourse shows how the Father assigned the elect to the Son but also contributes to the developing theme in John's Gospel about Jesus doing the Father's will. In John 6:35–40, Christ says,

> I am the bread of life; whoever comes to me shall not hunger, and whoever believes in me shall never thirst. But I said to you that you have seen me and yet do not believe. All that the Father gives me will come to me, and whoever comes to me I will never cast out. For I have come down from heaven, not to do my own will but the will of him who sent me. And this is the will of him who sent me, that I should lose nothing of all that he has given me, but raise it up on the last day. For this is the will of my Father, that everyone who looks on the Son and believes in him should have eternal life, and I will raise him up on the last day.

The Son expressly came down from heaven with the purpose of doing the will of the Father who sent him. First, his coming from heaven to earth in order to do the Father's will further confirms our Trinitarian starting point that the Son as God does not owe obedience to the Father.[18] The Son did not submit to the Father's will *in* heaven but came *from* heaven to obey the Father in human nature as part of his earthly mission for salvation.[19]

Second, Christ's teaching further clarifies that his incarnate obedience relates to the elect's salvation. The Father's will in sending the Son was that Christ would lose nothing that the Father had given him. The Father assigned the elect to the Son in the covenant of redemption as those whom he wills the Son not to lose but to raise on the last day. In this regard, Christ accepted the Father's will, coming to accomplish his assigned work in his mission for the elect's salvation.

Thus far, we have noted that John's Gospel emphasizes that the Father sent the Son, as a host of passages demonstrate.[20] This sending *into the world* had this express purpose: for the Son to accept the Father's will as

---

18. Anselm, *Why God Became Man*, 1.9.

19. Vidu, *Same God*, 217–46; Akala, "Sonship, Sending, and Subordination," 27–28.

20. John 3:34; 4:34; 5:23–24, 30, 36–38; 6:29–59; 7:18, 28–29, 33; 8:16–42; 9:4; 10:26; 11:42; 12:44–49; 13:16, 20; 14:24; 15:21; 16:5; 17:1–25; 20:21.

his mission in the covenant of redemption for the salvation of the elect (John 14:31).[21] Although we already looked some at John 10 and John 17 to show how the Father assigned the elect to the Son, these passages also confirm and explain how the Son came into the world as his mission in the covenant of redemption, specifically, as he accepted the mission that the Father had given him.

Jesus delivers two discourses in John 10 that highlight his work as the Good Shepherd of God's sheep, but our focus is on the specific portions informing how Jesus accepted his mission. John 10:17–18 says,

> For this reason the Father loves me, because I lay down my life that I may take it up again. No one takes it from me, but I lay it down of my own accord. I have authority to lay it down, and I have authority to take it up again. This charge I have received from my Father.

Jesus's words clarify the link between the Father assigning the elect to the Son and the Son accepting the Father's will by explaining that his accepted mission included laying down his life and taking it up again for the elect (John 10:11).[22] The Son had received specific sheep for whom he would accomplish salvation (John 10:25–30).

Christ's high priestly prayer also informs how Christ accepted the Father's will to accomplish salvation. In John 17:4, Jesus says, "I glorified you on earth, having accomplished the work that you gave me to do." Christ had just mentioned that he came to give everlasting life to those whom the Father had given him, and now he clarifies that he has accomplished this work. Presently not all of the elect have taken hold of their everlasting life, but only because the Spirit has not yet *applied* it. In reference to the Son's mission, Christ has *accomplished* redemption by completing the work that the Father had assigned to him, which brings new clarity to Christ's final words on the cross in John 19:30, "It is finished."[23] Christ finished not simply dying but his entire mission of redemption for his people, which the Spirit then applies.

---

21. Akala, "Sonship, Sending, and Subordination," 27–35.

22. Ridderbos, *John*, 365–66.

23. *VRD*, 2:85.

Christ's obedience for the elect, as described throughout John's Gospel, was not assigned to him upon his entry into the world, though, but charged to him in eternity in the covenant of redemption, as the use of Psalm 40:6–8 in Hebrews 10:5–10 shows. Although the whole psalm concerns trusting the Lord for deliverance from affliction, Psalm 40:6–8 focuses on obedience to God:[24]

> In sacrifice and offering you have not delighted,
>   but you have given me an open ear.
> Burnt offering and sin offering
>   you have not required.
> Then I said, "Behold, I have come;
>   in the scroll of the book it is written of me:
> I delight to do your will, O my God;
>   your law is within my heart."

The Hebrew idiom for obeying God was hearing God's voice, the ear then being the organ of obedience. Accordingly, God opened the psalmist's ear, enabling him to delight in doing God's will as given in the law.[25] Regarding the covenant of redemption, Hebrews 10:5–10 cites these words as belonging to the Son himself as our mediator.[26] In Hebrews' citation of Psalm 40:6, God does not open the Son's ear but prepares a body for him. The Westminster divines explain the difference between the Hebrew and Greek versions of Psalm 40:6, noting that this "proverbial manner of speech" indicates "the qualifying, or fitting a man unto obedience in service: the ear, or opening of the ear being an emblem or symbol, or a metaphorical sign of obedience."[27] Although hearing signifies obedience in Hebrew idiom, the divine Son needed a body if he were to obey, both since the Son as God cannot obey anyone and since the elect's mediator needed to render obedience in human nature.[28]

---

24. Goldingay, *Psalms*, 1:568.

25. Hodge, *Hebrews*, 96.

26. *CG*, 73–74; *CF*, 489–90.

27. Westminster Assembly, *Annotations upon all the Books of the Old and New Testament* (London: John Legatt and John Raworth, 1645), *ad loc* (italics original).

28. Ellingworth, *Hebrews*, 500; Michael Horton, "Obedience Is Better than Sacrifice," in *LNF*, 315–36; William L. Lane, *Hebrews 9–13* (Nashville: Thomas Nelson, 2000), 263.

Even though Hebrews explains that Psalm 40's words belong to the Son, the Gospel narratives never mention Christ speaking them during his incarnate life, suggesting that this is another intra-Trinitarian conversation between the Father and the Son *incarnandus* concerning his mission.[29] Still, is Psalm 40 a record of the Son's response as a reply from eternity or an indirect prophetic quote summarizing his incarnate ministry?

The better interpretation is that Hebrews discloses Psalm 40 as an eternal intra-Trinitarian "conversation" about the covenant of redemption. Hebrews characteristically interprets the Psalms not as summaries of the incarnation, but as interactions between the Father and Son *incarnandus*. So, Hebrews 7:15–22 clarifies that Psalm 110 records the Father's address to the Son in the covenant of redemption *from eternity*, since the words of this psalm themselves made the Son the mediator of God's people. For Psalm 40:6–8, Hebrews 10:5 notes that the Son said these words "concerning coming into the world," marking a preincarnate, extratemporal statement from the Son *incarnandus*.[30] Hence, the Son said, "Behold, I have come to do your will, O God," but said this to the Father in eternity, showing how the Father had assigned the mediatorial mission to the Son and the Son accepted that mission as part of the covenant of redemption.[31] Still, far from implying that the Son submitted to the Father as the divine Son, Hebrews explicitly designates the Son's words as pertaining to his coming into the world, so indicating that his performance of the Father's will was tied to his incarnation.[32] The Son's obedience was for us as our covenantal representative, so he "learned obedience" (Heb 5:8). The Son's office in the covenant of redemption is to accomplish salvation, first, by accepting the Father's will.

---

29. *VRD*, 2:85; Lane, *Hebrews 9–13*, 262, 265; Ellingworth, *Hebrews*, 499.

30. Most English translations do not clearly convey this sense suggested by the combination of the present participle "coming into the world" (εἰσερχόμενος) and the present tense verb "he says" (λέγει). This grammatical construction entails the *sense* that "he says concerning coming into the world," or even "by coming into the world he says," which—especially considering that absolutely no succession of moments occurs in eternity—suggests that this perspective is from outside time concerning the incarnation (*incarnandus*); Westminster Assembly, *Annotations, ad loc.*; also Ellingworth, *Hebrews*, 499–500.

31. Ellingworth, *Hebrews*, 505–6.

32. Peeler, "What Does 'Father' Mean?" 68–69.

The second aspect of the Son's mission in accomplishing redemption is *attaining* righteousness for the elect. Adam's potential to earn new creation life in his covenant with God crucially frames the covenant of redemption. He had the charge as humanity's first covenantal representative to fulfill the law and earn the right to eat from the tree of life. If he had passed his probation with the tree of knowledge of good and evil and had fulfilled the law, then he would have obtained citizenship in the new creation and indestructible life in richest communion with God for himself and for all those whom he represented. The Son accomplished salvation by accepting the Father's will, further specified as completing the Adamic task of meriting incorruptible and everlasting life for the elect whom the Father assigned to him in the covenant of redemption. In these respects, although the covenant of redemption secures grace for us, it was a covenant of works for the Son, as he assumed Adam's failed task to fulfill the law and the burden to pay the debt of penalty that Adam accrued for us all by his sin, which is death.[33] John Colquhoun argues that the covenant of redemption "was, indeed, in the strictest sense, a covenant of works, to Christ the second Adam" although "it is a covenant of the freest, the most unmerited grace, to sinners." This is because Christ as our representative "was himself the sole performer of the conditions of the covenant."[34] The following analysis presents the biblical evidence that Christ's part in the covenant of redemption in accepting the Father's will included attaining righteousness for the elect and so fulfilling the terms of the original covenant of works.[35]

The clearest passage outlining how Christ attained righteousness in his mission as our mediator is Romans 5:12–21. Many Reformed authors have thoroughly explored this passage already, so this discussion focuses merely on how it shows that Christ attained righteousness in a parallel fashion to how Adam should have.[36] Paul writes in Romans 5:

---

33. Louis Berkhof, *Systematic Theology*, comb. ed. (Grand Rapids: Eerdmans, 1996), 268; *VRD*, 2:86.

34. *CG*, 36.

35. *CRS*, 1:257.

36. E.g., *DIALIC*, 208–16; Murray, *Imputation of Adam's Sin*; Hodge, *Romans* 142–91.

> For if, because of one man's trespass, death reigned through that one man, much more will those who receive the abundance of grace and the free gift of righteousness reign in life through the one man Jesus Christ. Therefore, as one trespass led to condemnation for all men, so one act of righteousness leads to justification unto life for all men. For as by the one man's disobedience the many were made sinners, so by the one man's obedience the many will be made righteous. (Rom 5:17–19; my translation)

Paul contrasts the first and the last Adam's work by highlighting how Adam trespassed God's law, condemning all, but Christ attained full righteousness, resulting in justification unto life for everyone trusting in him. Christ's real obedience fulfilled all righteousness so that believers are pronounced righteous because of his righteousness. The parallel between the first and last Adams stands in their mission to achieve covenantal righteousness and reward for those whom they represented, differing because the first Adam fails but the last Adam is victorious for us.[37]

Christ also received a reward for attaining that righteousness. Although he acquired for us the rewards offered in the covenant of works, his personal reward was not identical to that offered to Adam—distinguishing the covenant of redemption from the covenant of grace, which gives Adam's potential reward to *us* through our mediator. The covenant of redemption established the reward that the Son would merit, thereby distinguishing it from Adam's potential reward. Just as God set the reward for Adam if he fulfilled the terms of the covenant, the Father set the Son's reward by the covenant's terms.[38] In one sense, it could not be otherwise. The Son already possessed indestructible, glorious life as God so had no need for it for himself as a reward. On the other hand, the Son wants a people for himself among whom he is exalted and glorified, so sensibly he would merit that exaltation and a people for himself (Ps 2:8).[39] The parallel between Christ and Adam is that both stood before God in a covenant of works with the prospect of earning universal and everlasting reward for themselves and those whom they represented.

---

37. *EC*, 2.10.15.

38. *CRS*, 1:260–61.

39. *CMT*, 76; Owen, "Exercitation XXVII," 1:456–60; *CG*, 185–86.

The passage most clearly connecting Christ's merit to his reward of exaltation and a redeemed people is Philippians 2:5–11. Several New Testament scholars note that this passage presents Christ as the second Adam, although it is lacking that explicit terminology, forging a clear link between the Son rendering obedience and obtaining his reward—exactly the structure of Adam's covenant of works.[40]

> Have this mind among yourselves, which is yours in Christ Jesus, who, despite existing in the form of God, considered his equality with God not something to be clutched but emptied himself by taking the form of a servant by coming in humanity's likeness. And so being found in human form, he humbled himself by becoming obedient culminating in death, namely, death on a cross. Therefore also [because of his obedience], God has highly exalted him and bestowed on him the name that is above every name, with the result that at the name of Jesus every knee should bow, in heaven and on earth and under the earth, and every tongue confess that Jesus Christ is Lord, to the glory of God the Father. (my translation)

Interestingly, Paul implements this intensely doctrinal section about the Son's incarnate mission and reward within a moral exhortation for believers to have the mind of Christ, whereby we would count others more significant than ourselves (Phil 2:3–4).[41] We can have this others-centered mindset because the Son humbled himself from his heavenly glory to achieve good for others. This passage provides a heavenly perspective on the incarnation by beginning with the Son having "the form of God," or his divine nature.[42] Still, Christ did not hold onto this equality with God but instead assumed "the form of a servant" by being born in human likeness.[43] Strikingly, the servant's form essentially equates with human nature,

40. N. T. Wright, *The Climax of the Covenant: Christ and the Law in Pauline Theology* (Minneapolis: Fortress Press, 1993), 86–97; Fee, *Pauline Christology*, 375–76.

41. Robert B. Strimple, "Philippians 2:5–11 in Recent Studies: Some Exegetical Conclusions," *WTJ* 41 no. 2 (Spring 1979): 252–56; Clark, "Do This and Live," 248–49.

42. Owen, "Exercitation XXVIII," 1:471–72; Butner, *Trinitarian Dogmatics*, 157–59; Ralph P. Martin, *An Early Christian Confession: Philippians 2:5–11 in Recent Interpretations* (London: The Tyndale Press, 1960), 16–18.

43. Ralph P. Martin, *Carmen Christi: Philippians ii.5–11 in Recent Interpretation and in the Setting of Early Christian Worship* (Cambridge: Cambridge University Press, 1967), 148–53, 174–77; Fee,

showing that the debt of full obedience properly belongs to our humanity (Luke 17:10).[44] In this case, true God became a true man, distinguishing Christ's identity as God's Son in terms of his existence as God, from his mission on earth as he assumed human nature.[45] More precisely, the Son has equality with God according to his procession within the Trinity's *ad intra* operations but is subordinate to the Father specifically according to his incarnate mission.[46]

In this respect, although it highlights the contrast between the Son's divine identity and his incarnate mission, Philippians 2:5–11 also contrasts Christ's work with Adam's.[47] Unlike the first Adam, who succumbed to the serpent's temptation that eating the fruit would mean "you will be like God" (Gen 3:5), Christ did not grasp even his natural and rightful equality with God but became obedient. In direct contrast with Adam's failure in trying to become like God and thus becoming a sinner, Christ assumed the servant's mantle thus becoming obedient.[48] Adam was not humble, as Paul exhorted the Philippians to be by using the mind of Christ to count others more significant than themselves, but haughty in thinking he could be like God. On the other hand, Christ exemplifies humility in prioritizing others precisely *by becoming obedient* in the incarnation.[49] God's eternally preexistent Son emptied himself by assuming a full human nature, so taking on Adam's mantle to serve God in perfect obedience.[50]

Pauline Christology, 376–90.

44. Fee, *Pauline Christology*, 387–89; Martin, *Carmen Christi*, 194–96, 226–28.

45. Wellum, *Person of Christ*, 78–80; Barrett, *Simply Trinity*, 246–48.

46. Owen, "Exercitation XXVIII," 1:465–66.

47. Many scholars recognize this second-Adam theme in Philippians 2, although not all properly relate it to traditional Christology. Christ's divine preexistence and the Adamic tone of his incarnate mission should not be set against each other as valid doctrines in this text, especially as the covenant of redemption unites these doctrines; see Ridderbos, *Paul*, 68–78; Oscar Cullmann, *The Christology of the New Testament*, rev. ed., trans. Shirley C. Guthrie and Charles A. M. Hall (Philadelphia: Westminster Press, 1963), 174–81; Martin, *Carmen Christi*, 119–20, 128–45, 161–64; James D. G. Dunn, *Christology in the Making* (Philadelphia: Westminster Press, 1980), 114–19; Morna D. Hooker, *From Adam to Christ* (Cambridge: Cambridge University Press, 1990), 88–102; Christopher M. Tuckett, *Christology and the New Testament: Jesus and His Earliest Followers* (Louisville: Westminster John Knox, 2001), 54–56; Lincoln D. Hurst, "Christ, Adam, and Preexistence Revisited," in *Where Christology Began: Essays on Philippians 2*, ed. Ralph P. Martin and Brian J. Dodd (Louisville: Westminster John Knox, 1998), 84–95.

48. Ridderbos, *Paul*, 74–75; Martin, *Early Christian Confession*, 22; Cullman, *Christology of the New Testament*, 177–78; Tuckett, *Christology and the New Testament*, 55.

49. Martin, *Early Christian Confession*, 30–31.

50. Cullmann, *Christology of the New Testament*, 188–92.

Christ fulfilled the covenant of works for the elect by humbling himself unto full obedience, succeeding where Adam failed.

The extent of Christ's obedience and its reward pivotally informs the covenant of redemption. After describing Christ's obedience, Paul infers ("therefore also") that it resulted in God highly exalting Christ and giving him the name above all names.[51] Whereas the Son did not grasp his equality with God but assumed a servant's form, in exchange the Father rewarded his obedience by highly exalting him—restoring and supplementing all the Son's glory that he set aside in his humiliation.[52] Christ merited his exaltation to be known again by the divine name itself, even though he first gave up his exalted status in his incarnation (Acts 2:36).[53] In regard to this exaltation, Paul quotes Isaiah 45:23, wherein God says,

> By myself I have sworn;
> from my mouth has gone out in righteousness
> a word that shall not return:
> "To me every knee shall bow,
> every tongue shall swear allegiance."

Notably, *God* swore that all people will bow *to him* and swear allegiance *to him*, meaning that Paul's citation underscores Christ's deity in that he obtains the ultimate worship that can go only to God.[54] This exaltation with the divine name and glory was part of Christ's reward for his obedience—certainly a difference from the reward Adam might have earned in the covenant of works. Moreover, Isaiah 45:25 further foretold that "in the LORD all the offspring of Israel shall be justified and shall glory." Accounting for the context of Paul's citation of Isaiah's prophecy reveals that God had decreed his own exaltation and the rescue of his people and

---

51. "Therefore also" translates διό καὶ. Although the word translated "bestowed" (ἐχαρίσατο) can refer to a free gift, it also commonly refers to the honors granted to public officials *for their good works*, which better fits the context here; see Walter Bauer, Frederick William Danker, W. F. Arndt, and F. W. Gingrich, eds., *A Greek English Lexicon of the New Testament and other Early Christian Literature*, 3rd ed. (Chicago: University of Chicago Press, 2001), 1078.

52. *CF*, 521–22; *EC*, 2.3.30–31; *TI*, 3.22.3; Daniel J. Treier, "Incarnation," in *CD*, 231–32; Matthew W. Bates, *The Hermeneutics of Apostolic Proclamation: The Center of Paul's Method of Scriptural Interpretation* (Waco, TX: Baylor University Press, 2012), 92.

53. *CG*, 72–78; *EC*, 2.3.32–34; Vos, "Alleged Legalism," 397–99; VanDrunen and Clark, "Covenant before the Covenants," 183–87; Fee, *Pauline Christology*, 396–98.

54. Treier, "Incarnation," 221–24; Fee, *Pauline Christology*, 398–401; Bates, *Hermeneutics*, 287–89.

bound these outcomes together (John 17:10). Christ obtained both these rewards by his perfect obedience as he rose from the grave in triumph, securing justification and full salvation for all those whom the Father had given to him, specifically acting, as *the servant*, foretold by Isaiah, who was crushed and "*poured out* [even emptied] his soul to death" to bear the sins of many (Isa 52:13; John 6:37).[55]

Importantly, Christ's death was part of this obedience whereby he earned his exaltation and earned his justified people. Commenting on Philippians 2:9, Thomas Aquinas wrote, "But he was glorified, not merely in Himself, but likewise in His faithful ones, as He says Himself (John 17:10). Therefore it appears that He merited the salvation of the faithful."[56] Although Adam was obligated to render perfect righteousness to God as the principal debt in the covenant of works, he also accrued the penalty debt by which he needed to die for his sin. Because Adam's sin was imputed to all people, we are all liable to death. Regarding Christ's death, he became a curse for us (Gal 3:13). It was, however, "the will of the LORD to crush him," indicating how the Father laid our curse upon Christ (Isa 53:10). The Father imputed our sins to the Son as our *expromissor* to bear their penalty (2 Cor 5:21), giving the cup of cursing to him to drink for us (Matt 26:39; Mark 14:36).[57] Still, the Son was not inactive in bearing that curse but obedient "unto death, even death on a cross." As Jesus explains in John 10:18: "No one takes [my life] from me, but I lay it down of my own accord. I have authority to lay it down, and I have authority to take it up again. This charge I have received from my Father." Jesus was fulfilling his missional obedience as he willingly laid down his life in exchange for the elect. He decided—since he had the authority to do so—to endure our suffering. According to the covenant of redemption, he accepted the Father's will that he would fulfill the terms of the covenant of works both in terms of its initial requirement of fulfilling the law (active obedience) and its penalty of death for breaking the law (passive obedience).

The Adam-Christ contrast then becomes startling in light of Philippians 2:8, namely, as Adam's *disobedience* led to death but Christ's *obedience* also

55. Baylor, "He Humbled Himself," 169–70; Strimple, "Philippians 2:5–11," 265–68; Martin, *Carmen Christi*, 182–90; Martin, *Early Christian Confession*, 26–27.

56. Thomas, *Summa Theologica*, 3.48.1.

57. *DIALIC*, 185–91.

led to death.[58] The same outcome occurred for both, despite opposing records concerning obedience, because Christ died in our place, enduring our curse, so to fulfill not only the original terms of the covenant of works for us but also its incurred penalty (2 Cor 5:21; Gal 3:10–14; Gal 4:4–5). As James Ussher explains, the parts of Christ's obedience and satisfaction are, first, "his sufferings, and his righteousness (Phil 2:5–8; 1 Pet 2:24) for it was requisite that he should first pay all our debt, and satisfy God's justice (Isa 53:5–6; Job 33:24) by a price of infinite value (1 Tim 2:6)." This two-fold understanding of Christ's obedience and satisfaction highlights how "by his suffering he was to merit unto us the forgiveness of our sins, and by his fulfilling the law he was to merit unto us righteousness, both which are necessarily required for our Justification."[59] The Father assigned Christ not only to live the perfect life, but also to die an obedient death, so that everything pertaining to the elect's everlasting salvation would be fulfilled.

This section explored Christ's office in the covenant of redemption in which he accomplished salvation for those whom the Father had given to him by accepting the Father's will and attaining righteousness for them. Christ not only attained righteousness by fulfilling the law but also by removing the penalty for our sin through dying in our place. Christ came to earth so that he could obey everything the Father commanded him to do, so securing citizenship in the new creation for the elect (Phil 3:20–21).

THE SPIRIT APPLIES REDEMPTION

This section completes the Trinitarian shape of the covenant of redemption by explaining the Spirit's office in fulfilling our salvation. Specifically, the Spirit *applies* redemption to us by *accompanying* Christ during his earthly ministry and *administering* Christ's benefits to the elect. Salvation comes to full fruition for the elect through the Spirit's work of application.[60]

The Spirit directly relates to the Son's mission in several ways, all expressing how he accompanies the Son. The Spirit's work in *accompanying*

---

58. Casper Olevianus, *In Epistolas Pauli Apostoli ad Philippenses, Colossense, notae* (Geneva: Eustathius Vignon, 1580), 19–20.

59. Ussher, *Body*, 171.

60. Scott R. Swain, "The Gospel in the Reformed Tradition," in *God's Two Words: Law and Gospel in the Lutheran and Reformed Traditions*, ed. Jonathan A. Linebaugh (Grand Rapids: Eerdmans, 2018), 98–100.

the Son in his mission is a necessary part of the Spirit's own mission in the application of redemption. By accompanying the Son in accomplishing redemption, the Spirit is bound into that work so that he can extend it to the elect for whom Christ procured it. The Spirit accompanied the Son to align his mission directly with the Son's so that, in application, he is extending the victorious results of the Son's mission.[61] Indeed, the Spirit takes what belongs to Christ and declares it to us (John 16:14).

The Spirit's mission in accompanying the Son is like time spent packing a plane full of care packages to distribute to people living in troubled lands. That time spent packing the plane gathers what is needed for the plane's proper mission, so it is *essential* preparation for the mission itself if the plane is to have the resources to distribute. The Spirit's mission of accompaniment resembles time packing the plane in that he has gathered all the benefits that the Son procured during that time of accompaniment and can then distribute them from Christ to the elect. From one perspective, then, the application of redemption is *Christ* applying the redemption he accomplished through the Spirit because he is the one who "loaded" those benefits into the Spirit and then "unloads" them through the Spirit too.[62] Still, the work of application properly terminates on the person of the Spirit.[63]

The Spirit's mission of accompaniment includes yet another subdistinction of two A's: *anointing* and *awarding*.[64] In regard to *anointing*, the Son is called the Christ because "Christ" is the Greek equivalent of the Hebrew word "Messiah," both meaning "anointed" (Ps 2:2). Throughout the Son's earthly ministry, the Spirit accompanies him by conceiving him in human nature in Mary's womb (Luke 1:26–35) and by resting upon him as the anointed Messiah (Matt 3:13–17; Isa 42:1; Luke 4:18; Isa 61:1; Acts 10:38).[65] The Spirit prepares a human nature for the Son to assume,

---

61. Letham, *Systematic Theology*, 88; see 86–91 for links between the Spirit and Son's earthly missions.

62. *BRD*, 4:524; Gaffin, "Work of Christ Applied," 269–70.

63. *BRD*, 4:569–73.

64. Owen, "Exercitation XXVIII," 1:472–73.

65. Vos, "Eschatological Aspect," 96; Horton, *Justification*, 2:269–73; Michael Horton, *Rediscovering the Holy Spirit: God's Perfecting Presence in Creation, Redemption, and Everyday Life* (Grand Rapids: Zondervan, 2017), 88–95; Wellum, *Person of Christ*, 52–53.

so to obey in our place (Ps 40:6–8; Heb 10:5–7; Luke 1:35).[66] Isaiah 42:1 includes the Father's promise to the Son in the covenant of redemption to use the Spirit to mark him as the chosen servant:

> Behold my servant, whom I uphold,
> my chosen, in whom my soul delights;
> I have put my Spirit upon him;
> he will bring forth justice to the nations.

Notably, the Father's promise comes within the context of giving the Son "as a covenant for the people," making the Spirit's mission, as well as the Son's, overtly covenantal (Isa 42:6).[67] The Spirit, then, had a covenantal task to accompany the Son by anointing him.[68]

The Spirit anoints the Son, so that the Spirit would be able to extend the benefits that the Son acquires to the elect—gesturing toward his mission of *administering*. This extension becomes clear in the overlap of the Spirit's presence with the Son and the Spirit's presence with the elect. Isaiah 11:1–2 records how the Spirit will rest upon the *shoot* from the stump of Jesse—indeed, the Branch of Zechariah 6:13:

> There shall come forth a shoot from the stump of Jesse,
> and a branch from his roots shall bear fruit.
> And the Spirit of the LORD shall rest upon him,
> the Spirit of wisdom and understanding,
> the Spirit of counsel and might,
> the Spirit of knowledge and the fear of the LORD.

Even though this promise of the Spirit's resting presence directly refers to the Messiah, 1 Peter 4:14 extends it to the church: "You are blessed, because the Spirit of glory and of God rests upon you." The Spirit's anointing of the Son as an abiding presence during the Son's mission is the reason that the Spirit abides with the church now. The Spirit then creates the church as the blessed place where "brothers dwell in unity" (Ps 133:1).

66. Horton, *Rediscovering*, 95–99.

67. Vidu, *Same God*, 31–33; *VRD*, 2:86, 95.

68. Irenaeus, *Demonstration*, §47.

The Spirit's mission to accompany the Son by anointing him during his mission is necessary for the Spirit to be able to pour out blessings from Christ to those whom the Father gave to Christ in the covenant of redemption. Upon the Son's ascension, the obvious completion of his mission to accomplish salvation, he distributes the Spirit, who abided with him, to abide now with the elect.[69] In John 16:12–15, part of the upper-room discourse, Jesus explains how the Spirit's ongoing ministry will extend from his own upon his ascension:

> I still have many things to say to you, but you cannot bear them now. When the Spirit of truth comes, he will guide you into all the truth, for he will not speak on his own authority, but whatever he hears he will speak, and he will declare to you the things that are to come. He will glorify me, for he will take what is mine and declare it to you. All that the Father has is mine; therefore I said that he will take what is mine and declare it to you.

In other words, the Spirit's mission concerning us extends from his mission concerning the Son. The Spirit comes to teach about matters that Christ himself did not fully explain during his time on earth.[70] Just as the Spirit rested on Christ at his baptism, so the Spirit was poured out to rest upon the church at Pentecost.[71] Just as the Spirit led Christ—God's natural and preeminent Son—into the wilderness to face his temptation (Matt 4:1), so then Christ helps us in our temptation (Heb 2:17–18), helping us as God's adopted children "led by the Spirit of God" (Gal 5:17–18; Rom 8:1–17). Even as the Spirit anoints *Christ*, the Heidelberg Catechism affirms that we are called *Christians* because each believer is a "partaker of his anointing" (HC 32).[72] The blessings that Christ obtains from the Spirit as the head are extended from Christ to his body, the church.[73] As Vos writes, "Consequently, it is not subject to any doubt that the bond between Christ and the members of His body is the Holy Spirit. … When Christ became the glorified Head, He took this gift and imparted it to all

69. *CF*, 533–35.

70. *CF*, 556–60.

71. Horton, *Rediscovering*, 99–100.

72. *COC*, 3:318.

73. Horton, *Rediscovering*, 146–47.

who are members of His body."[74] In *accompanying* the Son by *anointing* him, the Spirit identifies with the Son's mission of accomplishing redemption so that he might apply that redemption to the elect.[75]

The Spirit also accompanies the Son by *awarding* him in the culmination of his reward in the covenant of redemption. The Son did already have the Spirit by nature as God's eternal Son, but the Father awards the Spirit to the Son in a new manner of possession unto glorified life at his resurrection. As Acts 2:32–33 describes: "This Jesus God *raised up*, and of that we all are witnesses. Being therefore exalted at the right hand of God, and having received from the Father *the promise of the Holy Spirit*, he has poured out this that you yourselves are seeing and hearing." Since, as Acts 2:33 announces, Christ was "exalted at the right hand of God"—Philippians 2:9 likewise recounts Christ's exaltation as part of the covenant of redemption—he also received the Spirit as his promised reward. Glorification and the Spirit are then inseparably linked within the ultimate reward offered in God's covenants. Adam's potential reward in the covenant of works offered a spiritual body as a spiritual person, obviously somehow related to a new endowment of the Spirit's presence (1 Cor 15:42–45). The Spirit, as the Spirit of life (Rom 8:2), rewarded Christ with that same spiritual existence offered to Adam, namely, bodily life in glorified existence granted by the Spirit.[76] Although 1 Corinthians 15:45 respects Christ advancing from that natural condition which Adam had by creation to the spiritual condition, rather than specifically identifying Christ with the person of the Spirit, the outcome is still almost the same as that argued by those who understand a direct reference to the Spirit.[77]

---

74. *VRD*, 4:26.

75. Horton, *Rediscovering*, 131–37.

76. *EC*, 3.1.7; Vos, "Eschatological Aspect," 112–14; Horton, *Rediscovering*, 177–84; *BRD*, 3:577. The connection of the Spirit's mission to Christ's Adamic task helps resolve Vidu's reservations about the reward model, explaining why Christ could send the Spirit only after his ascension. As Vidu argued, there was a shift from Christ's humiliation to exaltation in the resurrection and ascension, which Vidu understood as the aspect of redemptive history necessary to unlock the Spirit's mission. Christ's role as second Adam, which Vidu highlights as part of the Son's journey to the fully transfigured state, includes that place for merit and reward that Vidu downplays. The Spirit as the Son's reward is not an ontological feature but an aspect of Christ's very Adamic task, which Vidu notes, whereby he earned that glorified state so to distribute the Spirit; see Vidu, *Same God*, 244, 247–78.

77. Gaffin, *By Faith, Not by Sight*, 44–45; Richard B. Gaffin Jr., "'Life-Giving Spirit': Probing the Center of Paul's Pneumatology," *JETS* 41 (1998): 473–89; Guy Prentiss Waters, "1–2 Corinthians," 212–14; Waters, "Covenant of Works in the New Testament," 84–84; Benjamin L. Gladd, "The Last

Since the Spirit brings about Christ's spiritual—bodily glorified—existence, the Spirit obviously connects directly to the Son's reward. Just as Adam's justification would have been spiritual—from the Spirit—so, too, Christ was "justified in the Spirit" by his resurrection (1 Tim 3:16 KJV; Rom 8:10–11), which grants to Christ a new possession of spiritual life—according to his mediatorial office—and so allows him in his exalted state to dispense the Spirit upon his people.[78]

The Spirit then serves a legal or judicial role in awarding Christ with the Father's pronouncement of righteousness.[79] The Spirit's mission in the covenant of redemption becomes directly related to Christ in the application of the accomplished redemption to the elect because Christ's earned reward of the glorified state so deeply links to the Spirit.[80] As Paul writes in Ephesians 1:13–14: "In him you also, when you heard the word of truth, the gospel of your salvation, and believed in him, were sealed with the promised Holy Spirit, who is the guarantee of our inheritance until we acquire possession of it, to the praise of his glory." In the covenant of redemption, the Spirit was the Son's reward, so that his spiritual and glorified existence is now indestructible and everlasting. The Spirit descended upon the Son at his baptism to anoint him for his incarnate mission, but the Son's reception of the Spirit in this manner did not grant full possession of the glorified, spiritual state that he has now after his resurrection. As the reward is so tied to this glorified condition, the Spirit as "the Spirit of Christ" can now be dispensed from the Son to the elect for whom he earned salvation as the pledge, the down payment guaranteeing and ensuring their full and final salvation (Rom 8:9).[81] So, as the Spirit

Adam as the 'Life-Giving Spirit' Revisited: A Possible Old Testament Background of One of Paul's Most Perplexing Phrases," *WTJ* 71 no. 2 (Fall 2009): 297–309.

78. Vos, "Eschatological Aspect," 108–10; Matthew Barrett, "Raised for Our Justification: The Christological, Covenantal, Forensic, and Eschatological Contours of an Ambiguous Relationship," in *Doctrine on Which the Church Stands or Falls*, 399–403; George W. Knight III, *The Pastoral Epistles* (Grand Rapids: Eerdmans, 2013), 184–85; *CG*, 183–84; *DIALIC*, 261–63; *VRD*, 2:86–87, 95, 96; 4:26; Gaffin, "Work of Christ Applied," 275; Gladd, "Last Adam as the 'Life-Giving Spirit' Revisited," 307, 308.

79. *EC*, 3.8.4; Horton, *Rediscovering*, 105–19.

80. Gaffin, *Resurrection and Redemption*, 119–22; *VRD*, 2:95; Gaffin, "Work of Christ Applied," 276–77; Gaffin, "Life-Giving Spirit," 578–79, 581–89. I am not sure that I interpret 1 Corinthians 15:45 *exactly* like Gaffin but do believe they are related understandings. Certainly, my argument is more a nuance to his view rather than an overturning.

81. *VRD*, 2:93; *BRD*, 3:499; Vidu, *Same God*, 33–35, 302–17.

accompanied Christ by anointing and awarding him, he was involved in the procurement of salvation (*historia salutis*).

The Spirit's part in Christ's exaltation makes other ways of explaining his relation to the glorified Christ besides that of a merited reward difficult to sustain. We already saw how Thomas Aquinas argues from Philippians 2:9 that Christ merited his glorification.[82] Paul connects this exaltation directly to Christ's resurrection and the Spirit's part in it, arguing that Christ "was declared to be the Son of God in power *according to the Spirit of holiness by his resurrection* from the dead" (Rom 1:4). The promised Holy Spirit then specially comes upon the Son to reward him with glorification at his resurrection because Christ has merited that exaltation.

The Spirit's mission to reward the Son with glorification is consistent with how the Son and Spirit relate according to their eternal processions as well. Augustine asks "whether the Holy Spirit was a gift also before he was given," arguing that just as the Son was absolutely the Son in eternity even though he was born into time at the incarnation, so, because the Spirit eternally proceeds, he is eternally the gift that was then given to Christ during the incarnation.[83] Augustine says that it should not trouble us that the Holy Spirit is said to be given in time "because the Spirit is eternally a gift but temporally given."[84] Aquinas agrees, writing, "To be the gift of the Father and the Son is proper to the Holy Ghost."[85] Because the Spirit is *eternally* gift, he can be given according to his mission to the Son in multiple ways, meaning his mission, although dependent upon the Son's logically, need not be entirely restricted to follow it chronologically as if there is no overlap.[86] Indeed, the Spirit proceeds from the Father as he anoints the Son and proceeds from the Son as his award, demonstrating the Spirit's double procession from Father and Son in his double mission to and from the Son.[87] Because the Spirit is eternally the gift for the Son because of his procession, he can have the mission to be given to the Son to anoint him even prior to the Son finishing his mission to award him

82. Aquinas, *Summa Theologica*, 3.48.1.

83. Augustine, *De Trinitate*, 5.15.16; in *PL*, 42:921–22.

84. Augustine, *De Trinitate*, 5.16.17 in *PL*, 42:922.

85. Aquinas, *Summa Theologica*, 3.3.8; 1.38.1–2.

86. Cf. Vidu, *Divine Missions*, 27–48.

87. Letham, *Systematic Theology*, 133–44.

on account of his completed work.[88] In this way, the Spirit's mission, just like the Father's and Son's, corresponds to and extends his procession.[89]

The Spirit extends his involvement in that accomplishment of salvation (*historia salutis*) in properly applying salvation by *administering* Christ and his benefits to the elect (*ordo salutis*). This work follows, as distributing goods to those in need follows from loading the plane, from the Spirit's role in rewarding Christ. Remember, Acts 2:33 states that because Christ was exalted and rewarded with the Spirit "he has poured out this that you yourselves are seeing and hearing"—namely, after Christ ascended, he gives salvation to his people by distributing the gospel to them through the Spirit's work. According to the Heidelberg Catechism, that the Spirit "is also given unto me, makes me *by a true faith partaker of Christ and all his benefits*, comforts me, and shall abide with me forever" (HC 53).[90] Two facets of the Spirit's contribution to the fulfillment of salvation are based in his office in the covenant of redemption. The Spirit, first, grants true faith to the elect through effectual calling and, second, makes believers partake of Christ and his benefits. Those facets go tightly together because by faith we are united to Christ and receive his benefits.

So, the first way that the Spirit administers salvation is through *effectual calling*. In effectual calling, the Spirit brings sinners to believe the gospel, so by faith unites us to Christ as our Savior. The Westminster Confession explains effectual calling, also linking it to the Spirit's work: "All those whom God has predestinated unto life, and those only, he is pleased, in his appointed and accepted time, effectually to call, *by his Word and Spirit*, out of that state of sin and death in which they are by nature, to grace and salvation by Jesus Christ (WCF 10.1).[91] Although the whole work of salvation must be accorded to the whole Trinity, the Spirit precisely holds the *appropriation* of the work of calling us to faith. Indeed, John Calvin

88. Harrison Perkins, "Reconciling the Divine Processions-Missions Relationship with Confessional Reformed Theology: An Engagement with Adonis Vidu's *The Divine Missions: An Introduction* (Part 4)," *The Heidelblog*, July 14, 2022, https://heidelblog.net/2022/07/reconciling-the-divine-processions-missions-relationship-with-confessional-reformed-theology-an-engagement-with-adonis-vidus-the-divine-missions-an-introduction-part-4/.

89. Vidu, *Divine Missions*, 27, et passim.

90. *COC*, 3:324 (emphasis added).

91. *COC*, 3:624 (emphasis added).

says that faith is the Spirit's "principal work."[92] This precision is necessary because whereas *the Father* draws us to the Son whom he sent (John 6:44), he does so *by the Spirit*, so preserving his inseparable operations. As we read in Titus 3:4–7, "But when the goodness and loving kindness of God our Savior appeared, he saved us, not because of works done by us in righteousness, but according to his own mercy, *by the washing of regeneration and renewal of the Holy Spirit*, whom he poured out on us richly through Jesus Christ our Savior, so that being justified by his grace we might become heirs according to the hope of eternal life." Even though the Father is the one who draws us to Christ in effectual calling, he issues and enacts this effectual calling through the Spirit's renewing work.[93] The Father pours out the Spirit on us "through Jesus Christ" precisely because the Spirit is now "the Spirit of Christ," having been tied to the Son's mission by accompanying him in it (Rom 8:9; 1 Cor 15:45).

The Spirit performs his mission, not spotlighting himself, but to point us to and make us partake of Christ. As the ascended Christ pours out the Spirit, the Spirit comes to glorify Christ (John 16:13–14). Whereas once we were dead in our sins and transgressions (Eph 2:1–3), so blind in our unbelief that we could never even bring ourselves to believe in Christ for salvation (2 Cor 4:4), the Spirit sovereignly shines gospel light into our hearts and effectively summons us to faith by using the proclamation of the gospel in the preaching of the Word (2 Cor 4:5–6; Rom 10:14–17). So, the Westminster Larger Catechism says, "The Union which the Elect have with Christ is the work of God's grace, whereby they are spiritually and mystically, yet really and inseparably, joined to Christ as their head and husband; which is done in their effectual Calling" (WLC 66).[94] In this way, the Spirit unites us to Christ so that Christ's benefits come to us.

That Spirit-wrought faith then brings us to communion in grace with Christ, the source of our life-giving benefits. So, the Westminster Larger Catechism says, "The Communion in grace, which the members of the Invisible Church have with Christ, *is*, their partaking of the virtue of his Mediation, in their Justification, Adoption, Sanctification, and whatever

---

92. Calvin, *Institutes*, 3.1.4.

93. *WWS*, 224–25; *CF*, 560–86.

94. *LC*, 78.

else in this life manifests their Union with him" (WLC 69).[95] As Titus 3:7 indicates, the Spirit works faith in us "so that being justified by his grace we might become heirs according to the hope of eternal life." Because Jesus by his perfect obedience and curse-bearing death earned our justification (Rom 4:24–25), and because the Spirit justified Christ by raising him from the dead based on his own perfect merits (1 Tim 3:16), the Spirit also extends Christ's own justification to us by faith. Just as Christ has been fully justified, so too as the Father imputes his record to us, we are *fully and completely* justified, now and forever, as we take hold of Christ by faith. As Paul writes in Romans 5:9, "Since, therefore, we have now been justified by his blood, much more shall we be saved by him from the wrath of God." On the premise of being justified, we are even more so guaranteed full salvation for the life to come. The two are bound together, justification ensuring the latter.[96] Since the Spirit takes up permanent residence in us upon our release from the curse of the law in justification (Gal 4:4–6), he is the guarantee of everlasting salvation (Eph 1:13–14). So, the Heidelberg Catechism affirms that "by his Holy Spirit, [God] also assures me of eternal life, and makes me heartily willing and ready henceforth to live unto him" (HC 1).[97] The Spirit administers redemption to us and so remains with us as the profound mark of believers in growing us in godliness as we live in the tension between being fully justified but not yet glorified (Rom 8:29–30).

CONCLUSION

Too often, we let ourselves imagine that God is far off and disconnected from his people's lives. Truly, God is outside time and acts for his own glory, but sometimes we disconnect those truths from other biblical teachings so that we develop an almost deistic mindset wherein God set things in motion and lets them run on their own. We sometimes believe—even if implicitly and accidentally—that lie that God works that way in our own lives as well, as if he has a general plan for our life but is not personally working in the events we experience to work them for our good.

95. *LC*, 78 (emphasis added).

96. Concerning how Romans 5:9 contributes to the proper interpretation of Romans 2:13 and the connection to justification, see the appendix.

97. *COC*, 3:308.

The missions of the Father, Son, and Spirit show how the Triune God has involved himself in history for his people's sake. The true God is immutable and founded his people's salvation on an eternal decree to bring about our redemption. Still, this God stepped into his creation and involved himself in the affairs of time to bring about salvation for his people. God is essentially outside time and is fundamentally distinct from creation. On the other hand, God shows, especially in the Son's incarnation, how he can overcome the supernatural gap between Creator and creation and involve himself in our affairs.

The pastoral application of this chapter's material is to note how God's involvement in creation for his people's benefit is not limited to the Son's incarnation. This involvement is particularly clear in the Spirit's ongoing presence for the further execution of the covenant of redemption. Despite being fully distinct from it, God remains active in the world to be good to his people. The Son's and Spirit's missions show how God participates in history to bring about wonderful things for those who belong to him.

Moreover, the covenant of redemption establishes the unconditional gracious foundations of our reception of redemption. The Triune God's work in the covenant of redemption grounds every aspect of the procurement and distribution of salvation. The decisive distinction between the covenant of redemption, as *God's* work to accomplish and apply salvation, and the covenant of grace, as God's way of distributing his covenantal blessings in history, pointedly focuses the foundations of our communion with God because God's own work in Christ precludes any way for us to add to his work. All the conditions for us to have full communion with God in everlasting life were laid upon Christ to fulfill for us, leaving nothing for the elect to accomplish. All the same, Christ earned the Spirit for his people and distributes him to us, so equipping us to live the Christian life powered by divine blessing. Thus, God, by virtue of the covenant of redemption, excluded both legalism and antinomianism from how he would grant everlasting life to us.[98]

---

98. Thanks to Ryan McGraw for his input on this application.

VII

The Last Adam and His People

For even the Son of Man came not to be served but to serve,
and to give his life as a ransom for many.
—*Mark 10:45*

Covenant theology clarifies how all Scripture finds its "yes" and "amen" in Christ as it highlights how Christ (*incarnandus*) was foreshadowed and (*incarnatus*) has completed his task for our salvation (2 Cor 1:20; Luke 24:44–47). The covenant of redemption as God's *eternal* plan ensured before the world began that Christ's work guarantees our salvation.

After addressing an historical question about the covenant of redemption in the Reformed confessions, this chapter thickens our description of the covenant of redemption by looking at the theme of Christ as the second Adam from the perspective of biblical theology and by thinking about the implications of Christ's appointment to represent specifically those whom the Father gave to him. The chapter closes with some reflections about how the covenant of redemption provides some points to help us interpret the whole Bible well.

CONFESSIONAL AND HISTORICAL CONSIDERATIONS

Readers possibly noticed that the chapters concerning the covenant of works quote Reformed confessions far more than those about the covenant of redemption. Admittedly, most Reformed confessions outline the covenant of redemption less explicitly than the covenants of works and grace. Still, that does not mean that this doctrine is not part of the confessional tradition. This covenant is less overt, even in the Westminster Standards, partly because of timing. David Dickson's speech at the Scottish General Assembly in 1638 was the first occurrence of the term "covenant of redemption."[1] The Westminster Assembly began its work in 1642, shortly after the term first appeared.

The Reformed confessions implicitly teach the covenant of redemption, plainly stating the Father, Son, and Spirit's roles in salvation, an integral aspect of the covenant of redemption. The Heidelberg Catechism says that Christ is called anointed "because he is *ordained of God the Father,* and *anointed with the Holy Ghos*t, to be our chief Prophet and Teacher, who fully reveals *the secret counsel* and *will of God* concerning our redemption; and our only High Priest, who by the one sacrifice of his body has redeemed us, and ever lives to make intercession for us with the Father; and our eternal King, who governs us by his Word and Spirit, and defends and preserves us in the redemption *obtained for us*" (HC 31).[2]

When the Westminster Confession discusses Christology, it first addresses how God appointed the Son as the mediator between God and men, which Hebrews 7 and Psalm 110 clearly link with covenantal themes. "It pleased God, in his eternal purpose, to choose and ordain the Lord Jesus, his only-begotten Son, to be the Mediator between God and man, the Prophet, Priest, and King; the Head and Savior of his Church, the Heir of all things, and the judge of the world; unto whom he did, from all eternity, give a people to be his seed, and to be by him in time redeemed, called, justified, sanctified, and glorified" (WCF 8.1).[3] Although the cov-

1. *TCR*, 30–31.
2. *COC*, 3:317–18 (emphasis added).
3. *COC*, 3:619.

enantal terminology does not appear outright, its constitutive ideas do.[4] The Savoy Declaration expands this statement to refer overtly to the covenant of redemption: "It pleased God in his eternal purpose, to choose and ordain, the Lord Jesus his only begotten Son, *according to a covenant made between them both,* to be the Mediator between God and man."[5] This additional phrase demonstrates that many Reformed theologians understood an inherent connection between the Son's appointment as mediator and the covenant of redemption, and they read the Westminster Confession accordingly.

The Westminster Larger Catechism is arguably more overt about Christ's office as mediator involving a covenant with the Father, stating, "The Covenant of Grace was made *with Christ,* as the second Adam, and, in him with all the elect, as his seed" (WLC 31).[6] In one sense, Christ was one of the parties in the covenant of grace since, as Patrick Gillespie (1617–1675) argues, God cannot covenant with sinners apart from Christ, so "Christ stands jointly with them."[7] Far from undermining the covenant of redemption's true distinction from the covenant of grace, he writes, "The covenant made with us, did spring out of that covenant made with Christ."[8] In this respect, the covenant of grace must include Christ in some sense since he is our mediator *in the covenant of grace* precisely because God cannot covenant directly with sinners unto blessing. Christ was, therefore, the "chief party" with all his blessings coming through him to believers in the covenant of grace.[9] Along these lines, Geerhardus Vos teaches, "The covenant of grace was established with the Son, not as *Logos* apart from His incarnation, but as the Son to-become incarnate."[10] Drawing on the category of the Son *incarnandus,* Vos grounds the covenant

---

4. J. V. Fesko, *The Theology of the Westminster Standards: Historical Context and Theological Insights* (Wheaton, IL: Crossway, 2014), 163–66; *VRD,* 3:10–13.

5. Savoy Declaration 8.1 in *A Declaration of the Faith and Order Owned and Practised in the Congregational Churches in England* (London: J. P., 1659), 10 (emphasis added).

6. *LC,* 71 (emphasis added).

7. Gillespie, *Ark of the Covenant Opened,* 454; also *CG,* 25–41, 50–61.

8. Gillespie, *Ark of the Covenant Opened,* 1.

9. Gillespie, *Ark of the Covenant Opened,* 455.

10. *VRD,* 3:2. In the Dutch tradition, many theologians combine the covenant of redemption and covenant of grace, arguing that the *pactum salutis* was simply the eternal aspect of the historical execution of the plan of salvation; see *VRD,* 2:83–84.

of grace in a relationship with the Son. He agrees with Gillespie, writing, "The counsel of peace is the secure foundation for the covenant of grace," noting that Christ is the chief party in the covenant of grace since "the first is between God and the Surety; the second between the Triune God and the sinner *in the Surety*."[11] In the Westminster Larger Confession, the covenantal relation between the Father and Christ is the eternal and decretal foundation of the covenantal application of salvation to the elect in Christ (WLC 31).[12]

Vitally, the Westminster Larger Catechism says that this covenant was made between the Father and Christ *as the second Adam*, importantly highlighting Christ's connection to the work of humanity's first covenantal representative. So, the covenant of redemption clarifies Christ's work precisely in how he succeeded where Adam failed and earned citizenship in the new creation for those whom the Father gave to him.[13]

Corresponding sources demonstrate that the covenant of redemption's implicit presence in the Westminster Standards is not an innovative reading. In its publication of the Westminster Standards, the Scottish church included *The Sum of Saving Knowledge*, whose doctrinal section about "the remedy provided in Jesus Christ for the Elect by the Covenant of Grace" treats the covenant of redemption at length. *The Sum*'s first point is that the covenant of redemption addresses humanity in our "woeful condition by nature through breaking the Covenant of Works" (hence, again, why this book explains the covenant of works before the covenant of redemption) so that God's plan of salvation is "according to the tenor of the Covenant of Redemption made and agreed upon, between God the Father and God the Son, in the counsel of the Trinity before the world began."[14] Given the conditions that the Son "humble himself so far as to assume the human Nature," including that he "submit himself to the Law as surety for them, and satisfy Justice for them, by giving obedience in their name, even unto the suffering of the cursed death of the Cross" so that "by virtue of the foresaid bargain made before the world began, he is

11. *VRD*, 2:92 (emphasis added).

12. *CMT*, 75–76; *WWG*, 252, 253–54; CG, 41–61.

13. Hodge, *Systematic Theology*, 2:359–61.

14. *Summe of Saving Knowledge*, in *The Confession of Faith, and the larger and shorter catechisms* (Edinburgh: Andrew Anderson, 1652), sig. L12r, L11r, L12v.

in all ages, since the fall of Adam, still upon the work of applying actually the purchased benefits unto the Elect."[15] That the Scottish Presbyterians published *The Sum* with their confessional documents demonstrates their intent that it clarify any ambiguity in the confession and catechisms about the covenant of redemption, namely, that this doctrine was fully part of the Reformed confessional heritage.

The term "covenant of redemption," or *pactum salutis*, most likely gained such quick popularity after its first use in 1638 because this new term so well encapsulated a set of ideas present within the confessional tradition. Even in the early sixteenth century, Johannes Oecolampadius (1482–1531) comments on Isaiah 55:3 that God "entered a covenant with his Son, our Lord Jesus Christ."[16] Later in the sixteenth century, Casper Olevianus (1536–87) also grounds the blessings of salvation in an eternal intra-Trinitarian covenant.[17] Olevianus even draws together the theme of Christ's appointment as high priest and exegesis of John 17, which the previous chapter argues is integral to the covenant of redemption.[18] The Belgic Confession, Heidelberg Catechism, Canons of Dort, and Westminster Standards all endorse these ideas, suggesting that the Reformed tradition quickly adopted the term "covenant of redemption" as the designation for these existing exegetical and confessional conclusions.[19]

THE LAST ADAM THEME

As the thrust of previous chapters makes clear, Christ's work performed for our salvation as our new covenant mediator concretely links to the covenant of works' structure. The New Testament explicitly connects Christ's office as savior to Adam's function as humanity's first covenantal representative, strengthening the case for the covenant of redemption itself.[20] In 1 Corinthians 15:45, Paul writes, "Thus it is written, 'The first

15. *Summe*, sig. L12v–M1r.

16. Johannes Oecolampadius, *In Iesaiam Prophetam Hypomnematōn* (Basel, 1525), 268r.

17. Casper Olevianus, *De substantia foederis gratuiti inter Deum et electos* (Geneva, 1585), 2.28.

18. Olevianus, *De substantia*, 1.2.1.

19. Muller, "*Pactum Salutis*," 11–65; VanDrunen and Clark, "Covenant before the Covenants," 167–78; Fesko, *Covenant of Redemption*; Richard, "The Covenant of Redemption," 44–45.

20. Barcellos, *Getting the Garden Right*, 133–37; VanDrunen and Clark, "Covenant before the Covenants," 189–92.

man Adam became a living being'; the last Adam became a life-giving spirit." Scripture definitely associates Adam and Christ as the two ultimate figureheads of the human race. In Romans 5:12–21, Paul outlines an extended parallel between Adam and Christ and how Adam brought condemnation and ruin upon humanity, but Christ brought justification unto life to the elect. Although the overt "first Adam" and "last Adam" terminology is absent, nevertheless, Paul's argued parallel makes the same point about how Adam and Christ stand as the two ultimate representatives available to humanity. Still, Paul is as direct as one could be when he says that Adam "was a type of the one who was to come," referring to how Adam's role foresignified Christ's office (Rom 5:14).[21]

Scripture also implicitly portrays Christ as recapitulating Adam's role but as the victorious covenantal representative. In the Gospel narratives, the authors provide little direct commentary to explain the theological significance of the stories and their details, but good reflection upon the Gospels' portrayal of Christ reveals a story-driven and thematic depiction of Christ as the second Adam. The theological relevance of these narrative elements in no way diminishes their historical accuracy or value but does show that the historical accounts are not simply records of *raw* events. They are records of events that have profound meaning within God's plan of salvation and within the way that God has authored Scripture in all places to point forward to Christ.[22] The Gospels, then, record, not simply Jesus's crucifixion with long introductions, but his entire obedient life, itself having significant theological value, not simply as a precursor to his death, but as an integral part of his saving mission.[23]

Some themes linked to Christ's office as second Adam may seem spurious at first, but the combination of motifs forms a powerful argument for Christ's work in recapitulating Adam's covenantal task. For example, Irenaeus argues that the reason that Christ was born of a virgin was because Adam was taken from the earth, creating a parallel that neither

21. Wellum, "Progressive Covenantalism," 81–82.

22. Matthew Barrett, *Canon, Covenant and Christology: Rethinking Jesus and the Scriptures of Israel* (Downers Grove, IL: IVP Academic, 2020); Craig A. Carter, *Interpreting Scripture with the Great Tradition: Recovering the Genius of Premodern Exegesis* (Grand Rapids: Baker Academic, 2018).

23. Crowe, *Last Adam*, 1–22, 83–116. On the nature of the Gospels, see N. B. Stonehouse, *Origins of the Synoptic Gospels: Some Basic Questions* (Grand Rapids: Baker, 1979); and N. B. Stonehouse, *The Witness of the Synoptic Gospels to Christ* (Grand Rapids: Baker, 1979).

Adam nor Christ had an earthly father.[24] On its own, Irenaeus's argument about the reason for the Son's virgin birth may not seem convincing according to many modern expectations, although perhaps it is worth contemplating.

Regardless, Irenaeus further mapped deeper parallels between the first and last Adams that substantiate his initial conclusion from the virgin birth. Irenaeus wrote of a covenant between God and Adam, and, although he did not call it the covenant of works, there are remarkable similarities to it.[25] He wrote concerning Adam's obedience that God "grants life, and incorruptibility, and eternal glory to the ones who follow and serve him, supplying benefit to his servants, on account of that they serve, and to his followers, on account of that they follow." Man's work does not help God but us, since "in as much as God in fact needs nothing, so much man needs of communion with God."[26] Irenaeus's point is remarkably close to the Reformed view of the covenant of works and the potential reward of incorruptible life for obedience. Further, Irenaeus linked this Adamic task to what Christ accomplished as Savior. "Indeed, we have shown the Son of God had no beginning because he was always existing with the Father. But when he became incarnate, and was made man, he recapitulated the long line of humanity in himself, supplying salvation to us in short fashion, so that we recover in Christ Jesus what we destroyed in Adam, specifically, to be according to the image and likeness of God."[27] Irenaeus clearly perceives a biblical link between Adam's role as humanity's first representative and Christ's as the Savior recapitulating and successfully fulfilling Adam's task.[28] Still, most of Irenaeus's view comes from extended

---

24. Irenaeus, *Against Heresies*, 3.21.10, in *PG*, 7.1:954–55; *ANF*, 1:454.

25. Horton, *Lord and Servant*, 173; Irenaeus, *Against Heresies*, 3.11.8 in *PG*, 7.1:889; *ANF*, 1:429.

26. Irenaeus, *Against Heresies*, 4.14.1 in *PG*, 7.1:1010; *ANF*, 1:478.

27. Irenaeus, *Against Heresies*, 3.18.1 in *PG*, 7.1:932; *ANF*, 1:446.

28. Minns, *Irenaeus*, 108–17; Kelly, *Early Christian Doctrines*, 170–74; Eric Osborn, *Irenaeus of Lyons* (Cambridge: Cambridge University Press, 2001), 97–140; Trevor Hart, "Irenaeus, Recapitulation and Physical Redemption," in *Christ in Our Place: The Humanity of God in Christ for the Reconciliation of the World: Essays Presented to James Torrance*, ed. Trevor Hart and Daniel Thimell (Exeter: Paternoster, 1989), 152–81; John VanMaaren, "The Adam-Christ Typology in Paul and Its Development in the Early Church Fathers," *Tyndale Bulletin* 64.2 (2013): 281–85; Irwin W. Reist, "The Christology of Irenaeus," *JETS* 13 no. 4 (Fall 1970): 247–49; Samuel George, "The Emergence of Christology in the Early Church—a Methodological Survey with Particular Reference to the Anti-Heretical Polemics of Irenaeus of Lyons," *Asia Journal of Theology* 24 no. 2 (October 2010): 219–53.

reflection upon Romans 5 and, although setting strong historical precedent for the doctrine, does not demonstrate how the Gospel narratives portray Christ as the second Adam. John Chrysostom (d. 407) and Cyril of Alexandria also interpret the Gospel narratives in light of a two-Adams view in a similar way to that presented below.[29]

The explicit statements in Romans 5 and 1 Corinthians 15 linking Adam and Christ prompt deeper thought about the Gospels' presentation of Jesus's life. The Gospels' use of historical events of Christ's life to portray him as the last Adam, whose obedience is inherently linked to procuring salvation for his people, should not be surprising.[30] Inasmuch as Christ rendered this obedience as his mission in the covenant of redemption, he performed his work of fulfilling the conditions of the covenant of works on our behalf.[31]

The Gospels are loaded with Old Testament connections that color the portrait of Christ as last Adam. Most basically, three of the four Gospels begin their narrative of Jesus's life by linking Christ's birth to Genesis (Matt 1:1; John 1:1).[32] Luke most directly connects Jesus's genealogy explicitly to Adam also as God's son, which forges an overt connection between them (Luke 3:38).[33] Moreover, Christ's life recapitulates Adam's role, although succeeding where the first failed. Genesis's creation account opens with God creating the heavens and the earth out of nothing except the power of his word (*ex nihilo*), resulting in a watery world over which the Spirit hovers (Gen 1:1–2). After dividing the waters, God formed Adam by a special creative act and breathed spiritual life into him (Gen 1:26–28; Gen 2:5–7). He then revealed the law to Adam and placed him in the garden where he would face his probation concerning the tree of knowledge of good and evil (Gen 2:8–17). Adam was then tempted by the serpent but failed his test (Gen 3:1–7). This outline of Adam in the covenant of works

---

29. Ashish J. Naidu, "The First Adam-Second Adam Typology in John Chrysostom and Cyril of Alexandria," *Perichoresis* 12 no. 2 (2014): 153–62.

30. Crowe, *Last Adam*, 55–82.

31. Stephen J. Wellum, *Christ Alone: The Uniqueness of Jesus as Savior* (Grand Rapids: Zondervan, 2017), 40–42.

32. Edward W. Klink III, "Genesis Revealed: Second Adam Christology in the Fourth Gospel," *Bulletin of Ecclesial Theology* 5.1 (2018): 27–42.

33. Richard, "Covenant of Redemption," 57–59; Crowe, *Last Adam*, 28–37, 118–19; *KTC*, 231.

sets important background for understanding the Gospels' presentation of Christ.

The Gospels recount the beginning of Christ's earthly ministry in a way that highlights his close resemblance to the first Adam. Jesus's public ministry properly began at his baptism (Matt 3:13–17; Mark 1:9–11; Luke 3:21–22; John 1:29–34). Just as Adam entered his commission as God's first covenantal priest by passing through the creation waters with the Spirit hovering overhead and being called God's son (Gen 1:1–2; Gen 5:1–2; Luke 3:38), so Christ entered his threefold ministry as mediator, with special emphasis on the priestly aspect, by passing through the waters of his baptism with the Spirit coming to rest upon him and God declaring that "This is my beloved Son, with whom I am well pleased" (Matt 3:16–17; Mark 1:10–11; Luke 3:21–22; John 1:32–33).[34] The Father properly commissioned the Son into his mission by directing him through the same entry process involving water, the Spirit, and sonship.

Christ's experiences directly after his baptism deepen that correspondence. The first Adam—after coming through the creation waters—heard the law, was placed in the garden for his probation, and was tempted by Satan. Christ also—immediately after his baptism—was sent into the wilderness to be tempted by Satan (Matt 4:1–11; Mark 1:12–13; Luke 4:1–13).[35] Christ's face-off against Satan's temptation reveals that his probation as the new Adam was far more intense than the first's.[36] Whereas Adam faced probation in paradise while having every tree save one for food, Christ's temptation took place in the desert after forty days of fasting. Whereas Adam was confronted by Satan as a serpent, Christ faced him under no pretense. Whereas Adam had one point of testing, in the tree, Christ endured three tests, as the devil increased his attempts to lure Jesus into sin. The overlap between Adam's story and Christ's is no mere coincidence, no invention of narrative creativity, nor accidental occurrence. Rather, God providentially orchestrated the events of Christ's earthly ministry to repeat the major points of Adam's initial covenantal assignment, so that Christ would legitimately fulfill every point of Adam's role in the covenant

34. *KTC*, 230–32; Crowe, *Last Adam*, 28–30, 34–35; Wellum, *Christ Alone*, 59–60.

35. Beale, *New Testament Biblical Theology*, 381–437; Crowe, *Last Adam*, 68–74.

36. *DIALIC*, 259–60.

of works.[37] God also inspired the Scripture to recount those events and the order that they occurred together, so that we could see Jesus's work as the second Adam clearly in the Gospel narrative, just as it is clearly explained in Paul's epistles.[38]

Christ's recapitulation of Adam's covenantal commission still extends further than the first events of his ministry. Jesus not only proved to be the faithful Son of God in the tasks that Adam obviously failed to complete, but also in the tasks that Adam never even really began to perform. Within the covenantal assignment that God gave to his image bearer, in Genesis 1:28, he directed Adam to exercise authority as his vice-regent, his locally delegated king: "Be fruitful and multiply and fill the earth and subdue it, and have dominion over the fish of the sea and over the birds of the heavens and over every living thing that moves on the earth." Adam's responsibility to exercise dominion was an expression of a royal office.[39]

In this respect, the continuation of Jesus's ministry shows that Christ executed Adam's assignment to spread the dominion of the kingdom of God throughout the world, namely, in executing his kingly duties as our mediator. As the period of Christ's wilderness temptation ends, the probation phase of Jesus's recapitulation of the covenant of works is fulfilled. Then, although Adam never got fully underway in spreading godly dominion throughout the world, Christ took up that task and began to make God's kingdom present.[40] So, Mark 1:15 tellingly records that Jesus initiated the public aspect of his ministry by declaring, "The time is fulfilled, and *the kingdom of God* is at hand; repent and believe in the gospel." Jesus was supremely aware that his earthly ministry would be about bringing God's kingdom into the world, even though Adam had failed to spread godly dominion in his covenantal commission.[41]

Thus, Jesus's kingly mission was more intense than Adam's. At creation, the world may have needed subduing, taming, and beautifying to

37. Michael J. Kruger, "Covenant in the Gospels," in *CT*, 216–18; Crowe, *Last Adam*, 23–34, 74–80.

38. Crowe, *Last Adam*, 52–53.

39. Wellum, *Christ Alone*, 145; *KTC*, 225–38; Crowe, *Last Adam*, 38–40.

40. *CF*, 525–26, 541–42.

41. Wellum, *Christ Alone*, 61–64; Wellum, "Progressive Covenantalism," 87–91; J. R. Daniel Kirk, "Mark's Son of Man and Paul's Second Adam," *Horizons in Biblical Theology* 37 (2015): 170–95; Crowe, *Last Adam*, 139–70.

widen the garden kingdom's dominion. On the other hand, at the outset of Jesus's ministry, the prince of the power of the air maintained his deception over the nations. Whereas Adam, as God's vice-prince, merely had to make a good creation pristine, Christ as the new Adamic King had to wage war on the kingdom of darkness. So, Christ's miracles of casting out demons, curing the sick, and healing the lame and blind assume richer meaning in the Gospel narratives since they are not merely impressive feats of godliness. They are incursions upon a godless kingdom and victories over the evil age, so expressing how Christ is taking dominion as the last, victorious Adam.[42]

Christ's miracles, then, serve several functions. Some aspects of Jesus's ministry reveal his deity.[43] Some miracles demonstrate Jesus's divine identity as he performs actions and roles proper only to God. For example, Christ's walking on water (Matt 14:22–33; Mark 6:45–56; John 6:16–20) was not simply an impressive feat but proof that he is divine since *God* "*alone* spreadeth out the heavens, and *treadeth upon the waves of the sea*" (Job 9:8 KJV, emphasis added). Other miracles, however, show how Christ was supremely anointed with the Spirit as the Messiah (Acts 10:38).[44] Further, many aspects of Christ's ministry recapitulate, even

---

42. *CF*, 545.

43. *VRD*, 3:59–60.

44. Horton, *Rediscovering*, 100–3; *CF*, 469. This point should not be pressed so far that Christ's miracles are disconnected from his divine identity, and he becomes simply the preeminent example of dependence upon the Spirit. Stephen Wellum has very helpfully noted a recent trend in evangelical theology to overemphasize Christ's dependence on the Spirit, gravitating in a kenotic direction; see Wellum, *God the Son Incarnate*, 395–419; and Wellum, *Person of Christ*, 54–55, 127–44. At least some of Christ's miracles serve the pointed purpose of demonstrating his divine identity, such as calming the storm (Mark 4:35–41; Ps 135:5–7), walking on water (Mark 6:45–52; Exod 33:18–23; Job 9:8), and healing the blind man (John 9:1–12; Ps 146:8). In this respect, the Spirit's necessary connection to the Son's incarnate works belongs to the Trinitarian principle of inseparable operations, wherein the whole Trinity acts together even as certain acts terminate upon one specific person; see Vidu, *Same God*, 158–79. Locating the Spirit's involvement with the incarnation in the doctrine of the Trinity, however, differs greatly from using the Son's dependence upon the Spirit to perform miracles as a soteriological point wherein the Son demonstrates dependence upon the Spirit for us to emulate; see Ivor J. Davidson, "Christ," in *OHRT*, 459–61; Robert Letham, *The Holy Spirit* (Phillipsburg, NJ: P&R, 2023), 128–30. This Trinitarian point is why John Owen emphasizes the Spirit's connection to the Son in the incarnation; see Suzanne McDonald, "John Owen's *Discourse on The Holy Spirit*," in *OHRT*, 270–71. Given the intertextual links between how the Old Testament describes God, and how Jesus takes on roles and actions attributed to God, we must assert that, in whatever way the Spirit was involved, *at least some* of Christ's miracles serve to show his own deity. Since the *person* of the incarnate Son performs these divine actions, his divine nature and human nature are not confused (*communicatio idiomatum*); Oliver D. Crisp, *Revisioning Christology: Theology in the Reformed Tradition*

intensify, and, most importantly, fulfill Adam's original covenantal role. Even if demonstrating his messianic anointing with the Spirit, Christ's miracles of healing, provision, and overcoming demonic powers highlight his mission as the king subduing the world under godly rule.[45] Christ's miraculous deeds were acts of making the kingdom of God present in the world today, even before its full arrival occurs at Christ's return.[46] In that regard, Christ's office links back to the covenant of redemption in reference to how the Father *covenanted* a kingdom to the Son (Luke 22:29).[47] Christ's messianic kingship, even as executed in his miracles, is a fulfillment or even heightened fulfillment of Adam's mission to spread dominion.

Even Christ's death and resurrection inform the last Adam motif. Whereas the first Adam faced probation with a tree, so Christ's suffering obedience culminated with a tree "by becoming obedient to the point of death, even death on a cross" (Phil 2:8). Whereas the first Adam accrued a curse from a tree, the last Adam endured our curse upon a tree (Gal 3:13). As Irenaeus writes, "And the trespass which came by the tree was undone by the tree of obedience, when, hearkening unto God, the Son of man was nailed to the tree thereby putting away the knowledge of evil and bringing in and establishing the knowledge of good: now evil it is to disobey God, even as hearkening unto God is good...So then by the obedience wherewith He obeyed even unto death, hanging on the tree, He put away the old disobedience which was wrought in the tree."[48] Then,

---

(Farnham; Burlington, VT: Ashgate, 2011), 100–7. This emphasis on how some of Christ's miracles demonstrate his divine identity counterbalances but does not eliminate how some of Christ's miracles also demonstrate his role as the Spirit-anointed Savior. So, even as "the LORD opens the eyes of the blind" (Ps 146:8), still God puts the Spirit on his servant and sends this anointed servant "to open the eyes that are blind" (Isa 42:1, 7). Jesus shows himself to be both God and the Spirit-anointed Messiah as he fulfills both roles in healing the blind (Mark 10:46–52; John 9:1–12). In other words, Christ's deity and messianic anointing should not be placed in competition, but appropriate emphasis should be placed on both so that neither eclipses the other. This balance reminds us that in all his miracles, regardless of their specific purpose, Christ is marked as the special divine emissary for our salvation, and certainly not merely as an example of faith, of how to walk in dependence on the Spirit; see Wellum, *Person of Christ*, 114–18, 156–58; and *RST*, 3:121–23. Indeed, an overstatement of the Spirit's relationship to the incarnation reverses the priority of the Son and Spirit's missions, also entailing a confusion of their eternal processions; see Vidu, *Divine Missions*, 33–36, 73–75.

45. Horton, *Rediscovering*, 103.

46. Herman Ridderbos, *The Coming of the Kingdom*, trans. H. de Jongste (1962; repr. Phillipsburg, NJ: P&R, 1992), 61–70, 104–21.

47. Crowe, *Last Adam*, 196.

48. Irenaeus, *Demonstration*, §34.

since Jesus proved himself to be the completely faithful Adam who fulfilled righteous obedience, he was rewarded with incorruptible life through his resurrection.[49] He has earned that glorification that our discussion of 1 Corinthians 15:42–45 showed was the reward that God offered to Adam in the covenant of works. Paul linked this discussion of indestructible life and Christ's resurrection explicitly to his understanding of the first and second Adams. So, the end of Christ's earthly ministry, just like its beginning, is marked with connections to the first Adam's commission in the covenant of works.[50] Jesus's earthly ministry displays his victorious work as the last Adam, as he completes the first Adam's covenantal mandate and attains righteousness for the elect by fulfilling the covenant of works in our stead.[51]

THE EXTENT OF CHRIST'S SATISFACTION

With the exploration of the missions that the Father, Son, and Spirit fulfill in the covenant of redemption from the previous chapter, as well as the biblico-theological theme of Christ's office as the second Adam in place, we can address a more systematic issue about Christ's work. Did Christ undertake his work for all of humanity or for only the elect? Christ's death and saving work is a centrally important issue because it is directly about our reconciliation with God—our restored and renewed communion with our covenant Lord.

The usual way that this question is framed concerns whether Christ died for the sins of the whole world or for the sins of only the elect. Usually, this issue has been described as concerning "the extent of the atonement" but is more clearly and helpfully framed as the extent of Christ's *satisfaction*. The concept of satisfaction needs explanation before we can consider its extent.

The reason for suggesting the terminology of "satisfaction" rather than "atonement," without wanting to overstate the criticism, is twofold. First, the language of "satisfaction" is the older way that Reformed writers

49. Crowe, *Last Adam*, 192–97.

50. Crowe, *Last Adam*, 61.

51. Crowe, *Last Adam*, 199–215.

address this issue.[52] The Reformed confessions speak almost universally about Christ's satisfaction. For example, the Belgic Confession uses biblical language, which the previous two chapters show are clearly part of the exegetical underpinnings for the covenant of redemption, to explain Christ's priestly work. So, Christ "is *ordained with an oath* to be an everlasting High-Priest" to appease God's wrath "by his *full satisfaction*" (BC 21).[53] The Heidelberg Confession says, as well, "By reason of the justice and truth of God, *satisfaction* for our sins could be made no otherwise than by the death of the Son of God" (HC 40).[54] The Westminster Standards also follow this pattern of describing Christ's work. In the chapter on Christ the Mediator, the Westminster Confession states that Christ, "by his perfect obedience and sacrifice of himself ... has *fully satisfied* the justice of his Father" (WCF 8.5).[55] So, the first reason for favoring the language of "satisfaction" is simply historical, in that familiarity with the Reformed confessions' preferred terminology furthers better understanding of the concepts and discussions in our tradition.

Second, "satisfaction" also clarifies Christ's work itself, becoming conceptually useful. The difference between the language of "satisfaction" and "atonement" may be one of degree rather than substance, but "satisfaction" helps explain Christ's work in fundamentally relational categories with more immediate reference to the covenantal structure of our relationship with God. More specifically, Christ *satisfied*—completed, fulfilled, and met—all the conditions of the covenant. So, "satisfaction" helps us more clearly understand that not merely Christ's death, but his incarnate work holistically brought about reconciliation—restored communion.[56]

Recently, there have been an increasing number of criticisms against the doctrine that Christ died as a penal substitute or as the one who suffered God's punishment for our sin. These criticisms reveal that discussion about the atonement easily fixates solely on Christ's death without

---

52. Richard A. Muller, *Calvin and the Reformed Tradition: On the Work of Christ and the Order of Salvation* (Grand Rapids: Baker Academic, 2012), 74–78.

53. *COC*, 3:406 (emphasis added).

54. *COC*, 3:320 (emphasis added).

55. *COC*, 3:621 (emphasis added). See also WLC 71; *LC*, 79.

56. *BRD*, 3:393–406; John Murray, *Redemption Accomplished and Applied*, 2015 ed. (Grand Rapids: Eerdmans, 1955), 14–48; *CF*, 492–501.

due justice to wider considerations about why Christ died *as our covenantal representative*.[57] In response to those criticisms, however, Christ's death *as our penal substitution* was certainly a central part of his work as our mediator ... but not the only part. As the second Adam theme shows, Christ obtained the status of the victorious Adam and is spreading his kingly dominion. Still, he achieved that victory in part by shouldering the consequences of our sin. Christ, as our covenantal representative, not only died for us but also fulfilled everything that was required in the first covenant of works to earn everlasting, new creation life.[58]

In the covenant of works, Adam and thereby all humanity owed a debt to God in order to obtain incorruptible life. This debt, however, predated Adam's fall into sin and was part of the covenant of works itself. Adam owed God a *principal debt* of obedience. By sinning, Adam also accrued another debt, a debt of *penalty*. Reformed theology has typically spoken about this same distinction in terms of Christ's active obedience (principal) and passive obedience (penalty), but debt categories help link this distinction into our discussion of satisfaction.[59] In a sermon delivered in London in 1648, James Ussher explained this twofold debt in connection to the traditional active-passive obedience distinction:

> Obedience is a Debt. And Sin is a Debt. There is the Principal, and the Penalty, which grows due to God upon our default. And, therefore, our Surety, who stands chargeable with all our debts. As He maketh Payment for the one, by his Active, so must He make Amends for the other. By his Passive obedience our mediator must perform that which we were to Perform.[60]

---

57. E.g. Oliver Crisp, *Approaching the Atonement: The Reconciling Work of Christ* (Downers Grove, IL: IVP Academic, 2020), 100–12, 131–45 163–79; cf. *DIALIC*, 266–69; Kevin J. Vanhoozer, "Redemption Accomplished: Atonement," in *OHRT*, 486–88; *CF*, 509–16; Wellum, *Christ Alone*, 213–19; and Harrison Perkins, "The Context of the Cross," *Modern Reformation* (blog), July 7, 2020, https://modernreformation.org/resource-library/web-exclusive-articles/the-mod-the-context-of-the-cross/.

58. Horton, *Justification*, 2:195–256; *CF*, 501–4.

59. *BRD*, 3:377–86; Crowe, "Passive and Active Obedience of Christ," 441–68; Letham, *Systematic Theology*, 551–53; *RST*, 2:1033–56.

60. CUL MS Mm. 6.55, fol. 53v (sermon on Philippians 2:8, dated January 9, 1647 [1648]). The original is quoted—with historical analysis—in Perkins, *Catholicity and the Covenant of Works*, 183–84.

Our principal debt is that we must obey God and fulfill the law. In the covenant of works, God kindly attached the promise of everlasting reward if we paid this debt, showing God's goodness in that he did not have to offer any reward for the payment of a debt that we already owed to him (Luke 17:10).

When Adam defaulted on his principal debt and rebelled against God in sin, he accrued a debt of penalty as well. Not only did Adam still owe the principal debt, which a sinner could never pay, but now he owed a debt to bear the curse for his disobedience. Ussher explains this twofold debt in another sermon, but in this case links it directly to the notion of satisfaction: "For there was on our part a Principal Debt to be paid, and a Penalty. The Principal Debt was obedience. And we were to be freed from this or to die in prison everlastingly. We were not able to pay this debt, therefore Christ Jesus, God's Fellow, as it is in Zachariah, did perform obedience, and by his sufferings, by his Active, and Passive obedience, did give just satisfaction."[61] Ussher makes the same point about the twofold debt of principal and penalty, this time explaining how these debts relate to Christ's work of *satisfaction*. Other Reformed theologians, such as William Perkins and Francis Roberts, likewise connect Christ's active and passive obedience to this principle of a double debt, stemming from the covenant of works.[62] The category of satisfaction is, then, more explicitly and clearly tied to our covenantal relationship with God because it highlights the obligations that the covenant of works imposed upon us, both before and after the fall.

Using satisfaction terminology highlights that Christ's death brings about reconciliation along with inbuilt reference to why we need that reconciliation with God. Practically speaking, in terms of our evangelistic efforts, unbelievers who have never been exposed to biblical teachings may be confused—since they suppress the truth in unrighteousness

61. CUL MS Mm. 6.55, fol. 54r (sermon on Philippians 2:8, dated January 16, 1647 [1648]). Ussher makes the same point in Bodleian Library, Oxford MS Eng. th.e.25, fol. 39v–40r, 55v–61v (two sermons on Hebrews 9:15, dated 1625 [1626]). For historical analysis of this point in both sets of sermons, see Perkins, *Catholicity and the Covenant of Works*, 183–84; Richard Snoddy, *The Soteriology of James Ussher: The Act and Object of Saving Faith* (New York: Oxford University Press, 2014), 45; Richard Snoddy, "'The Mysteries of Christ': James Ussher Among the Puritans, 1626," *Confessional Presbyterian* 16 (2020): 33–51.

62. *WWP*, 4:62 (commentary on Jude 3); *MMB*, 30–31.

(Rom 1:18)—about why they need to be reconciled to God. Certainly, our job includes explaining the law to them so that they know the greatness of their sin and misery. At the same time, we should use the terminology that most quickly and most effectively results in a clear explanation of that reality.[63] In this respect, "satisfaction" immediately points directly to our relationship with God. We are bound to our Maker by creation and by covenant, owe him our full obedience to his law simply as his creatures but also as those to whom he gave the covenant of works (Luke 17:10), and are guilty for breaking our relationship with God by sinning against God, thereby accruing a penalty for our transgression (Rom 5:12–14).[64] Again, "satisfaction," then, highlights how Christ fulfilled all the conditions of our covenantal relationship with God. It highlights that Christ's work as the second Adam was as much about his covenant-fulfilling obedience as it was about his curse-bearing death.

Satisfaction terminology is helpful in more immediately emphasizing our covenantal relationship with God, since God is the one who requires that satisfaction. We were meant to satisfy a principal debt of obedience to God both by creation and by covenant, but as sinners we must also satisfy a penalty debt to God for our transgressions. These debts are far from impersonal, despite their association with financial transactions, but are fundamentally relational. We were meant to express our full love for God in our creaturely and covenantal relationship with him by fully keeping his law (John 14:15; John 15:14) but defaulted on our relational debts. We failed to satisfy those payments of relational love which we should have *happily and joyfully* rendered to God for his goodness in making us and in further offering us even greater blessings simply for doing what we were supposed to do.

Since we failed to satisfy our principal debt and we accrued our penalty debt, we are left either to endure everlasting punishment by bearing our own penalty or we must find a new representative who is able to satisfy both debts for us.[65] Since God is just, and since breaking the moral

63. HC 2; *COC*, 3:308; WLC 30; *LC*, 71; WLC 72; *LC*, 79.

64. WSC 13–14 affirms that "our first parents, being left to the freedom of their own will, fell from the estate wherein they were created, *by sinning against God*" and "sin is any want of conformity unto, or transgression of, the law of God," *COC*, 3:678 (emphasis added).

65. *CG*, 93–100.

law is an assault upon and rebellion against God's holy and just character, God cannot let sin go unpunished (Rom 3:25).[66] The penalty for sin, after all, is not a matter of God's feelings, as if he is simply angry about being wronged. No, the "sting of death is sin, and the power of sin is the law" (1 Cor 15:56), meaning that death is the legal and just consequence for sin, "the curse of the law" that justice cannot arbitrarily set aside (Gal 3:13). God must be consistent with his own righteous character, so it is *necessary* that the covenantal curse for sin be inflicted. In other words, even according to God's *absolute power*, he cannot simply will to forgive sins without upholding the standards of justice. That would be out of accord with his nature. So, the means of reconciliation that God appoints according to his *ordained power* must cohere with his righteous character.[67] As Witsius put it, "If we could be saved any other way, than by the sufferings of the Son of God, the love of God would not shine with such luster in that method."[68] We must have both the principal *and the penalty* debts satisfied.

Household chores clearly demonstrate this need. Imagine a time when you were young, and your parents assigned you to mow the grass. Instead of doing this chore, however, you decide to go to the movies with your friends. When you return home, there sit mom and dad ... waiting. Now, two things will happen. First, you will be grounded and will endure a penalty for your disobedience. Second, you still must mow the grass. You are still liable for the principal debt even after accruing the penalty.

Perhaps, however, your older brother bounds into the room and steps between you and your parents. He informs them that he has actually mowed the lawn today, and so the task assigned to you as your principal obedience has been fulfilled. Further, he asks that he might endure whatever punishment that you were going to have to endure for your disobedience. Certainly, this is a tremendous older brother.

Yet, Christ has acted exactly this way for us as our older brother and new covenantal representative (Rom 8:29; Heb 2:11). We owed our

---

66. *CF*, 511–16; Wellum, *Christ Alone*, 32–35, 221–28; Murray, *Redemption Accomplished and Applied*, 3–13; *TI*, 14.10.1–29; *EC*, 1.5.19–39, 2.8.1–21.

67. On the distinction of God's absolute and ordained power, see *DLGTT*, 271. Concerning the medieval background of this category, see Heiko A. Oberman, *The Harvest of Medieval Theology: Gabriel Biel and Late Medieval Nominalism*, 3rd ed. (Grand Rapids: Baker Academic, 2000), 30–56.

68. *EC*, 2.8.9.

heavenly Father obedience as a principal debt but accrued everlasting punishment in hell as our penalty debt. Jesus Christ has satisfied both those debts on our behalf.

Reformed theologians have long thought that this twofold satisfaction is of monumental importance. Ussher helpfully explains how in Christ's work to reconcile God and man, Christ "should satisfy the first Covenant whereunto man was tied," namely, "in performing that righteousness which the Law of God did require of Man: and in bearing the punishment which was due unto Man for breaking of the same Law."[69] John Colquhoun also taught that even though Adam and Eve broke the law, it has not "ceased for a moment to demand from them, that perfect obedience which, as the condition of life, it at *first* required from man." After citing Luke 10:25–29, he explained, "Though the paying of the debt of punishment, could satisfy as to the *penalty* of the bond, yet the *principal* contained in the bond, namely the debt of perfect obedience to the law as a covenant, for eternal life, must likewise be paid." So, "The second Adam, then, substituting himself in their place, became surety for this their debt of perfect obedience to the law, in its covenant form, which was, and still is, the only obedience to it, that is meritorious of eternal life; obliging himself to discharge it, by obeying in their stead; and so fulfilling all that the preceptive part of the law required from them, as the proper condition of life."[70] Likewise, Vos preached that it is not sufficient for the punishment of sin to be borne because "the justice of the law must be fulfilled, that is to say, it must be perfectly obeyed and observed." In the case that God's wrath is satisfied, "the person would still be without citizenship and rights in God's kingdom, he would still remain a beggar who has no claim to anything. The unyielding law, with its 'Do this and you shall live' would still stand—with its accusation that it has not been fulfilled and its strict prohibition against giving life to the sinner." In sum, "God does not grant eternal life to either angels or men on any other condition than perfect keeping of the law."[71] Christ as the last Adam and our covenantal mediator has made satisfaction *to God for our covenantal debts.*

69. James Ussher, *The Principles of Christian Religion* (London: George Badger, 1653), 19–21.

70. CG, 94–95 (italics original).

71. Geerhardus Vos, "The Spiritual Resurrection of Believers," in *Grace and Glory: Sermons Preached at Princeton Seminary*, new ed. (London: The Banner of Truth Trust, 2020), 236–38.

We owed the principal and penalty debt *to God*. The Son of God came, therefore, *in human nature* so that he might pay those debts *to God* for us. The Westminster Larger Catechism outlines why our mediator had to be divine but also had to be human, helpfully showing that the one offering satisfaction for our debt had to have a life valuable enough to overcome our debt but also had to make satisfaction as a human.

> Why was it requisite that the Mediator should be God?
>
> It was requisite that the Mediator should be God, that he might sustain and keep the human nature from sinking under the infinite wrath of God, and the power of death; *give worth and efficacy to his sufferings, obedience and intercession*; and to *satisfy* God's justice, procure his favor, purchase a peculiar people, give his Spirit to them, conquer all their enemies, and bring them to everlasting salvation.
>
> Why was it requisite that the Mediator should be Man?
>
> It was requisite that the Mediator should be Man, that he might advance *our nature*, perform *obedience to the Law*, suffer and make intercession *for us in our nature*, have a fellow-feeling of our infirmities; that we might receive the adoption of sons, and have comfort and access with boldness unto the throne of grace.
>
> Why was it requisite that the Mediator should be God and man in one person?
>
> It was requisite that the Mediator, who was to reconcile God and man, should himself be both God and man, and this in one person, that the proper works of each nature might be accepted of God for us, and relied on by us, as the works of the whole person. (WLC 38–40)[72]

Reconciliation requires that we have fulfilled all our covenantal obligations to God, but Adam cast every human person into sin. Therefore, our effectual mediator had to be God. Still, *we* are the covenant breakers, so our mediator also must be human in order to pay *our* debts. The divine person, God's Son, assumed our nature so that he might assume our debts as well and pay them for us and thereby restore us to a right relationship with God and even earn all those things for us which Adam forfeited.[73]

72. LC, 72–73 (emphasis added).

73. EC, 2.4.4–23.

The considerations so far situate Christ's satisfaction in its proper covenantal context, itself a fruitful discussion, but have not yet addressed its extent. We have seen that Christ made satisfaction *to God for our covenantal debts* but now need to consider *for whom* he made this satisfaction. In this respect, we return to the previous chapter's argument that the Father's mission in the covenant of redemption was to *arrange* salvation by *appointing* the Son as mediator and *assigning* the elect to him so that he would lose none of them.[74] After all, when the Son *accomplished* redemption by *accepting* the Father's will, it was his will for the salvation of the elect (John 6:37–40; John 17:2–4). The Spirit *applies* redemption by not only *accompanying* the Son but also *administering* his benefits to the elect. The Canons of Dort, again, provide confessional summary, highlighting that "God the Father's sovereign counsel" ensures that "the quickening and saving efficacy of the most precious death of his Son should *extend to all the elect* for bestowing upon *them alone* the gift of justifying faith," fixing that "*those only*, who were from eternity chosen unto salvation and *given to him by the Father*" would receive "faith, which together with all the other saving gifts of the Holy Spirit, he purchased for them by his death" (Canons of Dort 2.8).[75] God's purpose for salvation was that the Son would actually save all those whom the Father gave to him in the covenant of redemption.[76]

God's decree significantly shapes the question of whether Christ died to pay for the sins of the whole human race or of only the elect. With this aspect of the covenant of redemption in place, Christ clearly died to pay for the sins of only the elect. In the first recorded instance of the term "covenant of redemption," David Dickson uses this doctrine to refute Arminianism precisely in regard to the extent of Christ's satisfaction.[77] Dickson explains that the covenant of redemption concerned the elect by "designing" and "condescending" "particularly upon their number and

74. *CF*, 518–20.

75. *COC*, 3:562 (emphasis added).

76. Donald Macleod, "Definite Atonement and the Divine Decree," in *From Heaven He Came and Sought Her: Definite Atonement in Historical, Biblical, Theological, and Pastoral Perspective*, ed. David Gibson and Jonathan Gibson (Wheaton, IL: Crossway, 2013), 401–35.

77. David Dickson, "Arminianism Discussed," in *Records of the Kirk of Scotland, containing the Acts and Proceedings of the General Assemblies, from the Year 1638 Downwards*, ed. Alexander Peterkin (Edinburgh: John Sutherland, 1838), 156–59; Fesko, *Covenant of Redemption*, 30–31.

names."[78] The Father's part in appointing the Son as the new covenantal head establishes the difference between the nature of the first and last of Adam's representative roles. God had appointed Adam as the covenantal representative of a set group of people, although that set group was all humanity. Likewise, the Father appointed the Son as second Adam to represent a set group of people, in this case only the elect, so discharging and satisfying the actual and entire debts of those given to him.[79]

Certainly, since Christ is God's infinitely valuable Son, his perfect life and death were sufficiently valuable to redeem the whole world *if God had intended such.*[80] As the Canons of Dort summarize, "This death of God's Son is the only and most perfect sacrifice and satisfaction for sin, being infinite in value and worth, abundantly sufficient to expiate the sins of the whole world" (2.3).[81] In other words, Christ would not have needed to do anything else or something more if God had chosen more people to be among the elect. As we saw above in the Westminster Larger Catechism, so, too, the Canons of Dort affirm that the mediator's life needed to be of infinite value—namely, divine—in order to overcome the debts that we owe to God by virtue of the covenant of works: "For that reason, moreover, this death is so great in value and worth, because the one who endured it is not only a true and perfectly holy man, but also God's only begotten Son, of the same eternal and infinite essence with the Father and the Holy Spirit, which qualifications were necessary to be our Savior" (2.4).[82] Still, we must consider how the Scripture clearly teaches that when the Father appointed the Son as mediator, he assigned to him the specific number of the elect so that Christ would perform his work specifically on their behalf (John 6:38–40; John 10:25–30; John 17:1–9).[83]

If Christ's appointment were simply to repeat Adam's role as it was originally grounded in nature, then Christ would have represented the

78. Dickson, "Arminianism Discussed," 159.

79. Samuel Maresius, *Collegium Theologicum* (Gröningen: Johanes Collenius, 1645), 10.5; *EC*, 2.9.1.

80. *EC*, 2.9.2, 5–6.

81. *COC*, 3:561.

82. *COC*, 3:561.

83. *EC*, 2.9.19–30.

whole human race, at least to some hypothetical capacity.[84] As it stands, however, the Son's last-Adam office as assigned to him in the covenant of redemption appointed him to represent a very specific group of people, namely, the elect whom the Father gave to the Son, and to merit reward *for them* according to the covenant of redemption's terms.[85] So, Colquhoun, who understood the covenant of grace to be made first with Christ and then the elect in him, argues that "the *Parties* of the covenant of grace" entail "that Christ *died* for those whom he represented, and for none else." Even if Christ's death would be valuable enough to save every sinner, because "of the covenant, and of the parties contracting," Christ became "the Representative of the elect and of them only" so that "the condition of the covenant, his obedience unto death, was performed for them, and for no other."[86] The covenant of redemption formed this relationship between Christ and the elect.

The covenant of redemption defined not only the Son's obligations to accept the Father's will and attain righteousness for the elect but also his rewards, not simply as exaltation and a *generic* redeemed people but a *specific* group of redeemed people, the sheep for whom Christ would lay down his life (John 10:15). Christ's merit and reward, like Adam's, was covenantally defined.[87] As Herman Witsius explains, "by virtue of a compact," Christ "owed obedience to God." Because Christ fulfilled the covenant, "God owed to Christ and to them who are Christ's the reward *promised by the compact*, which is given to Christ as a due debt."[88] Likewise, Herman Bavinck notes, "Christ became human and acquired salvation for his people in virtue of that pact."[89] In this respect, Christ performed

84. Dickson identifies this as precisely the Arminian argument for universal grace, Dickson, "Arminianism Discussed," 156. Some Reformed theologians who formulated their theology before the covenant of redemption came into prominence did not overcome this issue; see Perkins, *Catholicity and the Covenant of Works*, 185–88; Harrison Perkins, "Archbishop James Ussher (1581–1656): His Life and Work, the Scholarship about Him, and His Significance for Confessional Presbyterians," *Confessional Presbyterian* 16 (2020): 15–16; and Crowe, *Last Adam*, 201–6.

85. Carl R. Trueman, "Atonement and the Covenant of Redemption: John Owen on the Nature of Christ's Satisfaction," in *From Heaven He Came and Sought Her*, 213–22.

86. *CG*, 50 (italics original).

87. Daniel Chamier, *Panstratiae Catholicae*, 4 vol. (Geneva, 1626), 3:241–42; Owen, "Exercitation XXVIII," 1:473–75; *CRS*, 1:260–61; *EC*, 2.3.7, 14–15, 28–33.

88. *EC*, 2.2.13 (emphasis added).

89. *BRD*, 3:523.

his work as the second Adam specifically to make satisfaction to God in regard to the demands of the original covenant of works, specifically for those who were assigned to him in the covenant of redemption.

THE COVENANT OF REDEMPTION AND BIBLICAL INTERPRETATION

As part 1 closed with some reflections about how the covenant of works is relevant for our holistic understanding of Scripture, so too this section ends part 2 with some suggestions for how the covenant of redemption has more holistic significance for our Bible reading.

First, the covenant of redemption helps make clearer sense of how the New Testament interprets the Old Testament. There are instances wherein it might *seem* that the New Testament writers have played fast and loose with the original meaning of Old Testament passages. Our commitment to Scripture's inspiration and authority, however, reminds us that the biblical authors' interpretive strategies are truly better than ours. Perhaps we have overlooked something that they knew which clarifies how they can interpret Old Testament passages the way that they did, under the Spirit's guidance? The apostles' gospel was thoroughly shaped by the Scripture, which was only the Old Testament before they wrote the New. Christ's coming did not entirely replace their dependence on Scripture to know God but informed them about the proper way to read the Old Testament in the first place.[90] In the case of passages like Psalm 40 and Psalm 110, it may not immediately occur to us to interpret those as the words of the Son to the Father or the words of the Father to the Son, but that is exactly how the author of Hebrews understood them.[91] The covenant of redemption, as God's plan for salvation decreed even before the foundations of the world, helps us understand that the Son's appointment as mediator did not begin at his incarnation but in eternity.[92] He acts as mediator both *incarnandus* and *incarnatus*, clarifying why the New Testament can often read Old Testament passages as not simply pointing forward to Christ prophetically but as directly and immediately about Christ.

---

90. Watson, *Hermeneutics of Faith*, xx–xxvi, xiv–li, 12–22.

91. Richard, "Covenant of Redemption," 48–50.

92. Irenaeus, *Demonstration*, §48–53.

Second, the covenant of redemption explains *how* we find our rescue in Christ Jesus. Christians know that Christ is God the Son who is our Savior. Still, the covenant of redemption sheds deeper insight into the structure of his saving work on our behalf. Although Adam represented us before God in the first covenant and was supposed to render perfect obedience to merit our citizenship in heaven according to the covenantal terms, he failed. Our new representative, Jesus Christ, recapitulated Adam's role by rendering that perfect obedience and by bearing the curse for our disobedience. Because of Christ's perfect merits, he obtained renewed exaltation for himself but also purchased full redemption for those whom the Father had given to him to save. Believers belong to God's kingdom because Christ has earned our right to be there.

Finally, the covenant of redemption also helps us see more clearly how the whole Bible is about Christ. Since God decreed the plan of salvation from eternity, that he would choreograph historical events and inspire the Scripture in such a way as to teach about and give insight into that plan for our redemption should not surprise us. Even the relationship that God forged with Adam in the covenant of works foreshadowed Christ's work and established principles of covenant obedience and reward through a representative that set the stage for what Christ would do for the elect.[93] Those interruptions in portions of Scripture, such as in the Psalms or the Prophets, where we get a glimpse of some of those intra-Trinitarian conversations is also, in some ways, expected as the covenant of redemption was fixed before the world existed, and God is able and kind to reveal, even in advance, details about how he has woven the tapestry of our deliverance.

CONCLUSION

Whereas the first Adam broke the covenant of works, shattering our communion with God and forfeiting the possibility for even deeper communion by covenant, Christ as the last Adam in the covenant of redemption fulfilled the covenant of works for the elect, so earning everlasting blessings of our communion with God in indestructible life. The covenant of redemption establishes the foundation for how God can grant that

93. *BRD*, 2:564.

communion to us by grace, in that Christ as the last Adam and the new covenantal representative for the elect fulfilled the law on our behalf and paid the penalty for our sin. We should, then, remember the contrast between the two opposing covenantal principles—law and gospel—and how they are not opposed in themselves or in God but in regard to us as sinners. In this contrast, the covenant of works is never ultimately abrogated, even though sinners no longer have ability to obtain everlasting blessings of deeper communion with God by its terms. Rather, Christ fulfilled the covenant of works for us, facilitating God's offer of blessings to us by grace on the basis of someone else's works instead of our own.

The pastoral use of this chapter's material is to remind us that God is sovereign over history and is directing its events toward Christ's glory. More specifically, we can easily find ourselves troubled in our day when it seems that Christianity is increasingly disfavored in Western culture. We can readily let ourselves be overwhelmed and despair. Whether our work makes it hard to hold Christian commitments or our schools promote ungodly agendas, we must remember that God holds the whole scope of history in his hands and intends it to culminate in Christ's glory. As Christians, then, we remember that "If God is for us, who can be against us?" and that, when any sort of trial and struggle presents itself, "*in all these things* we are more than conquerors through him who loved us" (Rom 8:31, 37). We, then, do not lose hope but rejoice, knowing that as God has shaped history to point to Christ in the past, he will continue to direct global affairs for the exaltation of the one who intercedes for us now.

Part Three

THE SUBSTANCE OF THE COVENANT OF GRACE

VIII

The Unity of the Covenant of Grace in Christ

This is God, our God forever and ever. He will guide us forever.
—*Psalm 48:14*

The entire Bible is about Christ. Whereas the Old Testament foretold Christ's work by announcing what he would do for his people, the New displayed the Son as the Savior of all God's people, which holds true whether they lived before or after he executed his earthly mission. Boethius (d. 524) writes, "The Christian Faith is proclaimed by the authority of the New Testament and of the Old; but although the Old scripture contains within its pages the name of Christ and constantly gives token that he will come whom we believe has already come by his birth from the Virgin, yet the diffusion of that faith throughout the world dates from the actual miraculous coming of our Savior."[1] The covenant of grace is God's one plan of salvation whereby he effectively redeemed all his elect by the work of Christ.

The covenant of grace shows how we can have restored communion with God in Christ. As Francis Turretin teaches, the covenant of grace "is of the greatest importance in theology being as it were the center and bond of all

1. Boethius, "On the Catholic Faith," in *Theological Tractates, The Consolation of Philosophy*, trans. H. F. Stewart, E. K. Rand, and S. J. Tester (Cambridge, MA: Harvard University Press, 1973), 52–53.

religion, consisting in the communion of God with man and embracing in its compass all the benefits of God towards man and his duties towards God."[2] The covenant of grace provides hope as God offers everlasting fellowship with him in glory through it.[3] Just as once dinner is prepared, we still have to pick up a fork to deliver the food into our mouths, so too Christ has accomplished redemption as the Savior, but that salvation must still be made our own.

The covenant of grace is built on the gospel principle. Again, Scripture teaches about two kinds of covenantal principles—law and gospel, works and promise. So we can see that the covenants of works and redemption were both law covenants, in that God covenanted to require one person in each, Adam or Christ, to render perfect obedience for those whom they represented.[4] The covenant of redemption secured grace for us but was a covenant of works for the Son.[5] In the covenant of grace, God can promise grace, not because he has set aside his just requirements, but because Christ has fulfilled those requirements for us and, so, earned the blessings of grace on our behalf.[6]

This chapter argues that the covenant of grace is one in substance *because* Christ and his saving benefits are distributed to believers in every age, whether Old or New Testament. Readers from outside Reformed theology might easily misunderstand what we mean by arguing for one covenant of grace that is unified in substance, perceiving the point to be that each biblical covenant works that exact same way in redemptive history or that the covenants are the same, in that each provided salvation through the rituals of the covenant itself, such as circumcision or animal sacrifices. The chapters in part 3 elucidate the Reformed view that the one covenant of grace is unified in substance because, although the historical covenants function diversely in redemptive history, there has always been only one way of salvation since the fall, namely, *Christ and his benefits* received by faith.

---

2. *TI*, 12.1.1.
3. *TI*, 12.2.19–21.
4. *BRD*, 3:227–28.
5. *VRD*, 2:92–93.
6. *BRD*, 3:224–26.

WHAT IS THE COVENANT OF GRACE?

If Adam created the problem of putting all under the curse of sin, and Christ laid a foundation by his work for the solution to that problem, then the covenant of grace is the way that God brings that solution to completion in our lives. As the Westminster Larger Catechism explains, "God does not leave all mankind to perish in the estate of sin and misery, into which they fell by the breach of the first Covenant, commonly called the Covenant of Works; but, of his mere love and mercy, delivers his elect out of it, and brings them into an estate of salvation by the second Covenant, commonly called the Covenant of Grace" (WLC 30).[7] God made the covenant of grace as the mechanism to free us from sin's penalty and power by Christ's work. Our fallen condition means that we cannot have a right relationship with God on the basis of our works, so we must relate to him by grace rather than by the law.[8]

The covenant of grace is the arrangement in which God promises everlasting blessing to his people on the basis of grace and requires faith in Christ as the only condition. The Westminster Larger Catechism helpfully explains: "The Grace of God is manifested in the second Covenant, in that he freely provides and offers to sinners a Mediator, and life and salvation by him; and, requiring Faith as the condition to interest them in him, promises and gives his holy Spirit to all his elect, to work in them that Faith, with all other saving graces; and to enable them unto all holy obedience, as the evidence of the truth of their faith and thankfulness to God, and as the way which he hath appointed them to salvation" (WLC 32).[9] The covenant of grace offers Christ as the mediator for sinners. Since we are covenant breakers because of our sin, we need a mediator to reconcile us with God and fulfill the terms of our initial covenant for us.[10] The covenant of grace also promises the Spirit to believers.[11] The other aspects of the covenant in this section of the catechism are effects of the Son's and Spirit's work that we take hold of, blessings in the covenant of grace.

---

7. *LC*, 71.
8. *BRD*, 3:225–28; *TI*, 12.2.3–4, 10.
9. *LC*, 71–72.
10. *TI*, 12.9.2.
11. *TI*, 12.6.45.

The Westminster Confession outlines this doctrine well. "Man by his fall having made himself incapable of life by that covenant [of works], the Lord was pleased to make a second, commonly called the covenant of grace: wherein he freely offered unto sinners life and salvation by Jesus Christ, requiring of them faith in him that they may be saved, and promising to give unto all those that are ordained unto life his Holy Spirit, to make them willing and able to believe" (WCF 7.3).[12] The covenant of grace is God's promise to be God to us in Christ.[13] It focuses on how God offers life and salvation *by Jesus Christ* on the one condition of *faith in him.*[14]

Despite the Bible's long story of God's covenants with Adam, Noah, Abraham, Moses, David, and the new covenant, the confession condenses this story into the difference between the principles of the covenant of works and the one covenant of grace. That distinction between two basic covenants indicates that God has dealt with his people by only two principles throughout the human race's entire history: works and grace, law and gospel. We can relate to him by only one of those principles.

The covenant of grace offers salvation as the only alternative to the covenant of works, meaning *this* saving plan spans all human history and is *the* method of rescuing each of God's elect. More specifically, the covenant of grace offers salvation *by Jesus Christ* to everyone regardless of whether they lived during the Old Testament period, the New Testament age, or our era today until Christ returns. So, the Westminster Confession explains, "This covenant of grace is frequently set forth in the Scripture by the name of a testament, in reference to the death of Christ the testator, and to the everlasting inheritance, with all things belonging to it, therein bequeathed" (WCF 7.4).[15] Regardless of how we translate the Greek and Hebrew words that appear in our Bible as "covenant"—the translation issue is partly why the confession mentions "the name of a testament"—God's covenants all concern an inheritance for God's people.[16] Christ must

12. *COC*, 3:617.

13. Ussher, *Body*, 159; *TI*, 12.2.17; 12.5.9.

14. Hodge, *Systematic Theology*, 2:362–65.

15. *COC*, 3:617.

16. *CG*, 311–33.

be the reason for this inheritance for every believer throughout history, because he is "the only Mediator of the Covenant of Grace."[17]

Paul emphasizes Christ's office as the sole mediator in 1 Timothy 2:5–6: "For there is one God, and there is one mediator between God and men, the man Christ Jesus, who gave himself as a ransom for all, which is the testimony given at the proper time." Christ alone can reconcile a person to God, no matter whether that person lived before or after Christ wrought his work of redemption in history. He served as the true mediator of God's people *incarnandus* and *incarnatus* but was fully revealed as such "at the proper time" through the testimony of his saving death.[18] The real continuity in God's redeeming plan is salvation by grace through faith in Jesus Christ as "the only redeemer of God's elect."[19]

Christians have long recognized this continuity across God's covenants. For example, The Epistle of Barnabas is one of the earliest extant Christian writings outside the New Testament, most likely written between AD 70 and AD 132.[20] At the early end of this time frame, some apostles were still alive, but even the later end was close enough to their lifetimes that the author may have learned directly from them. After explaining how several Old Testament events point to Christ, Barnabas writes, "Now let us see whether this people or the former people is the heir, and whether the covenant is for us or for them."[21] Barnabas thought that there is only one covenant, belonging to the true people of God—the question being if that means national Israel or Christians.[22]

For Barnabas, the covenant concerns God giving an inheritance to his people. He writes, "Observe how by these means he [God] has ordained

---

17. WLC 36; *LC*, 72.

18. *CG*, 61–62. Even though the Greek phrase καιροῖς ἰδίοις is grammatically plural, Paul's use of this phrase elsewhere seems to indicate that the sense properly refers to a singular point of time (1 Tim 6:15; Titus 1:3; cf. Gal 6:9); see George W. Knight III, *The Pastoral Epistles* (Grand Rapids: Eerdmans, 1992), 123–24. Even if the plural is emphasized, the point about the unity of the covenant of grace is only strengthened, since Paul's point would then be that Christ's role as the only mediator between God and man would have testimony "at the proper times," namely, Christ's mediation is made known at other points in redemptive history before he even came in the incarnation.

19. WSC 21, in *COC*, 3:680; *TI*, 12.2.15(2), 17; 12.5.9–13.

20. *AP*, 373.

21. Barnabas 13.1; *AP*, 423.

22. Ligon Duncan, "Covenant in the Early Church," in *CT*, 297.

that this people should be first, and heir of the covenant."[23] This one covenant was established with Abraham by faith.[24] God did not give that one covenant to national Israel, because of their sins, but to Christians.[25] Although Moses received the covenant, "the Lord himself gave it *to us*, so that *we* might become the people of inheritance, by suffering *for us*." He worked through the Mosaic covenant so that "*we* might receive the covenant through the Lord Jesus who inherited it, who was prepared for this purpose, in order that by appearing in person and redeeming from darkness our hearts, which had already been paid over to death and given over to the lawlessness of error, he might establish a covenant *in us* by his word."[26] Barnabas recognized God's providential direction of Old Testament events to ensure that Christians received the covenantal inheritance (Gal 3:14).

Since the sixteenth century, the Reformed have explained the substance of the covenant of grace much like ancient theologians.[27] For Barnabas, Christ establishes the covenant in believers because of the Father's command—a basic premise of the covenant of redemption.[28] Strikingly, Barnabas and many other ancient writers appeal *readily* to the Old Testament to demonstrate the gospel.[29] In the sixteenth century, John Calvin writes, "The covenant made with all the patriarchs is so much like ours in substance and reality that the two are actually one and the same. Yet they differ in the mode of dispensation."[30] In the seventeenth century, James Ussher similarly writes that "the sum of the covenant of grace" is "that God will be our God and give us Life everlasting in Christ, if we receive him, being freely by his Father offered unto us."[31] Believers

---

23. Barnabas 13.6; *AP*, 423.

24. Barnabas 13.7; *AP*, 423.

25. Barnabas 14.1–4; *AP*, 425.

26. Barnabas 14.4–6; *AP*, 425 (emphasis added).

27. *CMT*, 80–81; *VRD*, 2:122–24.

28. *TI*, 12.2.14.

29. Andrew A. Woolsey, *Unity and Continuity in Covenantal Thought: A Study in the Reformed Tradition to the Westminster Assembly* (Grand Rapids: Reformation Heritage Books, 2012), 162–63; Duncan, "Covenant in the Early Church," 297, 299–302.

30. Calvin, *Institutes*, 2.10.2.

31. Ussher, *Body*, 159.

are the true heirs of God's one covenant, consisting in redemption from sin, which Christ establishes.[32]

The covenant of grace is unified, despite its long history prior to Christ's incarnation. So, Augustine writes, "Nevertheless, both the new covenant lies concealed in the old covenant, and the old stands revealed in the new."[33] In the old covenant, God's people had a very different outward form of life than the church today, including animal sacrifices and many other governing laws. Still, as Herman Bavinck explains, "The doctrine of the covenant of grace first emerged for the purpose of maintaining the essential unity of the Old and the New Testaments."[34] God has always saved us in exactly the same way: by grace alone through faith alone in Christ alone.

The distinction between the covenant's *substance* and its *administration* explains that continuity in salvation, despite God's people having different outward forms of worship.[35] The analogy of buying ice cream at an ice cream shop illustrates the relationship of substance and administration. When buying ice cream at a shop, you must decide whether you want it in a cup or in a cone. Regardless of the container, it is still ice cream. On the other hand, cups and cones deliver it in very different ways.

In this illustration, ice cream is the "substance," but cups and cones are the "administrations." Whatever way that you receive that ice cream, it is ice cream and remains what you actually want. The ice cream is the purpose, so, the substance. On the other hand, the cup and the cone are two different administrations of the substance. Cups and cones, although very different in appearance, both deliver ice cream. In the covenant of grace, Christ is the substance. Both the Old and New Testament administrations deliver Christ, although differing in appearance.

---

32. Duncan, "Covenant in the Early Church," 297.

33. Augustine, *Seven Questions Concerning the Heptateuch*, 2.73, in *PL*, 34:623; also Augustine, *Treatise on the Merits and Forgiveness of Sins, and on the Baptism of Infants*, 1.13, 54, in *NPNF1*, 5:20, 35; and Augustine, *On the Spirit and the Letter*, §18, 27, in *NPNF1*, 5:90, 95.

34. *BRD*, 3:227.

35. Reformed theologians have used various terms to designate the same distinction. Turretin refers to the *internal essence* and *external dispensation*, *TI*, 12.6.5. Witsius discusses *substance* or *essence* and *circumstantials*, *EC*, 3:2.1. Francis Roberts also refers to "essentials and substantials" in contrast to the "circumstantials," *MMB*, sig. a1r.

The covenant's unified substance is not a new idea. In the second century, Irenaeus understood the unity of the old and new covenants to be, at least partly, in Christ, as the Savior in all times who recapitulated Adam's role.[36] He explains,

> All things, therefore, have *one and the same substance*, that is, from one and the same God, just as also the Lord says to the disciples, "Therefore, every scribe who is taught in the kingdom of heaven is like the head of house, who brings forth new and old things from his treasure." He did not teach that the one who brought forth the old was a certain person but the one bringing forth the new is another, but that they are one and the same. In fact, the head of house is the Lord [Christ], who rules the entire house of the Father [Heb. 3:1–6].[37]

Further, Christ gives the law as moral guidance "to those who have been justified by faith, and opens his inheritance to those who are sons."[38] So, Irenaeus summarizes, "In fact there is one salvation and one God."[39] Irenaeus, one of our earliest theologians, saw unity across the whole canon of Scripture in who God is, in Christ as the Savior, and in salvation itself, including justification by faith.[40]

Although too easily overlooked, this unity was profoundly significant in the early church. In the church's infancy, Christians had to explain their identity as God's people to inquisitive believers, to Roman authorities, and to heretics trying to undermine the faith. Theologically, the covenant's unity emphasizes how Christ's coming was not God's brand-new work but the complete fulfillment of his ancient promises. This issue is imbedded in the New Testament writings as the apostles wrestled with the significance of God bringing gentiles to faith in Israel's Messiah (Acts 15:1–35; Rom 9–11). They concluded that God was extending salvation to the world by engrafting gentiles into God's covenant people (Rom

---

36. John Behr, *Irenaeus of Lyon: Identifying Christianity* (Oxford: Oxford University Press, 2013), 145–49.

37. Irenaeus, *Against Heresies*, 4.9.1 in *PG*, 7.1:996; *ANF*, 1:472 (emphasis added).

38. Irenaeus, *Against Heresies*, 4.9.1 in *PG*, 7.1:996; *ANF*, 1:472.

39. Irenaeus, *Against Heresies*, 4.9.3 in *PG*, 7.1:998; *ANF*, 1:473.

40. Horton, *Justification*, 1:39–74; Minns, *Irenaeus*, 47–67; Woolsey, *Unity and Continuity in Covenantal Thought*, 165–66.

11:17–24). As Paul writes in Ephesians 3:6, "This mystery is that the Gentiles are fellow heirs, members of the same body, and partakers of the promise in Christ Jesus through the gospel." Indeed, he says in Galatians 3:13–14 that Christ bore the curse of the law, "so that in Christ Jesus the blessing of Abraham might come to the Gentiles, so that we might receive the promised Spirit through faith." Christians have received the fulfilled inheritance of God's covenantal promises to the ancient fathers.[41]

Politically, Christians' unity with God's Old Testament people provided greater religious freedom under Roman law. Since the Roman Empire bound religious practices to cultural involvement, only governmentally approved belief systems were socially acceptable. Even if Rome never formally imposed empire-wide persecution upon Christians, local suppression occurred.[42] Although Judaism was sanctioned, Christianity was sometimes perceived as a new religion. Early Christian apologists then stressed Christianity's organic unity with Old Testament religion.[43] The Epistle to Diognetus emphasizes how Christ is the eternal God, whom Jews worshipped, now extending salvation to the rest of the world.

> This is why he sent the Word, namely, so that he might appear to the world; though dishonored by the chosen people, he was preached by apostles and believed in by Gentiles. This is the one who was from the beginning, who appeared as new yet proved to be old, and is always young as he is born in the hearts of saints. This is the Eternal One, who today is accounted a Son, through whom the church is enriched and grace is unfolded and multiplied among the saints.[44]

Christianity's unity with Judaism, as is the case if the covenant of grace encompasses God's Old and New Testament people, extended Rome's

41. Jaroslav Pelikan, *The Emergence of the Catholic Tradition (100–600)* (Chicago, IL: University of Chicago Press, 1971), 12–27.

42. Michael J. Kruger, *Christianity at the Crossroads: How the Second Century Shaped the Future of the Church* (London: SPCK, 2017), 40–54.

43. Kruger, *Christianity at the Crossroads*, 64–68.

44. Diognetus 11.3–5; *AP*, 715.

religious authorization to the church, so early Christians eagerly affirmed their unity with God's people of old.[45]

Early heretics sharply divided the Old and New Testaments, even regarding God's own identity.[46] For example, the gnostics claimed secret, newly revealed knowledge that the Old Testament God was a demiurge who fell from the spiritual realm and took control of this world, but Jesus was a compassionate, truly spiritual teacher.[47] Marcion (AD 85–160) rejected the Old Testament's description of God's moral character, arguing that it told of a demiurge who created evil, but Jesus revealed the philanthropic God.[48] These arguments for covenantal disunity not only contradicted orthodox teaching but also supported moral license.[49] Irenaeus, and others, such as Tertullian, fought against these heresies, emphasizing the unity of God's covenant and God's sameness in identity and saving plan throughout redemptive history.[50]

These historical points remind us that the covenant of grace's unity was a fundamental aspect of early Christian theology. In the medieval period, theologians continued to argue for the unity of the covenant of grace, even if not by that name. In the twelfth century, Hugh of St. Victor (c. 1096–1141) drew upon the distinction of Christ *incarnandus* and *incarnatus* to argue for one way of salvation in every era:

> It is certainly true, since Scripture repeatedly testifies, that no one even since the beginning has been saved without faith in Christ. So, the blessed Augustine, concerning this very point, thus argued: the same faith in the mediator has made those who are saved righteous, including the ancient ones—the insignificant along with the great. The old covenant that resulted in slavery did not save, nor the law which in this way was not given in order that it be able to

45. This point shows how theological systems like dispensationalism are utterly foreign to the Christian tradition, even at a merely historical level.

46. Henry Chadwick, *The Early Church*, rev. ed. (London: Penguin Books, 1993), 33–41; Pelikan, *Emergence of the Catholic Tradition*, 68–120; Kruger, *Christianity at the Crossroads*, 108–34.

47. Kelly, *Early Christian Doctrines*, 22–28; John Anthony McGuckin, *The Path of Christianity: The First Thousand Years* (Downers Grove, IL: IVP Academic, 2017), 32–41; Minns, *Irenaeus*, 19–25.

48. McGuckin, *Pathway of Christianity*, 41–48; Minns, *Irenaeus*, 25–27.

49. McGuckin, *Pathway of Christianity*, 39–41, 47.

50. *BRD*, 3:207; Duncan, "Covenant in the Early Church," 298n14, 306–7; Chadwick, *Early Church*, 85–90; McGuckin, *Pathway of Christianity*, 48–53; Minns, *Irenaeus*, 47–67.

give life, but God's grace through Jesus Christ. Because just as we believe Christ has come in the flesh, so they believed in Christ who would come; just as we believe he died, so they believed he would die; just as we believe he has certainly risen, so they believed he would rise; and we and they believe that he will come to judge the living and the dead.[51]

So too, with Heinrich Bullinger (1504–1575) we should take this non-negotiable theological point seriously.[52] The ancient church's focus on the unity of the covenant made the Reformers' use of covenant against Roman Catholic theology an obvious *and traditional* move. The Reformed development of covenant theology merely extended the ancient church's teaching to address new issues. To this point, Francis Roberts argues that all believers in the Old and New Testaments "were saved in the selfsame way for substance."[53] Christians embracing the Reformed understanding of covenant theology are aligned with the most ancient ideas of the Christian faith, as we have all reflected upon the Scripture as a record of God's one plan of salvation.[54]

CHRIST AS THE SUBSTANCE

Christ is the only mediator of the covenant of grace in every age. In John 14:6, Jesus declares, "*No one* comes to the Father except through me." Christ's claim, taken seriously, entails an absolute sense.[55] The Westminster Confession applies the covenant's unity in specific reference to Christ: "Although the work of redemption was not actually wrought by Christ till after his incarnation, yet *the virtue, efficacy, and benefits thereof were communicated unto the elect, in all ages* successively from the beginning of the world, in and by those promises, types, and sacrifices, wherein he was revealed, and signified to be the seed which should bruise the serpent's

51. Hugh of St. Victor, *Concerning the Mysteries of the Christian Faith*, 1.10.6, in *PL*, 176:336.

52. Heinrich Bullinger, "A Brief Exposition of the One and Eternal Testament or Covenant of God," in Charles S. McCoy and J. Wayne Baker, *Fountainhead of Federalism: Heinrich Bullinger and the Covenantal Tradition* (Louisville: Westminster John Knox, 1991), 117–30.

53. *MMB*, 67.

54. Hodge, *Systematic Theology*, 2:366–71; Woolsey, *Unity and Continuity in Covenantal Thought*, 161–83.

55. Maresius, *Collegium Theologicum*, 10.5.

head, and the lamb slain from the foundation of the world, being yesterday and today the same and forever" (WCF 8.6).[56] There is *no one*, regardless of the time and place, who rightly relates to God in some other way than through Jesus.[57] Even before he executed his saving work in history as the guarantor of the new covenant, God granted the efficacy of his work to old covenant believers by using their types and ordinances to direct them to trust in Christ *incarnandus*. As Bavinck explains, "The Old Testament is also one in essence and substance with the New Testament" because, "although Christ completed his work on earth only in the midst of history and although the Holy Spirit was not poured out till the day of Pentecost, God nevertheless was able, already in the days of the Old Testament, to fully distribute the benefits to be acquired and applied by the Son and the Spirit."[58] The Son had already been appointed as their mediator in the covenant of redemption, so he had taken on sin's penalty debt for every member of the elect, and forgiveness was granted to them by faith even before Christ paid that debt on the cross in history.[59] Christ's sponsorship was as *expromissor* rather than *fideiussor*, so that he became truly liable for every elect person's twofold debt by the covenant of redemption rather than leaving that debt credited to them until he paid it. The new covenant clearly exhibits Christ and his work, but the old used types and shadows as means of grace to communicate the eschatological reality of the virtue and effects of Christ's work to believers.[60]

Reformed writers attest that Christ alone is Savior, making his saving work the one way of salvation for those who live thousands of years before or after he walked on earth.[61] Herman Witsius explains that, to the elect from every era, "*one* and the same *eternal life* was promised" and "Jesus Christ was held forth as the *one* and the same *author* and bestower of

56. *COC*, 3:621–22 (emphasis added).

57. The Socinians, Arminians, and radical Anabaptists rejected that the redeemed in the Old Testament era were saved by Christ; *CRS*, 1:451; *TI*, 12.5.1–4.

58. *BRD*, 3:215–16.

59. *BRD*, 2:223–24, 3:491–95, 590, 4:215–19, 225–26; *VRD*, 2:88–89, 94; 3:112; *TI*, 12.2.21; 12.9.3–20.

60. Horton, *Rediscovering*, 152–54; Bryan D. Estelle et al., "Report to the 83rd (2016) General Assembly of the Committee to Study Republication" (Willow Grove, PA: The Committee on Christian Education of the Orthodox Presbyterian Church, 2016), 10–12.

61. *TI*, 12.9.1–20; *EC*, 3.2.39–40; *VRD*, 2:122–24; *CMT*, 89, 139–40, 148.

salvation," but that "they could not become partakers of it in any other way, but by a true and lively *faith* in him."[62] Turretin elaborates that "revelation of grace was somewhat obscure and sparing as to mode" but "was sufficient as to substance" even though "it did not differ as to substance."[63] The Reformed thought is in unison on this point.[64]

Far from a speculative leap, Scripture confirms this teaching. Even though God's old covenant had a different outward form than the new covenant, "these are a shadow of the things to come, but the substance belongs to Christ" (Col 2:17). In 1 Corinthians 15:20–22, Paul affirms: "But in fact Christ has been raised from the dead, the firstfruits of those who have fallen asleep. For as by a man came death, by a man has come also the resurrection of the dead. For as in Adam all die, so also *in Christ* shall *all* be made alive." Adam is the singular source of death for all humanity. In the same way, Christ is the singular source of life.[65] Every single human being received a death penalty because Adam represented us in the first covenant.[66] Just as Adam's work covers *all* the people who die, so in the same way Christ's work applies to *all* who will take part in everlasting life.[67]

Christ's position as the substance of the covenant of grace has several layers. First, Christ simply fulfills all Scripture, as in *redemptive-historical hermeneutics*.[68] The biblical narrative's scope and all God's promises culminate in Jesus Christ.[69] As Paul wrote in 2 Corinthians 1:19–20, "For the Son of God, Jesus Christ, whom we proclaimed among you, Silvanus and Timothy and I, was not Yes and No, but in him it is always Yes. For *all the promises of God* find their Yes *in him*. That is why it is through him that we

---

62. *EC*, 3.2.2 (italics original).

63. *TI*, 12.7.44.

64. Gillespie, *Ark of the Covenant*, 453–78.

65. *CC*, 20:2.24–25; Hodge, *Corinthians*, 323–26; Thiselton, *Corinthians*, 1224–29; Fee, *Corinthians*, 828–33.

66. *DIALIC*, 242–58.

67. Gaffin, *Resurrection and Redemption*, 34–36; *DIALIC*, 265–66.

68. Richard B. Gaffin Jr., "The Redemptive-Historical View," in *Biblical Hermeneutics: Five Views*, ed. Stanley E. Porter and Beth M. Stovell (Downers Grove, IL: IVP Academic, 2012), 89–110; *BTA*, 11–82, 186–90; Sidney Greidanus, *Preaching Christ from the Old Testament: A Hermeneutical Method* (Grand Rapids: Eerdmans, 1999); Graeme Goldsworthy, *According to Plan: The Unfolding Revelation of God in the Bible* (Downers Grove, IL: InterVarsity Press, 2003); Graeme Goldsworthy, *Christ-Centered Biblical Theology: Hermeneutical Foundations and Principles* (Downers Grove, IL: IVP Academic, 2012).

69. Stephen J. Wellum, "Christological Reflections in Light of Scripture's Covenants," *SBJT* 16 no. 2 (2012): 45–48.

utter our Amen to God for his glory." Every promise that God has made comes to fruition in Jesus Christ.[70]

This aspect of fulfillment assumes that God inspired the Scripture and intended its promises, even in their original meaning, to point to Jesus Christ. The story arc culminating in Jesus is not hard to follow. Just after Adam sinned, God cursed the serpent, saying in Genesis 3:15:

> I will put enmity between you and the woman,
> and between your offspring and her offspring;
> he shall bruise your head,
> and you shall bruise his heel.

Notably, the seed of *the woman* will crush the serpent's head.[71] Leaping ahead, God promised a sign of hope to King Ahaz in Isaiah 7:14: "Behold, *the virgin* shall conceive and bear a son, and shall call his name Immanuel." Isaiah's prediction that the Messiah would be born from a virgin renewed the promise of the descendant of *the woman*.[72] Finally, Paul explains in Galatians 4:4–5: "But when the fullness of time had come, God sent forth his Son, *born of woman*, born under the law, to redeem those who were under the law, so that we might receive adoption as sons." The woman's seed, the virgin's child, appeared in Jesus Christ, and he came to overthrow the penalty of sin, the principality of the devil, and power of death.[73] The Bible's story arc of redemption began by announcing Christ and culminates in Christ himself.

The second layer is that Christ completes God's part in saving his people, both by taking on God's role in salvation and by being the promised deliverer of God's people. For example, the theme of the royal shepherd runs throughout the Old Testament in reference both to God and to the messianic king. Famously, David announces in Psalm 23:1–3,

> The Lord is my shepherd; I shall not want.
> He makes me lie down in green pastures.

---

70. *TI*, 12.6.15–20.

71. Wenham, *Genesis 1–15*, 80–81; Collins, *Genesis 1–4*, 155–59; Robert S. Candlish, *Contributions towards the Exposition of the Book of Genesis*, 4th ed., 2 vol. (Edinburgh: Johnstone and Hunter, 1853), 1:99–103; *VRD*, 2:124–27.

72. E. J. Young, *The Book of Isaiah*, 3 vol. (Grand Rapids: Eerdmans, 1965), 1:286–91.

73. *MMB*, 210–16; *EC*, 4.1.17–20.

> He leads me beside still waters.
> He restores my soul.
> He leads me in paths of righteousness
> for his name's sake.

God cares and provides for his servants as the shepherd leads his sheep.

The theme of God as his people's shepherd intensifies as the prophets use it and deepen its application.[74] Most simply, Isaiah 40:11 declares that the Lord "will tend his flock like a shepherd; he will gather the lambs in his arms." More extensively, Ezekiel 34:11–16 explains how God will be the rescuing shepherd who delivers his people from exile.

> For thus says the Lord God: Behold, I, I myself will search for my sheep and will seek them out. As a shepherd seeks out his flock when he is among his sheep that have been scattered, so will I seek out my sheep, and I will rescue them from all places where they have been scattered on a day of clouds and thick darkness. And I will bring them out from the peoples and gather them from the countries, and will bring them into their own land. And I will feed them on the mountains of Israel, by the ravines, and in all the inhabited places of the country. I will feed them with good pasture, and on the mountain heights of Israel shall be their grazing land. There they shall lie down in good grazing land, and on rich pasture they shall feed on the mountains of Israel. I myself will be the shepherd of my sheep, and I myself will make them lie down, declares the Lord God. I will seek the lost, and I will bring back the strayed, and I will bind up the injured, and I will strengthen the weak, and the fat and the strong I will destroy. I will feed them in justice.

Although Psalm 23's moving description of God's general care for his people initiated the shepherd theme, the prophets developed it to demonstrate God's commitment to his people in *his* role in redemption.

---

74. The principle of heightening fulfillment of promises *and themes* is a rich way of seeing how the Scripture's divine author builds upon his own word to bring it to fulfillment in Christ; see Bryan D. Estelle, *Echoes of Exodus: Tracing a Biblical Motif* (Downers Grove, IL: IVP Academic, 2018), 19–60; and *KTC*, 120–21.

Scripture also develops the royal shepherd theme. When God sent Samuel to find the king of Israel who would follow Saul, David was tending *sheep* (1 Sam 16:11). The Spirit anointed this shepherd as king of God's people (1 Sam 16:12–13). In Ezekiel 37:24–27, God promised to provide a shepherd, a David-like king, who will secure an everlasting *covenant* of peace between the Lord and his people.

> My servant David shall be king over them, and they shall all have one shepherd. They shall walk in my rules and be careful to obey my statutes. They shall dwell in the land that I gave to my servant Jacob, where your fathers lived. They and their children and their children's children shall dwell there forever, and David my servant shall be their prince forever. I will make a covenant of peace with them. It shall be an everlasting covenant with them. And I will set them in their land and multiply them, and will set my sanctuary in their midst forevermore. My dwelling place shall be with them, and I will be their God, and they shall be my people.

Although God promised that he himself will shepherd his people, he still promised to provide a shepherd-king, who will fulfill the pattern of David's righteous reign. This Davidic king will bring about a covenant of peace between God and his people, securing God's presence with those who belong to him.

Unsurprisingly, Christ completes God's role as the shepherd of his people *and* fulfills God's promises about the royal shepherd like David. Since David, the shepherd boy, was anointed king in Bethlehem (1 Sam 16:1–13), Christ comes forth from Bethlehem to be the messianic king who will shepherd God's flock (Mic 5:2–4).[75] *God* the Son comes to earth and shepherds his people. This is precisely why Christ said, "I am the good shepherd" (John 10:11, 14). Only God is good, but Christ is the *good* shepherd (Mark 10:18). Moreover, in John 10:14–16, Christ explains his work as shepherd, "I am the good shepherd. I know my own and my own know me, just as the Father knows me and I know the Father; and I lay down my life for the sheep. And I have other sheep that are not of this fold. I must bring them also, and they will listen to my voice. So there will

---

75. Irenaeus, *Demonstration*, §63–66.

be one flock, one shepherd." Christ not only acts as shepherd but gathers the sheep given to him *by the Father* (John 10:27–29). In Ezekiel 34:11–16, God promised that he himself would be the shepherd to his people, gathering them from where they were scattered. Christ, God the Son, fulfills this divine role of shepherding God's people by gathering them into one flock.

On the other hand, the Davidic shepherd must be the king who secured a covenant of peace between God and his people. Christ laid down his life for the sheep because the covenant of redemption determined that the Son's obedient incarnate life and death would earn life for the elect. Through his merit, Christ secured that covenant of peace that guarantees God's presence among his people. Psalm 2 is a messianic psalm that tells of the Messiah's coronation. Psalm 2:7 establishes the covenantal work of the Messiah that is fulfilled in Christ.

> I will tell of the decree:
> The LORD said to me, "You are my Son;
> today I have begotten you.
> Ask of me, and I will make the nations your heritage,
> and the ends of the earth your possession.

The decree situates this promise in the covenant, installing the king over God's covenant people, even addressing the Son *incarnandus*.[76] God announces his faithful Son, who has finally fulfilled Adam's original mission.[77]

The Gospel writers emphasize Jesus's link to Adam (Luke 3:38) and to David (Matt 1:1) because the king fulfilled that same Adamic role of God's faithful son. The messianic king of Psalm 2 did that, so earning the nations as his inheritance. The Son not only undertook this mission and came forth as the one whom God appointed as both priest and king (Heb 5:5–6; Zech 6:13), but earned the nations as his inheritance by being the good shepherd who gathers God's people together.[78] This shepherd theme shows how Christ adopts God's role in being the covenant Lord to his people and fulfills God's promises for provision of the righteous

76. Owen, "Exercitation XXVII," 1:457–60.

77. *CF*, 452–55.

78. For extensive discussion about Psalm 2:7 in reference to the covenant of redemption, see *TCR*, 79–94.

Davidic king.[79] In this way, Christ's covenantal work brings together both his identity as the divine Son and as the faithful Adam.[80]

The final layer is that Christ is the substance of the covenant of grace since he was always its mediator. God saved his people in the same way before Christ's work of redemption was actually wrought, since the Son mediated for the elect *incarnandus* and *incarnatus*.

The Scripture marks Christ as the Savior across both Testaments in several ways. The covenant of redemption explains why the New Testament often interprets the Old Testament in specific reference to Christ and his work, implicitly indicating how the Old Testament is about Christ. Moreover, the New Testament explicitly designates Christ as the Savior who was active in the Old Testament. Peter confesses, regarding how the Old Testament fathers could not bear the burden of the law, "We believe that we will be saved through the grace of the Lord Jesus, *just as they will*" (Acts 15:11). So, grace from Christ extends as much to Old Testament believers as to Jews and gentiles after the resurrection.[81]

Paul highlights Christ as the Savior who was active during the Old Testament era in 1 Corinthians 10:1–4: "For I do not want you to be unaware, brothers, that our fathers were all under the cloud, and all passed through the sea, and all were baptized into Moses in the cloud and in the sea, and all ate the same spiritual food, and all drank the same spiritual drink. For they drank from the spiritual Rock that followed them, *and the Rock was Christ*." Paul interprets the exodus and Israel's time in the wilderness, arguing that the spiritual rock which followed and nourished them was Christ. Significantly, Paul specifically indicates that *Christ* was active as the source of their spiritual blessings in these Old Testament events.[82] More significantly, Paul writes to *gentile* Christians that these Old Testament believers are "our fathers," directly unifying God's old and new covenant people. Since Paul uses this event to illustrate the new

79. *CF*, 446–52.

80. In more technical terms, Christ's obedience as the last Adam *in some ways* harmonizes the approaches of Christology "from above" and "from below." See Horton, *Lord and Servant*, 159–77, 242–70. Concerning the methodological issues in Christology from above and from below in relation to biblical inerrancy, see Wellum, *God the Son Incarnate*, 79–104; and Wellum, *Person of Christ*, 21–34.

81. *EC*, 3.2.35.

82. Kim Riddlebarger, *First Corinthians* (Powder Springs, GA: Tolle Lege Press, 2013), 227–42.

covenant's spiritual blessings, this passage addresses our spiritual communion with God. In that respect, Christ was the source of that communion with God even *incarnandus*.[83] Just as Christ said that we must eat his flesh and drink his blood as the means of receiving him by faith (John 6:47–58), so Paul describes how Christ had already been the spiritual food and drink for God's people in the Old Testament. Paul's exhortation to New Testament believers, in its appeal to how Old Testament believers related to Christ, makes Christ's role as the substance of the entire covenant of grace markedly clear.[84]

Paul had this continuity precisely in view when he says that Old Testament truths were written down for the benefit of Christians, but he was not alone in affirming it (1 Cor 10:11; Rom 4:23–25; Rom 15:4). Jude 1:5 states, "Now I want to remind you, although you once fully knew it, that *Jesus, who saved a people* out of the land of Egypt, afterward destroyed those who did not believe."[85] Christ's death was for those Old Testament believers as much as for us today (Heb 9:15).[86] Jesus, the preexistent Son, was active as the Savior and was faithful to those who believed, just as today.[87] In this instance, Jude's exhortation, which clearly assumed Christ *incarnandus*, argued *from* the unity of God's old and new covenant people.

Further biblical evidence supports this point. In John 8:56–59, Jesus had a telling interaction with his opponents: "'Your father Abraham rejoiced that he would see my day. He saw it and was glad.' So the Jews said to him, 'You are not yet fifty years old, and have you seen Abraham?' Jesus said to them, 'Truly, truly, I say to you, before Abraham was, I am.' So they picked up stones to throw at him, but Jesus hid himself and went out of the temple." Abraham may have rejoiced out of expectation for the Savior's coming, which would still indicate Christ as Abraham's source of joy in salvation.[88] On the other hand, the Jews objected that Christ was too

83. Irenaeus, *Demonstration*, §43–55.

84. Fee, *Pauline Christology*, 94–97, 502–4; Fee, *Corinthians*, 487–97; Thiselton, *Corinthians*, 722–30; *CC*, 20:1.312–20; Hodge, *Corinthians*, 175–76.

85. Regarding the text critical issue in Jude 5 of whether the original text was Ἰησοῦς or κύριος, the evidence weighs decisively in favor of the former, especially considering the *lectio difficilior* rule; see Gene L. Green, *Jude and 2 Peter* (Grand Rapids: Baker Academic, 2008), 64–65, 77–78.

86. *EC*, 3.2.37.

87. Green, *Jude and 2 Peter*, 65.

88. Ridderbos, *John*, 320–23.

young for Abraham to have seen him, to which Jesus replied by affirming that he existed before Abraham, invoking his divine identity. By saying, "I am," Jesus was referring to God's own name revealed in Exodus 3:14, "I am who I am," or Yahweh, and applying it to himself.[89] Clearly, he was calling himself God, because his opponents wanted to kill him *because of how he named himself*. By appealing to his preexistence as the second person of the Trinity, Jesus explains how Abraham rejoiced at the day of Christ although living millennia prior to Christ.

This continuity is, to some degree, a necessary doctrine. Even as we focus on the literal, historical meaning of Scripture, we must recognize that it, in some way or other, points to Christ.[90] When they saw Christ in the Old Testament, the apostles did not change the text's original meaning.[91] Rather, they had previously not understood God's own intended and inspired meaning.[92] A proper view of inspiration affirms that Scripture is a product of God's sovereign providence.[93] The Triune God composed it to reveal himself to his people, so it inevitably, even with varying degrees, reveals his triunity throughout.[94]

Christians must read the Bible as though God wrote it, and God is Triune. The gospel always accords to the Scriptures (Acts 17:11). In John 5:39–40, Jesus rebukes his opponents, saying, "You search the Scriptures because you think that in them you have eternal life; and it is they that bear witness about me, yet you refuse to come to me that you may have life." Since Christ refers to the Old Testament, he must be in every part of Scripture as the way to everlasting life.[95] Indeed, "Jesus Christ is the

---

89. Richard Bauckham, "The Trinity and the Gospel of John," in *The Essential Trinity: New Testament Foundations and Practical Relevance*, ed. Brandon D. Crowe and Carl R. Trueman (Phillipsburg, NJ: P&R, 2016), 105–8.

90. Matthew W. Bates, *The Birth of the Trinity: Jesus, God, and Spirit in New Testament and Early Christian Interpretations of the Old Testament* (Oxford: Oxford University Press, 2015); Iain Provan, *The Reformation and the Right Reading of Scripture* (Waco, TX: Baylor University Press, 2017), 81–150; Carter, *Interpreting Scripture*, 31–60, 161–226; Sanders, *Triune God*, 209–37; Daniel J. Treier, *Introducing Theological Interpretation of Scripture: Recovering a Christian Practice* (Nottingham: Apollos, 2008), 39–77.

91. Dennis E. Johnson, *Him We Proclaim: Preaching Christ from All the Scriptures* (Phillipsburg, NJ: P&R, 2007), 1–22.

92. Watson, *Hermeneutics of Faith*, xix–xx, 1–26.

93. John Webster, *Holy Scripture: A Dogmatic Sketch* (Cambridge: Cambridge University Press, 2003), 30–39.

94. On the Triune God's revelation of himself in his word, see Barrett, *Canon, Covenant, and Christology*.

95. *EC*, 3.2.3.

same yesterday and today and forever" (Heb 13:8).[96] So as Roberts so well expresses this point: "This covenant is a golden cabinet, Christ as the most precious diamond or jewel in this cabinet."[97]

THE CONDITION OF FAITH

Throughout the covenant of grace, as the Westminster Confession says, God relates to his people by "requiring of them faith in him that they may be saved, and promising to give unto all those that are ordained unto life his Holy Spirit, to make them willing and able to believe" (WCF 7.3).[98] The condition of the covenant of grace has always been by faith alone, which the Spirit grants.

With respect to what faith is, the Heidelberg Confession says concerning true faith: "It is not only a certain knowledge whereby I hold for truth all that God has revealed to us in his Word, but also a hearty trust which the Holy Ghost works in me by the Gospel, that not only to others, but to me also, forgiveness of sins, everlasting righteousness and salvation, are freely given by God, merely of grace, only for the sake of Christ's merits" (HC 21).[99]

Or as the Westminster Larger Confession outlines,

> Justifying Faith is a saving Grace, wrought in the heart of a Sinner by the Spirit and Word of God, whereby he, being convinced of his sin and misery, and of the disability in himself and all other creatures to recover him out of his lost condition, not only assents to the truth of the promise of the Gospel, but receives and rests upon Christ and his righteousness therein held forth, for pardon of sin, and for the accepting and accounting of his person righteous in the sight of God for salvation. (WLC 72)[100]

Clearly, faith is not simply an inward welling up of positivity, as pop-culture often portrays it. Rather, it is, as John Murray (1898–1975) describes,

96. *CRS*, 1:453–54; *EC*, 3.2.36.

97. *MMB*, 108.

98. *COC*, 3:617.

99. *COC*, 3:313.

100. *LC*, 79.

"essentially extraspective."[101] It looks to something, namely, *someone*, outside of ourselves. Faith believes God, but more specifically as a saving grace, trusts in Christ as rescuer. Although we cannot put eyes on Christ in the flesh, faith believes that he lived, died, rose from the grave, and ascended, all to procure salvation for his people—even for me, personally and specifically (Gal 2:19–20).[102] Hebrews 11:1 describes faith, "Now faith is the assurance of things hoped for, the conviction of things not seen."[103] We may not see Christ, but faith is the soul's hand to grasp tightly to him as the only Redeemer of God's elect.

Faith binds us to Christ, so that we receive his benefits through that faith union. Too many have often imagined that God commands faith as something we do—a work or a new law—that he has accepted as an adequate achievement to warrant salvation. Faith, however, is not a personal accomplishment, especially since it is God's gift that he works in us (Eph 2:8–9).[104] Faith saves us, not in itself, but as the Spirit-wrought bond of our union with Christ.[105]

To illustrate, imagine taking a boat ride on the open ocean. If you fall overboard into storm-roused and shark-infested waters, you sense certain doom. Then, someone on the boat throws the end of a rope to you and drags you back to safety on board. In this case, the rope played a very specific role in saving you. If your rescuer threw the entire rope to you without holding one end to pull you, then the rope would have been useless. The rope saved you because it tied you to *a person* who saved you. When you get aboard, you do not proclaim thanks to the lifeless rope lying on the deck but embrace the person who held it, throwing your entire thanks and affection upon him.[106]

Faith is like that rope. Faith on its own—as a rope floating in the water with no one holding the other end—is of no use. Faith is instrumental in

---

101. John Murray, *The Epistle to the Romans* (Glenside, PA: Westminster Seminary Press, 2022), 131.

102. *VRD*, 4:128.

103. *VRD*, 4:77–78.

104. *VRD*, 4:79–81, 115, 132.

105. *TI*, 12.3.11–17; *BRD*, 4:209–12.

106. The rope illustration is meant to depict faith's *function*, not how we come to faith. Those who are dead in sin would not be able to do their part in taking hold of the other end of the rope. The point is about how faith ties us to Christ, rather than how we come to have that faith in the first place.

taking hold of Christ. Better, it is the *instrument*—the tool or mechanism—of receiving and resting upon the Savior.[107] It is the condition of the covenant of grace, not in that faith itself meets the requirements for inheriting everlasting life, but as it connects us to Christ, who has fulfilled the proper requirements of obtaining that inheritance for us.[108] So, the modern sentiment that you just need a little faith is a mindless platitude. Faith must be trust *in Christ*. He is at the other end of our faith.[109] Christ is our anchor in heaven, and we are bound to him as our rescuer by faith (Heb 6:19–20).[110] Faith is spiritual cement, fixing us to Christ the cornerstone.

Faith is that instrument of salvation throughout the covenant of grace, unifying it in substance, namely, Christ, and condition, namely, trust in Christ. In Romans 4:1–5, Paul writes,

> What then shall we say was gained by Abraham, our forefather according to the flesh? For if Abraham was justified by works, he has something to boast about, but not before God. For what does the Scripture say? "Abraham believed God, and it was counted to him as righteousness." Now to the one who works, his wages are not counted as a gift but as his due. And to the one who does not work but believes in him who justifies the ungodly, his faith is counted as righteousness.

The focal point is faith's role in justification *for Abraham*. Abraham lived long before the Son executed his incarnate mission on earth but still was justified by faith. Indeed, Paul quotes Genesis 15:6, Abraham "believed the Lord, and he counted it to him as righteousness."[111] Faith had been the instrument of being declared righteous long before God commissioned Israel as a nation and gave them the law at Mount Sinai (Exod 19–24). So, the claim that the covenant of grace is unified by the condition of faith is not an obscure inference. Rather, Paul's exact point is that Jew and gentile alike must be justified *by faith* because that has always been the case for every sinner who would be reconciled to God. This identical condition is

107. BC 22; *COC*, 3:407–8.

108. *CG*, 114–66.

109. *VRD*, 4:115–26.

110. *CMT*, 145.

111. *VRD*, 4:73.

why Paul, in Romans 1:16–17, can quote the Old Testament maxim from Habakkuk 2:4—"the righteous shall live by his faith"—to prove that the gospel of salvation is for anyone who believes in Christ.[112]

Inasmuch as God's call to faith is his sovereign work in decisively bringing us to trust in Christ, that coming to faith is our new birth.[113] In this respect, Jesus was very clear that faith and the new birth were not entirely new realities. In John 3:1–15, Nicodemus comes to Christ under the cover of night to inquire more about his teaching. Nicodemus was a Pharisee, a trained theologian, and a religious teacher in Israel.[114] Jesus's first response to him is, "Truly, truly, I say to you, unless one is born again he cannot see the kingdom of God" (3:3). Nicodemus, however, is taken aback by this claim and does not understand how someone can be born a second time (3:4). Jesus, however, doubles down on this teaching about the new birth, asserting that this is obviously a different kind of birth, one that is linked to the sovereign work of the Holy Spirit (3:5–8).[115] Still, Nicodemus does not get the point (3:9), which prompts Jesus's sharper response:

> Are you the teacher of Israel and yet you do not understand these things? Truly, truly, I say to you, we speak of what we know, and bear witness to what we have seen, but you do not receive our testimony. If I have told you earthly things and you do not believe, how can you believe if I tell you heavenly things? No one has ascended into heaven except he who descended from heaven, the Son of Man. And as Moses lifted up the serpent in the wilderness, so must the Son of Man be lifted up, that whoever believes in him may have eternal life. (3:10–15)

Jesus's response contains two aspects of the necessity of faith throughout every era of the covenant of grace.[116]

---

112. Hodge, *Systematic Theology*, 2:371–73; *TI*, 12.5.14; *EC*, 3.2.41.

113. *CF*, 560–77; *VRD*, 4:34–40; *CMT*, 147–48.

114. Ridderbos, *John*, 123.

115. *VRD*, 4:30–32; Ridderbos, *John*, 127–32.

116. The argument that the Spirit regenerated but did not indwell Old Testament believers is hard to substantiate theologically, for it separates blessings that belong together; see *RST*, 3:101–11.

First, John 3:5 is the only place in John's Gospel that mentions the kingdom of God, which marks this statement as an emphatic moment.[117] The future hope of Israel throughout the Old Testament looked forward to the coming of this kingdom, so even if that kingdom was not present then, they expected to be part of its everlasting installment on earth.[118] So, for Christ to join the new birth—which is coming to faith and entry into God's kingdom—is to underscore faith as the condition for all who would be citizens of heaven. The kingdom motif, then, binds the Old Testament people of God to the one condition of faith for receiving everlasting communion with God (Phil 3:19–20).

Second, Jesus's expectation that Nicodemus, *as a teacher of Israel* (John 3:9), should know about the Spirit's supernatural work of new birth indicates that the condition of faith should have been clear to those who had studied the Old Testament. Admittedly, from the Old Testament perspective, the arrival of God's kingdom was still future. Regardless, God's Old Testament people were still supposed to look forward to receiving it *in faith*.[119] That is the reason why Jesus draws on the event of Moses lifting up the bronze serpent from Numbers 21:4–9 as the biblical confirmation that "whoever believes in him [the Son] may have eternal life." As the people had to look upon a lifted-up bronze serpent as an act of trust in God for deliverance even from an earthly trial, so that demonstrates how God's people have always had to place their faith in God's promises to obtain his rescue. After all, Jesus reasoned from "earthly things" to "heavenly things" as he addressed Nicodemus.[120]

That limited deliverance from an infestation of serpents pointed ahead to God's ultimate deliverance from the curse of sin, which is received when we place our trust in the Savior. So, Augustine understood that the biting serpents are "sins coming from the mortality of the flesh" and the serpent on the pole is "the Lord's death on the cross." In the garden, death came from a serpent, so death is represented by a serpent with a lethal bite. In contrast, "the Lord's death is life-giving." So, Augustine continues, "Just as

117. Ridderbos, *John*, 125.

118. Ridderbos, *Coming of the Kingdom*, 3–17.

119. *VRD*, 4:81; Ridderbos, *John*, 125, 132.

120. Ridderbos, *John*, 134–37; *VRD*, 3:108.

those who gazed on that serpent did not die because of the serpent's bite, so those who gaze in faith on the death of Christ are healed of the bite of sins."[121] Likewise, the Epistle of Barnabas comments in regard to how the people were saved when they looked upon the bronze serpent: "Once again you have in these things the glory of Jesus, because all things are in him and for him" (1 Cor 10:9). [122] More importantly, Paul applies this event to the new covenant church. "We must not put *Christ* to the test, as some of them did and were destroyed by serpents." Paul clearly shows *Christ* as the one to whom the Israelites related as Savior—albeit the Savior not to be tested.[123] Christ, therefore, reasonably expected Nicodemus, a teacher of the Old Testament, to understand the new birth because the covenant of grace has always required faith as the condition to inherit everlasting life.

This condition of faith distinguishes the covenant of grace in principle from the covenant of works, again confirming our two covenantal principles of law and gospel. Because of these two covenantal principles, according to the Westminster Confession, the condition of faith marks this covenant that God made with us after man "made himself incapable of life by that covenant [of works]" by his fall (WCF 7.3).[124] Whereas the covenant of works required perfect obedience to obtain blessings, the covenant of grace requires trust in Christ as the last Adam who performed perfect and full obedience on our behalf.[125]

This difference concerns the covenant's *principle*, not its every detail. In the covenant of works, Adam needed to believe what God said, which is obvious in how the serpent tempted our first parents precisely by asking them to believe him rather than God's own words (Gen 3:1–7). Still, Adam's belief in God was not the condition for receiving blessings from God. That condition was his perfect obedience to the law.[126] Turretin explains this point that the covenant of works and the covenant of grace differ in "the prescribed condition," namely, the demand for perfect righteousness

121. Augustine, *John 1–40*, 238.

122. Barnabas 12.7; *AP*, 421.

123. Fee, *Corinthians*, 504–5. Regarding the text critical issue and the preference of Χριστόν over κύριον, see Thiselton, *Corinthians*, 740.

124. *COC*, 3:617.

125. *CMT*, 76.

126. *VRD*, 4:113.

contrasts with faith whereby perfect righteousness is received from Christ. In the covenant of works, "faith was required as a work and a part of the inherent righteousness to which life was promised." In the covenant of grace, however, "it is demanded—not as a work on account of which life is given, but as a mere instrument apprehending the righteousness of Christ (on account of which alone salvation is granted to us)." Works were required in the first "as an antecedent condition by way of a cause for acquiring life" but in the covenant of grace "are only the subsequent condition as the fruit and effect of the life already acquired."[127] Adam needed to trust God but did not need to trust in a mediator to fulfill the terms of the covenant for him. He was to fulfill the covenant's conditions by his own strength. Saving faith is then *distinctly* the condition of the covenant of grace in contrast to the covenant of works.

This distinct condition marks the vast difference between how God has related to humanity before and after Adam's fall. The covenants of works and grace do not parallel as if God's covenant with Adam was premised on faith followed by obedience and then the covenant of grace also requires faith followed by obedience with the caveat that we need more help to obey. Rather, the covenant of works and the covenant of grace rest upon two fundamentally different covenantal principles.[128]

The condition of faith also distinguishes the covenant of grace from the covenant of redemption. God requires nothing from us in the covenant of redemption, since believers are not one of its parties, but requires faith within the covenant of grace. More foundationally, the covenant of redemption enables faith to be the covenant of grace's condition without being a legal condition, by ensuring that this condition will be met. The reason is that Christ through his role in the covenant of redemption purchased the Spirit to give to the elect to make them willing and able to believe, making the condition of faith a gift that God grants to his people by consequence of the covenant of redemption.[129]

127. *TI*, 12.4.6–7.

128. *TI*, 12.3.6.

129. WLC 32; *LC*, 71–72; WCF 7.3; *COC*, 3:617.

Regarding the continuity of faith, the difference between faith before Christ's incarnation and after is not one of quality, but merely perspective.[130] As Irenaeus writes, "Our faith was anticipated in Abraham."[131] Faith may differ between the testaments in terms of degree, since the new covenant's greater revelation entails fuller and more explicit faith with greater fruit. The point is that Old and New Testament faith does the same action, namely, trusts in Christ.

If you and I are both looking at a statue, but you are standing in front of it and I am behind it, we are still doing the same thing, only from different angles. Saving faith for Old Testament believers took hold of the Christ who would come (*incarnandus*), whereas faith for us this side of the resurrection looks back to the Christ who has come (*incarnatus*).[132] In this sense, Old Testament faith received spiritual realities, not as in otherworldly, but specifically eschatological blessings, which Christ secured as guarantor of the new covenant, although he gave in advance to those who trusted in him under the old economy. So, Jacob confessed, "I wait for your salvation, O LORD" (Gen 49:18), and Job declared, "For I know that my Redeemer lives, and at the last he will stand upon the earth" (Job 19:25).[133] Moses himself, by faith "considered the reproach of *Christ* greater wealth than the treasures of Egypt" (Heb 11:26). Moses, as the other Old Testament saints, had faith not generically, but in Christ. Just as we look back to the cross with trust that God has there secured the forgiveness of our sin, so the Old Testament believers trusted God knowing that the Messiah would provide that forgiveness of their sins. So, Geerhardus Vos uses the category of the Son *incarnandus* to explain Old Testament faith: "Even before his incarnation, it was only possible to believe in Him as the one who would become flesh."[134] Faith has always been in the Savior and has always tied us to the Savior's work on our behalf.

There is also continuity in the way that believers come to faith. The Spirit's mission of effectual calling includes the task to bring the elect from their opposition to the truth unto faith in Christ. One of the clearest

130. *CRS*, 1:455; Horton, *Rediscovering*, 156–58.

131. Irenaeus, *Against Heresies*, 4.21.1, in *PG*, 7.1:1043; *ANF*, 1:492.

132. *CMT*, 83–84, 149.

133. *EC*, 3.2.16–23, 41–43.

134. *VRD*, 3:48; *EC*, 2.2.8, 2.3.2–4; *BRD*, 3:214; *DLGTT*, 169.

examples of effectual calling is how the apostle Paul was brought to faith on his way to Damascus to persecute Christians, but Christ's miraculous appearing to him effectively pulled him from unbelief to true faith (Acts 9:1–19). That sort of conversion experience through God's very explicit and direct work of effectual calling is not isolated to the New Testament. Abraham, the great father of promise, "served other gods" when God called him (Josh 24:2). In Genesis 12:1–3, while Abraham—then called Abram—still followed the gods of Ur, God summoned him to faith by announcing the great promise of blessing by faith (Heb 11:8).[135] This should not be radically disconnected from the New Testament understanding of faith. Paul wrote that, in Abraham's call, the Scripture "*preached the gospel* beforehand to Abraham" (Gal 3:8). This Genesis 12 event was a gospel-preaching event that was tied to the reality of justification by faith alone, which is why Paul consistently understood that when he "believed the LORD, and he counted it to him as righteousness" (Gen 15:6), it was the paradigm of how Jew and gentile alike are justified by faith apart from works because of Christ's work (Gen 15:6; Gal 3:5–9; Rom 4:1–8).

So, faith is the condition of the covenant of grace throughout each era of God's plan of salvation. There is no other way to receive salvation than in Christ, and there is no other way to receive Christ than by faith.[136] Faith is the condition of the covenant of grace precisely because it is receptive.[137] Faith believes that Christ as the last Adam has won our place in glory with him. Even then, upon the condition of faith, the covenant of grace remains entirely of grace because the Holy Spirit is the one who works faith in us as part of his mission in the covenant of redemption.[138] Even what God has required of us, he grants to us by grace.[139]

CONCLUSION

Faith leads us to a celebration of Christ because he is the only redeemer of God's elect. The covenant of grace marks how we are drawn into beautiful communion with our Lord. It is the way that we receive all that Christ

135. *MMB*, 287–303.

136. *CF*, 580–85, 624–25.

137. *MT*, 1.3.1; *TI*, 12.3.12, 15; 16.7.18; *VRD*, 4:164–66.

138. *VRD*, 2:120–21; 4:40–41; *CMT*, 77.

139. *TI*, 12.2.29–30.

has earned for us as the last Adam and is the location of our fellowship with God. It is not, however, new with the Son's incarnation, but has been God's one plan of salvation from the beginning, which further magnifies the glory of Christ as the one whose work is adequate to take effect even before he performed it. So, even when Christ was not overtly described as the Savior of God's people, he clearly was (Jude 1:5).[140]

The pastoral use of this chapter's material is to highlight why Reformed churches especially are characterized by preaching Christ from all Scriptures. Christ is truly at the heart of the whole Scripture—even though the focus has been more on how that point shapes our understanding of Christ, salvation, and to some degree interpreting the Bible. If the Scripture has unity in Christ because of the divine author's intent in the original meaning of the text, then the consequence is that we must explain the Bible along those lines. More specifically, Christ should be *preached* from every portion of Scripture.[141]

---

140. WLC 36; *LC*, 72.

141. On preaching Christ in all of Scripture, see Johnson, *Him We Proclaim*.

IX

The Unity of the Covenant of Grace in the Benefits of Christ

For all have sinned and fall short of the glory of God,
and are justified by his grace as a gift,
through the redemption that is in Christ Jesus.
—*Romans 3:23–24*

God communes with us by covenant, the covenant of grace having as its center, Christ, who restores our communion with God. Christ's mediation for all God's people, whether they lived before, during, or after his first coming, unifies the covenant of grace. The covenant of grace then historically executes the covenant of redemption, the source of Christ's unifying role as mediator, providing the means by which we participate in God's eternal plan for our salvation.[1]

As Christ mediates for the elect from all eras, as the one who procured salvation as the guarantor of the new covenant, the covenant of grace must be unified also in salvation, since Christ communicates *his* benefits even before he wrought salvation in history.[2] As Irenaeus writes in the second century concerning the unity of the old and new covenants, "In fact there

1. *BRD*, 3:523–24.
2. WCF 8.6; *COC*, 3:621–22.

is one salvation and one God."[3] In the fourth century, Augustine also comments on the righteousness from God in Romans 1:16–17, "This is the righteousness of God, which was veiled in the Old Testament, and is revealed in the New; and it is called *the righteousness of God*, because by His bestowal of it He makes us righteous, just as we read that 'salvation is the Lord's,' because He makes us safe."[4] Christians have long recognized the unity of God's plan not only in Christ but even in salvation itself.[5]

Our trip to the ice cream shop has illustrated the covenant of grace. In every trip to the ice cream shop, we aim to obtain ice cream. It may come in a cup or a cone but, nonetheless, remains ice cream. The ice cream is the substance with a cup or cone as the administration of the substance. Likewise, the substance of the covenant of grace is that God will be God to us in Christ, even as the outward form of life looks different for God's people in different times of administration. Still, ice cream as the substance can come in many flavors. So, as we continue considering the substance of the covenant, our focus is now on the multifaceted benefits that we receive from Christ.

This chapter, then, focuses on those benefits which we receive from Christ. Space and focus prevent a full defense of every aspect of Reformed teaching on salvation. Our attention, therefore, must stay tightly upon these doctrines in terms of the unity of the covenant of grace and how they connect to the wider aspects of covenant theology.[6]

UNION WITH CHRIST

In order to receive all the blessings that Christ procured as our mediator, we must be joined to him. Although he accomplished his work as the last Adam in a specific time and place in history, his cross-canonical role as Savior unifies the covenant of grace. All believers belong to Christ as our representative in his historical mission. Just as our federal union with

3. Irenaeus, *Against Heresies*, 4.9.3, in *PG*, 7.1:998; *ANF*, 1:473.

4. Augustine, *Spirit and the Letter*, §18 in *NPNF1*, 5:90.

5. *TI*, 12.5.15; *EC*, 3.2.2–3; *CRS*, 1:454–57.

6. This book then follows Witsius's pattern of discussing the benefits of the covenant of grace as to substance before progressing to discuss the differences of the covenant at the administrative level; *EC*, books 3–4.

the first Adam brought sin's curse upon us, so also we partake of Christ's benefits in union with him by faith.[7]

This section explores what the Westminster Larger Catechism describes: the elect have union with Christ by being joined to him as their head—their federal representative—and husband "in their effectual Calling" (WLC 66).[8] All the elect are then bound to Christ as God summons them to faith, unifying the covenant of grace in Christ as the one source of saving benefits. The Larger Catechism describes the content of our union with Christ in this life: "The Communion in grace, which the members of the Invisible Church have with Christ, is, their partaking of the virtue of his Mediation, in their Justification, Adoption, Sanctification, and whatever else in this life manifests their Union with him" (WLC 69).[9] The catechism continues to describe our union with Christ in the life to come by outlining how communion in glory is "perfected at the resurrection and day of Judgment" but "communicated to them in this life" so that we now "enjoy the sense of God's love, peace of conscience, joy in the holy Ghost, and hope of glory" (WLC 82–83).[10] Union with Christ is a rich and multifaceted reality that conveys a panoramic set of blessings to believers, centering on communion with him.

That union guarantees a host of diverse blessings for believers. At the personal and experiential level, the catechism affirms that our union with Christ brings about enjoying the sense of God's love, peace, and joy in the Spirit. How wonderful it is that God gives us a fulfilling and comforting sense of his loving presence with us! Most fundamentally, the catechism says communion with Christ is our "partaking of the virtue of his mediation." Union with Christ is most focused on the objective reality that the Son as the last Adam and mediator of the covenant of grace has obtained and secured every everlasting blessing possible in our covenantal communion with God.

This understanding of union with Christ as a partaking of the virtue of his mediation means that union with Christ *is* those benefits of

7. Gaffin, *By Faith, Not by Sight*, 40–45.

8. *LC*, 78.

9. *LC*, 78.

10. *LC*, 81–82.

communion with him that he obtained for us as our head and husband. In other words, the content of our union with Christ is not distinct from our justification, adoption, sanctification, and glorification, making this union "the summary of grace."[11] After all, the Westminster Larger Catechism says believers' communion with Christ is partaking of the virtue of his mediation "*in their* justification, adoption, sanctification, and whatever else in this life manifests their union with him." It is *in* these benefits from Christ that we partake of the virtues of his mediation, which partaking *is* our communion with him. Our union with Christ cannot be described apart from its saving aspects because there is no union with Christ that is not in his benefits. Our union with Christ overflows with the rich blessings of saving communion.[12]

---

11. *RST*, 3:227.

12. The primary import from this understanding of union with Christ is to push back against those who have used the category of union to confuse or eclipse Christ's benefits. Given a proliferation of uses of union with Christ, we must be specific about what we mean by it, especially if we are to leverage it properly within our theological system. Traditionally, Reformed theology has maintained an emphatic distinction between God's judicial and re-creative acts in salvation; see *VRD*, 4:5; Gaffin, *By Faith, Not by Sight*, 38–40. On the other hand, recent studies in Pauline theology have attempted to blend, displace, or even overturn this distinction by appealing to union with Christ. Albert Schweitzer's pivotal *The Mysticism of the Apostle Paul* set a trajectory of pitting eschatological themes *against* legal aspects of salvation, reducing justification to a "subsidiary crater" of Paul's soteriology. Schweitzer posed that "being in Christ" is the foundation of Paul's theology, and that view is driven by being caught in the eschatological tension between Christ's resurrection as the beginning of a general resurrection; Watson, *Hermeneutics of Faith*, 29–36. The effect of Schweitzer's view was to sideline the benefits of Christ's mediation in favor of a less specific mystical union related to resurrection power; see *The Mysticism of the Apostle Paul*, trans. W. Montgomery (Baltimore, MA: Johns Hopkins University Press, 1998). Further, E. P. Sanders' argument that Second Temple Judaism was a grace-oriented religion was based in a priority of "participation" over the forensic categories of justification by faith or works; see E. P. Sanders, *Paul and Palestinian Judaism: A Comparison of Patterns of Religion*, 40th anniversary ed. (London: SCM, 1977), 502–8, 519–20. More recently, Michael Gorman has argued for a blending of justification and sanctification within *theosis*—indeed, a category of union with Christ—so that justification is no longer forensic; here, re-creative categories displace the judicial; see *Inhabiting the Cruciform God: Kenosis, Justification, and Theosis in Paul's Narrative Soteriology* (Grand Rapids: Eerdmans, 2009). N. T. Wright, perhaps the most well-known proponent of the "New Perspective on Paul," has further argued that union with Christ makes the imputation of Christ's righteousness for justification superfluous, which enables Wright to distance justification from its location in soteriology; see *Justification: God's Plan and Paul's Vision* (Downers Grove, IL: IVP Academic, 2009), 150–51, 206, 217, 232–33. Matthew W. Bates similarly argues that the distinction between imputed and infused righteousness should be at least to some degree set aside; see *Salvation by Allegiance Alone: Rethinking Faith, Works, and the Gospel of Jesus the King* (Grand Rapids: Baker Academic, 2017), 185–89. In each of these cases, there is some measure where union with Christ indicates a confusion of the person of Christ and believers. These understandings of union, however, do not do justice to the Scripture's emphasis on Christ acting for us, nor to our union with him *as the second Adam*, which requires that we remain distinct from him as we partake of his mediation; see Gaffin, *Resurrection and Redemption*, 53–58; Gaffin, *By Faith, Not by Sight*, 40–45;

On the other hand, those benefits cannot be separated from our union with Christ. This link is necessary since Christ obtained justification and its resulting spiritual, glorified state first as the last Adam. We then receive those blessings by faith because Christ obtained them first.[13] We cannot speak of union with Christ apart from his saving benefits, but likewise we must never speak of those blessings without a clear focus on Christ as their source.[14] Union with Christ and the other benefits of salvation are mutually informing.[15]

Our union with Christ is holistically covenantal. First, just as we were bound to Adam by nature in the covenant of works, so, the elect are given to the Son in the covenant of redemption. Herman Bavinck describes this covenantal dimension of union with Christ as a bond "already forged between the mediator and those who were given to him by the Father in eternity, in election, and more precisely in the pact of salvation (*pactum salutis*)." By the decree about this union, the Son became the elect's substitute (*expromissor*) "precisely because he already was in communion with them and was their guarantor and mediator." Through his incarnate work, "all the benefits of grace therefore lie prepared and ready for the

---

and *CF*, 592–96, 602–5, 611. The understanding outlined in this book, that union with Christ *is* the partaking of the virtue of his mediation *in* our justification, adoption, sanctification, etc., underlines how Christ in his historical accomplishment of redemption is indeed the reason for our salvation, but also that our union with him is to be joined to him in his offices and is had through his benefits. In this way, "union with Christ is not actually an element of the *ordo salutis* but the umbrella-term (equivalent to the 'great exchange') for the *ordo* as a whole," Horton, *Justification*, 2:449. Regardless of the relationship between the benefits of Christ as we receive them, which the next chapter addresses, union with Christ should not be counted as one distinct step in the order of salvation as though it is separable from the benefits that we receive from Christ. This detaches Christ from those benefits. Rather, we are united to Christ in our effectual calling (WLC 66), and that union is our justification, sanctification, glorification, and every other blessing that Christ grants to us. For a longer discussion of how to frame union with Christ properly in contrast to these views that undermine Protestant soteriology, see J. V. Fesko, *Justification: Understanding the Classic Reformed Doctrine* (Phillipsburg, NJ: P&R, 2008), 264–80; *CF*, 588; Horton, *Justification*, 2:447–93; and R. Lucas Stamps, "Faith Works: Properly Understanding the Relationship between Justification and Sanctification," in *Doctrine on Which the Church Stands or Falls*, 505–30.

13. Vos, "Doctrine of the Covenant," 248; Horton, *Justification*, 2:257–80.

14. Billings, "Redemption Applied," 502–9; *VRD*, 4:25–28; *CF*, 587–91.

15. David VanDrunen, "A Contested Union: Union with Christ and the Justification Debate," in *Doctrine on Which the Church Stands or Falls*, 469–504.

church in the person of Christ."[16] Every blessing of our communion with God by covenant is then located "in Christ."[17]

Covenant theology is then gloriously connected to our salvation as Christ obtained every aspect of our communion with God as our new representative. To partake of the highest blessings of our relationship with God, we must be joined to Christ. James Ussher argues in regard to keeping our focus on the Savior rather than merely the gifts from the Savior that "not only Christ's benefits are ours, but Christ himself is ours."[18] Because salvation in Christ is the substance of the covenant of grace, we cannot forget that "God will be our God and give us Life everlasting *in Christ*."[19] Salvation cannot be separated from Christ, since he has won its benefits for us as our new covenant representative.

An illustration may clarify how to think about our union with Christ in terms of the benefits we receive from him, without focusing too much on Christ's gifts rather than Christ himself. When I was a kid, my father owned a stone patio table. This table had the base of a wide stone pillar, which supported a wide and sturdy stone tabletop. This table had parts that served distinct functions. The pillar held up the surface, which held our food as we ate. The parts, separately, were of little use. There may be times to inspect each part individually to make sure there was no crack in the base or no tilt in the tabletop. Still, the table was functional only as the parts work together. The whole table was always in focus, whether I hid behind the base during hide and seek or looked directly at the top while eating an afternoon meal.

Having described this union as the overarching blessing of covenantal communion with God, we need to examine how union with Christ is a blessing common throughout redemptive history. In Ephesian 2:11–13, Paul writes, "Therefore remember that at one time you Gentiles in the flesh, called 'the uncircumcision' by what is called the circumcision, which is made in the flesh by hands—remember that you were at that time

16. *BRD*, 3:523; *VRD*, 4:1.

17. The most thorough exegetical studies of union with Christ are Grant Macaskill, *Union with Christ in the New Testament* (Oxford: Oxford University Press, 2013); and Constantine R. Campbell, *Paul and Union with Christ: An Exegetical and Theological Study* (Grand Rapids: Zondervan Academic, 2015).

18. CUL MS Mm. 6.55, fol. 225r (sermon on John 6:57 dated June 8, 1651).

19. Ussher, *Body*, 159.

separated from Christ, alienated from the commonwealth of Israel and strangers to the covenants of promise, having no hope and without God in the world. But now in Christ Jesus you who once were far off have been brought near by the blood of Christ." This passage is addressed to gentile Christians needing to remember that they had been "separated from Christ." Certainly, this underscores Paul's understanding that salvation holistically comes in Christ.

More pointedly, gentile Christians were also once "alienated from the commonwealth of Israel and strangers to the covenants of promise."[20] This striking claim means that not being united to Christ was to be outside the people of Israel. Both realities entail lacking the covenants of promise and hope. All these descriptions relate to union with Christ because, in contrast to their former reality, "now in Christ Jesus you who once were far off have been brought near by the blood of Christ."

The profound point for the unity of the covenant of grace is that union with Christ includes participating in the *commonwealth of Israel*. God's Old Testament people were the heirs of the covenants of promise. To partake in this covenant identity also meant to have union with Christ. In no uncertain terms, Paul names union with Christ as a blessing that the old covenant people experienced and now gentiles were also receiving. This highlights union with Christ as a matter of the substance of the covenant of grace.

Other passages highlight the same point in more metaphorical language. For example, Galatians 3:16 and 29 connect the way that believers receive God's promise to the way that Abraham received it. "Now the promises were made to Abraham and to his offspring. It does not say, 'And to offsprings,' referring to many, but referring to one, 'And to your offspring,' who is Christ. ... And if you are Christ's, then you are Abraham's offspring, heirs according to promise." God promised Abraham an offspring, who would bring about the fulfillment of all the expected blessings. In context, these blessings are justification by faith and reception of the Spirit (Gal 3:7–14). Paul explained that this promised offspring was Christ. As it happens, if we "are Christ's"—that is, united to him—then believers are also Abraham's offspring. We are sons in the Son and heirs of

20. I take Paul's phrases here as epexegetical or appositional. The latter restates the former.

the promise, the same promise given to Abraham. Our union with Christ, therefore, is of the same promise that was given to Abraham.

The promise of our union, moreover, connects back even to the first promise of rescue made to Adam. In Genesis 3:15, God cursed the serpent by saying,

> I will put enmity between you and the woman,
> and between your offspring and her offspring;
> he shall bruise your head,
> and you shall bruise his heel.

Notice first that the promise of an *offspring* was included in even this first announcement of redemption, which grounds the Abrahamic promise of an *offspring* even further back in God's promises across the covenant of grace. The emphasis in that promise, however, was in what this offspring would accomplish in crushing the serpent's head. Christ fulfills that promise by returning, seizing the dragon, "that ancient serpent, who is the devil and Satan" (Rev 20:2), and destroying him (Rev 20:10; 2 Thess 2:8). Still, such is our union with Christ, even in this first promise to Adam, that Paul writes in Romans 16:20, "The God of peace will soon crush Satan under your feet."[21] Bound to Christ by faith, all his victories become ours, even those promised in the initial moments of the one covenant of grace.[22]

Union with Christ is, then, writ large across the entire Bible. All of God's true people are united to Christ for salvation. God's people are his temple (1 Cor 3:16–17), and Christ is the cornerstone so that "whoever believes in him will not be put to shame" (1 Pet 2:6). God did not begin a new temple after the Son came in the incarnation but always had his true people as his true temple joined to Christ the cornerstone (Eph 2:18–21).

JUSTIFICATION

Although communion with the Triune God, because of our union with Christ, is the *overarching* blessing diversely manifested in every aspect of salvation, justification is the primary *specific* benefit of the covenant of

21. Gladd, *Adam and Israel to the Church*, 123–24.

22. *MMB*, 196–97.

grace.[23] It is primary in the sense that it is the foundation of our right relationship with God. Christ is our salvation's ultimate cause, so no saving benefit can be uprooted from its soil in the person and work of Christ. In this way Christ is the material cause of our salvation. Still, justification is God's declaration that we are righteous in his sight, granting us peace with God (Rom 5:1).

Justification is the fundamentally legal aspect of our salvation, resting upon Christ's obedience credited to us. The Westminster Confession explains justification:

> Those whom God effectually calls, he also freely justifies; not by infusing righteousness into them, but by pardoning their sins, and by accounting and accepting their persons as righteous: not for any thing wrought in them, or done by them, but for Christ's sake alone; not by imputing faith itself, the act of believing, or any other evangelical obedience to them, as their righteousness; but by imputing the obedience and satisfaction of Christ unto them, they receiving and resting on him and his righteousness by faith; which faith they have not of themselves, it is the gift of God. (WCF 11.1)[24]

Justification emphatically excludes our works and includes the forgiveness of sin. As faith receives Christ, his obedience grounds our right standing with God. So, we are justified by faith. The aspects of justification that connect most directly with covenant theology concern Christ's obedience as its ground, and our receiving it under his representation.

Before examining justification's more specific features, we should consider the unity of the covenant of grace with respect to it. The Westminster Confession says, "The justification of believers under the Old Testament was, in all these respects, one and the same with the justification of believers under the New Testament" (WCF 11.6).[25] Although perhaps easily overlooked, Scripture clearly makes this point.

The New Testament appeal to Old Testament figures to demonstrate how Christians are justified by faith indicates that justification operates

---

23. *BRD*, 4:179; *EC*, 3.8.1; *TI*, 16.1.1.

24. *COC*, 3:626.

25. *COC*, 3:628.

the same way throughout every era of the covenant of grace. Paul writes concerning justification in Romans 4:1–6,

> What then shall we say was gained by Abraham, our forefather according to the flesh? For if Abraham was justified by works, he has something to boast about, but not before God. For what does the Scripture say? "Abraham believed God, and it was counted to him as righteousness." Now to the one who works, his wages are not counted as a gift but as his due. And to the one who does not work but believes in him who justifies the ungodly, his faith is counted as righteousness, just as David also speaks of the blessing of the one to whom God counts righteousness apart from works.

Paul could appeal to Abraham and David as examples of justification only if they were justified in the same way we are today. Even though Abraham lived around 2100 BC and David reigned over Israel around 1000 BC, Paul uses them as paradigms of the justification for New Testament readers. So, Irenaeus summarizes,

> For Abraham believed God and it was counted unto him for righteousness. In like manner we also are justified by faith in God: for the just shall live by faith. Now not by the law is the promise to Abraham, but by faith: for Abraham was justified by faith: and for a righteous man the law is not made. In like manner we also are justified not by the law, but by faith, which is witnessed to in the law and in the prophets, whom the Word of God presents to us.[26]

Christians today are justified by faith alone in Christ alone, but Paul asserts that these Old Testament saints were justified in the same way, which is, again, the only way that his appeal to them works.[27]

Justification also has broader relation to the structures of covenant theology. In the covenant of works, Adam was supposed to fulfill the law by his perfect obedience and so by that justification obtain indestructible life in glorified communion with God. Adam failed to attain that righteousness and his sin was credited to the whole human race. In the

26. Irenaeus, *Demonstration*, §35.

27. *TI*, 12.5.14–20; 16.8.10; 16.10.2–3.

covenant of redemption, the Son had the mission to attain that righteousness of the law needed to obtain justification, which results in everlasting life. As the last Adam, Christ fulfilled the covenant of works for the elect whom he represented. Just as Adam's covenantal transgression that resulted in condemnation was imputed to those whom he represented, so too Christ's covenantal righteousness that results in justification is imputed to everyone who believes in him.[28] In this way, the major themes explored in this book so far converge, and with pointed relevance, in the doctrine of justification.

A consideration of justification's ground or basis strengthens these connections. Even before Christ's incarnation, perfect life, death, resurrection, and ascension, his fulfillment of the principal debt (active obedience) and penalty debt (passive obedience) from the covenant of works were credited to everyone who was united to him by faith.[29] Christ was the guarantor in *expromissor* fashion for those who trusted in him *incarnandus*, as he remains for us who trust in him *incarnatus*. As Adam's obedience to the law would have been the basis for his justification unto life that would have been extended to those whom he represented, so too Christ's twofold covenantal obedience is the *only* basis for the justification unto life that God grants to believers.[30] In William Perkins's words, sinners "owe to God a double debt" because "we break the law and are bound to make satisfaction" but, more basically, "must fulfill the rigor of the law and perform what it requires." Being unable to pay, "we flee to our surety, who must pay both for us."[31] Adam defaulted on his principal debt, rendering the human race bankrupt of ability to pay the principal

28. *DIALIC*, 197–223; Clark, "Do This and Live," 229–65; *CF*, 630–40.

29. *WWP*, 2:113–17 (commentary on Galatians 2:15–16); *CG*, 119–22; Crowe, "Passive and Active Obedience of Christ," 441–68.

30. This point needs to be properly underscored because it highlights the specifically Protestant understanding of the ground of justification. The *relationship* of our union with Christ itself does not justify. Rather, Christ's imputed righteousness grounds our justification. By faith, that righteousness is imputed to us, which means it cannot be separated from our union with Christ by faith. Still, Christ's righteousness itself, rather than our relationship to Christ, is the foundation of our justification; see *TI*, 16.2.2, 6; 16.3.1–31; *EC*, 3.8.37–42; Fesko, *Justification*, 241–63; *CF*, 635–40; Horton, *Justification*, 2:321–66; Gaffin, *By Faith, Not by Sight*, 57–59; and VanDrunen, "Contested Union," 490–96; contra Marcus Peter Johnson, *One with Christ: An Evangelical Theology of Salvation* (Wheaton, IL: Crossway, 2013), 72. Johnson argues that justification occurs on the basis of union, and then God imputes Christ's righteousness to us on the basis of that justifying declaration.

31. *WWP*, 4:62 (commentary on Jude 3).

or penalty debt. So, we need a new Adam as our guarantor, rich beyond measure but willing to become poor for our sake to settle our debts, reconcile us to God, and provide an inheritance in God's kingdom (2 Cor 8:9).

Just as it would have been in the original covenant of works, someone else earned our justification. Since the last Adam fully and finally earned that justification for us, it is the unshakeable and permanent reality for believers. The justification that comes to us by faith is the guarantee of everlasting life (Rom 5:9–10).[32] Justification, then, establishes our citizenship in God's kingdom.

An illustration may clarify that link between justification and citizenship. I used to pastor in the United Kingdom, where almost everyone has a passport. When someone has a passport, it guarantees his access to all the rights and privileges of his country. He may go abroad, but his passport ensures his safe return through his country's borders. It proves the claim that he has the legal right to reside in his homeland. Paul raised this point in Ephesians 2:18–21: "For through him we both have access in one Spirit to the Father. So then you are no longer strangers and aliens, but *you are fellow citizens* with the saints and members of the household of God, built on the foundation of the apostles and prophets, Christ Jesus himself being the cornerstone, in whom the whole structure, being joined together, grows into a holy temple in the Lord." Christ has granted full access to God, which means that we are no longer strangers and aliens in God's kingdom but are citizens there.

If you move to a new country, you must pass a citizenship test to prove you deserve to live there indefinitely with all the rights and privileges of full inclusion. That citizenship test is like the covenant of works. God set a citizenship test of perfect obedience for Adam so he could prove that he deserved to reside in God's new creation. Adam failed, but Jesus Christ passed, earning the right to everlasting life for all whom he represents.[33] Just as naturalized citizens pass their citizenship on to their children, so too Jesus passes the citizenship he earned in his incarnation on to his adopted brothers and sisters who have faith in him.

32. Stamps, "Faith Works," 527.

33. *TI*, 17.1.16–17; *VRD*, 4:154.

The Scripture draws clearly upon this notion of citizenship to describe the identity of believers. In Philippians 3:8–9, Paul emphasizes that he wants to receive *righteousness* through faith in Christ, rather than to depend on his own works. So, he asserts that our right standing with God is based on Christ's righteousness—justification. Then, he connects his point to believers' heavenly citizenship in Philippians 3:19–21: "Their end is destruction, their god is their belly, and they glory in their shame, with minds set on earthly things. But our citizenship is in heaven, and from it we await a Savior, the Lord Jesus Christ, who will transform our lowly body to be like his glorious body, by the power that enables him even to subject all things to himself." Some will go to everlasting destruction, but believers' citizenship is in heaven. Clearly, heavenly citizenship grants the privilege that believers never endure everlasting destruction.

Our heavenly citizenship also points forward to our reception of that full spiritual existence offered to Adam if he had fulfilled the covenant of works (Rom 5:18; 1 Cor 15:44–46). Paul indicates how we presently wait for Christ to return so that he will transform our bodies to be like his glorious body. This is the Christian hope because we are waiting for him to come from heaven *where our citizenship presently is*. Citizenship, like justification, is a secure reality for believers, guaranteeing the reception of even further blessings in the future.

The covenant of works is an underlying structure for the certainty of our salvation as it intersects with the covenant of redemption. There is no distinction between our present justification and our right to future entrance into heaven, since our righteousness from Christ makes us heavenly citizens. The explored combination of various strands of biblical theology shows that Christ as the second Adam has merited justification for us, which *is* our citizenship in heaven.[34] As John writes in Revelation 22:12–14: "'Behold, I am coming soon, bringing my recompense with me, to repay each one for what he has done. I am the Alpha and the Omega, the first and the last, the beginning and the end.' Blessed are those who wash their robes, so that they may have the right to the tree of life and that they may enter the city by the gates." The context, as in

34. *VRD*, 4:154.

Philippians 3:19–21, is the present period of waiting for Christ's return. The eternal Christ will come soon to bring judgment.[35]

Throughout the Scripture, God grants clean garments to signify the forgiveness of sin (Zech 3:1–5), linking that symbolism to justification.[36] It connects back to Revelation 7:14 about those who have "washed their robes and made them white in the blood of the Lamb." So, those who are blessed in Revelation 22:14 are the justified.[37] They have been justified, "so that they may have the right to the tree of life and that they may enter the city by the gates."[38] The tree of life, as it functioned in the covenant of works, is that sacrament of receiving glorified, spiritual life. That blessing, which goes to the justified, is accompanied by entrance into God's city. This parallels the blessing of being welcomed and cared for before God's throne that goes to the justified in Revelation 7:13–17.[39] Entrance into God's city is a matter of citizenship, recognized because these blessed ones are justified. As in Philippians 3:19–21, then, justification and heavenly citizenship are clearly tied together with Christ having earned both for his people.

Justification, which grants heavenly citizenship as its consequence, is, then, a matter-of-fact reality, guaranteed now and for everlasting life. If citizenship is a present reality, so that we will enter God's city by the gates, then justification is already firmly and completely in place to secure it. Paul cannot be clearer on this issue than he is in Romans 5:6–11:

> For while we were still weak, at the right time Christ died for the ungodly. For one will scarcely die for a righteous person—though perhaps for a good person one would dare even to die—but God shows his love for us in that while we were still sinners, Christ died for us. Since, therefore, we have now been justified by his blood,

---

35. Beale, *Revelation*, 1134–38.

36. *DIALIC*, 264; *CF*, 642; Beale, *Revelation*, 1137–39.

37. Beale links this point well to the context of coming judgment: "Works demonstrate that a person has already met the ultimate, causal, necessary condition for salvation, which is redemptive justification from sin by Christ's death (so also Eph. 2:6–10)." *Revelation*, 1138. This explanation coheres well with my argument that justification plays a causal role in making us citizens of heaven.

38. Whether the ἵνα clause grammatically marks purpose or result makes no material difference to the outcome of this argument. The purpose is clearly not hypothetical but fulfilled.

39. Beale, *Revelation*, 1139–40.

> much more shall we be saved by him from the wrath of God. For if while we were enemies we were reconciled to God by the death of his Son, much more, now that we are reconciled, shall we be saved by his life. More than that, we also rejoice in God through our Lord Jesus Christ, through whom we have now received reconciliation.

Christ died not to rescue godly people, but to justify the ungodly, supremely indicating God's love for his people. Further, Paul uses three "more than" statements, which demonstrates that if we are presently justified because of Christ, then that blessing of justification even more so ensures that Christ will rescue us from God's last-day wrath. So, glorified spiritual life is justification's consequent reward, as would have been the case for Adam in the covenant of works and was for Christ in the covenant of redemption (Rom 5:18–21). The implications for our assurance of salvation should make our hearts soar as we contemplate the unshakable reality of God's love for his people and how he brought that into irreversible fruition through our Savior.

These themes from biblical theology intersect to show how God offers Christ and his benefits to us in the covenant of grace. The unity of the covenant is clear in that the gospel about justification was preached beforehand to Abraham (Gal 3:7–8), meaning Christ's imputed righteousness was the basis of justification throughout every age of the covenant of grace. Moreover, we become partakers of Christ as the Spirit unites us to him by faith (Rom 4:1–6). Faith itself does not save us. As the Belgic Confession describes, faith's role is "only an instrument with which we embrace Christ our Righteousness." So, "faith is an instrument that keeps us in communion with him in all his benefits, which, when they become ours, are more than sufficient to acquit us of our sins" (BC 22).[40] Similarly, the Heidelberg Catechism explains how we say that we are righteous only by faith: "Not that I am acceptable to God on account of the worthiness of my faith," since "only the satisfaction, righteousness, and holiness of Christ is my righteousness before God," and "I can receive the same and make it my own in no other way than by faith only" (HC 61).[41] Faith is the beautiful life rope that ties us to Christ, the trustworthy and sure Savior.

---

40. *COC*, 3:408.

41. *COC*, 3:327.

In light of everything that we have considered so far, faith is clearly not the condition of the covenant of grace in the same way that works were the condition of the covenant of works for Adam and the covenant of redemption for Christ. Faith is not a "new law" as if God has simply changed his standard for entering his kingdom.[42] Rather, we are represented before God by one of the two ultimate covenant heads, Adam or Christ. By nature, we are in Adam and so stand condemned by his failure in the covenant of works.

Faith, however, is the God-appointed mechanism to transfer us from Adam's representation to Christ's. To reinforce the previous chapter's life rope illustration, the rope is the device that pulls us from the domain of shark-infested waters and binds us to our rescuer who drags us to safety aboard the ship. The covenant of grace transfers us from being in Adam to being in Christ. Even in the second century, the Epistle to Diognetus celebrates this point.

> But when our unrighteousness was fulfilled, and it had been made perfectly clear that its wages—punishment and death—were to be expected ... in his mercy he took upon himself our sins; he himself gave up his own Son as a ransom for us, the holy one for the lawless, the guiltless for the guilty, the just for the unjust, the incorruptible for the corruptible, the immortal for the mortal. For what else but his righteousness could have covered our sins? In whom was it possible for us, the lawless and ungodly, to be justified, except in the Son of God alone? O the sweet exchange, O the incomprehensible work of God, O the unexpected blessings, that the sinfulness of many should be hidden in one righteous person while the righteousness of one should justify the many sinners.[43]

Faith is that which unites us to Christ so that we might have communion with him in grace to partake of the virtue of his mediation.[44] *Jesus* saved believers in the Old Testament, even if he destroyed those who did not

42. *TI*, 16.2.9; 16.7.9–10; *EC*, 3.8.48–56; 4.3.23.

43. Diognetus 9.2–5; *AP*, 709–11.

44. WLC 69; *LC*, 78.

believe (Jude 1:5). *Christ* was the Rock who provided spiritual blessings to Old Testament believers (1 Cor 10:1–6).

The Son of God has always been the mediator for believers, whether they trusted in the mediator *incarnandus* or *incarnatus*. From God's eternal perspective, the Lamb was slain before the foundation of the world (Rev 13:8), so, even though the Son needed to perform his work in history, he had already become the guarantor to pay the principal and penalty covenantal debts for all the elect. Again, the Son became the elect's sponsor as *expromissor* rather than *fideiussor*. As Irenaeus writes, in some sense, that which God has "determined to take place, is reckoned as having already taken place."[45] In this respect, the Westminster Confession explains, "Christ, by his obedience and death, did fully discharge the debt of all those that are thus justified, and did make a proper, real, and full satisfaction of his Father's justice in their behalf" (WCF 11.3).[46] In terms of the eternal perspective, the Confession adds, "God did, from all eternity, decree to justify the elect, and Christ did, in the fullness of time, die for their sins and rise again for their justification: nevertheless, they are not justified until the Holy Spirit does, in due time, actually apply Christ unto them" (WCF 11.4).[47] There is continuity throughout the covenant of grace in terms of its substance regarding the Savior, the justification that the Savior grants to us, and the way that we take hold of the Savior and receive justification from him.

SANCTIFICATION

The communion with God that we have because of Christ is not limited to the *restoration* of a right relationship but continues in the *development* of that relationship. Just as a marriage relationship begins with the legal vows that bind bride and groom in covenant, so too justification secures the legal beginning of our peace with God. In addition, the marriage is not limited to its legal dynamic, but develops in every aspect of relational communion as the couple learn to live with and for one another. Likewise,

45. Irenaeus, *Demonstration*, §67.

46. *COC*, 3:626–27.

47. *COC*, 3:627.

our communion with God develops as we walk by the Spirit and grow in our ability to live for him in this life.[48]

This aspect of the Christian life wherein we grow in holiness is called sanctification. The Westminster Larger Confession explains,

> Sanctification is a work of God's grace, whereby they, whom God has before the foundation of the world chosen to be holy, are in time, through the powerful operation of his Spirit applying the death and resurrection of Christ unto them, renewed in their whole man after the Image of God, having the seeds of Repentance unto life, and of all other saving graces put into their hearts, and those graces so stirred up, increased, and strengthened, as that they more and more die unto sin and rise unto newness of life. (WLC 75)[49]

Sanctification concerns our moral renovation, namely, overcoming spiritual death and increasing in the present reality of our spiritual life.

Sanctification is something that God does to us. It is "a work of God's grace" through the Spirit living in believers.[50] Herman Witsius explains, it is "that real work of God, by which they, who are chosen, regenerated, and justified, are continually more and more transformed from the turpitude of sin, to the purity of the divine image."[51] The nature of our union with Christ demands that we recognize Christ as the primary actor in our sanctification: "I have been crucified with Christ. *It is no longer I who live, but Christ who lives in me.* And the life I now live in the flesh I live by faith in the Son of God, who loved me and gave himself for me" (Gal 2:20).[52] Since sanctification concerns the renovation of our moral life, focus easily shifts to us, emphasizing radical and vibrant efforts to transform ourselves. This approach to sanctification can quickly devolve into a type of legalism, at least by focusing on ourselves more than on Christ.[53]

---

48. *CG*, 180.

49. *LC*, 79–80.

50. *BRD*, 4:252–54.

51. *EC*, 3.12.11.

52. Horton, *Rediscovering*, 216–20; *VRD*, 4:25–26; Gaffin, *By Faith, Not by Sight*, 87–89.

53. Grant Macaskill, *Living in Union with Christ: Paul's Gospel and Christian Moral Identity* (Grand Rapids: Baker Academic, 2019), 8–10, 17–26.

The better approach emphasizes how our union with Christ constitutes our moral transformation.[54]

A proper emphasis on union with Christ in relation to sanctification recognizes that there is no "I," even if energized by the Spirit, left in the Christian life. Paul is clear: "It is no longer I who live, but Christ who lives in me" (Gal 2:20). Sanctification does not help us increase our own personal goodness, which is not very good in sinners, but makes us a participant in Christ's "radically other goodness."[55] Paul contrasts his old impressive record of accomplishments, which he counted as loss, with "the surpassing worth of knowing Christ Jesus my Lord" and being "found in him," precisely in order to experience "the power of his resurrection" (Phil 3:8–10).[56] It is not as though justification is God's part in salvation and sanctification is ours. Rather, God sanctifies his people, and God's work of sanctification produces newness of life in them so that they increasingly die unto sin and live unto righteousness.[57]

Sanctification is, further, real newness of life that results in our good works.[58] When Adam sinned, he brought the verdict of condemnation upon himself and us, but that verdict also brought the effect of corruption in its wake. Adam was legally declared a sinner, and also truly became a sinner (Rom 5:12–21). On the other hand, the last Adam won justification unto life as the verdict for those whom he represents (Rom 5:18).[59] Just as condemnation brought corruption in its wake, so too righteousness brings renewal in its wake (Rom 5:21). That spiritual life that is the consequent reward of justification does not have to wait for our life in the age to come but begins here and now in sanctification. So, the Heidelberg Catechism says,

> *86. Since, then we are redeemed from our misery by grace through Christ, without any merit of ours, why must we still do good works?*

---

54. Macaskill, *Living in Union with Christ*, 16–17.
55. Macaskill, *Living in Union with Christ*, 40–41, 50–57.
56. Macaskill, *Living in Union with Christ*, 43–50.
57. *VRD*, 4:212–13; Horton, *Rediscovering*, 216–17.
58. *BRD*, 4:256–60.
59. *CG*, 209–11.

> Because Christ, having redeemed us by his blood, renews us also by his holy Spirit after his own image, that with our whole life we may show ourselves thankful to God for his blessing, and that he may be glorified through us; then, also, that we ourselves may be assured of our faith by the fruits thereof, and by our godly walk may win our neighbors also to Christ.[60]

Sanctification is then a blessing of the covenant. Importantly, sanctification is not a condition added after we are justified for gaining everlasting life but is itself truly a reward that Christ has earned for us. God sanctifies us because Christ merited that renewal for his people.

The emphasis on sanctification as the transformative blessing of salvation magnifies that distinct work of God throughout the Christian life. Those who want to make justification both legal and transformative ask justification to carry more weight than God intended.[61] Although they intend to highlight sanctification's importance by incorporating it into justification, they actually dilute it. They imply that for something to be truly important, it must be justification, so they smuggle transformation into the legal aspect of salvation. In contrast, the Reformed strong distinction between justification and sanctification insists that God cares for both legal and transformative aspects of our salvation. Sanctification need not be justification to be important, since God has given it to us in Christ as a distinct and independently wonderful blessing.

Sanctification is our present experience of that spiritual life that we will have with God in the new creation. Paul writes in Romans 6:1–4: "What shall we say then? Are we to continue in sin that grace may abound? By no means! How can we who died to sin still live in it? Do you not know that all of us who have been baptized into Christ Jesus were baptized into his death? We were buried therefore with him by baptism into death, in order that, just as Christ was raised from the dead by the glory of the Father, we too might walk in newness of life." Sanctification is our present experience of resurrection life. Christ currently has that life by perfection, but we have it in measure as we wait to receive it in completion at our resurrection.

---

60. *COC*, 3:338.

61. E.g., deSilva, *Galatians*, 223–24, 250, 252.

Denying that Christians should walk in holiness because we are saved by grace is a monstrosity, even if our strides toward holiness in this life are incomplete and stumbling.[62] As John Calvin comments on Romans 6:1: "Those who, in a false and perverse manner, imagine that our Redeemer has conferred upon us gratuitous justification without imparting newness of life divide and tear Christ into pieces."[63] Sanctification is a non-negotiable part of the Christian life because Christ has earned it for us. We cannot have only part of Christ, as if we can pick among his benefits, but we receive the whole Christ by faith for justification and sanctification.[64]

Regarding sanctification's unity throughout the covenant of grace, God has always required his people to be holy. The major issue is to explain the manner of this obligation, which raises the question of how we relate to God's law. Vos notes that one sense of the law indicates "a natural obligation toward God that is incumbent on us and must always be incumbent on us."[65] This is the law given *as a rule* rather than *as a covenant*. Our natural obligation to obey God's law as a rule never goes away, explaining why Christians remain responsible to grow in holiness even after our relationship with God is restored in justification. Still, because Christ fulfilled the covenant of works on our behalf, believers cannot relate to the law as a condition—as a covenant—for inheriting everlasting life, as that would confuse the law and the gospel.

So, we must consider our obligation to holiness in some other way than as a condition for entering Christ's kingdom. It is our rule. In this sense, "The law of God lays claim to the entire life of man and to every act in it. It also lays claim to the relationship in which man is faced with the gospel." As we relate the law as a rule to the covenant of grace we can "maintain that there is law in the gospel ... *only if it is clearly understood how here there is no thought of the law as an instrument of the covenant of works*. Of itself the law cannot yield the covenant of grace, for it knows of no grace." In the gospel, the law is not given as a covenant but as a rule "by which the law establishes the norms for our life."[66] There is continuity

62. *VRD*, 4:205–12, 205–12.

63. *CO*, 49:103; *CC*, 19:2.217.

64. Calvin, *Institutes*, 3.1.1–3.

65. *VRD*, 5:86.

66. *VRD*, 5:86–87 (emphasis added).

in our remaining obligation to obey God's law, even though its manner is very different in the covenant of works and the covenant of grace.

As justified Christians, God's law is no longer a prerequisite condition for obtaining a reward from God. Works are not an *antecedent condition* as a cause of reward, but a *subsequent condition* as the evidence of possessing the reward.[67] They are not a condition for maintaining or finalizing our salvation but the condition for showing that we are saved. Believers were already judged at the cross (Gal 2:19–20), so there is no future review of our works—no slideshow of our failures before the heavenly court—to determine whether we truly measure up. So, the Heidelberg Catechism confesses that, "concerning the forgiveness of sins," we believe "that God, for the sake of Christ's satisfaction, will no more remember my sins, neither the sinful nature with which I have to struggle all my life long; but graciously imparts to me the righteousness of Christ, that I may nevermore come into condemnation" (HC 56).[68] Christ's work has accomplished everything needed to secure our place in his heavenly kingdom.

Works, being the consequent condition as fruits and evidence of salvation, do not serve to complete or fulfill our salvation. Rather, they are the condition of showing our gratitude. To illustrate, imagine that a father gives his daughter a car as a gift after she has learned to drive. The car is a completely free gift and there are no terms that might result in it being taken away. As she celebrates her new prized possession, she asks "Daddy, how can I ever thank you?" He replies, "It would be very helpful if you cleaned the dining room once a month." In this situation, cleaning is not a condition of obtaining or keeping the car but for expressing gratitude for a free gift. That is how consequent conditions operate in the covenant of grace as well. Works do not obtain or maintain our salvation but serve to demonstrate our experience of salvation. The standard for those evidentiary works can be none other than God's law, which abides as the guide—the *rule*—to direct our lives of holiness in the covenant of grace.

Further, sanctification is a benefit experienced across the covenant of grace. The Scripture provides one crystal clear passage that attests to this reality. Hebrews 11 is often called "the hall of faith" because it records

67. *TI*, 12.4.6–7.

68. *COC*, 3:325. Thanks to Scott Clark for noting the usefulness of Heidelberg 56 at this point.

examples from the Old Testament of faithful believers. This catalogue begins, "Now faith is the assurance of things hoped for, the conviction of things not seen. For by it the people of old received their commendation" (Heb 11:1–2). The chapter then recounts how Old Testament believers lived faithfully to God, even though imperfectly. Abel, Enoch, Noah, Abraham, Moses, the judges, and David are all commended for the things they accomplished *by faith*.[69]

Hebrews portrays faith as resulting in new obedience unto God. Hebrews did not replace holiness for justification as the benefit of faith, since the epistle also thoroughly explains how those who trust in Christ are cleansed by his death (Heb 2:10–18). Rather, faith that justifies also sanctifies.[70] Indeed, Hebrews 11 commends the Old Testament saints for their acts of faithfulness that flow from hearts full of faith. This record should inspire us in our lives of sanctification too, since all of God's people strive to live holy lives, imperfect as they may be, as we wait for the full reception of the promise, together as one people from old and new covenants, at the last day (Heb 11:39–40).

As Christ is the Savior throughout the covenant of grace, so sanctification is a benefit that believers receive from Christ regardless of the era in which they live. Certainly, there are differences between the old and new covenants in the way that believers experience the full measure of the Spirit's indwelling presence.[71] Still, the Spirit has been active throughout the whole covenant of grace to work in God's people to bring them to faith and produce newness of life in them.[72] Irenaeus writes, "Because for those who died before Christ appeared there is hope that in the judgment of the risen they may obtain salvation, even such as feared God and died in righteousness and *had in them the Spirit of God*, as the patriarchs and prophets and righteous men."[73] Clement of Alexandria also writes against the Valentinians that "the Paraclete, who works immediately in the Church, is of the same substance and power with him who was working under

69. *BTA*, 159–82.

70. *VRD*, 4:201–5.

71. Horton, *Rediscovering*, 138–69.

72. *TI*, 12.5.45; Crowe, *Path of Faith*, 92–94.

73. Irenaeus, *Demonstration*, §56 (emphasis added); cf. *KTC*, 142n91; and James M. Hamilton Jr., *God's Indwelling Presence: The Holy Spirit in the Old and New Testaments* (Nashville: B&H, 2006), 1–24.

the Old Testament."[74] More importantly, 1 Peter 1:10–11 explains that the Old Testament prophets searched to know what "the Spirit *of Christ* in them was indicating when he predicted the sufferings of Christ and the subsequent glories." Note that not merely the Spirit but *Christ's* Spirit was at work, on the basis of the Son's work distributed *incarnandus*, to inspire the prophets before the incarnation. In the new covenant, believers may be universally called into special Spirit-filled service, but that does not mean that the Spirit did not grant all of Christ's benefits that are necessary aspects of salvation to every believer in every period of salvation history.[75] Sanctification is a benefit of Christ common to all believers alike.

GLORIFICATION

Glorification is the full possession of that indestructible, spiritual life that is the ultimate reward for those who fulfill all righteousness. It is our full conformity to Christ in his exalted and glorious state, both in soul and body, to be perfected at the resurrection.[76] It too is a benefit common to all believers across the covenant of grace. This commonality is easy to prove since it remains future for all believers of every age. Those who have died are presently with the Lord in heaven, perfected in their souls (2 Cor 5:8). As the Westminster Larger Catechism explains, "The Communion in glory with Christ, which the members of the invisible Church enjoy immediately after death, is, in that in their souls are then made perfect in holiness, and received into the highest heavens, where they behold the face of God in light and glory, waiting for the full redemption of their bodies, which even in death continue united to Christ, and rest in their graves as in their beds, till at the last day they be again united with their souls" (WLC 86).[77] Believers who have died are in full communion with God in their souls but wait to be reunited with their bodies at the resurrection.[78]

The Scripture is plain that all believers will be raised from their graves and glorified at the same time. In 1 Thessalonians 4:16–17, Paul describes Christ's return and the resurrection. "For the Lord himself will

74. Clement of Alexandria, *Excerpta ek Theodotou*, §24, in *PG*, 9:671–72.

75. Beale, *New Testament Biblical Theology*, 733–37.

76. WLC 82; *LC*, 81.

77. *LC*, 82.

78. *EC*, 3.14.11–33.

descend from heaven with a cry of command, with the voice of an archangel, and with the sound of the trumpet of God. And the dead in Christ will rise first. Then we who are alive, who are left, will be caught up together with them in the clouds to meet the Lord in the air, and so we will always be with the Lord." This resurrection at the last trumpet is when believers are translated into the glorified state, as Paul explains in 1 Corinthians 15:51–52: "We shall not all sleep, but we shall all be changed, in a moment, in the twinkling of an eye, at the last trumpet. For the trumpet will sound, and the dead will be raised imperishable, and we shall be changed." So, every believer will be translated into the glorified state at the same event.[79] Those who are dead will be raised to glory, and those who are living will be changed. Since all believers are raised or changed to this glorified state at the same future event, it is a blessing common to every true member of the covenant of grace.

That glorification is future for all believers is a crucial piece of the puzzle in explaining the unity of the covenant of grace. The stress upon the sameness of saving benefits for believers of every age may trouble some readers who want to make sure that a theological grid is not imposed upon the text, especially in regard to what makes the new covenant *new* in contrast to how God dealt with his people before Christ's coming. Still, believers have always looked forward to the promise of the resurrection. Despite God's covenantal curse of death upon Adam (Gen 2:17; Rom 5:17–19), Adam named his wife "Eve" "because she was the mother of all *living*" (Gen 3:20). Even at the beginning of the covenant of grace, Adam's resurrection life was in store. Paul, indeed, saw Christ's resurrection, which was for our justification, as the fulfillment of the promise to Abraham (Rom 4:20–25).[80] The resurrection of the body, as our glorification, is nothing more than the completion of the promise that believers have always trusted would occur. If the resurrection has always been the hope throughout God's saving plan, it should alleviate any reservations we might have about the other aspects of salvation also being granted before and after Christ came.

79. *BRD*, 4:693–94.

80. Barrett, "Raised for Our Justification," 395–97.

CONCLUSION

The pastoral use of this chapter's material is that God has not left us in the dark about what our communion with him by covenant is like but has told us about the profound blessings for those who have faith in Christ. Whereas so many of our relationships are unsure or disappointing, believers are bound to Christ as our sure Savior, who guarantees our everlasting life in beautifully abundant communion with God. Although our struggle to overcome the flesh and live faithfully for God in this life can at times be frustrating, we should take heart that even the smallest evidence of growth in holiness is evidence of the Spirit's work in us. Those dim rays of transformation that creep across the horizon of our heart will not be dim forever. Because we are justified in Christ, it is guaranteed that that sun of transformation will eventually burst over the skyline and we will have the fullness of glory. That glory is good because we will be entirely freed from sin and in complete and undiluted communion with the Triune God. We will be as we were meant to be: truly human, living fully according to the law as the expression of our full love for God, and able to commune face-to-face with our covenant Lord.

X

The Time of Tension

And we know that for those who love God all things work together
for good, for those who are called according to his purpose.
For those whom he foreknew he also predestined to be conformed
to the image of his Son, in order that he might be the firstborn among
many brothers. And those whom he predestined he also called,
and those whom he called he also justified,
and those whom he justified he also glorified.
—*Romans 8:28–30*

Believers should rejoice and be filled with wonder at knowing who Christ is, what he has done for us, and the blessings which he grants to us in salvation. Still, we do not presently possess all those Christ-earned benefits. In our present age, believers live in a time of tension wherein we have received salvation but wait to see its completion at Christ's return when he will raise us bodily to new life and bring about the new creation. This season, therefore, includes contented joy but also expectation and hardship as we anticipate the full redemption of our bodies.

Covenant theology provides tools to explain this already/not yet dynamic of our salvation. Gathering the implications from how God promised rewards to his people by his covenants, this chapter explores how we presently experience salvation and how various aspects of our salvation relate to one another.[1]

ESTABLISHING THE TIME OF TENSION

The time of tension between the former age and the age to come forges the context for our experience of salvation, especially concerning how the saving benefits which we presently possess and those which we will receive at Christ's return all relate to one another (Gal 1:4; Eph 2:7). The last days have begun, but they have not been entirely fulfilled, in what theologians often call the "already/not yet" (Heb 1:1–2).[2] Christ's first coming changed the world by fulfilling centuries of prophecy of the messianic Savior rescuing God's people. As the fulfillment of the promise for the redeemer king in David's line, he inaugurated the kingdom of God on earth (Rom 1:3–4). So, he began his preaching ministry by declaring, "The time is fulfilled, and *the kingdom of God is at hand*; repent and believe in the gospel" (Mark 1:15). Presently, Christ possesses "all authority in heaven and on earth" (Matt 28:18) and "must reign until he has put all his enemies under his feet" (1 Cor 15:25). Inasmuch as God's kingdom's ultimate form is the new creation, its total fulfillment is still future.[3]

This tension has more specific reference to Christ's resurrection, especially regarding our salvation. Christ has been raised as "the firstfuits" from the dead (1 Cor 15:20–23). A rosebush's first blossom helps illustrate Christ as the firstfruits of the resurrrection. That first bud's full blossoming assures us that the whole bush is alive and that more blossoms will surely follow. Much like individual blossoms are joined within one rosebush, the elect are joined with Christ. Christ's rising from death showed that he had fulfilled the covenant of works *for those whom he represented* and had taken possession of the reward that he merited for himself *and for*

1. This chapter, admittedly, pulls together implications of preceding arguments but is not integral to the book's central argument. It applies previous conclusions to a specific discussion in contemporary Reformed theology.

2. Beale, *New Testament Biblical Theology*, 88–116, 129–84; O'Brien, *Hebrews*, 50.

3. Ridderbos, *Coming of the Kingdom*, 61–184; Richard B. Gaffin Jr., *In the Fullness of Time: An Introduction to the Biblical Theology of Acts and Paul* (Wheaton, IL: Crossway, 2022), 65–80; Kim Riddlebarger, *A Case for Amillennialism: Understanding the End Times*, expanded ed. (Grand Rapids: Baker Books, 2013), 83–145; S. M. Baugh, *The Majesty on High: Introduction to the Kingdom of God in the New Testament* (CreateSpace, 2017).

them. Since Christ's incarnate work was so tied to the fate of those given to him by the Father, his resurrection was that first blossom, guaranteeing that others will surely follow. In another metaphor, as a locomotive is the powerful engine that pulls all the train cars bound to it, so Christ's resurrection will drag all those united to him from our graves into the glorified state as well.[4]

Further, Christ's resurrection was his justification and glorification *as the last Adam*. He was justified in his resurrection because he had fulfilled the covenant of works but also was "raised for our justification" (Rom 4:25).[5] Christ was also glorified so that he "will transform our lowly body to be like his glorious body" (Phil 3:21). Our justification and glorification are bound to Christ's, but whereas Christ received both in full measure at his resurrection, we must wait until the last day to experience both together. The time of tension is, then, that Christ has earned every saving benefit for those whom he represented but we do not yet possess them all.

CHRIST'S REWARDS IN RELATIONSHIP TO ONE ANOTHER

Covenant theology's structure, as this book argues it, explains how Christ was justified and glorified in one event at his resurrection, while we wait to experience them both together. Specifically, the covenant of works established that perfect obedience would obtain the status of justification which would further result in the consequent reward of glorified life, so binding justification to glorification in a specific relationship (Rom 5:18–21). Both properly belong to the final judgment, which now awaits Christ's return. Already, however, he has guaranteed every saving blessing for the elect and is distributing those blessings in the present age even as we wait for those that cannot be possessed until the age to come. Our union with Christ guarantees that we will take part in every benefit that he has earned for us, including glorification. As the Westminster Larger

4. Vos, "Eschatological Aspect," 92–93; Gaffin, *Resurrection and Redemption*, 33–41; Gaffin, *By Faith, Not by Sight*, 67–70.

5. *BRD*, 4:216–17; VanDrunen, "Contested Union," 490; Gaffin, "Work of Christ Applied," 275; Gaffin, *Resurrection and Redemption*, 122–24.

Catechism says, every saving blessing that the saints receive from Christ "manifests their Union with Him" (WLC 69).[6]

Since the covenant's blessings had specific relationships to one another in Christ's experience of obtaining them, they must still relate to one another in a specific way in our experience of receiving them in union with Christ.[7] Christ's historical procurement of those blessings, then, models how we receive them, and so the *historia salutis* sets the pattern of the *ordo salutis*. For us, effectual calling is prerequisite to every other aspect of salvation because only those who believe in Christ are justified, sanctified, and glorified.[8] As Geerhardus Vos incisively argues, "The subjective application of the salvation obtained by Christ does not occur at once or arbitrarily." Rather, "there are a multiplicity of relationships and conditions to which all the operations of grace have a certain connection."[9]

---

6. *LC*, 78.

7. *RST*, 3:267–82; Stamps, "Faith Works," 506, 518–30; VanDrunen, "Contested Union," 499–502; Letham, *Systematic Theology*, 615–16.

8. *TI*, 16.1.1; 16.9.4; *VRD*, 4:162; *BRD*, 4:179.

9. *VRD*, 4:1–2. Vos's major concern was again likely Albert Schweitzer (1875–1965), who used mystical union with Christ as the foundation of Paul's theology to undermine the relevance of Christ's more specific benefits. This chapter likewise emphasizes how the mechanics of Reformed covenant theology better explain that eschatological tension. Schweitzer sidelined salvation's legal aspects, namely, justification as a "subsidiary crater," in favor of more general participation in the eschatological power of Christ's resurrection. Also, potentially, Vos was concerned from a dogmatic perspective with the challenge that Karl Barth (1886–1968) posed to the traditional Reformed formulation of the *ordo salutis*, as Barth favored only union with Christ in the *historia salutis* and contended that justification and sanctification should not presuppose illumination, conversion, and faith "rather than themselves being as already accomplished in Jesus Christ." Arguing so, Barth eclipsed an ordered reception of Christ's benefits behind generic union with Christ in the *historia salutis*, disjoined from the modes in which Christ procured and distributes his benefits; see Karl Barth, *Church Dogmatics*, 14 vol. trans. G. W. Bromiley, ed. G. W. Bromiley and T. F. Torrance (Peabody, MA: Hendrickson, 2010), IV.3.2. §71.2 (505–7). More recently, Bates rejects the notion of an ordered relationship between the benefits of Christ in favor of the primacy of union with Christ. He argues that Christ's benefits, especially justification and sanctification, are not distinct in the way that Reformed theology understands them. Rather, salvation is essentially incorporation into Christ's eschatological resurrection, rendering every aspect of our salvation—justification, sanctification, and glorification—in some ways already accomplished but in other ways incomplete. In Bates's view, our final salvation ultimately depends upon our conformity to Christ at the end of our lives; see Bates, *Allegiance Alone*, 166–76, 196–98, 207–10.

Vos, however, specifically rejects that union with Christ is the basis of our legal relationship with God, emphasizing Christ's imputed righteousness as the *sole* ground of our justification; see *VRD*, 4:21–24; and Vos, "Alleged Legalism," 384. In other words, union is not a "more basic" reality separate and prior to justification. Rather, justification is part of and manifests our union with Christ. As Vos writes, "Concerning the legal relationship, being reckoned in Christ precedes, and only from that does being the Mediator follow. The mystical union is not the basis on which I appear just before God but a gift that is extended to me from God's justification." See *VRD*, 4:22; and Fesko, *Justification*, 299–331, 264–80; cf. Johnson, *One with Christ*, 72, 75.

Our salvation's every aspect manifests our union with Christ but not as if God grants all Christ's benefits in the same way or even all entirely at the same time. Rather, God distributes Christ's benefits to us in an ordered way, protecting the connections between those benefits, precisely so that his various acts of grace would be seen in their distinct relation to one another, and God's multifaceted grace would be overtly experienced.[10] Can we then explain the specific ways that justification, sanctification, and glorification relate to one another?

The answer requires more reflection upon the earlier discussion about the reward that Adam could have earned in the covenant of works, the covenant in which he would have been justified if he had fulfilled the law. To illustrate, when a student fulfills all the assignments for their degree, the school *designates* them as a "graduate." Similarly, if Adam fulfilled the covenant of works, God would have *designated* him as "righteous" or "justified." But when a student earns the designation of "graduate," they receive the consequent reward of a diploma. The status warrants its accompanying reward. So too, justification is "unto life" as this legal status entails its consequent reward of spiritual, glorified life (Rom 5:18; 1 Cor 15:42–44).[11] Adam's justified status would have had its accompanying reward of a new creation body in indestructible life, namely, glorification.

This graduation illustration also illumines how Christ, as the last Adam, received his justification and glorification. Typically graduating students are declared graduates *through* the act of conferring their diploma. Their status is made known *by* granting that status's consequent reward. The status is the legal ground for receiving that reward, even though the two are received in the same act. For Christ, his resurrection was both his justification and glorification.[12] Although the event itself of Christ's resurrection was both forensic and renovative, his perfectly righteous status remained the legal ground for his resurrection's renovative aspect—glorification. As Vos explains, "Our first principle is that the judicial relationships are the

10. Gaffin also forcefully argues that the blessings of the *ordo salutis* "are not received as an arbitrary or chaotic mix but in a set pattern with fixed connections among them" which prevents "misrepresenting individual aspects or acts and so distorting the work of Christ applied as a whole." Gaffin, "Work of Christ Applied," 270.

11. *VRD*, 4:154.

12. Gaffin, "Work of Christ Applied," 275–76; Gaffin, *Resurrection and Redemption*, 119–24, 126–27.

basis on which the moral acts of re-creation rest in their entirety."[13] Christ's justification and glorification came simultaneously in his resurrection but remain conceptually different.

Although Christ is already justified and glorified, believers do not receive both in this age. Still, because the covenant of works and Christ's fulfillment of it in the *historia salutis* established the relationship between them, glorification remains justification's consequent, ensured reward.[14] Christ grants both benefits to us but not at the same time. Christ in his resurrection is the firstfruits that have blossomed, but Christ's second coming will produce the full harvest. God declares believers justified in the present age, even though that status properly belongs to the final judgment.[15] If believers did not presently possess a full and final justification, then our justification would not correspond to Christ's. So, God can grant and has granted blessings that belong to the final judgment before its occurrence.

Even though believers are presently fully justified in this age, God does not yet grant glorification. Still, since glorification is justification's consequent reward and we are fully justified, we have the right to glorification, despite not yet experiencing it.[16] As Vos writes, "Justification serves to take away the guilt of sin and to replace it with *the right to eternal life* in relationship with God."[17] God has granted the status of "justification that entitles to eschatological life in the Spirit" but delays in bestowing its consequent reward until the last day.[18]

This is as if our graduation ceremony officially and fully declared us graduates but with a promise to send our diplomas later. The declaration ensures that the reward must be sent, but receiving it is delayed.

---

13. *VRD*, 4:6–7; also Vos, "Alleged Legalism," 384. Gaffin also affirms the priority of the legal aspects of salvation: "While these two [forensic and renovative] aspects are inseparable, the judicial aspect has an essential and decisive priority. Because his [Christ's] obedience unto death is the requisite judicial ground for his resurrection, his becoming the life-giving Spirit presupposes his being justified in the Spirit, not the reverse." Gaffin, "Work of Christ Applied," 278–79.

14. *VRD*, 4:154.

15. Longenecker, *Paul, Apostle of Liberty*, 106–15, 131–39; Barrett, "Raised for Our Justification," 403–5; Gaffin, *By Faith, Not by Sight*, 74–76.

16. *BRD*, 4:224; *VRD*, 4:154; Barrett, "Raised for Our Justification," 403–5.

17. *VRD*, 4:138 (emphasis added).

18. Gaffin, *Fullness of Time*, 220.

Believers have a full share in Christ's justification because his righteousness is imputed to us, but we wait to partake of *his* glorification.

This tension for believers as we live between having already received the justified status from Christ but not yet sharing in his fully glorified condition has highest relevance for how we ourselves experience salvation in relationship to Christ. Our justification, as Herman Bavinck writes, "carries life with it (Rom 5:18)."[19] Christians should, then, be supremely hopeful people because, even though we do not yet possess that glorified life, justification still presently pushes its reward onto us so that our everlasting life bleeds forward into the present age.[20]

THE RELATIONSHIP OF JUSTIFICATION TO GLORIFICATION FOR BELIEVERS

Although the relationship between Christ's justification and glorification has been established, we must consider how those blessings relate to one another for believers. Our hopefulness is fueled when we realize that the connection between justification as the status that guarantees its consequent reward of glorification is why believer's works cannot contribute to their salvation at the last day.[21] As Paul has so clearly said in Romans 5:9–10, "*Since*, therefore, we have now been *justified* by his blood, *much more* shall we be saved by him from the wrath of God. For if while we were enemies we were reconciled to God by the death of his Son, *much more*, now that we are reconciled, shall we be saved by his life." Because Christ's imputed perfect righteousness grounds our justification, the principle from Romans 2:13 that "the doers of the law ... will be justified" becomes the real *present* experience for believers. In this respect, as Vos notes, "justification that takes places under the covenant of grace is not different from that justification under the covenant of works" because "gospel justification did not differ from legal justification *quoad essentiam*, 'as to essence,' but *quoad circumstantias*, 'as to circumstances.' " Specifically, our justification requires perfect righteousness as to its essence, but someone else can supply that righteousness for us as to its circumstances. Since

19. *BRD*, 4:186, 210–11; *VRD*, 4:154; Crowe, "Passive and Active Obedience of Christ," 449–50.

20. *BRD*, 3:595; *TI*, 12.3.17; 17.1.3, 11; 17.3.14–15.

21. Stamps, "Faith Works," 526–28.

Christ's merit is the basis of our justification, "we have justification in the strict sense of the word."[22] Indeed, God has done what the law could not do *because of our weak, sinful condition* by sending the Son in human nature to fulfill the law's requirement of righteousness for us (Rom 8:3–4; Gal 3:21; 2 Cor 3:6; Gal 4:4–5).[23] Even though justification properly belongs to the last judgment, we experience it fully and *already* in the present since Christ has fully and *already* done the law and brought that declaration belonging to the last day forward into the present for those who trust in him.[24]

Another justification for believers, not even another part or aspect of our justification, with an evaluation of our works then cannot wait in the future. As Vos explains, "Once declared, justification remains secure forever."[25] So, "it is completely unthinkable that the one Christ, who surely becomes ours in justification, would only be imparted to us by degrees and in parts. We receive Him completely, and therefore our justification must be complete from the outset."[26] If God "re-justified" us by considering even our Spirit-enabled good works, then his declaration—because of Christ—would no longer contradict our condition.[27]

The Reformed have long affirmed this point. Confessionally, the Heidelberg Catechism says our good works cannot "be the whole or part of our righteousness before God" because "the righteousness which can stand before the judgment seat of God must be perfect throughout, and wholly conformable to the divine law; whereas even our best works in this life are all imperfect and defiled with sin" (HC 62).[28] The Westminster Confession also affirms that "any thing wrought in them, or done by them ... *or any other evangelical obedience*" cannot be the reason for that verdict of justification—now or in the future (WCF 11.1).[29] Individually, Francis Turretin argues that holiness and obedience "do not have causality

22. *VRD*, 4:151.

23. Moo, *Romans*, 481–85; MMB, 30–31.

24. Vos, "Alleged Legalism," 388–90; *VRD*, 4:22; Longenecker, *Paul, Apostle of Liberty*, 106–15; Longenecker, *Romans*, 694–96; Thielman, *Romans*, 380–82.

25. *VRD*, 4:139.

26. *VRD*, 4:159.

27. *WWP*, 4:64 (commentary on Jude 3); *TI*, 16.10.8; Vos, "Alleged Legalism," 384–87; *VRD*, 4:142–43, 158, 170–71; *BRD*, 4:191, 209; cf. *EC*, 3.8.63–77.

28. *COC*, 3:327. Thanks to R. Scott Clark for recommending HC 62 on this point.

29. *COC*, 3:626 (emphasis added); *VRD*, 4:143.

either with respect to justification or eternal life flowing from [them]," even though good works do inseparably accompany faith.[30] There can, therefore, be no time when God takes consideration of our works *for justification itself* (now or in the future).[31] Vos confirms, "Justification excludes that in our sanctification there could ever be any mention of obtaining rights to eternal life. Sanctification remains completely outside the legal sphere."[32] The justification that believers presently possess by faith is then sufficient to grant them the right to everlasting life.[33]

We might think about an awards ceremony, such as the Oscars or the Grammys. The winners are selected and recorded well in advance of the ceremony. Their names are written down on cards kept in sealed envelopes. The presenters later open these envelopes and read the cards aloud at the ceremony itself. Once the winner's name has been publicly announced, their award statue is handed to them. Because they already had the right to that statue, winners still receive it even if unable to attend the ceremony. The ceremony serves as the moment to announce the winner's status and bestow its accompanying reward. Still, that event does not change that the winners were already unalterably decided.

The illustration's point is that being justified means that our names are recorded on those winning cards. At the last judgment, the names of the justified will be read aloud, thereby informing the entire universe about the identity of the justified. In the event of our resurrection, which corresponds to the awards ceremony, the award itself, our glorification, will be bestowed upon us, as the award statue is bestowed. Just as in the case of an awards ceremony when the winners are decided, recorded, and have the right to their award well before they are announced, so too those who will receive glorification are fully justified when they place their faith in Christ for salvation. Just because the announcement has yet to be made and the award itself is still to be bestowed does not mean that our status as justified, as "winners," is not fully settled in the present. As Turretin writes, "That final judgment is nothing else than a public and solemn

30. *TI*, 12.3.16; 16.9.7.

31. *TI*, 16.10.5.

32. *VRD*, 4:194, 171; *BRD*, 4:179.

33. *VRD*, 4:154.

manifestation of preceding judgments."[34] The difference between our situation and an entertainment award ceremony is that we know the verdict before the award is bestowed, whereas no one knows the winners of an award until the event. In our case, God has told us that those who believe in Christ are truly justified here and now because Christ's imputed righteousness ensures that status for us. We are fully justified in the present by faith alone, and so its consequent reward of glorified life will certainly be bestowed upon us at the "ceremony"—better, at Christ's return.

Regarding the final judgment where God renders to everyone according to what they have done, there is no reason to think that believers will receive anything other than what accords with the justification and glorification that they receive by faith in Christ. Concerning how James's epistle mentions a justification "by works," James was very clear about the timing of this justification. He stated this justification by works happened for Abraham "*when* he offered up his son Isaac on the altar" (Jas 2:21) and for Rahab "*when* she received the messengers and sent them out by another way" (Jas 2:25). Since James clearly noted *when* these justifications occurred and both happened thousands of years ago, it would be absurd to suggest that he was talking about a justification by works at the last judgment. The past is not the future. Especially in the case of Abraham, since his test regarding Isaac occurred well after he believed God and it was counted to him as righteousness (Gen 15:6; Gen 22), it becomes clear that James wrote about proving our faith, a vindication or support of our profession of faith.[35] His point, after all, was that "faith by itself, if it does not have works, is dead" (Jas 2:17). Certainly, even though James is not about a future justification by works, we should still note well his point that believers must demonstrate their faith by good works.[36]

Regarding passages that refer to God rendering to each according to their works at the last day, timing is again significant (Rom 2:6; 2 Cor 5:10; Rev 20:12–13). The final judgment occurs at Christ's return when he comes back to earth *in his body* (1 Thess 4:16). At the moment Christ

34. *TI*, 16.9.7; 16.8.21.

35. *CC*, 22:2.314–16; *EC*, 3.8.25; Dan McCartney, "An Epistle of Straw? Reconciling James and Paul," in *Doctrine on Which the Church Stands or Falls*, 288–91; Luke Timothy Johnson, *The Letter of James* (New Haven: Yale University Press, 2007), 58–63.

36. *TI*, 16.8.22–24.

returns, he will raise believers in their bodies to join him (1 Thess 4:15–17). At *this* resurrection, believers will be raised in their imperishable, glorified bodies (1 Cor 15:50–56). Clearly, when we appear before Christ's judgment seat (2 Cor 5:10), we are already glorified; the Westminster Shorter Confession summarizes how "at the resurrection, believers *being raised up in glory*, shall be openly acknowledged and acquitted *in the day of judgment*" (WSC 38).[37] Thus, we appear for this judgment *after* we are already glorified.[38] The sheep and the goats are distinctly different when Christ separates them as such (Matt 25:31–46). So, whatever happens at this judgment cannot affect the outcome of our everlasting reward of glorification, since we possess that reward as we come to the judgment.[39]

Even a need for inherent righteousness to enter heaven would be met because of Christ's work apart from ours, since glorification wipes out every vestige of sin in us.[40] So, "the holiness without which no one will see the Lord" (Heb 12:14) is quite separate from our good works as individual acts but is God's work of making us completely holy for himself. Thus Vos contends, "Perfect holiness *in the glorified state* always remains the fruit of the merits of the mediator."[41] The holiness required to see the Lord is not works that we render *unto glorification* but God's work of glorification *unto that holiness* that enables us to see him fully. As Vos further argues, "Scripture nowhere teaches that no one can be saved without good works. Certainly, on the other hand, without sanctification no one shall see the Lord. There is a difference between sanctification and good works. The former can occur at once without any passage of time, as in a crisis moment; for doing the latter, time is necessary."[42]

There is then no reason to doubt that the last judgment is anything other than an open recognition of what God has already provided in Christ.[43]

---

37. *COC*, 3:684 (emphasis added).

38. *BRD*, 4:693–94.

39. Horton, *Justification*, 2:367–94; Fesko, *Justification*, 299–331; Stamps, "Faith Works," 520; Longenecker, *Paul, Apostle of Liberty*, 109–11.

40. *VRD*, 4:171–72.

41. *VRD*, 4:172 (emphasis added).

42. *VRD*, 4:211; *EC*, 3.12.7–9; *BRD*, 4:252–60.

43. *BRD*, 4:698–702; Harrison Perkins, "What Is Required to See God? The Beatific Vision and the *Ordo Salutis*," *Credo Magazine* 13 no. 3, December 5, 2022, https://credomag.com/article/

SPIRITUAL LIFE

That connection between justification and glorification is why believers *must* grow in sanctification in this life. Believers must pursue sanctification because it is our present experience of that spiritual life resulting from justification. Paul, therefore, writes in Romans 6:14, "For sin will have no dominion over you, since you are not under law but under grace." Being freed from the law's curse—justification—is the reason that sin will not have dominion in believers' lives.[44]

God's justifying act frees us from the law's curse with the purpose that we would walk in the Spirit for new life. So, Paul describes in Romans 7:6: "But now we are released from the law, having died to that which held us captive, *so that* we serve in the new way of the Spirit and not in the old way of the written code." The "so that" marks a result clause, indicating something that truly comes about because of the previously mentioned reality. This result establishes, in Vos's words, that "the rule is firm that there cannot be genuine Christian sanctification that does not grow on the root of justification."[45] Justification results in walking in the Spirit, or sanctification.[46]

The biblical evidence for this relationship between justification and sanctification is more extensive. In Hebrews 8:8–13, the application of the new covenant from Jeremiah 31 to the superiority of Christ's priesthood emphasizes God's promised work of moral renewal. God's reason for that moral renewal is, "For I will be merciful toward their iniquities, and I will remember their sins no more" (Heb 8:12). In the forgiveness of sin, justification grounds God's transformative work as God writes his law on our hearts so that we might walk in it.[47] In Romans 6:6–7, after arguing for justification by faith alone, Paul has to assert the necessity of our sanctification: "We know that our old self was crucified with him in order that the body of sin might be brought to nothing, so that we would no longer be enslaved to sin. For one who has died has been set free from sin." God's purpose for our justification is clear in that we were

---

what-is-required-to-see-god/.

44. Hodge, *Romans*, 205–6; Thielman, *Romans*, 311–12.

45. *VRD*, 4:68.

46. Vos, "Eschatological Aspect," 108–10; VanDrunen, "Contested Union," 500.

47. Allen, *Sanctification*, 182.

crucified with Christ—the legal ground of our forgiveness in justification (Gal 2:19–20)—so that we would be free from sin's power.[48] The one who has been counted as having died with Christ, that is, justified, is free from the enslaving grip of sin's corruption.[49] Justification provides an arena of freedom in which we are no longer bound to the law's cursed burden but enabled to perform the duties it describes so that we might be good to our neighbor and glorify God (Rom 6:9–10).[50]

There is, then, a link between the freedom granted to us in justification and the resulting progress in sanctification. James Ussher emphasizes sanctification's necessity: "I grant Justification doth lead the way, but sanctification must be joined and follow after. They must go together. If the one follows not, the other is but a false imagination."[51] Bavinck also indicates how sanctification accompanies justification: "But this objective judicial benefit of forgiveness is not the only one; it is followed by the ethical and mystical benefit of sanctification."[52] Even though glorification awaits the future, God grants us a taste of that spiritual life now in our sanctification (2 Cor 4:16).

Sanctification is the tension between what Christ has already given us and what he has not yet bestowed. We so easily fluctuate in our experience of godliness precisely because we are caught in between the secure and complete declaration that we are justified and the guaranteed renovation of hearts and bodies in glorification.[53] Justification is granted in full by faith to believers from Christ, which guarantees glorification, but sanctification is the process of slowly, and unfortunately at times even minimally, experiencing the holy renewal of our glorification in this life.

Causal relationships, then, exist among justification, sanctification, and glorification because the covenant of works established that justification results in the consequent reward of glorification. As Vos affirms,

---

48. *BRD*, 3:505.

49. Horton, *Rediscovering*, 216; Allen, *Sanctification*, 185–87.

50. R. Michael Allen, *Justification and the Gospel: Understanding the Contexts and Controversies* (Grand Rapids: Baker Academic, 2013), 127–51; *CF*, 709.

51. Balliol College, Oxford MS 259, II fol. 288v (undated sermon on 1 John 3:9); for quote with original spelling and historical analysis of Ussher's view of the *ordo salutis*, see Perkins, *Catholicity and the Covenant of Works*, 245.

52. *BRD*, 3:505.

53. Horton, *Rediscovering*, 209–20; *TI*, 17.1.10, 21.

"According to Romans 8:30, glorification is connected directly to justification as a link in the chain of salvation; it is *the consequent fruit* of justification."[54] Since justification obtains entitlement to spiritual life, it grants us the privilege of possessing sanctification here and now as the present inbreaking of our future glorification.[55] In this way, sanctification, *in terms of its cause*, is not so much pressing forward in hope of achieving glorification as it is being gripped by glorification—grounded in Christ's own resurrection—and being pulled forward. It is like being shot upward from the bottom of a canyon by a bungie cord, Christ's glorious resurrection being the locomotive dragging us along the tracks of sanctification toward our own glorification.[56]

Sanctification is, therefore, caused in different ways by both justification and glorification, leaving our present moral identity shaped by both the past and the future.[57] Paul indicates how Christ's imputed righteousness brought about the possession of the power of Christ's resurrection in Philippians 3:9–11: "And I would be found in him, thereby not having my own righteousness by the law but righteousness through faith in Christ [which is] the righteousness from God that depends on faith, *with the result of* knowing him, and the power of his resurrection, and the participation in his sufferings, thereby being conformed to his death, if perhaps I will

54. *VRD*, 4:156 (emphasis added).

55. Vos, "Eschatological Aspect," 114–16; *EC*, 3.8.9; *BRD*, 4:253; Gaffin, *Fullness of Time*, 220.

56. New Testament eschatology's already/not yet dimension has not always been precisely applied to soteriology. More specifically, the relationship between sanctification and glorification has at times been explained, as the former is striding toward the latter, as the reward for achieving the proper amount of holiness in this life, rather than glorification breaking into the present in sanctification. That explanation, however, does not match the pattern of inaugurated New Testament eschatology. In Hebrews 8:1–7, the author outlines how God established the typological worship of the old covenant as a limited copy of the ultimate worship that belongs to the last day and has been brought about in Christ. Although that point is about typology in the old covenant, the principle that the ultimate things of the last day ground what God does in the present in a limited way surely has some explanatory power for the relationship between sanctification and glorification. God has guaranteed our ultimate glorification at the last day by justifying us through faith on the basis of Christ's perfect obedience. In light of that ultimate reality of the last day, God is presently working a limited copy of that transformation in us. Just like the old covenant priesthood did not lead up to the eschatological priesthood of Christ, but Christ was foreshadowed in those types, so too sanctification does not lead up to eschatological glorification but rather glorification is the eschatological ground of God working a limited copy of that holiness in his people during this age. See Vos, *Hebrews*, 49–68.

57. Grant Macaskill, *Living in Union with Christ: Paul's Gospel and Christian Moral Identity* (Grand Rapids: Baker Academic, 2019), 115.

arrive at the resurrection from the dead."[58] To be found in Christ, to have received and rested upon him by faith, is to have Christ's righteousness imputed as the ground of our justification, so that we stand before God on the basis of his record rather than our own.[59] Being found with his righteousness rather than our own, however, has the consequent result of knowing Christ, the power of his resurrection, and participation in his sufferings.

The three things that Paul would know because of being found with Christ's righteousness are significant. First, in this instance, "to know him" does not mean that initial union with Christ by faith, since this knowing him is a benefit of being found "in him" already. Rather, this seems to be the use of "know" as in having intimate relational knowledge. In that sense, Paul's statement is essentially the same as when he writes, "having been justified by faith, we have *peace* with God" (Rom 5:1, my translation). As John Calvin explains, "Unless you first of all grasp what your relationship to God is and the nature of his judgment concerning you, you have neither a foundation on which to establish your salvation nor one on which to build piety toward God."[60] The good and dynamic relationship of loving intimacy and peace grows out of that restored legal relationship of

---

58. My translation. The translation emphasizes τοῦ γνῶναι as a true result clause ("with the result of knowing") because the articular infinitive, especially in the genitive, regularly marks this grammatical function; see Wallace, *Greek Grammar*, 592. The (genitive) articular infinitive of purpose is followed by the complex object that Paul would know Christ, the power of resurrection, and participation in Christ's death; see Macaskill, *Living in Union with Christ*, 47. It should be noted that the genitive serves this same result function to mark the reward of δικαίωσιν in Romans 5:18. There is, then, a similarity in the syntactical relationships of righteousness language followed by a genitive that designates the result of that righteousness. It also so happens that, as righteousness resulted in life (ζωῆς) in Romans 5:18, it results in knowing Christ, the power of his resurrection, and participation in his sufferings in Philippians 3:9–10. The conceptual overlap is profound. For Adam, simply obtaining justification through his own righteousness would have resulted in eschatological life. For those in Christ, imputed righteousness grants the same goal but that life is represented, as perhaps expected, by Christ with his death and resurrection. Regarding the final clause of verse 11, the normal translation of εἴ πως with the future indicative is "if perhaps," which in this case must represent a result that is not truly in doubt. After all, Paul has just stated that Christ's imputed righteousness makes him know the power of Christ's resurrection, and Christ's resurrection is the guarantee of ours, as the firstfruits of the harvest; see Gaffin, *Resurrection and Redemption*, 33–41; and Gaffin, *By Faith, Not by Sight*, 67–70.

59. *DIALIC*, 263–66; *VRD*, 4:21–24, 138, 150–51, 164–66, 178; VanDrunen, "Contested Union," 490–96; Horton, *Justification*, 2:321–66; *CF*, 611; Gaffin, *By Faith, Not by Sight*, 57–59; *TI*, 16.7.8–9; *BRD*, 4:211; Macaskill, *Living in Union with Christ*, 45–47.

60. Calvin, *Institutes*, 3.11.1.

justification, just as the relational dynamics of marriage thrive on the basis of having made those legal vows at the wedding.[61]

Second, knowing the power of Christ's resurrection is the consequence of imputed righteousness. In this case, that resurrection power seems to be the full import of spiritual resurrection life. Just as Romans 5:18–21 indicates that life results from justification, so Philippians 3:10 shows that spiritual life here and now, even as we are conformed in that spiritual life to Christ's sufferings, follows as the consequent reward of imputed righteousness. Righteousness—so justification—then, has a causal relationship to spiritual life, even as we have it during the present age in sanctification.[62]

Lastly, knowing participation in Christ's sufferings is the way that Paul would be conformed to Christ's death and then arrive at the resurrection from the dead. Seemingly, "being conformed to his death" specifically links to participation in Christ's sufferings. This conformity to Christ's death is about Paul's own experience of suffering during his ministry (Col 1:24–26; Phil 1:29). In that suffering, he conforms to the pattern of Christ's humiliation during his earthly ministry—a ministry that culminated in obedience unto death (Phil 2:8).

Christian experience of suffering is, then, a testimony to how we belong to Christ, as we follow him from humiliation to exaltation (Rom 5:3–5; Rom 8:16–17). Since Paul himself wrote about how Christ's own resurrection is the firstfruits and guarantee of the resurrection of believers (1 Cor 15:20–23), he would not have doubted that he will arrive at the resurrection from the dead. Since the body follows the head, our pattern of following Christ in his pattern of earthly suffering means only that we will follow him into heavenly glory.[63] Paul puts off his old man to be renewed as he puts on Christ according to the power of his resurrection.[64] Sanctification is both putting off the old man in Adam and putting on the new man in Christ.[65] Having been counted righteous in Christ, Paul now becomes active in pursuing holiness through humility rather than glory,

---

61. *VRD*, 4:193–94; *BRD*, 4:249–52; Stamps, "Faith Works," 526.

62. *CG*, 225–27.

63. Robert L. Plummer, "The Role of Suffering in the Mission of Paul and the Mission of the Church," *SBJT* 17.4 (2013): 6–19.

64. Macaskill, *Living in Union with Christ*, 64–67.

65. *CF*, 661–62.

since glory is for the future rather than the present.[66] As we walk through hardship in this life, we take heart that it means that we are joined to Christ in his pattern of suffering before triumphant glory.

Sanctification as the present spiritual life is not passive. Justification results in peace with God once and for all (Rom 5:1), but sanctification as an ongoing battle with sin must then come after that peace. We are always both at peace and at war with something.[67] If we have peace with our sin, then we are God's enemies. If we have peace with God, then we must wage war on our fleshly desires. Being reconciled to God and having peace with him because of justification means that our sinful nature, which we once loved, has become our enemy for the rest of the Christian life. The legal change in justification effects a change of allegiance that, in that moment, begins our war against our old nature. So, William Perkins says, "Justification brings peace of conscience, so does not sanctification, but follows that peace. Thus, the apostle has them distinct: 'Ye are washed, ye are justified and sanctified' (1 Cor 6:11). Christ is made to us righteousness and sanctification (1:30). Secondly, because justification goes with sanctification. Though justification be before in nature, yet they are wrought at the same time."[68] The Westminster Confession also well describes this war between the Spirit indwelling us and our old sinful nature that refuses to die in full during this age: "In which war, although the remaining corruption for a time may much prevail, yet, through the continual supply of strength from the sanctifying Spirit of Christ, the regenerate part does overcome; and so the saints grow in grace, perfecting holiness in the fear of God" (WCF 13.3).[69] Still, sanctification is far more than "getting used to our justification" or simply reflecting upon it. It is distinct from justification yet inseparable from it because our growth in godliness is actually part of the reward of spiritual life that we receive because we have been justified in Christ.[70] God's work of sanctification, his gift of grace to us,

66. Macaskill, *Living in Union with Christ*, 47–50.

67. *EC*, 3.9.1–28.

68. *WWP*, 4:31 (commentary on Jude 1).

69. *COC*, 3:629–30.

70. *TI*, 17.1.16.

enables, powers, and causes our labors toward deeper godliness as we "endeavor after new obedience."[71]

That sanctification is this tension between full justification and the inbreaking reward of new life is exactly why our good works are, as the Westminster Confession says, "fruits and evidences of a true and lively faith" (WCF 16.2).[72] Sanctification does not need the goal of obtaining future rewards at the last judgment since, indeed, it should be cherished for itself as the consequent reward of our restored relationship with God through Christ.[73] The new life we have in Christ, lived out in sanctification, is *itself* the consequent reward of being justified in Christ. Indeed, justification restores our communion with God *so that* he might dwell among his people and by that communion we might grow in holiness.[74] We should treasure that new life as a prized reward rather than as a means to an end.

This experience of sanctification as the tension in between justification and glorification links to justification's role in making us citizens of heaven (Phil 3:20–21). To illustrate, I am an American but lived for a while in the United Kingdom. When I moved abroad to my new country of residence, I had to obtain a residence permit, fancily called a "biometrics card." This card declared my legal right to reside in my new home. This legal right to reside means that I could not be arbitrarily deported. Justification is like that biometrics card. As our legal right to eat from the tree of life and enter God's city by the gates (Rev 22:14), justification guarantees our right to reside in God's kingdom.

Still, obtaining the legal right to reside in the United Kingdom was not everything involved in living here. As an American, I had to learn to drink more tea, to talk a lot about the weather, and to pronounce many words in a new way. This experience of acclimatizing was certainly distinct from

71. WSC 87; *COC*, 3:695.

72. *COC*, 3:633; *TI*, 17.3.14–15; 20.6.20.

73. *VRD*, 4:170. This notion of sanctification as our present possession of the spiritual life, being the consequent reward of our justification, helps answer the unusual objection, despite the long history of Reformed theologians arguing otherwise, that this cause-effect relationship between justification and sanctification blends the two blessings as in Roman Catholic theology; cf. Johnson, *One with Christ*, 112–13. On historical evidence, see J. V. Fesko, *Beyond Calvin: Union with Christ and Justification in Early Modern Reformed Theology (1517–1700)* (Göttingen: Vandenhoeck & Ruprecht, 2012); and Muller, *Calvin and the Reformed Tradition*, 161–243.

74. Allen, *Sanctification*, 190–97.

gaining the legal right to live abroad but was a necessary part of being part of the culture. On the other hand, I could not have joined the culture had I not had the full legal right to be there.

Likewise, sanctification is an essential part of the Christian life, even though it depends upon justification as the legal right to be in God's kingdom. When we are transferred from the kingdom of darkness into the kingdom of light, we must learn how to live there. That is what it means to be a citizen. Since citizens of God's kingdom love their new home, we indeed must engage in this process of increasingly dying unto sin and living unto righteousness.

PRIORITIES BETWEEN BENEFITS

Regarding sanctification as an *essential* part of the Christian life, justification and sanctification are both "more important" from different perspectives.[75] The previous chapter illustrates how our union with Christ relates to our possession of Christ's benefits by describing how a stone patio table comprises its parts of a supporting pillar and the tabletop. The whole table is manifested in its pillar and tabletop, but those parts have a specific relationship to one another within the whole fixture. From one perspective the supporting pillar is most important because it is the basis of the whole unified structure. Without the pillar, the table would collapse. From another perspective the tabletop is most important because it fulfills the table's design. If that basis supported no surface off which to eat, it would serve no purpose.

Similarly, the benefits of our union with Christ relate to one another and are more important from different perspectives. Justification is the basis of our union with Christ like the central pillar is the basis of the table. Note well that justification is *not* separate from our union with Christ but is the basis *within* that union, and so supports the whole structure of union while remaining a part and benefit of it.[76] A table's pillar fulfills its distinct purpose as part of the whole table in this way, as justification is the legal basis *within* our union with Christ. On the other hand, as that table's stone pillar would not fulfill its design if it were not holding up the

75. *TI*, 17.1.19.

76. *VRD*, 4:21–24.

tabletop as the surface for our food, so that basis of justification would not fulfill its design *as part of union with Christ* if it were not supporting the transformative aspects of union.

Just as a complete table includes a supporting pillar, union with Christ has the *internal* basis of justification. That basis supports *other parts* of our union with Christ because God designed it to function in this capacity within the full manifestation of that union.[77] Importantly, *internal basis* means that it plays the foundational role *within* union rather than *to* union, as it would if it were an external foundation, such as when a desk supports a computer or an end table holds a houseplant.[78] Just like a complete table needs a supporting basis but is designed to hold food, so too our union with Christ needs the supporting basis of a restored relationship with God but is designed to blossom in a transformed life of holiness.[79]

How then are these benefits more important from differing perspectives? Justification has a type of priority because it makes us right with God. Without being justified, we do not have the gift of the Holy Spirit, which Paul explains in Galatians 4:4–7:

> But when the fullness of time came, God sent forth his Son, by being born from a woman, by being born under the law, with the result that he would redeem those under the law, with the further

77. As Vos argues, "The essence of the organic consists in the fact that there is a reciprocal connection of goal and means between the differing parts of a things that nonetheless has an abiding significance in itself." *VRD*, 4:25.

78. Justification as the *internal* basis of our union with Christ should alleviate the concerns that justification as the basis of sanctification or union with Christ holistically somehow divorces justification from Christ. The suggestion that union with Christ is one, singular point among the benefits of salvation in the *ordo salutis* rather than as an encompassing category for all the benefits causes much confusion. If union were a punctiliar benefit, then it would be highly problematic to ascribe an internal basis to it. On the other hand, if union with Christ occurs in our effectual calling (WLC 66), is the overarching category for partaking of the virtue of Christ's mediation (WLC 69), and is manifested *in* our justification, adoption, sanctification, then those manifestations (blessings) can have varying functions in relation to one another and to the whole. As Vos affirms, "Sanctification not only flows from the merits of Christ as its *judicial* wellspring, but also from the living Christ as its fountain," *VRD*, 4:203 (italics original). Justification's role as a basis is not external to our union with Christ, but internal to it and so then supports those other blessings that also come to us in union with him; Horton, *Covenant and Salvation*, 129–30, 143–44; Horton, *Justification*, 2:449; *CF*, 597, 599; *VRD*, 4:6–7, 9, 21–24; cf. G. C. Berkouwer, *Faith and Justification* (Grand Rapids: Eerdmans, 1954), 31–33; Sinclair B. Ferguson, *The Holy Spirit* (Downers Grove, IL: InterVarsity Press, 1996), 97–100; and Ridderbos, *Paul*, 205–6.

79. Stamps, "Faith Works," 525–30.

> result that we would receive the adoption as sons. Now, because you are sons, God sent forth the Spirit of his Son into our hearts, who is crying "Abba, Father!" The result is that you are no longer a slave, but a son, but if you are a son, then you are also an heir through God. (my translation)

God's purposes in Christ's mission have a clear progression that establishes relationships between the benefits that we receive from Christ.[80]

In his mission, Christ was born from the virgin, but also born under the law. The result of Christ's birth under the law was to redeem those under the law, which is directly about our justification.[81] Galatians 3:23–24 has already made that point: "Now before faith came, we were held captive *under the law*, imprisoned until the coming faith would be revealed. So then, the law was our guardian until Christ came, in order that we might *be justified by faith*." The first step in what Christ grants to believers is justification.[82]

Christ's benefits do not end with justification. Christ redeemed us from under the law—justified us—"with the result that we would receive the adoption as sons." As Vos explains: "The guilt of the covenant of works must first be cleared away before the blessings of the covenant can be imparted."[83] So, with the law's curse removed, we becomes God's sons.[84] The royal Son merited full possession of heavenly inheritance and shares it with his adopted siblings (Rom 8:14–17; Eph 2:18–19).[85] John 1:12 is important in this connection: "But to all who did receive him, who believed in his name, he gave the right to become children of God." William Ames argues that calling and justification ground adoption because "the right of adoption is obtained by faith and the righteousness of faith. ... Adoption of its own nature requires and presupposes the reconciliation found in justification."[86] Vos infers that John 1:12 entailed

80. Macaskill, *Living in Union with Christ*, 98–105.

81. Fesko, *Galatians*, 103.

82. Longenecker, *Galatians*, 170–72.

83. *VRD*, 3:106.

84. Longenecker, *Galatians*, 172.

85. *CF*, 644–45.

86. *MT*, 1.28.5–6; *EC*, 3.10.13.

adoption as the second aspect or part of justification.[87] Although making adoption part of justification may be imprecise, the justification of a sinner "places him forever in the status of a child."[88] We are God's adopted children because we are justified.[89]

God also sends the Spirit of his Son into the hearts of his adopted sons. Two points are notable in this respect. First, specifically the Spirit *of the Son* is sent to indwell the adopted. The Son's possession of the Spirit in this sense is inherently linked to his mission in the covenant of redemption. Second, God sends the Spirit "*because* you are sons."[90] The Spirit indwells believers because of our adoption.[91]

Christ's fulfillment of the covenantal requirement, which is imputed to us in justification, is the legal reason that the Spirit takes up sanctifying residence in our hearts (Ezek 36:25–27).[92] Charles Hodge explains, "The imputation of his righteousness consequent on faith secures the indwelling of the Holy Spirit as certainly, and for the very same reasons (the covenant stipulations), that it secures the pardon of our sins."[93] Hodge further argues that as soon as we exercise faith, we receive Christ's righteousness, so that "God's justice is thereby satisfied, and the Spirit comes and takes up his dwelling in the believer as the source of all holy living. There can therefore be no holiness until there is reconciliation with God, and no reconciliation with God except through the righteousness imputed to us and received by faith alone. Then follow the indwelling of the Spirit, progressive sanctification, and all the fruits of holy living."[94] Certainly, the Spirit's indwelling presence *in* us is not identical with the Spirit's work *upon* us in effectual calling, which simply means that this progression of benefits does not encompass all the Spirit's saving activity.[95]

87. *VRD*, 4:152, 155–56; *MT*, 1.28.4–5; *BRD*, 4:226.
88. *VRD*, 4:221; *BRD*, 4:224.
89. *BRD*, 4:226–27; *TI*, 16.4.5–9; 16.6.1; 17.1.18.
90. Macaskill, *Living in Union with Christ*, 100, 102.
91. Longenecker, *Galatians*, 173–74; *CF*, 591.
92. Allen, *Sanctification*, 180–83.
93. Hodge, *Systematic Theology*, 3:171.
94. Hodge, *Systematic Theology*, 3:172.
95. *MT*, 1.28.22–24.

So, the sum of Galatians 4:4–7, again, shows that Christ's historical mission sets the pattern for our experience of salvation. More technically, the relationships among Christ's rewards in the *historia salutis* are recapitulated in the *ordo salutis*'s shape.[96] Although God's eternal Son by nature, Christ also obtained the recognized status of God's faithful Son in power upon his fulfillment of his role as the last Adam, who was also God's son (Luke 3:38; Rom 1:1–4).[97] Christ's historical mission progressed from being born under the law to attaining justification with its reward of glorification and new possession of the Spirit, which is simply the difference between his humiliation and exaltation (1 Cor 15:45; Acts 2:33; 1 Tim 3:16).[98] Following this pattern of the *historia salutis*, our experience of the *ordo salutis* includes that our justification secures our possession of the indwelling Spirit.[99]

The Spirit's residence in us is a multifaceted work related to all aspects of our salvation.[100] His indwelling is "the guarantee of our inheritance until we acquire possession of it" (Eph 1:13–14). Since the covenant of works' reward was *spiritual* existence, the Spirit's presence confirms our fully justified status, which is why he is the seal and guarantee of our redemption.[101] He is the guarantee as a down payment on a home is the guarantee that the rest of the payment will follow.[102] This legal aspect of the Spirit's work is why Jesus said that he would send "another advocate" to help his people (John 14:16–17 NIV). The Spirit does not *simply* renovate us but ratifies our legal status as our advocate.[103] "The Spirit himself bears

---

96. *VRD*, 3:91.

97. Vos, *Hebrews*, 68–87; *CF*, 458–67; Horton, *Justification*, 2:262–73; Gaffin, *Resurrection and Redemption*, 98–113; Macaskill, *Living in Union with Christ*, 99, 102–3.

98. Gaffin rightly argues that Karl Barth's rejection of the *ordo salutis* as a series of distinct acts of appropriating Christ's benefits collapses redemption accomplished and applied by undermining the redemptive-historical shift from Christ's humiliation to exaltation. To extend Gaffin's critique, because Christ experienced the rewards of the covenant of works in specific relationship to one another, the connection between the *historia salutis* and the *ordo salutis* requires that we experience Christ's benefits in specific relationship to one another as well; see Gaffin, "Work of Christ Applied," 271–72; Vos, "Alleged Legalism," 397–99; and *CF*, 629.

99. *VRD*, 4:154.

100. *BRD*, 4:227.

101. Horton, *Rediscovering*, 198–201, 206–9.

102. Vos, "Eschatological Aspect," 102–3; *EC*, 3.13.32; Horton, *Rediscovering*, 118–19, 187, 199–200; Gaffin, *Resurrection and Redemption*, 68–70.

103. Horton, *Justification*, 2:278–80; Horton, *Rediscovering*, 105–19, 125–31.

witness with our spirit that we are children of God" as a legal testimony to what is true (Rom 8:16). As the guarantee of glorification, the Spirit's indwelling can only have a renovating effect as he begins to radiate the life-giving effects of Christ's resurrection power within us now.[104] In this age, we experience new life only according to our inner man in ongoing sanctification but will one day possess that full inheritance of glory in soul and in body at the resurrection (2 Cor 3:18; 4:16–18).[105]

We must, therefore, see how rich and beautiful our full salvation is and understand that there are multiple ways in which we might consider each aspect of Christ's benefits to be important. From *one* perspective, justification has a more important priority because it secures and enables other facets of our salvation.[106] On the other hand, God designed justification as a means to the higher end of those other resulting benefits.[107] After all, God elected those whom Christ redeemed before the foundations of the world "that we should be holy and blameless before him" (Eph 1:4). Further, "we are his workmanship, created in Christ Jesus for good works, which God prepared beforehand, that we should walk in them." (Eph 2:10) In Romans 6:2, Paul rhetorically asks, "How can we who died to sin still live in it?" Calvin answers that "we are justified for this end" of regenerate new life "that we may afterwards worship God in purity of life."[108] God's purpose for our growth in godliness and eventual full conformity to Christ shows that, although justification has a priority in our salvation by ensuring other aspects of salvation will come to us, God has higher purposes than simply making us legally right with him and has designed our salvation with the purpose of growing us in conformity to his Son (Rom 8:29–30).[109]

Reformed theologians have traditionally argued that God saves us *for* and *unto* holiness and good works but not *by* those things.[110] Ussher writes that justification, as the "former grace," differs from sanctification "in the Order, not of time, wherein they go together, (Rom. 8.30.) nor

104. Horton, *Rediscovering*, 119–21.

105. Gaffin, *Resurrection and Redemption*, 109, 126–27; Horton, *Rediscovering*, 219–20.

106. Contra deSilva, *Galatians*, 216–24.

107. Horton, *Covenant and Salvation*, 248.

108. *CO*, 49:104; *CC*, 19:2.219.

109. VanDrunen, "Contested Union," 499–502; Letham, *Systematic Theology*, 613.

110. *TI*, 17.1.17.

of Knowledge and Apprehension, wherein this latter hath precedence, (1 Cor. 6.11.) but of Nature, wherein the former is the ground of this latter, 2 Cor. 7.1."[111] Ussher further preached, "After justification then comes the righteousness of sanctification, to do righteousness. He that has healed me, does not mean that I should sin afresh. I am not under the Law in the point of Sanctification."[112] Turretin affirms the same point that justification and sanctification differ "as to order. That [justification] is prior at least in the order of nature because God sanctifies those only who are reconciled and justified by faith; this [sanctification], however, follows."[113] Wilhelmus à Brakel also follows this pattern:

> Justification is the fountain of sanctification. Sanctification is exceedingly precious to believers, for it consists in humbly walking with God, honoring Him with holy reverence, loving Him, fearing Him, and pleasing Him in our walk. ... Justification is the means to this. Since justification is the fountain, it therefore defines the proper manifestation of sanctification and its true essence. One must, therefore, with all his might endeavor to attain to justification and to being assured of this. He who endeavors to attain to sanctification upon another foundation has gone astray, will never attain to it, and will never make progress in it.[114]

Likewise, Vos explains how being saved *for* and *unto* holiness "makes works a consequence of justification."[115] In other words, the proper view of our good works "demands a sanctification under which the indispensable foundation of justification" is fully emphasized.[116]

As our salvation is bound thoroughly into Christ's resurrection, still our resurrection life is not a nebulous experience of the rewards that Christ earned in his mission and obtained in his resurrection.[117] Rather,

---

111. Ussher, *Body*, 202.

112. CUL MS Mm. 6.55, fol. 90v (sermon on Romans 6:14–15 dated September 3, 1648). For quote with original spelling with historical analysis of Ussher's view of the *ordo salutis*, see Perkins, *Catholicity and the Covenant of Works*, 244–46.

113. *TI*, 17.1.10.

114. *CRS*, 2:405.

115. *VRD*, 4:8.

116. *VRD*, 4:9.

117. Gaffin, "Work of Christ Applied," 270.

we take part in salvation as God distributes some aspects here and now but waits to grant others until the end of all things. Still, justification's role as the basis of sanctification does not entail or even suggest a time delay between them.[118] Rather, even as some benefits of Christ come simultaneously, yet they are specifically related to one another. As Hodge puts it, "That logical order and chronological succession are different things or that the order of nature and order of time are not to be confounded. Many things are contemporaneous or co-instantaneous which nevertheless stand in a certain logical, and even causal relation to each other."[119] Or in Vos's words, "The various saving acts of God, however much they can and must be distinguished logically, nevertheless may not be separated from one another as if they did not affect each other. Rather, they involve each other at every point and are interwoven with each other."[120] There is then an ordered relationship among the blessings that we receive in union with Christ and in the order of salvation.

In this way, every individual aspect of our salvation does not have an "already" and a "not yet" dimension.[121] Rather, the ordered relationships between the blessings that we have in Christ explain our experience of this tension of salvation as an "already/not yet" reality.[122] Effectual calling, justification, and adoption are already realized and completed blessings granted to us by faith here and now. Glorification lies fully in the future.

---

118. Allen, *Sanctification*, 182–83.

119. Hodge, *Systematic Theology*, 3:173.

120. *VRD*, 4:68.

121. *WWP*, 2:126 (commentary on Galatians 2:15–16); *VRD*, 4:159; Horton, *Justification*, 2:274–78, 451, 465–66.

122. Although it is an overstatement to call justification the center of Paul's thought, Vos astutely notes: "Naturally the problem becomes most accentuated where it touches the center of Paul's teaching. This, we may still insist, is the doctrine of justification. Recent attempts to dislodge it from this position, and to make the mystical aspect of the believer's relation to Christ, as mediated by the Spirit, entirely coordinated with it—so that each of the two covers the entire range of religious experience, and becomes in reality a duplicate of the other in a different sphere—we cannot recognize as correct from the apostle's own point of view. In our opinion Paul consciously and consistently subordinated the mystical aspect of relation to Christ to the forensic one. Paul's mind was to such an extent forensically oriented that he regarded the entire complex of subjective spiritual changes that take place in the believer and of subjective blessings enjoyed by the believer as a direct outcome of the forensic work of Christ applied in justification. The mystical is based on the forensic, not the forensic on the mystical." Vos, "Alleged Legalism," 384; also Gaffin, "Work of Christ Applied," 278–79; *CF*, 708–10; cf. Green, *Covenant and Commandment*, 105–45; Bates, *Allegiance Alone*, 165–92, 207–13; Beale, *New Testament Biblical Theology*, 469–526; and Gaffin, *By Faith, Not by Sight*, 93–114.

Presently, we live the life of sanctification as the tension between these already and not yet blessings of Christ.[123] So in 2 Corinthians 4:16–18, Paul describes the tension of this life, "We do not lose heart. Though our outer self is wasting away, our inner self is being renewed day by day. For this light momentary affliction is preparing for us an eternal weight of glory beyond all comparison, as we look not to the things that are seen but to the things that are unseen." Given how this emphasis on the outer man concerns the body, focusing clearly on the future resurrection (1 Cor. 4:13–5:10), Paul's point was about longing for full glorification but having to be content with the present renewal of sanctification. In the time of tension, we must be content with incomplete spiritual renewal, in godliness that increasingly molds us in personal holiness that will be completed in our glorification at our bodily resurrection.

This view of our salvation, as charged with the tension between the already and not yet of receiving everything that Christ has earned for us, is precisely why God *must* grant to us the specific aspects of our salvation that we receive in union with Christ as distinct acts, namely, calling, justification, sanctification, and glorification.[124] Because Christ's justification brought about his glorification, even as they occurred simultaneously, according to the pattern of rewards in the covenant of works, so our justification on the basis of Christ's imputed righteousness guarantees our glorification.[125]

The tension of the time is the delay of execution between those two connected blessings. Glorification has a future legal relevance because it is the consequent reward for justification.[126] Since justification is, in Turretin's words, an "undivided act," what happens on the last day "is not so much justification, as a solemn declaration of the justification once made and an adjudication of the reward, in accordance with the preceding justification."[127] In this connection, Vos argues that justification bestows "a legal entitlement from God to all the benefits of the covenant of grace"

123. Longenecker, *Romans*, 616; Horton, *Rediscovering*, 211; *CF*, 657–61, 689, 703–8.

124. *VRD*, 4:1–2; Gaffin, "Work of Christ Applied," 270; cf. Gaffin, *Resurrection and Redemption*, 130–34, 137–39.

125. *DIALIC*, 261–63.

126. Crowe, "Passive and Active Obedience of Christ," 449–50; *CF*, 703–10.

127. *TI*, 16.9.11, 12; *VRD*, 4:157.

so that it is "not the imparting of those benefits, but the granting of the right to them."[128] Similarly, William Ames wrote that glorification "is a real deliverance from the evils of punishment, which is actually nothing but *the carrying out of the sentence of justification*. For in justification we are pronounced just and awarded the judgment of life. In glorification the life that results from the pronouncement and award is given to us: We have it in actual possession."[129] At the resurrection, the perishable puts on the imperishable because Christ's victory has swallowed death, but that victory over death owes to Christ's having dealt with our sin which has power because of *the law* (1 Cor 15:50–57). As small but obvious streaks of light crack the darkness as dawn awakens, so our imperfect steps forward in the life of holiness are small guarantees that there is a full and bright day ahead when we are perfectly conformed to Christ when he returns for us.[130]

CONCLUSION

The communion that we have with God by covenant has a specific shape in that it restores every aspect of our relationship with God because of Christ's work and our partaking of his mediation.[131] Our salvation takes that shape because it follows the pattern of Christ's own work and the way that he obtained those blessings for us. In that way, the *historia salutis* and the *ordo salutis* remain properly related and mutually informing.

The pastoral use of this chapter's material is to motivate us in patience. We live in an age of instant gratification, but God distributes the blessings of Christ in such a way as to remind us that this world is not our home. We are pilgrims in this age and cannot possess every benefit of our inheritance while we travel here. God teaches us expectation, anticipation, endurance, and contented waiting even by filling us with joy at having received some of Christ's benefits in full but delaying to let us taste the full measure of the goodness that he promises to us.

---

128. *VRD*, 4:156.

129. *MT*, 1.30.4 (emphasis added). Although Ames began this sentence "Redemption is," the context, especially the previous section, shows that he teaches glorification "is called redemption," so he uses the two terms somewhat synonymously in this discussion.

130. *TI*, 17.2.1–26.

131. WLC 69; *LC*, 78.

Part Four

THE ADMINISTRATION OF THE COVENANT OF GRACE

XI

God's Multifaceted Plan of Salvation

When you read this, you can perceive my insight into the mystery of Christ, which was not made known to the sons of men in other generations as it has now been revealed to his holy apostles and prophets by the Spirit. This mystery is that the Gentiles are fellow heirs, members of the same body, and partakers of the promise in Christ Jesus through the gospel.
—*Ephesians 3:4–6*

Life in the present world waiting on the world to come raises questions for God's people about how to relate to our God well. The covenant of grace's substance in redemptive history's every era is that God will be God to us in Christ, but we still need a way to experience those heavenly blessings in our present earthly existence. So, how does God distribute those blessings to his people?

Perhaps expectedly, God grants blessings to his people by using the features of the covenant. Our communion with God is not limited to the intangible realities of our union with Christ through effectual calling and in justification, adoption, sanctification, and glorification. Rather, it takes concrete form as God ordains features of worship and piety for our lives so that we might experience those heavenly realities in connection to earthly ways of life.

Part 4 concerns the covenant of grace's administration, each chapter contributing to one extended argument that God works grace in his people by the activities that he has given to his church. Certainly, God's blessings come to us personally, as the discussion about the substance of the covenant demonstrated. Nonetheless, God has appointed ordinances for us to do *as the church* because he has promised to use *those things* to work salvation, comfort, and holiness in his people. In sum, the church matters because God distributes Christ and his benefits through the means that he has appointed in the church.[1]

Although the substance of salvation in Christ remained the same throughout each era of the covenant of grace, as God's plan of salvation developed historically, people received it through various administrations, with different outward features. Our ongoing illustration of a trip to the ice cream shop highlighted how whether you choose a cup or a cone, you always get ice cream, resembling how Christ and his benefits are always the covenant of grace's substance, even when that substance is delivered in various ways or by different administrations.

So, part four traces how God has given Christ to his people through the various administrations of the covenant of grace. This chapter outlines what an administration is and the major difference between Old and New Testaments, arguing that God always delivers communion with himself in the administrations that he instructs us to use. The following chapters unpack how the various means that God appointed in different eras of redemptive history all delivered Christ to his people, closing with reflection on the shape of the covenant community today and how we are to live in it.

WHAT IS AN ADMINISTRATION?

In principle, an administration is a way that God delivers the substance of the covenant of grace to his people, as our ice cream shop metaphor illustrates. Nevertheless, the specific application and outworking of that principle needs explanation.

1. Clark, *Recovering the Reformed Confession*, 326–37.

The covenant's administration has a twofold sense. First, the *internal administration* truly applies the substance of the covenant to believers so that they genuinely receive Christ and his benefits. This internal administration is faith. James Ussher outlines how God offers Christ's satisfaction through "the internal manner"—meaning "that by which the Gospel covenant is received," namely, faith as the instrument to take hold of Christ.[2] Faith then internally and truly administers Christ to God's people.

Since faith's role in the covenant of grace has been explored already, the present focus is on the covenant's *external administration*. Casper Olevianus explains, "The covenant must be grasped in a twofold manner: first, according to the substance of the covenant itself or according to the thing itself promised by God, but then according to its administration in the visible Church."[3] Ussher also helpfully captures this sense as "the external ministry of the covenant."[4] Specifically, "there are two parts of Gospel ministry: The Word and the sanctions that are attached in the Word."[5] In other words, God ordained the Word and the sacraments in various forms throughout redemptive history as the *outward* means to bring his people to faith and externally distribute Christ and his benefits.

God uses an administration to apply blessings to his people. The external administrations of the covenant all communicated the same substance, although looking very different in various eras of redemptive history.[6] Broadly, when the gospel was first promised to Adam (Gen 3:15), preached to Abraham (Gal 3:8), and present for Israel (1 Cor 10:1–4; Jude 1:5), God's people did not have the same clarity about it as we do after Christ's coming. Neither did those believers gather *in the same way* each Lord's Day to worship God through the exposition of Scripture and reception of baptism and the Lord's Supper, under the oversight of pastors and elders. Still, they had knowledge of God's promises and an outward form of life that directed their walk with God. That outward practice of faith is the external administration.

---

2. Queen's College, Oxford MS 217, fol. 40r; Ussher, *Body*, 193.
3. Casper Olevianus, *De Substantia Foederis Gratuiti inter Deum et Electos* (Geneva, 1585), 1.1.2.
4. Queen's College, Oxford MS 217, fol. 38v.
5. Queen's College, Oxford MS 217, fol. 39r.
6. WCF 8.6; *COC*, 3.621.

More specifically, an administration is *God's appointed* means for applying his promises, which we must use to walk well with him. John Colquhoun explains that the administration includes "the exhibition, or offer of the covenant, together with all that is necessary to be done, in order to make those sinners of mankind, who were represented by Christ, *partakers* of the purchased and promised benefits of it."[7] The administration is how we experience communion with God. Christ ascended to heaven and sits at the right hand of the Father. We cannot, therefore, see him directly, nor lay physical hands on him, nor hear his own bodily voice.

The various administrations of the covenant of grace do more than just apply Christ and his benefits to believers. At the *historia salutis* level, the historical covenants drive redemptive history toward its fulfillment in Christ and his new covenant work. In this respect, on the one hand, they issue and further God's promises about Christ and set forth types that depict him and his work so that believers know what to expect of their Messiah and his work. On the other hand, the covenants also remind God's people of the tension that exists in redemptive history, namely in the demand of a faithful Adam to satisfy our twofold debt from the covenant of works for us, so that we can be forgiven, and God can remain just (Rom 3:21–26). The structures tied to the historical covenants show an anticipation of the coming Messiah, particularly as the promise to Eve guaranteed the Savior who would crush Satan, the Noahic covenant depicted the universal judgment that will befall all who are not in the Savior, the Abrahamic covenant promised that God would grant the provisions of salvation by grace alone, the Mosaic covenant displayed the plight of all sinners under the law as we cannot maintain God's blessings by our works, and the Davidic covenant focused messianic expectation in the coming king. While affirming that the historical covenants involve all this diversity and forward motion at the *historia salutis* level, post-fall covenants simultaneously serve the same function at the *ordo salutis* level concerning individual believers. Precisely, the covenants include the ordinances the God used for creating and confirming faith in the elect, so that

7. CG, 278.

they trust in Christ for salvation according to whatever revelation they had, given through the means of grace in the covenant under which they lived.[8]

In that respect, although Old Testament believers trusted in Christ *incarnandus* and we trust in him *incarnatus*, we are in the same situation in terms of knowing Christ through the means of grace of our covenant administration. Christ was only briefly present physically on earth, so all believers have simply had to trust God's promises. Such was Paul's exact point in 2 Corinthians 5:6–7: "We know that while we are at home in the body we are away from the Lord, for we walk by faith, not by sight." As we pilgrims and sojourners traverse this world, we cannot directly experience God himself or even Christ in the flesh, so we must locate our communion with God in the activities that God has promised to use to meet and bless us.[9]

We must then devote ourselves to the means that God promises to use for furthering our communion with him. We very easily chase activities that induce exciting religious experiences, or wish our churches would behave more relevantly to the society at large. We should take care to seek God in the way that he has invited us to do so.[10] If I were to leave a note saying, "I'll meet you at 3 p.m. by the hardware shop on Main Street," it would be foolish to look for me on Second Avenue at 4 p.m. So, we should consider how God himself says he will meet us rather than trying to invent new ways to find him.

This approach, although sounding boring to some, truly provides immense comfort. God has told us where to find him and how he will commune with us. God is dependable and has made promises, so we should cherish those ways of experiencing communion with him. Christians are blessed, as we need not search for ways to meet God. We need not read tea leaves or mark astrological patterns, hoping for God's coded message. Rather, God has told us how to find him, so we rejoice that church leaders do not need to be immensely creative people to point us to Christ. We merely need pastors and elders who submit to God's word. Just as faith is

---

8. *KTC*, 118–37, 670–72, 680–85 (even with overall agreement of this discussion, see chapters 15–16 in this book concerning the differences regarding progressive covenantalism's refutation of the so-called genealogical principle and view on the moral law).

9. Clark, *Recovering the Reformed Confession*, 71–116; *BRD*, 4:443–46; *VRD*, 5:79–80.

10. See further Ligon Duncan, *Does God Care How We Worship?* (Phillipsburg, NJ: P&R, 2020).

receptive when it comes to claiming Christ and his benefits personally, so faith is receptive in listening to how to commune with God as his people.

In the new covenant, we commune with God as he summons us into his throne room each Lord's Day. Many Christians reduce church to a place to "fuel up" or "get energized" for spiritual endeavors. Notice *reducing* church means that church should have those effects but is also much more. When we do the activities to which God has attached his promises, we are guaranteed communion with God. That is not a guarantee based on quantitative research but on God's categorical promise. How do we put this into practice?

To commune with God, we look for how Scripture reveals that God meets us. In Ephesians 2, Paul addresses church unity concerning Jew and gentile, writing, "But now in Christ Jesus you who once were far off have been brought near by the blood of Christ. For he himself is our peace. … And *he came and preached peace to you* who were far off and peace to those who were near. For through him we both have access in one Spirit to the Father" (Eph 2:13–14, 17–18). Christ brings peace between Christians because he reconciles us all to God by his blood. If I personally am reconciled to God despite my sin against him, then I should have peace with those who likewise have peace with God alongside me.

Two points are worth noting about Christ preaching peace to the Ephesians. First, Psalm 85:8 tells of God speaking peace to his covenant people: "Let me hear what God the Lord will speak, for he *will speak peace to his people,* to his saints; but let them not turn back to folly." From the psalmist's standpoint, a day would come when God himself would address his saints with peace. That day has arrived in Christ's present ministry since Christ, who is God, preaches peace to his people, reconciling them to God and to one another as a unified church. Paul's claim that Christ preached peace to his people directly but implicitly asserts Christ's deity as he fulfills the role that God promised to perform for his people.

Second and more pointedly for the means of grace, how is it that *Christ* "came and preached peace to you," although he never travelled to Ephesus? Christ himself preached to the Ephesians as their pastor explained God's promises from the Scripture.[11] He continues to do so through pastors today.

11. *CF*, 751–63.

Thus, the Second Helvetic Confession: "So then, when this Word of God is now preached through legitimately called preachers, we believe that God's very Word is proclaimed and received by believers" (1.4).[12] God himself acts for our benefit through those activities which he has appointed for us to do as the church.[13]

Christ has ordained the Word and sacraments as these means. In John 4:1–2, the Pharisees "heard that *Jesus was* making and *baptizing* more disciples than John," but John importantly qualified, "Jesus himself did not baptize, but only his disciples." Jesus baptized through his disciples who applied the water. Just as Christ continues to preach through his ministers, he continues to baptize and to teach us to obey all that he commanded *through* his disciples who pastor.[14]

True spiritual care, therefore, happens in the church as the covenant community. In John 21:15–19, Christ's encounter with Peter after the resurrection has twofold importance. Christ asked Peter three times, "Do you love me?" Each time Peter responded affirmatively. One significance of Jesus's threefold questioning is that he was restoring Peter regarding his threefold rejection of Christ before the crucifixion. Second, Jesus commissioned Peter three times to care for his sheep, namely, as a representative of the apostles, who were the foundation of the church, to take spiritual care of God's people.

The church's officers, then, provide this spiritual care. In Acts 20:28, Paul charges the Ephesian elders to the proper care they should exercise in the church: "Pay careful attention to yourselves and to all the flock, in which the Holy Spirit has made you overseers, *to care for the church of God*, which he obtained with his own blood." God appointed pastors and elders to care for his people, working through them on earth even though Christ himself is in heaven. Jesus feeds his sheep through office bearers, hence Paul addressed Philippians, "To all the saints in Christ Jesus who are at Philippi, *with the overseers and deacons*" (Phil 1:1). The church is the group under the exercise of spiritual care. Paul's comfort to the Philippians does not apply to those who neglect to meet together (Heb 10:25). In Titus 1:7,

12. *COC*, 3:237.

13. Michael Horton, "The Church," in *CD*, 319.

14. Horton, "Church," 313–17.

Paul charges those office bearers to be of good character: "For an overseer, *as God's steward*, must be above reproach." The office bearer in the church acts as God's own steward over the church. Far from being a position of power to abuse, this authority is one of care and stewardship, which is exactly why office bearers must be above reproach.

Spiritual care, moreover, occurs through the church's activities. The phrase "in the name of Christ" (and its variations) has a specific use indicating official churchly actions. For example, 1 Corinthians 5:4–5 is about the enactment of negative church discipline: "When you are *assembled in the name of the Lord Jesus* and my spirit is present, with the power of our Lord Jesus, you are to deliver this man to Satan for the destruction of the flesh, so that his spirit may be saved in the day of the Lord."

The assembly gathers in Christ's name and conducts its official activities as the church. In 2 Thessalonians 3:6, Paul invokes that same capacity for authority in Christ's name: "Now we command you, brothers, *in the name of our Lord Jesus Christ*, that you keep away from any brother who is walking in idleness and not in accord with the tradition that you received from us." The official invocation of Christ's name is clear.

This churchly sense of operating in the Lord's name extends to preaching the word and administering the sacraments. The apostles were scolded for speaking in Jesus's name (Acts 5:40). Preaching happened in Christ's name (Acts 9:27–28). Baptism is "in the name of the Father and of the Son and of the Holy Spirit" (Matt 28:19). Scripture even often abbreviates this formula to being baptized "in the name of the Lord Jesus Christ," although we must maintain the fully trinitarian version when we baptize someone (Acts 2:38; 8:16; 10:48; 19:5). The Lord's Supper is conducted in remembrance of Christ (1 Cor 11:24–25). The church has an official capacity to act in Christ's name.

The church is then the place where Christ works through those whom he commissions to work in his name. Matthew 18:15–20 is crucial in that respect:

> If your brother sins against you, go and tell him his fault, between you and him alone. If he listens to you, you have gained your brother. But if he does not listen, take one or two others along

> with you, that every charge may be established by the evidence of two or three witnesses. If he refuses to listen to them, tell it to the church. And if he refuses to listen even to the church, let him be to you as a Gentile and a tax collector. Truly, I say to you, whatever you bind on earth shall be bound in heaven, and whatever you loose on earth shall be loosed in heaven. Again I say to you, if two of you agree on earth about anything they ask, it will be done for them by my Father in heaven. For where two or three are gathered in my name, there am I among them.

Christ's instruction for addressing problems between Christians includes his presence when the church officially gathers in his name. If someone refuses to repent when individuals confront him or her, those involved must "tell it to the church" as those under the overseers. Christ gave "the power of the keys" to the church so that discipline for the positive building up and for difficult correcting belongs to the church's formal capacity. The church's pronouncement is bound in heaven *because* "where two or three are gathered *in my name*, there am I among them." Christ's promise to be with two or three concerns not his mystical presence at an informal Bible study or hymn sing, but how, when the church of any size gathers formally under his name to do the things that he has commanded, he is personally present to work through them.[15]

The activities that Christ ordained for his church and through which he promised to work are called *the outward means of grace*.[16] The Westminster Larger Catechism states, "The outward and ordinary means whereby Christ communicates to his Church the benefits of his mediation, are, all his ordinances; especially the Word, Sacraments, and prayer: all which are made effectual to the elect for their salvation" (WLC 154).[17] God's Word commands four specific activities for when Christ's church assembles in fellowship (Acts 2:42): preach the word (Matt 28:20; Rom 10:14–17; 1 Cor 1:23; 1 Tim 5:17; 2 Tim 4:2), baptize in God's Triune name (Matt 28:19; Acts 2:38), eat the Lord's Supper (Luke 22:14–20; 1 Cor 11:23–25),

15. Letham, *Systematic Theology*, 616–18.

16. *WWS*, 274–81.

17. *LC*, 102.

and pray (Acts 6:4; 1 Thess 5:16–18).[18] When we do these appointed activities, God promises to distribute his blessings to believers.

During my high school summer breaks, I worked in a mechanic's shop. My job was to disassemble engines upon arrival, so that people who knew what they were doing could repair and reassemble them. I put the engines on a table to work on them, but the problem was getting them from the ground to the tabletop. I never quite managed to lift a complete small block Chevrolet engine from floor to table. I used a crane to hoist them. The crane was a *means* that I used when I could not directly take hold and do it myself. It was the instrument that I used to convey the engine from floor to table.

God's word, the sacraments, and prayer are like that crane. We cannot take direct hold of Christ himself in a physical sense because he is bodily in heaven. We are not directly surrounded by his physical kingdom in the new creation yet, even though he reigns in heaven. So, his promises must be given to his people by some means. He has appointed word, sacraments, and prayer as those means. Certainly, we receive Christ by faith as the internal administration. Still, the outward means of the external administration communicate those promises so that we can believe in Christ and thereby receive him. As Calvin writes, a sacrament's visible sign "has not indeed that efficacy of itself, but from the will of God, as it is instituted for this end."[19] The means of grace are like that crane in that God uses them to convey Christ and his benefits from where he is in heaven to believers on earth.[20] The outward means create and confirm faith in Christ.

---

18. Singing is an act of congregational prayer.

19. Q. 311, John Calvin, *The Catechism of the Church of Geneva*, trans. Elijah Waterman (Hartford, MA, 1815), 87.

20. Although contemporary evangelicalism tends to be suspicious of the Reformed emphasis on the means of grace as earthly means that God uses to convey Christ truly to us, their preference for personal experientialism is not new. In the medieval period, Franciscan theologians, such as Bonaventure (1221–1274) and John Duns Scotus (1266–1308), denied that God uses creaturely things as instruments to give grace, arguing instead that the sacraments particularly were merely *occasions* for grace. God might use the moment of administration as his opportunity to convey grace personally to a believer but did not use the sacrament itself. Reformation theology often more resembled Dominican theology, represented by Thomas Aquinas, which emphasized preaching and also understood the sacraments as God's instruments of grace. Certainly, the Reformed modified Dominican sacramental theology, but the point is that they sided with the tradition that understood the means of grace as true instruments rather than *mere* signs of grace; see Richard Cross, *Duns Scotus* (New York: Oxford University Press, 1999), 136–38; Clark, *Recovering the Reformed Confession*, 71–116.

We should, therefore, cherish the word, sacraments, and prayer because God commissioned them as means for communion with him. Reformed theology has long recognized that God works through the church. The Heidelberg Catechism asks,

> 55. *What do you understand by the* communion *of saints?*
> First, that believers, all and every one, as members of Christ, have part in him and in all his treasures and gifts. Secondly, that each one must feel himself bound to use his gifts, readily and cheerfully, for the advantage and welfare of other members.[21]

In more specific respect to the official activities of the church, the same catechism asks,

> 65. *Since, then we are made partakers of Christ and all his benefits by faith only, whence comes this faith?*
> The Holy Ghost works it in our hearts by the preaching of the holy Gospel, and confirms it by the use of the holy Sacraments.[22]

The Westminster Larger Catechism explains concerning God's appointed function for his word: "The Spirit of God makes the Reading, but especially the Preaching of the Word, an effectual means of enlightening, convincing, and humbling sinners, of driving them out of themselves, and drawing them unto Christ, of conforming them to his Image, and subduing them to his will, of strengthening them against temptations and corruptions, of building them up in grace, and establishing their hearts in holiness and comfort through faith unto salvation" (WLC 155).[23] Whereas wider evangelicalism sometimes promotes constant hunting for the Spirit's mystical work disconnected from God's word, the Reformed, although keeping the Spirit and the word distinct, have emphasized that the Spirit inseparably works through the power of the word (Rom 10:8–17).[24]

---

21. *COC*, 3:325 (italics original).

22. *COC*, 3:328.

23. *LC*, 102.

24. J. V. Fesko, "Preaching as a Means of Grace and the Doctrine of Sanctification: A Reformed Perspective," *American Theological Inquiry* 3 no. 1 (2010): 35–54; *CF*, 758; Letham, *Systematic Theology*, 623–34.

Perhaps surprisingly to some, the Larger Catechism affirms that the sacraments are also *effectual for our salvation*. "The Sacraments become effectual means of salvation, not by any power in themselves, or any virtue derived from the piety or intention of him by whom they are administered; but only by the working of the holy Ghost, and the blessing of Christ by whom they are instituted" (WLC 161).[25] Word and sacrament together are used by God for our communion with him. As the Heidelberg Catechism indicates:

> 67. *Are both these, then, the Word and Sacraments, designed to direct our faith to the sacrifice of Jesus Christ on the cross as the only ground of our salvation?*
> Yes, truly; for the Holy Ghost teaches us in the Gospel, and by the holy Sacraments assures us, that our whole salvation stands in the one sacrifice of Christ made for us on the cross.[26]

God works through the sacraments as earthly means to accomplish his heavenly purposes.

Certainly, the sacraments' efficacy requires clear explanation, specifically as they do not work independently of God's word. Herman Bavinck affirms, "The first and most important means of grace is the word of God."[27] The word is preeminent because its description of God's promises is "an automatic given," but water, bread, and wine do not inherently by nature seal Christ and his benefits. God must declare that connection in his covenant.[28]

Still the word and sacrament have the same exact content, namely, Christ. The sacraments do not impart any grace to believers that is absent in the word. "The two contain the same Mediator, the same covenant, the same benefits, the same salvation, the same fellowship with God."[29] In this respect, the sacraments cannot be administered without the word preached. Normal water, bread, and wine receive their holy significance

---

25. *LC*, 103–4.
26. *COC*, 3:328–29.
27. *BRD*, 4:448.
28. *BRD*, 4:481.
29. *BRD*, 4:479.

during the worship service because the word gives, assigns, and effects that meaning.[30]

The sacraments are then not sacraments without the word. Geerhardus Vos writes, "The word that accompanies the sacraments belongs essentially to them and is a part of the sacramental actions; it may not be omitted."[31] Further, "The word of institution as it was originally spoken by Christ is the basis of the sacrament as sacrament. This is the sole guarantee by which we are assured that God wills to have His grace joined with these means."[32] The preached word does not change the elements' substance but sets them apart for holy use, co-opting them as a sacramental sign and seal.[33] So, the word gives the meaning and efficacy to the sacraments, which are not means of grace if not connected to the ministry of the word.

The sacraments *confirm* rather than supplement the word preached, which in no way makes them expendable or diminishes the importance of their role. The sacraments may not be necessary inasmuch as God can, has, and does save true believers who have not had opportunity to receive them. Still, they are necessary in that God has appointed them for us to use as means through which we receive that salvation by faith alone.[34]

To illustrate this type of necessity of means, an envelope is not a letter, but postal services have appointed envelopes as the means that we are to use to convey our letters through the mail. Other means besides an envelope could convey a letter, but envelopes are the ordinary way. Then to illustrate the nature of how the means of grace confirm, a marriage ceremony for taking vows and being pronounced husband and wife is supremely important, but the accompanying marriage certificate recording that the vows and pronouncement happened is also necessary to prove and *confirm* that ceremony's reality in an objective way. Just because something is not *most* important does not mean it is not *crucially* important.[35]

30. *TI*, 19.6.1–14.

31. *VRD*, 5:98.

32. *VRD*, 5:99.

33. *VRD*, 5:100.

34. *TI*, 19.13.3–18, 22–23; *BRD*, 4:476; *VRD*, 5:91.

35. As Turretin indicates, it was the Socinian heretics who diminished the sacraments to mere external badges of profession rather than true means of grace; *TI*, 19.8.1.

God's word comes both in preaching and in the sacraments, so that it remains that which creates and builds the church. At the same time, God delivers his word through means that are both *heard* and *held*. Francis Turretin pointedly explains that "What is offered to and apprehended by many senses at the same time is more certain to us than what is perceived by the hearing alone."[36] God has made his promises audible and tangible.[37] On that point, Vos exhorts seminary students to consider how, even though the word makes the sacraments effective, the meaning of the sacraments should inform our preaching so that we remember that a sermon's primary purpose is the proclamation of Christ:

> And in order to find out whether you are doing this, whether your preaching meets this requirement or not, a good test to apply is the frequent comparison of the purport of your sermon with the purport of the sacrament. The word and the sacrament as means of grace belong together: they are two sides of the same divinely instituted instrumentality. While addressing themselves to different organs of perception, they are intended to bear the identical message of the grace of God—to interpret and mutually enforce one another.[38]

When the church gathers in Christ's name, God uses his word heard in preaching and held in the sacraments as means or instruments to convey Christ as we receive those means with true faith. The grace offered in the sacraments has an objectivity in the consecrated water, bread, and wine, but these elements do not truly convey Christ to the recipient for salvation unless received by faith.[39] The sacraments do not work by magic but because God pledges in his word to use them for confirming the word's promises and because the Spirit makes them effective.[40]

By way of illustration, my wife gave me my wedding ring when we got married. That ring did not do anything on its own. I tried it on before our wedding, but it did not effect our marriage. In the ceremony, however,

---

36. *TI*, 19.2.2.

37. *CF*, 756–61, 785.

38. Geerhardus Vos, "The Gracious Provision," in *Grace and Glory*, 251.

39. *WWS*, 302–7.

40. *TI*, 19.8.5–28; Letham, *Systematic Theology*, 634–47.

she gave it to me, saying, "*With this ring*, I thee wed." Regardless of the ring, we would have been married because the pastor pronounced it and the marriage license legally confirmed it. She gave my ring to me as tangible confirmation of legal vows she made to me as we covenanted in marriage. Although the ring did not marry us, it was "*with this ring*" that we married. Likewise, God gives the sacraments as signs to demonstrate, confirm, and convey his promises in a tangible way.[41] As the Westminster Larger Catechism affirms, the sacraments are not effectual in themselves for salvation, but only by the Spirit's work as he uses them to confirm the word's promises and establish faith through them.[42]

God has always instructed his people to use certain features of outward life precisely as these means. The word, the sacraments of baptism and the Lord's Supper, and prayer are those means for the new covenant community, but God instructed his covenant community in the past to use other means, such as circumcision and animal sacrifices. Even though God appointed other means, he still delivered the same promises, the same substance of the covenant, which is that he will be our God and give us everlasting life in Christ.

Admittedly, the means that God appointed under the old covenant look very different from ours, possibly suggesting that they delivered different promises, necessitating that distinction between substance and administration. While in college, I worked a few summers at a fast-food Mexican restaurant. My favorite meal was the nachos, but I problematically never had enough tortilla chips for all the toppings. Thankfully, extra chips were free! Sometimes when I got more chips for scooping meat and cheese, a new batch had been fried. This new batch may have stayed in the fryer too long and ended up brown and tough. Regardless of how they differed, they did not look and taste exactly like the previous batch, they still effectively scooped the same toppings.

Across the Testaments, God's variously appointed means work similarly to those chips. God instructed Abraham to use circumcision and

41. *CF*, 777–85.

42. Scott R. Swain, "Lutheran and Reformed Sacramental Theology: Seventeenth-Nineteenth Centuries," in *The Oxford Handbook of Sacramental Theology*, eds. Hans Boersma and Matthew Levering (Oxford: Oxford University Press, 2015), 366–68; Todd Billings, "Sacraments," in *CD*, 339–62; Horton, "Church," 313–17.

Moses to keep the Passover and ceremonial laws. Despite how different these appear, God used them to distribute the same promises of salvation by faith in Christ. God's people across history receive the same matchless grace in Christ, no matter how their outward form of worship looks.

Our outward forms of worship inform how believers have communion with God. That communion cannot be reduced to external ceremonies, as if going through religious motions without genuine faith is effective. On the other hand, in ordinary circumstances we cannot disconnect the practice of our faith from the external forms of worship that God has given us. For instance, God said to Abraham in Genesis 17:9–10: "As for you, you shall keep my covenant, you and your offspring after you throughout their generations. *This is my covenant*, which you shall keep, between me and you and your offspring after you: Every male among you shall be circumcised." God commanded Abraham to keep the covenant, but the covenant *is* circumcision. God's covenant with Abraham was equated with the outward act, the sacrament, of circumcision. Certainly, this covenant keeping depends on how Abraham already believed God and it was counted to him as righteousness (Gen 15:6). Still, God equated Abraham's life in the covenant with the sacrament.[43]

The principle carries into the new covenant. In Luke 22:19–20, Christ instituted the Lord's Supper: "And he took bread, and when he had given thanks, he broke it and gave it to them, saying, 'This is my body, which is given for you. Do this in remembrance of me.' And likewise the cup after they had eaten, saying, 'This cup that is poured out for you *is the new covenant* in my blood.' " Like God explained his covenant with Abraham, Christ directly linked the new covenant and its sacrament. Faith is still essential to have true communion with God in the sacraments since the meal is kept *in remembrance* of Christ. On the other hand, a bare act of recalling Christ is foreign to the text.

Paul emphasizes this aspect of the Lord's Supper when he recounts its institution. "This is my body, which is for you. Do this in remembrance of me." In the same way also he took the cup, after supper, saying, 'This cup is the new covenant in my blood. Do this, as often as you drink it, in remembrance of me.' For as often as you eat this bread and drink

43. *CF*, 780–83.

the cup, you proclaim the Lord's death until he comes" (1 Cor 11:24–26). Christ's command for remembrance occurs after both the bread and the cup, underscoring the dimension of a conscious relationship to Christ. Whoever eats this meal without incurring judgment must "discern the body" (1 Cor 11:29). Regardless of whether one understands this as comprehending who Christ himself is or fathoming who the church as Christ's body is, the implication remains that we must be aware of Christ and his work among his people to receive the Supper in the right manner.

In 1 Corinthians 10:16, the observance of the Supper explicitly concerns our communion with God: "The cup of blessing that we bless, is it not a *participation* in the blood of Christ? The bread that we break, is it not a *participation* in the body of Christ?" Whereas "the blood of the covenant" was drawn from the sacrificed animals when God made the Mosaic covenant with Israel (Exod 24:8), Christ said of the wine of the Lord's Supper, "This is my blood of the covenant, which is poured out for many for the forgiveness of sins" (Matt 26:28). Although the Mosaic covenant began as sacrificial blood was put upon the people, now the wine of the Lord's Supper is that sacrificial blood—wine being that blood because it stands for Christ's blood once for all shed for the forgiveness of sin—binding the church to God.[44] So, the celebration of this meal *is* the new covenant as our communion with the Triune God.[45]

The means of grace are empty without faith, counting for nothing toward our relationship with God if we participate in them faithlessly (Rom 2:25–29). Emphatically, the means of grace are not the substance of the covenant. At the same time, in ordinary circumstances we cannot participate in communion with God apart from his given means for experiencing that communion. These outward means *are* the covenant, specifically its administration. Although remaining distinct from it, the external administration delivers the substance, constituting our participation in the covenant. Substance and administration cannot be conflated nor separated. The means of grace are not the basis of our relationship with God, since that is only Christ and his work, but are the way we experience that

44. *VRD*, 5:218–19.

45. *VRD*, 5:222–39.

covenant fellowship. So, to walk with God requires that we make use of the ordinary means of grace.

The church serves as the point of contact between God and his people. The church, therefore, is properly considered one of God's own works. The church is where God's works flow to his people, and that directional stream cannot be reversed. Even as we worship God in the assembly, God is at work in his people through their acts of worship. The church is a theological, more than a social, reality. When the church forgets its role primarily as the place where God distributes his promises through the means of grace, it inevitably shifts its primary focus to social issues. It reconsiders itself as a working, rather than a receiving, assembly. Properly understanding the church as one of God's works establishes the church's primary role in God's economy of grace as the place where Christ's blessings are simultaneously received and distributed.[46]

This theological understanding of the church has profound application. Practically, as we think about our life with God, the church is where the action is. The typical, if unspoken or even subconscious, conception of the church in evangelical theology today is that the institutional church exists mainly to support wider causes, such as parachurch organizations. After all, *these* groups accomplish agendas in the world. Without denying that parachurch groups have accomplished some good things, God's people cannot shift our focus from encountering the living God to outside affairs. Our first priority must be to find ourselves in God's presence rather than in the world's eye. Whatever we hope to achieve for our neighbor's well-being, we will find it hopelessly unfulfilling if we do not meet our highest purpose of communing with our God. This communion occurs in the church's assembly as we engage the means that God has given us.[47]

ONE COVENANT, DIVERSELY ADMINISTERED

The assorted external administrations of the covenant of grace each contributes something distinctly important to God's history-spanning plan of salvation. Our emphasis on the covenant of grace's unity sometimes

46. John Webster, "'In the Society of God': Some Principles of Ecclesiology," in *GWM1*, 177–94.

47. D. G. Hart, *The Lost Soul of American Protestantism* (Lanham, MD: Rowman & Littlefield, 2002), xv–xxiv, 1–56, 141–86; D. G. Hart, *Recovering Mother Kirk: The Case for Liturgy in the Reformed Tradition* (Grand Rapids: Baker Academic, 2003), 21–65, 203–8.

tempts Reformed theologians to describe the various eras of redemptive history in a way that does not do justice to the real differences between the shape of communion with God in the Old and New Testaments. God himself ordained a diversely administered covenant of grace, so we should reflect well upon those changes in redemptive history.[48] This section unpacks *the twofold economy* of the covenant of grace as the pivotal difference between Old and New Testaments.

Reformed theology has long recognized the significant differences between how God met with his people during different eras of the covenant of grace. The Westminster Larger Catechism states, "The Covenant of Grace was not always administered after the same manner, but the administrations of it under the Old Testament were different from those under the New" (WLC 33).[49] The Westminster Standards elaborate those differences, helpfully explaining Old and New Testaments in turn. Whereas paragraph 8.6 of the Westminster Confession expounds Christ as the substance of the covenant of grace conveyed through old economy means, paragraph 7.5 more specifically applies this principle to the external administration.

> This covenant was differently administered in the time of the law and in the time of the gospel: under the law it was administered by promises, prophecies, sacrifices, circumcision, the paschal lamb, and other types and ordinances delivered to the people of the Jews, all fore-signifying Christ to come, which were for that time sufficient and efficacious, through the operation of the Spirit, to instruct and build up the elect in faith in the promised Messiah, by whom they had full remission of sins and eternal salvation; and is called the Old Testament.[50]

The Westminster Larger Catechism summarizes the same point: "The Covenant of Grace was administered under the Old Testament, by promises, prophecies, Sacrifices, Circumcision, the Passover, and other types and ordinances, which did all fore-signify Christ then to come, and were for

48. *MT*, 1.38.1; *BOC*, 18.

49. *LC*, 72.

50. *COC*, 3:617–18.

that time sufficient to build up the elect in faith in the promised Messiah, by whom they then had full remission of sin, and eternal salvation" (WLC 34).[51] So, the Westminster Standards use the category of Christ *incarnandus*—Christ-to-come—to affirm both that the covenant's substance is identical and that the life of believers during Old Testament times looked significantly different than ours does.[52]

That different appearance of communion with God in ages past does not displace the unity of the covenant of grace, even in those differences. The Standards mention "types and ordinances" as features of Old Testament religious life. A type is something that God built into an earlier part of redemptive history that would provide an advance depiction of Christ and his work. For example, God appointed David as the shepherd king over God's people (1 Sam 16:11–13), which pointed forward to how Christ would be the Good Shepherd who is the ultimate king over God's people (Ps 23; Ezek 37:24–27; John 10:14–16). David was even crowned in Bethlehem to mark its royal significance for when Christ would be born there. In his providence, God orchestrated these events concerning David, which occurred during the old covenant, so that we would more forcefully understand Christ's role as the divine shepherd, the ultimate king, and the true Savior when he came. More directly, God appointed animal sacrifices as part of Israel's worship, not because those animals actually procured the forgiveness of sin for them, but because the sacrifices taught them that someone—the Savior—has to die in their place and bear the penalty of God's justice if they are to be forgiven. In 1 Corinthians 10:6, Paul reflects upon events in Israel's past, their time during the wilderness wandering, writing: "Now these things took place as examples for us, that we might not desire evil as they did." God brought about events in Israel's history, including roles people played as well as features of religious worship, to instruct Christians about faith. These Old Testament events, people, and worship served as types foresignifying Christ, although there were still far

51. *LC*, 72. WLC 34, as well as writers contemporary with the Westminster Assembly analyzed below, shows that the Reformed use the phrase "under the law" to designate the whole period before Christ's coming—namely "under the Old Testament"—which had further specified covenants within it, rather than only the Mosaic covenant; cf. James M. Renihan, "Covenant Theology in the First and Second London Baptist Confessions," in *Recovering a Covenantal Heritage*, 67.

52. Estelle et al., "Report to … Study Republication," 10–13.

more types and ordinances under the old covenant that also pointed to Christ.[53] These covenantal features and ordinances, at the *historia salutis* level, created structures and furthered tensions in redemptive history that anticipated and indicated our need for Christ but, at the *ordo salutis* level, created and confirmed faith in Christ so that Old Testament believers received his benefits just like we do in the new covenant.

God's major purpose for these types and ordinances centered in Christ as the substance of the covenant of grace. He intended that they would "all fore-signify Christ then to come." Further, they were "to instruct and build up the elect in faith in the promised Messiah, by whom they had full remission of sins, and eternal salvation." So, just as the preached word offers and directs us to Christ, these types and ordinances, even though they were far less clear, likewise directed the old covenant believers to Christ. Vos explains: "The Old Testament sacraments portray a Christ who was to come and they sealed benefits of salvation that still had to be obtained, although certainly those benefits were already granted to believers at that time by virtue of the suretyship of Christ, which is eternally valid. The New Testament sacraments signify and seal the benefits of salvation that have already been obtained."[54] Again, faith differed for old and new covenant believers only in perspective, not quality. Old Testament saints trusted in Christ *incarnandus* but nevertheless trusted in Christ. That identical faith was then confirmed by sacraments of various kinds, all communicating the same substance, as the Westminster Confession affirms: "The sacraments of the Old Testament, in regard of the spiritual things thereby signified and exhibited, were, for substance, the same with those of the New" (WCF 27.5).[55] Believers today need the preaching of the gospel and the sacraments to build our faith and grow us in communion with Christ. Old covenant types and ordinances intended "to instruct and build up the elect in faith in the promised Messiah" so that believers then would grow in their trust in the Savior and in communion with him.

---

53. *EC*, 4.6.1–12; *CG*, 29–31; Johnson, *Him We Proclaim*, 198–238; *KP*, 340–55; Wellum, "Progressive Covenantalism," 82–87; *KTC*, 129–37; *BTA*, 190–96; Renihan, *Mystery*, 27–35; G. K. Beale, *Handbook on the New Testament Use of the Old Testament: Exegesis and Interpretation* (Grand Rapids: Baker Academic, 2012), 13–25, 58–66, 95–102.

54. *VRD*, 5:103.

55. *COC*, 3:661.

THE COVENANT UNDER THE LAW

Reformed theology understands that life "under the law," or "under the Old Testament," looked very different from life in the New Testament, or "under the gospel, when Christ the substance was exhibited."[56] This section addresses the main difference between the Old and New Testament periods of the covenant of grace.

This book intentionally emphasizes aspects of covenant theology other than the historical outworking of God's saving plan, not because this issue is unimportant, but because it has already received the most attention in recent years. Most books about covenant theology, written by theologians from every perspective, have focused on tracing the development of the covenant idea across the progress of redemptive history.[57] That approach is a necessary feature of covenant theology, explaining why so many books address it.

On the other hand, this book aims to revive our interest in other aspects of covenant theology besides the biblical narrative of redemptive history, focusing more on the *ordo salutis* than the *historia salutis*. Most often, those studies in biblical theology focus on the covenants' theological significance for the doctrine of the church, mainly concerning the differences between Baptist and Reformed ecclesiologies. By contrast, this book prioritizes the covenants' value for understanding the doctrines of Christ and salvation, how to articulate the law and the gospel, and how to fit God's future new creation into the scope of Scripture from Genesis to Revelation. Although a discussion of unfolding redemptive history is inevitable in a full treatment of covenant theology, this volume's distinct contribution is to focus on how the changes across redemptive history relate specifically to the means of grace.

Christ is the only redeemer of God's elect, so the elect must all partake of Christ to be saved. Old Testament believers needed not only to

---

56. WCF 7.6; *COC*, 3:618.

57. *CT*; VanDrunen, *Divine Covenants*; Michael G. Brown and Zach Keele, *Sacred Bond: Covenant Theology Explored*, 2nd ed. (Middleville, MI: Reformed Fellowship, Inc., 2017; repr. 2018); Jonty Rhodes, *Covenants Made Simple: Understanding God's Unfolding Promises to His People* (Phillipsburg, NJ: P&R, 2014); Robertson, *Christ of the Covenants*; Williamson, *Sealed*; *VBT*; John Murray, *The Covenant of Grace: A Biblico-Theological Study* (Phillipsburg, NJ: P&R, 1992); Belcher, *Fulfillment*; Schreiner, *Covenant*; *KP*; *KTC*; and Renihan, *Mystery*. Some exceptions are *TCR*; *ACW*; Horton, *Covenant Theology*; Horton, *Lord and Servant*; Horton, *Covenant and Salvation*; and Barcellos, *Covenant of Works*.

know about the promise of the Savior but to receive the Savior himself. Christ and his benefits had to be applied to them, just as to new covenant believers. Of course, the internal administration under the old economy was faith, so that Christ was applied personally to each who trusted in him *incarnandus*. The Reformed view that the old economy's external administration delivered the same substance as the new simply indicates that God truly applied Christ and his benefits to old covenant believers through faith by using creaturely means distinct to their time to create and strengthen their trust in the coming Savior.[58] God applied the virtue and efficacy of Christ's historical work to believers before Christ actually wrought that work of redemption, conveying it through means of grace, much like he fully applies the verdict of justification to believers in the present even though that declaration properly belongs to the future last day.[59] The eternal God can distribute the efficacy of his decreed acts before they occur in history. The Reformed confession that the substance was administered through the old economy simply affirms that God *truly gave* Christ and his benefits to Old Testament believers, not making them wait until the incarnation to experience those blessings, by using the outward means they had in their age to form their faith.

In summarizing the Old Testament as the covenant of grace "under the law," Reformed theology has not collapsed everything in the Old Testament into one administration of the covenant of grace. There are several administrations during the time "under the law" or during the *old economy*, which is the term we will use to refer collectively to the covenant administrations prior to Christ's coming. Ussher helpfully unpacks these differences, noting that the gospel, as to substance, "always has been the same: but in regard of the manner proper to certain times, it is distinguished into two kinds: the Old and the New." The old ministry was delivered to the fathers "to continue until the fulness of times; wherein by the coming of Christ it was to be reformed." During this time "the commandments of the Law were more largely, and the promises of Christ

58. *VRD*, 5:102–4.

59. WCF 8.6; *COC*, 3.621.

more sparingly and darkly propounded."[60] Types and shadows characterized this era.

Despite varying characteristics throughout the old economy, Ussher clearly indicates that the Old Testament was a time of ministry *for the gospel*, marking unity in substance. The old ministry of the gospel, however, had a different manner in that it "more sparingly and darkly" explained those promises about Christ. The new covenant ministry is certainly more explicit about Christ and his work. As Ussher teaches, "This ministry is common for every generation and time, and that ministry pertains to the substance of the Gospel covenant (which is Christ). Now, it pertains as much to the time before Christ was made man as to the time after his incarnation."[61] Despite the difference of clarity, the substance is the same.

The old economy can be further subdivided in at least one way. Ussher argues, "The parts of this ministry are defined by certain periods of time, which are, first, from Adam to Moses, then, from Moses to Christ. There are likewise two parts in the period just mentioned. From Moses to Solomon and from Solomon to Christ."[62] Ames also divides Old Testament history primarily into that before Moses and that from Moses to Christ.[63] Regardless of exactly how one may decide to divide the Old Testament era, or into how many distinct periods, the point is that the old economy as a unit contains several administrations of the covenant of grace.[64] Most Reformed theologians, as we will follow, describe several dispensations of the covenant of grace under Adam to Noah, Noah to Abraham, Abraham to Moses, Moses to Christ, and Christ to the last day.[65]

Reformed theology has called this division of Old Testament and New Testament that administers the same substance of the covenant of grace the *twofold economy*. An economy is simply a way of doing things, particularly a way that God has worked.[66] The *old economy* included every dispensation of the covenant that God gave to his people prior to Christ's

---

60. Ussher, *Body*, 409.
61. Queen's College, Oxford MS 217, fol. 38v.
62. Queen's College, Oxford MS 217, fol. 38v.
63. *MT*, 1.38.11.
64. *MMB*, 189–90; *EC*, 3.3.11–15.
65. *DLGTT*, 239–40.
66. *DLGTT*, 94.

coming in the incarnation.[67] The *new economy* obviously encompasses God's covenant with us since Christ came *incarnatus*. Reformed theology, then, confesses that the main difference between the Old and New Testaments is that Christ is revealed through *types and shadows* in the Old and that he is revealed with profound and direct clarity in the New.[68]

Even in this difference between the twofold economy with the old pointing forward to Christ *incarnandus* through promises, types, and symbols but the new looking back to Christ *incarnatus* with sharp clarity, we can still see the unity of God's people across time in the one covenant of grace. In Ephesians 2:11–13, Paul writes, "Therefore remember that previously you, the Gentiles in the flesh, who are called 'Uncircumcision' by the so-called 'Circumcision' *which is* performed in the flesh by human hands—*remember* that you were at that time separate from Christ, excluded from the people of Israel, and strangers to the covenants of the promise, having no hope and without God in the world. But now in Christ Jesus you who previously were far away have been brought near by the blood of Christ" (NASB, italics original). The predominantly relevant phrase is "the covenants of the promise," indicating multiple covenants all having the same, singular promise. In context, the contrast is between how the Ephesians were once "separate from Christ, excluded from the commonwealth of Israel and strangers to the covenants of the promise" but ho v they are "now in Christ" (my translation). Belonging to *any* of the apparently several "covenants of promise," then, is contrary to being "separated from Christ."[69] All the covenants of promise include union with Christ by faith, so the promise is singular and the promise is Christ.[70]

---

67. *EC*, 3.3.2; *TI*, 12.7.1.

68. *MT*, 1.38.3–5.

69. *MMB*, 73–76, 185–90.

70. The distributive role of the singular genitive "of the promise" in the phrase τῶν διαθηκῶν τῆς ἐπαγγελίας is debatable, but this understanding implies that that each covenant in question is individually a promise covenant. Baptistic theology seemingly requires the distributive view. On the other hand, Reformed theology can account for the phrase's sense regardless of whether the singular genitive is distributive; see S. M. Baugh, *Ephesians* (Bellingham, WA: Lexham Press, 2016), 185n27. Roberts interestingly distinguishes the covenants of promise, all of which point ahead to Christ's work, from the one "covenant of performance," which is the new covenant that exhibits Christ as the substance. He certainly sees each administration as related to one singular promise and bases that point on the grammatical and theological argument; see *MMB*, 185–90.

So, Christ is in all the covenants. In Ephesians 2:11–13, to be a stranger to any of the covenants of promise is to be separated from Christ. The promise associated with each covenant is to be "now in Christ," whether literally a citizen of theocratic Israel or now a member of "the Israel of God," which is the church (Gal 6:16). Charles Hodge comments that God entered repeatedly into multiple covenants with his people but Paul wrote of "a *covenant of promise*, or rather of *the* promise, because the promise of redemption was connected therewith."[71] Indeed, "the Scripture, foreseeing that God would justify the Gentiles by faith, preached the gospel beforehand to Abraham" and preached the gospel to Adam before that as well (Gal 3:8; Gen 3:15).[72] Wherever Christ is promised, the covenant of grace is present as to its substance. As Herman Bavinck puts it, "The covenant of grace is everywhere and at all times one in essence, but always manifests itself in new forms and goes through differing dispensations. Essentially and materially it remains one, whether before, or under, or after the law. It is always a covenant of grace."[73] The covenant of grace may be diversely administered but has centered entirely and always on taking hold of God's one promise about salvation in Christ by faith.[74]

CONCLUSION

Christians know that there is no more fundamental reality than our communion with God. This communion grips us personally as we take hold of Christ by faith as the internal administration of the covenant and its blessings. Still, God puts his people in the external administration of the covenant, although that looks different in various periods of redemptive history, so that our communion with him is lived out in the concrete reality of the covenant community. The major claim of this discussion, then, also becomes its own supremely important pastoral use: the church matters because God distributes Christ and his benefits through the means that he has appointed in the church. In our ice cream shop illustration, cups or cones with ice cream in them are not magically appearing in people's

71. Charles Hodge, *A Commentary on the Epistle to the Ephesians* (New York: Robert Carter and Brothers, 1860), 127 (italics original). Thank you to Ligon Duncan for alerting me to this quote.

72. Baugh, *Ephesians*, 184–85.

73. *WWG*, 256.

74. Waters, "Covenant in Paul," 238.

hands as they walk on the beach. An individual is not madly running about lugging a duffle bag full of ice cream. There is a *shop*, a physical place, containing and distributing the substance in its means of administration. So too, God appointed the church as the real place distributing heavenly realities on earth through the means of grace. The church, then, matters.

Another crucial pastoral use of this chapter's material highlights our dependence upon God's revelation to know him and upon the church to walk with him. The modern era celebrates rampant individualism. New spiritualities, even as held by those claiming to be Christians, insist that we can know God by means of our own invention. This mindset is treasonous against the God of the universe because it suggests that we are so special that God is subject to our demands and desires concerning how we might meet with him. The means of grace highlight how we are subject to God and the ways that he ordains to meet us, thereby highlighting our need to submit to God in all things. This submission intrinsically furthers our overall sanctification by teaching us that we are meant to listen to God rather than instruct him.

The simple pastoral point is that we can have confidence in our relationship with God because God has revealed the reasons for our assurance. As we depend on the means by which he makes his truth known and delivers Christ to his people, we know that we are in a thriving relationship with the holy God. Although too often reduced to a children's song, some of the most profound words ever written are: "Jesus loves me, this I *know, for* the Bible tells me so." I have assurance of Christ's love for *me* personally *because* God reveals it in Scripture and appointed preaching and sacraments to deliver that assuring word to his people (Gal 2:19–20).

XII

From Adam to Moses

Long ago, at many times and in many ways,
God spoke to our fathers by the prophets, but in these last days
he has spoken to us by his Son, whom he appointed the heir of all things,
through whom also he created the world.
—Hebrews 1:1–2

Despite the differing appearances of the covenant of grace's various administrations, God has always provided communion with himself through them. God's people have always experienced our communion with God in concrete form through the means he has granted for encountering him. God has always given us a way to meet him and to meet him in Christ. The old and new economies both offered Christ through their ordinances.

Within the old economy, more specific dispensations each contributed their own promises, types, and symbols pointing forward to Christ. In our ice cream shop illustration, the ice cream is the purpose of the trip, so Christ is the substance, but cups or cones, as different kinds of administration, grant that substance. The principle difference between cups and cones resembles that the difference between old and new economies as they foresignified or now directly exhibit Christ. Still, there may be the further choice between a plain or waffle cone. Within the old economy, several "flavors" of administration each distinctly advanced the development of the covenant of grace as it built toward the revelation of Christ, the substance.

This chapter examines the development of the old economy administrations as they point toward Christ, specifically in the periods from Adam until Moses. Our reflection remains focused on paragraph 7.5 of the Westminster Confession:

> This covenant [of grace] was differently administered in the time of the law and in the time of the gospel: under the law it was administered by promises, prophecies, sacrifices, circumcision, the paschal lamb, and other types and ordinances delivered to the people of the Jews, all fore-signifying Christ to come, which were for that time sufficient and efficacious, through the operation of the Spirit, to instruct and build up the elect in faith in the promised Messiah, by whom they had full remission of sins, and eternal salvation, and is called the Old Testament.[1]

The confession does not address how each administration contributes to the one covenant of grace but merely points to their general features that offered Christ by pointing forward to him. Although perhaps not often adequately stated, there is no singular confessional view of each individual administration.[2] These chapters unpack each administration within the confessional framework, not aiming for a full account of each administration's redemptive-historical relevance, but at demonstrating how each distinctively offered and displayed Christ.[3] This discussion is not meant to replace or displace the many works in biblical theology that unpack the full significance of the covenants but remains focused on issues of

1. *COC*, 3:617–18.

2. Letham is, therefore, incorrect to argue that WCF 7.5 specifically interpreted the Mosaic covenant; *Systematic Theology*, 457.

3. In this respect, Peter Gentry and Stephen Wellum's proposed "progressive covenantalism" correctly argues that "the Bible presents a *plurality* of covenants that *progressively* reveal our triune God's *one* redemptive plan for his *one* people, which reaches its fulfillment and terminus in Christ and the new covenant." *KTC*, 35 (italics original). The question is whether this unity is merely historical progress toward the goal or if it runs deeper as God distributed salvation in Christ through each of the covenants. The issue is, then, not primarily ecclesiology, as is progressive covenantalism's emphasis, but soteriology. Rather than arguing contrary to the Reformed view of Old Testament salvation, progressive covenantalism does not extensively address the soteriological issues. One need not overturn the entirety of Gentry and Wellum's exegesis to confirm covenant theology, but merely establish, additionally, that redemptive history is unified as to the substance of the covenants. For more elaborate reflection upon how progressive covenantalism relates to classic Reformed covenant theology, see Harrison Perkins, "*Kingdom Through Covenant*—Round Two," *The Heidelblog*, August 10, 2021, https://heidelblog.net/2021/08/kingdom-through-covenant-round-two/.

systematic theology as it connects to redemptive history. The argument remains that, throughout redemptive history, God communicated—truly applied—Christ and his benefits to believers through the means of grace.

THE START OF THE PROMISE

This section explores how God offered the gospel to Adam directly after the fall. God's pronouncement in Genesis 3:15, after Adam's fall, that the woman's seed would crush the serpent's head was the first announcement of the gospel, Christ being the woman's seed.[4] Reformed theologians affirm that this promise began the one covenant of grace. Francis Roberts links the curse upon the serpent to Christ: "Though the same Christ was under the Old Testament represented as promised, under the New Testament as performed. Under the Old Testament darkly and typically, under the New clearly and fully. Yet in both sufficiently for salvation."[5] If the essence of the old economy was to communicate Christ through promises and types, then God's first promise fits that category.[6]

After the serpent successfully tempted Adam and his wife regarding the tree of knowledge of good and evil, God confronted all the parties involved. Although he pronounced curses that would afflict the ongoing situation for each, he cursed the serpent first. In Genesis 3:15, God said to the snake,

> I will put enmity between you and the woman,
>   and between your offspring and her offspring;
> he shall bruise your head,
>   and you shall bruise his heel.

Satan, as this snake, approached Adam to lure him into sin and succeeded, but God promised the snake that the woman's future offspring would destroy him. In that regard, Christ's role as the last Adam is highly relevant, since Christ picked up the exact challenge against Satan that

---

4. *KTC*, 653; Renihan, *Mystery*, 75–76; Schreiner, *Covenant*, 13; Williamson, *Sealed*, 51.

5. *MMB*, 216.

6. *MMB*, 210–40; *EC*, 4.1.4–6; *CMT*, 83; Wellum, "Progressive Covenantalism," 91; John D. Currid, "Adam and the Beginning of the Covenant of Grace," in *CT*, 99–110; Belcher, *Fulfillment*, 38–41.

Adam failed, fulfilling the promise of the woman's descendant who would destroy Satan.[7]

Christ's confrontation against Satan ties to the covenants. Satan's act of tempting Adam was linked to the covenant of works' probationary command. Adam's failure was not a mere mistake but a covenant transgression. When Christ fulfilled the task to destroy Satan as the seed of the woman and the last Adam, he was resuming Adam's covenantal task.[8] Adam named his wife "Eve" because the Hebrew word affirmed her connection to life, justification's consequent reward, as the mother of all the living (Gen 3:20).[9] Upon Adam's profession of faith, God clothed him and his family as a sign that he would provide reconciliation by covering their sin, promising Christ would pass the very probation set for humanity in the covenant of works (Gen 3:21).[10]

Reformed theology, therefore, reasonably understands this promise as the beginning of God's unified dealings with his people, the covenant of grace. It begins the economy "under the law" precisely by delivering the message of Christ through a forward-pointing promise, the same message of Christ that we preach today, right in the wake of Adam's triggering the law's curse. This point confirms the previous chapter's argument that "the covenants of the promise" from Ephesians 2:11–13 indicate that multiple covenants all have the same, singular promise—that although once "separate from Christ," all believers of any administration are "now in Christ."[11]

Since Christ is the promise in every covenant, the substance of the covenant is present every time he is promised. The bruise to the woman's offspring's heel, an injury ultimately proving nonfatal, was Christ's crucifixion, which was unable to hold him in death.[12] So, "the Scripture, foreseeing that God would justify the Gentiles by faith, preached the gospel beforehand to Abraham" and preached the gospel to Adam before that as well (Gal 3:8).[13] Even if one does not count God's first promise about

7. Waters, "Covenant in Paul," 230–32; *TI*, 12.7.13–17; *EC*, 4.1.9–15.

8. *CRS*, 1:451–52; *EC*, 4.1.17–20.

9. *CMT*, 84; *EC*, 4.1.27–32.

10. *KP*, 143–53; Belcher, *Fulfillment*, 41–42; *EC*, 4.1.22; *MMB*, 245.

11. Hodge, *Ephesians*, 127; Williamson, *Sealed*, 200.

12. *MMB*, 224–32.

13. Baugh, *Ephesians*, 184–85.

the woman's seed as a formal covenant, God certainly announced his one plan of salvation, promising the redeemer in whom Adam, Eve, and everyone else who would be saved must trust.[14] So, this promise, at the *historia salutis* level, created the historical tension anticipating Christ as the Messiah who would destroy the serpent but, at the *ordo salutis* level, applied Christ and his benefits to everyone who had faith in that coming seed of the woman.

NOAH'S UNIVERSAL BLESSING

God made two covenants with Noah, one before the flood concerning his family's rescue (Gen 6:9–8:22), and one after about preserving the world from another universal catastrophe (Gen 9:1–19). Although some understand these two accounts as one continuous covenant, the better interpretation recognizes that God's rescue of Noah and his family in the Ark fulfilled his covenant promises in Genesis 6:13–21.[15] In this respect, 1 Peter 3:21–22 explains this covenant's role in the covenant of grace: "Baptism, which corresponds to this [event of God bringing Noah and his family "safely through water" in the flood], now saves you, not as a removal of dirt from the body but as an appeal to God for a good conscience, through the resurrection of Jesus Christ, who has gone into heaven and is at the right hand of God, with angels, authorities, and powers having been subjected to him." God's first covenant with Noah, then, foresignified Christ in that the ark itself, as the rescue from God's universal judgment, depicts our rescue in Christ from God's coming wrath at the last day.[16] Baptism appeals to God to save us *through the resurrection of Christ* by shielding us in Christ from his wrath, just as he shielded Noah's family in the ark from his flood. God's *first* covenant with Noah then administered the covenant of grace through the ark typifying Christ as the redeemer from God's final judgment.[17]

14. *VRD*, 2:124–27; *MT*, 1.38.14–19; Brown and Keele, *Sacred Bond*, 62–68; *MMB*, 241–48; *EC*, 4.1.25–37; Belcher, *Fulfillment*, 42–46.

15. Miles V. Van Pelt, "The Noahic Covenant of the Covenant of Grace," in *CT*, 111–32; *KP*, 212–20; cf. *KTC*, 199.

16. *EC*, 4.6.21–23; *MMB*, 249–55, 267–70, 274–81; *KP*, 225–41.

17. Thanks to Scott McDermand for his help clarifying how God's first covenant with Noah administered the covenant of grace.

God's other covenant with Noah contributes to redemptive history not by making a redemptive promise concerning Christ, but by promising that God will not destroy the world again. In Genesis 9:9–11, just after the flood, God said to Noah, "Behold, I establish my covenant with you and your offspring after you, and with every living creature that is with you, the birds, the livestock, and every beast of the earth with you, as many as came out of the ark; it is for every beast of the earth. I establish my covenant with you, that never again shall all flesh be cut off by the waters of the flood, and never again shall there be a flood to destroy the earth." God designated the rainbow as this covenant's sign, reassuring every creature that he would not bring such great judgment upon the world again until he fully installs the new creation (Gen 9:12–17).[18] This covenant primarily established a lasting foundation for "common grace," meaning it does not itself offer salvation but confirms the dependability of the world's general order so that the gospel can spread among the human race without God destroying us all.[19] This covenant's promise is not limited to those who believe in the Savior, since everyone benefits from God withholding universal judgment.[20] The Noahic covenant in Genesis 9:1–17 does not properly administer the covenant of grace but facilitates its purpose by upholding the world as the stage for God's unfolding plan.[21]

Nonetheless, Christ was active as Savior throughout Noah's time. Although a difficult passage, 1 Peter 3:18–20 reveals the Son's activity *incarnandus*.

> Because Christ also suffered once for all for sins, the righteous for the unrighteous, in order to bring us to God, being put to death in the flesh but made alive by the Spirit, through whom [the Spirit] also going, he [Christ] preached to the spirits in prison, at the time that they disobeyed, when God's patience waited in Noah's

18. *MMB*, 256–57, 260–62; *EC*, 4.7.21–26.

19. *KTC*, 686; Horton, *Covenant Theology*, 111–28; VanDrunen, *Living in God's Two Kingdoms*, 76–81; *KP*, 153–60; Belcher, *Fulfillment*, 56–57; Schreiner, *Covenant*, 89–90.

20. Van Pelt, "Noahic Covenant," 127–30, VanDrunen, *Divine Covenants*, 95–132; Letham, *Systematic Theology*, 294–95; *KTC*, 199–208; Wellum, "Progressive Covenantalism," 91–92; Schreiner, *Covenant*, 34–38.

21. *VRD*, 2:127; Williamson, *Sealed*, 67–69; *KP*, 244–62; Brown and Keele, *Sacred Bond*, 75–85; Renihan, *Mystery*, 78–84; cf. Belcher, *Fulfillment*, 47–59.

> days while the ark was being built, in which a few, that is, eight souls, were brought safely through water. (my translation)

By virtue of his once-and-for-all death by which he gives life to all believers, *Christ* through the Spirit went and preached to imprisoned spirits *in Noah's days*. Lively interpretations abound for Christ's preaching to imprisoned spirits, but the best suggests that he preached to those imprisoned *in their sin by the law* (Gal 3:21–24).[22]

Several reasons favor this interpretation. First, our discussion of the covenant of redemption showed that the Holy Spirit justified Jesus by making him alive at the resurrection, so our reading of this passage should take into account that the Spirit's work in Christ's resurrection is the premier biblical connection between the Spirit and Christ's being made alive (Rom 1:4). Second, by the Spirit who made him alive, Jesus preached to imprisoned spirits, who were not dead spirits, since Peter also referred to Noah's living family, whom God saved, as "souls." Third, Peter identified the time of Christ's preaching by the Spirit as "*at the time that they disobeyed,* when God's patience waited *in Noah's days while the ark was being built.*"[23] The Triune God's common eternal decree for the Son to save the elect from every age of redemptive history undergirds his ability to preach, by the Spirit's power and task to apply salvation, to bring to faith those given to him in the covenant of redemption.

Just as Paul said that *Christ* preached to the Ephesians without ever going to Ephesus (Eph 2:17), Christ himself likewise preached by the Spirit's power to those under spiritual imprisonment in Noah's time. Christ preached through Paul in Ephesus but through Noah in Noah's day. Christ has always preached through the Spirit through his ministers on earth. Herman Witsius comments,

> The Lord Christ, says he, who was raised from the dead by the infinite power of his Spirit, formerly *went,* came out of heaven, not indeed in the flesh assumed, and personally united to himself, but

---

22. *CG*, 370; *TI*, 12.11.15.

23. For the phrase, ἀπειθήσασιν ποτε, ὅτε ἀπεξεδέχετο, ποτε and ὅτε are both distinctly *temporal* markers, not carrying logical force that many English translations give them in this passage; F. Blass, A. DeBrunner, and Robert W. Funk, *A Greek Grammar of the New Testament and Other Early Christian Literature* (Chicago: University of Chicago Press, 1961), §105; Wallace, *Greek Grammar*, 677, 762.

> in the demonstration of his *Spirit*, by which he formed the prophets, and among them also Noah. By the ministry of these prophets, who were stirred up by his Spirit, he *himself preached*. ... By that preaching, he invited the *spirits* to faith and repentance, that is, those souls of men, which are now separated from the body, and such are usually called *spirits* (Heb.12:23) and are *in prison*. ... Peter therefore declares, that Christ formerly, and especially in the days of Noah, preached by his Spirit, by the prophets; and what else did he preach, but himself, and faith and repentance, whereby they might come to him?[24]

It could not be otherwise since Christ is always the substance of the covenant of grace.

THE PARADIGM OF ABRAHAM

Reformed theology emphasizes the role of God's covenant with Abraham in redemptive history's development. After all, God preached *the gospel* to Abraham so that people from every nation would be justified by faith (Gal 3:8).[25] Abraham is "the father of all who believe," the realization of his salvation by faith recorded specifically for our benefit (Rom 4:11, 22–24). God had promised the seed of the woman to crush the serpent (Gen 3:15), laying special claim to one branch of Noah's line, one offspring, through the lineage of Shem, who was Abraham's ancestor (Gen 9:26–27; Gen 10:10–26).[26] To be a Christian is to be Abraham's offspring and an heir of his inheritance (Gal 3:29). So, God's dealing with Abraham is crucial for how God distributed the gospel in the world.

With Abraham, God covenantally formalized his saving promise. He first called Abraham from paganism, resulting in personal blessing for Abraham and making him a blessing to the whole world (Gen 12:1–3).[27] Abraham became that universal blessing because the gospel itself was announced to him, yet he struggled to have firm confidence in God's

24. *EC*, 4.2.8 (italics original).

25. *CRS*, 1:452–53.

26. *EC*, 4.2.16–21; *CMT*, 84; *KP*, 263–69, 279–89, 292, 327–32; O. Palmer Robertson, "Israel and the Nations in God's Covenants," in *CT*, 509.

27. *EC*, 4.3.11.

promise, particularly of the promised offspring, because he too lived by faith and not by sight (Gen 15:1–8; 2 Cor 5:7). So, God ratified his promise with a covenant, confirming his commitment to provide Abraham with the one heir who would make him the father of many nations (Gen 15:9–21).[28] To this covenant promise, God added the sign of circumcision (Gen 17:1–14).[29] God's dealings with Abraham, then, sharpen his promises about an offspring to rescue fallen humanity into new specificity through a covenant.[30]

The Abrahamic covenant pivotally administers the covenant of grace. At the *historia salutis* level, the promise of Abraham's offspring advances the promise of an offspring from Genesis 3:15, confirming and progressing the promise of the coming redeemer. Through this offspring, Abraham became the father of many nations. Isaac initially realized that promise, but Christ ultimately fulfills the seed of the woman and the seed of Abraham, uniting all believers under Abraham's fatherhood (Rom 4:11; Gal 3:29).[31] So, the Abrahamic covenant carries forward God's promise by preserving a specific line through which the ultimate offspring of the woman came.[32]

The Abrahamic covenant also indicates how, regardless of other blessings God bestowed on the nation of Israel, he always intended the gospel for people from all over the world.[33] In Genesis 12:1–3, God's initial promise included that "all the families of the earth shall be blessed" in Abraham. In Genesis 17:4–8, God sealed that promise by giving Abraham the covenant sign of circumcision to seal his faith:

> Behold, my covenant is with you, and you shall be the father of a multitude of nations. No longer shall your name be called Abram, but your name shall be Abraham, for I have made you the

---

28. John Scott Redd, "The Abrahamic Covenant," in *CT*, 138–41; *KP*, 295–300; Belcher, *Fulfillment*, 63–65, 70; Brown and Keele, *Sacred Bond*, 92–93.

29. *MMB*, 545–46; Redd, "Abrahamic Covenant," 141–42; *KP*, 312–14; *KTC*, 312–18; Belcher, *Fulfillment*, 68; Renihan, *Mystery*, 89–94; Schreiner, *Covenant*, 48–50; cf. Williamson, *Sealed*, 89–91.

30. *KP*, 292–93; Brown and Keele, *Sacred Bond*, 87.

31. Gordon, *Promise, Law, Faith*, 134–37; *EC*, 4.3.24–25; Belcher, *Fulfillment*, 72–73; Brown and Keele, *Sacred Bond*, 88–89, 94–97; Schreiner, *Covenant*, 43–44.

32. *TI*, 12.7.20; *MMB*, 361–66; *EC*, 4.3.16–19; Waters, "Covenant in Paul," 232–34.

33. *EC*, 4.3.15.

> father of a multitude of nations. I will make you exceedingly fruitful, and I will make you into nations, and kings shall come from you. And I will establish my covenant between me and you and your offspring after you throughout their generations for an everlasting covenant, to be God to you and to your offspring after you. And I will give to you and to your offspring after you the land of your sojournings, all the land of Canaan, for an everlasting possession, and I will be their God.

God restated the promise to make Abraham the father of many nations, ultimately fulfilling this promise in the gospel, as he always intended, by justifying gentiles by faith, just like he had Abraham (Gal 3:6–9).[34]

At the *ordo salutis* level, the New Testament directly links the Abrahamic covenant to spiritual blessings that we still receive in the new covenant.[35] Galatians 3:7–14 directly relates this promise to the gospel.[36] This promise not only preached the gospel (Gal 3:8) but also confirmed that "it is those of faith who are the sons of Abraham" because Christ's work was "so that in Christ Jesus the blessing of Abraham might come to the Gentiles, so that we might receive the promised Spirit through faith" (Gal 3:7, 14).[37] The promise of Genesis 12:3, about "all the nations" being blessed in Abraham, is fulfilled when "God would justify *the Gentiles* by faith" (Gal 3:8). Acts 3:18–26 likewise recounts the prophets foretelling that Christ would suffer for the forgiveness of sin, highlighting that Moses spoke about Christ and that Christians are the sons of the covenant that God made with the fathers. Peter specifically referred to the covenant with Abraham in the promise God made in Genesis 12:1–3 and repeated in Genesis 22:18 (Gal 3:25).[38] So, the apostles understood this promise about nations to regard personal salvation.[39]

Abraham's fatherhood always primarily referred to personal salvation in Christ. In Genesis 17:7, God confirmed his promise that "I will establish

34. *MMB*, 356–61.

35. *KTC*, 332–37.

36. "The life pledged in the Abrahamic administration, however, was real eschatological life" Gordon, *Promise, Law, Faith*, 152.

37. Watson, *Hermeneutics of Faith*, 176–77.

38. Williamson, *Sealed*, 185–86.

39. Watson, *Hermeneutics of Faith*, 170–77.

my covenant between me and you and your offspring after you throughout their generations for an everlasting covenant, to be God to you and to your offspring after you." John Calvin comments on the phrase "to be God to you":

> In this single word we are plainly taught, that this was a spiritual covenant, not confirmed in reference to the present life only; but one from which Abraham might receive the hope of eternal salvation, so that being raised even to heaven, he might lay hold of solid and perfect bliss. ... Let us then mark this as the principal part of the covenant, that He who is the God of the living, not of the dead, promises to be a God to the children of Abraham.[40]

God sealed this promise to Abraham through the sign of circumcision, given to Abraham because he had faith.[41] Abraham's fatherhood has always been foremost about the spiritual promise of justification by faith and reception of the Spirit (Rom 4:11–12; Gal 3:7–14).[42]

In Genesis 17:8, God also promised the land of Canaan to Abraham. This promise is also partially fulfilled when God brought Israel out of Egypt into the land (Neh 9:7–8). Abraham himself, however, understood that promise to be truly about far more than a plot of land in the Middle East.[43] Hebrews 11:8–10 says, "By faith Abraham obeyed when he was called to go out to a place that he was to receive as an inheritance. And he went out, not knowing where he was going. By faith he went to live in the land of promise, as in a foreign land, living in tents with Isaac and Jacob, heirs with him of the same promise. For he was looking forward to the city that has foundations, whose designer and builder is God." By his faith, the same as new-covenant saving faith, Abraham knew that this land of inheritance signified something greater. He lived in tents rather than building cities because he understood that God, through the gospel, promised him "the city that has foundations," the new creation itself (Heb 11:13–16).[44] Abraham recognized that this land was just a type

40. *CC*, 1:1.450.

41. *TI*, 12.7.21.

42. *EC*, 4.3.14–19; Schreiner, *Covenant*, 46.

43. *EC*, 4.3.26; Brown and Keele, *Sacred Bond*, 94–97.

44. *CC*, 22:1.280; *CC*, 1:450–51; *KTC*, 828–38.

pointing to the ultimate offspring's capturing the world through salvation. So, Paul writes in Romans 4:13: "For the promise to Abraham and his offspring that he would be heir of the world did not come through the law but through the righteousness of faith." God's promise of land for Abraham and his family always concerned Abraham as the father of faith having a global family in the new creation.[45]

In that light, even God's covenant promises to Abraham about earthly blessings cannot be reduced to their earthly significance or limited to his biological descendants.[46] Paul, explaining how the old covenant no longer applies to believers, directly links Abraham and our experience in the new covenant precisely because the emphasis for Abraham, even in the types that foreshadowed Christ and his benefits, was on the *spiritual* realities.[47] Even circumcision as the Abrahamic covenant's sacrament was not simply about following a genealogical family line.[48] Specifically, "He received the sign of circumcision as a seal of the righteousness that he had by faith while he was still uncircumcised" (Rom 4:11). Circumcision acted as a sign that sealed his righteousness by faith, which would "make him the father of all who believe" (Rom 4:11). Abraham's circumcision marked the spiritual reality that he was the forefather of faith to all who trust in Christ.

Fundamentally, circumcision was a type, *chiefly* foresignifying Christ's crucifixion and the spiritual reality that comes to us by his death. Throughout the Old Testament, God's prophets exhorted the people about their need for the circumcision of their hearts, which the New Testament confirms was always a reality symbolized in physical circumcision (Deut 10:16; 30:6; Jer 4:4; 9:25–26; Rom 2:28–29). Physical circumcision, therefore, *always* signified heart circumcision, making it the *sacrament* of the new heart during the old economy but a sacrament whose further role as a *type* taught about how Christ's work procured that new heart for his people.[49] In Colossians 2:11–12, Paul writes: "In him also, you have been circumcised with circumcision made without hands through the putting

---

45. *BTA*, 168–75; *KP*, 336–40.

46. *MMB*, 371–89; *EC*, 4.3.20.

47. *TI*, 12.7.18–19; *KP*, 302–7, 332–40.

48. Belcher, *Fulfillment*, 70–71.

49. *MT*, 1.38.25; *CMT*, 87; *EC*, 4.7.15; *KP*, 314–18; *BOC*, 39–49.

off of the body of the flesh in Christ's circumcision, by being buried with him in baptism through which also you have been raised together [with him] by faith in God's work of raising him from the dead" (my translation). Most crucially, this passage concerns not primarily the circumcision of our hearts, but Christ's death. "Christ's circumcision" was his crucifixion, since his "body of the flesh" was put off in that circumcision when he was killed.[50]

More specifically, in his circumcision-crucifixion, Christ was cut off for his people, highlighting how circumcision was most foundationally a type of Christ and his work, rather than a type of God's spiritual work in our hearts.[51] The Christian's experience of being circumcised with this handless circumcision is not God's work of regeneration but the reality of being "crucified with Christ" in his crucifixion-circumcision unto the forgiveness of sin (Gal 2:19–20). Although Colossians 2:11–12 is relevant again when we consider the new covenant, the primary point here is that, even though the circumcision of our hearts in renewal is based upon Christ's death to secure our new life, Abrahamic circumcision most fundamentally typified Christ's future work for us rather than his work in us. It was a means of grace to administer Christ and his benefits by foresignifying Christ's death rather than *merely* an external sign of an inward work. So, John Davenant (1572–1641) comments, "Abraham by submitting to this sign declared and confirmed his faith concerning Christ, to be born of his seed, free from all sin; but we do not look for Christ to be born, but believe that he is born."[52] By pointing to the reality of righteousness by faith directly connected to Christ's cross, Abraham's circumcision, which *was the covenant* between him and God, administered the promise about Christ, thereby the substance of the covenant of grace.[53]

---

50. This interpretation takes the genitive in τῇ περιτομὴ τοῦ Χριστοῦ as objective. The phrase certainly relates to the preceding clause, ἐν τῇ ἀπεκδύσει τοῦ σωματος τῆς σαρκός, and the only other usage of the phrase "the body of the flesh" occurs in Colossians 1:22 as an obvious reference to Christ's human body. So, in Christ's circumcision his body of flesh is put off, which refers to when he died on the cross; *WWS*, 239–40; Peter T. O'Brien, *Colossians, Philemon* (Mexico City: Thomas Nelson, 2000), 116–17; *BOC*, 45–47, 70–73.

51. Cf. John D. Meade, "Circumcision of Flesh to Circumcision of Heart: The Typology of the Sign of the Abrahamic Covenant," in *Progressive Covenantalism*, 127–58.

52. John Davenant, *An Exposition of the Epistle of Paul to the Colossians*, trans. Josiah Allport, 2 vol. (London: Hamilton, Adams, and Co., 1831), 1:436.

53. *BRD*, 4:526–27; Horton, "Covenant Theology," 60–65.

THE MOSAIC COVENANT'S RELATIONSHIP TO THE ABRAHAMIC

God's covenant with Israel under Moses must be considered, not just abstractly, but within God's already-begun story. At the end of Genesis, God had certainly been good to Abraham's descendants, specifically the line of Jacob. Joseph had become a high-ranking official in Pharaoh's court and had made provisions for his extended family to live well in part of Egypt called Goshen (Gen 50). After Joseph had faded from Egyptian memory, Pharaohs began to oppress and use his people as slaves because they had become so plentiful (Exod 1). When the people had been in captivity for four hundred and thirty years, God acted on his covenant promises to Abraham's family. Moses recounts: "During those many days the king of Egypt died, and the people of Israel groaned because of their slavery and cried out for help. Their cry for rescue from slavery came up to God. And God heard their groaning, and God remembered his covenant with Abraham, with Isaac, and with Jacob. God saw the people of Israel—and God knew" (Exod 2:23–25). Because of his promises to Abraham, God rescued Israel from Egyptian captivity.[54] Notably, this passage indicates that *Israel* was a people, one connected to the Abrahamic promise, before they were constituted as a legal nation covenanted with God.[55] Their rescue from slavery became a paradigm for how God's people understood the pattern of salvation.[56] Once God redeemed Israel from Egypt, he made a covenant with them at Mount Sinai, constituting them as a theocratic and geopolitical nation, establishing the nature of his relationship to this nation, and defining Israel's redemptive-historical purposes in providing types and symbols about Christ and his work.[57]

In some ways, the Mosaic covenant built upon the Abrahamic. Fundamentally, salvation in Christ remains the same for the true believer under the Mosaic economy (Matt 17:1–13; Rom 4:6–8; 1 Cor 10:1–4; Heb 3:1–6; Jude 1:5). Individual Israelites were saved by believing in the coming Messiah, namely, as God appointed the Mosaic covenant's ordinances

54. Belcher, *Fulfillment*, 75–77; *KTC*, 442; Williamson, *Sealed*, 94–96.

55. *MMB*, 649–50.

56. Estelle, *Echoes of Exodus*.

57. *VRD*, 2:129; Brown and Keele, *Sacred Bond*, 104–8.

fundamentally as means of grace. The animal sacrifices were sacramental types foresignifying Christ's sacrifice on the cross as our substitute (Lev 16), and the thanksgiving offerings foresignified Christ's active obedience as the one who fulfilled the law in our place (Lev 7; Hos 6:4–6).[58]

Even before ratifying the Mosaic covenant at Sinai, God instituted the Passover as a sacrament. The initial meal commemorated God's mercy in sparing those whose doors were covered in the blood of the lamb from losing their firstborn in the final plague against Egypt (Exod 11–12). Regarding this seal upon God's saving grace, Roberts argues,

> This sacrament was instituted before the giving of the law on Mount Sinai, a little before Israel's departure out of Egypt, and was first celebrated on that very night when they went out of Egypt, at the end of 430 years to a day from God's first covenant and promise to Abraham in Ur of the Chaldees. Therefore, though this sacrament was ordained in the days of Moses, yet being ordained before the Sinai covenant was made about three months, it cannot belong to the Sinai covenant which was not then in being but must needs be most properly annexed to God's last federal dispensation foregoing, which was God's covenant with Abraham and his seed. So then the Passover was added for confirming of God's covenant with Abraham and his seed.[59]

The meal was repeated annually as a memorial of God accepting the blood of the lamb in place of taking lives from Israelite families (Exod 12:12–14).

The sacrificial lamb foresignified Christ as the lamb of God who bears the sins of the world (John 1:29).[60] In 1 Corinthians 5:7–8, Paul drew the connection explicitly to Christ: "Cleanse out the old leaven that you may be a new lump, as you really are unleavened. For Christ, our Passover lamb, has been sacrificed. Let us therefore celebrate the festival, not with the old leaven, the leaven of malice and evil, but with the unleavened bread of sincerity and truth." His point is that as Israel cleared its homes of leaven in preparation for the Passover lamb, all the more Christians

---

58. Horton, "Obedience Is Better than Sacrifice," 315–36.

59. *MMB*, 546.

60. *EC*, 4.9.36–40; *MMB*, 547–50.

should urgently set aside sin because Christ is the total of the Passover lamb. The Passover was a memorial of Israel's rescue from Egypt, but that rescue itself pointed forward to how Christ would liberate his people from slavery to sin.[61] Importantly, however, the Passover along with circumcision, as repeatable sacraments given prior to and distinct from the Mosaic administration, pointed directly to spiritual promises about Christ. The Passover, at the *historia salutis* level, deepened the anticipation of God's once-and-for-all Lamb who would come to make satisfaction for his people's sin but, at the *ordo salutis* level, was a typological sacrament wherein believers truly received Christ and his benefits.

Further, the Mosaic covenant picked up the promises to Abraham concerning nations coming from him and concerning the land (Gen 17:4–8). In connection with those promises, God brought Israel from Egypt, declared them to be his people, and gave Canaan to them (Exod 6:2–8). In making his covenant with Abraham, God promised that Abraham's descendants would be as many as the stars (Gen 15:5). He added to that promise for Isaac that his offspring would be as many as the sands on the shore (Gen 22:16–18). In the Mosaic covenant, "Judah and Israel were as many as the sand by the sea" (1 Kgs 4:20). The nation took possession of Canaan, at least for a time (Deut 32:49). Even though the Abrahamic covenant focused on spiritual realities, God kept his promises to Abraham even at an earthly level by making Israel his nation and giving Canaan to them.[62] This unified network of provisional promise fulfillment served as types of Christ.

This fulfillment of the Abrahamic covenant, however, was only provisional and the Mosaic covenant did not serve as the ultimate fulfillment of the promises to Abraham.[63] The Mosaic covenant itself distinctly focused on earthly aspects of fulfilling God's promises.[64] Augustine goes so far as to write, "In that testament, however, which is properly called the Old, and was given on Mount Sinai, only earthly happiness is expressly promised."[65] Whereas Abraham focuses on spiritual realities with some

61. *VRD*, 5:202–3.

62. *MMB*, 654–56; Belcher, *Fulfillment*, 87–88.

63. Cf. *KTC*, 442.

64. Michael J. Glodo, "Dispensationalism," in *CT*, 544–45; Brown and Keele, *Sacred Bond*, 113.

65. Augustine, *On the Proceedings of Pelagius*, §14, in *NPNF1*, 5:189.

earthly implications, Moses latches onto those earthly implications to emphasize their *typological* value, which *primarily* taught about what the heavenly realities signified.[66] The next chapter explores the typology of the Mosaic covenant more thoroughly, but this discussion demonstrates already the Mosaic covenant's links to the Abrahamic respecting God's promises and spiritual realities.

CONCLUSION

God does not change as time passes in creation but remains eternally faithful, dependable, and true. Directly after the fall, he promised to provide redemption for his people. He kept, preserved, and extended his promise throughout redemptive history. Moreover, his people did not have to wait for the historical fulfillment of the promise of the redeemer to take part in his blessings. God provided salvation through faith in Christ *incarnandus* to those who lived before Christ came *incarnatus*.

The pastoral use of this chapter's material is to see how God always fully provides for his people, even though sometimes that provision is not fully clear to us as we experience it. God gave to Old Testament saints promises and types, which "were for that time sufficient and efficacious, through the operation of the Spirit, to instruct and build up the elect in faith in the promised Messiah, by whom they had full remission of sins, and eternal salvation, and is called the Old Testament."[67] Those believers may often have wished for greater clarity than they had, but God gave them what they needed to be sufficient so that they could believe in Christ and walk with him. When we wish for greater clarity about God's provision in our lives too, we ought to trust that what God has given is sufficient for the moment.

66. Gordon, *Promise, Law, Faith*, 151–52; Belcher, *Fulfillment*, 93–95.

67. WCF 7.5; *COC*, 3:618.

XIII

The Mosaic Covenant

For the law was given through Moses;
grace and truth came through Jesus Christ.
—*John 1:17*

The Old Testament narrative predominantly focuses on the Mosaic covenant, suggesting its deserved amount of attention among God's various administrations for distributing Christ and his benefits to his people. Reformed theologians have disagreed most about the Mosaic covenant, making it hardest to discuss. Anthony Burgess (1600–1664) approaches this topic with charitable care, noting that more theologians end up "being like Abraham's Ram, hung in a bush of briars and brambles by the head" concerning the Mosaic covenant than any other issue.[1] Some readers may consider this discussion stuck in that bush too, but at least it shares company with the genuinely learned men Burgess says struggled as well. This chapter outlines how the Mosaic covenant, as the covenant of grace's administration most predominated by legal features, exhibited Christ and his work by providing types that display Christ's obedience for us. So, the Mosaic covenant is identical in substance with the other administrations of the covenant of grace but differs significantly in its outward and typological features.[2] It

1. Anthony Burgess, *Vindiciae Legis* (London: Thomas Underhill, 1646), 219; *MMB*, 738.

2. Estelle et al., "Report to ... Study Republication," 30–31, 40–44, 50–51.

was the covenant of grace as to its substance but uniquely administered the covenant of grace in a way appropriate for that stage in redemptive history so that its legal features demonstrate our need for Christ to satisfy the covenant of works for us.[3] Nonetheless, this chapter contributes to the ongoing argument that God communicated Christ and his benefits to believers through the means of grace in each covenant administration.

THE MOSAIC COVENANT RESEMBLED THE COVENANT OF WORKS

The Mosaic covenant's types make it in some ways resemble the original covenant of works. Despite some continuity, the Mosaic covenant does not merely extend the Abrahamic. In Deuteronomy 5:1–3, Moses emphasized the difference: "Hear, O Israel, the statutes and the rules that I speak in your hearing today, and you shall learn them and be careful to do them. The LORD our God made a covenant with us in Horeb. *Not with our fathers did the LORD make this covenant*, but with us, who are all of us here alive today." After highlighting God's statutes and rules, which the people had said "we will do" (Exod 24:3), Moses noted that this covenant differed from the covenant God had made with their ancestors.[4]

The Mosaic covenant required Israel *as a nation* to obey the law.[5] The principle of grace alone remains for each individual's salvation, but a real works principle operated for the nation holistically, meaning Israel's obligations had sanctions attached for blessing or curse.[6] Salvation was only by grace, but the nation's obedience maintained earthly blessings.[7]

When God gave the law, the surrounding events showed the nature of the Mosaic covenant. In Exodus 19:3–8, the people of Israel have escaped

---

3. Estelle et al, "Report to ... Study Republication," 39–40. In this report's language, the Mosaic covenant was "in substance a covenant of grace" so that its "legal elements belong to the administrative level."

4. *VRD*, 2:132; *LG*, 67; Brown and Keele, *Sacred Bond*, 108–16; Michael G. McKelvey, "The New Covenant as Promised in the Major Prophets," in *CT*, 192–94; cf. Renihan, *Mystery*, e.g. 97, 108.

5. For the covenant as between God and the nation, see *MMB*, 790–800; *LG*, 72–85; *WWG*, 257.

6. "The Sinai covenant is an administration of the covenant of grace. ... The Sinai covenant was never an alternative way of salvation: by law rather than by promise." Horton, *Rediscovering*, 140n4; *KP*, 321; Estelle et al., "Report to ... Study Republication," 6–8.

7. Michael Horton, "Kingdom of God," in *CD*, 364–69; *KP*, 109; Brown and Keele, *Sacred Bond*, 104–8.

Pharoah's army and make camp at Sinai where Moses has ascended the mountain. There, God said to him,

> "Thus you shall say to the house of Jacob, and tell the people of Israel: 'You yourselves have seen what I did to the Egyptians, and how I bore you on eagles' wings and brought you to myself. Now therefore, if you will indeed obey my voice and keep my covenant, you shall be my treasured possession among all peoples, for all the earth is mine; and you shall be to me a kingdom of priests and a holy nation.' These are the words that you shall speak to the people of Israel." So Moses came and called the elders of the people and set before them all these words that the LORD had commanded him. All the people answered together and said, "All that the LORD has spoken we will do."

God reminded Israel about his judgment upon Pharaoh's army, grounding his exhortation that "*if you will indeed obey my voice* and keep my covenant, you shall be my treasured possession among all peoples."[8] God initiated this covenant in light of judging his enemies, hence, calling for obedience. The elders confer, and Israel says together, "All that the LORD has spoken we will do," accepting the conditions.[9]

Even as God revealed the moral law in light of this works principle, we cannot lose sight of the Mosaic covenant's fundamental identity as part of the covenant of grace. God's preface to the Decalogue reminds of redemption: "I am the LORD your God, who brought you out of the land of Egypt, out of the house of slavery" (Exod 20:2).[10] Centering this preface within God's fatherly relationship to his people, the Westminster Shorter Catechism explains its significance, stating, "Because God is the Lord, and our God and redeemer, therefore we are bound to keep all his commandments" (WSC 44).[11] This covenant, even with its legal focus, refracts through the covenant of grace.[12] No matter the national covenant's

---

8. Gladd, *Adam and Israel to the Church*, 42–43; Belcher, *Fulfillment*, 77–79.

9. *EC*, 4.4.46.

10. Belcher, *Fulfillment*, 80, 87.

11. *COC*, 3:685.

12. *LG*, 55–56, 58–59.

shape for typological and redemptive historical purposes, God provided salvation itself only by grace alone.[13]

Further, not only is the Mosaic covenant's substance Christ and his benefits, as in all the covenant of grace's administrations, but its core condition to receive its spiritual efficacy is faith alone.[14] Its core condition, after all, pertained specifically to its primary substance, namely, Christ. Hence James Buchanan (1804–1870) contended that "the addition of the law was not intended to alter either the ground or the method of a sinner's justification" but was promulgated to make known sinners' need for free grace.[15] The Mosaic covenant was, fundamentally, the covenant of grace, since Christ was its "essential parts." Buchanan outlined the Mosaic covenant's two distinct aspects: "*first*, as a system of religion and government" in which case Christ and the substance were the administration's *primary* focus. Then, only *secondarily* at the redemptive-historical level, "*secondly*, as a scheme of preparation for another and better economy," one in which the substance was displayed directly rather than by types and shadows.[16] Accordingly, "The economy of Moses, whatever prominence it gave to the law, was unquestionably a dispensation of the covenant of grace."[17] Any conditions that resembled the works principle were typological conditions pertaining to typological benefits, meaning that these conditions and benefits belonged to the covenant secondarily, both being "accidentals" not belonging to the covenant's substance or essence but only its administrative level.[18] The Mosaic covenant then demanded faith in Christ (Ps 78:21–22; Isa 28:14–16; 43:8–10; Jude 1:5).

Even at the redemptive-historical level, the Mosaic covenant was fundamentally about grace, although perhaps not in a direct fashion. Its outward ordinances were frightening as the works principle informed its typological features—not its substance—but God appointed even these typological ordinances as a teacher unto Christ so that all would be justified by faith in him (Gal 3:23–26), reviving a *reflection* of the covenant

13. Hodge, *Systematic Theology*, 2:374–76; Brown and Keele, *Sacred Bond*, 116–18.

14. Estelle et al, "Report to ... Study Republication," 11–12.

15. Buchanan, *Justification*, 36.

16. Buchanan, *Justification*, 35 (italics original).

17. Buchanan, *Justification*, 37.

18. *TI*, 12.5.5.

of works "in the interests of the covenant of grace continued at Sinai."[19] As every sacrament marks a reality beyond itself, old covenant types, as Vos said, "led the people to something better" by delivering the reality of the good things to come in shadowy form.[20] Because Mosaic ordinances' forward-looking typological content and their symbolic significance for their own day was identical, namely, Christ and his benefits, they simultaneously typified, at the *historia salutis* level, and sacramentally applied, at the *ordo salutis* level, Christ and all his benefits for old covenant believers.[21] God had no mixed purposes for the Mosaic covenant, using it to promote grace substantially and historically, albeit in different manners. Its substance is not works even if its types have a legal tenor. As Westminster Assemblyman Robert Baillie (1599–1662) explained, the covenant of grace under Moses "had adjoined to it upon Mount Sinai the old covenant of works to be a severe pedagogue for the pointing out the way to Christ."[22] Although the new covenant presents the same substance under sacraments that clearly display its grace, none of Moses's legal shadows "change the state and nature of the principall; it remains ever a covenant of pure grace without any mixture."[23] Moses's substance was Christ, although he was given through shadowy ordinances that drive believers to him through sacramental reminders of the covenant of works.

Those legal features appear quickly despite God's fatherly preface as the people reacted uncomfortably when God recounted the moral law. Exodus 20:18–21 recounts:

> Now when all the people saw the thunder and the flashes of lightning and the sound of the trumpet and the mountain smoking, the people were afraid and trembled, and they stood far off and said to Moses, "You speak to us, and we will listen; but do not let God speak to us, lest we die." Moses said to the people, "Do not fear, for God has come to test you, that the fear of him may be before

19. Vos, "Doctrine of the Covenant," 255.

20. Vos, *Hebrews*, 65–68.

21. *VBT*, 144–48. Thanks to Carlton Wynne for this passage.

22. Robert Baillie, *Anabaptism the True Fountaine of Independency, Brownisme, Antinomy, Familisme, and the Most of the Other Errours, Which for the Time Doe Trouble the Church of England, Unsealed* (London: Samuel Gellibrand, 1647), 141.

23. Baillie, *Anabaptism*, 142; Estelle et al., "Report to ... Study Republication," 16–17.

> you, that you may not sin." The people stood far off, while Moses drew near to the thick darkness where God was.

The view that, in every context, God's law *simply* regulates life under grace, as if the whole Mosaic law *merely* guided sanctification, overlooks the Scripture's negative assessment of the law.[24] The law always abides as a rule to direct our lives but, *as a covenant* to Israel, does not *simply* regulate life under grace.

The storms, noise, and fire accompanying the law terrified the people. Herman Witsius notes that the Sinai law "was a repetition of the covenant of works" since "those tremendous signs of thunders and lightenings, of an earthquake, a thick smoke and black darkness, were adapted to strike Israel with great terror."[25] The frightened people wanted distance from God.[26]

Pivotally, the people cried for Moses to mediate between them and God.[27] As Adam hid from God when he broke the law, so Israel wanted distance from God as he announced the law.[28] The Heidelberg Catechism unpacks reasons for this Mosaic revelation wherein "God so strictly enjoin[ed] upon us the ten commandments," so that "all our life long we may learn more and more to know our sinful nature, and so the more earnestly seek forgiveness of sins and righteousness in Christ" and "may continually strive and beg from God the grace of the Holy Ghost, so as to become more and more changed into the image of God, till we attain finally the full perfection after this life" (HC 115).[29] From its first moment, the Mosaic covenant accentuated God's people's need for a mediator.

The people's fear, prompting their desire for a mediator, illumines the Mosaic covenant's resemblance to the covenant of works. Just as God gave the law about the tree to Adam *for probation*, he gave the law to Israel at Sinai *for probation*, as Moses said: "Do not fear, for *God has come to test you*, that the fear of him may be before you, that you may not sin" (Exod

24. Letham, *Systematic Theology*, 349–65.

25. *EC*, 4.4.48.

26. *LG*, 64–66; *EC*, 4.4.12.

27. *MMB*, 678.

28. *MMB*, 910–13.

29. *COC*, 3:349.

20:20). The fear-inducing law made the Mosaic covenant resemble the covenant of works because both had a law to test God's covenant people. Nonetheless, critical redemptive-historical reasons undergird Moses's appeal to the law's testing role to exhort the people not to fear before their God.

The Mosaic administration's demand for national obedience related not to their salvation, but to their blessings in the land, specifically for the sake of typology. In Deuteronomy 28:1–2, God said to the people: "And if you faithfully obey the voice of the LORD your God, being careful to do all his commandments that I command you today, the LORD your God will set you high above all the nations of the earth. And all these blessings shall come upon you and overtake you, if you obey the voice of the LORD your God." God then recounted rewards for their obedience pertaining to life in the land, such as blessings on the cities and fields (28:3, 7), children (28:4), and farming (28:5). God's blessing would touch every area of life *if* the people would obey his voice. Markedly, even when God called Abraham to obedience in the covenant (Gen 17:1–2), he never imposed this "if-then" sort of condition upon Abraham's reception of any of the promises.[30]

This aspect of Mosaic typology functioned to highlight what is often called the law's second use, namely, to teach people about their need for a Savior as they realize their inability to keep God's law. In years long past, high school home economics classes would give eggs to students to test how well they were able to care for a baby ... as if those are the same. Recognizing that eggs greatly differ from babies, the exercise had a sort of reasonability: if you cannot protect an egg for a week, you are likely not ready for a baby. The egg as a lesser version of the higher reality it symbolized, namely, a baby, revealed that students weren't ready for the real thing. In a similar manner, the Mosaic covenant taught Israel about what it takes to obtain heavenly everlasting life. When Israel failed to keep the law, God sent them into exile. In the way that inability to care for an egg shows how someone is not ready for the greater responsibility of caring for a baby, Israel's inability to keep the merely *earthly* dwelling by their covenant's demands for obedience teaches us all how our works are then certainly not adequate to obtain life in *heavenly* blessing. If their

30. Watson, *Hermeneutics of Faith*, 173.

obedience could not keep them in the promised land, it certainly would not get them into heaven. This point built into the Mosaic covenant was meant to teach us as well as them.

The nation's legal conditions for maintaining earthly blessings highlight this administration's major types. The Mosaic covenant preserved the Abrahamic covenant's use of the promised land as a type of the new creation (Heb 3:7–4:13; 11:8–10, 13–16).[31] With Moses, the nation's obligation to keep the land by their obedience taught about Christ by showing the requirement to earn the right to live in the new creation by perfect law keeping.[32] God called Israel out of Egypt as his son (Exod 4:22–23; Hos 11:1), giving this legal covenant that taught that obedience obtains the promised land in God's presence.[33] Jesus is God's natural Son, whom God also called out of Egypt (Matt 2:13–15), who was born under the law (Gal 4:4) but proved successful in earning the new creation. The Mosaic covenant's conditional aspect most distinctly contributes to typology precisely in its emphasis on national Israel's covenantal relationship to those earthly features of God's promises to Abraham. Israel as a covenanted nation would reap blessings or suffer curses depending on their corporate obedience. The nation's legal conditions were a type, teaching about Christ's active obedience in fulfilling the law as the covenant of works to obtain new creation life for his people.[34] All these aspects of typological obedience differentiate the Mosaic covenant from the new covenant, which has no conditions of *typological* obedience to maintain blessings but only the call to Spirit-powered sanctification.

The Mosaic covenant, then, has significant points of similarity with the covenant of works. Most generally, Adam and Israel were God's sons (Luke 3:38; Hos 11:1). Adam lived in the garden paradise and Israel lived in the promised land, often described like Eden (Gen 2:8–15; Num 24:5–9; Joel 2:3). God dwelt in the temple in the garden and in Jerusalem (Gen 2:8–15; 1 Kgs 8:13). Both Adam and Israel were exiled from their holy space.[35] The Mosaic covenant even widely corresponds to the covenant

31. *MT*, 1.38.28; *LG*, 67.

32. *EC*, 4.4.54; Brown and Keele, *Sacred Bond*, 113–16.

33. Wellum, "Progressive Covenantalism," 84.

34. Gladd, *Adam and Israel to the Church*, 47–49, 61–63.

35. Horton, *Justification*, 2:66–76.

of works, Israel functioning as a corporate Adam.[36] In this respect, Hosea 6:7 compared Israel's breaking the Mosaic covenant to Adam's covenant violation, saying they broke it in the same manner as he did.[37]

Further, the Mosaic covenant more specifically resembles the covenant of works. Even in its original context, Leviticus 18:5, which the Reformed understand to summarize the covenant of works' "do this and live" premise, establishes a works principle for the nation regarding their earthly blessings. In Leviticus 18:24–29, God explained,

> Do not make yourselves unclean by any of these things, for by all these the nations I am driving out before you have become unclean, and the land became unclean, so that I punished its iniquity, and the land vomited out its inhabitants. But you shall keep my statutes and my rules and do none of these abominations, either the native or the stranger who sojourns among you (for the people of the land, who were before you, did all of these abominations, so that the land became unclean), lest the land vomit you out when you make it unclean, as it vomited out the nation that was before you. For everyone who does any of these abominations, the persons who do them shall be cut off from among their people.

This conclusion to Leviticus 18's commandments shows that the law's "do this and live" principle does not *simply* guide believers in holiness.[38] Witsius argues that the Mosaic administration included "a repetition of the doctrine concerning the law of the covenant of works" because "the very same precepts are inculcated, on which the covenant of works was founded, and which constituted the condition of that covenant." Further, "the terror of the covenant of works is increased by repeated comminations." The result was "as the requirement of obedience was rigid under the ministry of Moses, the promises of spiritual and saving grace were more rare and obscure."[39] Israel was ejected from the land because they did not keep God's law according to the legal principle of God's covenant with them.

---

36. Gladd, *Adam and Israel to the Church*, 36–56; Crowe, *Last Adam*, 56–67; VanDrunen, "Israel's Recapitulation," 304–6; Fesko, "Republication," 204; Schreiner, *Covenant*, 67.

37. Curtis, "Hosea 6:7," 170–209.

38. Estelle, "Leviticus 18:5 and Deuteronomy 30:1–14," 109–146; Fesko, "Republication," 206.

39. *EC*, 4.4.47.

Israel's exile repeated Adam and Eve's ejection from the garden upon Adam transgressing the covenant law. Notably, Adam's first sin was not properly against the moral law but against the probationary command regarding the tree. Adam possessed the garden most pointedly by obedience to a *symbolic* law. Israel also possessed the promised land most pointedly by their obedience to a body of legal material that was far more extensive than the moral law (Exod 21–24). Francis Gomarus (1563–1641) explains how the Mosaic covenant repeated the covenant of works by noting it had "added a special and handwritten test of obedience, namely the yoke of ceremonies, the jagged burdens (as Tertullian called them), and this concerns the natural covenant."[40] The Mosaic covenant, then, resembles the covenant of works as possession of the holy space depends most pointedly on obedience to symbolic laws.[41]

The prophets invoked Leviticus 18:5's works principle. In Ezekiel 20:10–13, the prophet recounts how God rescued Israel from Egypt and gave them the covenant based on the "do this and live" principle:

> So I led them out of the land of Egypt and brought them into the wilderness. I gave them my statutes and made known to them my rules, by which, if a person does them, he shall live. Moreover, I gave them my Sabbaths, as a sign between me and them, that they might know that I am the LORD who sanctifies them. But the house of Israel rebelled against me in the wilderness. They did not walk in my statutes but rejected my rules, by which, if a person does them, he shall live; and my Sabbaths they greatly profaned.

Even framed against Israel's redemption from Egypt and the promise of personal salvation by grace alone, the Mosaic covenant's application of "do this and live" is not itself grace and guidance.[42] It brings judgment for breaking, specifically, the symbolic laws of the system of annual

40. Francis Gomarus, "Oration concerning God's Covenant," in *Opera Theologica Omnia* (Amsterdam: Johannes Janssonius, 1664), sig. (*)2v.

41. Horton, *Justification*, 2:81–86; Roberts rejects this understanding of the Mosaic covenant; see *MMB*, 734–89.

42. Watson, *Hermeneutics of Faith*, 296; *ACW*, 204–6.

Sabbaths. Moses's "do this and live" principle reveals the people's need for the Savior.[43]

God himself explained why he imposed the "do this and live" principle that resulted in exile. To this effect, God said in Ezekiel 20:23–26:

> Moreover, I swore to them in the wilderness that I would scatter them among the nations and disperse them through the countries, because they had not obeyed my rules, but had rejected my statutes and profaned my Sabbaths, and their eyes were set on their fathers' idols. Moreover, I gave them statutes that were not good and rules by which they could not have life, and I defiled them through their very gifts in their offering up all their firstborn, that I might devastate them. I did it that they might know that I am the LORD.

God explicated that their disobedience concerning the Sabbaths caused exile, and, shockingly, that he gave them "statutes that were not good and rules by which they could not have life." God aimed to defile them to devastate them, so they would know he is Lord.[44] Again, the law reveals our need for a mediator. Further, the *nation's* experience of the Abrahamic blessing, noting again that the Mosaic covenant only provisionally fulfilled the Abrahamic, was conditional upon their obedience: "But this command I gave them: 'Obey my voice, and *I will be your God, and you shall be my people*. And walk in all the way that I command you, that it may be well with you.' But they did not obey or incline their ear, but walked in their own counsels and the stubbornness of their evil hearts, and went backward and not forward" (Jer 7:23–24). National Israel needed to keep the covenant to remain the recipient of the Abrahamic blessings. Their failure, as God intended, taught that we need to receive the Abrahamic blessings by faith rather than by works of the law (Gal 3:15–29).

The sign attached specifically to the Mosaic administration was the Sabbaths, as God emphasized in Exodus 31:12–27:

---

43. Walter C. Kaiser Jr., "Leviticus 18:5 and Paul: Do This and You Shall Live (Eternally?)," *JETS* 14 no. 1 (1971): 20–28.

44. Fesko, "Republication," 206–7.

> And the LORD said to Moses, "You are to speak to the people of Israel and say, 'Above all you shall keep my Sabbaths, for this is a sign between me and you throughout your generations, that you may know that I, the LORD, sanctify you. You shall keep the Sabbath, because it is holy for you. Everyone who profanes it shall be put to death. Whoever does any work on it, that soul shall be cut off from among his people. Six days shall work be done, but the seventh day is a Sabbath of solemn rest, holy to the LORD. Whoever does any work on the Sabbath day shall be put to death. Therefore the people of Israel shall keep the Sabbath, observing the Sabbath throughout their generations, as a covenant forever. It is a sign forever between me and the people of Israel that in six days the LORD made heaven and earth, and on the seventh day he rested and was refreshed.'"

The command for the plural Sabbaths indicates that this sign involves the system of annual festivals, rather than one day of the week. This designation of the Sabbath as the Mosaic administration's sign culminates God's instruction about the tabernacle system, so the Sabbath was the pinnacle of Israel's religious worship (Exod 25:1–30:11).[45] The Mosaic covenant should not be sacramentally linked to circumcision or the Passover because God designated the Sabbath as its sign. As other covenants were identified with their sacrament (Gen 17:10; Luke 22:20), so keeping the system of Sabbaths *is* the Mosaic covenant.

This administration's connection to the Sabbath further confirms its resemblance to the covenant of works. The creation Sabbath offered everlasting rest in the new creation to Adam as his reward if he fulfilled the covenant's terms. The ceremonial Sabbath seals the Mosaic covenant because the nation's rest in the land depended on their obedience. Even sacramentally, the Mosaic covenant resembled the covenant of works.

This republication created a type, foresignifying Christ's work as the last Adam. Herman Bavinck explains that the Mosaic law "was not a covenant of works in disguise and did not intend that humans would obtain justification by their own works," since "the impossibility of keeping the

45. Williamson, *Sealed*, 100–5.

Sinaitic covenant and of meeting the demands of the law made another and better dispensation of the covenant of grace necessary."[46] Christ fulfilled the true covenant of works by being born under the Mosaic law as the situation most resembling it.[47]

Mosaic typology thoroughly signified Christ's obedience. Reformed theologians seem to agree universally that the animal sacrifices signify Christ's passive obedience, but surely the Mosaic covenant also teaches Christ's active obedience.[48] Some object that it would be unfitting for human deeds of righteousness to be types of Christ's active obedience.[49] This objection overlooks that the Israelites themselves offered the animal sacrifices, which certainly did not themselves truly remove sin (Heb 9:11–14). The Mosaic covenant itself emphasized active obedience above sacrifices, as in Jeremiah 7:21–26:

> Thus says the LORD of hosts, the God of Israel: "Add your burnt offerings to your sacrifices, and eat the flesh. For in the day that I brought them out of the land of Egypt, I did not speak to your fathers or command them concerning burnt offerings and sacrifices. But this command I gave them: 'Obey my voice, and I will be your God, and you shall be my people. And walk in all the way that I command you, that it may be well with you.' But they did not obey or incline their ear, but walked in their own counsels and the stubbornness of their evil hearts, and went backward and not forward. From the day that your fathers came out of the land of Egypt to this day, I have persistently sent all my servants the prophets to them, day after day. Yet they did not listen to me or incline their ear, but stiffened their neck. They did worse than their fathers."

Jeremiah indicted their lack of active obedience.[50] The people's actions, albeit imperfect, were no more problematic as types of Christ's active obedience than his passive obedience.

---

46. *BRD*, 3:222.
47. *KP*, 352–55; VanDrunen, "Israel's Recapitulation," 323–24.
48. Wellum, "Some Christological Reflections," 48–52; Fesko, "Republication," 210–11.
49. Venema, *Christ and Covenant Theology*, 126–29.
50. Schreiner, *Covenant*, 62–65.

The Mosaic administration offered Christ through these types contained in the law. The animal sacrifices depict Christ's death for our sins. On the other hand, the law's demands for obedience to live in the holy space demonstrate how Christ would merit citizenship in the heavenly kingdom for his people. Even though the nation was under a covenant of works, those types sufficiently instructed believers about their Savior. Even though the terms of the Mosaic covenant cannot be merit since sinners cannot perform perfect obedience, these terms are *types* of Christ's merit. As means of grace for that time, God's people experienced Christ through those sacrifices. The animal sacrifices themselves could never truly purify sin, since the Levitical system in itself merely cleansed the sanctuary of impurities and pollutions concerning violations of the ceremonial law pertaining to Israel's possession of the land, but Christ forgave sin as he was given sacramentally through those offerings (Heb 9:11–14).[51] As we try to learn about what the Mosaic covenant teaches us even today as we walk with Christ, those types remain infinitely valuable for us as their resemblance to the covenant of works instructs not only about how the law cannot provide our means to obtain heaven but also how Christ has met those conditions for us.

THE MOSAIC COVENANT IN THE REFORMED TRADITION

Although Reformed theologians hold diverse opinions about the Mosaic covenant, some provide historical precedent for the view argued, demonstrated here by a sample of Reformed statements to this effect.[52]

Even confessional statements include some degree of this teaching, albeit these are open to more than one understanding. The Westminster Confession teaches, "God gave to Adam a law, *as a covenant of works*" (WCF 19.1).[53] The Confession then refers again to that law, which was the covenant of works: "This law, after his fall, continued to be a perfect rule of righteousness; and, as such, was delivered by God upon mount

51. Jacob Milgrom, *Numbers* (Philadelphia, PA: Jewish Publication Society, 2003), 444–47.

52. *ACW*, 107–58; Brenton C. Ferry, "Works in the Mosaic Covenant: A Reformed Taxonomy" in *LNF*, 76–106; Estelle et al., "Report to ... Study Republication," 30–86.

53. *COC*, 3:640.

Sinai in ten commandments" (19.2).[54] So, the law that was the covenant of works for Adam was given at Sinai, serving a different capacity, but still presenting the covenant of works' content in the Mosaic administration.[55] Accordingly, the Westminster Larger Catechism confesses, "The Moral Law is the declaration of the will of God to mankind, directing and binding every one to personal, perfect, and perpetual conformity and obedience thereunto ... promising life upon the fulfilling, and threatening death upon the breach of it" (WLC 93).[56] The Confession then follows Ursinus's *Catechism*: "The law contains the natural covenant ... and requires from us perfect obedience toward God, and promises everlasting life to those who keep it but threatens everlasting death to those who do not keep it."[57] The moral law was a perfect rule of righteousness for Adam in the covenant of works, even as it covenantally demanded obedience from him to obtain reward. As Robert Rollock explains, "The law, which is the rule of those works which were properly and principally required in the covenant of works, remains but now has another special use, abiding presently as the rule and standard for works of grace and sanctification."[58] The law remained the perfect rule of righteousness in each of its iterations, having the same promises and threats in some sense embedded, even when refracted through the covenant of grace.[59]

The moral law's application within the covenant of grace must maintain both its use to drive sinners to Christ and its use as a perfect rule of righteousness to direct our lives in holiness. When the Westminster Confession notes that God joined the ceremonial and civil laws to the moral law for national Israel, one purpose was "prefiguring Christ, his graces, actions, sufferings, and benefits" (WCF 19.3–4).[60] Certainly this includes teaching about how Christ would fulfill the covenant of works for his people. Even as the moral law is a good and perfect rule of righteousness abiding for believers in the covenant of grace, the combination

---

54. *COC*, 3:640.

55. *MMB*, 686–87.

56. *LC*, 84.

57. Ursinus, *Summa*, in *Opera Theologica*, 1:14.

58. Rollock, *Tractatus*, 14; Rollock, *Treatise*, 10.

59. Horton, "Covenant Theology," 41–48.

60. *COC*, 3:641.

of the moral, ceremonial, and civil laws together *as the Mosaic administration* resembles the covenant of works to foreshadow Christ.[61] Certainly, the Mosaic covenant was an administration of the covenant of grace, so its substance was Christ and his benefits received by faith alone, even while its typological features resembled the covenant of works. This understanding of the Mosaic covenant, as resembling the covenant of works, then, pointedly concerns types of Christ, not salvation for individual Israelites. The Mosaic covenant joined a repetition of the moral law with civil and ceremonial commandments, announcing the embedded demand of obedience with its corresponding consequences, to provide types of Christ's fulfillment of the covenant of works so that people would be directed to faith in him. The Mosaic covenant's ordinances that resembled the covenant of works never functioned as an alternative means of salvation apart from Christ's work given sacramentally through them (Gal 3:21). The confession does not require this reading but permits it.[62]

Individual theologians argue more specifically that the Mosaic covenant repeated the covenant of works. Regarding Galatians 4:24–25, William Perkins comments: "The two testaments are the covenant of works and the covenant of grace, one promising life eternal to him that does all the things contained in the law, [and] the other to him that turns and believes in Christ."[63] Perkins distinguished the Mosaic administration from the gospel in that "here lies the difference between the law and the gospel. The law is from Sinai; the gospel, from Zion or Jerusalem."[64] Perkins links the covenant of works and the covenant at Sinai so much that he essentially equates them.[65]

Rollock also argues that the Mosaic covenant repeated the covenant of works to the nation of Israel, explaining:

> For that reason as well, when this covenant of works was repeated to the people of Israel, first he gave the law written on stone tablets,

61. Longenecker, *Paul, Apostle of Liberty*, 112–15, 123–39.

62. Estelle et al., "Report to ... Study Republication," 17–19, 29–30, 41–42; Gordon, *Promise, Law, Faith*, 151–54.

63. *WWP*, 2:302.

64. *WWP*, 2:303.

65. Harrison Perkins, "Reconsidering the Development of the Covenant of Works: A Study in Doctrinal Trajectory," *CTJ* 53.2 (2018): 302–9; Estelle et al., "Report to ... Study Republication," 34–35.

> then he struck his covenant with them, "Do this," it says, "and you will live." Therefore, the foundation of the covenant of works was certainly not Christ, nor the grace of God in Christ, but the nature of man in the first creation, holy and perfect, and being fashioned with knowledge of the law.[66]

Rollock elsewhere affirms that the covenant of works "was continually repeated from the creation and fall of man up until the coming of Christ," significantly, as "it was handed down and inscribed by Moses."[67] Rollock then also links the covenant of works and the Mosaic covenant.

Amandus Polanus (1561–1610) likewise calls the Mosaic covenant a repetition of the covenant of works. After defining the covenant of works, he argues, "God repeated this same covenant with the people of Israel through Moses, which is why the same is called 'the covenant of Moses,' 'the covenant of the law,' and commonly 'the old covenant.' " In this covenant, "God stirred man towards rendering obedience by this repetition," so that "every mouth would be stopped and the whole world would be liable to God's condemnation because they did not render perfect obedience (Rom. 3:19)." Nevertheless, "the Israelites did not persevere in the repetition of the covenant (Heb. 8:9)."[68] Polanus clearly articulates that the Mosaic administration repeated the true covenant of works, emphasizing obedience to the law.

Gomarus too argues that the Mosaic covenant repeated the covenant of works by repeating the natural law. After explaining what he calls "the natural covenant," he writes that "then this covenant was repeated to the Israelites through the mediator Moses and related in the two tables of the Decalogue (which contain the express form of the natural covenant)."[69] Still, Gomarus affirms that the Mosaic covenant repeated the covenant of grace, having a twofold redemptive-historical purpose: that is, "primarily to promulgate the certain law or natural covenant (whence most regard synecdochally in this way) but secondarily to renew the memory of the

66. Rollock, *Tractatus*, 9–10; Rollock, *Treatise on God's Effectual Calling*, 7.

67. Rollock, *Some Questions*, 25.

68. Amandus Polanus von Polansdorf, *Syntagmatis Theologiae Christianae*, 2 vol. (Hanau, 1609), 2:2906.

69. Gomarus, "Oration concerning God's Covenant," sig. (*)2v.

supernatural and gracious covenant begun once with Abraham and the Israelites as they examine the Mosaic promises."[70] So, Gomarus views the Mosaic covenant as administering the covenant of grace while simultaneously announcing the covenant of works' demands again.

James Ussher further exemplifies this view. After arguing that under the old ministry "the commandments of the Law were more largely, and the promises of Christ more sparingly and darkly propounded" with "a multitude of types and figures," he describes the special property of the old ministry "from Abraham to Christ" as having "joined with it a solemn repetition and declaration of the first covenant of the Law."[71] The "solemn repetition and declaration of the first covenant of the Law" was *added* to the old ministry revealed to Abraham's family.

Similarly, Francis Turretin explains how the Mosaic administration was added to the old economy rather than supplementing or replacing the prior promises. He argues, "The Israelites with whom God stipulates were already under the Abrahamic covenant (which was a covenant of grace)."[72] The old covenant "denotes the covenant of works or the moral law given by Moses—the unbearable burden of legal ceremonies being added, absolutely and apart from the promise of grace."[73] Within a "twofold relation" of this covenant, the legal aspect was "a new promulgation of the law and of the covenant of works."[74] According to its external economy, "the Mosaic covenant would seem to be legal because only under the condition of one's own obedience (and that too perfect without any forbearance) did it promise life," even though, "as to the intention of the lawgiver and as to the end of the law again promulgated, it led to the coming Messiah—and so it is rightly said to belong to the covenant of grace."[75] On the other hand, the evangelical aspect included "the internal truth of the gospel promise" lying under the legal veneer of the external

70. Gomarus, "Oration concerning God's Covenant," sig. (*)3r.

71. Ussher, *Body*, 409; for further analysis of Ussher's view of the Mosaic covenant in conversation with other early modern voices, see Perkins, *Catholicity and the Covenant of Works*, 116–24.

72. *TI*, 12.12.12.

73. *TI*, 12.8.4.

74. *TI*, 12.7.31.

75. *TI*, 12.5.33.

administration.[76] Turretin, while clearly maintaining its power to apply Christ and his benefits to believers through its means of grace, recognizes the Mosaic covenant's typology included a legal dimension.[77]

John Colquhoun called the Mosaic covenant "a *mixed* dispensation." Although it "*repeated* and *published*" the covenant of grace, "the covenant of works was awfully *displayed*." So, as Ussher and Turretin held, he writes the "national covenant between God and the Israelites" was "an *appendage* to the covenant of grace." Although the moral law guides believers, "the same law was repeated and displayed to Israelites in the form of the covenant of works."[78] By calling the Mosaic covenant "a mixed dispensation," Colquhoun did not mean that the principles of law and gospel were confused regarding salvation. As he writes later, "Although the Sinaitic transaction, was a *mixed dispensation*; yet the covenant of grace and the covenant of works, were *not blended together* in it. The latter as well as the ceremonial law, was *added* to the former; and was added to it, in order that, the Israelites might be so convinced of their sinfulness and misery, as to see their extreme need, of embracing the promise, or covenant of grace."[79] So, although the Mosaic administration is part of the covenant of grace in terms of the way that individuals receive salvation, its appearance was like that of the covenant of works for the nation of Israel.[80]

Finally, Geerhardus Vos writes, "The covenant with Israel served in an emphatic manner to recall the strict demands of the covenant of works. To that end, the law of the Ten Commandments was presented so emphatically and engraved deeply in stone. The law was not, as Cocceius meant, simply a form of the covenant of grace. It truly contained the content of the covenant of works. But—and one should certainly note this—it contains this content as made serviceable for a particular period of the covenant of

---

76. *TI*, 12.7.31–32.

77. *TI*, 12.7.32.

78. *LG*, 53–54 (italics original).

79. *LG*, 70 (italics original). Colquhoun's view is, then, not the "mixed" view concerning substance described in Estelle et al., "Report to ... Study Republication," 35–37; cf. Baillie, *Anabaptism*, 141–42.

80. Watson, *Hermeneutics of Faith*, 190–91.

grace."[81] The Reformed tradition, then, contains precedent for connecting the Mosaic covenant and the covenant of works.[82]

NEW TESTAMENT REFLECTION ON THE MOSAIC ADMINISTRATION

This section explores the apostolic interpretation of the Mosaic administration, importantly, establishing its typological contribution. In 2 Corinthians 3:6–7, Paul interpreted the Mosaic administration as "the ministry of death" because of its works principle. Charles Hodge highlights how Paul links Moses to the covenant of works in that "the apostle often speaks of the Mosaic law as he does of the law considered as a covenant of works; that is, presenting the promise of life on the condition of perfect obedience." The problem is that Paul "calls it a ministration of death and condemnation" and "denies that it can give life."[83] The Mosaic covenant causes tension in redemptive history because salvation remains the same throughout the covenant of grace.[84]

The Mosaic administration's typological features ease this tension. True, as Hodge, perhaps following Buchanan, contended, "The law of Moses was, in the first place, a re-enactment of the covenant of works" but "the Mosaic economy was also a national covenant." The important perspective is that its "purely legal" aspect concerned "national promises on the condition of national obedience."[85] The gospel was, after all, also present as the types taught how Christ would fulfill the covenant of works for his people.[86]

This reading accounts for Paul's interpretation of the unfolding Old Testament story. Paul knew that the Pentateuch composed an overarching narrative, even as he digested the principles of law and grace from them. That story grounds his interpretation of the Mosaic administration

---

81. *VRD*, 2:130; *EC*, 4.4.45.

82. This historical evidence demonstrates that Pascal Denault erroneously overgeneralized by claiming that paedobaptists "reject the unity and continuity between the covenant of works and the Old Covenant" simply to defend the unity of the covenant of grace. Although the Reformed do not explain that continuity as Baptists do, Denault inadequately wrestles with the historical evidence; see "By Farther Steps," 74–75.

83. Hodge, *Corinthians*, 432–33.

84. *TI*, 12.8.8.

85. Hodge, *Corinthians*, 433–34; Buchanan, *Justification*, 36–37.

86. *TI*, 12.12.22–25; Hodge, *Corinthians*, 434; Watson, *Hermeneutics of Faith*, 271.

as a "ministry of death."[87] As Old Testament prophets and Jewish readers in Paul's day understood, the Mosaic law contained the "do this and live" principle in Leviticus 18:5. When the law was given, this principle offered life on the condition of obedience, but the unfolding story revealed a much different outcome. Two censuses of military-age men bookend the book of Numbers (Num 1; 26), the second revealing that the whole first generation of those numbered to enter the promised land had died. Numbers' specific contribution to Moses's five-book narrative demonstrates that death, rather than life, was the Mosaic covenant's outcome (Rom 8:3).[88]

This deathly perspective from Numbers is not limited to Israel's time in the wilderness. In Deuteronomy 27–34, Moses's final speeches as the people were poised to enter the promised land were not optimistic, repeatedly foretelling the curse that would come upon Israel for their unfaithfulness.[89] God's people under the Mosaic covenant would die.

Paul and Jude both clearly state that the wilderness generation died because of God's punishment. Paul writes how they were overthrown in the wilderness because "with most of them God was not pleased" (1 Cor 10:5). Jude argues, "Jesus, who saved a people out of the land of Egypt, afterward destroyed those who did not believe" (Jude 1:5). God judged the people under the Mosaic covenant, inflicting death. Despite the Mosaic administration's offer of life, the people's sin earned the wages of death (Lev 18:5; Rom 6:23). The Mosaic covenant, precisely according to its terms, resulted in death rather than life for the nation, just as the covenant of works with Adam resulted in spiritual (and eventual bodily) death for him and his posterity.[90] So Paul writes in Romans 7:10: "The very commandment that promised life proved to be death to me."[91] As

---

87. Burnside, *God, Justice, and Society*, 63–64; Vos, *Hebrews*, 65; Horton, *Rediscovering*, 139–46; *KP*, 108–10.

88. *EC*, 4.4.47–49; Watson, *Hermeneutics of Faith*, 325–27, 371–78.

89. Watson, *Hermeneutics of Faith*, 391–416, 464–72.

90. Rosner, *Paul and the Law*, 145–46; Watson, *Hermeneutics of Faith*, xxxiii, 274. 285–88, 325–78.

91. Chapter 3 indicates that one very plausible reading of Romans 7:7–12 is that Paul writes from Adam's perspective concerning how the law was delivered in the garden with the offer of life attached. Another common reading is that Paul writes from Israel's perspective concerning how the law was delivered at Sinai with the promise of life attached. The argued interpretation of the Mosaic covenant resolves the opposition between these readings. Paul's point would be that when God delivered the law *as a covenant* that includes the promise of life, which occurred both in Eden and at Sinai. The actual result has been death for those under said covenant, harmonizing well

God delivered a commandment that promised life to Adam in Eden in the covenant of works, so he did the same at Mount Sinai, with both covenants resulting in death.

The redemptive-historical shift from the Mosaic covenant to the new covenant is fundamental in New Testament thought. Paul writes that God's righteousness has been manifested apart from the law (Rom 3:21–26). The law and the prophets taught that righteousness would be given to believers by faith. The substance of the old and new economies is not different, since God "had passed over former sins." That forgiveness, however, was not because of the law, so not because of the Mosaic administration.[92] Rather, the Mosaic administration as the law covenant taught via its types how Christ would fulfill the original covenant of works' terms in our place.

Adam was "a type of the one who was to come," revealing even in his failure in the covenant of works what Christ achieved (Rom 5:14). Still, under the law "death reigned from Adam to Moses" (Rom 5:14), so Israel under the Mosaic covenant taught about Christ's fulfillment of the covenant of works as well. Christ was the end of the law "unto righteousness for everyone who believes," in that he fulfilled the law's demands—natural and Mosaic—with the result of justification for those who receive him by faith (Rom 10:4).[93]

In Galatians 3:15–4:7, Paul undeniably sees tension between grace and works as they connect to the Abrahamic and Mosaic administrations, relating them in terms of two covenantal principles.[94] He argues that God cannot undo or alter a covenant after ratifying it, entailing that the Mosaic law could not add conditions to the Abrahamic promise, since it was holistically delivered four hundred and thirty years after God covenanted

with the argued interpretation of Romans 5:13–14 that sin was counted even in between Adam and Moses because the law was first given to Adam in the covenant of works before it was given to Israel at Mount Sinai; see VanDrunen, "Israel's Recapitulation," 310–12; N. T. Wright, "Romans" in *The New Interpreter's Bible*, 12 vol. (Nashville: Abingdon Press, 2002), 10:553, 562–63; N. T. Wright, *The Climax of the Covenant: Christ and the Law in Pauline Theology* (Minneapolis, MN: Fortress Press, 1992), 197; Wright, *Paul: In Fresh Perspective* (Minneapolis, MN: Fortress Press, 2005), 31; Watson, *Hermeneutics of Faith*, 325–48, 466–69.

92. Rosner, *Paul and the Law*, 149–55.

93. *CMT*, 90; Longenecker, *Paul, Apostle of Liberty*, 116–41; Watson, *Hermeneutics of Faith*, 305–7.

94. Watson, *Hermeneutics of Faith*, 179–85; Gordon, *Promise, Law, Faith*, 1–7, 28–39, 132n54.

with Abraham (Gal 3:15–18).[95] In other words, the *administration* with legal conditions for the nation, although genuinely differing in principle *concerning the nation's blessings*, could not alter the covenant of grace's true *substance* of salvation by grace alone in Christ for individuals (Gal 3:2–3).[96]

Although Paul argues that the historical covenants connected to Abraham and Moses differed, that argument's relevance to redemptive history's development is that these historical covenants represent theological principles of promise and law—or grace and works.[97] Bavinck argues, "Although in a broad sense the terms 'law' and 'gospel' can indeed be used to denote the old and the new dispensation of the covenant of grace, in the actual significance they definitely describe two essentially different revelations of the divine will."[98] Petrus van Mastricht likewise connects theological principles to Paul's historical points by affirming that prooftexts about the Mosaic covenant help prove the covenant of works because the covenant of works "was repeated and renewed upon Sinai with Israel in the Decalogue, which had proof of the covenant of works."[99] The Mosaic covenant, then, as a distinct administration represented the legal principle not for obtaining the Abrahamic promise, but for another pedagogical purpose.[100]

The Mosaic covenant's purpose, at least partly, was to make God's people aware of their need for a Savior and to teach them about the Savior's work. God gave promises directly to Abraham because the promise required no mediator.[101] On the other hand, the Mosaic administration required Moses—and the priests after him—to mediate between God and the people.[102] The Mosaic law was given "because of transgressions"

95. Watson, *Hermeneutics of Faith*, 251–58; Horton, *Justification*, 2:86–95; Gordon, *Promise, Law, Faith*, 1–7, 132–33, 137–40.

96. Kline, *God, Heaven, and Har-Mageddon*, 96–97; *KP*, 109–10.

97. Gordon, *Promise, Law, Faith*, 7–25. Although Gordon's exegesis of Galatians 3–4 is often persuasive concerning the historical level of Paul's argument, he should have further argued that the historical covenants represent the theological reality of the law-gospel distinction; *BTA*, 90–98; Bruce, *Galatians*, 83.

98. *BRD*, 4:453.

99. Mastricht, *Theoretica-Practica Theologia*, 3.12.23.

100. Longenecker, *Paul, Apostle of Liberty*, 112–13; Estelle et al., "Report to ... Study Republication," 54–72.

101. Cf. Renihan, *Mystery*, 88.

102. Waters, "Covenant in Paul," 235–36; Gordon, *Promise, Law, Faith*, 132n53, 149–51.

(Gal 3:19–20).[103] It is not contrary to the promise because it cannot give life, only the promise can (Gal 3:21; Rom 8:3).[104] God used the Mosaic law to *imprison* "so that the promise by faith in Jesus Christ might be given to those who believe" (Gal 3:22). The law was given to show how it imprisons, entailing our need for a Savior to redeem us from its curse.[105]

The Mosaic law cannot serve *simply* to guide God's people in living faithfully because sanctification is lasting freedom rather than temporary imprisonment.[106] The Mosaic covenant was, after all, explicitly *temporary*, functioning "before faith came" only "until the offspring should come" (Gal 3:19, 23).[107] In Galatians 3:24–26, Paul further explains that "the law was our guardian *until Christ came*, in order that we might be justified by faith." Now "we are no longer under a guardian, for in Christ Jesus you are all sons of God, through faith."[108] If the Mosaic law *simply* functioned for guidance in holiness, its temporary nature would suggest, "now that faith has come," that the law's guiding role no longer applies and its imprisoning role would imply that sanctification is bondage. These antinomian implications of a consistent application of the view that the Mosaic law *simply* guides holiness are unacceptable.[109] The Mosaic covenant's resemblance to the covenant of works for the nation of Israel helps uphold the doctrine of sanctification.

All the same, the Mosaic law as republishing the covenant of works makes good sense of its imprisoning role.[110] As becomes clear in Galatians 4:1–7, although believers have always had an inheritance—the substance—in Christ, believers under Moses were *in a typological way* treated like a slave because they were imprisoned under the guardian.[111] The Mosaic covenant was supposed to serve a temporary instructive purpose "in order

103. *CMT*, 90.

104. Gordon, *Promise, Law, Faith*, 140.

105. Watson, *Hermeneutics of Faith*, 184; *LG*, 63–72; *CW*, 5–6; *EC*, 4.4.41.

106. *EC*, 4.4.52–57.

107. Waters, "Covenant in Paul," 236–37; Gordon, *Promise, Law, Faith*, 146–60.

108. *BTA*, 98–105, 111–13.

109. *EC*, 4.4.33–37.

110. Richard N. Longenecker, "The Pedagogical Nature of the Law in Galatians 3:19–4:7," *JETS* 25 no. 1 (March 1982): 53–61.

111. Michael Horton, "Church," 317–22.

that we might be justified by faith" (Gal 3:24).[112] Its purpose was not simply to guide holiness but explicitly to promote justification by faith. So, the Westminster Confession says, "Although true believers be not under the law as a covenant of works, to be thereby justified or condemned; yet it is of great use to them, as well as to others; in that as a rule of life, informing them of the will of God and their duty, it directs and binds them to walk accordingly" (WCF 19.6).[113] The law functions primarily as a rule for holiness only for those who are justified by faith.[114]

The law's universal relevance also indicates the Mosaic covenant's resemblance to the covenant of works. In Romans 5:12–14, death is the consequence of transgressing the law but was also universal from Adam until Moses.[115] The time passing *between* Adam and Moses somehow differs from the times *under* Adam and Moses, yet this period's dissimilarity highlights the similarity of life *for* Adam and Moses, namely, under the covenant of works and Mosaic administration.[116] In this respect, Israel's plight under the Mosaic covenant widens to a universal significance for gentiles. Galatians 3:23–29 describes how the Mosaic law imprisoned Israel, but Christ brought freedom from its imprisoning effects. Following this explanation of specifically the Mosaic covenant, Galatians 4:1–11 reveals that this plight somehow has wider significance for Jew *and gentile* concerning their need for redemption in Christ. Particularly, those who lived under the Mosaic covenant were treated "in the same way" as children under a guardian by being "enslaved to the elementary principles of the world" until "the fullness of time had come" when "God sent forth his Son" (Gal 4:3–4).

Although the meaning of "the elementary principles of the world" is debated, the phrase strikingly universalizes the Mosaic law's imprisoning/enslaving effects.[117] These elementary principles ground both Israel's imprisonment under Mosaic law *and* the gentiles' enslavement,

---

112. Crowe, *Path of Faith*, 50–51; VanDrunen, "Israel's Recapitulation," 322–24.

113. *COC*, 3:642.

114. Belcher, *Fulfillment*, 91; *EC*, 4.4.42.

115. Gordon, *Promise, Law, Faith*, 153.

116. VanDrunen, "Israel's Recapitulation," 306–10.

117. Neil Martin, "Returning to the *stoicheia tou kosmou*: Enslavement to the Physical Elements in Galatians 4.3 and 9?" *Journal for the Study of the New Testament* 40 no. 4 (2018): 434–39.

necessitating redemption in Christ for them both, since gentile Christians need to ask themselves, "How can you turn back again to the weak and worthless *elementary principles of the world*, whose slaves you want to be once more?" (Gal 4:9) Although gentiles were never under the Mosaic covenant, the elementary principles enslaved them before they were Christians, just as these principles enslaved Israel under Moses before Christ's arrival. So, the elementary principles' imprisoning function has the same effect in the Mosaic law for Israel as for the whole world.[118] Something about these elementary principles that can enslave gentiles corresponds to Israel's enslavement under the Mosaic covenant.[119]

These elementary principles are the law that enslaves every sinner, Jew or gentile, under its curse. In Colossians 2:8–15, these same "elementary principles of the world" (2:8, my translation) are part of humanity's general plight, leaving gentile readers "dead in [their] trespasses" (2:13). God addressed this plight for us in Christ "by canceling the record of debt that stood against us with *its legal demands*" (2:14). Paul's point in Colossians 2:20, that "with Christ you died to the *elementary principles of the world*" removing any need to "submit to regulations," links Christ's death to our freedom from condemnation much like in Galatians 2:19–20: "For through the law I died to the law, so that I might live to God. I have been crucified with Christ."[120] Christ's death provides freedom, in Galatians, from the law's curse and, in Colossians, from the elementary principles.[121]

The elementary principles of the world, then, relate at least to the law's effects, if not the law itself. Paul's reference to being enslaved "to those that by nature are not gods" (Gal 4:8) easily refers to angels, whom he closely associated with giving the law (Gal 3:19).[122] Classical writers, such as Philo, Xenophon, and Plutarch, use this phrase to refer to "the

118. Ernest de Witt Burton, *The Epistle to the Galatians* (Edinburgh: T&T Clark, 1921), 215–16; Longenecker, *Galatians*, 165–66; Schreiner, *Galatians*, 267–69; deSilva, *Galatians*, 346–53; Bruce, *Galatians*, 29, 193–94; *EC*, 4.13.10–11; 4.15.19.

119. F. F. Bruce, *The Epistles to the Colossians, to Philemon, and to the Ephesians* (Grand Rapids: Eerdmans, 1984), 99–100; *BTA*, 100–3; *KP*, 108–17.

120. Bruce, *Colossians, Philemon, Ephesians*, 125–26.

121. James D. G. Dunn, *The Epistles to the Colossians and to Philemon* (Grand Rapids: Eerdmans, 1996), 150–51, 189–90; Douglas J. Moo, *The Letters to the Colossians and to Philemon* (Grand Rapids: Eerdmans, 2008), 189–90; Martin, "Returning to the *stoicheia tou kosmou*," 448–50.

122. Bruce, *Colossians, Philemon, Ephesians*, 99; cf. Moo, *Colossians*, 190–93.

fundamental principles or rules of life," readily resonating theologically with the idea of God's natural law.[123] Even when ancient writers use the phrase to refer to the universe's supposed constitutive elements—earth, air, fire, water—they often discuss a priest working to bring harmony between these elements to remove cosmological strife.[124] In this respect, from the Christian perspective, Christ by his priestly work removed the cursed effects of the elementary principles by being born under the law on our behalf. As John Chrysostom explains, since these elementary principles defined the period of enslavement before Christ was "born under *the law*" (Gal 4:4–5), they reasonably describe the law itself.[125] The elementary principles then relate to the legal demands upon every sinner—Jew or gentile—from which Christ's death frees us.[126]

The Mosaic covenant imprisoned Israel under the law to show their need for a Savior as a type of how the natural law—the principles of the world—imprisons everyone under sin.[127] So, Turretin explains,

> Meanwhile it pleased God to administer the covenant of grace in this period *under a rigid legal economy*—both on account of the condition of the people still in infancy and on account of the putting off of the advent of Christ and the satisfaction to be rendered by him. A twofold relation ought always to obtain: the one legal, more severe, through which *by a new promulgation of the law and of the covenant of works*, with an intolerable yoke of ceremonies, *he wished to set forth what men owed and what was to be expected by them on account of duty unperformed.*[128]

---

123. Burton, *Galatians*, 510–18; Schreiner, *Galatian*, 267.

124. Eduard Schweizer, "Slaves of the Elements and Worshipers of Angels: Gal 4:3, 9 and Col 2:8, 18, 20," *Journal of Biblical Literature* 107 no. 3 (1988): 455–68.

125. John Chrysostom, *Commentary on the Epistle of St. Paul the Apostle to the Galatians* in *NPNF1*, 13:30; Ridderbos, *Galatia*, 154–56; Longenecker, *Galatians*, 165; Bruce, *Galatians*, 193–94; DeSilva, *Galatians*, 352–53.

126. *ACW*, 270–76; Bruce, *Galatians*, 29–31; Longenecker, *Galatians*, 165–66; deSilva, *Galatians*, 363–66.

127. Bruce, *Galatians*, 194; Gordon fails to draw the connection from those historical covenants to the theological principles of law and gospel because, he admits, he remains "completely flummoxed" about these elementary principles—*στοιχεῖα τοῦ κοσμοῦ*—which is the exact premise that connects the Mosaic covenant and the covenant of works; see Gordon, *Promise, Law, Faith*, 16n34, 167.

128. *TI*, 12.7.31 (emphasis added).

The Mosaic covenant re-presented the covenant of works, showing that first covenant's requirements upon humanity.[129]

The Mosaic law, then, uses the local example of Israel—the microcosm—to display the effects of the covenant of works at the universal level—the macrocosm.[130] To illustrate, sometimes famously designed or historic buildings have a smaller scale model of the whole building in its foyer. Although the whole building's grand scope makes it beyond your capacity to see at once, this model encapsulates the full architectural design in one easily digestible snapshot. It gives perspective on the bigger picture when that bigger picture is too large to absorb fully. The Mosaic covenant functions similarly in relation to the covenant of works. The covenant of works' universal scale makes its significance easily lost as we live under its widespread effects and fallout. The Mosaic covenant encapsulated the covenant of works' details in a local snapshot, making its effects easy to perceive. In this way, the Mosaic covenant served as a scale model—a microcosm—within the universal macrocosm of the covenant of works' demands. Narrowly, those who inhabited Canaan prior to Israel, although not having covenanted with God at Sinai, suffered the same covenant penalties as Israel endured on account of the Mosaic covenant. More widely, the inhabitants of the whole world, despite also not belonging to the Mosaic covenant, have defiled the earth, as Israel defiled the promised land, by transgressing the covenant (Lev 18:6–23; Isa 24:5).[131] No one on earth is beyond the scope of the covenantal curse that remarkably resembles those under the Mosaic covenant. The reason is that the Mosaic covenant served as a microcosmic illustration of the plight affecting the whole world under the broken covenant of works.

This relationship between the covenant of works and the Mosaic law is why Paul writes in Galatians 3:13 to gentile Christians that "Christ redeemed *us* from the curse of the law"—the "us" being all believers formerly cursed by the law and needing salvation.[132] Bavinck cites the elementary principles as a revelation of God's abiding ethical demands as taught

129. *LG*, 67–68 (italics original).

130. *KTC*, 831–34.

131. *ACW*, 202–4; 217–37.

132. For this grammatical point about the referent of Paul's pronouns in Galatians, see deSilva, *Galatians*, 296–302.

under the Mosaic law, arguing these demands were not "the imperfect, preparatory, Old Testament dispensation of the covenant of grace" but "a religious/ethical requirement and demand, as the God-willed regulation of the revelation between him and human beings."[133] As the covenant of works, founded on the natural law, enslaves the whole world under sin, so the Mosaic covenant imprisoned Israel under its law by making their sinful inability obvious.[134] The Mosaic covenant was a temporary and local administration that reveals and represents permanent and universal theological principles, such as the demands of the covenant of works.[135]

Paul elsewhere reasons from the Mosaic covenant's local curse to humanity's universal condemnation for sin, confirming our interpretation of the elementary principles. In 2 Thessalonians 1:3–12, he comforts a church suffering under the prospect of persecution surprisingly by reminding them that God will reap vengeance upon those who wrong his people.[136] In this context, Paul describes that judgment. "They will undergo the punishment of everlasting destruction coming from the face of the Lord as well as from the glory of his might when he comes on that day to receive glory from his saints and to be admired by all who have believed because our testimony to you was believed" (2 Thess 1:9–10; my translation). In what may seem like a rather simple statement, that the Lord will inflict everlasting judgment upon those remaining in sin, Paul shows skillful, nuanced biblical interpretation by reasoning from the Mosaic covenant's curse to universal judgment.

In 2 Thessalonians 1:9–10, Paul extends the application of Old Testament passages about judgment under the Mosaic covenant to God's *universal* last day judgment, resembling how he understood the Mosaic covenant's correlation to the elementary principles. In Isaiah 2:5–19, the

---

133. *BRD*, 4:450–51.

134. David VanDrunen, "Natural Law and the Works Principle under Adam and Moses," in *LNF*, 283–314; Horton, *Justification*, 2:69–70, 85–86; Longenecker, *Paul, Apostle of Liberty*, 140–41.

135. "The covenant of creation provides the widest cosmic horizon, while the Sinai covenant is specific to Israel. Yet both require the successful completion of the probation by the covenant servant." Horton, "Kingdom of God," 372; Watson, *Hermeneutics of Faith*, 191; Gordon, *Law, Promise, Faith*, 173–79.

136. Gordon D. Fee, *The First and Second Letters to the Thessalonians* (Grand Rapids: Eerdmans, 2009), 252–53; Gene L. Green, *The Letters to the Thessalonians* (Grand Rapids: Eerdmans, 2002), 278–79, 293–94; Charles A. Wannamaker, *The Epistles to the Thessalonians* (Grand Rapids: Eerdmans, 1990), 215.

prophet indicted Israel for their idolatry and told of God's coming judgment.[137] Paul cites the Septuagint wording of Isaiah 2:10, which interestingly includes an additional final phrase compared to the Hebrew text. In the Septuagint reading, Isaiah exhorts Israel to hide "from the face of the fear of the LORD as well as from the glory of his might when he arises to break the land" (my translation). Paul cites the Greek of this phrase almost exactly, except for "when he arises to break the land," which is the Septuagint's additional phrase not in the Hebrew.[138] This inserted phrase specified that God's judgment was coming upon *the land,* namely, the covenant people, emphasizing the threat of impending exile under the Mosaic covenant.

Paul, recognizing that the "when" phrase was not in the original Hebrew, reworked it to fit his purposes. Whereas the Septuagint said God would act with the glory of his might in judgment *when* he rose against the people of the Mosaic covenant, Paul substitutes citations from the Psalms to indicate universal judgment. He combines "being glorified in the council of his saints" (Ps 89:7) with "admired by his saints" (Ps 68:35) as the timing of God's outpoured judgment.[139] That Paul overtly ascribes this worship to Christ when God was its recipient in the Old Testament highlights Paul's thoroughly Trinitarian theology.[140] Nevertheless, Paul extends the Septuagint's interpretation of Isaiah 2:10 about the threat of exile under the Mosaic covenant to Christ's second coming and universal judgment.[141]

Paul's application of Isaiah's prophecy assumes that the Mosaic covenant's threats pertain to the whole world. Even within their own writings, the prophets also tended to widen God's threats of judgment against his covenant people to the nations. This move itself presumes that the

---

137. Young, *Isaiah,* 115–16, 119–23; Green, *Thessalonians,* 292–93.

138. Jeffrey A. D. Weima, "1–2 Thessalonians," *Commentary on the New Testament Use of the Old Testament,* eds. G. K. Beale and D. A. Carson (Grand Rapids: Baker Academic, 2007), 885; Wannamaker, *Thessalonians,* 229; Fee, *Thessalonians,* 259.

139. Paul used the Septuagint Greek, versified as Psalm 88:8 and Psalm 67:36; my translations above are based on the Septuagint. See Fee, *Thessalonians,* 261–62; Green, *Thessalonians,* 294–95; and Wannamaker, *Thessalonians,* 230–31.

140. WLC 11; *LC,* 68; Fee, *Pauline Christology,* 57–61; Fee, *Thessalonians,* 252–53, 259–60, 262; Green, *Thessalonians,* 294; Wannamaker, *Thessalonians,* 229; Weima, "1–2 Thessalonians," 885–86; Young, *Isaiah,* 1:97–100.

141. G. K. Beale, *1–2 Thessalonians* (Downers Grove, IL: IVP Academic, 2003), 191.

covenant people and the nations are accountable before God according to similar standards, namely that the moral law in the Mosaic covenant corresponds to the natural law that binds the whole world.[142] Paul also overtly modifies the threatened curse of exile for *the land* to apply to gentile oppressors in Thessalonica, requiring a correspondence between the Mosaic curses and the broader world. Paul's interpretive modification of Isaiah 2:10 indicates how he saw the curses of the Mosaic covenant that pertained to national Israel as linked to the broader principle of retribution built into the covenant of works, which remains active as an entailment of the natural law.[143]

Paul's point in Galatians 4:1–11, therefore, comes to fuller force, namely, that in the fullness of time—meaning, when God had made his point through the Mosaic administration that the works principle leaves everyone enslaved as under the covenant of works—Christ came to free everyone who believes from the law's curse.[144] He came under the Mosaic covenant *because* it resembled the covenant of works, so that it would be obvious to everyone that he was fulfilling the principle of works and earning our citizenship in the true heavens. In this way, when Christ fulfilled the Mosaic covenant and the nation was freed from the burden of its works principle to obtain inheritance, that historical change to the new covenant also symbolized how each believer transitions from being under the law's curse from the covenant of works to having full heavenly inheritance by faith in Christ.[145]

When Paul reflects upon the law as given through Moses, he says that "Moses writes about the righteousness that is based on the law, that the person who does the commandments shall live by them" (Rom 10:5). That legal righteousness explicitly contrasts with the righteousness by faith (Rom 10:6–13), again distinguishing the two opposing covenantal principles of law and grace.[146] Paul *at least* to some degree associated Moses with that law principle, making it similar in premise *as an administration* to the covenant of works.

---

142. VanDrunen, *Divine Covenants*, 164–208.

143. Fee, *Thessalonians*, 255; Wannamaker, *Thessalonians*, 224, 227.

144. Schreiner, *Galatians*, 269–71; deSilva, *Galatians*, 353–57.

145. Horton, *Justification*, 2:89–95; *EC*, 4.13.9.

146. Fesko, "Republication," 207–8; Estelle, "Leviticus 18:5 and Deuteronomy 30:1–14," 109–146.

The resemblance of the Mosaic covenant's types to the covenant of works explains why the new covenant administration so blessedly orders believers lives today. The new covenant clearly displays Christ and his benefits while the Mosaic covenant's features typologically obscured that substance. As Hebrews 10:1 says: "Because the law, since having a shadow of the coming good things, not the exact appearance of these realities, is never able to perfect those who draw near by the annual sacrifices themselves, which they continually offered" (my translation). Because its types resembled the covenant of works, the Mosaic covenant did not have the likeness or form of the covenant of grace's substance—Christ and the benefits of the new covenant. Nonetheless, the covenant of redemption stands behind the bestowal of spiritual blessings in every age, making Christ and his benefits the ground of God's relationship to his people under Moses too. The covenant of redemption has its direct reflection in the new covenant but was revealed with shadowy appearance in the Mosaic ordinances, which could not in themselves perfect anyone but gave the coming good realities of Christ and his benefits to believers by imposing constant reminders of the demands that Christ fulfilled for us.[147] In other words, the Mosaic covenant had the substance—which is Christ—by shadow, not as a clear picture.[148]

Recalling Christ's role as the last Adam, we can now add a third layer of biblical theology to the types about everlasting life that began even with Adam. Adam came through the creation waters with the Spirit hovering over them, was given the law, put in paradise, proved disobedient, and was then exiled from Eden. Israel similarly came through the waters of the Red Sea with the Spirit leading in a pillar of smoke and fire, was given the law, put in the promised land, proved disobedient, and so was exiled from Canaan.[149] Climactically, Christ came through the baptismal waters of the Jordan with the Spirit descending like a dove, was given his mission by the Father in the covenant of redemption to be born under the law, was put in the wilderness for testing, but proved fully obedient, and so has passed into the heavenly places as our great high priest who

147. TI, 12.7.31.

148. Vos, *Hebrews*, 55–65.

149. Wellum, "Progressive Covenantalism," 94.

sympathizes with our weaknesses, but even more so has earned our citizenship in heaven for us.[150] As the New Testament reflection upon the Mosaic covenant shows, the types and requirements tied to the Mosaic administration display Christ's active and passive obedience, so that the gospel would be thickly understood as even Old Testament faith took hold of the promised Savior.

CONCLUSION

The Mosaic covenant's typology and redemptive-historical relevance, admittedly complex, importantly concern Christ in the old economy.[151] Still, these matters of interpreting Mosaic typology are very specific and even niche, rendering overly vitriolic disagreement about parsing these delicate issues inappropriate when our varying interpretations fall within the confessional boundaries.[152] Perhaps especially those who are concerned to thwart antinomianism should be the first to lead winsomely with a twinkle in the eye rather than with the elbows, since gentleness and kindness are Christian virtues.

Despite the Mosaic covenant's redemptive-historical complexity, its value in the biblical storyline and for God's people can still be recognized. At the *historia salutis* level, the Mosaic covenant heightened the redemptive-historical tension concerning the demand for a faithful Adam by showing Israel's failure under the law. Further, it created a structure reflecting the world's plight under the original covenant of works so that, when Christ was born under it, his fulfillment of the law's demand for

150. For a more extensive and thorough defense of this position, see Fesko, "Republication," 197–212; J. V. Fesko, "The Republication of the Covenant of Works: The Accommodated Scriptures: A Response to Cornelis Venema," *Confessional Presbyterian* 9 (2013): 178–87, 285; *ACW*, 339–56; *LNF*; Horton, *Covenant Theology*, 35–50; Horton, *Covenant and Salvation*, 11–101; Horton, *Justification*, 2:57–96; VanDrunen, "Israel's Recapitulation," 303–24; VanDrunen, *Divine Covenants*, 346–65. For criticism, see Cornelis Venema, "The Law of Moses: Not a Disguised Covenant of Works: A Response to J.V. Fesko's 'The Republication of the Covenant of Works,' " *Confessional Presbyterian* 8 (2012): 212–27; Cornelis Venema, "The Mosaic Economy and the Covenant of Grace," *Confessional Presbyterian* 9 (2013): 157–78; Venema, *Christ and Covenant Theology*, 37–144; Belcher, *Fulfillment*, 88–95. Letham's criticism that this view of the Mosaic covenant undermines the doctrine of God itself is not only overstated, but also rests on his flawed assumption that law always regulates grace in every relationship between God and humanity; *Systematic Theology*, 459–60. His reservation is not the same as that outlined in Estelle et al., "Report to ... Study Republication," 47.

151. Estelle et al., "Report to ... Study Republication," 1–2.

152. Writing with other conclusions, Belcher exemplifies charitable and gentlemanly engagement, see *Fulfillment*, 75–95, 165–97.

perfect obedience would be more clearly perceived. At the *ordo salutis* level, the very covenantal features that furthered those tensions in redemptive history served as blessings to believers by teaching of Christ's active and passive obedience, so that believers partook of Christ and his benefits through those types and ordinances.

The pastoral use of this chapter's material is to reemphasize how Christ is writ large throughout the Scripture, even when the issues are complicated and require extended thought. The richness of the Mosaic covenant's contribution to redemptive history should not frustrate us into thinking these matters are too complicated. Rather, the depth of God's word should invigorate us as we see how we can never exhaust what we learn from it or run out of new things to find as we reread it repeatedly. In all its details, the Bible directs us to Christ.

XIV

From Moses to Christ

Now these things happened to them as an example,
but they were written down for our instruction,
on whom the end of the ages has come.
—*1 Corinthians 10:11*

The covenant of grace is one in substance but diversely administered, continuing to unfold throughout the Old Testament but coming to true fulfillment in Christ. The purpose of unpacking the old economy's administrations is to explore how those covenants demonstrate the point in the Westminster Confession that the covenant of grace's administrations under the old economy offer Christ by pointing ahead to him and his work.

> This covenant was differently administered in the time of the law and in the time of the gospel: under the law it was administered by promises, prophecies, sacrifices, circumcision, the paschal lamb, and other types and ordinances delivered to the people of the Jews, all fore-signifying Christ to come, which were for that time sufficient and efficacious, through the operation of the Spirit, to instruct and build up the elect in faith in the promised Messiah, by whom they

> had full remission of sins, and eternal salvation, and is called the Old Testament. (WCF 7.5)[1]

This chapter furthers that same purpose by exploring the covenant that God made with David, the interaction of the various old economy administrations, and, lastly, the new covenant, which fully exhibits the covenant of grace's substance. Again, the goal is not an exhaustive explanation of redemptive history's developing aspects but an account of each administration's contribution to redemptive history as it offers Christ. The focus remains on the argument that, throughout redemptive history, God communicated Christ and his benefits to believers through the means of grace in each covenant administration.

THE DAVIDIC KING

During the Mosaic covenant, God made a covenant with David as the king over Israel. This covenant concerned the preservation of David's line in the monarchy over God's people. In 2 Samuel 7:8–16, Nathan the prophet delivered God's message to David about God's covenant with him to make a house for him and "raise up your offspring after you, who shall come from your body, and I will establish his kingdom." God "will establish the throne of his kingdom forever" and "be to him a father" so that "he shall be to me a son" (2 Sam 7:12–14). Perhaps most astonishingly, God promised about this Davidic son: "When he commits iniquity, I will discipline him with the rod of men, with the stripes of the sons of men, but my steadfast love will not depart from him, as I took it from Saul, whom I put away from before you. And your house and your kingdom shall be made sure forever before me. Your throne shall be established forever" (2 Sam 7:14–16). God's covenant with David is then tied to David's lineage and preserving the kingdom.

As for its contribution to redemptive history's progress and anticipating Christ, the Davidic covenant primarily establishes the paradigm of the king for God's people. Despite how God rejected David's plan to build the temple (2 Sam 7:4–7), God used David to further his redemptive-historical purpose, building on his previous covenants, especially since he

1. *COC*, 3:617–18.

has always used them to administer his kingdom on earth.[2] As God's son, Adam had been charged with a royal role in exercising dominion within creation. Further, God had promised Abraham that kings would descend from his line (Gen 17:6). Humanity's role as God's image bearers then always had a royal aspect, which God had preserved in connection to his promise of the seed of the woman, confirmed to Abraham in the promise of an heir.[3]

In this connection, especially given the lack of initiation ceremony or additional covenant sign, the Davidic covenant is an extension of the Abrahamic covenant.[4] The Abrahamic covenant directly connected the promise of the offspring with a promise concerning royalty. God had provisionally fulfilled the promise to Abraham concerning nations by constituting Israel as his covenant people. In David, he began to fulfill his promises about royalty. God, therefore, covenanted with David that the promise of the offspring would be focused in David's royal lineage.[5] Even though David was king within the Mosaic covenant, the fulfillment of God's covenant with David transcends that context.

The kingly pattern culminates in Christ. In 1 Chronicles 17:1–15, the retelling of God's covenant with David explicitly connects David's throne and God's: "I will confirm him in my house and in my kingdom forever, and his throne shall be established forever" (17:14).[6] The discussion of the covenant of redemption showed how Christ is the royal priest sitting on God's throne in the temple (Zech 6:13). Additionally, David was the shepherd-king, anointed in Bethlehem (1 Sam 16:11–13). Christ was born in Bethlehem as David's royal city (Mic 5:2) and announced as the Good Shepherd for those given to him by the Father (John 10:10–16). Christ completes that kingly role begun in the Old Testament.

He is also the final reigning king over God's people. He has all authority in heaven and on earth (Matt 28:18). He is the Son of God in power

2. *KTC*, 446–64; Williamson, *Sealed*, 125–28; Richard P. Belcher Jr., "The Davidic Covenant," in *CT*, 181–83; Belcher, *Fulfillment*, 108–12; *BOC*, 36–38; *KP*, 1–7; Baugh, *Majesty on High*, 105–36; Renihan, *Mystery*, 99.

3. Schreiner, *Covenant*, 73, 75–76.

4. *KTC*, 481–85; Williamson, *Sealed*, 120–22, 144–45.

5. Belcher, "Davidic Covenant," 173–79, 188; Belcher, *Fulfillment*, 97–105; Schreiner, *Covenant*, 74–75, 78–79; Williamson, *Sealed*, 128–31; Brown and Keele, *Sacred Bond*, 123–28.

6. Belcher, "Davidic Covenant," 180, 184–85; Belcher, *Fulfillment*, 107–8, 113–14.

(Rom 1:3–4). According to his humanity, he descended from David, whose heir was promised to be the everlasting king, and from Abraham, who God assured would also father kings in his line (Matt 1:1; Rom 1:3–4).[7] He is the seed of the woman (Gen 3:15), the heir of Abraham (Gen 17:3–8), but also the Son given to Israel whose name is Mighty God and who bears the weight of government by establishing righteousness upon David's throne (Isa 9:6–7). As Adam was God's son on earth and Christ the Son is the last Adam, so too God most fittingly promised to be Father to David's heir since Christ as God's true Son would be that heir. So, the Westminster Larger Catechism well describes Christ's role as our king:

> Christ executes the Office of a King, in calling out of the world a people to himself, and giving them Officers, Laws, and Censures, by which he visibly governs them; in bestowing saving grace upon his elect, rewarding their obedience, and correcting them for their sins, preserving and supporting them under all their temptations and sufferings, restraining and overcoming all their enemies, and powerfully ordering all things for his own glory and their good; and also in taking vengeance on the rest, who know not God, and obey not the Gospel. (WLC 45)[8]

Christ then fulfills all God's promises about a king for his people, descending from the promised lineages as the offspring born of the woman who would crush Satan.[9] Whereas the Mosaic covenant primarily shone a typological light on Christ's priestly duties, the Davidic provides covenantal context and teaching for his kingly duties.

THE RELATIONSHIP BETWEEN OLD ECONOMY ADMINISTRATIONS

Although the one covenant of grace was diversely administered even under the old economy, Scripture draws connections among those various administrations. Most discussions about redemptive-historical development consider passages wherein God initiated covenants but neglect

---

7. Letham, *Systematic Theology*, 461.

8. *LC*, 74.

9. *MMB*, 1072–78; *CMT*, 136–38; Belcher, *Fulfillment*, 112–14; Wellum, "Progressive Covenantalism," 95–96; Schreiner, *Covenant*, 79–87; Williamson, *Sealed*, 141–45.

later accounts of how these covenants affect one another in God's ongoing relationship with his people through them.[10] The narrative of the nation under the Mosaic covenant during the time of the kings confirms that God's promises to Abraham and to David were the reason for all of God's mercies—concerning heavenly and earthly blessings—but that the Mosaic covenant provided the rationale for their judgment. This underemphasized development within the Old Testament narrative clarifies the Mosaic covenant as resembling the covenant of works for the nation.

Although God's promise appears unconditional for David, its fulfillment seems conditional for his heirs.[11] When 1 Chronicles 17:1–15 recounts God's covenant with David, the writer omits God's commitment to forgive the iniquity of David's heir. This difference indicates not contradictions of the accounts but merely that Chronicles emphasizes the responsibility for David's line. Even in 2 Samuel 7:13, God had said that David's heir "shall build a house for my name, and I will establish the throne of his kingdom forever." David's heir must build God's house for God to establish his kingdom forever.[12] 1 Kings 9:4–7 emphasizes the conditions upon David's heir:

> And as for you, *if you will walk before me,* as David your father walked, with integrity of heart and uprightness, *doing according to all that I have commanded you,* and keeping my statutes and my rules, *then I will establish your royal throne over Israel forever,* as I promised David your father, saying, "You shall not lack a man on the throne of Israel." But *if* you turn aside from following me, you or your children, and *do not keep my commandments and my statutes that I have set before you,* but go and serve other gods and worship them, *then I will cut off Israel from the land* that I have given them, and the house that I have consecrated for my name I will cast out of my sight, and Israel will become a proverb and a byword among all peoples.

---

10. The best discussions are Brown and Keele, *Sacred Bond,* 129–34; and Belcher, "Davidic Covenant," 185–88.

11. *MMB,* 1052–64; Belcher, "Davidic Covenant," 176–77, 187; Belcher, *Fulfillment,* 102–3; Schreiner, *Covenant,* 76–78, 83; Williamson, *Sealed,* 133.

12. Brown and Keele, *Sacred Bond,* 129.

The conditions for David's heir appear in many other places too (1 Kgs 2:2–4; 6:11–13; 14:7–10; 2 Kgs 10:28–31; 1 Chr 17:12–14; 28:7–8; 2 Chr 6:16; 7:17–20).[13] Although God unconditionally promised an everlasting throne to David through his lineage, that promise's fulfillment depended upon an heir being truly obedient to God's commands.[14] In this regard, it becomes very clear as the narrative develops that the works principle for the whole nation becomes most focused upon the king as the people's representative (2 Kgs 23:25–27; 24:3–4; 2 Chr 12:1–2; 33:7–9).[15]

This concentration of the works principle in the king ultimately unites some features of redemptive history and provides the means for someone to fulfill not only the original covenant of works but also the Mosaic administration as a repetition of the covenant of works for God's nation. God promised an everlasting heir to David but set conditions for that heir because Christ was always going to fulfill the promise and condition by his perfect obedience. In Jeremiah 33:14–18, God explained this very point:

> Behold, the days are coming, declares the LORD, when I will fulfill the promise I made to the house of Israel and the house of Judah. In those days and at that time I will cause a righteous Branch to spring up for David, and he shall execute justice and righteousness in the land. In those days Judah will be saved, and Jerusalem will dwell securely. And this is the name by which it will be called: "The LORD is our righteousness."
>
> For thus says the LORD: David shall never lack a man to sit on the throne of the house of Israel, and the Levitical priests shall never lack a man in my presence to offer burnt offerings, to burn grain offerings, and to make sacrifices forever.

---

13. Brown and Keele, *Sacred Bond*, 129–32.

14. Regarding Psalm 2's relationship to 2 Samuel 7, John Goldingay comments, "God made a permanent commitment to David that his line would always reign. Yhwh would have a father-son relationship with him, defeat his enemies, make him the greatest king in the world, and thus make him a witness to Yhwh's might and purpose. This commitment represents a form of *fulfillment of God's promise to Abraham* that he would be blessed in such a way that people would covet the same blessing, while people who belittled him would be cursed (Gen. 12:1–3). As the family becomes a people, a nation, and a state, God's promise becomes more politicized. The nation is destined to rule the world on God's behalf. The introduction of the monarchy means *God's undertaking comes to focus on the king*. God promises the king victory over his enemies and submission from them; when he experiences attack from them, God gives him victory over them." Goldingay, *Psalms*, 1:95 (emphasis added).

15. Belcher, *Fulfillment*, 91.

Christ as the final and ultimate Davidic heir would fulfill every need for obedience in order to bring about the completion of God's promise to David (Ezek 37:24–28; Jer 33:14–26).[16] So, Irenaeus writes:

> The Lord sware truth unto David, and he will not disappoint him: Of the fruit of thy body will I set on thy throne: if thy children shall keep my covenant and my testimonies, which I covenanted with them, their sons for evermore (shall sit upon thy throne.) But none of the sons of David reigned for evermore, nor was their kingdom for evermore; for it was brought to nought. But the king that was born of David, He is Christ.[17] Christ fulfills every condition to bring about God's everlasting kingdom through David's line.

The promise about and conditions for David's heir mark God's covenant with David as driving history pointedly toward Christ. At the *historia salutis* level, by concentrating his promise on David's royal heir, God advances the promise of the woman's seed who would crush the serpent and the offspring of Abraham who would inherit the earth. This offspring will now come through David's kingly line. Moreover, since the Mosaic covenant repeated the principle of the covenant of works with Adam and concentrated that requirement for obedience on David's heir, the conditions upon David's heir prepare the way for Christ to fulfill the covenant of works, both in its Adamic and Mosaic manifestations, for his people's salvation. Although the promise of the Davidic king extended the Abrahamic promise of a royal seed, its relationship to the Mosaic covenant climactically heightened the tension in redemptive history for the demand of a faithful Adam by creating the structure wherein this kingly Messiah would be born under the law to fulfill requirement of obedience while being specially qualified to rule over his earned kingdom. At the *ordo salutis* level, the promise of this king directed faith toward Christ, the ultimately faithful king, saving his people, so granting him and his benefits to every believer who trusted in him through the promise.

The ongoing narrative of Israel's history reveals further ways that the biblical authors appealed to the various covenants. Every time God

16. *KTC*, 468–75.

17. Irenaeus, *Demonstration*, §64.

mentions his covenant with David, he appealed to it to explain why he was *delaying* judgment or *doing good* to his people (1 Kgs 2:33, 45; 15:4–5; 2 Kgs 8:18–19; 20:5–6; 2 Chr 6:16), as in 2 Chronicles 21:7: "Yet the LORD was not willing to destroy the house of David, because of the covenant that he had made with David, and since he had promised to give a lamp to him and to his sons forever." Even regarding the conditions upon David's heirs, despite their failures, God withheld condemnation because of his promise to David (1 Kgs 11:9–13, 32–39). God's covenant with David is an anchor point in the story for God's blessing upon the people.[18]

Alternatively, biblical authors appealed to the Mosaic covenant always to explain *judgment*. In stark contrast to the Davidic covenant, God never mentioned Moses as the reason for withholding punishment (1 Kgs 8:55–58; 2 Kgs 13:1–3; 17:7–23, 34–40; 18:11–12; 21:14–15; 22:13–20; Neh 9:26–30; Jer 9:13–16; 16:10–13; 22:4–9; 25:8–14; 34:13–22; 44:22–23). Nehemiah 10:28–29 provides a pointed example:

> The rest of the people, the priests, the Levites, the gatekeepers, the singers, the temple servants, and all who have separated themselves from the peoples of the lands to the Law of God, their wives, their sons, their daughters, all who have knowledge and understanding, join with their brothers, their nobles, and *enter into a curse and an oath to walk in God's Law that was given by Moses* the servant of God, and to observe and do all the commandments of the LORD our Lord and his rules and his statutes.

As the people commit to *do* God's commandments as given to Moses, the ratification ominously highlights their curse. The Mosaic administration emphasized obedience as the condition to have the land (2 Kgs 21:7–8; 23:1–3; Jer 11:1–11). The only exceptions to the Mosaic covenant as a cause of judgment are God's delay of exile *because the king obeyed* the Mosaic

18. Michael G. McKelvey comments on Psalm 89:38–39, "The Babylonian exile challenged Israel's understanding of their status and future. Exile marked the end of human kingship in the land, and their nationhood was terminated. Nevertheless, this question still remained: What about God's promise to David? ... Even with the monarchy destroyed, God's covenant with David was still valid, and the psalmist called upon Yahweh to remember that covenant. Psalm 89 provides a vivid example of the profound connection between the Davidic covenant and God's redemptive purposes." Michael G. McKelvey, "1–2 Samuel," in *A Biblical-Theological Introduction to the Old Testament: The Gospel Promised*, ed. Miles V. Van Pelt (Wheaton, IL: Crossway, 2016), 217.

law, dramatically confirming the works principle's connection within the Davidic covenant (2 Kgs 18:6; 23:25–27; 2 Kgs 24:3–4).[19] The Mosaic administration was never a point of appeal for mercy or promise.[20]

When Israel's narrative reaches its worst, the final point of appeal for hope is always God's covenant with Abraham. This was true even before they entered the land. In Leviticus 26:40–42, God grounded his ongoing mercy in the Abrahamic promise: "But if they confess their iniquity and the iniquity of their fathers in their treachery that they committed against me, and also in walking contrary to me, so that I walked contrary to them and brought them into the land of their enemies—if then their uncircumcised heart is humbled and they make amends for their iniquity, then I will remember my covenant with Jacob, and I will remember my covenant with Isaac and my covenant with Abraham, and I will remember the land." Abraham remained the cause for hope as they entered the land (Deut 4:31). Under the monarchy as well, Abraham remained the last hopeful cause to know that God would not totally destroy the people (2 Kgs 13:22–23; 1 Chr 16:14–18). Even though God gave the land to the nation because of Abraham and continued with them for some time because of Abraham and David, they lost those blessings because they disobeyed the Mosaic covenant (Jer 32:22–23).[21]

The appeals to the various covenants throughout the ongoing biblical narrative confirm that God's promises to Abraham and David were continual reasons for hope, but the Mosaic administration required obedience to maintain the people's earthly blessing.[22] In every era, the people were

---

19. Commenting on the author's theological purpose for composing 1–2 Kings, William Fullilove writes, "The content and shape of the book allow the reader to infer its goal: to justify that Yahweh's exile of his people was, in fact, a just punishment since they broke the Mosaic law." He further explains, "Instead, the author is arguing that God's people were in exile because God had willed it as a judgment for their disobedience to the law, especially as presented in Deuteronomy." William B. Fullilove, "1–2 Kings," in *Biblical-Theological Introduction to the Old Testament*, 224, 225.

20. Horton, *Justification*, 2:72–73.

21. *VRD*, 2:132. God's withholding the consequences of the Mosaic covenant precisely because of his promises to David and Abraham shows how the claim that "the Mosaic covenant controls both the Abrahamic and the Davidic Covenants" is at least overly simplistic if not fundamentally mistaken by incorrectly conflating all the old economy's covenants, thereby wrongly transposing the biblical contrast between the old covenant, specifically the Mosaic, and the new, onto the new covenant's difference from the whole Old Testament; see Micah Renihan and Samuel Renihan, "Reformed Baptist Covenant Theology and Biblical Theology," in *Recovering a Covenantal Heritage*, 482.

22. Horton, *Justification*, 2:76–80.

saved by grace alone through faith alone in Christ alone, but each administration contributed its own set of types or promises that applied Christ and his work before he came. Those administrations, however, cannot be mixed as if they all perform the same exact function since Scripture appeals to them for different purposes as they drive history toward Christ.

THE NEW COVENANT

The new covenant fulfills every promise and type as Christ's arrival and completed mission abrogate every previous symbolic ordinance, directly revealing the covenant of grace's substance. This covenant not only grants the reality of eschatological blessings but also has the exact appearance and form, rather than shadowy types, of those realities (Heb 10:1). The Westminster Confession describes this administration's distinct features:

> Under the gospel, when Christ the substance was exhibited, the ordinances in which this covenant is dispensed are the preaching of the word and the administration of the sacraments of Baptism and the Lord's Supper; which, though fewer in number, and administered with more simplicity and less outward glory, yet in them it is held forth in more fullness, evidence, and spiritual efficacy, to all nations, both Jews and Gentiles; and is called the New Testament. There are not, therefore, two covenants of grace differing in substance, but one and the same under various dispensations. (WCF 7.6)[23]

Whereas Christ was previously communicated namelessly through ordinances signifying his work, now his name is clearly announced, displaying his life as the fulfillment of the law and his death as the once-and-for-all sacrifice for our sin.[24] Turretin explains,

> It is called "new" not as to the substance of the covenant (which is the same in both) but: (1) as to the circumstances and mode, being manifested without a veil and the law (in which way the covenant appeared as if new or renewed), also because it sets forth Christ not to be exhibited but as exhibited, in which way it can be called

23. *COC*, 3:618; WLC 35; *LC*, 72.

24. *CG*, 377–78.

> new both intensively as to degree of light and extensively as to amplitude, extending itself indiscriminately to all nations.[25]

The new economy's means of grace plainly, not typologically, divulge the substance they offer.[26] The new covenant, compared to the old economy, is thoroughly new *as an administration* by setting forth Christ in full clarity, though it is not new in substance.[27]

To clarify, the new covenant is the same in substance with the previous covenants as Christ always grounded true forgiveness of sins during every administration of the covenant of grace. The substance is the same because other administrations' means of grace never in themselves procured forgiveness of sin but communicated forgiveness *in Christ*. Physical circumcision itself never removed spiritual uncleanness from God's people (Jer 9:25–26; Rom 2:25–29). Mosaic sacrifices in themselves never covered sin before God (Heb 9:13–14; 10:2).[28] Each administration's outward means never in themselves procured salvation, although they granted it *in Christ*, functioning sacramentally to apply it *from Christ*. The previous covenants conveyed the same substance as the new, not by obtaining justification and sanctification in themselves, but through the means of grace appointed for communicating *Christ and his benefits*.[29]

Moreover, the new covenant differs *in administration* in that Christ historically wrought his work of redemption as its guarantor, thereby clearly exhibiting the substance of every administration and permanently securing

---

25. *TI*, 12.7.46.

26. *MMB*, 1229–32.

27. Crowe, *Path of Faith*, 92–94.

28. Block, *Covenant*, 272, 502–11.

29. To be explicit about these clarifications, my confessional Baptist friends sometimes say that "the blood of bulls and goats cannot purify the conscience," as if genuinely refuting the Reformed view of the covenant of grace. That supposed critique always confuses me since no Reformed source of which I am aware argues that animal sacrifices *themselves* provided forgiveness before God. This section states as clearly as possible that Mosaic ceremonies provided grace only inasmuch as they served as means of grace to communicate *Christ and his benefits*, not procuring salvation in themselves. For an attempt to account for confessional Baptist covenant theology concerning these issues, see Harrison Perkins, "Engaging Confessional Baptists on Covenant Theology Part 1: Typology," *The Heidelblog*, September 13, 2022, https://heidelblog.net/2022/09/engaging-confessional-baptists-on-covenant-theology-part-1-typology/; and Harrison Perkins, "Engaging Confessional Baptists on Covenant Theology Part 2: Unity of Salvation in the Old and New Testaments," *The Heidelblog*, September 20, 2022, https://heidelblog.net/2022/09/engaging-confessional-baptists-on-covenant-theology-part-2-unity-of-salvation-in-the-old-and-new-testaments/.

this administration as the communication of his work's virtue, efficacy, and benefits. The substance is clearly exhibited in that whereas God formerly spoke through the prophets about the Son, now he speaks directly in the Son (Heb 1:1–2). The new differs from the Mosaic as forgiveness now comes from the guarantor of our own administration rather than from the future work of our mediator foresignified in our ordinances—noting that true forgiveness never came from within the Mosaic sacrifices themselves but always from Christ (*expromissor*) communicated and applied through the Mosaic covenant's ordinances. Still, this difference is simply now receiving the virtue of Christ's work *incarnatus* through our administration rather than as previously believers received it *incarnandus* through theirs. The new covenant is the external administration, having outward ordinances that most completely display the covenant of grace's substance, truly exhibiting salvation's guarantor. The tensions of redemptive history created by the structures and types of the old economy's administrations have given way simply to the tension between being fully justified and waiting to be fully glorified, as chapter 10 discussed.

What confirms the new covenant as an outward administration? First, as Christ instituted the Lord's Supper, he said of the wine, "This cup is the new covenant in my blood" (1 Cor 11:25; see also Luke 22:20). Jesus inherently links the new covenant to this outward rite, a means of grace. Second, Paul refers to himself and the apostles as "*ministers* of a new covenant" (2 Cor 3:4). The new covenant cannot, therefore, be reduced to its blessings, as if it is simply forgiveness of sin by Christ's blood. Its outward form necessarily includes sacraments and ministers.

The new covenant's sacraments and shape of ministry, not its blessings, differ from the old economy. Peter explains, "To him all the prophets bear witness that everyone who believes *in him* receives forgiveness of sins through his name" (Acts 10:43). The prophets preached forgiveness through faith *in Christ*. David likewise announces, "Blessed is the one whose transgression is forgiven, whose sin is covered" (Ps 32:1). Old covenant saints truly received this forgiveness in Christ. The new covenant differs as an administration with new sacraments and new ministers but applies the same blessings from Christ that believers had received under the old economy.

The prophets announced the new covenant in the Old Testament. In Deuteronomy 18:15–19, even at the Mosaic covenant's renewal before Israel entered Canaan, Moses foretold:

> The LORD your God will raise up for you a prophet like me from among you, from your brothers—it is to him you shall listen—just as you desired of the LORD your God at Horeb on the day of the assembly, when you said, "Let me not hear again the voice of the LORD my God or see this great fire any more, lest I die." And the LORD said to me, "They are right in what they have spoken. I will raise up for them a prophet like you from among their brothers. And I will put my words in his mouth, and he shall speak to them all that I command him. And whoever will not listen to my words that he shall speak in my name, I myself will require it of him."

Moses knew that God's people needed the final prophet, whom they would truly hear. The people were right to be afraid of the Lord's declarations at Sinai, since this law covenant could not in itself effectively secure the grace that they needed for salvation.

In his new covenant arrival, Christ is this culminating prophet, rounding out the full scope of his threefold duties as mediator. Moses foretold that some would not listen to this prophet, Christ being the one who "came to his own, and his own people did not receive him" (John 1:11). Still, Christ is the final emissary, completing covenant history. Whereas Sinai offered a frightening message through Moses, in the final prophet, "the Word became flesh and dwelt among us, and we have seen his glory, glory as of the only Son from the Father, full of grace and truth" (John 1:14). In Acts 3:18–26, Peter used Moses's exact prophecy to show that the prophets foretold Christ would suffer to forgive his people's sin.[30] The new covenant promises were always built into the old economy.

Jeremiah 31:26–40 announces the clearest promise of the new covenant:

30. Williamson, *Sealed*, 185–86.

> Behold, the days are coming, declares the LORD, when I will make a new covenant with the house of Israel and the house of Judah, not like the covenant that I made with their fathers on the day when I took them by the hand to bring them out of the land of Egypt, my covenant that they broke, though I was their husband, declares the LORD. For this is the covenant that I will make with the house of Israel after those days, declares the LORD: I will put my law within them, and I will write it on their hearts. And I will be their God, and they shall be my people. And no longer shall each one teach his neighbor and each his brother, saying, "Know the LORD," for they shall all know me, from the least of them to the greatest, declares the LORD. For I will forgive their iniquity, and I will remember their sin no more. (Jer 31:31–34)

This prophecy prompts three major reflections pertinent to our considerations.

First, this new covenant concerns the houses of Israel and Judah.[31] Unless we are *in some way* part of that old covenant people, we have no share in the new covenant (Matt 15:21–28; Mark 7:24–30).[32] In this respect, Jeremiah 31:33–34 invokes the Abrahamic promise "And I will be their God, and they shall be my people. ... They shall all know me, from the least of them to the greatest, declares the LORD" (cf. Gen 17:7).[33] God's commitment that even the least members *within the covenant* would know him did not revise the entry requirement but strengthened and intensified the spiritual expectation in his Abrahamic promise to be God to us and our children. The new covenant deepens God's Abrahamic commitments, heightening expectation of his regenerating work within the covenant rather than altering the structure of the new covenant community.[34]

---

31. *MMB*, 1292–1303.

32. Block, *Covenant*, 280–81; *KTC*, 539–47.

33. Jack R. Lundbom, *Jeremiah 21–36* (New York: Doubleday, 2004), 469.

34. Accordingly, the argument that the new covenant changed the nature of membership in the community fundamentally misunderstands the nature of Jeremiah's prophecy; *KTC*, 749–55, 807–24; Christopher W. Cowan, "The Warning Passages of Hebrews and the New Covenant Community," *Progressive Covenantalism*, 196. Many have criticized this Baptistic interpretation's over-realized eschatology, meaning that total fulfillment of Jeremiah's prophecy of completely regenerate covenant membership belongs to the consummation but not to this age of inaugurated fulfillment; see, e.g., Scott R. Swain, "New Covenant Theologies," in *CT*, 566–69; Richard L. Pratt Jr., "Infant Baptism in

For precisely this reason, Peter applies the Abrahamic promise to his hearers during his first *new covenant* sermon, noting that the new covenant promise "is for you and for your children and for all who are far off" (Acts 2:39). This connection necessarily demonstrates how God's covenant with Abraham was always primarily spiritual in nature, so that all nations are blessed as the promise of justification by faith and receiving the Spirit extends globally (Gen 12:3; Gal 3:8, 14).[35] Reflecting Galatians 4:21–31, Irenaeus argues that Abraham began the Mosaic covenant *and the new covenant*:

> It was necessary that some things were announced in advance by the fathers in a paternal manner, but others anticipated by the prophets in a legal manner, and others delineated according to the fashion of Christ—by those who have received adoption—even though the one God reveals all things. Since, for instance, Abraham was one, yet anticipated in himself two covenants [the Mosaic and the new], in which some have sown, but others reaped: "For in this saying, 'the word is true, that one people shall sow but another shall reap,'" [Jn. 4:37] but one God supplies what is fitting to both, seed to the sower but bread to the reaper. As one plants and another waters, but God is the one who gives the increase. For the fathers

the New Covenant," in *The Case for Covenantal Infant Baptism*, ed. Gregg Strawbridge (Phillipsburg, NJ: P&R, 2003), 158–73. Although true, this critique still underplays how the Baptistic interpretation understands the prophecy's eschatology in entirely the wrong direction. Specifically, it is not as though the new covenant revised the covenant community's structure but presently falls short of an ideal fulfillment. Rather, the new covenant intensifies the old Abrahamic promise to be God to us and our children after us so that the extent of those who partake of the covenant's substance while participating in the administration within the same structure has expected increase, completed at the consummation. Progressive covenantalism fails to read the new covenant in light of the previous covenants which shaped how Jeremiah's original audience would have understood his prophecy as furthering Abrahamic expectations, not as forging Baptistic ecclesiology; see Robert J. Cara, "Covenant in Hebrews," in *CT*, 264–66.

35. Lundbom, *Jeremiah 21–36*, 475–76: "Moreover, the Mosaic covenant contains the law, which is now a burden to everybody—Jew and Gentile. In Paul's view the law only brings people under its curses. But Christ, by dying on the cross, becomes himself a curse redeeming those under the law who have faith in him (Gal. 3:10–14). The new covenant, therefore, contains only blessings, making it just like the Abrahamic covenant. The Mosaic covenant serves Paul only for the purpose of making a contrast with the Abrahamic covenant. In his allegory in Gal. 4:21–31, Paul sees the Abrahamic covenant (fulfilled through Sarah) leading to freedom, sonship, and the Jerusalem above; the covenant made at Sinai (called Hagar) leads to present Jerusalem—i.e., the Jews and Judaizers, and thus slavery."

> and the prophets sowed the word about Christ, but the Church has reaped, that is, received the fruit.[36]

The new covenant completes the Abrahamic covenant, being fundamentally like it.[37] Christ "helps the offspring of Abraham" (Heb 2:16).[38] The church is, then, simply the true fulfillment or "fruition" of Israel but under the new administration, rather than the Mosaic administration, of the covenant of grace.[39]

In Acts 15:12–21, the church clearly fulfills promises to Israel, even as an extension of Israel. At this Jerusalem Council, Paul and Barnabas recount gentiles coming to faith in Christ, which James explains by quoting Amos 9:11–12:

> "In that day I will raise up
> the booth of David that is fallen
> and repair its breaches,
> and raise up its ruins
> and rebuild it as in the days of old,
> that they may possess the remnant of Edom
> and all the nations who are called by my name,"
> declares the Lord who does this.

God promised to rebuild David's exile-crumbled tent. The new covenant people composed of Jews and gentiles with faith in Christ fulfilled Israel's restoration, showing how the church has some part in Judah and Israel as recipients of Jeremiah's new covenant.[40]

Second, God promised that the new covenant would be "*not like* the covenant that I made with their fathers on the day *when I took them by the hand to bring them out of the land of Egypt*, my covenant that they

---

36. Irenaeus, *Against Heresies*, 4.25.3, in *PG*, 7.1:1051–52; *ANF*, 1:496.

37. Lundbom, *Jeremiah 21–36*, 474–79; Burnside, *God, Justice, and Society*, 62: "The New Testament claims that with the death and resurrection of Jesus the Messiah, the full expression of the covenant formula—"I will be their God, and they shall be my people"—has finally opened up. Jesus's new covenant is not only a revision of the Abrahamic covenant but also an incorporation of a new body of people."

38. Cara, "Covenant in Hebrews," 252.

39. Horton, *Covenant Theology*, 129–36; Swain, "New Covenant Theologies," 560–61; Glodo, "Dispensationalism," 545–47; Williamson, *Sealed*, 188–92.

40. Robertson, "Israel and the Nations," 522–23.

broke, though I was their husband, declares the LORD" (Jer 31:32). The new covenant contrasts specifically and directly with the Mosaic covenant.[41] Irenaeus comments, "Moreover, the laws of bondage were separately taught to the people through Moses, adapted for their instruction as Moses himself declared, 'And the Lord commanded at that time to teach to you statutes and judgments.' *These things* [of Moses], therefore, which were given to them unto bondage and for a sign were cancelled by the new covenant of liberty."[42] The new covenant *as an administration* of the covenant of grace radically differs from, specifically, the Mosaic administration.[43]

Christ's priesthood, as explained in Hebrews 7:11–22, confirms the new covenant differs precisely from the Mosaic covenant. That the Levitical priesthood was inadequate for salvation is markedly part of the Mosaic covenant (Heb 7:11–14).[44] So, the effective priest must be from a priesthood of Melchizedek's order, rather than Aaron's (Heb 7:15–19). The Mosaic priesthood's inadequacy necessitated a mediator who can intercede "by the power of an indestructible life" (Heb 7:16). Notably, Melchizedek's priesthood connected to the *Abrahamic* covenant (Heb 7:1–10), specifically, distinguished from the Mosaic priesthood.[45] Climactically, God's pronouncement in Psalm 110:4 made Jesus the guarantor of a better covenant (Heb 7:20–22). Christ's priesthood is better than the *Mosaic* priesthood, since it connects to the Abrahamic covenant.

This connection certainly applies to the superiority of Christ's self-sacrifice over the animal sacrifices (Heb 9:11–15). Certainly, "it is impossible for the blood of bulls and goats to take away sins" (Heb 10:4). Those sacrifices never effected salvation. Christ, however, "is the mediator of a new covenant, so that those who are called may receive the promised eternal inheritance, since a death has occurred that redeems them from

---

41. Hodge, *Systematic Theology*, 2:376–77; Lundbom, *Jeremiah 21–36*, 466–67; Cara, "Covenant in Hebrews," 261–63; McKelvey, "New Covenant as Promised in the Major Prophets," 194, 187; Brown and Keele, *Sacred Bond*, 137–40; Williamson, *Sealed*, 152–57; contra Renihan and Renihan, "Reformed Baptist Covenant Theology and Biblical Theology," 479–85; and Renihan, *Mystery*, 98. Here, Renihan too closely associates the Abrahamic and Mosaic covenants so that the new covenant differs fundamentally from them both.

42. Irenaeus, *Against Heresies*, 4.16.5, in *PG*, 7.1:1018; *ANF*, 1:482 (emphasis added).

43. *EC*, 4.13.5–8; *TI*, 12.12.18–21; *MMB*, 1257, 1267–69; Letham, *Systematic Theology*, 462–63; Belcher, *Fulfillment*, 199–258.

44. Ellingworth, *Hebrews*, 370, 373–74, 381.

45. Johnson, *Hebrews*, 175–81, 183–93; Ellingworth, *Hebrews*, 360, 363–64.

the transgressions committed under the first covenant" (Heb 9:15). This first covenant is the Mosaic, contrasting Christ's priestly appointment and the efficacy of his sacrifice with the *Mosaic* priesthood.[46] As Charles Hodge comments, "This covenant is called *new* in reference to the Mosaic covenant. The latter was ratified by the blood of animals; the new, by the blood of the eternal Son of God; the one in itself could secure only temporal benefits and the remission of ceremonial offenses; the other secures eternal redemption, and the remission of sin in the sight of God."[47] As means of grace, those Mosaic sacrifices communicated the virtue, efficacy, and benefits of Christ's work to believers but did not themselves procure true forgiveness of sin.

Christ's priestly work is, then, not Mosaic but after that order of Melchizedek, the priestly order connected to Abraham. This priest for Abraham was tied so pointedly to the new covenant that Hebrews argues Melchizedek in "*resembling the Son of God* he continues a priest forever" (Heb 7:3). The connection between Abraham's priest and the new covenant could hardly be tighter. Hebrews' covenantal logic concerning Abraham and Moses follows the same pattern as Paul's in Galatians 3:15–4:31, differentiating precisely the new and Mosaic covenants.

Reformed theologians, following Irenaeus, repeatedly affirm that the new covenant differs from the old economy only as to administration, not substance. John Calvin argues that the Abrahamic and new covenants are so similar "in substance and reality, that the two are actually one and the same."[48] Francis Junius (1545–1602) argues, "But the conditions were demanded from the people under the old covenant, but from Christ under the new, and were fulfilled in Christ for our good and salvation."[49] In other words, the types that burdened God's people with the law—hence "my covenant that they broke"—disappear, fully manifesting the substance in Christ as the law fulfiller.[50] There is no "*if* you obey,

46. Lane, *Hebrews 9–13*, 217–19, 225–26, 233–42; Ellingworth, *Hebrews*, 452–54, 456, 460–62, 465, 470, 471–74.

47. Hodge, *Corinthians*, 227.

48. Calvin, *Institutes*, 2.10.2.

49. Francis Junius, "De Federe et Testamento Dei in Ecclesia Vetere," in *Opera Theologica*, 2 vol. (Heidelberg, 1608), 28.

50. *VRD*, 2:131–32.

then I will" in the new covenant. Rather, the new differs in that, unlike Israel's potential to lose the land by breaking the covenant, the church can never lose its blessings.[51] William Ames explains, "The testament is new in relation to what existed from the time of Moses and in relation to the promise made to the fathers. But it is new not in essence but in form. In the former circumstances the form of administration gave some evidence of the covenant of works, from which this testament is essentially different. Since the complete difference between the new covenant and the old appeared only in the administration which came after Christ, this administration is properly termed the covenant and testament which is new."[52] Or Witsius's point, "The difference of the economies consists in this, that the same inheritance is held forth different ways: in the New Testament clearly and without any vail; in the Old, wrapped up in many types and earthly pledges."[53] The new covenant, therefore, repudiates not everything in the old economy, but its types, fulfilling its promises. The substance is the same, but the administration, thoroughly new.[54]

Third, the new covenant administration directly displays the covenant of grace's substance. This newness is clearest, as God promised, "I will forgive their iniquity, and I will remember their sin no more" (Jer 31:34) Still, God had always provided his people with forgiveness of sins according to the substance of the covenant. David writes in Psalm 103:2–4:

> Bless the Lord, O my soul,
> and forget not all his benefits,
> who forgives all your iniquity,
> who heals all your diseases,
> who redeems your life from the pit.

God forgave *all* his people's iniquities under the old economy. Paul uses David as an example of how our sins are forgiven (Rom 4:6–8), clearly stating that God's promises to Abraham were the gospel (Gal 3:8). Even God's promise to make the law internal to his people is new only in a

51. Williamson, *Sealed*, 153–54.

52. *MT*, 1.39.4.

53. *EC*, 4.10.6.

54. *MMB*, 1365–67; Swain, "New Covenant Theologies," 551–55.

specific way, since old covenant believers internally possessed the law as God sanctified his people (Deut 10:16; 11:18; 30:6).[55] This internalizing promise is new, not as though the Spirit had not always worked regeneration and holiness in God's people, rather in that now our piety consists not in external sacrifices and offerings, but in presenting our own bodies "as a living sacrifice, holy and acceptable to God, which is your *spiritual* worship" (Rom 12:1).[56] So, the new covenant's substance is not its newness.[57]

The newness of the new covenant is in its administration. The Mosaic covenant's types had not themselves provided the forgiveness of sins. The animal sacrifices had reminded people of their sin, rather than actually forgiving it: "But in these sacrifices there is a reminder of sins every year. For it is impossible for the blood of bulls and goats to take away sins" (Heb 10:3–4). God had forgiven his people's sin under the Old Testament but because Christ was already their mediator rather than because of animal sacrifices merely typifying Christ (Rom 3:24–26).[58] Whereas the Mosaic administration taught about Christ through animal sacrifices and the other requirements of obedience, the new covenant preaches about Christ by name in detail about his work, offering him in the gospel message, the waters of baptism, and the elements of the Lord's Supper.[59] All these features directly exhibit the substance of the covenant of grace.[60]

Christ confirmed the new covenant in his blood. The Mosaic administration officially began when Moses made a sacrifice; applied the blood to the people; and the elders, representing the people, ate a meal with God in his presence (Exod 24). So too, the new covenant began when the apostles ate a meal in God's presence—the last supper at which the Lord himself was present—when Christ sacramentally applied his blood to his followers, all in light of his sacrifice (Luke 22:14–20). In this instance, Christ pointed to the cup and said, "This cup that is poured out for you *is* the new covenant in my blood" (Luke 22:20). As in every administration, God

55. Williamson, *Sealed*, 153–57; Rosner, *Paul and the Law*, 165–83; Swain, "New Covenant Theologies," 561–62; Horton, *Justification*, 2:473–74.

56. Burnside, *God, Justice, and Society*, 57–60.

57. Block, *Covenant*, 283–86.

58. *EC*, 4.14.21–22.

59. Horton, "Kingdom of God," 364–69.

60. *MT*, 1.39.6–9; Swain, "New Covenant Theologies," 562.

appointed his people to do certain things, which *are* the covenant. Now, however, the cup that is the new covenant in Christ's blood directly and overtly exhibits Christ, who has always been the substance.

Even though Christ is the guarantor of a better covenant—namely, the new—this mediation again contrasts specifically with the Mosaic covenant (Heb 7:11–24). Christ's new covenant work effectively secured everlasting blessing for his people because he is mediator for all the elect by virtue of the covenant of redemption. Even though he historically wrought his work at a particular time as the guarantor of the new covenant, he communicated the virtue, efficacy, and benefits of that work to believers under the old economy from the future by using the means of grace given to them in their various administrations.[61] Christ's new covenant blessings were delivered proactively or in advance through the old economy's types and ordinances.

The last supper as the event instituting the Lord's Supper highlights the continuity between the old and new economies. Confessional Protestants agree that baptism is prerequisite for receiving the Lord's Supper. When Christ instituted the Supper, however, none of the disciples had received *Christian* baptism. Those who received John's baptism before Christ's ascension still had to receive Christian baptism in the name of the Triune God, which Christ instituted after his resurrection (Acts 19:1–7; Matt 28:19).[62] As Calvin notes, Christ timed his institution of the Lord's Supper on the night of his betrayal to connect it to its significance—the proclamation of his death (1 Cor 11:23, 26).[63] Likewise, he timed institution of Christian baptism after his resurrection to connect it to its

---

61. WCF 8.6; *COC*, 3.621. This understanding of forgiveness in the Old Testament, again, rests on Christ's role as mediator understood in the sense of *expromissor* rather than *fideiussor*. God imputed the elect's twofold covenantal debt (principal and penalty) to the mediator in the covenant of redemption, so that he became the one liable for that debt. Christ did not leave this debt upon his people during the old economy until he paid it at his coming but took responsibility for it from eternity. Old Testament believers received the full remission of sin (ἄφεσις) in their time, not a mere passing over (πάρεσις), as if their sin still lay upon them until Christ paid for it in his new covenant work; see *BRD*, 2:223–24; 3:491–95, 590; 4:215–19, 225–26; *VRD*, 2:88–89, 94; 3:112; 4:144–50, 160–66; *TI*, 12.2.21; 12.9.3–20; 16.9.2–6, 8; *EC*, 4.12.27–43; 4.13.2–4; *DLGTT*, 33–34, 116, 120, 254, 342; and Van Asselt, "Expromissio or Fideiussio," 37–57.

62. *EC*, 4.16.8–11; *BOC*, 50–65.

63. *CC*, 20:1.373.

significance—new life (Matt 28:16–20). How do these institutions help us see the continuity of circumcision and baptism?

The disciples could receive the Supper before Christ instituted Christian baptism because they had received the Abrahamic covenant's sign of initiation, namely, circumcision. They bore the mark of entry into the covenant community, which baptism would replace as the sign of *the same promises of the gospel* (Gal 3:8), meaning they could partake of the Supper. Remembering with Francis Roberts that the Passover was added prior to the Mosaic covenant as the sacrament of continuation in the Abrahamic covenant, the debate about baptism replacing circumcision takes on new light.[64] Since the Lord's Supper was replacing the Abrahamic meal of continuation, the disciples could eat it with Christ because they had received the Abrahamic sign of initiation. As Calvin argued that "circumcision was for Jews their first entry into *the church*," so "baptism has taken the place of circumcision to fulfill the same office among us."[65] Soon after, baptism did replace circumcision.[66]

Paul explains the correspondence between what circumcision was and what baptism is in Colossians 2:11–12: "In him also, you have been circumcised with circumcision made without hands through the putting off of the body of the flesh in Christ's circumcision, by being buried with him in baptism through which also you have been raised together [with him] by faith in God's work of raising him from the dead" (my translation). Circumcision and baptism both describe our union with Christ. The circumcision without hands happens to us "in him" while our baptism is being buried "with him." Both, then, concern our relationship with Christ.[67]

Paul uses baptism to describe union with Christ in two ways. First, as chapter 12 argues, Christ's circumcision was his crucifixion. Regarding the current point, baptism is the means God uses to circumcise us into Christ's death.[68] As Vos argues,

64. *MMB*, 546.

65. Calvin, *Institutes*, 4.16.4.

66. *EC*, 4.16.46; Robertson, "Israel and the Nations," 523.

67. Paul habitually strings together "in him" statements, syntactically functioning with locative sense, as descriptions of our union with Christ; see Constantine R. Campbell, *Paul and Union with Christ: An Exegetical and Theological Study* (Grand Rapids: Zondervan, 2012), 196.

68. The main verb, περιετμήθητε, is aorist passive indicative followed by aorist passive participle συνταφέντες. Aorist participles following the main verb, especially when the tenses match, tend to be

> The "circumcision" of the Christian is not to be understood as following his baptism. Instead, the two actions are to be regarded as simultaneous. The rite of cleansing found in the old covenant finds its fulfillment in the rite of cleansing ordered in the new. ... The meaning of the passage would be communicated best by a rendering such as "when you were buried with him in baptism, you were circumcised"; or "by being buried with him in baptism you were circumcised." ... In the fullest possible sense, baptism under the new covenant accomplishes all that was represented in circumcision under the old. By being baptized, the Christian believer has experienced the equivalent of the cleansing rite of circumcision.[69]

Being buried with Christ in baptism is the transfer into his circumcision-death, so that our receiving his circumcision means "I have been crucified with Christ" (Col 2:11–12; Gal 2:19–20).[70] Water baptism on its own does not make us partakers in Christ's death since *by faith* we receive baptism's benefits, even if our coming to faith is not at the moment of our baptism.[71]

Second, baptism is a sign that we are joined to Christ in his death (Rom 6:3; Gal 2:19–20).[72] Baptism *and circumcision* describe the spiritual realities that we possess in Christ.[73] Indeed, as Paul refers to Christ's crucifixion as his circumcision, Jesus elsewhere calls it his baptism (Luke 12:50), demonstrating how circumcision and baptism both signify and depict the same reality of his death, as he was cut off in our place, resulting in God washing us clean from sin by his blood unto newness of life (Heb 13:12; Heb 9:14; 1 John 1:7; Rom 6:4; Titus 3:5).[74] So, to be circumcised in Christ is to be baptized into him.

---

contemporaneous. In this case, the participle of means best expresses that syntactical relationship; see *WWS*, 239–40; *CC*, 21:2.185; Bruce, *Colossians, Philemon, Ephesians*, 104–5; and Dunn, *Colossians and Philemon*, 156–58; cf. John D. Meade, "Circumcision of Flesh to Circumcision of Heart: The Typology of the Sign of the Abrahamic Covenant," in *Progressive Covenantalism*, 149–51.

69. Geerhardus Vos, "Hebrews, the Epistle of the Diatheke," in *RHBI*, 165–66; quoted in *CF*, 790.

70. *WWS*, 240–42; Bruce, *Colossians, Philemon, Ephesians*, 125–26.

71. Longenecker, *Galatians*, 155–56; *WWS*, 281–84.

72. Campbell, *Paul and Union with Christ*, 197.

73. *BRD*, 4:526–27.

74. Letham, *Systematic Theology*, 707–8; *WWS*, 241–42, 339–45.

This idea that circumcision and baptism signify the same spiritual realities is ancient. As early as the second century, Justin Martyr saw the similarity between Abraham and Christians in respect to circumcision: "We also, who have come near to God through this one [Christ], have received not fleshly but spiritual circumcision, which Enoch and those like him observed. Now we received the same through baptism, since we were sinners, because of mercy from God, and it is proper for all to receive it in the same manner."[75] It would be difficult to connect the spiritual realities of both covenant signs more closely.[76] Further, Justin seemingly endorses infant baptism by arguing that "it is proper *for all* to receive" baptism "in the same manner" as circumcision because of the corresponding spiritual realities.[77] Many ancient theologians—such as Irenaeus, Hippolytus of Rome (c. AD 170–c. AD 235), Cyprian of Carthage (d. AD 258), Gregory of Nazianzus (AD 329–390), and John Chrysostom—promoted infant baptism, arguably in the second century and certainly by the third.[78]

Reformed theologians, following the ancients, argued the unity of the covenant of grace from the identity of the sacraments in the old and new economies. Turretin extensively described the link between old and new sacraments, claiming that they "were the same in both testaments as to substance, signifying and sealing Christ and his benefits." The names of the sacraments have changed, as has the sign itself, but "the thing signified" or the substance "in all the sacraments was always the same (namely, Christ with his benefits; in whom the types and sacraments, no less than the promises, are yea and amen, i.e. obtain their realization and fulfillment)."[79]

---

75. Justin Martyr, *Dialogue with Trypho*, §43, in *PG*, 6:568; *ANF*, 1:216.

76. *WWS*, 228–48.

77. *VRD*, 5:160.

78. Irenaeus, *Against Heresies*, 2.22.4, in *ANF*, 1:391; Irenaeus, *Fragments* 34, in *ANF*, 1:574; Hippolytus of Rome, *The Apostolic Tradition*, 21:4, in Burton Scott Easton (ed.), *The Apostolic Tradition of Hippolytus* (Cambridge: Cambridge University Press, 1934), 45; Cyprian of Carthage, *Epistle 58*, §2 in *ANF*, 5:353–54; Gregory of Nazianzus, *Oration on Holy Baptism*, §17, §28, in *NPNF2*, 7:365, 370; John Chrysostom, *Sermo ad Neophytos*, §6, in Antoine Wenger (ed.), *Huit Catéchèses Baptismales Inédites: Introduction, Texte Critique, Traduction et Notes* (Paris: les Éditions du Cerf, 1957), 170; Council of Carthage (AD 401), Canon 7, in *NPNF2*, 14:478. For defense of Hippolytus's authorship of *Apostolic Tradition*, see Hippolytus, *On the Apostolic Tradition*, ed. Alistair Stewart-Sykes, 2nd ed. (Crestwood, NY: St. Vladimir's Seminary Press, 2015), 28–38; Allen Brent, *Hippolytus and the Roman church in the Third Century: Communities in Tension before the Emergence of a Monarch-Bishop* (Leiden: Brill, 1995).

79. *TI*, 12.5.21; also *VRD*, 5:102–4.

Any application—however figurative—of circumcision to Christians would mark the new covenant people's unity with the Abrahamic legacy.[80] The promises and signs in the old economy, even if less clearly, set forth the same special grace of Christ and his benefits to be received by faith.

Respectively, under the old economy, physical circumcision was a sacrament signifying the inward reality of circumcision of the heart. *In this sense,* circumcision signified a present, not future, spiritual reality. Moses exhorted the people: "Circumcise therefore the foreskin of your heart, and be no longer stubborn" (Deut 10:16). Still, the outward sign of the spiritual reality was still tied to the inclusion of children: "And the LORD your God will circumcise your heart and *your children's* heart to love the LORD your God with all your heart and all your soul so that you will live" (Deut 30:6; my translation). God never condoned that his covenant people would have the external sign without its inward reality, since he announced, "The days are coming, declares the LORD, when I will punish all those who are circumcised merely in the flesh" (Jer 9:25; also Jer 4:4; Rom 2:28–29). As circumcision indicates, God's covenants with his people *always* required each member to have faith in Christ, flowing from a regenerate heart.[81] Accordingly, baptism, in signifying a renewed heart, indicates the same spiritual reality as circumcision.

In addition to its sacramental role, circumcision served as a type of how Christ would be cut off in his crucifixion for his people to procure forgiveness of their sin, as chapter 12 argues. This typological role united this sign of new spiritual life to the application of Christ through the Old Testament ordinance. This link between new life and Christ, combined with the old economy's exhortation that each member of the covenant needed to possess the reality symbolized in the sign, aligns circumcision's meaning with baptism's. In the new covenant, baptism signifies our renewed heart and the cleansing we receive in Christ. Just like in the old economy, this sacrament has a close connection with its signified spiritual reality. In all these ways, as the Westminster Shorter Catechism says, in all old and new sacraments "Christ and the benefits of *the new covenant*

80. Dunn, *Colossians and Philemon*, 154–55.

81. As even Baptistic theologians argue; David Kingdon, *Children of Abraham: A Reformed Baptist View of the Covenants*, revised and updated (London: Grace Publications, 2021), 28.

are represented, sealed, and applied to believers" (WSC 92).[82] Across the Testaments the sacraments effectually apply Christ's new covenant work to only those who receive them with true faith, bringing continuity to how God used his sacraments throughout the various covenants.[83]

If the blessings of the new covenant were always communicated to believers in the covenant of grace, then was a new administration needed? More specifically, why did the covenant's signs and sacraments need to change?[84] The administration needed to change to exhibit Christ the substance fully. Again, Augustine claims, "In that testament, however, which is properly called the Old, and was given on Mount Sinai, only earthly happiness is expressly promised." Importantly, Augustine highlights the Mosaic covenant's *express and explicit* promises concerned earthly blessing, saying nothing about its implicit promises, which is why the new covenant is much superior in directly exhibiting the substance of the covenant of grace. He continues,

> But then the happy persons, who even in that early age were by the grace of God taught to understand the distinction [between children of the Mosaic covenant and of the new] now set forth, were thereby made the children of promise, and were accounted in the secret purpose of God as heirs of the New Testament, although they continued with perfect fitness to administer the Old Testament to the ancient people of God, because it was divinely appropriated to that people in God's distribution of the times and seasons.[85]

The old economy's believers obtained the promises of Christ through types and ordinances, which had "perfect fitness" to distribute Christ and his benefits in their time. Now that Christ is clearly perceived, the typological and shadowy administrations are no longer fitting. The signs and sacraments also needed to change because the new covenant's clarity was not properly displayed in the old economy's signs that had such inbuilt

82. *COC*, 3:696 (emphasis added).

83. *TI*, 19.9.1–18; cf. Jeffrey D. Johnson, "The Fatal Flaw of Infant Baptism: The Dichotomous Nature of the Abrahamic Covenant," in *Recovering a Covenantal Heritage*, 223–56.

84. *KTC*, 104.

85. Augustine, *Proceedings of Pelagius*, §14, in *NPNF1*, 5:189.

typological and pedagogical functions.[86] The new covenant requires sacraments that plainly seal the clearly exhibited realities without any typological or forward-pointing function. So, the administration changes to correspond to its place in redemptive history.

How then does the new covenant administration differ from the old economy? First, it differs in extent.[87] The new covenant's expansion applies first to the inclusion of the nations in God's people.[88] According to James Ussher, the whole period from Abraham to Christ had the "special properties" of being "more specially restrained unto a certain Family and Nation."[89] Roberts expands, "The Covenants of Promise were before Christ, and limited peculiarly to one sort of people."[90] This limitation demanded exclusivity for Israel, confining promises to one lineage and prohibiting intermarriage with other nations.[91] By contrast, Ussher characterizes the new covenant's properties as "propounded indifferently to all people, whether they be Jews or Gentiles; and in that respect is catholic or universal."[92] Likewise, Roberts writes, "The Covenant of Performance, or New Covenant is since Christ, and extended to all sorts of people and Nations, is no less evident."[93] In the new covenant, God broke the genealogical bonds, not by excluding believers' children from the covenant administration but by including believers of any bloodline, along with their children, in it.[94] As seen in each covenant, God dealt with families in every administration: Adam and Eve (when Adam believed), Noah and

86. McKelvey, "New Covenant as Promised in the Major Prophets," 194n8.

87. WCF 7.6; *COC*, 3:618.

88. Wellum, "Progressive Covenantalism," 96–97.

89. Ussher, *Body*, 409; Ussher, *Principles*, 117.

90. *MMB*, 187.

91. *MMB*, 187–89.

92. Ussher, *Body*, 410; Ussher, *Principles*, 118–19.

93. *MMB*, 188.

94. In this respect, progressive covenantalism correctly rejects the "genealogical principle" but wrongly locates it in connection to the family rather than in relation to national and ethnic bonds; see *KTC*, 151–57, 659–60. Indeed, they rightly argue that "the genealogical principle is *transformed* across the covenants; it does not remain unchanged." See *KTC*, 816 (italics original). Gentry and Wellum misunderstand this transformation to apply to family relationships in the community rather than the new covenant's new international scope, whereas the old covenant was limited to one *ethnic* people—noting that an ethnic genealogical principle, expiring in the new covenant, is not identical to God dealing with his people according to individual families as he has done in *every* covenant, not just the Abrahamic.

his family in the ark, Abraham and his children, and Israel as a nation. The inclusion of believers' children is not a fluke for one covenant but laced into the fabric of God's redemptive history.[95] The new covenant promise "is for you and for your children and for all who are far off, everyone whom the Lord our God calls to himself" (Acts 2:39). This expansion applies also to those in the covenant because knowledge of revealed truths extends past the priestly office to the people themselves.[96]

Second, the new covenant differs by being unbreakable. This unbreakability does not undermine the difference between truly partaking of the covenant's substance by the internal administration of faith and outwardly participating in its external administration by involvement in the means of grace, as if the visible and invisible church are entirely conflated.[97] Those who leave the church, forsaking even a profession of faith, were never truly of the church, "for if they had been of us, they would have continued with us. But they went out, that it might become plain that they all are not of us" (1 John 2:19). This apostasy is not breaking the new covenant in the sense of losing a true possession of the covenant's benefits since they never truly partook of the substance of the covenant of grace by faith.[98] Rather, the new covenant is unbreakable because types and their

---

95. In this respect, progressive covenantalism's argument concerning the "genealogical principle," that only specific aspects of the Abrahamic covenant still apply in the new covenant, fails to reckon with God's unbroken pattern of dealing with families throughout the covenant of grace; see *KTC*, 661–62, 690–93, 706–9.

96. Beale, *New Testament Biblical Theology*, 733–37.

97. Progressive covenantalism seems to understand the visible-invisible church distinction entirely in relation to their concern to refute the church as a "mixed community" of believers and unbelievers; see *KTC*, 754–55. WCF 25.1 shows that distinction's fundamentally different point: "The catholic or universal Church, which is invisible, consists of the whole number of the elect, that have been, are, or shall be gathered into one, under Christ the head thereof; and is the spouse, the body, the fullness of him that fills all in all." *COC*, 3:657. The invisible church comprises every *elect* person. Baptists and Reformed alike agree that we cannot see the saints who are presently in heaven or those who have not yet been born, which is the distinction's major emphasis.

98. Colin G. Kruse, *The Letters of John* (Grand Rapids: Eerdmans, 2000), 102; *KTC*, 810–11. Progressive covenantalism seemingly misunderstands how covenant theology distinguishes substance and outward administration, since, at least I agree, "no one disputes the *fact* that apostasy takes place in the new covenant age. What is at dispute is the *status* of those apostates. Should they be viewed as 'new covenant breakers' (assuming they were once full covenant members) or as those who *professed* faith, who identified with the church, but who, by their rejection of the gospel, demonstrated that *they were never one with us* (see 1 John 2:19)?" *KTC*, 810 (italics original); also Wellum, "Progressive Covenantalism," 105n60. In Reformed churches, "full covenant members" are only those who have explicitly professed faith and, often previously baptized as infants, then receive the Lord's Supper. Still, we recognize that an apparently credible profession of faith can later be undermined, indicating

obligations have disappeared. The typological blessings of the promised land and God's presence in the Jerusalem temple, which had to be maintained by obedience, are gone. Unlike the Sinai covenant, the true church cannot lose her blessings. She will always belong to Christ and have his presence, having no types pointing to a greater reality than she possesses.[99]

This difference importantly helps make sense of Old Testament prophecies about the new covenant. In Jeremiah 31:38–40, the promise of a restored Jerusalem is attached directly to the new covenant's spiritual promises. Likewise, Amos 9:11–12 promises the renewal of the city walls and Israel's possession of Edom. The apostles understood those promises about Jerusalem in Amos to be fulfilled as the nations came to Christ (Acts 15:12–21), which applied as much to the restoration of the city as to the mention of Edom. In the same way, the promises about the old covenant's earthly blessings in Jeremiah's new covenant prophecy are fulfilled in the church's spiritual realities as well. So, those earthly aspects of the old economy's various administrations always had a spiritual function to provide an idiom for the prophets to explain future blessings, eventually giving way to the spiritual realities, which they always signified, in their new covenant fulfillment.

Last, but perhaps most importantly, we must repeat that the new covenant differs in offering the spiritual reality of Christ and his benefits far more directly than the old. Types and ordinances foresignifying Christ have given way and we understand him and his work clearly. In the new covenant sacraments, Christ, the substance of the covenant of grace, "is held forth in more fullness, evidence, and spiritual efficacy, to all nations," marking how the law is now written on more people's hearts than before (Isa 51:7), the Spirit's mission is much fuller on account of the Son completing his mission (John 7:37), and we know the Triune God with profoundly new *explicitness*.[100] Still, as Francis Gomarus explains, the differences among the various administrations of the covenant of grace "are not absolute differences but must be assigned to the natural covenant repeated through Moses, and the supernatural covenant sanctioned

---

that the church mistakenly received that profession and that the person had never truly partaken of the covenant's substance.

99. Beale, *New Testament Biblical Theology*, 731–32, 737–40; Renihan, *Mystery*, 34–35.

100. WCF 7.6; *COC*, 3:618. Thanks to Ryan McGraw for his suggestions on this point.

through Christ's coming."[101] Likewise, Turretin affirms that the new covenant's promises are more excellent "relatively, not simply," namely, "*with regard to the mode* of setting them forth more clearly, of enlarging them and more efficaciously impressing them and of extending them to the Gentiles also."[102] We still take hold of Christ by faith through the administration, but the administration clearly and explicitly exhibits the substance.

CONCLUSION

The covenant of grace has not always looked the same as it unfolded across history, but communion with God has always been based on the same foundation. God's people have always been in communion with him by grace alone through faith alone in Christ alone. That substance has been constant throughout the covenant of grace in every era. On the other hand, Christ has not always been offered explicitly or clearly, like he is in the new covenant. Each administration of the covenant of grace has, however, always pointed to Christ and taught about our communion with God because of Christ in some way.

The pastoral use of this chapter's material is that we should rejoice to live in the new covenant and be thankful for the ways that God instructs us to practice our faith in it. Too many professing Christians do not value the means of grace as we have them in the new covenant and even claim that it is legalistic to insist that participation in the church is necessary for the true Christian life. These claims do not reckon with how light the new covenant yoke of worship is. We do not have to offer daily animal sacrifices. We do not have to go through endless purification rituals. We do not have ongoing yearly festivals besides the weekly Lord's Day to beleaguer our worship practices. When someone claims that they meet with God better by walking in the forest or playing with their grandchildren, they have not understood that God is the sovereign who appoints the means by which we commune with him. Those good blessings are certainly wonderful and should prompt us to praise God, but they are not sacramental. They do not directly convey Christ to us. We should

101. Gomarus, "Oration concerning God's Covenant," sig. (*)3r.

102. *TI*, 12.5.34.

value our new covenant worship for its simplicity and direct exhibition of Christ while knowing that it sets the necessary ways for us to live out our communion with God.

Part Five

LIVING IN GOD'S COVENANT OF GRACE

XV

The Covenant Community

To me ... this grace was given ... to bring to light for everyone what is the plan of the mystery hidden for ages in God, who created all things, so that through the church the manifold wisdom of God might now be made known to the rulers and authorities in the heavenly places. This was according to the eternal purpose that he has realized in Christ Jesus our Lord.

—*Ephesians 3:9–11*

The means of grace always communicated Christ to believers in the covenant of grace and also structured the covenant community. In the new covenant, word and sacraments make the covenant community tangible in our worship and experience of communion with God. The means of grace are, then, inherently covenantal. God has always appointed and still appoints features of life for his covenant community to experience communion with him. This chapter explores the shape of the covenant community today in the covenant of grace's present and final administration. Most simply, we are meant to live out our communion with God through life in the church.

In this respect, part 5 holistically draws upon the principles about God's external administration of the covenant of grace to sketch their relevance for Christians walking in communion with God today. The purpose is to press this book's theological concepts as far into use for discipleship and

Christian formation as possible. This chapter, therefore, reflects on the covenant of grace's implications at the more corporate level for the church, and the next probes its implications more for individuals in the church.

THE UNITY OF GOD'S PEOPLE

God's people throughout the ages have a commonality together in receiving the promises of Christ through whatever feature of life God appointed for distributing the gospel. That commonality extends beyond how we have all received Christ through the means of grace to the covenant people itself. According to Herman Bavinck, "However unchangeable the covenant of grace is in its essence, it changes in its form, and takes several shapes in the several dispensations."[1] The old and new economies, although looking very different, ultimately include God's one people.

Scripture plainly teaches that God's people in all ages are part of God's *one* house, as in Hebrews 3:1–6:

> Therefore, holy brothers, you who share in a heavenly calling, consider Jesus, the apostle and high priest of our confession, who was faithful to him who appointed him, just as Moses also was faithful in all God's house. For Jesus has been counted worthy of more glory than Moses—as much more glory as the builder of a house has more honor than the house itself. (For every house is built by someone, but the builder of all things is God.) Now Moses was faithful in all God's house as a servant, to testify to the things that were to be spoken later, but Christ is faithful over God's house as a son. And we are his house, if indeed we hold fast our confidence and our boasting in our hope.

The theme of Christ's preeminence develops, presenting him as faithful in a greater way than God's other servants because he himself is God and is over God's people in every age. Moses has some glory as a servant inside God's house, but Christ has supreme glory as the Son and builder over God's house.

Despite increasing Roman pressure upon Christianity, Hebrews argues that Christians should not return to the Mosaic covenant but remain

1. *WWG*, 257.

faithful to their confession of Christ, seeing his greater glory and rejoicing to belong to him. The Mosaic covenant's practices harm rather than help Christians because *now* they are no longer *types* functioning as means of grace. As God's appointed types and ordinances, they once meaningfully nourished believers by conveying Christ. When Christ established the new covenant, he displaced the previous administration, nullifying its means of grace. Those ordinances, previously serving as means of grace, become a covenant of works upon the institution of a better covenant administration. Hebrews' rationale not only explains the superiority of the new covenant but also supports how the old economy's ordinances truly administered the covenant of grace when they were appointed to do so.

Moses's ministry contrasts with Christ's position in God's plan. In Numbers 12, Miriam and Aaron spoke against Moses, but God responds, "He is faithful in all my house. With him I speak mouth to mouth, clearly, and not in riddles, and he beholds the form of the LORD" (Num 12:7–8). Moses had direct contact with the Lord as a faithful servant. Despite this privileged status, Christ has even higher place than Moses. Christ is not a *servant* but the *Son* and is not faithful *within* but *over* the house.[2]

Two points in Hebrews 3:1–6 pertain to the unity of God's people. First, Christ's divine identity is implicit in his role as the builder of the house. He is worthy of more glory than Moses, "as much more glory as the builder of a house has more honor than the house itself." Christ's glory is *qualitatively* greater than Moses's since he is the builder.[3] Further, the title "the builder" belongs to God, but Christ is "the builder" of God's own house.[4] Christ's glory is then God's, and God's house is Christ's.

Second, Christ's role as divine builder of the house that includes Moses's ministry unifies God's old and new covenant people. Christ's house contains Christians and those under the Mosaic covenant since salvation in Christ is the substance of the covenant of grace in every administration.[5] God's people under Moses are God's house, but Christians can likewise say, "We are his house" (Heb 3:6). So, God has *one house*

2. Johnson, *Hebrews*, 108.

3. Ellingworth, *Hebrews*, 203; Johnson, *Hebrews*, 109.

4. Vos, *Hebrews*, 76–77.

5. Vos, *Hebrews*, 67.

including God's old and new covenant people with Christ as its builder.[6] The unity of the covenant of grace and the unity of God's people in old and new economies shine in Christ's role as the *one mediator* between God and man in every age. Very plainly, God's people even in the Mosaic covenant had a relationship *to Christ* as they lived within Christ's covenantal house.

Christ's oversight of God's one old-and-new economy-spanning house means that Christ's federal headship spans old and new covenants. Geerhardus Vos asks "how the Old Covenant can be identical in substance with the New, what is the common essence, that notwithstanding the great progress from one to the other, makes them two coherent stages in the expression and conveyance of the same spiritual reality," answering:

> The same world of heavenly spiritual realities, which has now come to light in the Person and work of Christ, already existed during the course of the Old Covenant, and in a provisional typical way through revelation reflected itself in and through redemption projected itself into the religious experience of the ancient people of God, so that they in their own partial manner and measure had access to and communion with and enjoyment of the higher world, which has now been let down and thrown open to our full knowledge and possession. In other words, the bond that links the Old and the New Covenant together is not a purely evolutionary one, inasmuch as the one has grown out of the other; it is, if we may so call it, a transcendental bond: the New Covenant in its preexistent, heavenly state reaches back and stretches its eternal wings over the Old, and the Old Testament people of God were one with us in religious dignity and privilege; they were, to speak in a Pauline figure, sons of the Jerusalem above, which is the mother of all.[7]

Christ is the one saving mediator between God and man, given *incarnandus* under the old economy but fully manifest *incarnatus* in the new covenant. His eschatological new covenant work was applied to believers in advance under the old covenant, making the substance of the old and new identical.

---

6. Ellingworth, *Hebrews*, 196; Johnson, *Hebrews*, 110.
7. Vos, "Hebrews, the Epistle of the Diatheke," 199.

Christ's role over God's one house informs other passages also attesting the unity of God's people. It further supports that Ephesians 2:11–15 teaches that gentiles join the actual commonwealth of Israel by faith in Christ. God's Israel is no longer a geopolitical nation but the church. In Romans 11:11–24, when Paul discusses God's purpose for saving gentiles in relation to Israel's status as God's chosen people, he affirms that gentile believers "although a wild olive shoot, were grafted in among the others and now share in the nourishing root of the olive tree" (11:17).[8] Christ builds God's one house of old and new covenant believers and nourishes the old and new branches on God's one tree as their common root.[9]

Christ himself testifies to this unity. In Matthew 22:1–14, Jesus's parable of the wedding feast explicitly concerns inclusion in God's kingdom. The kingdom is like a king's feast for his son's wedding where the originally invited guests refuse the call to attend, so the king sends servants to invite new guests. The parable depicts how, when God sent his Son, Israel should have joyously attended his honor but did not receive him. God then invited gentiles, who did receive him (John 1:9–13). God's kingdom across the covenant of grace is unified because God invites Israel and gentiles to the *same* feast. So, Irenaeus comments:

> So, the Lord, who has called us from every place through the apostles, is the same who called those who were of old through the prophets, as is clear from the Lord's words. And the prophets were not from one Lord but the apostles from another even though they preached to different peoples. Rather, they were from one and the same as some announced the Lord, others proclaimed the Father, and others foretold the arrival of God's Son, but then others preached him as now present to those who were far off.[10]

Irenaeus recognizes this unity as a recurring theme in Christ's parables.[11] Since Christ was the content of the message from God's servants in every

8. *KTC*, 545–46.

9. Hodge, *Romans*, 368.

10. Irenaeus, *Against Heresies*, 4.36.5, in *PG*, 7.1:1095; *ANF*, 1:517.

11. Irenaeus, *Against Heresies*, 4.36.1–8 in *PG*, 7.1:1090–99; *ANF*, 1:514–18.

era, even given their differing perspectives on his coming, God's people are one throughout the covenant of grace.[12]

THE STRUCTURE OF GOD'S PEOPLE

Given the unity of God's people across each administration of the covenant of grace, does their structure remain the same? As is stressed throughout this book, God delivers his promises *to his people* and does so through the means of grace. These external means create the space of participating in the covenant and the ordinary avenue for people to come to faith and profess it. Some in the old covenant participated in its administration but never truly partook of its substance by faith. Concerning Israel's corporate election, Herman Witsius explains that the "very close but yet external covenant" contained "those who were actually chosen to grace and glory," who "enjoyed the saving favor of God, and the privilege of the mystical covenant."[13] Since the *external administration* comprises the outward ordinances, some possibly participate in it without truly partaking of its substance.[14] The point is, then, not that someone can "break" the new covenant, but that not everyone who participates in the church's affairs proves to be a true believer (1 John 2:19). Even though not ideal

12. Longenecker, *Romans*, 891–94; Thielman, *Romans*, 540–541.

13. *EC*, 4.10.4.

14. As progressive covenantalism argues: "No doubt, it is true that not all those who profess faith in Christ are regenerate and that some who are admitted into membership in the church later show themselves not to have belonged. ... The New Testament knows of false professions and spurious conversions; in fact, the Scripture exhorts us to examine ourselves (see 2 Pet. 1:10). Yet the New Testament also assures us that all those united to Christ and born of the Spirit will be kept to the end. This contrasts with covenant theology, which affirmed a mixed view of the church or asserts that the visible church is constituted by believers and unbelievers until the end of the age." *KTC*, 755. Gentry and Wellum incorrectly claim a contrast with covenant theology's ecclesiology, since we affirm that the visible church includes those who participate in the outward administration without truly partaking of Christ and his benefits by faith. Covenant theology does not argue that the church is "constituted by believers and unbelievers," as if we purposefully put unbelievers in church membership. Even infants baptized into the covenant community must profess faith to receive the Lord's Supper, marking how Reformed churches recognize that covenant children are not automatically believers, although having a real place in the church. Baptism marks someone as being in the covenant community—the external administration—but "full covenant membership," often called "communicant membership," requires a credible profession of faith to receive the Supper; cf. *KTC*, 810. Despite modifications to account for credobaptism, progressive covenantalism does affirm the previous section's argument that God has one people, rejecting that Israel and the church are God's two entirely distinct peoples; see *KTC*, 748–65.

or desired, the church as a covenant community does contain believers and unbelievers.[15]

The church's structure and the parallel between the old and new covenant communities forms the necessary context for any discussion of the sacraments. Tellingly, the New Testament describes the church's structure in the same way as the old covenant people.[16] Jude exhorts his readers "to contend for the faith that was once for all delivered to the saints" so that Christians would persevere in the truth (Jude 1:3), also urging them to "keep yourselves in the love of God" (Jude 1:21). In that regard, he uses Christ's actions for his old covenant people as an example for his new covenant readers, writing, "Now I want to remind you, although you once fully knew it, that Jesus, who saved a people out of the land of Egypt, afterward destroyed those who did not believe" (Jude 1:5). Jesus rescued a people, but *unbelievers*, whom he later destroyed, were among them.

Jude uses this example to exhort new covenant Christians by connecting the church's present problems to that previous situation where unbelievers participated in the administration but did not partake of the substance by faith. He wrote that *Jesus* "destroyed those who did not believe" after he saved the people out of Egypt (Jude 1:5). Their personal destruction was not a matter of disobedience but unbelief. The covenant community tied to Jesus in the old economy warns the new covenant community about taking part in the church without truly believing in Christ, since this apostasy under the old economy prefigured unbelievers entering the church.[17] Jude understood that *Jesus's* covenant community is structured the same way in the old and new economies.[18] Pointedly, Jude's problem with unbelief under the Mosaic covenant indicates that God's covenants always obligated each member to have personal and saving

---

15. *CF*, 791.

16. The apostolic appeal to the old covenant community's structure to exhort the new covenant church demonstrates that the structural similarity across the Testaments is an *exegetical* reality, not merely an inference from covenant theology's supposed assumption concerning continuity. In other words, New Testament texts overtly portray the structural continuity between God's old and new covenant people, which undermines the claim that Reformed theology has presumed this continuation because of a hermeneutical implication; cf. *KTC*, 94–101, 706–9, esp. 708n105, 807–12.

17. Green, *Jude and 2 Peter*, 62.

18. Richard Bauckham, *Jude–2 Peter* (Grand Rapids: Zondervan, 1983), 50.

faith in Christ, even while acknowledging that some among the covenant's ranks never fulfilled this obligation.

In the same vein, Peter expresses the new covenant community's continuity with the old economy by applying descriptions of Israel to the church. Isaiah had declared that God laid a cornerstone as a sure foundation in Zion (Isa 28:16), a promise clearly issued to the old covenant people. Peter still explains that new covenant members are being joined to this same cornerstone, who is Christ, and that we are living stones being added to God's spiritual house (1 Pet 2:4–8). Further, God called Israel his kingdom of priests and a holy nation, but Peter applies this language to the church too (Deut 7:6; 10:15; Exod 19:6; 1 Pet 2:9). For Peter, the church fulfilled Israel.

Paul also appeals to the old covenant people to exhort the new covenant church to faithfulness (so revealing their similar structure) when he writes in 1 Corinthians 10:1–6 about how all the fathers were baptized into Moses through the Red Sea's cloud and drank the same spiritual drink, since Christ was the Rock nourishing them. Even with Christ's presence, "Nevertheless, with most of them God was not pleased, for they were overthrown in the wilderness. Now these things took place as examples for us, that we might not desire evil as they did" (1 Cor 10:5–6). Paul appeals to the same events as Jude, likewise marking the covenant community's inclusion of true believers as well as those who participate in only the external administration.[19] Although *Christ* was the spiritual reality in the Rock that followed them, unbelievers in the covenant were destroyed. With more specificity than Jude, Paul explains that these old covenant events "took places as *types* for us," meaning God appointed these events to signify future realities (10:6; my translation). The covenant community in the wilderness exemplified not only ethical choices that Israel and the church faced but also the structure of God's new covenant community.[20] After all, God *baptized* all Israel as they crossed the Red Sea. This old-economy type occurred as examples for the new covenant community,

19. *BOC*, 67–70.

20. Fee, *Corinthians*, 499–501.

so that all who participate in the external administration would be warned to partake of the substance by faith.[21]

In several instances, the apostles appeal to the *structure* of God's old economy people to exhort new covenant readers, showing that the old economy's structure extends to the new. If that continuity were not so, the apostles' claim that features of old covenant life "took place as examples for us" would be illegitimate. Paul insists that this structure is not only expected but necessary, since he believed that the Corinthian congregation contained divisions: "For there must be factions among you in order that those who are genuine among you may be recognized" (1 Cor 11:18–19).[22] The church must encounter conflict so that the true believers will be made clear among those who are not truly partaking of the substance of the covenant. Strikingly, Paul's assertion addresses those who were all participating in the Lord's Supper. God's old and new covenant community, therefore, include those who truly partake of the substance by faith along with those who participate in only the external administration.[23]

THE SACRAMENTS

The covenant of grace's structural continuity pointedly applies to the sacraments. As God's people themselves find their identity in the covenant, so the covenant grounds their sacraments. God appoints creaturely signs for holy use that are not means of grace apart from the covenant. The tree of life offered life to Adam only as appointed to that use in the covenant of works. The rainbow marks nature's stability only by designation in God's covenant with Noah. Circumcision sealed God's promises about an eschatological heir only as God appropriated it as the sign of the Abrahamic covenant. For the church, water is not baptism except in connection to our covenant actions, so also with bread and wine in the Supper.[24]

God's covenants commandeer earthly things to distribute heavenly realities among God's people. Peter Lombard writes, "All teaching concerns things or signs." The covenants prove him right, especially as some

21. *WWS*, 206–13; Riddlebarger, *First Corinthians*, 227–42.

22. Fee, *Corinthians*, 596–97.

23. R. Scott Clark, "Baptism and the Benefits of Christ: The Double Mode of Communion in the Covenant of Grace," *Confessional Presbyterian* 2 (2006): 3–19.

24. *CF*, 777–85.

signs "not only signify, but also confer what may be of interior aid, as is the case with the sacraments of the Gospel."[25] God uses earthly things as "holy signs" to signify a spiritual reality, making a sacrament, namely, "to represent Christ and his benefits and to confirm our interest in him" (WCF 27.1).[26] The sacraments in every covenant embody the spiritual reality of God's promises by using an earthly means to convey those promises tangibly to embodied creatures, so also, they mark the community who belongs to God with physical signs.[27]

The sacraments, then, visibly structure God's covenant people. In Acts 2:38–39, as he concludes the first post-ascension sermon, Peter preaches: "Repent and be baptized every one of you in the name of Jesus Christ for the forgiveness of your sins, and you will receive the gift of the Holy Spirit. For the promise is for you and for your children and for all who are far off, everyone whom the Lord our God calls to himself." Peter's exhortation obviously picks up God's promise to Abraham, "I will establish my covenant between me and you and your offspring after you throughout their generations for an everlasting covenant, to be God to you and to your offspring after you" (Gen 17:7). Peter further expands that promise from the hearers and their children to those who are "far off," namely, gentiles.[28] Far from altering the Abrahamic covenant, this expansion fulfills God's promise to Abraham that "in you all the families of the earth shall be blessed" (Gen 12:3). The gentiles' justification by faith was always God's intention, meaning the Abrahamic covenant always concerned God's spiritual promises that would include believers, their children, and the nations (Gal 3:7–9).[29] Peter summons his hearers to baptism, *explicitly* including their children as recipients of the promise and expanding the promise's reception to all families of the earth in fulfillment of the Abrahamic promise.[30]

---

25. Peter Lombard, *The Sentences Book 1: The Mystery of the Trinity*, trans. Giulio Silano, (Ontario: Pontifical Institute of Medieval Studies, 2007), 1.1.1.

26. *COC*, 3:660; *WWS*, 292–97.

27. *WWS*, 297–302, 345–51; Hodge, "Visibility of the Church," 670–85.

28. *KTC*, 502–4.

29. *VRD*, 5:161–64.

30. *VRD*, 5:167. The Babylonian Talmud demonstrates that infants were baptized even in the Jewish practice, referring to the ritual washing applied to a "little one" (קָטָן) who is a proselyte—since children were admitted to the covenant with their parents as converts—and admitting to the

As chapter 14 argues, the new covenant promise that everyone will know the Lord *intensifies* rather than overturns the Abrahamic promise to be God to us and our children, as other prophecies confirm by explicitly affirming the new covenant's continual inclusion of believers' children. In Isaiah 59:20–21, God foretold concerning the new covenant:

> "And a Redeemer will come to Zion,
> to those in Jacob who turn from transgression," declares the LORD.
>
> "And as for me, this is my covenant with them," says the LORD:
> "My Spirit that is upon you, and my words that I have put in your mouth, shall not depart out of your mouth, or out of the mouth of your offspring, or out of the mouth of your children's offspring," says the LORD, "from this time forth and forevermore."[31]

In Romans 11:26–27, Paul applies this prophecy to new covenant salvation, showing its relevance for God's people today.[32] God announces that the coming Redeemer will come to Zion, which was fulfilled when Christ came to earth, literally entered Jerusalem, and dealt with his people's sin.[33] God further describes the covenant he would have with his people after the Redeemer's coming—namely, the new covenant—as the promise of the Spirit's presence. Pointedly, this very covenant includes "your offspring" and "your children's offspring." In prophetic explanation of the new covenant, God explicitly includes believers' children, overtly tying them to this *everlasting* covenant.[34] After all, Christ rebukes his disciples for trying to prevent *parents* from bringing their children for him to lay hands on them and pray for them when he said: "Let the little children come to me and do not hinder them, for to such belongs the kingdom of heaven" (Matt 19:13–15). Believing parents have always been meant to place their children

---

possibility of him growing up to reject his conversion, further supporting that Peter was overtly including children in his summons to receive baptism as existing Jewish practices had a place for infant baptism; see Bab. Keth. 11a.3, 8–9.

31. *KTC* classifies Isaiah 59:21 as a new covenant prophecy but does not address how it explicitly includes children. See *KTC*, 509.

32. Waters, "Covenant in Paul," 241–42.

33. Young, *Isaiah*, 3:440–41.

34. Young, *Isaiah*, 3:441–42.

under Christ's authority within the church, even explicitly according to Christ in the new covenant.[35]

The prophetic announcements of the new covenant consistently state that intensification of the Abrahamic promise that God will be God to us and to our children after us. In Isaiah 54, God announces the new covenant, promising "All your children shall be taught by the LORD, and great shall be the peace of your children" (Isa 54:13).[36] The connection to Jeremiah 31, that *all* will be taught *by the Lord* rather than a neighbor, is obvious, and is applied this time explicitly to believers' children. The lens of biblical theology suggests that Isaiah explicitly restates the Abrahamic promise to be God to us and our children after us *within a prophecy of the new covenant.*[37] Jeremiah 32:36–41 also promises the new covenant, likewise including concern for children.[38] The pattern of restating the Abrahamic promise within new covenant prophecy continues: "And they shall be my people, and I will be their God. I will give them one heart and one way, that they may fear me forever, for their own good and the good of their children after them" (Jer 32:38–39). The Abrahamic maxim to be our God is clear, as is God's commitment to work on behalf of our children *in the new covenant.*[39] Even the prophecy of the new creation in Isaiah 65:17–25 includes the promise that "they shall be the offspring of the blessed of the LORD, and their descendants with them" (Isa 65:23). As God's people wait on Christ to return, God's promise to be God to us and our children abides.[40] The prophets announced the continuation and intensification of the Abrahamic promise to be God to us and to our children even in the new covenant.

In that respect, the new covenant continues the Old Testament principle that spiritual promises must be received by faith, but the external administrations include believers' children. Even in the first announcement of Christ, upon *Adam's* profession of faith, God gave a sign of provision to Adam *and Eve,* clothing them both with the skins of sacrificed

35. *BOC,* 90–102.

36. *KTC,* 495–500; Young, *Isaiah,* 3:360–61.

37. Cf. *KTC,* 498–99.

38. McKelvey, "New Covenant as Promised in the Major Prophets," 198–200; *KTC,* 570–72.

39. Lundbom, *Jeremiah 21–36,* 518–19; John Bright, *Jeremiah* (New York: Doubleday, 1965), 295.

40. Young, *Isaiah,* 3:516.

animals (Gen 3:20).[41] Noah *and his family* were included in the ark, but only Noah was said to have favor in God's sight (Gen 6:8). Abraham was commanded to include his children in the covenant (Gen 17:7–14). Isaiah and Paul directly connect the Abrahamic covenant to new covenant promises, since *Abraham* and Sinai distinguish freedom and slavery (Isa 65:15–16; Gal 3:15–4:31).[42] The church's structure consistently resembles the makeup of the old covenant community.[43] Peter's summons to baptism because the promise concerns his hearers *and their children* aligns with the full thrust of Scripture and the New Testament's other explicit teachings.[44] After all, the Apostles explicitly addressed children when they wrote to the churches, treating them as responsible participants in the covenant community (Eph 6:1–4; Col 3:20; 1 John 2:13).

In this regard, Hebrews 6:1–8 clarifies that sacramental structure of life in the covenant of grace.

> Therefore, leaving the discussion of the elementary principles of Christ, let us go on to perfection, not laying again the foundation of repentance from dead works and of faith toward God, of *the doctrine of baptisms*, of laying on of hands, of resurrection of the dead, and of eternal judgment. And this we will do if God permits. For it is impossible for those who were once *enlightened*, and have *tasted the heavenly gift*, and have become partakers of the Holy Spirit, and have *tasted the good word of God* and the powers of the age to come, if they fall away, to renew them again to repentance, since they crucify again for themselves the Son of God, and put Him to an open shame. For the earth which drinks in the rain that often comes upon it, and bears herbs useful for those by whom it is cultivated, receives blessing from God; but if it bears thorns and briers, it is rejected and near to being cursed, whose end is to be burned. (NKJV; emphasis added)

41. *MMB*, 1306–7.

42. *KTC*, 332–37, 516–21; Ridderbos, *Galatia*, 132–34, 172–83; deSilva, *Galatians*, 394–404; Gordon, *Promise, Law, Faith*, 174–79.

43. Billings, "Sacraments," 358.

44. Swain, "New Covenant Theologies," 566–69.

This passage describes not falling away from true salvation, but how the sacraments in part facilitate life within the church as blessings that produce good spiritual fruit in the elect.[45] If this passage is properly read as addressing the covenant community rather than merely individuals in it, this point is clear.[46] The external administration is our experience of the covenant, but only those with faith truly partake of its substance.[47]

Several features from Hebrews inform the sacraments' recipients. Christians should pursue doctrinal maturity beyond basic principles, which includes teaching about "baptisms." Further, the outlined blessings go to people within the church, as the first blessing of "being enlightened" refers to Christian baptism. Justin Martyr writes during the second century, "Now this washing of baptism is called enlightenment, since those who learn of these things are the ones being enlightened in understanding."[48] The text supports Justin's understanding of this enlightenment as a reference to baptism, since the author had just signaled "instruction about baptisms" as one relevant issue.[49] Clement of Alexandria (c. 150–c. 215) made the same connection: "By being baptized, we are enlightened."[50] William Perkins likewise understood this enlightenment as baptism.[51] The imposition of hands, which Hebrews mentions, was also often connected

45. Gentry and Wellum argue concerning the warning passages and their relevance for the sacraments that "proponents [of covenant theology] must first prove that the nature of the covenant communities is essentially the same," *KTC*, 809. The previous section argues this exact point by noting the apostolic appeal to Israel's structure in application to the church. This discussion about the sacraments, which gives concrete visible-church features to the community, including appeals to the warning passages, *confirms* the argument for explicit apostolic warrant concerning ecclesiology structure. In other words, progressive covenantalism incorrectly argues that covenant theology's view of infants in the visible church rests most strongly on an arguable interpretation of the warning passages; *KTC*, 809–12. Rather, at least Hebrews 6:1–8 *corroborates* explicit New Testament teaching about the church's structural continuity with God's people under the old economy *with specific application to the sacraments.*

46. Ellingworth, *Hebrews*, 323; *BOC*, 79–83.

47. Notably, a proponent of Baptistic theology also argues a similar interpretation, precluding accusations of special pleading or Reformed eisegesis; see Wayne Grudem, "Perseverance of the Saints: A Case Study from the Warning Passages in Hebrews," in *Still Sovereign: Contemporary Perspectives on Election, Foreknowledge, and Grace*, eds. Thomas R. Schreiner and Bruce A. Ware (Grand Rapids: Baker Books, 2000), 133–83.

48. Justin Martyr, *First Apology*, §61, in *PG*, 6:421; *ANF*, 1:183.

49. Ellingworth, *Hebrews*, 315; Johnson, *Hebrews*, 159.

50. Clement of Alexandria, *Paedagogus*, 1.6, in *PG*, 8:281; *ANF*, 2:215.

51. *WWP*, 2:222 (commentary on Galatians 2:27).

to the baptism ritual.[52] Although baptism itself does not create new life, it signifies that reality of being enlightened when God effectually calls us (2 Cor 4:6). The blessings received in the church also include "tasting the heavenly gift," referring to the Lord's Supper. If, as most commentators conclude about Jude 1:12, the false teachers' participation in the church's "love feasts" refers to the Lord's Supper, it confirms the danger of illegitimate faith professors managing to participate fully, albeit illicitly, in the covenant's outward administration, while lacking true belief.[53] Being a "partaker of the Holy Spirit" indicates not a sure personal indwelling, but simply sharing blessings that come from him, as happens to everyone in the church. They *encounter* the Spirit in the church, even if they reject him. The last blessing is receiving the word of God, as everyone who hears preaching does. This preaching is God's means to call unbelievers to faith, which is the power of the age to come, visible to even those not themselves called.

Hebrews' agricultural illustration depicts life in the covenant of grace, confirming that the blessings mentioned belong to the external administration but not necessarily to every participant. Rain falls on the land generally, portraying how the blessings of church life fall upon everyone in it. This rain—blessings of church participation—falls on everyone, producing useful crops in some but thorns and thistles in others. God, who sovereignly brings about his desired effects through outward means, uses the rain—the word, *the sacraments*, and fellowship in the church—to bring some people to faithful fruition. That *same* rain produces the worthless crop of not trusting in Christ in those who are not elect.[54] Nonmetaphorically, God uses the sacraments to fence his covenant community, bringing some to true faithfulness and manifesting unbelief in others.[55]

---

52. Johnson, *Hebrews*, 159.

53. *WWP*, 4:177 (commentary on Jude 12); Bauckham, *June–2 Peter*, 84–85; Green, *Jude and 2 Peter*, 93–94.

54. *VRD*, 5:97; Robert A. Peterson, *Our Secure Salvation: Preservation and Apostasy* (Phillipsburg, NJ: P&R, 2009), 163–65.

55. Michael Horton, "A Classical Calvinist View," in *Four Views on Eternal Security*, ed. J. Matthew Pinson (Grand Rapids: Zondervan, 2002), 21–42; Horton, "Covenant Theology," 63–65; Crowe, *Path of Faith*, 144–49.

So, the sacraments belong to the external administration of the covenant of grace, which sometimes includes unbelievers, even as God implements it to bring his elect to faith and strengthen them in their walk with Christ. Francis Turretin explains how the "covenant may be regarded in two ways: either as to internal essence; or as to external dispensation." Although the internal essence concerns true calling for the elect, the external dispensation—or outward administration—"is regarded only as to promulgation and presentation by the external call; and as to external benefits, which flow from that presentation, in the preaching of the word; the administration of the sacraments and the participation in sacred things (of which as many as in the people or in the church retain the same profession, become partakers; and thus it is extended even to many reprobates who remain in the visible church)." The outward administration pertains only to the elect inasmuch as they alone receive "internal communion with Christ by faith" and truly receive "the benefits of the covenant."[56] Members of the covenant community must rightly use every feature of the covenant's administration by receiving them with true faith to partake of the substance, lest they profane the sacrament and incur judgment.[57] So Hebrews explains this issue about mere participation in the external administration of the covenant as a warning to believers, which God sovereignly uses to preserve them in faith.[58]

Baptism is the sacrament of entry into the covenant community.[59] Although not itself guaranteeing that we partake of the blessings of renewal in Christ, it conveys the blessings of new life and forgiveness to all who trust Christ by faith.[60] Baptism is, after all, "for the forgiveness of sins" (Acts 2:38).[61] In 1 Peter 3:21–22, after noting how Noah and his family were saved from the flood in the ark, Peter explains that "baptism, which corresponds to this, *now saves you*, not as a removal of dirt

56. *TI*, 12.6.5.

57. Horton, *Covenant Theology*, 182–86; *WWS*, 228–58, 294–95, 351–56; *CF*, 683, 778; Riddlebarger, *First Corinthians*, 228, 238–42.

58. CC, 22:1.136–38. The sacramental understanding of the warning passages is then compatible with the core premises of the "means of salvation" view; see Cowan, "Warning Passages," 198–210.

59. *EC*, 4.16.18.

60. Letham, *Systematic Theology*, 705–18; *KTC*, 571.

61. Letham, *Systematic Theology*, 709–10.

from the body but as an appeal to God for a good conscience, *through the resurrection of Jesus Christ,* who has gone into heaven and is at the right hand of God, with angels, authorities, and powers having been subjected to him." Strikingly, baptism saves, easily bristling Protestant sensibilities, but clearly not by the physical action of applying water.[62] Rather, it saves "through the resurrection of Jesus Christ," who is the mediator standing in heaven to intercede for us.[63]

God uses baptism as a means to grant that reality *when we take hold of it by receiving Christ in faith.*[64] Calvin writes concerning the water of baptism: "I consider it to be a figure, but at the same time, it has the substance connected with it. For God, in promising us his gifts, does not deceive us. Therefore, as forgiveness of sins and newness of life are offered to us in baptism, so it is certain that they are received by us."[65] Scripture describes baptism as the tool that brings us "into Christ." In Romans 6:3–4, Paul writes, "Do you not know that all of us who have been baptized into Christ Jesus were baptized into his death? We were buried therefore with him *by baptism* into death, in order that, just as Christ was raised from the dead by the glory of the Father, we too might walk in newness of life." Baptism does not automatically regenerate but is a feature of the covenant's administration that God uses to make us into fruitful crops, even if some who receive it will become worthless thistles.

According to Romans, God uses baptism to join us to Christ in the divine community. Just as Abraham received circumcision as the sign and seal of his faith after he believed but circumcised both Isaac and Ishmael before they believed (Rom 4:11), so also baptism belongs to those who come to faith from outside the covenant community and their children.[66] The new covenant differs foremost from the Mosaic covenant but

62. Notably, Noah and his family remained dry through the flood, and their experience corresponds to baptism. In the flood, God fully immersed his enemies but kept his people out of the water in an event that typifies baptism, which is a significant problem for Baptist theologians who insist that baptism requires full immersion in water. The same problem is true in Paul's assertion in 1 Corinthians 10:2 that God baptized all Israel as they passed through the Red Sea, since God kept Israel totally dry but fully immersed his enemies.

63. Letham, *Systematic Theology*, 710–16.

64. *TI*, 19.8.12, 17–28; 19.19.3–11.

65. Q. 328, Calvin, *Catechism of … Geneva*, 93.

66. Perkins, "Engaging Confessional Baptists on Covenant Theology (Part 1)."

primarily grows out of the Abrahamic.[67] The Abrahamic covenant's focus on God's spiritual promises rather than earthly and national blessings cannot be overemphasized, and this spiritual covenant included believers and their children. God has always marked the children of his people with the sign of the covenant, thereby designating them as heirs of his promise to be God to us and our children (Gen 17:7; Acts 2:39).[68] Since the children of believers are holy (1 Cor 7:14), their holiness according to the administration of the covenant entitles them to the sacrament of entry.[69] So the Canons of Dort say, "The children of believers are holy, not even by nature, but by right of the covenant of grace" (1.17).[70] Because God includes and Christ's authority extends over believers and their children within the sphere of his promises, namely, the church, those children have a right to baptism.[71]

God uses baptism to bind believers and their children into the covenant community and confirm his promises to them, delivering the very promises it signifies. Although some have abused this truth, we need not fear bare ceremonialism. The Westminster Confession explains: "The efficacy of baptism is *not tied to that moment of time wherein it is administered*; yet, notwithstanding, *by the right use of this ordinance* the grace promised is not only offered, but *really exhibited and conferred* by the Holy Ghost, to such (whether of age or infants) as that grace belongs unto, according to the counsel of God's own will, in his appointed time (WCF 28.6)"[72] God genuinely uses baptism to convey blessings of new life to those who are elect but does not necessarily bind that effect to the moment of application.[73] The Heidelberg Catechism outlines,

> 72. *Is, then, the outward washing of water itself the washing away of sins?*

---

67. *MMB*, 1313–17; *KTC*, 520–21.

68. *MMB*, 1303–6; *EC*, 4.16.41–43.

69. *VRD*, 5:167–68; *MMB*, 1307–13; *EC*, 3.12.3–5; *WWS*, 349–51.

70. *COC*, 3:556.

71. Jonathan D. Moore, "The Westminster Confession of Faith and the Sin of Neglecting Baptism," *WTJ* 69 (2007): 63–86; *BRD*, 4:528–30; *EC*, 4.16.45; *MMB*, 1317–38; *CF*, 794–98; Letham, *Systematic Theology*, 718–22; *BOC*, 90–102; *WWS*, 356–61.

72. *COC*, 3:663 (emphasis added).

73. *WWP*, 2:221–34 (commentary on Galatians 2:27); *TI*, 19.19.3; *CF*, 790–91; Letham, *Systematic Theology*, 715.

> No; for only the blood of Jesus Christ and the Holy Ghost cleanse us from all sin.
>
> 73. *Why, then, does the Holy Ghost call Baptism the washing of regeneration and the washing away of sins?*
> God speaks thus not without great cause: namely, not only to teach us thereby that like as the filthiness of the body is taken away by water, so our sins also are taken away by the blood and Spirit of Jesus Christ; but much more, that by this divine pledge and token he may assure us that we are really washed from our sins spiritually as our bodies are washed with water.[74]

God is not forced to distribute the blessings signified in baptism when the sacrament is applied, since they are granted only through faith, but makes a pledge of assurance in baptism, using baptism as a means to his spiritual ends. The sacrament of entry into God's people always signified new spiritual life but never guaranteed that its external application ensured its internal reality, as the Old Testament exhortations for those who were physically circumcised to have circumcised hearts shows (Deut 10:16; 30:6; Jer 4:4; 9:25–26; Rom 2:28–29). This situation, where the external mark of the covenant does not necessarily grant its spiritual reality at the time of its application, continues to be a feature of the new covenant community.

On the other hand, the Lord's Supper seals nourishment and continuation. God uses the Supper to convey Christ. As Paul writes in 1 Corinthians 10:16, "The cup of blessing that we bless, is it not a participation in the blood of Christ? The bread that we break, is it not a participation in the body of Christ?" God grants participation in Christ through the Supper, but not by magically transforming the bread and wine physically into Christ's body and blood.[75] The Westminster Confession explains that worthy receivers of the Supper "really and indeed, yet not carnally and corporally, but spiritually, receive and feed upon Christ crucified, and all benefits of his death" since Christ's body and blood are "really, but spiritually, present to the faith of believers in that ordinance, as the elements

---

74. *COC*, 3:330–31.

75. Hodge, *Corinthians*, 224–28; *TI*, 19.22.2–3, 12–16.

themselves are to their outward senses" (WCF 29.7).[76] God does truly offer Christ to us in the Supper to be received by faith.[77]

In contrast to baptism, the Supper requires a personal profession of faith, confirming not only that those who receive it are within the administration but also profess to partake of its substance.[78] One must eat with faith because "anyone who eats and drinks without discerning the body eats and drinks judgment on himself" (1 Cor 11:29). Receiving the Supper requires that you have already been part of the baptized community. As the Didache states, "Let no one eat or drink of your Eucharist except those who have been baptized into the name of the Lord, for the Lord has also spoken concerning this: 'Do not give what is holy to dogs' " (Did. 9.5).[79] After being discipled in the baptized community to the point of making a credible profession of faith, a person is eligible to receive the Supper properly.

God has not given his people an abstract experience of our salvation in Christ. He places us in his church, so that we might concretely meet Christ in the preached word, the sacraments, and relationships with other believers. In baptism, he binds us to Christ but also to one another. Baptism makes us accountable in the community of faith to profess faith and to walk worthily of the God who calls us (Eph 4:1). In the Supper, God strengthens our souls as food nourishes the body, even or especially when we are weak and struggling. The Supper is not our *mere* remembrance of God but a meal by which God feeds his people. God uses it to frame our life in the covenant of grace. A credible profession of faith grants us access to the Supper, but unrepentant sin prompts corrective church discipline, removing our right to this meal with the communion of saints. God has met our ultimate spiritual needs in providing us with the unsurpassable Savior, Jesus Christ, but also meets us as creatures who exist in bodies by giving us words of assurance on the page and from the pulpit, pouring baptismal waters on us to promise cleansing of our sin, and spreading a table for us to show how he feeds us.

---

76. *COC*, 3:666.

77. EC, 4.17.39–43.

78. *WWS*, 361–65; *WWG*, 523; *BRD*, 4:583–85; *VRD*, 5:244–45; Letham, *Systematic Theology*, 765; cf. Billings, "Sacraments," 358–61.

79. *AP*, 359.

THE NECESSITY OF THE PEOPLE OF GOD

Because God has diversely delivered Christ and his benefits through the variously appointed means in the covenant of grace, God's people *needed* their administration. As Vos affirms, "That effectual grace only works where the means of grace are present."[80] Although God is not dependent on earthly signs to accomplish his purposes, we creatures cannot escape our need for God to communicate his purposes to us through earthly means.[81] God appointed means in every administration to make his way of salvation known, entailing we are to depend on those means to hear of God and be reminded of his promises.[82]

God addresses his promises to his people today, working in us to walk well with him in the world through the means of grace that he has appointed in *the church*. Are individual Christians able to read and understand God's word? Yes, of course. Can each pray directly to God confessing sin and seeking mercy? Yes, of course. Still, God has given pastors and elders to help us understand his word, to pray at length for us, and to guide us in the faith. That some find this provision intrusive is odd, since God kindly gives these leaders so that we do not have to fumble blindly and alone as we seek the Lord. God generously appoints men to come alongside us in the church as a gracious provision.

So, God provides help for his people *in the church*. He gave pastors and teachers—officers in the church—"to equip the saints, to do the work of ministry, for building up the body of Christ, until we all attain to the unity of the faith and of the knowledge of the Son of God, to mature manhood, to the measure of the stature of the fullness of Christ" (Eph 4:12–13; my translation).[83] Bavinck explains,

> The church is the communion, and hence also the mother, of believers. God establishes his covenant with the parents and in them with their children. He distributes his benefits in the way of the covenant. In that sense it is true that the church as the communion of saints is the great means of grace that Christ in his good

80. *VRD*, 5:82.

81. *TI*, 19.2.8–10.

82. *MMB*, 1671–90.

83. T. David Gordon, "'Equipping' Ministry in Ephesians 4," *JETS* 37 no. 1 (March 1994): 69–78.

> pleasure uses to gather his elect from the beginning to the end of the world. In that sense the church definitely aims at the salvation of the elect.[84]

God then has commissioned workers for the sake of his people and put them in the church. Our union with Christ as our head cannot be disconnected from union with his body, the church (John 17:11–12, 20–23; Eph 4:15).[85]

The covenant of grace's administration must be connected to the means of grace because Christ works through them. Remember, Paul writes to the Ephesians that *Christ* "came and preached peace to you who were far off and peace to those who were near" (Eph 2:17), even though Jesus never travelled to Ephesus, because Christ personally preaches through his ordained ministers. So, Bavinck emphasizes the priority of the preached Word:

> The first and most important means of grace is the word of God. … But the word of God, both as law and gospel, is the revelation of the will of God, the promulgation of the covenant of works and the covenant of grace. It concerns all human beings and all creatures and so has universal significance. The sacrament can only be administered by a lawfully called minister in the assembly of believers, but the word of God also has a place and life outside of it and also there exerts many and varied influences. As a means of grace in the true sense alongside the sacraments, the word of God only comes up for discussion insofar as it is publicly preached by the minister. The emphasis falls on the Word as proclaimed in God's name and by virtue of his mission.[86]

In more succinct fashion, Vos writes, "In what sense is God's Word a means of grace? In the sense in which we use it of the whole of Scripture. It is then usually differentiated into two parts, namely law and gospel."[87] If we know with Peter that Christ alone has the words of everlasting life (John 6:68), then we should also know that Christ is still preaching in the

84. *BRD*, 4:447.
85. Horton, *Justification*, 2:455–56, 458–59.
86. *BRD*, 4:448 (first italics added).
87. *VRD*, 5:84.

church as properly ordained pastors open the Scripture to explain and apply it each Lord's Day.[88] Further, just as Jesus was baptizing, although not personally but through his apostles (John 4:1–2), so he continues to baptize his followers today through the baptism that pastors apply in the church. As we partake of the Lord's Supper, which is bread and wine broken and blessed *together* in the church, we participate in Christ's body and blood (1 Cor 10:16–17). As Bavinck writes, "It is Christ himself who baptizes and celebrates the Lord's Supper in his church. … He alone administers the Word as the prophet, so also he is the only administrator of the sacrament, even though it is true that in this connection he also employs humans as his instruments."[89] Christ is active in the word and sacraments as means of grace.

The church is necessary as the present external administration of the covenant of grace. We cannot have the substance except through the administration. In the Abrahamic covenant, the forerunner of the new, God equated the sign of circumcision with the covenant itself: "This *is* my covenant, which you shall keep, between me and you and your offspring after you: Every male among you shall be circumcised" (Gen 17:10). If someone did not take part in this administration of the covenant, then they also were not partaking of the substance: "Any uncircumcised male who is not circumcised in the flesh of his foreskin shall be cut off from his people; he has broken my covenant" (Gen 17:14). The administration was necessary to receive the substance.

Paul's discussion in Ephesians 2:11–13 about the union of Jew and gentile in Christ clarifies that it remains necessary to participate in the covenant's administration to partake of the substance. Paul's overall point is that Christ has brought Jew and gentile together as one people of God, so those who were formerly far off are united to Christ in the commonwealth of Israel and the covenants of the promise. How does this indicate the church's necessity?

The answer easily comes if we simply further ask: Would any Israelite have been able to fathom the possibility of a relationship with God apart from the structures of community life that God had revealed in the old

88. *CF*, 755–56.

89. *BRD*, 4:474; Billings, "Sacraments," 341.

covenant? To be specific: Would any faithful Israelite have accepted the notion that someone could be in a true relationship with God apart from taking part in the divinely commanded features of Old Testament religious life, such as the sacrificial system, participation in the mandated gatherings of God's people, and Sabbath observance? Plainly, no. If any Israelite had suggested that they were in a true relationship with God but had simply realized that they can walk faithfully with God in a new way that they had discovered apart from the things that God had appointed for his people to do, that would not have ended well for them. God had told Abraham that not to be included in the sign of the covenant was to be cut off from the covenant entirely (Gen 17:14). Certainly, no one within God's people would have acknowledged them as a true believer, and they obviously would have been inventing their own religion to suit themselves, merely pretending to love God.

The same principle holds true in the new covenant administration of the covenant of grace. The Belgic Confession affirms, "In the mean time we believe, though it is useful and beneficial, that those who are rulers of the Church institute and establish certain ordinances among themselves for the maintaining of the body of the Church; yet they ought studiously to take care that they do not depart from those things which Christ, our only master, hath instituted" (BC 32).[90] The new covenant differs from the old covenant, not by now permitting people to relate to the true God in any way they choose, but as types and shadows that have expired so that the realities are clearly exhibited. Too many dream that Christ's pronouncement in John 4:23–24, that new covenant people worship "in spirit and in truth," means that we decide how we want to worship, as if riding my horse or watching the sunset are equally viable forms of relating to God as attending Lord's Day worship.

Freedom in the new covenant, rather than doing away with defined ways to relate to God, pertains to the clarity with which our means exhibit the *substance*. Not regarding the requirements for becoming right with God in the first place, but in terms of our ongoing Christian life, anyone wanting to walk in relationship with God must do so according to the mode of community practice that God himself has revealed to us. God has

90. *COC*, 3:423.

revealed that we need to be under the discipline of ministers and elders, to hear the preaching of the gospel, and to receive the sacraments. There are many facets of the Christian life, but the institutional church is the apparatus in which those facets are supposed to take place.

The Christian tradition affirms the church's necessity. In the ancient period, Cyprian of Carthage formulated the maxim, "There is no salvation out of the Church."[91] Likewise Augustine argues against the Donatists, "This Church is the body of Christ, as the Apostle said: 'for the sake of his body, which is the Church' (Col. 1:24). From that it is certainly obvious that the one who is not among the members of Christ, cannot have Christian salvation."[92] True Christians participate in the institutional church since Christ appointed it as his body on earth. Being part of Christ's body requires being connected to the apostles, prophets, teachers, and gifts that God grants to individual believers (1 Cor 12:12–31). The Lord left no other way to be his people and so take part in his blessings than in the church.

Although the idea that salvation is ordinarily not available outside the church has roots in the ancient period, Reformed churches have formally confessed it too. Long before the Reformation even, the Apostles' Creed affirms as a fundamental point of the faith that, "I believe in the Holy Ghost; *the holy catholic Church; the communion of saints*; the forgiveness of sins; the resurrection of the body; and the life everlasting."[93] Our most basic doctrinal statement links the Spirit's work, the church, and personal salvation together. Further, the Belgic Confession pronounces,

> We believe, since this holy congregation is an assemblage of those who are saved, and *out of it there is no salvation*, that no person of whatsoever state or condition he may be, ought to withdraw himself to live in a separate state from it; but that all men are in duty bound to join and unite themselves with it; maintaining the unity of the Church; submitting themselves to the doctrine and discipline thereof; bowing their necks under the yoke of Jesus Christ; and as

91. Cyprian, *Epistle LXXII*, §21 in *ANF*, 5:384.

92. Augustine, *Letter to the catholics against the Donatists generally concerning the Unity of the Church, Book One*, §2, in *PL*, 43:392.

93. *COC*, 2:45 (emphasis added).

> mutual members of the same body, serving to the edification of the brethren, according to the talents God has given them. (BC 28)[94]

The emphasis on our responsibility to join a church is because the church is where God distributes blessings to us, but also because it is where we have the opportunity to serve our neighbors. The Westminster Confession makes a similar point: "The visible Church, which is also catholic or universal under the gospel (not confined to one nation as before under the law) consists of all those, throughout the world, that profess the true religion, and of their children; and is the kingdom of the Lord Jesus Christ, the house and family of God, *out of which there is no ordinary possibility of salvation*" (WCF 25.2).[95] As we consider how Christ has earned our citizenship in heaven, we should also realize that the present manifestation of his kingdom is the church. Unless we participate in his kingdom, we are not properly exercising citizenship in it.[96]

Christ works in his people, administering the substance of the covenant of grace in the church. In Matthew 28:19–20, Christ commands the apostles to make disciples *by baptizing and teaching*, tying Christ's people to word and sacrament ministry. These means of grace are also tied to the Lord's Day as the Christian Sabbath. God's people gather at a particular time to take part in the administration of the covenant. The Sabbath always points to eternal rest with God in worshipful communion. Christ has entered his rest as the reward of the covenant of works, but we wait to join him at the last day. We keep the Sabbath in the meantime as our opportunity to receive the means of grace and participate in the covenant.[97]

CONCLUSION

Communion with God is churchly, so that our life with God plays out among his people. The church is then necessary for our lives as the place where God meets us. He distributes his promises to us through the structures that he appointed for our lives as "those sanctified in Christ Jesus, called to be saints *together* with all those who in every place call

94. *COC*, 3:418 (emphasis added).

95. *COC*, 3:657 (emphasis added).

96. Letham, *Systematic Theology*, 616–23.

97. Clark, *Recovering*, 293–342; Barcellos, *Getting the Garden Right*, 231–59.

upon the name of our Lord Jesus Christ" (1 Cor 1:2). He binds us together as those who are reconciled to God "in one body through the cross, thereby killing the hostility" (Eph 2:16). He knits us together under "one Lord, one faith, one baptism" (Eph 4:5), so that faith and the outward administration that conveys God's promises to us unites us. In that body of Christ, he calls us to new holiness, not because it secures our entry into heaven, but because it is who he re-created us to be.

The pastoral use of this chapter's material is to value our church community. God could have left us to walk the Christian life in the world alone. For our fulfillment as creatures who need community, and often for our sanctification as sinners increasingly learn to love and get along with other sinners, God saves us into the church. The church is the place where the Father answers Christ's prayer that his people become one even as the Father and Son are one (John 17:11). The church is truly a family to one another, but the family that is fundamentally and foremost related to God. We then should learn to treasure what it means to belong to God in the church.

XVI

The Shape of Covenantal Life with God

I appeal to you therefore, brothers, by the mercies of God,
to present your bodies as a living sacrifice, holy and acceptable to God,
which is your spiritual worship. Do not be conformed to this world,
but be transformed by the renewal of your mind, that by testing
you may discern what is the will of God, what is good
and acceptable and perfect.
—*Romans 12:1–2*

God has always had communion with his people by way of covenant. In covenant, we find fellowship with God, joyful assurance, friendship in the community of faith, and great reasons for comfort. This chapter draws out two major ways in which the covenant shapes our everyday living for the Lord, connecting it to a more specific vision for our daily life of sanctification.

The Christian life, after all, must be lived. Despite its obviousness (and bordering on tautology), Christians most struggle precisely in this lived experience of wrestling for assurance of the Lord's presence, searching for wisdom to process issues that confront them in the Christian life, questioning how their faithfulness in the Christian life relates to their relationship with the Lord, and then, at times, lacking the strength or even desire to do the right thing, even when they know exactly what it is. Believers need renewed and increasing strength, help, and comfort for all these facets of the Christian life. Whereas chapter 15 explores how God applies Christ to his people *externally* through the outward means of grace, this chapter now looks at how God does his renewing work of sanctification *internally* within us. So, these final reflections focus upon the inward effects of those outward means of grace.

A COVENANTAL ETHIC

The way we live as Christians is shaped by our understanding of who God is, our relationship to Christ, our justification, our sanctification, and our place in the church. Because we are bound to God as his image bearers and as those in covenant with him, we must not invent how to live the Christian life. The covenantal shape of our lived experience of sanctification fittingly concludes our exploration of covenant theology.

This book stresses how covenant theology reinforces the certainty of our salvation and how Christ irrevocably secured everlasting life for his people, because both Christians and pastors who teach Christians sometimes find it difficult to maintain that assurance. This difficulty magnifies when reckoning with the Scripture's genuine call for God's people to live holy lives. The easiest way to motivate people to pursue holiness is by convincing them that their salvation is at stake. In this case, the easiest way is not the best or truly effective way.

The structure of covenant theology shows that a true believer's everlasting life cannot be at stake in keeping the law. True, humanity is responsible by creation in the covenant of works to fulfill the law and so earn heightened communion with God, entailing an inherent relationship to God's law (*realiter*). Christ as the last Adam fulfilled the law for us, imputing his perfect righteousness to us. So, the law *as a covenant* has been fulfilled for us and can no longer serve as such. Although even some within Reformed and evangelical churches have suggested that our works play a role in a so-called "final justification," covenant theology shows how our full justification by faith, which believers presently possess, guarantees our unending communion with God. There must then be another motivation for holiness other than making salvation dependent on it.[1]

Our ethics should instead begin with our reality of belonging to God. In 1 Corinthians 6:19–20, Paul explains how Christians do not belong to themselves but to God, since Christ purchased us with his own life and the Spirit indwells us as his temple: "Or do you not know that your body is a temple of the Holy Spirit within you, whom you have from God? You are not your own, for you were bought with a price. So glorify God in your body." John Calvin concludes that "we are consecrated and dedicated to God in order that we may thereafter think, speak, meditate, and do, nothing except to his glory."[2] Because Christ is our new representative and has definitively earned everlasting blessings for us, we are his. We are in his hands in grace because he has been so richly good to us. Our understanding of the Christian life should be fundamentally shaped by an awareness that we belong to Christ.[3]

If this belonging drives our ethics, prayer should be the chief factor of our Christian life. The Heidelberg Catechism affirms that prayer is necessary "because it is the *chief part* of the thankfulness which God requires of us, and because God will give his grace and Holy Spirit only to such as earnestly and without ceasing beg them from him and render thank unto him for them" (HC 116).[4] The Westminster Shorter Catechism confesses prayer as a means of grace "made effectual to the elect for salvation" (WSC 88).[5] Unlike word and sacraments, prayer is not an objective token that God gives to us to convey grace. Rather, "Prayer is an offering up of our desires unto God, for things agreeable to his will, in the name of Christ, with confession of our sins, and thankful acknowledgment of his mercies."[6] Prayer is, then, subjective as our action toward God but nonetheless still divinely appointed to convey blessings to us. As Paul writes in

1. This section includes material revised and expanded from Harrison Perkins, "Virtue is Its Own Reward," *Modern Reformation*, September 8, 2020, https://modernreformation.org/resource-library/web-exclusive-articles/the-mod-virtue-is-its-own-reward/. Used with permission.

2. Calvin, *Institutes*, 3.7.1.

3. Philip G. Ziegler, "Reformed Ethics," in *OHRT*, 581–83.

4. *COC*, 3:350 (emphasis added).

5. *COC*, 3:695.

6. *COC*, 3:698.

Philippians 4:6–7: "Do not be anxious about anything, but in everything by prayer and supplication with thanksgiving let your requests be made known to God. And the peace of God, which surpasses all understanding, will guard your hearts and your minds in Christ Jesus." Praying results in God's incomprehensible peace flowing into our hearts because God designed it that way.

Moreover, God uses prayer to accomplish spiritual good in our lives. Jude instructs readers to "keep yourselves in God's love," surrounded by three ways to accomplish this direction (Jude 1:20–21; my translation). The way revelant for our discussion is "by praying in the Holy Spirit," indicating how God uses prayer as his means to keep us in his love, which is effective for "the called ones, who have been loved by God the Father and are certainly kept for Jesus Christ" (Jude 1:1; my translation). Prayer is the reflex, reaction, recognition, and repose of belonging to God by grace alone. Although it is our action, God nonetheless uses prayer as his instrument—his means of grace—to fill us with grace and apply Christ to us as we drink from him by conversing with the Lord. Hence, it is *by prayer* that, in light of Christ's high priesthood on our behalf, we "with confidence draw near to the throne of grace, that we may receive mercy and find grace to help in time of need" (Heb 4:16). If we come near to God's throne *by prayer* to *receive grace to help*, then prayer is a means of grace that deserves constant and unceasing use. So, we need to see that, although it is not an external administration of the covenant of grace in the way that word and sacrament are (or the types and ordinances of the old economy were), prayer is nonetheless a means of grace whereby God does something to us and in us to build us up in Christ. If word and sacrament are like funnels that pour Christ upon us objectively, prayer is like a straw whereby, in our action of sipping, we drink of Christ.

By contrast to this grounding of the Christian life primarily in an awareness of belonging to God, some attempt to motivate holiness by teaching that the last judgment includes rewards for our Spirit-induced good deeds. They suggest that not emphasizing these rewards is due to a lack of concern for obedience. This challenge tests our understanding of the Christian life by confronting us with whether we take the Scripture's call to holiness seriously. This view raises the question of whether an insistence that we grow in Christian obedience *requires* a link to final rewards.

Is there another way to explain the necessary pursuit of godliness? Many seemingly assume that the prospect of personally getting something in return is the only motivation for doing good works. Truly, I would not exercise if it did not result in better health. I would not pay bills if I did not want utilities for my home. Should we think this way concerning godliness though? Our covenant theology provides a richer account of our continuing need for holiness in the Christian life than stoking a desire for personal rewards in heaven.

A full understanding of the issue requires a consideration of ethical paradigms. Over the centuries, Christians have diversely explained our ethical principles, suggesting differing reasons for the Christian pursuit of holiness. In the modern era, a view called *divine command theory* has been a major, if not the predominant, ethical model.[7] Crassly put, divine command theory teaches that we are required to do something *simply* because God commanded it. On the surface, that seems well and good, since we certainly should do as God instructs. On further inspection, one of this theory's underlying premises is that there is not necessarily a reason for God's command. Most pertinently, divine command theory often neglects that God's image bearers were made with God's law hardwired into us as the ethical standard.[8]

Special revelation certainly discloses God's will for ethics. The Second Helvetic Confession affirms that "truly good works flow out of living faith through the Holy Spirit, and are done by believers *according to the will or rule of God's Word*" (16.5)[9] The Westminster Confession likewise avows: "Good works are only such as God has commanded in his holy Word, and not such as, without the warrant thereof, are devised by men out of blind zeal, or upon any pretense of good intention" (WCF 16.1).[10]

7. E.g., Richard J. Mouw, *The God Who Commands* (Notre Dame: University of Notre Dame Press, 1990).

8. Cross, *Duns Scotus*, 89–95; Stephen J. Grabill, *Rediscovering the Natural Law in Reformed Theological Ethics* (Grand Rapids: Eerdmans, 2006), 1–53, 175–91; Kirk J. Nolan, *Reformed Virtue After Barth: Developing Moral Virtue Ethics in the Reformed Tradition* (Louisville: Westminster John Knox, 2014), 37–61; David F. Wells, *Losing Our Virtue: Why the Church Must Recover Its Moral Vision* (Grand Rapids: Eerdmans, 1998), 13–19; Dorothea Frede, "The Historic Decline of Virtue Ethics," in *The Cambridge Companion to Virtue Ethics*, ed. Daniel C. Russell (Cambridge: Cambridge University Press, 2013), 124–48.

9. *COC*, 3:269 (emphasis added).

10. *COC*, 3:633.

The confessions preclude demanding works from God's people that God himself has not required. But does special revelation originate God's law or describe the law built into God's image bearers? Divine command theory tends to the former.[11]

The principle in divine command theory has an easy illustration in a common experience of parents and children. When a mother instructs her son to clean his room, his potentially endless questioning about why he should obey may eventually prompt her to conclude, "Because I said so." Although not itself wrong, this response may suggest that the instruction is arbitrary.[12] Evangelicals, however, often seem to think that God acts like a frustrated parent, so that his commands are ultimately binding *simply* because he said so. God's commands are considered events, God's announcement of the actions that he requires, rather than explanations of the character we should have.[13]

This view rightly affirms God reveals his moral will but wrongly downplays that his commands correspond to his creational purpose for us. God's moral law summarizes his own character, unbreakably linking the Lawgiver and his law.[14] Since the law is "in" God precisely as his character, it binds his image bearers to him by being imprinted on our nature.[15] Divine command theory explains God's law more as his chosen will than as an expression of his nature.

Questions do not necessarily stop because the "I said so" principle is asserted, especially when a deeper reason than arbitrary choice is not yet clear.[16] People are prone to ask why specific deeds are required if they

---

11. A recent example of this approach is found in Paul T. Nimmo, "The Law of God and Christian Ethics." For example, he writes, "The law of God is not to be sought in the creation or in the conscience. On a common account of the matter, there is implanted in humanity in the divine act of creation a moral law—a so-called law of nature—that provides humans with knowledge of the will of God and with awareness of the obedience or disobedience with which that will has been followed." He continues, "Yet this understanding of the once implanted and still effective moral law is to be at least marginalized and at best resisted." See "The Law of God and Christian Ethics" in *CD*, 291–310. Although better than Karl Barth on the law-gospel distinction and its significance for soteriology, Nimmo's presentation represents a Barthian approach to the law, most easily called divine command theory.

12. Cf. Calvin, *Institutes*, 2.8.8.

13. Grabill, *Rediscovering the Natural Law*, 204–5n16–17.

14. John Webster, "The Dignity of Creatures," in *GWM2*, 29–38.

15. Grabill, *Rediscovering the Natural Law*, 216–17n40.

16. Carl R. Trueman, *The Rise and Triumph of the Modern Self: Cultural Amnesia, Expressive Individualism, and the Road to the Sexual Revolution* (Wheaton, IL: Crossway, 2020), 76–80, 82–88.

feel that "because God said so" is a shallow answer. One plausible supplement adds the prospect of final rewards as *the reason* to pursue holiness.

In contrast to divine command theory, *virtue ethics* suggests that the image of God entails that we are made for certain ends, namely, to reflect the holy God's *good* character. This ethical paradigm affirms that there need not be a higher reason, such as personal rewards, for good works besides their inherent goodness.[17] We do not need a deeper reason to spend time with our loved ones besides the intrinsic good of enjoying loved ones. So, godliness does not require a deeper motivation than the intrinsic good of godliness.[18]

Although the Reformed confessions explicate no ethical paradigm, virtue fits their ethical principles.[19] They clearly affirm that our works do not secure everlasting life, that continued obedience is nevertheless necessary, and that God both created and redeemed us for good works. For example, the Belgic Confession explains the Spirit's sanctifying work promotes a desire for good works, since "without it they would never do anything out of love to God, but only out of self-love or fear of damnation." Still, good works "from the good root of faith, are good and acceptable in the sight of God," but "are of no account towards our justification." Yes, "God rewards our good works, but it is through his grace that he crowns his gifts." Although striving after good works, "we do not found our salvation

---

17. Sebastian Rehnman, "Moral Philosophy and Moral Theology in Vermigli," in *Church and School in Early Modern Protestantism: Studies in Honor of Richard A. Muller on the Maturation of a Theological Tradition*, eds. Jordan J. Ballor, David S. Sytsma, and Jason Zuidema (Leiden: Brill, 2013), 204–12; Jean Porter, "Virtue Ethics in the Medieval Period," in *Cambridge Companion to Virtue Ethics*, 70–91; Rachana Kamtekar, "Ancient Virtue Ethics: An Overview with an Emphasis on Practical Wisdom," in *Cambridge Companion to Virtue Ethics*, 29–48; P. J. E. Kail, "Virtue and Vice," in *The Oxford Handbook of Philosophy in Early Modern Europe*, eds. Desmond M. Clarke and Catherine Wilson (Oxford: Oxford University Press, 2011), 363–78.

18. John Webster, "Mortification and Vivification," in *GWM2*, 103–21; Grant Macaskill rightly raises a concern that a recent emphasis on virtue ethics in Pauline studies has promoted an understanding of sanctification as the formation of simply a better version of myself rather than conformity to Christ. His concern does not undermine the present use of virtue ethics, since this use underscores the deontological aspect that godliness is inherently good as part of the *imago Dei*. The argument then dovetails with and supports Macaskill's concern to avoid legalism in our soteriology and ecclesiological identity by using virtue ethics to refute the notion that our growth in holiness is aimed at obtaining blessings from God; see Grant Macaskill, *Living in Union with Christ: Paul's Gospel and Christian Moral Identity* (Grand Rapids: Baker Academic, 2019), 131–39.

19. David B. Hunsicker, "The Westminster Standards and the Possibility of a Reformed Virtue Ethic," *Scottish Journal of Theology* 71 no. 2 (2018): 180–86.

upon them" (BC 24).[20] As William Perkins writes, "If it be considered as an instrument to apprehend Christ to our salvation, we are only saved by faith in this manner. Yet if faith be considered as a way, we are not only saved by faith. For all other virtues and works are the way to life as well as faith, though they be not causes of salvation."[21] Believers should not pursue holiness out of "self-love or fear" as if our works establish our standing before God.[22]

The pursuit of holiness, therefore, requires other motivating factors. Virtue ethics affirms that God designed us for holiness. If we lack holiness, we are not functioning in a properly human manner, nor in the manner that the Spirit's sanctifying work promotes.[23]

A virtue is our inherent disposition for doing a particular good, strengthened as God sanctifies us. According to William Ames, "Virtue is a condition or habit [*habitus*] by which the will is inclined to do well.... It is called a habit because it is in general a state of mind of various degrees of perfection."[24] Correspondingly, the practice of muscle strengthening illustrates virtue ethics' premise.[25] God created his image bearers with ability to live uprightly with capacities for love, joy, peace, patience, kindness, goodness, and so forth as inherent goods. Our capacity for each good is a virtue, functioning like a muscle because, as physical muscles are trained by lifting increasingly heavy objects, a virtue, such as kindness, strengthens as we exercise it by being kind. The fall atrophied our virtue muscles, but Christ gives virtue-muscle transplants so that believers draw upon his grace to restrengthen them.

Although often weak, practicing our regenerate capacities for virtue increases them. Paul endorses this very outlook on growth in godliness in exhorting the churches: "Rather train yourself for godliness; for while bodily training is of some value, godliness is of value in every way, as it holds promise for the present life and also for the life to come"

20. *COC*, 3:410–12.

21. *WWP*, 2:123 (commentary on Galatians 2:15–16).

22. R. C. Sproul, *Getting the Gospel Right: The Tie That Binds Evangelicals Together* (1999; repr. Grand Rapids: Baker, 2017), 178.

23. Ziegler, "Reformed Ethics," 587–89.

24. *MT*, 2.2.4–5.

25. This illustration is most fitting because the Latin word *virtus* means "strength."

(1 Tim 4:7–8); in another passage, he writes, "But I discipline my body and keep it under control, lest after preaching to others I myself should be disqualified" (1 Cor 9:27). In this way, virtue ethics helps us account for the possibility of genuine growth in the Christian life better than divine command theory can.[26] The Spirit's sanctifying work in us conforms us to Christ's image to restore us to what it truly means to live as God's image bearers and yet we strive after holiness by practicing it with increasing discipline.[27]

This notion of virtue as spiritual muscle training, whereby believers strengthen their capacity for certain good habits as the Spirit sanctifies us, coheres with the confessional tradition's affirmation of infused grace, confirming virtue ethics as the probably assumed ethical paradigm.[28] In the Westminster Larger Catechism, one way that justification differs from sanctification is having the sole ground of Christ's imputed righteousness. On the other hand, "in Sanctification his Spirit *infuses grace*, and enables to the exercise thereof" (WLC 77).[29] By contrast, the Council of Trent (1546) describes "advancing from virtue to virtue" as through "faith cooperating with good works, they increase in that righteousness received through Christ's grace and are justified to a higher degree."[30] Further, "whereas Christ himself continually infuses his virtue into the said justified," this virtue precedes its accompanying good works to make them meritorious before God, so that the justified "by those very works which have been done in God, fully satisfied the divine law according to the state of this life,

---

26. Stanley Hauerwas, *Character and the Christian Life: A Study in Theological Ethics* (Notre Dame: University of Notre Dame Press, 1994), 1–10.

27. John Webster, "'Where Christ Is': Christology and Ethics," in *GWM2*, 5–27; Webster, "Dignity of Creatures," 38–47.

28. Sebastian Rehnman, "Virtue and Grace," *Studies in Christian Ethics* 25 no. 4 (2012): 473–81, 488–90; Luca Baschera, "Ethics in Reformed Orthodoxy," in *A Companion to Reformed Orthodoxy*, ed. Herman Selderhuis (Leiden: Brill, 2013), 519–52; Pieter Vos, "Calvinists among the Virtues: Reformed Theological Contributions to Contemporary Virtue Ethics," *Studies in Christian Ethics* 28 no. 2 (2015): 201–4; cf. Alasdair C. MacIntyre, *A Short History of Ethics: A History of Moral Philosophy from the Homeric Age to the Twentieth Century*, 2nd ed. (London: Routledge, 1998), 118, 122; Alasdair MacIntyre, *After Virtue: A Study in Moral Theory*, 3rd ed. (Notre Dame: University of Notre Dame Press, 2007), 53; Brad S. Gregory, *The Unintended Reformation: How a Religious Revolution Secularized Society* (Cambridge, MA: Belknap Press of Harvard University Press, 2012), 269; and Daniel Westberg, "The Influence of Aquinas on Protestant Ethics," in *Aquinas Among the Protestants*, Manfred Svensson and David VanDrunen (Hoboken, NJ: Wiley Blackwell, 2018), 267–83.

29. *LC*, 80.

30. Session 6, chapter 10; *COC*, 2:99.

and *to have truly merited* everlasting life."[31] Trent insists on merit precisely in connection to biblical passages where believers receive rewards at the final judgment.[32] Rome holds that God infuses grace so that believers can increase *in justification* by their growing virtues to merit final glory, but the Reformed insist that God infuses grace *only for sanctification.*[33]

On this point, the Reformed followed Peter Lombard in naming the indwelling Spirit himself as our infused grace.[34] Thomas Aquinas furthered Lombard's point, as well, arguing that "the Holy Ghost is possessed by man, and dwells within him, in the very gift itself of sanctifying grace."[35] In our confessional tradition, the Canons of Dort affirm that after he "not only causes the Gospel to be external preached to them [the elect] and powerfully illumines their minds by the Holy Spirit," God "enters a person's innermost parts by the same regenerating Spirit's efficacy" and "infuses new qualities into the will" (Canons of Dort 3/4.11).[36] By the Spirit's indwelling presence, his sanctifying work infuses grace, continually enabling us to exercise those strengthening virtues with "heartfelt joy in God" so that we "take delight in living according to the will of God in all good works."[37] God's infused grace pumps strength into our spiritual muscles, our virtues, so that we can increasingly live in gratitude-fueled godliness.[38] Christ earned new creation life for his people, not only legally guaranteeing future glorification, but also cultivating present sanctification as the Spirit's indwelling increasingly enables us to live unto righteousness.[39]

---

31. Session 6, chapter 16; *COC*, 2:108.

32. Joseph P. Wawrykow, *God's Grace and Human Action: Merit in the Theology of Thomas Aquinas* (Notre Dame: University of Notre Dame Press, 2016), 276–78.

33. WCF 11.1–2; *COC*, 3:626; *WWP*, 2:116–17 (commentary on Galatians 2:15–16); Rollock, *Treatise*, 36–38, 183–87, 201, 237; John Owen, *The Doctrine of Justification by Faith through the Imputation of the Righteousness of Christ, Explained, Confirmed, and Vindicated* (London: R. Boulter, 1677), 82; cf. deSilva, who blends transformation into justification itself so that righteousness is not imputed to but wrought in us. See *Galatians*, 221n278, 220–2.

34. J. V. Fesko, "Aquinas's Doctrine of Justification and Infused Habits in Reformed Soteriology," in *Aquinas Among the Protestants*, 257–58.

35. Thomas, *Summa Theologica*, 1.43.3.

36. *COC*, 3:566.

37. HC 90; *COC*, 3:339.

38. Fesko, "Infused Habits," 249–63; Vos, "Calvinists among the Virtues," 204–8; Rehnman, "Virtue and Grace," 481–93.

39. WSC 35; *COC*, 3:683.

This outlook highlights how Christians should cherish our sanctification for its own inherent goodness. Believers, who love their Savior, should delight in being more like their Savior, regardless of what rewards may be in store. Lombard distinguishes things that are to be *enjoyed,* things that are to be *used,* and things to be enjoyed and used.[40] He quotes Augustine, "To enjoy is to adhere in love to some thing for its own sake; but to use is to apply whatever comes into one's hand in order to obtain that which is to be enjoyed."[41] Believers should consider godliness as virtues for *enjoying and using.* You should enjoy a glass of good lemonade and use that lemonade for the sake of enjoying it. Likewise, we should deeply delight in our sanctification, not for prospective rewards, but because living out God's own goodness by extending it to our neighbors is itself something to cherish and enjoy. So, we use our Spirit-enlivened virtues, thereby also strengthening them, because we enjoy godliness itself.[42] Linking enjoyment back to the Spirit as God's indwelling presence of infused grace, Aquinas highlights how, to increase in our sanctification is to increase delight in the Spirit himself: "By the gift of sanctifying grace the rational creature is perfected so that it can freely use not only the created gift itself, but *enjoy also the divine person Himself*; and so the invisible mission takes place according to the gift of sanctifying grace; and yet the divine persons Himself is given."[43] In the life of sanctification in this age, we enjoy in a limited way, hoping for more of, the renewal and freedom that we will see clearly and experience fully in the future.[44]

The Genesis 1 narrative emphasizes humanity's purpose to display God's character, recording God's self-deliberation only regarding his creation of humanity in his image: "Then God said, 'Let us make man in our image, after our likeness' " (Gen 1:26). God's image is embedded in human nature but also includes a functional dimension to reflect God's image in creation. After all, God is the sovereign Lord, which humanity reflects by exercising (responsible) dominion within creation (Gen 1:27).

---

40. Lombard, *Sentences Book 1*, 1.2.1–5. Thanks to John Fesko for alerting me to Lombard's distinction.

41. Lombard, *Sentences Book 1*, 1.2.3; citing Augustine, *De Doctrina Christiana*, 1.4.4.

42. Lombard, *Sentences Book 1*, 1.3.7–10.

43. Thomas, *Summa Theologica*, 1.43.3 (emphasis added).

44. Lombard, *Sentences Book 1*, 1.3.2–3.

The role of bearing God's image informs our understanding of God's law. Since the Decalogue *summarizes* rather than exhaustively details the moral law, ethical obligations cannot be reduced to each commandment's bare statement. The commandments as individual mandates certainly stand, but their implications and entailments are also binding. The commandments are not exhaustive legislation but encapsulate wisdom principles to be further applied.[45] The Westminster Larger Catechism employs this principle by explaining what each commandment of the Decalogue both requires and forbids (WLC 91–152).[46] The law captures a wider understanding of virtuous character that should belong to God's image bearers.[47]

In this regard, the image of God is an investiture with goodness as such. Throughout the creation narrative, God sees that the things that he has made are good (Gen 1:4, 10, 12, 18, 21, 25), and that the completed creation is "very good" (Gen 1:31). In Colossians 3:10, Paul writes, "Put on the new self, which is being renewed in knowledge after the image of its creator." He affirms a similar point in Ephesians 4:24: "Put on the new self, created after the likeness of God in true righteousness and holiness." Humanity's function is at least partly to reflect God's goodness within creation.

How does humanity's purpose motivate holiness? Our role to reflect God's holiness and righteousness means we are being properly human only as we instantiate his goodness. Creation was "very good" only once God placed his own image in it. God's purpose that we refract his goodness into creation means that God ordered us by nature to be good. Sin is not only a lack of conformity unto or transgression of God's law but is functioning in a truly less-than-human manner.

Goodness is then itself our end. Final rewards are an unnecessary, even if real, prospect for motivation because they are displaced by an awareness of our created purposes and by our gratitude for belonging to

45. Walton and Walton, *Lost World of the Torah*, 89–94, 104–11. Walton and Walton's argument errs in many features but helpfully makes the specific point that Old Testament law is not modern legislation, and so should be understood in light of the categories of covenant and wisdom.

46. Crowe, *Path of Faith*, 120; Hunsicker, "Westminster Standards and the Possibility of a Reformed Virtue Ethic," 186–89.

47. David VanDrunen, "Wisdom and the Christian Life," (paper presented at the WSC 2015 Annual Conference, Escondido, California, January 21, 2015, https://www.wscal.edu/resource-center/wisdom-and-the-christian-life).

Christ.[48] Since Christ is the exact imprint of God's nature (Heb 1:3), and God has predestined us to be conformed to his Son's image (Rom 8:29), our highest goal simply is to be more like our Savior.[49]

Christ, therefore, provides the model for our thinking about obedience. Christ is God's Son, who by nature did not have to obey the Father but learned obedience for us (Heb 5:8). The Son had perfect equality with God but relinquished it to learn obedience precisely to benefit others (Phil 2:3–11). Christ's assumed servant role supports an ethical point: "Do nothing from selfish ambition or conceit, but in humility count others more significant than yourselves. Let each of you look not only to his own interests, but also to the interests of others" (Phil 2:3–4). He became obedient for others' sake, setting our example.[50]

Christ is not merely our example but the Savior who has earned everlasting blessings for his people. We are new creations in Christ Jesus (2 Cor 5:17). Virtue ethics focus attention on sanctification as a matter not of trying our hardest but of growing into our identity as those who have put on Christ, who enables us by grace to pursue new obedience.[51]

Still, Christ has provided this new creation life not simply to secure our everlasting life, but to commandeer us for good works in this age. Paul writes in 2 Corinthians 5:14–15: "For the love of Christ controls us, because we have concluded this: that one has died for all, therefore all have died; and he died for all, that those who live might no longer live for themselves but for him who for their sake died and was raised." The Father chose us in Christ "that we should be holy and blameless before him" (Eph 1:4), marking our holiness as God's purpose for our salvation. According to Ephesians 2:10: "For we are his workmanship, created in Christ Jesus for good works, which God prepared beforehand, that we should walk in them." In other words, God does not save us by our good works but for them.

God recreates us for holiness, then works in us to strengthen our capacity for good, not for self-motivated gain but because godliness is

---

48. Ziegler, "Reformed Ethics," 583–84.

49. John Webster, *Holiness* (London: SCM Press, 2002), 77–98.

50. Allen, *Sanctification*, 264–75.

51. Allen, *Sanctification*, 227–55; Macaskill, *Living in Union with Christ*, 39–58.

inherently virtuous. Our present possession of new life in Christ, and the fact that our good deeds result from this spiritual life, defines our relationship to the law. The absolute necessity of our pursuit of new obedience does not make the law an *antecedent condition* unto life. We do not live "under the law" *as a covenant* as if it were a condition for our communion with God (Rom 6:14; 7:1–6; 1 Cor 9:20–21; 2 Cor 3:7–9; Gal 2:19–20; 5:18). In light of Christ's work, the law as a covenant, be it creational or Mosaic, is totally fulfilled. Rather, believers have God's moral law *as a rule*, plaited naturally into our constitution as God's image bearers, as the guide to living faithfully as those who represent our God.[52]

THE ABIDING RULE FOR LIFE

God's moral law, as summarized in the Ten Commandments, remains the abiding rule for Christians as the guide to the Christian life. The moral law, even as given to us by nature, describes those good virtues that Christians should cultivate.[53] The Westminster Confession affirms: "The moral law does forever bind all, as well as justified persons as others, to the obedience thereof; and that not only in regard of the matter contained in it, but also in respect of the authority of God the Creator who gave it. Neither does Christ in the gospel any way dissolve, but much strengthen, this obligation" (WCF 19.5).[54] The Mosaic law as such no longer obligates Christians. The ceremonial laws are totally abrogated in

52. Rosner, *Paul and the Law*, 45–109; *ACW*, 278–79; Ziegler, "Reformed Ethics," 585–87; cf. *KTC*, 782–98; Wellum, "Progressive Covenantalism and the Doing of Ethics," in *Progressive Covenantalism*, 215–33; Jason C. Meyer, "The Mosaic Law, Theological Systems, and the Glory of Christ," in *Progressive Covenantalism*, 87–89. Progressive covenantalism omits the Bible's "intrasystematic" category of natural law that explains why the moral law is distinct from the other Mosaic laws, as well as the distinction between the law as a covenant and as a rule. Nonetheless, progressive covenantalism approximates the covenant-rule distinction by distinguishing the law as a *covenant* and as *Scripture*. Still, natural law remains the missing premise in their argument, which would support more cogently why they can reach similar ethical conclusions as covenant theology.

53. The point here being that virtue ethics and natural law ethics are complementary within a Reformed understanding of creation, law, regeneration, and sanctification, although philosophers often juxtapose these paradigms. The harder contrast is between virtue ethics and *strict* divine command theory. The divide between virtue and natural law developed later with the political discussions of natural law, primarily associated with Thomas Hobbes, John Locke, and Hugo Grotius; see Vos, "Calvinists among the Virtues," 208–12; Rehnman, "Virtue and Grace," 481–93; Fesko, "Infused Habits," 255–62; and Ian Hunter, "Natural Law as Political Philosophy," in *Oxford Handbook of Philosophy in Early Modern Europe*, 475–96; cf. Kail, "Virtue and Vice," 363–64, 369–74; and Frede, "Historic Decline of Virtue Ethics," 139–40.

54. *COC*, 3:641.

Christ's work and have no continuing role in our present practice.[55] The civil laws have expired and bind no person or country except inasmuch as they contain principles that correspond to "general equity" or natural law.[56] On the other hand, the moral law is distinct because it was given to Adam by nature, not originating at Sinai like the other kinds of laws in the Mosaic covenant.[57]

Even the accounts of the Mosaic covenant distinguish the Decalogue from the rest of the Mosaic law. These commands were given twice, whereas the other civil and ceremonial laws were revealed only once (Exod 20; Deut 5). God speaks these commandments directly to the people "face-to-face," motivating the people's request that Moses act as their mediator, but gave the others through Moses (Deut 5:4; Exod 20:18–19).[58] Herman Witsius explains, "The foundation of the moral laws, whose perpetuity and unchangeableness is an unquestionable truth, is of a quite different nature, from that of the ceremonial institutions ... because the former are founded on the natural and immutable holiness of God, which cannot but be the exemplar to rational creatures; and therefore cannot be abolished, without abolishing the image of God: but the latter are founded on the free and arbitrary will of the lawgiver."[59] In the covenant of grace, the moral law is not our condition for obtaining life but is our guide for living out the life we have in Christ.

Salvation places us beyond the demands of the moral law as a condition for obtaining everlasting life but not beyond obligation to the moral law absolutely. Since the moral law reveals what it means to conduct

---

55. WCF 19.3; *COC*, 3:640–41; *KTC*, 796.

56. WCF 19.4; *COC*, 3:641; *KTC*, 796; Meyer, "Mosaic Law," 91–93.

57. Burnside, *God, Justice, and Society*, 67–100; cf. *KTC*, 791. Still, Gentry and Wellum come very close to affirming the continuity of the moral law: "The term תּוֹרָה (inappropriately translated 'law') shows that God's direction and instruction for appropriate relationships (divine-human, human-human, human-creation) will not change. The new covenant does not mean a change in God's standards of righteousness, of right and wrong, of what is appropriate in a covenant relationship." This is thoroughly consistent with Reformed theology's commitment to the continuity of God's moral law. Gentry and Wellum cannot explain that continuity as clearly or with as much force as the Reformed because they have not yet reckoned with the Reformed understanding of natural law and its connection to the covenants.

58. Swain, "New Covenant Theologies," 562–64.

59. *EC*, 4.14.2.

ourselves in a truly human way, we can never entirely transcend it.[60] Herman Bavinck explains, "Freedom from the law, therefore, does not mean that Christians no longer have anything to do with that law, but that the law can no longer demand anything from them as a condition for salvation and can no longer judge and condemn them."[61] Christ's work in fulfilling the law as the last Adam fully frees Christians from the law as a condition for obtaining everlasting communion with God, but that freedom does not mean that we entirely dispose of the law.

Our freedom in Christ, then, enables us to use the law as a mirror for living faithfully rather than as a tool to try to earn blessings from him. Too many have reduced Christian liberty to an openness to drinking alcohol when it is foremost "freedom from the guilt of sin, the condemning wrath of God, [and] the curse of the moral law."[62] Evangelical freedom is not the ability to determine ourselves and decide what is right in our own eyes but the comfort that the gospel liberates us from the shackles of sin and death so that we can hear God commission us for holy service in fellowship with him without fear that the instructions for that service will put us back under God's curse and condemnation.[63]

The moral law binds us as the standard for living well before God even if it is no longer our condition for life with him. As a description of God's character, it cannot change since God cannot change (Jas 1:17). The moral law is inherently tied to God as our king, which is why James writes, "If you really fulfill the royal law according to the Scripture, 'You shall love your neighbor as yourself,' you are doing well" (Jas 2:8). Crucially, James summarizes this royal law with the command to love your neighbor as yourself. This command appears in multiple contexts throughout the Scripture. The Mosaic law uses it to encapsulate the law's requirement for our relationship with other people (Lev 19:18). Further, Christ likewise uses this command to summarize the Ten Commandments that regulate holiness regarding fellow humans (Matt 19:16–19). More pointedly, Christ

60. Swain, "New Covenant Theologies," 565–66.

61. *BRD*, 4:455.

62. WCF 20.1; *COC*, 3:643. Credit to Bryan Estelle who powerfully highlighted this point in classes at Westminster Seminary California.

63. John Webster, "Evangelical Freedom," in *Confessing God: Essays in Christian Dogmatics II* (London: T&T Clark, 2016), 215–26; *WWP*, 2:128 (commentary on Galatians 2:19).

also ties this very command to the "do this and live" principle of the covenant of works by which we would earn justification (Luke 10:25–29). James, however, who clearly still saw this command as summarizing the Ten Commandments, which concern our obligations toward other people (Jas 2:8–11), cited it as instruction for the new covenant community who are already saved in Christ. In other words, God gave the same moral law—which can be summarized as love the Lord your God with all your heart, soul, mind and strength and love your neighbor as yourself—in the covenant of works, the Mosaic covenant, and still in the new covenant.

Even though the content of the moral law is the same in all covenants, our relationship to the moral law in the covenant of grace is not as a covenant of works. God gave this moral law to Adam as the natural law in the covenant of works where it certainly regulated how God's people lived holy lives but also offered the reward of everlasting spiritual life if Adam fulfilled it. In the Mosaic covenant, the moral law again regulated how God's people ought to live but was further linked into the whole Mosaic legislation by which the nation was bound to obedience in order to maintain the possession of the land. In the covenant of grace, holistically speaking (not in *full* contrast to the Mosaic covenant), concerning how God relates to individuals for salvation in every administration, the moral law is delivered as the royal law (Jas 2:8) or the law of Christ (1 Cor 9:21; Gal 6:2) to direct how those who belong to King Jesus should conduct themselves as faithful citizens of his kingdom. As the substance of the covenant of grace is fully exhibited in the new covenant, the moral law no longer imposes itself as a condition for obtaining the blessing of salvation from God, since this is fully granted to us in Christ, but comes to us as the sure and faithful guide for how to live holy lives that are pleasing to our God who rescued us.[64]

This change in how we are able to relate to the same moral law in different ways in different covenants is based on how God has connected the law to the priesthood. Priests are charged with driving the religious life of God's people. In the covenant of works, Adam was the priest who represented all of humanity before God with the task to fulfill God's commands to earn new creation life for us all. In the Mosaic covenant, the priests

64. Allen, *Sanctification*, 275–86.

were those tasked to conduct the sacrifices and lead worship to facilitate the nation's relationship with God. In the covenant of redemption, Christ was appointed as the final high priest who would fulfill the covenant of works for all the elect and ensure our everlasting life in the new creation.

These differences in the various priesthoods are important to how we understand the law because Hebrews 7:11–12 explains: "Now if perfection had been attainable through the Levitical priesthood (for under it the people received the law), what further need would there have been for another priest to arise after the order of Melchizedek, rather than one named after the order of Aaron? For *when there is a change in the priesthood, there is necessarily a change in the law* as well." The law changes when the priesthood changes.[65] Adam received moral law as the natural law as our first priest but failed to keep its terms. The Levitical priests received the moral law as the Mosaic law, but that whole covenant merely proved the need for a priest who could obtain perfection for God's people.

Under Christ's priesthood, the same moral law guides what it means to be Christ's faithful citizen and what it means to be truly human. The content of the moral law remains the same for believers under Christ's priesthood as when it was given to us by nature. Although that natural law cannot change, Christ's priesthood displaced the Levitical priesthood, fulfilling the ceremonial laws and expiring the civil laws from the Mosaic covenant.[66] Those *positive laws*, divine commands not directly summarizing the natural law, are not binding anymore under Christ's priesthood, but the moral law is the abiding rule for believers.[67]

In Psalm 119, the psalmist reflects upon his love for God's law. He declares, "I will delight in your statutes; I will not forget your word" (Ps 119:16). He does not speak of the law as a condition but as his guide to what is truly good, a good which he longed to live out.

---

65. Vos, "The Priesthood of Christ in the Epistle to the Hebrews," in *RHBI*, 126–60; Ellingworth, *Hebrews*, 372–74.

66. WCF 19.3–4; *COC*, 3:640–61.

67. *TI*, 11.2.1–34; 11.23–26; James Ussher, "Ussher to William Twisse, c. 1636," in Elizabethanne Boran (ed.), *The Correspondence of James Ussher, 1600–1656*, 3 vol. (Dublin: Irish Manuscripts Commission, 2015), 2:706–14; James Ussher, "Ussher to John Ley, partial letter," in *Correspondence*, 2:715–16; *CO*, 30:1106; Simon J. G. Burton, "Samuel Rutherford's *Euthyphro Dilemma*: A Reformed Perspective on the Scholastic Natural Law Tradition," in *Reformed Orthodoxy in Scotland: Essays on Scottish Theology 1560–1775*, ed. Aaron Clay Denlinger (London: Bloomsbury, 2014), 123–39.

Incline my heart to your testimonies,
and not to selfish gain!
Turn my eyes from looking at worthless things;
and give me life in your ways. (Ps 119:36–37)

He saw that the believer relates to the law, and so can love the law, in light of our salvation.

Behold, I long for your precepts;
in your righteousness give me life!
Let your steadfast love come to me, O LORD,
your salvation according to your promise. (Ps 119:40–41)

The psalmist speaks so joyfully about the law because he understood that our salvation changes the law from our condition for obtaining life with God into the guide to how to live well the life we have with God: "Your word is a lamp to my feet and a light to my path" (Ps 119:105).[68]

Perhaps Christians should think far less about potential final rewards and more about how Christlikeness pursues obedience to benefit others. Indeed, the parable from Matthew 20:1–16 concerning the laborers in the vineyard seems to indicate that in the kingdom of heaven the same gift of everlasting life will be granted to every believer in equal amounts no matter what their contribution in life was. Unlike the workers who objected to the master's equal distribution of rewards at the end of the workday, Christians' godliness should not be about personal ambition but about looking out for neighbors (1 Cor 10:33; Phil 2:3–4). In Philippians 4:8, Paul exhorts: "Finally, brothers, whatever is true, whatever is honorable, whatever is just, whatever is pure, whatever is lovely, whatever is commendable, if there is any excellence, if there is anything worthy of praise, think about these things." Christians should think about true, honorable, and just things because these things are "worthy of praise." Unsurprisingly, since being properly human includes reflecting God's goodness as those made in his image, we tend to find that we are more joyful when we are properly ordered in our walk with God in a pattern of obedience. In that respect, virtue truly is its own reward because the

68. Allen, *Sanctification*, 263–64.

reward is an unfettered enjoyment of our relationship with Christ, who guarantees our everlasting life by grace alone.

THE PROCLAMATION OF LIFE

The scope of covenant theology also provides a pattern for how to proclaim the offer of life with God and live it out in communion with him. The biblical means for expanding and strengthening God's covenant people is God's word heard in preaching and held in the sacraments, but covenant theology shapes how we preach, so that the proclamational force of God's word—whether we are delivering or receiving that word—in our covenantal encounters with the Lord in worship is well understood.[69]

Both faithful preachers and faithful listeners have several simultaneous concerns for preaching. We want clear commitment to that great Reformation doctrine of justification by faith alone, plainly and unapologetically stating that none of our works can contribute anything at all to the procurement of our salvation. In Romans 6:1–2, the apostle Paul seems to know that the freeness of grace he describes in Romans 4–5 might open the door to an abuse of grace, so denies that such free grace means we can sin as we wish. If we do not at times preach grace so free that we must add that qualification afterwards, then we are not preaching biblical grace. At the same time, we certainly do not want to omit that qualification that we are not free *to* sin even though we are free *from* sin. We need to commit to absolutely free justification and to thriving sanctification.

Covenant theology clarifies how we might faithfully preach (and hear preaching) with a proper balance in that works-grace relationship by providing the structures for clearly announcing how we relate to God and his law. It provides the framework to know how each preached word addresses God's people according to law and gospel.

There is then the looming question of whether the law is our friend or foe and how we explain that in preaching. In Galatians 5:1–4, Paul writes, "For freedom Christ has set us free; stand firm therefore, and do not submit again to a yoke of slavery. Look: I, Paul, say to you that if you

---

69. This section includes material revised from Harrison Perkins, "The Covenant of Works and the Christian Life, Part 3," *Evangelical Presbyterian Magazine* (Summer 2019): 8–10. Used with permission.

accept circumcision, Christ will be of no advantage to you. I testify again to every man who accepts circumcision that he is obligated to keep the whole law. You are severed from Christ, you who would be justified by the law; you have fallen away from grace." Taking Paul's lead, we should preach the law in a twofold way. In light of everything explored about the covenant of works and the covenant of grace, we see that the law is our foe if used to earn God's favor but our friend if used as a guide to faithfulness in the Christian life.

To clarify this point, if we detach the law from its place within the covenant of grace as a rule, then we return to the law as a covenant, in which case it demands perfection as Paul writes in Galatians 5:1–4.[70] God does not accept our best efforts when it comes to justification, so we are "severed from Christ" if we seek to be right with God by works (Gal 5:4). In sum, the law is always a condemning slaveowner over us *if we try to use it to earn God's favor*.[71] Rather than treating the law this way, we should realize that Christ has set us free for freedom's sake, so we should not use—or proclaim—the law as a condition, even though we do not abuse that freedom as a reason to sin.[72] How does this help us think about sermons?

As we preach, we must frame our discussion about God's law in reference to whether we relate to it as the covenant of works or in the covenant of grace. Nearly every text of Scripture makes some sort of demand upon us.[73] How do we relate to that demand?[74] We must always first consider that there is a way that we could relate to that demand as if it were part of the covenant of works. Consider, for example, the responsibilities for husbands and wives in Ephesians 5:22–33. Certainly, Christians should vigorously endeavor to do everything in this passage. What if, however, we consider this passage apart from how Christ has forgiven our failures? What if, for the sake of argument, we contemplate ourselves *as if* we need to do these things to try to earn God's favor? If we think about

---

70. Fesko, "Preaching as a Means of Grace," 52.

71. Kelly M. Kapic, "The Law-Gospel Distinction in Reformed Theology and Ministry," in *God's Two Words*, 131–35.

72. Allen, *Sanctification*, 275–86.

73. Fesko, "Preaching as a Means of Grace," 52.

74. Kevin Vanhoozer, "Continuing the Conversation: A Reformed Reflection," in *God's Two Words*, 228–29.

these demands as if we are under the covenant of works, apart from the consideration that Christ's cross has covered our sins, then every one of these obligations would condemn us. For the unmarried, the same reasoning applies to Ephesians 6:1–3, since no one has perfectly obeyed their parents. None have succeeded perfectly in fulfilling even the Scripture's basic exhortations.

Preachers should proclaim the law so that people know that, considered apart from Christ, it condemns us. People need to see that they are sinners in need of a Savior. They need to see that God's standards are not set according to our best efforts and so if we fail at any point, we stand condemned. That is the first way we can consider the law, which should drive us to hope not at all in our own works but to flee to Christ for redemption.

Hearers of sermons should keep this clearly in mind, that your preacher, when he thunders the law's terrors, is not being mean or legalistic but setting forth your need for a Savior. The people of Israel clearly perceived these terrors of the law when, directly after God declared the Ten Commandments, "the people were afraid and trembled" and asked Moses, rather than God, to speak to them (Exod 20:18–19). But this recognition of the depths of our sin only makes the glories of our Savior sweeter when we realize how much he has done for us. In sum, firstly, covenant helps us to proclaim the freeness of grace by showing that we cannot earn God's favor by the law and must flee to him only in the gospel of Christ, never mixed with our works.

Then, if grace is so free, how does covenant help avoid license to sin? The moral law still binds us to obedience because we are still made in the image of God. The difference is that now we do not consider the law as our condition for inheriting everlasting life but as the guide to how to live for God. The law considered in light of Christ's work to forgive our sins takes on a new dimension. Now that we do not have to fulfill that law personally perfectly to enter heaven, since Christ has done that for us, we can look to the law as a faithful guide to how we might please God in the Christian life as an expression of gratitude for what he has done for us in Christ. In other words, the covenant of works and the covenant of grace categorically help our preaching to describe more clearly on which side of the law that we live. Do we live under it as a *covenant* to life or as a *rule* for life?

The sermon experience has two sides. Preachers must keep diligent awareness of whether they are announcing the law as a covenant of works to drive their people to Christ for salvation, or if they are speaking about it as a guide to faithfulness once their people have been forgiven. The first way must be spoken in preparation for the gospel to drive hearers to repent and feel the need for the Savior. The law in this sense should be preached with (conceptual) ferocity and all the fires and terrors that the people felt at Sinai (Exod 20:18–19). As Martin Luther (1483–1546) writes, "Commands, to be sure, teach what is good, but what is taught is not thereby done. For the commands show what we ought to do but do not give the power to do it. They were instead established for this: so that they may reveal individuals to themselves. Through the commands they know their inability to do good, and they despair of their own powers."[75] So, the first way that our preaching must appropriate the gospel is to prepare hearers to receive the gospel.

The second way must be spoken tenderly with attention to how the Spirit helps us even when we are immensely weak as we "endeavor after new obedience" (WSC 87).[76] On the other side, those who hear sermons must also be careful to think clearly about the law and whether they hear it as a covenant of works or from within the covenant of grace. For example, your pastor might tell you that you must keep the fourth commandment, to remember the Sabbath to keep it holy. This is legalism *only if* your pastor said that you must do this to earn or keep God's favor. Certainly, he should not batter you with its requirements so that you feel ill-equipped for the Christian life. On the other hand, if he said simply that you must do this as an expression of the obedient life, then he is faithfully explaining the content of sanctification.

Reflecting on covenant theology and preaching in this way helps us to understand why Paul can refer to the law as a "ministry of condemnation" (2 Cor 3:9) and James can refer to it as "the law of liberty" (Jas 1:25). The law condemns in reference to justification, and in that case brings nothing but death. On the other hand, if you are in Christ and there is no

75. Martin Luther, *The Freedom of a Christian 1520*, ed. Timothy J. Wengert (Minneapolis, MN: Fortress Press, 2016), 494.

76. *COC*, 3:695.

condemnation for you because you are saved by faith alone, then the law is the sweet guide to the faithful Christian life. In that case, we can say with the psalmist, "Your testimonies are my delight; they are my counselors" (Ps 119:24). Therefore, whether we are delivering or digesting sermons, we must do well in thinking about how we relate to the law, and covenant theology helps us do so.

The gospel distinguishes our twofold proclamation of the law. When the law has been announced as a terror to drive us to Christ, then Christ must be set forth as the hope for sinners. In light of the gospel, God's people will delight in their salvation but also long to live faithfully for him. As Luther also explains, "For the inner person—conformed to God and created in the image of God through faith—is joyful and glad on account of Christ, in whom all good things have been conferred upon such a one. Because of this, that person has only one concern: to serve God joyfully, with boundless love and with no thought of earning anything."[77] So, we must explain the law as our guide to sanctification. The law and the gospel are always distinct and must not be confused. The law commands what we must do, but the gospel promises what Christ has done. The indicatives of our identity in Christ lead to but never become the imperatives for the Christian life.[78] Still, even though the law remains distinct from the gospel, the gospel changes our relationship to the law. In Christ, we are set free. Preaching must announce why we need freedom and must use the law to do so. Preaching must also announce how Christ has made that freedom available to all who come to him in faith. That freedom has a particular shape, though, and God still directs us in the paths of faithfulness as we seek after him as those who are guaranteed everlasting life in Christ.

As we live in covenant with God, specifically as those who belong to him by faith in Christ, we must keep in mind that our communion with him is gospel shaped. That shape needs to be clear in our preaching. The law as a condition for life drives us to the Savior for rescue since sinners cannot earn God's favor by our works. The gospel must, then, be clearly announced as the solution to our plight. The gospel resolves our

77. Luther, *Freedom of a Christian*, 511.

78. Fesko, "Preaching as a Means of Grace," 49–50.

alienation from God as it declares that Christ has fulfilled the law for us. The free grace of the gospel should never be qualified by anything besides the summons to true faith in the Savior. Every sermon from any text of Scripture must set forth the glory of Christ, describing some facet of his saving work for us, so that God's people might be assured and equipped to trust their Savior and treasure his love for them throughout the week. The gospel cannot be a sideshow, a tack on, or merely a concession for potentially unbelieving attenders. The gospel of Jesus Christ must be the core and climax of covenantal preaching.[79]

Application then helps us to see how the moral law guides our lives as we live in communion with God. This application should not be guilt filled, as when the law is described as a condition, but gratitude filled. The Christian life of sanctification, even as it requires prayer and effort, is one of joyous communion with God as we live with him in covenant. Although we do not earn blessings from God by our works, trenchant sin interferes with our communion with him. Guilt lays heavier when we will not turn away from our sin. Still, application is not about guilt but about guiding our lives of gratitude that are grounded in, informed by, and fueled from the gospel and the gospel clearly announced. We ought to remember that the law always describes the proper way to express our love for God—even when it was a condition in the covenant of works; how much more does it help us know how to show love for God and neighbor now that it is no longer a condition for our relationship with God (John 14:21–23)?[80]

These categories should help with preaching, whether we deliver or digest the announcement of the law and the gospel. If we are preparing sermons, we must know exactly how we are addressing God's people with every sentence.[81] Is this law? In what manner am I delivering the law? Is this the gospel? Are both law and gospel with right uses present in my sermon? On the other hand, if we are processing sermons, we must be aware that there is a dynamic interplay between the law and the gospel throughout a sermon and I need to go through the entirety of that process. Perhaps I do feel guilty halfway through the sermon. That does not

79. Fesko, "Preaching as a Means of Grace," 44–48.

80. Kapic, "Law-Gospel Distinction in Reformed Theology and Ministry," 140–48.

81. Fesko, "Preaching as a Means of Grace," 53.

mean the gospel is not preached but just that it is still to come. On the other hand, just because there is instruction about how to live for Christ does not signal legalism if that application is grounded in the reality of the gospel. Truly, the contours of condemnation under law, freedom in the gospel, and how, then, we might live is nothing more than the confessional categories of guilt, grace, and gratitude (HC 2).[82] This dynamic of preaching is what drives forward the Christian life.[83]

This shape of preaching, however, is governed by the covenant and focused on the covenant's aims. Preaching cannot be disconnected from all that we have considered before, as if a simple afterthought for application, but must be the extension and expression of how we understand God's whole dealings with us. The law-gospel dynamic shapes our preaching, and so ties our preaching to the structure of the covenant because the basic premises of the covenants of works and grace establish this paradigm. Further, preaching as a means of grace is thoroughly linked to our virtue ethics, in that, rather than simply a renewed statement of God's commands, it is God's own covenantal address to his people to shape us by his promises and reformat our character as the people of Christ. Preaching, moreover, channels God's word in its heard medium to install significance in the sacraments as its held medium.

Sermons must then have a robust proclamational force. The dynamics of the law and the gospel should work out often in our preaching as God addresses to kill our old self by the law and enliven the new self by the gospel. So, preaching should include exegetical observations to teach the point of a given passage with application but must do more than simply teach and give advice. It must confront the hearer with the glory and splendor of the holy God who will judge sinners but has offered life to believers. On that note, Geerhardus Vos reminds seminary students that,

> It is quite possible that both to the intention and the actual performance of the preacher any departure from the historical faith of the church may be entirely foreign. And yet there may be such a failure in the intelligent presentation of the gospel with the proper emphasis upon that which is primary and fundamental as to bring

82. *COC*, 3:308.

83. Fesko, "Preaching as a Means of Grace," 148–51.

> about a result almost equally deplorable as where the principles of the gospel are openly contradicted or denied. There can be a betrayal of the gospel of grace by silence. There can be disloyalty to Christ by omission as well as by positive offence against the message that he has entrusted to our keeping. *It is possible, Sabbath after Sabbath and year after year, to preach things of which none can say that they are untrue and none can deny that in their proper place and time they may be important, and yet to forego telling people plainly and to forego giving them the distinct impression that they need forgiveness and salvation from sin through the cross of Christ.*[84]

Worship, particularly as it is carried along by God's word, is, then, more than an activity but is our covenantal encounter with God himself. Church is not as much a play as it is an event where God summons his people to receive his justifying and renewing promises as gifts from his glorious throne. The church, being the community of grace, then, finds its existence as the place where we live in communion with God by covenant.[85]

CONCLUSION

The main point of covenant theology is that God has established fellowship with his people. He *designed* our communion with him in the covenant of works as the way to claim everlasting life. He *determined* our communion with him in the covenant of redemption to ensure his elect enjoy that spiritual communion forever. He now *delivers* our communion with him to us in the covenant of grace as the place where we encounter our God in worship and are shaped for our commission to serve our neighbors. God is richly good to come to his people to commune with us and we have that communion by covenant.

84. Geerhardus Vos, "The Gracious Provision," in *Grace and Glory*, 249–50 (emphasis added).

85. Webster, *Holiness*, 53–76.

XVII

Theses on Covenant Theology

He sent redemption to his people; he has commanded his covenant forever. Holy and awesome is his name!
—*Psalm 111:9*

This conclusion synthesizes this book's main themes into crystalized statements of Reformed covenant theology's major ramifications. The purpose here is to condense the wide-ranging aspects of the book's arguments into digested formulations about the intersection of theological reflection and our personal relationship with God in churchly discipleship.

SIX THESES ABOUT REFORMED COVENANT THEOLOGY

1. God's covenants with us are the axis between dogmatic reflection and relational discipleship.

2. God's covenants with us acknowledge mystery about God in himself but reckon deeply with how he has revealed himself to us.

3. God's covenants with us are the *historically conditioned* hermeneutical tool for relating the Old and New Testaments.

4. God's covenants with us center his revelation and our relationship with him in Jesus Christ.

5. God's covenants with us clarify the relationship of grace and works in salvation.

6. God's covenants with us underscore the church's essential nature as the location of the Christian life.

These tersely stated theses require some further explanation to tease out their meaning and significance. The following explanation then provides one final attempt at summing up this book's major, broadly stated, contributions to our theological and discipling endeavors.

THESES ON COVENANT THEOLOGY EXPLAINED

1. God's covenants with us are the axis between dogmatic reflection and relational discipleship.

This book has stressed both scholastic, theological precision and pastoral warmth and application. Too often, writers prefer one of these emphases to the other, neglecting either focused precision or how that precision aids Christians in their walk with God. Covenant theology provides the grid to integrate precision and piety because the categories of covenant facilitate and demand calibrated theological formulations but the covenant itself entirely pertains to how we live with God.

2. God's covenants with us acknowledge mystery about God in himself but reckon deeply with how he has revealed himself to us.

Academic theology tends to swing between the poles of emphasizing *theologia*, God in himself, and *oikonomia*, God's works in the world, often discarding the traditional doctrines that belong to the other category. The twentieth century was forcefully focused on *oikonomia* at the expense of *theologia*, looking repeatedly at redemptive history, so creating a correlative theology proper, or theistic mutualism. Presently, the academy is full tilt amidst a recovery of classical theism, which in itself is a wonderful thing.

All the same, the focus on *theologia* is beginning to diminish our output concerning doctrines such as anthropology, soteriology, eschatology, and, to some degree, ecclesiology.

Reformed covenant theology provides the matrix to emphasize both *theologia* and *oikonomia,* allowing us to ponder the mysteries of God as God but also make firm and precise statements about what he has told us about our relationship with him. Some doctrines are mysterious because they transcend finite human minds, others because we do not have (or have not discovered) enough data in general or special revelation to clarify them further, and others have rich supply of material, particularly in Scripture, so that we can outline rather fully what God has said on the matter. In contrast to a tendency to abstract *theologia* and *oikonomia,* Reformed covenant theology highlights how we meet the transcendent God in the place which he has ordained, namely, his covenants. We can thereby do full justice to the majestic doctrines of theology proper, maintaining a right focus on God as he is, while also maintaining traditional Protestant concerns for soteriology and ecclesiology.

3. *God's covenants with us are the* historically conditioned *hermeneutical tool for relating the Old and New Testaments.*

Reformed covenant theology was never "invented," as if we can trace the origins of this hermeneutic and its doctrinal categories to a clear-cut moment in church history. Rather, Reformed covenant theology aligns with concerns and interpretive strategies nascent in even the earliest post-apostolic period, arguably because it reflects the apostolic interests themselves. The doctrines that most characterize Reformed covenant theology are latent throughout the ecumenical legacy, being codified with a new set of terminology in our confessional tradition. Nonetheless, the Reformed understand our conclusions and hermeneutics, specifically in our appeal to the covenants for soteriology and ecclesiology, to be, by and large, in continuity with patristic theology.

Although itself not a guarantee of truth, this point concerning antiquity explains why Reformed theologians are often hard to dissuade from our viewpoints. When new hermeneutical strategies are proposed, even those centering on covenant, we struggle to see why we need something brand new when we believe our approach has been working well to construct Christian orthodoxy for more than two millennia now. Although Scripture is always the ultimate authority, new theologies of the covenants often appear superficial to those holding to confessionally Reformed theology, precisely in the desire to construct something original and new.

4. *God's covenants with us center his revelation and our relationship with him in Jesus Christ.*

Reformed covenant theology's three doctrinal covenants each place the spotlight on Christ, entailing that the covenants are ultimately about Christ. So to meet God in covenant is to meet him in Christ. Even before Adam fell, when he had no need for a savior, his federal role and the structures of his covenant were forging the makeup of Christ's work for his people. Adam was, after all, a type of the one to come. The covenant of redemption centers on appointing the Son as our mediator and applying his work to us.

5. *God's covenants with us clarify the relationship of grace and works in salvation.*

Reformed covenant theology presents the law and the gospel as clearly distinct principles, founded in two different types of covenants. This categorical clarity establishes why grace and works cannot be mixed *as the basis of* our relationship with God. This emphasis on the premises by which we relate to God relates directly to our understanding of the covenants and their conditions. This clarity about the law-gospel distinction, however, also facilitates a clearer presentation of why works are necessary *as part of the Christian life*. God's law is always good because it expresses God's character. It is not a sinner's friend when used as the ground for receiving blessings from the holy God. It is, on the other hand, the friend to believers on the path of sanctification looking for a rule to holiness in the life God has freely granted rather than a covenant to obtain that life.

6. God's covenants with us underscore the church's essential nature as the location of the Christian life.

Reformed covenant theology underscores that God relates to his people and distributes his blessings to us through means that he has appointed as features of each of his covenants. These means are our interface for meeting with the Lord and experiencing his goodness. In the new covenant, God has appointed his outward and ordinary means of grace—namely word, sacrament, and prayer—as the way by which we know him and have Christ and his benefits applied to us. In this regard, covenant theology demonstrates the church's necessity for us to thrive spiritually. We are not free to invent our own ways to meet with God, since he is not so cruel as to leave us to our own devices for finding him. He has promised to meet us in the activities and features of church life, pointing us into the community where we have communion with God by covenant.

Appendix
Romans 2:13 and the Doers of the Law

For it is not the hearers of the law who are righteous before God,
but the doers of the law who will be justified.
—*Romans 2:13*

Romans 2:13 has become a point of dispute, even within Reformed circles, concerning whether Paul describes how people relate to God according to the principle of the law as such, or a real future of experience for believers in which they will face a second justification, a future part of their justification, or a completion of their present justification determined on the basis of or in accord with their works. Since divided opinion about how to understand Paul's point can make conclusions based upon it controversial, some extended exegetical support seems warranted so that there is at least some justification (!) for understanding this passage in the way it is understood in this work. At the same time, detailed arguments about one short passage can clutter the book's main arguments if they appear in the main text, so they seem better gathered in this separate section so that they do not distract from the central point and need not burden readers who find them too technical, extraneous, or superfluous.

This appendix argues that the understanding that says Romans 2:13 expresses how justification according to works demands perfect obedience to stand before God righteously has the stronger exegetical support.[1] More specifically, Romans 2:6–16 truly expresses how justification functions under the law. Geerhardus Vos refers to this as "the forensic system" wherein Paul outlines "the method of gaining eternal life by works as retaining its validity in the abstract," although sinners can no longer fulfill it. With respect to the exegesis of the passage in question, Vos outlines,

> In the second chapter of the epistle to the Romans this is set forth at considerable length. God will recompense obedience to the law with eternal life (vss. 7, 10); the doers of the law shall be justified (vs. 13); if the uncircumcision keep the ordinances of the law, his uncircumcision shall be reckoned for circumcision, i.e., he shall be treated as entitled to all the privileges of the people of God (vs. 26); the circumcision of the heart, i.e., the inward doing of the law, has praise of God (vs. 29). … But inasmuch as Paul nowhere says that he recognizes this theory against his own better conviction, but on the contrary speaks of it with a degree of pathos, we are constrained to believe that besides its dialectic value it also possessed to his mind a certain hypothetical value within the limits of his own system—that, discounting the objectionable spirit with which, on their part, it was applied, he found himself at one with the Jews in the recognition of its formal principle. … If a man were able to satisfy the conditions imposed, he would receive the reward promised.[2]

In Romans 2:6–16, then, Paul described the mechanics of the covenant of works.

The interpretations of this passage are often categorized as either *hypothetical* or *real* views. The hypothetical interpretation suggests that people could theoretically obtain justification by works but they are in practice unable to meet the condition. This justification by works is, then, hypothetical because the premise of the works principle is hypothetically true, but it is not possible to fulfill the condition. On the other hand, the real interpretation suggests that Paul describes a situation in which believers

1. Vos, "Alleged Legalism," 393–98; Waters, *The Mouth of the Lord Has Spoken*, 22–26, 30–31.
2. Vos, "Alleged Legalism," 393–94.

will go through the experience of being justified at the last day according to their imperfect but Spirit empowered good works. This justification by works is, then, *real* because it truly occurs exactly as described for believers.

The interpretation argued in this appendix does not precisely fit either of these categories, although it is somewhat closer to the hypothetical view. Still, even though believers do not personally go through the process of being justified by works on the last day, "hypothetical" is a misleading label.[3] True, if the condition is met, then a person will be justified, but this is more of a contingency than a hypothetical premise. It is hypothetical only inasmuch as *sinners* are unable to fulfill the terms. Romans 2:6–16 describes a real situation, however, in that everyone who has the required record of perfect righteousness will be truly justified, although everyone who falls short of the law's conditions will be condemned.

Romans 2:6–16, then, describes how justification functions under the law. This principle is not hypothetical because believers have the required perfect record of righteousness to warrant justification under the law because Christ's perfect righteousness is imputed to us by faith. The premise of justification by works is *real* even for believers, not because God accepts their imperfect works of sanctification toward final justification, but because they stand before God according to the law with a genuinely pristine, spotless, and perfect righteousness, which they have received from Christ.[4]

What exegetical evidence supports this interpretation? First, it best fits the scope of Paul's wider argument. The major section of Romans 1:18–3:20 focuses on humanity's condemnation. Paul began the argument of this first section: "For the wrath of God is revealed from heaven against all ungodliness and unrighteousness of men, who by their unrighteousness suppress the truth" (1:18). In the following argument, he aims to prove that every human being stands condemned before God for our sin. He summarizes the point of this first section: "Now we know that whatever the law says it speaks to those who are under the law, so that every mouth may be stopped, and the whole world may be held accountable to

3. Longenecker, *Paul, Apostle of Liberty*, 110–11.

4. Rollock, *Treatise*, 31–38.

God. For by works of the law no human being will be justified in his sight, since through the law comes knowledge of sin" (3:19–20).

Contextually, Paul's clear emphasis throughout 1:18–3:20 is to show why sinners are condemned before God. The law leaves them inexcusable, accountable, and condemned in God's sight.[5] No sinners will be justified before the holy God. Romans 2:13's principle that the doers of the law will be justified is the middle premise between God's coming wrath (1:18) and our condemnation (3:19–20).

Second, in closer context, Paul's first assertion that God "will render to each on according to his works" grounds why those with hard and impenitent hearts are "storing up wrath for yourself on the day of wrath when God's righteous judgment will be revealed" (Rom 2:5–6). So, Romans 2:13 explains why no one will be justified in God's sight by the law precisely because "the doers of the law will be justified." Paul's major point is then to articulate, not the future experience of believers, but the reason why everyone stands condemned before God: they have not done—completely kept—the law.[6]

Third, and more specifically, Paul notably does *not* speak anywhere else of Christians "doing" (ποιέω, πράσσω), "keeping" (φυλάσσω), or "obeying" (τελέω) the law. He reserves those specific terms for Jews in relation to the Mosaic covenant. Rather, Paul uses language like "fulfill" (πληρόω) in reference to Christians' relationship to the law or to speak of obedience to the gospel.[7] In Galatians 5:3, Paul clearly intends that "doing" the law means perfectly and completely keeping it (ὀφειλέτης ἐστιν ὅλοω τὸν νόμον ποιῆσαι). When Paul cites Deuteronomy 30:11–14 in Romans 10:6–10 as applicable to Christians, he notably omits the very terms for doing the commands (ποιήσει, ποιήσομεν) from his quotations.[8] So, within his own linguistic patterns, Romans 2:13 would be an extraordinary departure from Paul's typical way of talking about the issue if he were referring to Christians truly becoming successful doers of the law.

---

5. Watson, *Hermeneutics of Faith*, 323–34.
6. Longenecker, *Paul, Apostle of Liberty*, 106–15.
7. Rosner, *Paul and the Law*, 83–109, 127–28.
8. Rosner, *Paul and the Law*, 139–42; Estelle, "Leviticus 18:5 and Deuteronomy 30:1–14," 109–146.

From the standpoint of biblical theology, this aspect of the structure of Paul's theological thinking is a remarkable difficulty to overcome for those who would understand Paul to mean a real future process of justification for Christians. Those who interpret Romans 2:13 to indicate a future experience of believers where Christians will actually be justified—a second time or in a completionary sense—according to the law have seemingly not accounted for how Paul's statement fits within his wider argument and for how his language accords with his own usage of the Greek verbs. We should then not interpret passages in a fragmented way, as if the Apostle does not maintain a consistent and linear argument.[9] The condemnation that comes because justification depends on perfect keeping of the law (1:18–3:20) is precisely what sets the stage for the surprise of justification by faith alone apart from works (3:21–26). A statement about a future justification for believers on the basis of their works would be a very odd interruption in this argument.[10]

The most proximate context confirms this same point. Romans 2:12–13 reads, "For all who have sinned without the law will also perish without the law, and all who have sinned under the law will be judged by the law. For it is not the hearers of the law who are righteous before God, but the doers of the law who will be justified." Paul argues in verse 12 that the law makes sinners perish, whether they possessed the written law or merely the natural law (2:12–14). In verse 13, he then states the reason for this *condemnation*, which returns to his point from verse 5. The explanatory γὰρ establishes that condemnation comes by the law *because* doing is the criteria for justification under the law.[11] As Frank Thielman summarizes, "In other words, God will declare them what they already are—righteous and therefore exempt from punishment—because of their obedience to the law. The verb is future because the declaration will happen on 'the day of the wrath and the revelation of the righteous judgment of God'" (2:5), and it is passive because God, as judge, will make the declaration. Because God is a just judge (2:5), he will declare to be righteous only those who

9. Cf. Richard B. Hays, *Echoes of Scripture in the Letters of Paul* (New Haven: Yale University Press, 1993), 41.

10. Longenecker, *Romans*, 268–69, 357–77; Thielman, *Romans*, 188–90; Horton, *Justification*, 2:75–76.

11. Thielman, *Romans*, 134–35.

actually are righteous."[12] In this case, then, the law "promises life to those who do it (10:5; cf. Lev 18:5)."[13]

As Richard Longenecker highlights, reading the future tense verb for justification (δικαιωθήσονται) as though it must bear the weight of actual and unquestionable future situation demands too much of the grammar. Rather, "Here all that Paul wants to do is to challenge any comfortable understanding, such as was proposed by his imaginary interlocutor of 2:1–5, regarding who is accepted by God and on what basis that reconciliation takes place—hearing God's law, knowing its contents, and approving of its judgments, or obeying and doing God's will."[14] The sense of the future tense is then gnomic, expressing a general truth. Even if the gnomic use of the future tense verb is rare, that Paul's argument throughout Romans 1:18–3:20 is that the condemnation of the law applies *generally* and impartially to Jews and gentiles demands the gnomic focus on a generic situation.[15]

Longenecker convincingly argues that Paul was tying his point to the same theological outlook that he explains in Galatians 3:10–14, where Leviticus 18:5 is cited. Reformed theologians have often understood Galatians 3:12, Romans 10:5, and Leviticus 18:5, in general, to express the principle of the covenant of works in its demand for perfect obedience unto justification.[16] Longenecker draws together significant exegetical and contextual warrant to show that Romans 2:13 is about the demand for perfect obedience in order to obtain eschatological life by our works.[17]

The exegetical arguments have biblico-theological import that is especially relevant for the nature of the covenant of works as articulated in chapter 3 but also thoroughly pertains to the discussion about Christ's work as the last Adam in chapter 7. Longenecker well summarizes this biblico-theological connection:

---

12. Thielman, *Romans*, 135.

13. Thielman, *Romans*, 136.

14. Longenecker, *Romans*, 266.

15. Wallace, *Greek Grammar*, 571.

16. *WWP*, 1:244 (commentary on Matthew 5:17); Owen, *Hebrews*, 3:715–16; *MT*, 1.10.32; Rollock, *Some Questions*, 21–22; Mastricht, *Theoretica-Practica Theologia*, 3.12.28; *TI*, 5.12.4, 8.3.7, 8.5.4, 11.3.4; *EC*, 1.2.1; *CRS*, 1:360; *BRD*, 2:565; 3:174, 182–85, 224–28; 4:601–2; *VRD*, 2:41, 94, 130; Muller, "Either Expressly Set Down ...," 69–81; *ACW*, 13–42.

17. Longenecker, *Romans*, 266–72.

> That the law was fulfilled by Jesus in his earthly ministry (his "active obedience") and by his death on the cross (his "passive obedience"), in order that all people might come to God "by faith" and so be declared righteous, is a truth that must never be diminished or perverted in any way by stray thoughts regarding justification by works—that is, by "works of the law (ἔργα νόμου)." But the law of God still exists as God's standard for all of his created universe and for the lives of all his people.[18]

Still, Longenecker and Thielman are not alone in recognizing the exegetical evidence favors the view that Romans 2:13 is about the standard of the law to be justified by works, as if only some niche Reformed interpreters come to this conclusion. Joseph Fitzmyer, a Roman Catholic exegete, also argues that this was Paul's point: "Paul may seem to introduce the motif of judgment according to deeds not to warn the Christian reader as such, but because he wants to undermine the smugness of the Jewish interlocutor. And yet, it is precisely the motif of God's judgment that must be retained for the sake of the message of justification by grace through faith."[19] Paul's argument, then, continues to aim at the specific target of undermining presumptuous confidence that a person has in fact performed well enough to warrant justification on the last day.

Those who would interpret Romans 2:13 to indicate another, future justification (or future aspect to it) rob present justification of its eschatological value. Justification itself does not have already and not yet aspects but is given in the present as the last-day verdict that Christ has merited for his people. Jesus has already *fully* granted that justified status to them by faith, even though the rewards that belong to justification have not yet been enacted. Christ by his perfect obedience has done the law and has earned the reward of the law that was offered in the covenant of works. Now, in the gospel, he offers that reward to those who would come to him by faith. God does not justify those who imperfectly try their best to do the law, as some read Romans 2:13. Rather, God "justifies the ungodly" by faith (Rom 4:5).

18. Longenecker, *Romans*, 286–87.

19. Joseph A. Fitzmyer S.J., *Romans: A New Translation with Introduction and Commentary* (New Haven: Yale University Press, 2008), 307.

Paul's later arguments in Romans prove relevant for his point in Romans 2:6–16. He writes in Romans 5:9, "Since, therefore, we have now been justified by his blood, *much more* shall we be saved by him from the wrath of God." His logic requires that the justification that we have in the present by faith alone is permanent and does not need to be supplemented by a future second justification or second part of justification according to works. Since we are justified now by Christ, Paul's *a fortiori* argument clarifies that it is even more the case that we will pass through God's wrath at the final judgment.[20]

This theological import of Romans 5:9 confirms the interpretation of Romans 2:13 argued for in this appendix. First, the justification that ensures our safety at the last judgment is explicitly the one that we have *now*. Paul draws an inference (οὖν), from the reality of having been now justified (δικαιωθέντες νῦν), that our outcome at the last judgment is secure. The "now" is then an eschatological νῦν, which indicates that the last day reality of our need for justification in order to enter into God's everlasting kingdom has to be granted to us ahead of time in the present by faith.[21] As Thielman argues, "Because of Christ's atoning death, those who believe the gospel are 'now' justified. Although God will punish in the future those whose hearts are hard and unchanged (2:5), the present justification of believers should assure them that they will not experience God's wrath on that day. God will save believers 'through' Christ at that time, just as God has justified them in the present by his atoning death."[22] The last day simply makes public what was already true ahead of time. Believers' status as the justified has been confirmed and set already. That reality will be made public, and the privileges that follow from justification will be enacted on the last day. This enactment, however, is precisely of the

20. *CC*, 19:2.196–97; Thielman, *Romans*, 271. DeSilva, *Galatians*, 218, esp. n268 argued that theologians have not properly distinguished between initial and final justification in part because they have not reckoned with the way that Paul wrote of justification's already aspect in Romans but its future aspect in Galatians. DeSilva overlooked that, rather than a differentiation between present and future justification, Paul likely used affirmative language in Romans because his audience was standing firm in the gospel but used more hypothetical language in Galatians because his audience was infringing upon the very doctrine of justification by their practices. DeSilva mistakenly attributes Paul's varying verb tenses to distinct theological meaning rather than to the two letters' very different contexts.

21. Longenecker, *Romans*, 566.

22. Thielman, *Romans*, 271.

privileges that follow from justification rather than a completion of justification itself.

Second, it is also clear that the justification that already ensures our standing before God at the last day does not include our works. In other words, the aorist passive participle with its temporal adverb "having been now justified" (δικαιωθέντες νῦν) cannot refer to the supposed future justification according to works that some see in Romans 2:13. The reason is that justification in 5:9 is explicitly by Christ's blood (ἐν τῷ αἵματι). It is Christ's work on the cross for the forgiveness of our sins that ensures our deliverance at the last judgment. As Longenecker puts it, "The forensic reality of having been 'justified by his [Jesus'] blood' in this present time of eschatological fulfillment (the eschatological 'now') also involves the greater personal hope that believers in Jesus 'will be saved through him [Jesus] from God's wrath.' "[23]

Paul, though, has not limited justification and the certainty of our standing at the final judgment to Christ's passive obedience (debt of penalty). He continues the argument in Romans 5:10, "For if while we were enemies we were reconciled to God by the death of his Son, much more, now that we are reconciled, shall we be saved by his life." In other words, our full reconciliation with God, which we have despite our previous identity as God's enemies, is another eschatological reality brought forward into the present. This full reconciliation confirms that we will be saved at the last day because of Christ's life (ἐν τῇ ζωῇ αὐτοῦ). Paul, then, draws attention not merely to Christ's suffering on our behalf, but also to his active obedience as our new representative who fulfilled the law on our behalf. On the one hand, the future tense δικαιωθήσονται in Romans 2:13 was gnomic, given the context of Paul's argument of the general reality of condemnation on the basis of God's impartial judgment of our works. On the other hand, the future tense σωθησόμεθα in Romans 5:9–10 is the genuine and certain eschatological event concerning how believers' present justification and reconciliation by faith on the basis of Christ's perfect obedience in life and curse-bearing death ensures the certainty that

23. Longenecker, *Romans*, 565–66.

we will be raised unto life and that we have the guarantee of full last-day salvation in the present.[24]

Paul's point in Romans 2:13 that "the doers of the law will be justified" then refers to the way that justification works under the law. Although sinners cannot ever fulfill the conditions to be right with God, believers truly stand before God justified according to works because Christ's perfect righteousness is imputed to us by faith.

24. Hodge, *Romans*, 138–40.

Bibliography

Allen, R. Michael. *Reformed Theology*. Doing Theology. London: T&T Clark, 2010.

______. *Justification and the Gospel: Understanding the Contexts and Controversies*. Grand Rapids: Baker Academic, 2013.

______. *Sanctification*. New Studies in Dogmatics. Grand Rapids: Zondervan, 2017.

Allen, Michael, and Scott R. Swain, eds. *Christian Dogmatics: Reformed Theology for the Church Catholic*. Grand Rapids: Baker Academic, 2016.

______. eds. *The Oxford Handbook of Reformed Theology*. Oxford: Oxford University Press, 2020.

______. *Reformed Catholicity: The Promise of Retrieval for Theology and Biblical Interpretation*. Grand Rapids: Baker Academic, 2015.

Ames, William. *The Marrow of Theology*. Translated by John Dykstra Eusden. Grand Rapids: Baker, 1968.

Augustine. *Homilies on the Gospel of John 1–40*. The Works of Saint Augustine: A Translation for the 21st Century. Translated by Edmund Hill. Edited by Allan D. Fitzgerald. Hyde Park, NY: New City Press, 2009.

Baillie, Robert. *Anabaptism, the True Fountaine of Independency, Brownisme, Antinomy, Familisme, and the Most of the Other Errours, Which for the Time Doe Trouble the Church of England, Unsealed*. London: Samuel Gellibrand, 1647.

Ball, John. *A Treatise on the Covenant of Grace*. London: Edward Brewster, 1645.

Barcellos, Richard C. *The Covenant of Works: Its Confessional and Scriptural Basis*. Recovering Our Confessional Heritage. Palmdale, CA: RBAP, 2016.

______. *Getting the Garden Right: Adam's Work and God's Rest in Light of Christ*. Cape Coral, FL: Founders Press, 2017.

Barrett, Matthew. *Canon, Covenant, and Christology: Rethinking Jesus and the Scriptures of Israel*. New Studies in Biblical Theology. Downers Grove, IL: IVP Academic, 2020.

______, ed. *The Doctrine on which the Church Stands or Falls: Justification in Biblical, Theological, Historical, and Pastoral Perspective*. Wheaton, IL: Crossway, 2019.

______. *None Greater: The Undomesticated Attributes of God*. Grand Rapids: Baker, 2019.

______. *Simply Trinity: The Unmanipulated Father, Son, and Spirit*. Grand Rapids: Baker, 2021.

Bates, Matthew W. *The Birth of the Trinity: Jesus, God, and Spirit in New Testament and Early Christian Interpretations of the Old Testament*. Oxford: Oxford University Press, 2015.

______. *The Hermeneutics of the Apostolic Preaching: The Center of Paul's Method of Scriptural Interpretation*. Waco, TX: Baylor University Press, 2012.

______. *Salvation by Allegiance Alone: Rethinking Faith, Works, and the Gospel of Jesus the King*. Grand Rapids: Baker Academic, 2017.

Bauckham, Richard. *Jude–2 Peter*. Word Biblical Commentary. Grand Rapids: Zondervan, 1983.

Baugh, S. M. *Ephesians*. Evangelical Exegetical Commentary. Bellingham, WA: Lexham Press, 2016.

Bavinck, Herman. *Reformed Dogmatics*. Edited by John Bolt. Translated by John Vriend. 4 vols. Grand Rapids: Baker Academic, 2003–2008.

______. *The Wonderful Works of God: Instruction in the Christian Religion according to the Reformed Confession*. Translated by Henry Zylstra. Glenside, PA: Westminster Seminary Press, 2019.

Beale, G. K. *1–2 Thessalonians*. IVP New Testament Commentary Series. Downers Grove, IL: IVP Academic, 2003.

______. "Adam as the First Priest in Eden as the Garden Temple." *Southern Baptist Journal of Theology* 22.2 (2018): 9–24.

______. *The Book of Revelation*. New International Greek Testament Commentary. Grand Rapids: Eerdmans, 1999.

______. *A New Testament Biblical Theology: The Unfolding of the Old Testament in the New*. Grand Rapids: Baker Academic, 2011.

______. *The Temple and the Church's Mission: A Biblical Theology of the Dwelling Place of God*. New Studies in Biblical Theology. Downers Grove, IL: IVP Academic, 2004.

Beale, G. K., and D. A. Carson, eds. *Commentary on the New Testament Use of the Old Testament*. Grand Rapids: Baker Academic, 2007.

Beeke, Joel R., and Paul M. Smalley. *Reformed Systematic Theology*. 4 vols. Wheaton, IL: Crossway, 2019–.

Belcher, Richard P., Jr. *The Fulfillment of the Promises of God: An Explanation of Covenant Theology*. Fearn, UK: Mentor, 2020.

Bird, Michael F., and Scott Harrower, eds. *Trinity without Hierarchy: Reclaiming Nicene Orthodoxy in Evangelical Theology*. Grand Rapids: Kregel Academic, 2019.

Blocher, Henri. *In the Beginning: The Opening Chapters of Genesis*. Downers Grove, IL: InterVarsity Press, 1984.

Block, Daniel I. *Covenant: The Framework of God's Grand Plan of Redemption*. Grand Rapids: Baker Academic, 2021.

Bower, John R. *The Larger Catechism: A Critical Text and Introduction*. Principal Documents of the Westminster Assembly. Grand Rapids: Reformation Heritage Books, 2010.

Brakel, Wilhelmus à. *The Christian's Reasonable Service*. Translated by Bartel Elshout. Edited by Joel R. Beeke. 4 vols. Grand Rapids: Reformation Heritage Books, 1992.

Brown, Michael G., and Zach Keele. *Sacred Bond: Covenant Theology Explored*. 2nd ed. Middleville, MI: Reformed Fellowship, Inc., 2017; repr. 2018.

Bruce, F. F. *The Epistle to the Galatians*. New International Greek Testament Commentary. Grand Rapids: Eerdmans, 1982.

Bruno, Chris, Jared Compton, and Kevin McFadden. *Biblical Theology According to the Apostles: How the Earliest Christians Told the Story of the Old Testament*. New Studies in Biblical Theology. Downers Grove, IL: IVP Academic, 2020.

Buchanan, James. *The Doctrine of Justification: An Outline of Its History in the Church and of its Exposition from Scripture*. London: The Banner of Truth Trust, 2016.

Burgess, Anthony. *Vindiciae Legis: or A Vindication of the Moral Law and the Covenants*. London: James Young, 1646.

Burnside, Jonathan. *God, Justice, and Society: Aspects of Law and Legality in the Bible*. New York: Oxford University Press, 2011.

Burton, Ernest DeWitt. *The Epistle to the Galatians*. International Critical Commentary. Edinburgh: T&T Clark, 1921.

Butner, D. Glen, Jr. "Eternal Functional Subordination and the Problem of the Divine Will." *JETS* 58 no. 1 (2015): 131–49.

______. *Trinitarian Dogmatics: Exploring the Grammar of the Christian Doctrine of God*. Grand Rapids: Baker Academic, 2022.

Calvin, John. *Calvin's Commentaries*. 22 vols. Grand Rapids: Baker, 2009.

______. *The Catechism of the Church of Geneva*. Translated by Elijah Waterman. Hartford, MA: Sheldon and Goodwin, 1815.

______. *Institutes of the Christian Religion*. Translated by Ford Lewis Battles. Edited by John T. McNeill. 2 vols. The Library of Christian Classics. Louisville: Westminster John Knox, 1960.

______. *Opera quae superunt omnia*. Edited by Edouard Cunitz, Johann-Wilhem Baum, and Eduard Wilhem Eugen Reuss. 58 vols. Corpus Reformatorum. Brunsigae: C. A. Schwetschke, 1863.

Cara, Robert J. *Cracking the Foundation of the New Perspective on Paul: Covenantal Nomism Versus Reformed Covenantal Theology*. Reformed Exegetical and Doctrinal Studies. Fearn, UK: Mentor, 2017.

Carter, Craig A. *Interpreting Scripture with the Great Tradition: Recovering the Genius of Premodern Exegesis*. Grand Rapids: Baker Academic, 2018.

Clark, R. Scott. "Baptism and the Benefits of Christ: The Double Mode of Communion in the Covenant of Grace." *Confessional Presbyterian* 2 (2006): 3–19.

______, ed. *Covenant Justification and Pastoral Ministry*. Phillipsburg, NJ: P&R, 2012.

______. *Recovering the Reformed Confession: Our Theology, Piety, and Practice*. Phillipsburg, NJ: P&R, 2008.

Clement of Alexandria. *Paedagogus* 1.6, in *PG* 8.

Collins, C. John. *Genesis 1–4: A Linguistic, Literary, and Theological Commentary*. Phillipsburg, NJ: P&R, 2006.

Colquhoun, John. *A Treatise on the Covenant of Grace*. Edinburgh: Thomsons Brothers, 1818.

______. *A Treatise on the Covenant of Works*. Edinburgh: Thomsons Brothers, 1821.

______. *A Treatise on the Law and the Gospel.* Edinburgh: J. Ogle, 1816.

Crisp, Oliver D. *Approaching the Atonement: The Reconciling Work of Christ.* Downers Grove, IL: IVP Academic, 2020.

______. *The Word Enfleshed: Exploring the Person and Work of Christ.* Grand Rapids: Baker Academic, 2016.

Crowe, Brandon D. *The Last Adam: A Theology of the Obedient Life of Jesus in the Gospels.* Grand Rapids: Baker Academic, 2017.

______. *The Path of Faith: A Biblical Theology of Covenant and Law.* Essential Studies in Biblical Theology. Downers Grove, IL: IVP Academic, 2021.

Cullmann, Oscar. *The Christology of the New Testament.* Translated by Shirley C. Guthrie and Charles A. M. Hall. rev. ed. Philadelphia: Westminster Press, 1963.

Currid, John D. *Genesis.* 2 vol. EP Study Commentary. Holywell, UK: Evangelical Press, 2003.

Damascus, John of. *The Orthodox Faith* 2.22, in *The Fathers of the Church: Saint John of Damascus: Writings.* Translated by Frederic H. Chase Jr. Washington DC: The Catholic University of America Press, 1958.

Davison, Andrew. *Participation in God: A Study in Christian Doctrine and Metaphysics.* Cambridge: Cambridge University Press, 2019.

DeSilva, David. *The Letter to the Galatians.* New International Commentary on the New Testament. Grand Rapids: Eerdmans, 2018.

Dolezal, James. *All That Is in God: Evangelical Theology and the Challenge of Classical Theism.* Grand Rapids: Reformation Heritage Books, 2017.

Dunn, James D. G. *Christology in the Making.* Philadelphia: Westminster Press, 1980.

Ellingworth, Paul. *The Epistle to the Hebrews.* New International Greek Testament Commentary. Grand Rapids: Eerdmans, 1993.

Estelle, Bryan D., J. V. Fesko, and David VanDrunen, eds. *The Law Is Not of Faith: Essays on Works and Grace in the Mosaic Covenant.* Phillipsburg, NJ: P&R, 2012.

Fee, Gordon D. *The First Epistle to the Corinthians.* rev. ed. New International Commentary on the New Testament. Grand Rapids: Eerdmans, 2014.

______. *The First and Second Letters to the Thessalonians.* New International Commentary on the New Testament. Grand Rapids: Eerdmans, 2009.

______. *Pauline Christology: An Exegetical-Theological Study.* Grand Rapids: Baker Academic, 2007.

Fesko, J. V. *Adam and the Covenant of Works*. Fearn, UK: Mentor, 2021.

______. *The Covenant of Redemption: Origins, Development, and Reception*. Göttingen: Vandenhoeck & Ruprecht, 2016.

______. *The Covenant of Works: The Origins, Development, and Reception of the Doctrine*. New York: Oxford University Press, 2020.

______. *Death in Adam, Life in Christ: The Doctrine of Imputation*. Reformed Exegetical and Doctrinal Studies. Fearn, UK: Mentor, 2016.

______. "The Republication of the Covenant of Works." *Confessional Presbyterian* 8 (2012): 197–212.

______. "The Republication of the Covenant of Works Part 2." *Confessional Presbyterian* 9 (2013): 178–87, 285.

______. *The Trinity and the Covenant of Redemption*. Fearn, UK: Mentor, 2016.

______. *Word, Water, and Spirit: A Reformed Perspective on Baptism*. Grand Rapids: Reformation Heritage Books, 2010.

France, R. T. *The Gospel of Matthew*. New International Commentary on the New Testament. Grand Rapids: Eerdmans, 2007.

Gaffin, Richard B., Jr. *By Faith, Not by Sight: Paul and the Order of Salvation*. 2nd ed. Phillipsburg, NJ: P&R, 2013.

______. *In the Fullness of Time: An Introduction to the Biblical Theology of Acts and Paul*. Wheaton, IL: Crossway, 2022.

______. *Resurrection and Redemption: A Study in Paul's Soteriology*. Phillipsburg, NJ: P&R, 1987.

Gentry, Peter J., and Stephen J. Wellum. *Kingdom through Covenant: A Biblical-Theological Understanding of the Covenants*. 1st ed. Wheaton, IL: Crossway, 2012.

______. *Kingdom through Covenant: A Biblical-Theological Understanding of the Covenants*. 2nd ed. Wheaton, IL: Crossway, 2018.

Gibson, David, and Jonathan Gibson, eds. *From Heaven He Came and Sought Her: Definite Atonement in Historical, Biblical, Theological, and Pastoral Perspective*. Wheaton, IL: Crossway, 2013.

Gillespie, Patrick. *The Ark of the Covenant Opened: or A Treatise on the Covenant of Redemption*. London: Thomas Parkburst, 1677.

Gladd, Benjamin L. *From Adam and Israel to the Church: A Biblical Theology of the People of God*. Essential Studies in Biblical Theology. Downers Grove, IL: IVP Academic, 2019.

Goldingay, John. *Psalms*. 3 vols. Baker Commentary on the Old Testament Wisdom and Psalms. Grand Rapids: Baker Academic, 2006–2008.

Gomarus, Franciscus. *Opera Theologica Omnia*. Amsterdam: Johannes Janssonius, 1664.

Gordon, T. David. *Promise, Law, Faith: Covenant-Historical Reasoning in Galatians*. Peabody, MA: Hendrickson Academic, 2019.

Green, Bradley G. *Covenant and Commandment: Works, Obedience and Faithfulness in the Christian Life*. New Studies in Biblical Theology. Downers Grove, IL: IVP Academic, 2014.

Green, Gene L. *Jude and 2 Peter*. Baker Exegetical Commentary on the New Testament. Grand Rapids: Baker Academic, 2008.

______. *The Letters to the Thessalonians*. Pillar New Testament Commentary. Grand Rapids: Eerdmans, 2002.

Hagner, Donald A. *Matthew 14–28*. Word Biblical Commentary. Dallas, TX: Word Books, 1995.

Heidegger, Johann Heinrich. *The Concise Marrow of Theology*. Translated by Casey Carmichael. Grand Rapids: Reformation Heritage Books, 2019.

Helm, Paul. *Calvin at the Centre*. New York: Oxford University Press, 2010.

Hodge, Charles. *1 & 2 Corinthians*. Geneva Series of Commentaries. London: The Banner of Truth Trust, 1974.

______. *Commentary on the Epistle to the Ephesians*. New York: Robert Carter and Brothers, 1860.

______. *Exegetical Lectures and Sermons on Hebrews*. Edited by William VanDoodewaard. London: The Banner of Truth Trust, 2019.

______. *Romans*. Geneva Series of Commentaries. London: The Banner of Truth Trust, 1972.

______. *Systematic Theology*. 3 vols. New York: Scribner, Armstrong, and Co., 1877.

Honert, Taco Hajo van den. *Dissertationes Historicae 1. de Creatione Mundi 2. de Situ Edenis et Horti …* . Leiden: Apud A. Kallewier, 1738.

Hooker, Morna D. *From Adam to Christ*. Cambridge: Cambridge University Press, 1990.

Horton, Michael. *The Christian Faith: A Systematic Theology for Pilgrims on the Way*. Grand Rapids: Zondervan, 2011.

______. "A Classical Calvinist View." Pages 21–42 in *Four Views on Eternal Security*. Edited by J. Matthew Pinson. Grand Rapids: Zondervan, 2002.

———. "Covenant." Pages 434–45 in *The Oxford Handbook of Reformed Theology*. Edited by Michael Allen and Scott R. Swain. Oxford: Oxford University Press, 2020.

———. *Covenant and Salvation: Union with Christ*. Louisville: Westminster John Knox, 2007.

———. *Introducing Covenant Theology*. Grand Rapids: Baker Books, 2006.

———. *Lord and Servant: A Covenant Christology*. Louisville: Westminster John Knox, 2005.

———. *People and Place: A Covenant Ecclesiology*. Louisville: Westminster John Knox, 2008.

———. *Rediscovering the Holy Spirit: God's Perfecting Presence in Creation, Redemption, and Everyday Life*. Grand Rapids: Zondervan, 2017.

Irenaeus. *The Demonstration of the Apostolic Preaching*. Translated by J. Armitage Robinson. London and New York: Aeterna Press, 2015.

Johnson, Luke Timothy. *Hebrews: A Commentary*. New Testament Library. Louisville: Westminster John Knox, 2012.

Kelly, Douglas F. *Systematic Theology*. 3 vols. Fearn, UK: Mentor, 2008–2021.

Kelly, J. N. D. *Early Christian Doctrines*. 4th ed. London: Adam and Charles Black, 1968.

Kidner, Derek. *Genesis*. Tyndale Old Testament Commentaries. Downers Grove, IL: IVP Academic, 1967.

Klauber, Martin I. "The Helvetic Consensus Formula (1675): An Introduction and Translation." *Trinity Journal* 11 (1990).

Kline, Meredith G. *By Oath Consigned: A Reinterpretation of the Covenant Signs of Circumcision and Baptism*. Grand Rapids: Eerdmans, 1968.

———. *God, Heaven, and Har Magedon: A Covenantal Tale of Cosmos and Telos*. Eugene, OR: Wipf & Stock, 2006.

———. "Gospel until the Law: Rom 5:13–14 and the Old Covenant." *Journal of the Evangelical Theological Society* 34 no. 4 (Dec 1991): 433–46.

———. *Kingdom Prologue: Genesis Foundations for a Covenantal Worldview*. Overland Park, KS: Two Age Press, 2000.

Kruger, Michael J., ed. *A Biblical-Theological Introduction to the New Testament: The Gospel Realized*. Wheaton, IL: Crossway, 2016.

Lehner, Ulrich L., Richard A. Muller, and A. G. Roeber, eds. *The Oxford Handbook of Early Modern Theology, 1600–1800*. New York: Oxford

University Press, 2016.

Letham, Robert. *Systematic Theology.* Wheaton, IL: Crossway, 2019.

Linebaugh, Jonathan, ed. *God's Two Words: Law and Gospel in the Lutheran and Reformed Traditions.* Grand Rapids: Eerdmans, 2018.

Lombard, Peter. *The Sentences Book 2: On Creation.* Translated by Giulio Silano. Ontario: Pontifical Institute of Medieval Studies 20.6.2 (2008).

Longenecker, Richard N. *Galatians.* Word Biblical Commentary. Grand Rapids: Zondervan, 1990.

______. "The Pedagogical Nature of the Law in Galatians 3:19–4:7." *Journal of the Evangelical Theological Society* 25 no. 1 (March 1982): 53–61.

Martin, Ralph P. *An Early Christian Confession: Philippians 2:5–11 in Recent Interpretations.* London: The Tyndale Press, 1960.

______. *Carmen Christi: Philippians ii.5–11 in Recent Interpretation and in the Setting of Early Christian Worship.* Cambridge: Cambridge University Press, 1967.

Martin, Ralph P., and Brian J. Dodd, eds. *Where Christology Began: Essays on Philippians 2.* Louisville: Westminster John Knox, 1998.

McGrath, Alister E. *Iustitia Dei: A History of the Christian Doctrine of Justification.* 4th ed. Cambridge: Cambridge University Press, 2020.

McGraw, Ryan M. *By Good and Necessary Consequence.* Grand Rapids: Reformation Heritage Books, 2014.

McKeown, James. *Genesis.* Two Horizons Old Testament Commentary; Grand Rapids: Eerdmans, 2008.

Migne, Jacques Paul, ed. *Patrologia Cursus Completus: Series Graeca.* 161 vol. Paris: Amboise, 1857–66.

______. *Patrologia Cursus Completus: Series Latina.* 221 vols. Paris: Amboise, 1844–1864.

Muller, Richard A. *Dictionary of Latin and Greek Theological Terms Drawn Principally from Protestant Scholastic Theology.* 2nd ed. Grand Rapids: Baker Academic, 2017.

Murray, John. *The Covenant of Grace: A Biblico-Theological Study.* Biblical and Theological Studies. Phillipsburg, NJ: P&R, 1992.

______. *The Epistle to the Romans.* Glenside, PA: Westminster Seminary Press, 2022.

______. *Imputation of Adam's Sin.* Phillipsburg, NJ: P&R, 2012.

______. *Collected Writings of John Murray*. 4 vols. Edinburgh: The Banner of Truth Trust, 1982.

Oberman, Heiko A. *The Harvest of Medieval Theology: Gabriel Biel and Late Medieval Nominalism*. 3rd ed. Grand Rapids: Baker Academic, 2000.

O'Brien, Peter T. *Colossians, Philemon*. Word Biblical Commentary. Mexico City: Thomas Nelson, 2000.

______. *The Letter to the Hebrews*. Pillar New Testament Commentary. Grand Rapids: Eerdmans, 2010.

Ortlund, Gavin. *Theological Retrieval for Evangelicals: Why We Need Our Past to Have a Future*. Wheaton, IL: Crossway, 2019.

Owen, John. *An Exposition of the Epistle to the Hebrews*. 4 vols. London: Thomas Tegg, 1839.

______. *The Works of John Owen*. Edited by William H. Goold. 16 vols. Edinburgh: T&T Clark, 1862.

Parker, Brent E., and Richard J. Lucas, eds. *Covenantal and Dispensational Theologies: Four Views on the Continuity of Scripture*. Downers Grove, IL: IVP Academic, 2022.

Penman, Thomas George. "There Is a Covenant of Redemption and By It We Are Blessed: A Dissertation in Support of Its Retrieval for the Contemporary Church." BTh diss., Edinburgh Theological Seminary, 2019.

Perkins, Harrison. *Catholicity and the Covenant of Works: James Ussher and the Reformed Tradition*. New York: Oxford University Press, 2020.

______. "*Meritum ex pacto* in the Reformed Tradition: Covenantal Merit in Theological Polemics." *Mid-America Journal of Theology* 31 (2020): 57–87.

______. "Reconsidering the Development of the Covenant of Works: A Study in Doctrinal Trajectory." *Calvin Theological Journal* 53.2 (Nov 2018): 289–317.

______. *Righteous by Design: Covenantal Merit and Adam's Integrity*. Reformed Exegetical and Doctrinal Studies. Fearn, UK: Mentor, forthcoming.

Perkins, William. *The Works of William Perkins*. 10 vols. Grand Rapids: Reformation Heritage Books, 2014–2020.

Peterson, Robert A. *Our Secure Salvation: Preservation and Apostasy*. Explorations in Biblical Theology. Phillipsburg, NJ: P&R, 2009.

Rehnman, Sebastian. "Moral Philosophy and Moral Theology in Vermigli." Pages 199–214 in *Church and School in Early Modern Protestantism: Studies in Honor of Richard A. Muller on the Maturation of a Theological Tradition*. Edited by Jordan J. Ballor, David S. Sytsma, and Jason Zuidema. Leiden: Brill, 2013.

______. "Virtue and Grace." *Studies in Christian Ethics* 25 no. 4 (2012): 473–93.

Renihan, Samuel. *From Shadow to Substance: The Federal Theology of the English Particular Baptists (1642–1704)*. Centre for Baptist History and Heritage Studies. Oxford: Regents Park College, 2018.

______. *The Mystery of Christ: His Covenant and His Kingdom*. Cape Coral, FL: Founders Press, 2020.

Rhodes, Jonty. *Raiding the Lost Ark: Recovering the Gospel of the Covenant King*. Leicester, UK: Inter-Varsity Press, 2013.

Roberts, Alexander, and James Donaldson, eds. *Ante-Nicene Fathers*. 10 vols. Buffalo: The Christian Literature Publishing Co., 1885.

Roberts, Francis. *Mysterium & Medulla Bibliorum: The Mysterie and Marrow of the Bible, viz. God's Covenants with Man*. London: George Calvert, 1657.

Robertson, O. Palmer. *The Christ of the Covenants*. Phillipsburg, NJ: P&R, 1981.

Rollock, Robert. *Analysis Logica in Epistolam Pauli Apostoli ad Galatas*. London: Felix Kyngston, 1602.

______. *Analysis Dialectica ... in Pauli Apostoli Epistolam ad Romanos*. Edinburgh: Robert Waldgrave, 1594.

______. *Some Questions and Answers about God's Covenants and the Sacrament That Is a Seal of God's Covenant: with Related Texts*. Translated by Aaron Clay Denlinger. Eugene, OR: Pickwick, 2016.

______. *Tractatus de Vocatione Efficaci*. Edinburgh: Robert Waldgrave, 1597.

______. *A Treatise of God's Effectual Calling*. Translated by Henry Holland. London: Felix Kyngston, 1603.

Rosner, Brian S. *Paul and the Law: Keeping the Commandments of God*. New Studies in Biblical Theology. Downers Grove, IL: InterVarsity Press, 2013.

Sanders, Fred. *Fountain of Salvation: Trinity and Soteriology*. Grand Rapids: Eerdmans, 2021.

______. *The Triune God*. New Studies in Dogmatics. Grand Rapids: Zondervan, 2016.

Sanders, Fred, and Scott R. Swain, eds. *Retrieving Eternal Generation.* Grand Rapids: Zondervan, 2017.

Schaff, Philip, ed. *Nicene and Post-Nicene Fathers, Series 1.* 14 vols. New York: Christian Literature Company, 1887.

______. *The Creeds of Christendom.* 3 vols. New York: Harper and Brothers, 1877.

Schreiner, Thomas R. *Covenant and God's Purpose for the World.* Short Studies in Biblical Theology. Wheaton, IL: Crossway, 2017.

______. *Galatians.* Zondervan Exegetical Commentary on the New Testament. Grand Rapids: Zondervan, 2010.

Strong, William. *A Discourse of the Two Covenants: Wherein the Nature, Differences, and Effects of the Covenant of Works and of Grace Are Distinctly, Rationally, Spiritually and Practically Discussed.* London, 1678.

Sutanto, N. Gray. "Consummation Anyway: A Reformed Proposal." *Journal of Analytic Philosophy* 9 (Summer 2021): 223–37.

Svensson, Manfred, and David VanDrunen, eds. *Aquinas Among the Protestants.* Hoboken, NJ: Wiley Blackwell, 2018.

Thiselton, Anthony C. *The First Epistle to the Corinthians.* New International Greek Testament Commentary. Grand Rapids: Eerdmans, 2000.

Thomas Aquinas. *Compendium of Theology.* Translated by Richard J. Regan. New York: Oxford University Press, 2009.

______. *Summa Theologica.* Translated by Fathers of the English Dominican Province. 5 vols. New York: Benziger Bros., 1948. Reprinted by Notre Dame: Christian Classics, 1981.

Tuckett, Christopher M. *Christology and the New Testament: Jesus and His Earliest Followers.* Louisville: Westminster John Knox, 2001.

Turner, David L. *Matthew.* Baker Exegetical Commentary on the New Testament. Grand Rapids: Baker Academic, 2008.

Treier, Daniel J. *Introducing Theological Interpretation of Scripture: Recovering a Christian Practice.* Nottingham, UK: Apollos, 2008.

Trueman, Carl R. *Grace Alone: Salvation as a Gift of God.* The Five Solas Series. Grand Rapids: Zondervan, 2017.

Turretin, Francis. *Institutes of Elenctic Theology.* Translated by George Musgrave Giger. Edited by James T. Dennison Jr. 3 vols. Phillipsburg, NJ: P&R, 1992–1997.

Ussher, James, *A Body of Divinitie.* London: Thomas Downes and George Badger, 1645.

______. *The Principles of Christian Religion*. London: George Badger, 1653.

Van Asselt, Willem J. "The Doctrine of the Abrogations in the Federal Theology of Johannes Cocceius (1603–1669)." *Calvin Theological Journal* 29 no. 1 (1994): 101–16.

______. "Expromissio or Fideiussio?: A Seventeenth-Century Theological Debate between Voetians and Cocceians about the Nature of Christ's Suretyship in Salvation History." *Mid-America Journal of Theology* 14 (2003): 37–57.

VanDrunen, David. *Divine Covenants and Moral Order: A Biblical Theology of Natural Law*. Grand Rapids: Eerdmans, 2014.

______. "Israel's Recapitulation of Adam's Probation under the Law of Moses." *Westminster Theological Journal* 73 no. 2 (Fall 2011): 303–24.

______. *Living in God's Two Kingdoms: A Biblical Vision for Christianity and Culture*. Wheaton, IL: Crossway, 2010.

Vermigli, Peter Martyr, and Heinrich Bullinger, et al. *Epistolae Duae, Ad Ecclesias Polonicas*. Zurich: Christoffel Froschouer, 1561.

Vidu, Adonis. *The Divine Missions: An Introduction*. Eugene, OR: Cascade Books, 2021.

______. *The Same God Who Works All Things: Inseparable Operations in Trinitarian Theology*. Grand Rapids: Eerdmans, 2021.

Vos, Geerhardus. *Biblical Theology: Old and New Testaments*. New ed. London: The Banner of Truth Trust, 1975.

______. *Redemptive History and Biblical Interpretation: The Shorter Writings of Geerhardus Vos*. Edited by Richard B. Gaffin Jr. Phillipsburg, NJ: P&R, 1980.

______. *Reformed Dogmatics*. 5 vols. Bellingham, WA: Lexham Press, 2012–2014.

______. *The Teaching of the Epistle to the Hebrews*. Grand Rapids: Eerdmans, 1956.

Vos, Pieter. "Calvinists among the Virtues: Reformed Theological Contributions to Contemporary Virtue Ethics." *Studies in Christian Ethics* 28 no. 2 (2015): 201–12.

Wace, Henry, and Philip Schaff, eds. *Nicene and Post-Nicene Fathers, Series* 2. 14 vols. New York: The Christian Literature Company, 1895.

Waltke, Bruce K., with Cathi J. Fredericks. *Genesis: A Commentary*. Grand Rapids: Zondervan, 2001.

Walton, John H. *The Lost World of Adam and Eve: Genesis 2–3 and the Human Origins Debate*. Downers Grove, IL: IVP Academic, 2015.

______. *The Lost World of Genesis One: Ancient Cosmology and the Origins Debate.* Downers Grove, IL: IVP Academic, 2009.

Walton, John H., and J. Harvey Walton. *The Lost World of the Torah: Law as Covenant and Wisdom in Ancient Context*. Downers Grove, IL: IVP Academic, 2019.

Wannamaker, Charles A. *The Epistles to the Thessalonians.* New International Greek Testament Commentary. Grand Rapids: Eerdmans, 1990.

Warfield, Benjamin B. "The Idea of Systematic Theology." Pages 49–87 in *Studies in Theology.* Oxford: Oxford University Press, 1932.

Waters, Guy Prentiss. *For the Mouth of the Lord Has Spoken: The Doctrine of Scripture*. Reformed Exegetical and Doctrinal Studies. Fearn, UK: Mentor, 2020.

Waters, Guy Prentiss, J. Nicholas Reid, and John R. Muether, eds. *Covenant Theology: Biblical, Theological, and Historical Perspectives.* Wheaton, IL: Crossway, 2020.

Watson, Francis. *Paul and the Hermeneutics of Faith*. 2nd ed. London: T&T Clark, 2016.

Webster, John. *The Culture of Theology*. Edited by Ivor J. Davidson and Alden C. McCray. Grand Rapids: Baker Academic, 2019.

______. *God and the Works of God.* Vol. 1. God without Measure: Working Papers in Christian Theology. London: T&T Clark, 2016.

______. *Holiness*. London: SCM Press, 2003.

______. "Theologies of Retrieval." Pages 583–99 in *The Oxford Handbook of Systematic Theology.* Edited by John Webster, Kathryn Tanner, and Iain Torrance. New York: Oxford University Press, 2007.

______. *Virtue and Intellect*. Vol. 2. God without Measure: Working Papers in Christian Theology. London: T&T Clark, 2016.

Wellum, Stephen J. "Baptism and the Relationship between the Covenants." Pages 105–70 in *Believers Baptism: Sign of the New Covenant in Christ.* Edited by Thomas R. Schreiner and Shawn D. Wright. NAC Studies in Bible and Theology. Nashville: B&H Academic, 2006.

______. *Christ Alone: The Uniqueness of Jesus as Savior*. The Five Solas Series. Grand Rapids: Zondervan, 2017.

______. "Christological Reflections in Light of Scripture's Covenants." *Southern Baptist Journal of Theology* 16 no. 2 (2012): 44–55.

———. *God the Son Incarnate: The Doctrine of Christ*. Foundations of Evangelical Theology. Wheaton, IL: Crossway, 2016.

———. *The Person of Christ: An Introduction*. Short Studies in Systematic Theology. Wheaton, IL: Crossway, 2021.

Wellum, Stephen J., and Brent E. Parker, eds. *Progressive Covenantalism: Charting a Course between Dispensational and Covenant Theologies*. Nashville: B&H Academic, 2016.

Wenham, Gordon J. *Genesis 1–15*. Word Biblical Commentary. Grand Rapids: Zondervan, 1987.

Williamson, Paul R. *Sealed with an Oath: Covenant in God's Unfolding Purpose*. New Studies in Biblical Theology. Downers Grove, IL: IVP Academic, 2007.

Witsius, Herman. *The Economy of the Covenants between God and Man, Comprehending a Complete Body of Divinity*. Translated by William Crookshank. 2 vols. Edinburgh: Thomas Turnbull, 1803.

Young, E. J. *The Book of Isaiah*. 3 vols. Grand Rapids: Eerdmans, 1965.

Author Index

Subject Index

Confessions Index

Westminster Larger Catechism

Westminster Shorter Catechism

Scripture Index

Old Testament

Genesis

Exodus

New Testament

Acts

Romans

1 Corinthians

2 Corinthians